BLÜCHER

C&C

CAMPAIGNS & COMMANDERS

GREGORY J. W. URWIN, SERIES EDITOR

CAMPAIGNS AND COMMANDERS

GENERAL EDITOR

Gregory J. W. Urwin, *Temple University, Philadelphia, Pennsylvania*

ADVISORY BOARD

Lawrence E. Babits, *East Carolina University, Greenville*

James C. Bradford, *Texas A&M University, College Station*

Robert M. Epstein, *U.S. Army School of Advanced Military Studies, Fort Leavenworth, Kansas*

David M. Glantz, *Carlisle, Pennsylvania*

Jerome A. Greene, *Denver, Colorado*

Victor Davis Hanson, *California State University, Fresno*

Herman Hattaway, *University of Missouri, Kansas City*

J. A. Houlding, *Rückersdorf, Germany*

Eugenia C. Kiesling, *U.S. Military Academy, West Point, New York*

Timothy K. Nenninger, *National Archives, Washington, D.C.*

Bruce Vandervort, *Virginia Military Institute, Lexington*

BLÜCHER

Scourge of Napoleon

Michael V. Leggiere

UNIVERSITY OF OKLAHOMA PRESS | NORMAN

Also by Michael V. Leggiere

The Fall of Napoleon: Volume 1, The Allied Invasion of France, 1813–1814
  (Cambridge, 2007)
Napoleon and Berlin: The Franco-Prussian War in North Germany, 1813
  (Norman, 2002)

Publication of this book is made possible through the generosity of
Edith Kinney Gaylord.

Library of Congress Cataloging-in-Publication Data

Leggiere, Michael V., 1969–
 Blücher : scourge of Napoleon / Michael V. Leggiere.
    pages cm. — (Campaigns and commanders)
  Includes bibliographical references and index.
  ISBN 978-0-8061-4409-2 (hardcover : alk. paper)
  1. Blücher, Gebhard Leberecht von, 1742–1819. 2. Marshals—Germany—Prussia—
Biography. 3. Prussia (Germany)—History—1740–1815. 4. Prussia (Germany)—
History, Military. 5. Napoleon I, Emperor of the French, 1769–1821—Adversaries.
6. Wars of Liberation, 1813–1814—Campaigns—Germany. I. Title.
  DD418.6.B6L44 2013
  940.274092—dc23
  [B]

                          2013019314

Blücher: Scourge of Napoleon is Volume 41 in the Campaigns & Commanders
  series.

1 2 3 4 5 6 7 8 9 10

Interior layout and composition: Alcorn Publication Design

In memory of my father,
Thomas R. Leggiere (1943–2007)

Contents

Illustrations

Figures

Maps

Preface

Of all the characters in the Napoleonic pantheon, Gebhard Leberecht von Blücher is one of the most colorful. Affectionately nicknamed "Marshal Forward" by his troops, the images we have of Blücher are that of the brash hussar who was cashiered by Frederick the Great, the gambler who loved the bottle, the reckless general who squandered his cavalry in futile attacks against the French at Auerstedt, the conquered Prussian who passionately hated Napoleon, and the half-crazed co-victor of Waterloo who claimed to be pregnant with an elephant. One of his Russian subordinates, the French émigré general Louis Alexandre de Langeron, thus described him as commander of the Army of Silesia in 1813:

> General Blücher, to whom the Army of Silesia was confided, was over seventy years old, but his spirit and body had lost none of their vigor. He was an old Hussar in the clearest sense of the word: he drank and debauched; he had all the faults that one takes pains to excuse in a young man. But he redeemed them by many qualities; an intrepid soldier, an ardent patriot, frank, loyal, possessing a martial figure . . . , he knew how to inspire in his troops the most complete confidence, and won the love of his soldiers: he would soon be as adored by the Russian soldiers as he was by the Prussians.
>
> His activity was prodigious, he was always on horseback; on the battlefield, he had the experience and routine of a veteran soldier; his *coup d'œil* (tactical vision) was excellent, his heroic bravery carried the troops, but his talent as a general was limited to these qualities. It was a great deal, but not enough if he was not seconded; he had little strategic ability, could not find himself on a map, and was incapable of making a campaign plan or disposition. He left all military and political details to the three people given and attached to him to direct him.[1]

The 1903 judgment of Major Rudolf Friederich of the Historical Section of the Great German General Staff seems to confirm Langeron's assessment of these limitations:

> Although endowed with keen insight and able to see the whole picture with tremendous insight, Blücher lacked everything that

today we combine in the term *Generalstabswissenschaften* (the science of General Staff work). He clearly knew and keenly recognized the decisive moment of a tactical situation, but he was completely incapable of strategic combinations; his view was always directed only upon the most obvious and he never looked at a map. He was like a chess player who only understands to play move by move, but who during the course of the game does not think a few moves ahead to be in position to pursue any special idea, any special objective. Thus, in strategic vision and in the technique of army leadership, in the arrangement and calculation of marches, the drafting of dispositions—overall in command leadership—Blücher's General Staff had to intervene by supplementing and helping.[2]

Do these descriptions tell Blücher's full story? We will begin answering this question by reviewing what we know of him. Thanks in part to Blücher, the conflict that started in 1813 expanded from a war for Prussia's liberation from Napoleon's control to a war for the liberation of all of Germany from French hegemony. His operations ensured that a battle of epic proportions—the Battle of Nations—took place at Leipzig on 15–19 October 1813. This victory after four brutal days of combat broke Napoleon's control of central Europe, ended French rule in Germany, and sent the French army retreating across the Rhine River. Having rid his people of the French, Blücher received universal acclaim as Germany's savior. Nineteenth-century nationalist and romantic writers eulogized his feats. The Prussian and later German General Staffs examined every aspect of his operations, concluding that Blücher devised a new way of warfare that eclipsed Napoleon's. Marshal Forward came to symbolize Prussia's modern way of war: an ominous portent for the brave men who marched to war in 1914.

We know much about Blücher's generalship. He harbored absolutely no fear of Napoleon and possessed an endless drive to fight a decisive battle and to win a decisive victory. This prompted him to conduct operations that have drawn criticism from civilian and military historians, both contemporary and modern. Contemporaries accused Blücher of imprudence, rashness, and irresponsibility. Some concluded that his impetuosity produced a two-fold result: exhausted, ill-supplied troops and considerable combat casualties. Thus, critics have summarized his command style as negligent, inefficient, imprudent, and at times careless. The record suggests that, up to his last major battle at Waterloo, Blücher was far from a cautious general. Yet careful examination of his campaigns in 1813–15 demonstrates the exact opposite. In fact, Marshal Forward went backward more than he advanced.

Criticism of Blücher is generally eclipsed by the positive aspects of his generalship. We know that his coolness, steadfastness, and leadership could not be replaced. Like Napoleon, he too realized that his mere presence served as a force multiplier. We know that he provided the unity that held his army together and arguably the Sixth and Seventh Coalitions. His profound service to the internal cohesion of the army he commanded started with his staff. Despite the differences and egos of the numerous members of his entourage, Blücher possessed the uncanny knack of maintaining harmony. All accounts attest to the cheerful nightly gatherings for dinner at his quarters. Whether through a timely joke or thoughtful inquiry about a loved one back at home, he managed his people well. For example, during the invasion of France in 1814, one of his staff officers suggested marching the army to the plateau of Langres. Blücher listened quietly as the officer eagerly explained that the plateau served as the key to France. When the officer finished, Blücher looked at a map and declared: "I can see that if I stand on the plateau and piss to the north it will drain into the Atlantic, while if I piss to the south it will drain into the Mediterranean. But I don't see how that will help me win the war."

On numerous occasions he struggled with a disgruntled or irreconcilable subordinate. The commander of the Prussian corps of the Army of Silesia during the 1813 and 1814 campaigns, General Hans David von Yorck, threatened to resign numerous times. He actually submitted a letter of resignation to Prussian king Frederick William III in August 1813 and one to Blücher in March 1814. In addition, the commander of one of his two Russian corps, Langeron, disobeyed Blücher so many times in 1813 that the Prussian had to physically remain with him to guarantee the prompt execution of orders.[3] Great was Blücher's service to the internal cohesion of his army.

We also know that Blücher established an exemplary relationship with the Russian soldiers of his Army of Silesia. Not seeing the magnanimity of Tsar Alexander I's decision to distribute his forces among the three Allied armies, the Russian generals felt slighted by their posting to the Silesian Army. Wishing to fight in their master's presence, these Russian officers believed their opportunity to earn

glory drastically if not fatally diminished. That one of their countrymen had not been selected to command one of the Allied armies
likewise irked the Russians; some even opposed Alexander's decision to carry the war into central Europe. Regardless, Blücher took
a very pragmatic approach in his relations with the Russians. One
contemporary, Friedrich Karl von Müffling, claimed that merely
avoiding discord was not his ultimate goal, but "establishing broth-
erly harmony" so the Russians would execute the war "if not with
pleasure, at least without reluctance."

Blücher rejected the opinion shared by many Prussians that the
Russians should adopt German customs while in Germany. Instead,
he believed the Prussians should conform to the Russians. As a firm
principle, Blücher maintained that the Prussian army should "earn
and preserve the respect of its allies through great actions." Thus, in
his opinion, Prussian troops should receive the most difficult tasks,
march on the worst roads, and lead every attack. Yorck eventually
protested, yet Müffling asserts that this belief formed "the funda-
mental condition" of Blücher's command. "Without the assistance
of the Russians, we were unable to crush the colossus that threatened us with degradation and eternal slavery; but to desire more
than assistance, where our own strength did not suffice, would be
unfair." No fan of Blücher, Müffling concludes: "Russia had freed
itself in 1812; our turn had now come, and General Blücher harbored
an overly exalted notion of national honor to balance it against a
policy that might teach us cunningly to shift on others the heavy
labors of which we hoped to reap the advantages."[4]

The Russians grew to love and adore Blücher. They appreciated
that he led from the front and that he always displayed a fatherly
care for them as well as his own troops. It was the Russians who
bestowed upon him the nickname "Marshal Forward"; wherever he
appeared, they greeted him with a hurrah. The Cossacks especially
venerated him. They claimed he had been born on their Steppes as
part of their clan but as a child had been snatched from their midst.
Blücher's 1814 farewell to the Cossack detachment assigned to his
headquarters brought tears to everyone's eyes; the Russian warriors
vowed to pray for him at the Don.[5] But the Russian officers wished
Blücher did more to contain the arrogance of their Prussian counterparts. "During the entire war," notes Langeron, "every individual
in the Prussian army—princes, generals, officers, soldiers, militia-
men—covered themselves in glory; one could not carry military

honor further than them; but they left to be desired a greater degree of modesty: their boasting was truly insufferable. They remembered too much of the Seven Years War, too little of the war of 1806. Our officers were required to display a highly meritorious prudence and self-abnegation, dictated by the circumstances and the orders of our sovereign."[6]

Many misperceptions about Blücher's abilities also exist. To begin, Blücher could read a map and did understand strategy. His correspondence suggests that he could sufficiently discuss campaign planning and operations. The elaboration of orders, march routes, and timetables did not fall under the jurisdiction of the commander in chief but that of the chief of staff and quartermaster general. For this reason, contemporaries and historians have argued that Blücher served as a mere figurehead while his chief of staff, August von Gneisenau, actually commanded the Silesian Army in 1813 and 1814 and then the Army of the Lower Rhine in 1815. Without question, Gneisenau exerted a decisive influence on the conduct of Blücher's two armies. He most likely made the decisions in terms of operational planning, yet they still required Blücher's understanding and approval. For this reason, the chief of staff always conducted exhaustive talks with his commander; operations simply could not commence without Blücher's complete understanding, agreement, and support. Conversely, Gneisenau complained more than once about the general's incessant demands to advance.

As this book will suggest through an analysis of Blücher during the 1807–12 period, his ego and constant concern over his manly image made him a force to be reckoned with. Although they were friends, it is difficult to imagine that Blücher, as commander of the Silesian Army and later the Army of the Lower Rhine, obediently and blindly deferred to Gneisenau, basically abdicating the role he had craved since 1807. A warrior like Blücher understood that only leadership earned respect. If he could not lead, if he could not make decisions, he would rather resign than act as a mere figurehead. Two glaring examples provide proof. The first occurred after Blücher fell extremely ill during the 1814 battle of Laon in France. With the general bedridden and incapacitated, Gneisenau halted operations rather than surreptitiously direct the army. The second example occurred when Blücher was wounded during the 1815 battle of Ligny. With Blücher among the missing, Gneisenau still executed his commander's wish to have the army abandon its line of communication and march north to link with the Duke of Wellington's Anglo-Dutch army.

Blücher and Gneisenau must be viewed as a team. Individually, neither would have achieved the success they did together. Friederich adequately summarizes their military marriage:

> In later times, it is understandable to place excessive high esteem on theoretical knowledge and general education so that all the great results of the Silesian Army are attributed exclusively to the person of Gneisenau and, on the contrary, to see Blücher as a coarse old warhorse, who used the efficiency of his General Staff to gain renown that went far beyond his actual merit. This is completely untrue! Without doubt, Gneisenau surpassed his old commander in genius of comprehension, in width of view, in theoretical and practical knowledge. But it is certainly very doubtful that Gneisenau could have brought his bold ideas to fruition if they were not always echoed by Blücher, if he was not their advocate, if Blücher's powerful personality did not always stand behind them to eliminate the friction, which especially in the Silesian Army threatened to bring the machinery that drove it to a standstill. While it is always and generally a difficult task to compare and establish the share of the success between the commanding general and his General Staff, in the Silesian Army it is completely impossible. Bound closely together by the spirit of high command, the mutuality of military and political convictions, the burning love and respect for King and Fatherland, and the burning hatred of all things French, similar to each other in desires, insight, energy, and stamina, Blücher and Gneisenau belonged together, one cannot think of one without the other.[7]

Although we have much information on Blücher's private life and know much about his generalship, his influence on Napoleon has yet to be analyzed fully or satisfactorily. Thus, a second goal of this study is to evaluate the effect of Blücher's operations on Napoleon. This book will explain how the Prussian played the most decisive role in the campaigns of 1813, 1814, and 1815. Not a rash, overemotional hatred of Napoleon or an irrational desire to reach Paris earned Blücher this distinction. Instead, the bold, unorthodox, and unexpected moves he made bewildered and frustrated the emperor, who found himself reacting to his enemy rather than seizing the initiative. He chased shadows, exhausting his men through back-and-forth marches between Saxony, Silesia, and Bohemia in

1813, then fruitless chases in France and Belgium in 1814 and 1815. Blücher, often the butt of Napoleon's jokes, outwitted and outran him in 1813, 1814, and 1815. Consistently hoodwinking his adversary by abandoning his own line of communication, Blücher appears more like the General Bonaparte of the First Italian Campaign (1796–97) than does Emperor Napoleon in in the later stages of his career.

In addition to this operational analysis, this book also uses Blücher's own words to reveal the true man. While tough as nails on the outside, Blücher was actually a thoughtful, loving family man. As a commander he hated war, comparing it to committing murder. The gruesome side of the soldier's trade weighed heavily on him. In his conversations he often referred to the horrors of war. While riding with the monarchs across the battlefield the day after the struggle at La Rothière, he lectured the Prussian crown prince, the future Frederick William IV, that in an unjust war, each drop of bloodshed must be like boiling oil on the conscience of the regent.[8] In all of his major campaigns as a commander, he looked forward to the day he could return home to his wife and family. Blücher's love for his children burned just as fiercely as his hatred of Napoleon. His heart broke after his eldest son, Franz, lost his sanity after receiving several head wounds. In the circle of friends and the members of his staff, Blücher alternately served as the kind grandfatherly type and the stern father figure. Always a friend of women, alcohol, and gambling, he never freed himself of the wild habits of camp life. Yet, while on campaign, he demonstrated his energy and determination, never losing control of himself or neglecting his duties. Until the entry into Paris, he never touched cards and did not tolerate card playing at his headquarters.[9]

The early and final chapters of the book go to great lengths to uncover Blücher the man, the Junker, the husband, and the father. Sandwiched in between is the story of Blücher the warrior, the hero, the general, and the victorious field marshal and prince. As much as possible, Blücher's own words are used to capture his essence. While space does not allow for the retelling of every tail or witty quote, the material produced here will provide a complete picture of the real man.

Surprisingly, few attempts have been made to write a scholarly work on Blücher. The destruction of much of the Prussian General Staff archives during World War II makes the task seem daunting.

But the Geheime Staatsarchiv Preußischer Kulturbesitz in Berlin does contain much of the documentary record of the armies commanded by Blücher between 1813 and 1815. Just as crucial, the historians of first the Prussian and then the German General Staff published much of the official correspondence coming from the headquarters of Blücher and Gneisenau during this period in their exhaustive studies of the Army of Silesia and the German wars of liberation, respectively. Thanks to the historiographic war between the German General Staff and Hans Delbrück, this prolific historian likewise published vast quantities of the official correspondence in his massive five-volume biography of Gneisenau. In addition, most of Blücher's private correspondence was published before the war. Moreover, in 1796 Blücher published his journal of the 1793 and 1794 campaigns in the Rhineland. Thus, we have much in terms of primary sources.

While several German-language biographies exist, they mostly follow one of two storylines established by the initial biographers. *Feldmarschall Fürst Blücher von Wahlstatt*, written in 1878 by Dr. Friedrich Wigger, is the authoritative work on Blücher's early life. Carl Blasendorff's 1887 work, *Gebhard Leberecht von Blücher*, is a close second.[10] Yet the Germans and all other interested parties had to wait until General Wolfgang von Unger published the two-volumes of his *Blücher* in 1907 and 1908 to read the authoritative work on Blücher's military career. Incidentally, Unger expanded on the volume of correspondence published in 1876 by the descendants of the field marshal's second wife, *Blücher in briefen aus den feldzügen 1813–1815*, to produce the 1913 work *Blüchers Briefe*. Sadly, German biographers either follow the personal history as described by Wigger, attempt to condense Unger's two-volumes into one, or blend the two, such as Walter Görlitz attempted in 1940 with his *Fürst Blücher von Wahlstatt*.[11] Thus, not one German biography is definitive, and they all disappoint to a greater or lesser degree. Such is the case with Roger Parkinson's *The Hussar General: The Life of Blücher, Man of Waterloo* (1975). Although extremely entertaining, Parkinson takes too many liberties with literary creativity, and his book blurs the line between fact and fiction.[12] Based on German, Russian, and French sources, this book will combine the best of both approaches to provide a total picture of Blücher.

I have many, many friends and colleagues to whom I owe much gratitude. First, I must thank Alexander Mikaberidze for his untiring assistance in acquiring and translating Russian documents. Moreover, his thoughts and insight have made this book much better than it would have been had I not heeded his erudite advice. At the University of North Texas, I have three senior colleagues who I am fortunate to call friends: Geoff Wawro, Rob Citino, and Rick McCaslin. The endless well of knowledge of Prusso-German history provided by Geoff and Rob saved me from despair at many turns, while Rick's steadfast support was much appreciated. I am also indebted to UNT's Department of History for its generous financial support. Alex Mendoza made the battle maps for this book, enduring with humor the countless revisions I requested. I must also thank Simone de Santiago Ramos for assistance with acquiring some of the illustrations and with translations. I must note a deep debt of gratitude to my mentor, Donald D. Horward, for teaching me how to be a passionate historian. Lastly, I must thank my graduate students Jon Abel, Chad Tomaselli, Jordan Hayworth, Nate Jarrett, Casey Baker, and Eric Smith for their support and encouragement.

Dear friends such as Rick Schneid, Huw Davies, and Jack Gill likewise provided much support, encouragement, and technical advice. I also want to thank Dennis Showalter, Sam Mustafa, Mike Pavkovic, Llew Cook, Chuck White, and Peter Hofschröer for their assistance, support, and advice over the years. I wish to offer my deep appreciation to Peter Harrington of the Anne S. K. Brown Military Collection at Brown University for providing the vast majority of the artwork that accompanies the text posthaste. I must thank the 5th Count Bülow von Dennewitz, Joachim-Albrecht, as well as his son, Hasso, for their kindness. For several years, both provided a constant stream of documents and information. Also, Anne-Dorte Krause of the Bildarchiv at Berlin's Stiftung Deutsches Historisches Museum and Ines Pannek of the Stiftung Stadtmuseum Berlin aided my search for illustrations. I must give special thanks to Bertrand Fonck as well as the staff of the Service historique de l'armée de terre at Vincennes for patiently handling my requests to exceed the daily limit of cartons. I also express my gratitude to the helpful staff of Berlin's Geheimes Staatsarchiv Preußischer Kulturbesitz for producing repositorium from the former German General Staff archive previously thought to have been lost during the Second World War. I also want to thank Chuck Rankin and Greg Urwin for their patience, support, and advice during this long project. Also I extend my appreciation to Kevin Brock and to Alice Stanton and the rest of the production crew at the University of Oklahoma Press. Many others have contributed in several ways. To them, thanks and an apology for any omission. Whatever merits this work has are due in part to their contributions; whatever faults may lie here are those of the author.

No words suffice to state my deep appreciation for my wife of fourteen years and companion of twenty, who patiently endured my absence during numerous research trips to Europe and coped with endless days of my short temper due to sleep deprivation. Our beautiful children, Jordyn and Nicholas, likewise endured countless hours of having to entertain themselves while I was writing. Finally, I wish to thank my mother, Rosalie, who is always a source of solid support. I dedicate this volume to my father, Tom, who died on 29 December 2007 at the age of sixty-four from complications of primary amyloidosis. Many can claim to be a "good man," but my father actually was in every sense of the phrase: a good father, husband, and son. I will forever miss his kindness, thoughtfulness, gentleness, and understanding. If I can be half the father he was, I will consider myself lucky.

I wrote this book with Google maps displayed on a secondary computer monitor at all times. While this resource greatly enhanced my understanding of Blücher's campaigns, it drove home the need to provide the reader with informative maps. With few exceptions, every population center mentioned in the book can be found on the maps. I included roads where space permitted. As much as possible, I employ native, modern spellings of villages, towns, smaller cities, and geographic features. Larger cities, capitals, and rivers are in English. I also provide at first mention the modern Polish, Russian, Lithuanian, and Czech names of population centers and geographic features in regions that once belonged to Prussia or Austria. Names of persons are likewise native, except for monarchs, whose names are in English. To avoid confusion, all general officers are referred to simply as "general." Lastly, I use "imperials" to refer to the French and their allies after 1804.

MAPS

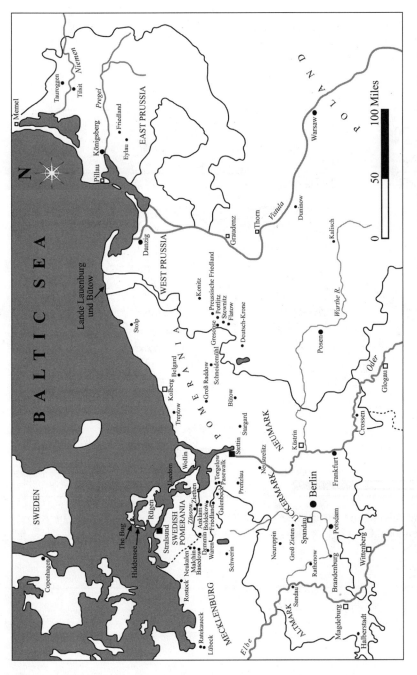

The North German and Polish Theaters of War, 1760–62, 1770–72, and 1806–1807. Map drawn by Alex Mendoza. Copyright © 2014 by the University of Oklahoma Press.

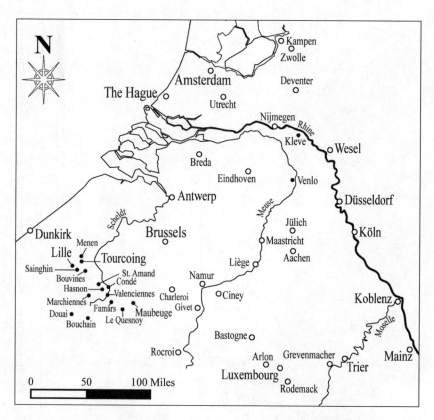

The Belgian and Dutch Theaters of War, 1787 and 1793. Map drawn by Alex Mendoza. Copyright © 2014 by the University of Oklahoma Press.

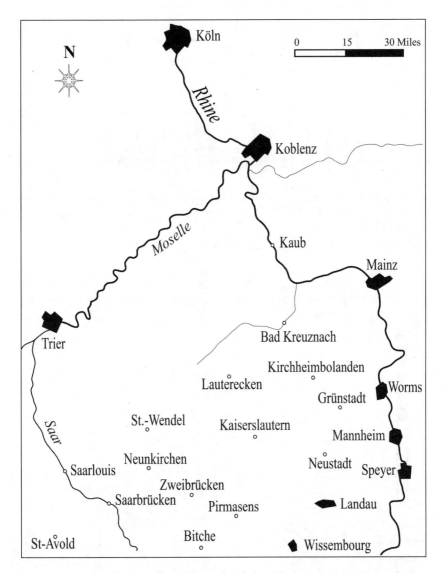

N

Köln

0   15   30 Miles

Rhine

Koblenz

Moselle

Kaub

Mainz

Trier

Bad Kreuznach

Kirchheimbolanden

Lauterecken

Grünstadt

Worms

Saar

St.-Wendel

Kaiserslautern

Mannheim

Neunkirchen

Neustadt

Speyer

Saarlouis

Zweibrücken

Saarbrücken

Pirmasens

Landau

St-Avold

Bitche

Wissembourg

The Theater of War on the Left Bank of the Rhine, 1793–94. Map drawn by Alex Mendoza. Copyright © 2014 by the University of Oklahoma Press.

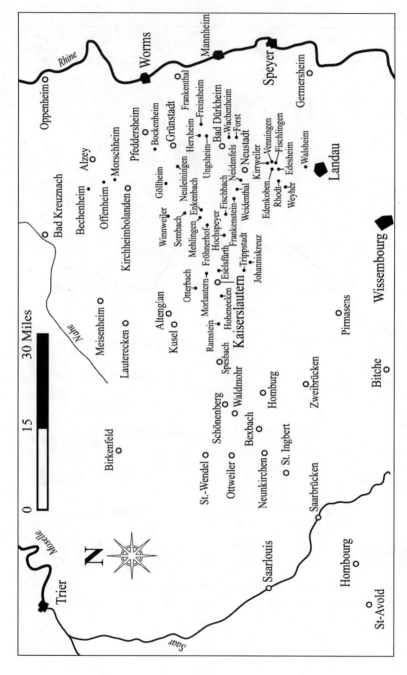

The Theater of War between the Rhine and the Saar, 1793–94. Map drawn by Alex Mendoza. Copyright © 2014 by the University of Oklahoma Press.

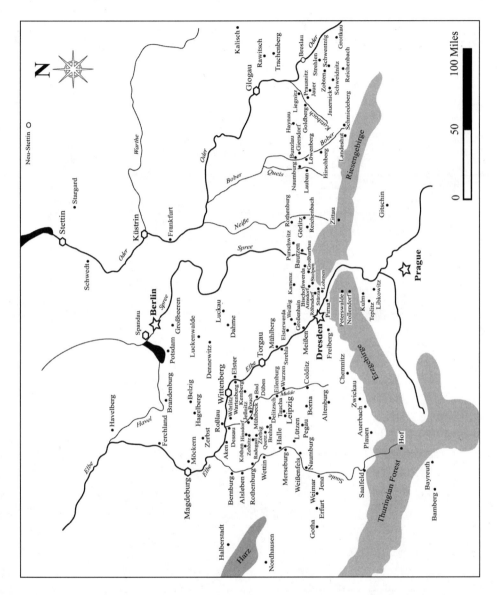

N

Neu-Stettin O

The German
Theater of War,
1762, 1806,
and 1813. Map
drawn by Alex
Mendoza.
Copyright
© 2014 by the
University of
Oklahoma Press.

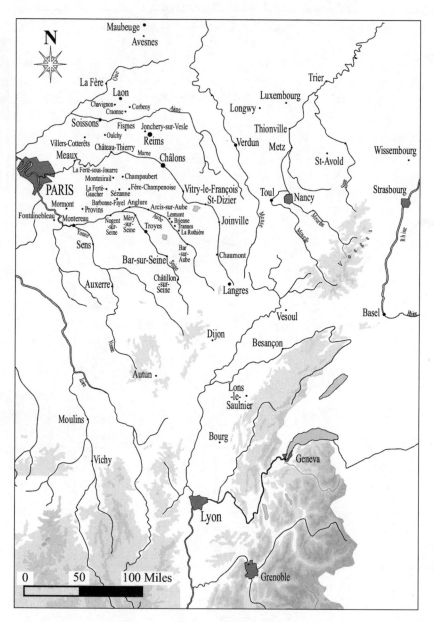

The French Theater of War, 1814 and 1815. Map drawn by Alex Mendoza. Copyright © 2014 by the University of Oklahoma Press.

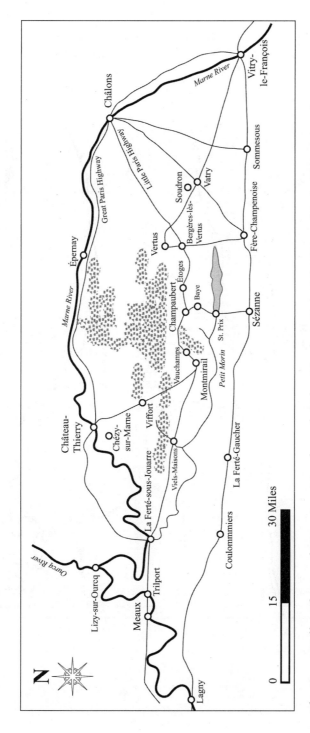

The Marne Valley Theater of War, 1814. Map drawn by Alex Mendoza. Copyright © 2014 by the University of Oklahoma Press.

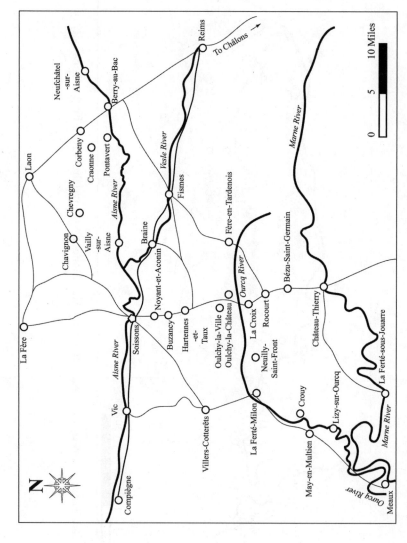

The Aisne Valley Theater of War, 1814. Map drawn by Alex Mendoza. Copyright © 2014 by the University of Oklahoma Press.

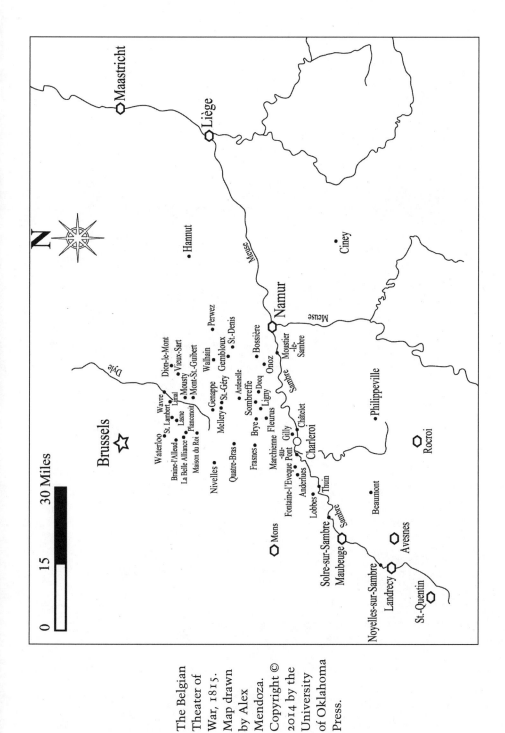

The Belgian Theater of War, 1815. Map drawn by Alex Mendoza. Copyright © 2014 by the University of Oklahoma Press.

BLÜCHER

PRUSSIA

At the Baltic port of Rostock in the German duchy of Mecklenburg, Dorothea Maria von Blücher gave birth to the youngest of six boys—Gebhard Leberecht—on Sunday, 16 December 1742. Her husband, Christian Friederich, a former captain in the cavalry of Hesse-Kassel, numbered among the landless minor nobility.[1] He left the service in 1737 after participating as a second in a duel that ended with a fatality. Life only became harder for Christian. Receiving no pension from Hesse-Kassel, he found himself forced to serve Duke Karl Leopold of Mecklenburg as a mediator in his dispute with the guilds. This earned him an annual pension of 200 thaler, which fell far short of satisfying the needs of his large family.[2] Various requests to serve in Mecklenburg's army or receive a position in the forestry service remained unfulfilled. Money remained tight, and Gebhard never forgot how it felt to number among the starving nobles of Germany.

We know little about the future field marshal's childhood. He seldom spoke of his youth, but the few hints he gave suggests it passed happily. Blücher once said that he spent "nine full years in the exemplary care of his father's house" but also admitted that "he lacked everything he was supposed to learn."[3] Although he attended the Rostock city school until age fourteen, books did not interest him, and his parents did not pressure him to complete his studies. At a time when proficiency exams for the civil and military services did not exist, the nobility placed little value on formal education.

The nineteenth-century historian Johannes Scherr proclaims that for all of his life, Blücher "remained an archenemy of German grammar, spelling, and style."[4] Fault for this did not reside solely with Blücher. Not only did the family still speak *Plattdeutsch* (Low German) but also the Rostock city school, a Latin academy that prepared students for the university, did little to help Blücher master *Hochdeutsch* (High German). Conversely, Blücher learned enough Latin to prevent him from ever forgetting a few words and phrases that sometimes surfaced in his letters.[5] Despite taking French lessons until the age of forty, he never mastered the language of his great foe. Blücher himself admitted that his handwriting was not legible.[6]

Although Blücher complained in old age that he learned little while growing up, contemporaries disagreed. General Georg Wilhelm von Valentini, a Prussian staff officer and chief of the army's military training and education system, maintained that "concerning his education, and compared to the majority of his peers, [Blücher] was in no way inferior. In both oral and written form, he knew how to express himself." Blücher addressed his fellow countrymen in Low German and employed much military jargon. Once, when leaving a group of elegant ladies, he jokingly said goodbye with the following words: "well, every one of you 'Frölens' [*Fräuleins*] has to kiss me now." His personal physician, Dr. Carl Bieske, emphasized that Blücher "knew how to express himself, especially around women." A skilled orator, he frequently gave moving speeches, especially to his fellow Freemasons. His main German biographer, General Wolfgang von Unger, admirably summarizes that Blücher "was vulgar around friends; exuberant and emotional with his lodge brothers; flirtatious with lady friends; and reverent and formal when presenting to his king."[7]

All five of Blücher's brothers pursued military careers. His oldest, Berthold, retired from the Prussian service as an infantry lieutenant at the end of the Seven Years War (1756–63) but died shortly after from the lingering effects of wounds received at the 18 June 1757 battle of Kolin. The second oldest, Gustav, enjoyed a successful career in the Danish army. A testament to the solid education Gustav received at the Rostock city school, he rose to the rank of *Generaladjutant* before transferring to the civil service; he died at Copenhagen in 1808. Burchard, the third son, first served in the Duchy of Schwerin's army before transferring to the Prussian service, for which he fought in the Seven Years War as an infantry officer and then as a dragoon. Wounded at the 5 December 1757 battle of Leuthen, Burchard fell at the 12 August 1759 battle of Kunersdorf. The fourth brother, Siegfried, entered Swedish service along with Gebhard. The brother closest to Gebhard in age, Hans, followed Gustav into the Danish service; poor health forced him to resign. After spending several years recovering, Hans joined the Russian army and died fighting the Turks.

In addition to his five brothers, Gebhard had two sisters, ten and eight years older than him. The oldest, Dorothee, never married and died at the Malchow convent in 1812 at age eighty. Gebhard's other sister, Margarete, married a former captain in Mecklenburg's army, Hans Friedrich von Krackevitz, who possessed the small estate of Ventz on the northwestern part of the island of Rügen, a Swedish possession.[8] After watching four sons enter the military, Christian hoped Gebhard would pursue farming. In 1756 he decided to send his son to live with Margarete so she could supplement his lack of education either personally or through private lessons with the local preacher. Moreover, Hans would teach him the fundamentals of estate management. Thus, at age fourteen the future Prussian field marshal exchanged his father's house for his brother-in-law's at Ventz.

That same year, 1756, the Seven Years War erupted; Sweden and Mecklenburg joined Austria, Russia, France, and the states of the Holy Roman Empire to destroy Prussia.[9] For the Mecklenburgers as well as the Swedish subjects living on Rügen, the war remained very close to home. Dubbed the "Pomeranian War," the fighting in this region occurred between Prussian and Swedish forces from 1757 to 1762 in Swedish Pomerania, Prussian Pomerania, northern Brandenburg, and eastern Mecklenburg. After the Swedes did not fare well in the 1757 campaign, they withdrew toward the end of the year to Stralsund—just across the water from Rügen—where the Prussians besieged them. A large Swedish garrison quartered on Rügen's neighboring island of Hiddensee. With the war moving much closer to home, Rügen's inhabitants became concerned.[10]

Instead of hitting the books, Gebhard spent his days riding, hunting, hiking, rowing, and sailing. Loving physical exertion, he developed a powerful body. Blücher established a close friendship with two of the sons of Johann Adolfs von Bohlen, whose estate stood one hour from Ventz. The son of a tenant farmer named Dierck also numbered among Blücher's friends. While on holiday from Schwerin's *Pageninstitut*, Siegfried, Blücher's brother, joined them to hunt.[11] Often possessing only one musket, the youths roamed about for miles. Sometimes the teens rode on horses they found in isolated pastures—never bothering to ask permission from the owner. Most of all, they loved to take trips to the fishing village of Schaprode on the western side of Rügen, from where they could take scenic boat rides to Hiddensee or to a part of the island

called The Bug, which was a breeding ground for seabirds that the
boys liked to hunt.[12] On The Bug they often mingled with Swedish
cavalry troopers, who no doubt filled the youths with wild stories.
Dierck's eldest son served in General Johann Sparre's *Svenska hussarregementet* and so provided the introductions.

No doubt awed by the hussars and their brilliant uniforms,
Gebhard and Siegfried wanted to join the regiment. Their brother-
in-law, Krackevitz, refused to grant them permission to join the
hussars, whose lack of discipline had earned them a sinister reputation. But he did not oppose their decision out of principle. In fact, he
recognized that they had little choice in vocation. Military or civil
service provided the only viable careers for the younger sons of the
impoverished minor nobility. As the Blücher brothers lacked financial assets as well as the education and desire to be civil servants,
the army appeared to be their only salvation. Two of their older sib-
lings, Berthold and Burchard, already were serving in the Prussian
army, and Gustav had entered the Danish army as an ensign that
same year. Krackevitz considered service in Mecklenburg's army
for the two teens, especially because Siegfried already attended the
Pageninstitut at Schwerin. But to avoid provoking further invasions by Prussian forces, Duke Frederick II of Mecklenburg sought
to limit the size of his military establishment and thus froze commissions. With Rügen being a Swedish possession, the choice for
the Blüchers remained obvious, but Krackevitz cautioned his young
brothers-in-law against becoming hussars.[13]

Insufficient light cavalry had hindered Swedish operations during the campaign of 1757. To increase these numbers, the Swedes
attempted to hire Russian Cossacks and Hungarian hussars. In addition, two of Rügen's nobles sought to raise two hussar squadrons of
one hundred troopers each by the end of April 1758. As the recruit-
ers made their rounds, Gebhard and Siegfried could not resist the
promise of adventure. Krackevitz finally gave in. Despite the continued objections of his parents, Gebhard enrolled as a cornet in
Sparre's Svenska hussarregementet at age fifteen.[14]

After the Prussians lifted the blockade of Stralsund in June
1758 and marched to confront the Russians in East Prussia, Cornet
Blücher's regiment ventured forth along with the rest of the
Swedish army. Having little information on Blücher himself during this campaign, we can only relate the major events. After establishing a line that extended one hundred miles from Pasewalk to

Treptow-am-Riga (Trzebiatów), the Swedish commander, General Gustav David Hamilton, finally ordered an advance southeast toward Berlin on 11 September. On reaching Neuruppin, only forty-two miles northwest of the capital, Hamilton learned of the return of Prussian forces from East Prussia following another successful defense of that province. After ordering the army to turn around, Hamilton resigned on 23 November. His successor, General Jacob Albrecht von Lantingshausen, retreated back to Stralsund in early 1759, pursued by the Prussians. Another Russian invasion of East Prussia in May 1759 took the pressure off the Swedes, but again they lacked the funds to immediately begin a campaign.[15]

With 15,000 men, Lantingshausen finally marched into Prussian Pomerania on 21 August, hoping to take Stettin. After detaching 4,000 men to drive the small Prussian garrisons from the islands of Usedom and Wollin at the mouth of the Oder River, he led the rest of his forces to the Uckermark district north of Berlin.[16] Believing he would not find any Prussian troops there, Lantingshausen unexpectedly encountered militia commanded by a retired Prussian officer, a Major Stülpnagel. Forced by the Swedes to evacuate Pasewalk and Torgelow on 1 September, Stülpnagel turned around on the following morning to surprise them at Pasewalk, where young Blücher's squadron passed the night. After sustaining 200 killed, wounded, and captured, the Swedes retreated. "That man," Blücher later expressed, "hit us Swedes hard at Pasewalk, where I was almost taken captive."[17]

King Frederick II then permitted General Heinrich von Manteuffel to form a few battalions from convalescents and assigned to him a small force commanded by Colonel Wilhelm Sebastian von Belling consisting of two infantry battalions, five squadrons of the 8th Belling Hussar Regiment, and five dragoon squadrons totaling 4,500 men. By the end of October 1759, Manteuffel had pushed Lantingshausen's army back to Swedish Pomerania. On 20 January 1760 Manteuffel commenced an offensive across the frozen Peene River—the border between Swedish and Prussian Pomerania—with some 10,000 men, prompting Lantingshausen to counter with 15,000 troops. On 23 January he stopped the Prussian advance at Züssow, some thirty miles southeast of Stralsund. After camping on the icy battlefield, lack of adequate winter gear forced the Prussians to withdraw nine miles southeast the next day to the village of Ziethen, though they still held the suburbs north of the Peene at Peenedamm. During the night of 27–28 January, the Swedes surprised Manteuffel's post at Anklam. The general was wounded and captured during the engagement. During the fighting, Cornet Blücher received a foot wound courtesy of the Belling Hussars. Despite Lantingshausen's success, lack of supply and funds prevented him from capitalizing. Thus, the situation at the river remained quiet until August, when the Swedish commander pushed south with 16,000 men. His adversary, General Otto Ludwig von Jung-Stutterheim, commanded approximately 6,000 soldiers for the defense of the Peene.[18]

After seven months and with his foot healed, Blücher looked forward to his third campaign. On 17 August Swedish forces crossed the Peene and advanced on Demmin, driving the Prussians thirty miles east toward the border of Pomerania and Mecklenburg. On 27 August Sparre's regiment led the Swedish advance guard to the Kavelpaß, prompting the Prussians to withdraw south toward Friedland. Two days later, on the twenty-ninth, Blücher participated in a reconnaissance mission through the pass to Friedland, where they encountered the Belling Hussars, likewise reconnoitering.[19] After a sharp contest, the Swedes drove the Prussians into a defile but inflicted few casualties. Yet after the Swedes broke off the skirmish and began the return ride to the Kavelpaß, the Prussians pursued them. The chase continued through the pass and then two and one-half miles northeast toward Boldekow. Near that village, the Prussians surrounded young Blücher. He defended himself as best he could, but his wounded and rearing horse threw him off. One Prussian trooper, purportedly Sergeant Siegfried Landeck, grabbed the slender teen and hoisted him onto his horse, purportedly stating: "You dam'd little tenderfoot, you come along and fight for us!"[20] The official report of the skirmish made to Frederick by General Joachim Friedrich von Stutterheim stated the day's catch to be ten prisoners, including one French lieutenant and one Swedish ensign—Blücher.[21]

Today the Blücherstein, a boulder roughly seventeen feet long, thirteen feet wide, and eleven feet high located near Boldekow in the Vorpommern-Greifswald district, commemorates the spot where the Prussians captured Blücher. Although the field marshal's descendants in the early twentieth-century credited Landeck as the captor, some uncertainty surrounded his actual identity during Blücher's lifetime. According to the German historian Friedrich

Wigger: "Later, after several including Landeck, Pfennig, and others claimed the credit for capturing the future Prussian field-marshal, it became difficult to determine who the lucky one was because Blücher himself could no longer remember the name of his 'solo captor.' Anyone who claimed to be so received an invitation to dine with General Blücher or presents from him, for while it might not have been the actual Hussar who captured him, it was still an old Hussar. When Siegfried Landeck, the one most insistent with his claim, retired in old age, he received a private pension from the General himself."[22] According to Bieske, Blücher always credited Landeck with his capture. Landeck served in the regiment until he retired in 1798, having earned a gold service medal during the Rhine campaigns. In 1808, forty-nine years after capturing the young Blücher, he stopped at the general's headquarters in Pomerania. Blücher invited the old veteran to stay for dinner, giving him the seat of honor at the table. During the dinner, he referred to Landeck as the trooper who had single-handedly captured him. From 1798 until 1814, Landeck worked as an estate manager at Gramenz near Neu-Stettin in Pomerania. After the estate changed hands in 1814, he retired for good, supported in part by a six-thaler-per-month pension from Blücher. Following Landeck's death, the field marshal supported his widow with four thalers each month.[23]

Awe inspiring, the Belling Hussars, or "Der Ganze Tod (Death)" Hussars, wore buff-colored trousers with black *Schalavary* (over-trousers) edged green, black dolmans with collars and cuffs of black-edged green velvet—the cuffs sporting a green chevron—accented by yellow buttons and twelve green braids, and a black pelisse slung over the left shoulder trimmed with black fur, twelve rows of green braids, and yellow buttons. They adorned their black mirliton with white cords, knots, and tassels, decorating the front with the image of a full skeleton reclining and holding a scythe in its right hand and having its left elbow leaning on an hourglass to thus prop it up. Under the blade of the scythe was the regiment's motto, "Vincere Avt Mori (Victory or Death)."[24] Like the uniform, the regiment's commander, Colonel Belling, was larger than life. At age forty-three, Belling already had twenty-nine years of service in the Prussian army under his belt.[25] He purportedly prayed for insubordinate officers, rode to battle singing hymns, and in times of peace called on the Almighty: "Thou seest, dear Heavenly Father, the sad plight of thee servant Belling. Grant him soon a nice little war so

The Total Death Hussar insignia.

that he may better his condition and continue to praise thy name. Amen."[26] Belling's personality combined openness and trust with piety, devotion to duty, and a commitment to honor.

Landeck led his young captive to the colonel's headquarters at the estate of Galenbeck. Belling took a liking to the eighteen-year-old. No doubt he looked even more favorably on Blücher after learning that the young Mecklenburger in Swedish service was the brother-in-law of Hans von Krackevitz, a close relation of Belling's wife. Thus, he encouraged the prisoner to change sides and join his hussar squadron. At that time, Belling considered forming a second hussar battalion and so mentioned to Blücher that a promotion would quickly follow his transfer to Prussian service.[27] He also questioned him over his loyalty to Sweden, wanting to know why he felt bound to the Swedish service. He asked if the young man's loyalty was worth a long imprisonment. Blücher hesitated, but so confident was Belling that on the next day he wrote to King Frederick suggesting that "Ensign von Blücher," who he did not characterize as a prisoner of war, be commissioned as a cornet in the Prussian service.

Although changing service from one state to another was common practice for both officers and soldiers in eighteenth-century Europe, the strong-willed Blücher placed conditions on his transfer. First, he sought to resign from Swedish service and "exchange" himself by having Belling release a captured Swedish officer. Second, he sought his father's permission. Less than one month later, these conditions were met, and Blücher exchanged his Swedish uniform for that of the Belling Hussars. On 20 September 1760 he received a royal-cabinet order commissioning him as a cornet in the Prussian army.[28] According to the November 1760 *Rangliste* of the Belling Hussars, the seventeen-year-old Blücher stands out as the youngest of the regiment's five cornets; two twenty-three-year-olds came next.[29]

Belling became quite a mentor to the young man. "From that time on," Blücher once expressed, "the unforgettable Belling was a true father to me and loved me so unconditionally that it took the real effort of youthful escapades to provoke his anger."[30] Later in life, in Blücher's darkest hours, he could always be cheered by recalling his days with Belling. The colonel helped him attain the accoutrements necessary for a junior officer of the hussars: the brilliant uniform, fur-lined pelisse, and saber. Belling instinctively knew how to win over and curb young Blücher's impetuous disposition, impressing on him the idea that discipline formed the core of all military efficiency. He stressed the absolute necessity of training and developing each individual soldier. Lastly, he provided him an excellent model of a military leader coping with difficult circumstances and insufficient resources. After the cornet proved himself, the colonel made him his adjutant, sharing with him his plans, views, and thoughts. Much of Blücher's future leadership style—a mixture of paternalism, piety, and ferocity—can be traced to Belling.[31]

Blücher participated in the ensuing campaign against the Swedes. On 6 September 1760 the Swedes reached Prenzlau. Stutterheim ordered a general retreat, leaving the enemy in possession of the Uckermark to live off the land at Prussia's expense. Frederick relieved Stutterheim of his command on 25 September, appointing Duke Frederick Eugene of Württemberg in his place. In addition, a Prussian force commanded by General Hans Paul von Werner would advance west from Stettin to attack Lantingshausen's rear. Although an Austro-Russian raid on Berlin prevented Frederick Eugene from participating, Werner attacked the Swedish position at Pasewalk on 2 October. Despite being repulsed twice and then returning to Stettin, Werner's operation caused Lantingshausen to withdraw from Prenzlau to Pasewalk. After learning that the Austrians and Russians had withdrawn from Berlin, the Swedish commander decided to retreat north across the Peene in mid-October, eventually returning to Swedish Pomerania.

With only five hussar squadrons, ninety dragoons, and two infantry battalions, Belling cautiously followed all the way to Blücher's home of Rostock. Frederick redeployed both Werner and Duke Frederick Eugene, thus leaving only Belling's 900 infantry and 600 cavalry to guard Prussia's northern frontier west of the Oder and collect requisitions from the now-neutral Mecklenburg duchies. At their expense, the Prussians spent a cozy winter and spring.[32] In this last regard, Blücher, the native Mecklenburger, returned to his homeland. Having to view his former country-men as the enemy supposedly pained him so much that he refused to execute orders. Although the gentry shunned the Prussians, Blücher joined his young cousin Helmuth von Blücher at Suckow and formed a circle of friends with several other noble landowners.[33]

Neither side launched an offensive during the winter of 1760–61. During this time, Belling raised the second battalion of his regiment, likewise consisting of five hussar squadrons. In the spring of 1761, he started organizing a third. Blücher himself served in the 1st Battalion, commanded by Major Johann von Podscharly. With the expansion of the regiment, promotions steadily came for Blücher just as Belling had promised. On 4 January 1761, he became an eighteen-year-old second lieutenant, reaching first lieu-tenant on 4 July.[34] He also had the good fortune of serving with family.[35] Two of his mother's cousins, Captain Berthold Hans von Zülow and Lieutenant Claus Ferdinand von Zülow, received pro-motions and posts in the 2nd Battalion as major and captain respec-tively. Unfortunately for Blücher, sorrow eclipsed this pleasantry. On 18 June 1761 his father died at age sixty-five while the son was home on leave.

Meanwhile, after Lantingshausen resigned in June 1761, his successor, General Augustin Ehrensvärd, managed to assemble 14,000 men and launch an offensive to drive the Prussians from Mecklenburg in July. Although Stutterheim returned to the the-ater with 1,600 men from the army of the king's younger brother, Prince Henry, the Swedes slowly drove back Belling's outnumbered forces in minor engagements over the course of two months. Despite this success, Ehrensvärd ran out of steam and returned to Swedish Pomerania in October. Two months later he commenced a winter campaign in response to Prussian incursions deeper into Mecklenburg. Less than fifty miles south of Stralsund, a Swedish force under Jacob Magnus Sprengtporten drove the Prussians from Malchin and occupied the neighboring *Schloß* (manor) of Basedow on 22 December. On the following day, Belling's counterattack on the Schloß failed. According to an unsubstantiated story, Blücher purportedly set the farmhouse ablaze by wantonly firing his pistol at its dry thatched roof.

Belling and Stutterheim simply did not have the numbers to stop Ehrensvärd. Fortunately for the Prussians, Frederick Eugene arrived on 26 December with several detachments of regulars, increasing Prussian troop strength to 5,000 men.[36] With Sprengtporten isolated at Malchin, Belling attacked one week later on New Year's Eve, but the Swedes again held their position. Seeking to break through to Malchin, Ehrensvärd moved south. On 2 January 1762 his advance guard repulsed Belling seven miles north of Malchin at Neukalen and opened the road to Sprengtporten's forces. Instead of exploiting his victory, Ehrensvärd ordered a general retreat to Swedish Pomerania, leaving Mecklenburg to Belling. Nothing more occurred in that theater until the Swedish commander proposed an armistice, which the Prussians accepted on 7 April 1762.[37]

The following month Belling's troops moved to Saxony to join Prince Henry's army—Blücher again missed the opportunity and honor of fighting under the direct supervision of King Frederick. Regardless, he found several opportunities to shine. Assigned to the wing of Henry's army commanded by the famed cavalry commander General Friedrich Wilhelm von Seydlitz, Belling's troopers helped drive Austro-German forces toward the Bavarian frontier. During an engagement at Auerbach, Blücher's platoon captured five hundred prisoners. Based on this success, he led sixty hussars on an incursion into Austrian territory at the beginning of September as part of the "small nuisance raids" launched by Henry.[38] Not far from Libkowitz (Libkovice), itself less than thirty miles north of Prague, an Austrian force of two hundred hussars attacked him. Despite being outnumbered, Blücher repulsed three assaults, taking thirty prisoners.

Recalled to Henry's main body, Blücher arrived in time to participate in the 29 October 1762 battle of Freiberg, twenty-two miles southwest of the Saxon capital Dresden, that pitted 22,000 Prussians against 29,000 Austrians and Germans. Although numerous redoubts and abatis protected the front of the enemy position, its right flank was "in the air" and thus vulnerable. Henry planned to exploit this oversight by fixing the Austrians with a small detachment while his main force outflanked and crushed the Germans of the Reichsarmee (imperial army)—the forces provided by the states of the Holy Roman Empire. While the Germans showed more skill and the Austrians provided more resistance than Henry expected, a timely attack by Stutterheim breached the enemy line. Belling's hussars and other Prussian cavalry units charged through, breaking the defending infantry and precipitating their general retreat. Henry sustained 1,400 casualties, while the Austrians and Germans lost 7,400 men, including 4,000 dead, and twenty-eight guns. This victory proved to be the last major engagement of the Seven Years War.[39]

Unfortunately for Blücher, he could not participate in the pursuit after the battle. A cannonball smashed through a building close to him, sending a shard of wood deep into one of his feet. He went to the Saxon city Leipzig to convalesce. Blücher remained in the Prussian service after the signing of the Treaty of Hubertusburg on 15 February 1763 ended the war. Afterward, Belling's hussars mainly quartered in Prussian Pomerania at Stolp (Słupsk) and the surrounding region. They exchanged their black uniforms for the red (oxblood) of the former Gersdorf Regiment. Demobilization led to reductions that shrank the regiment to two battalions. Fortunately for Blücher, he remained at Stolp with Belling, the regimental staff, and four squadrons.[40]

Now a general major, Belling continued to instruct his officers over the fear of God, piety, and the necessity of strictly performing their duty. Regardless of this preaching, peacetime garrison life provided many idle hours, and Blücher had no interest in passing them by praying or studying the art of war. Nor did he show any inclination to increase his chances for promotion other than through seniority. "In my youth," he once admitted, "I cared for nothing except having fun; instead of studying, I gambled, drank, caroused with the ladies, hunted, and pulled hilarious pranks on my friends. That is why I now know nothing. Indeed, otherwise I would be a very different chap!"[41] Although receiving no subsidy from home, being short on cash did not limit Blücher's pursuit of pleasure nor curb his vanity. In fact, for some time, he chose to live quite poorly rather than forsake his vices. Despite his meager salary, he could not resist a beautiful horse, taking pride in distinguishing himself through a majestic steed. In social situations his humor, wit, and fine manners carried him through when his wallet came up short.[42]

Except when on active duty, Blücher did not provide a shining example of discipline. All evidence points to an extremely wild, impulsive, and carefree junior officer. Nevertheless, Belling appreciated his personality, especially his cheerful and saucy nature. That Blücher's pistol sat very loose in its holster reminded him of his own youthful duels in the defense of honor; Belling numbered among the officers who still loved the *Mensur* (the distance between duelists). But one day Blücher overstepped his bounds, responding to the general's fatherly admonitions with arrogant, open defiance. Consequently, the wise master found it necessary to separate from his young apprentice before lasting damage could be done to their relationship. Belling sent him back to his squadron at Bütow, likewise the 1st Battalion's headquarters. Its commander, Major Podscharly, had a well-deserved reputation for being a stern disciplinarian.[43] This shot across Blücher's bow helped the young officer mature. By his own admission, he enjoyed a comfortable relationship with Podscharly, who considerably advanced the future field marshal's development as an officer.[44]

Lieutenant Blücher spent seven years enduring the monotony of garrison life, which was only broken by the annual exercises before the king near Stargard (Szczeciński) or by visiting his relatives. Not all the trips home proved to be pleasant. While two of his brothers married during this time, his sister Margarete died in 1766, and his mother passed on 6 January 1769.[45] Blücher's loving and thoughtful disposition toward his own children suggests that the passing of his parents aggrieved him considerably. Yet these personal setbacks and those that followed did not appear to influence his religiosity. Not strictly religious nor interested in the confessional debate between the Christian denominations, he harbored a suspicion of the clergy in general and rarely attended public service. The Bible always served as the source of his faith and the sustenance of his religious life. His experiences on the journey through life only reinforced and strengthened this conviction.[46]

Outside of Prussia, Russia went to war with the Ottoman Empire in 1768 in a conflict known as the Russo-Turkish War

(1768–74). After several victories, the Russians secured the Danubian provinces of Moldavia and Wallachia. Such expansion alarmed the Austrians, who considered the Balkans their sphere of influence. Not only did Vienna target the Balkans for future expansion but also considered Moldavia, which bordered Austrian territory, vital to its national security. In Prussia King Frederick likewise grew concerned over Russia's success and the resulting effect on the balance of power in eastern Europe. To compensate for Russia's expansion in the Balkans, he secretly negotiated with Vienna for both Austria and Prussia to take territory from Poland, itself weakened by internal strife between the pro-Russian King Stanisław August Poniatowski and his nobility. To make matters worse for the Poles, Russian troops occupied districts in eastern Poland.

Prussian forces massed in Pomerania, poised to add the Polish-controlled province of West Prussia to the kingdom.[47] In late 1770 the Belling Hussars took quarters at Deutsch-Krone (Wałcz) and Konitz (Chojnice), with Blücher at the former. To avoid Russian suspicion, the troops claimed to be taking measures to prevent the bubonic-plague epidemic of 1770–72 from reaching Prussia.[48] Originating in the Moldovan theater of the Russo-Turkish War in January 1770, the epidemic had swept northward through Ukraine and Russia and into Poland before the end of the year. This was the last massive outbreak of the plague in eastern Europe, claiming between 50,000 and 100,000 lives just at Moscow, where the epidemic peaked in September 1771. With the disease raging in some Polish provinces, Frederick conveniently found pretext to have his army close his eastern border. Moreover, from 1769 to 1771, the Prussians incorporated the Polish border region of Lande Lauenburg und Bütow (Ziemia lęborsko-bytowska) in eastern Pomerania, while Austrian forces moved into the county of Szepes (Spisz) in northern Hungary.[49]

Blücher saw action thanks to internal unrest in Poland. In 1768 Polish nobles opposed to King Stanislaus and his pro-Russian policy united at the fortress of Bar in Podolia to defend their nation's internal and external independence. Known as the Bar Confederation, its creation led to a civil war. Not only did the rebels engage the king's forces but they also attacked Prussian and Russian forces whenever the opportunity arose. According to Blücher, "when the Polish disturbance started, a troop of 300 men, so called rebels, moved to the Pomeranian border; I was in charge of guarding the border with 40

Hussars. During a patrol, I encountered the enemy at Schneidemühl [Żerdno]. Because they advanced toward me, I attacked. Despite their great advantage, I punished them, taking four so-called captains and eighty men prisoner." In accordance with Prussian policy, the lieutenant sent them to Küstrin (Kostrzyn) for fourteen days of internment. Following their incarceration, thirty-eight men capable of service went to Berlin to be processed into the Prussian army. During the next revue at Stargard, Frederick declared his "highest satisfaction" with Blücher's conduct and recognized him as an "efficient officer." Blücher later boasted that "Generals Belling and Lölhöffel told all the other officers."[50] His next promotion came on 3 March 1771, when he made *Stabsrittmeister* (staff captain), an intermediate post between first lieutenant and *Rittmeister*, likewise a captain but designating a squadron commander.[51]

Despite the animosity between the Prussians and the Polish nobles, Blücher made the acquaintance of the local gentry, at least those who would talk to him. He soon met Franz Leopold von Mehling, who joined the Belling Hussars as a cornet after they recruited in his hometown of Pottlitz (Potulice). Becoming friends, Franz brought Blücher home to meet his family. His father, Baron Friedrich Wilhelm von Mehling, the son of a former Saxon-army captain, owned estates in West Prussia between Flatow (Złotów) and Preussisch Friedland (Debrzno) not far from the border with Pomerania. To Blücher, this wealthy man seemed different than the other nobles in the region. Although a former colonel in the Polish army, Baron von Mehling did not disguise his preference for Prussian rather than Polish rule. As soon as the Belling Hussars arrived, he forced Franz to enroll. His wife, Ernestine Bojanowska, the daughter of the Polish governor of Gniezno, Ernest Wilhelm Bojanowski, harbored no enmity toward the Prussians, perhaps because her mother was Prussian. The Mehlings made Blücher feel welcome in their home, so much so that he fell in love with their beautiful young daughter Karoline.[52]

Continued unrest in Poland prompted Frederick to advance his troops from the border districts deeper into the country. Belling led a division of hussars—his own 8th Regiment as well as another— south to the region of Posen (Poznańska) and occupied Kalisch (Kalisz). Blücher reluctantly said farewell to the Mehlings and joined his troop. Violence increased, and a bloody guerilla war with accompanying reprisals ensued. With a partition appearing imminent, the Poles' hatred toward the occupation forces increased tenfold. Raids, assassinations, and open combat spread. The situation vexed King Frederick. Wanting to win the support of his new subjects, he demanded restraint by his troops.

In February or March 1772, the Poles attacked one of Blücher's posts, torturing the Prussians to death purportedly with scorn. Enraged at the sight of his comrades' mutilated bodies, the officer swore bloody revenge. Although he could not prove it, Blücher arrested a priest suspected of being the instigator of these atrocities. To extort a confession, he held a mock trial. Blücher condemned the priest, sentencing him to be executed by firing squad. The Prussians dug a pit and blindfolded the clergyman. Blücher gave the order to fire, but the executioners had received only powder and no lead. Regardless, the unfortunate priest fainted and then fell seriously ill, purportedly due to this maltreatment.[53]

Meanwhile, after continued Russian success in the Balkans, Austria threatened war. To prevent a general conflagration that would certainly include Prussia, Frederick suggested a general partition of Poland by all three powers. In return for Polish territory, the Russians agreed to evacuate Moldavia. In February 1772 the Prussians, Russians, and Austrians concluded their negotiations, signing treaties at Saint Petersburg on the sixth and Vienna on the nineteenth. Known in history as the First Partition of Poland, Prussian, Austrian, and Russian troops moved into their zones of occupation in early August. Despite being massively outnumbered, the forces of the Bar Confederation controlled some of Poland's key fortresses and refused to submit. Regardless, the Russians broke the confederates by December, exiling some 5,000 men, women, and children to Siberia.

News of Blücher's treatment of the priest eventually reached Frederick, but he initially made light of the case. Yet after complaints from Polish officials over this incident and other excesses committed by the regiment increased, he summoned Belling to make an official report. Although the general's statements concerning the priest satisfied Frederick, the crotchety king believed other allegations claiming that officers of the regiment committed extortion and other acts of dishonesty. He recalled Belling from the field and transferred command of the hussar division to General Daniel Friedrich von Lossow with orders to treat the Poles better.[54]

Lossow's command style differed significantly from that of Belling, and the hussars did not like the restrictions he imposed on their conduct toward the inhabitants, especially because the Poles continued to commit atrocities. Lossow did not much like Blücher but did task the captain with purchasing a horse that caught his eye. The transaction began with the parties agreeing to the sale price of fifty gold pieces. Blücher randomly mentioned that the buyer was actually General Lossow. Upon hearing that the buyer was a Prussian general, the seller demanded one hundred gold pieces for the steed. Blücher abruptly terminated the negotiations but, in so doing, earned the general's ire for failing to acquire the horse.[55]

To further punish the Belling Hussars for their alleged crimes, Frederick ordered his inspector of the Pomeranian cavalry, General Friedrich Wilhelm Lölhöffel von Löwensprung, to produce a list of officers to cashier. After Lölhöffel failed to find any officers guilty of the supposed infractions, the king demanded a list of officers who had "participated in plundering or extorting, and similar vile acts in Poland." Either unable or unwilling to find officers guilty of these charges, Lölhöffel suggested that the task be delegated to Lossow. Frederick agreed but harbored a grudge against the 8th Regiment, possibly due to the political headaches it had caused him with the Poles. He passed over its commander, Major August von der Schulenburg, as well as several other officers for promotion. In September 1772 Schulenburg petitioned the king for promotion to lieutenant colonel. Frederick responded by scribbling in the margin of the document: "This regiment has done nothing in Poland but loot and disgrace the army. He is to blame for its negligence and disorder, and if he does not restore order I will appoint another commander rather than promote him."[56]

Captain Blücher likewise did not escape the king's wrath. Now the senior staff captain in the 8th Regiment, he became eligible to receive command of a squadron. In addition, he had enough time served to be promoted to major. As luck had it, the squadron commanded by his cousin needed a new commander after Major Zülow, who had succeeded Podscharly some years back, received a requested discharge on 10 October 1772. Most believed that Blücher would fill the vacancy. Being Zülow's cousin increased the captain's confidence that he would receive command of the squadron.

Committed to marrying Karoline von Mehling, he counted on the promotion to improve his standard of living.[57] Despite Blücher's seniority in the regiment, Frederick passed him over and appointed First Lieutenant Georg Wilhelm von Jägersfeld (1725–97) from the Czettritz Regiment.[58] Aside from Blücher, Jägersfeld jumped over five majors and two other staff captains in the 8th Regiment. Not only did the king deny Blücher command of the squadron but also refused to promote him to major.

At age forty-four, Jägersfeld was both considerably older than the twenty-nine-year-old Mecklenburger and had served three years longer. His promotion impelled an outraged Blücher to complain directly to Frederick. Insisting that Jägersfeld received the promotion only because he was the bastard son of Margrave Frederick William of Brandenburg-Schwedt, the captain requested a discharge.[59] While some historians assert that the disrespectful language in this complaint landed Blücher in jail for nine months, purportedly to give him time to cool off and come to his senses, the documentary evidence does not exist.[60] The summary of a cabinet meeting held on 31 October 1772 states: "Staff Captain Blücher of the Belling Hussars humbly requests a discharge because he was passed over by First Lieutenant Jägersfeld for the vacancy in the Zülow squadron and, convinced of his own irreproachable conduct, the pain caused by this is intolerable." Suggesting that the slight was not personal but instead an indictment of the 8th Regiment in general, Frederick responded by writing in the margin of this summary that the regiment consisted not of hussars but gypsies, none of whom deserved promotion.[61] On Christmas Day 1772 Lölhöffel informed Blücher that the king had released him from service.[62]

Furthermore, in January 1773 Lossow produced his list, and Blücher's name was on it. Titled "Generalliste der pommerschen Kavallerie-Inspektion für Januar 1773," the document records Blücher as "cashiered." Upon receiving the list, Frederick uttered his famous declaration that Blücher "can go to the devil," which appears to be more a sign of the king's confirmation of his fate rather than a personal attack.[63] In the end, the irascible Frederick called Blücher's bluff. The captain requested a discharge, and a discharge he received. Yet this was not an ordinary dismissal. Being cashiered meant that Blücher received a dishonorable discharge. Not only did he lose the honor of wearing his uniform in public, but he also had to surrender his uniform altogether. With no other choice, Blücher reluctantly left the army on 3 February 1773.[64] Believing Lossow had railroaded him, he did request a formal hearing. On 13 February the king's secretary reported that Staff Captain Blücher, "cashiered because of imputed excesses," requested an investigation of his case and outright dismissal. Although Frederick never accused him of an actual crime, he allowed the request to go unfulfilled.[65]

Dishonorably discharged from the army at age thirty, Blücher probably could have found a place in the Danish service through his brother Gustav, a royal chamberlain, or his cousin Karl von Blücher, a colonel in the Danish army. Instead, it appeared that he wanted to hang his hussar saber on the wall for good. Accompanied by Franz von Mehling, he returned to Pottlitz in search of a new career as well as a wife; one complemented the other. Baron Mehling did not view Blücher's discharge as reason to prevent him from marrying Karoline. Consequently, a Protestant minister married Blücher and the seventeen-year-old Baroness Mehling at her family's estate in Pottlitz on 21 June 1773, the summer solstice.[66]

The newlyweds lived with the Mehlings for the next eleven months. Although having learned little from Krackwitz, Blücher decided to join the ranks of the minor landed gentry. Baron Mehling provided his son-in-law sound financial and agrarian advice. To begin his career, Blücher leased two farms from him on 1 July 1774. He and Karoline moved to the first, located at Gresonse (Stare Dzierzążno), four miles north of Flatow; the second farm, Stewnitz (Stawnica), was less than two miles southeast of Gresonse. In three years Blücher accumulated enough cash to purchase the estate of Groß Raddow (Radowo Wielkie) in Pomerania, thirty-five miles northeast of Stargard, on 28 August 1777 for 14,500 thaler.[67] "I was put in the utmost happy circumstances because of my marriage to the Colonel Baron von Mehling's daughter from West Prussia so that I was able to buy land and I have no worries about my subsistence," he recalled.[68]

Joy and sorrow visited the Blüchers in rapid succession. Karoline gave birth to a son on 30 April 1774, Ernst Friedrich Gustav von Blücher. Unfortunately, he died in infancy, as did her next two children, both boys, Wilhelm and Friedrich. Their next two children, again both boys, survived infancy: Bernhard Franz Joachim, born on 10 February 1778, and Georg Ludwig, born on 3 March 1780. Although Karoline gave birth to five sons, only Franz and Georg accompanied their parents to Groß Raddow. Despite his rough exterior and vices, Blücher proved to be a most loving father and husband.

Blücher's success as an estate owner continued, but the conquests of the plow meant little to a warrior who lived for conquests of the sword. After Prussia declared war on Austria in the War of Bavarian Succession (July 1778–May 1779), Blücher realized what he had to do. On 9 June 1778 he petitioned Frederick to return to the service: "Please Your Royal Highness, please recall me to your cavalry as a major. I can count on the testimony of all my superiors, but mostly on that of General Belling, that I used my sword only in honor of the King and that I did my duty on every occasion; hence, I graciously request with the deepest devotion to be Your Royal Highness's obedient servant."[69] An answer never came.

Not only did Blücher itch to grasp the saber but he also became bored with the monotonous life of a country gentleman. Fortunately, business trips to Stargard and Stettin provided a distraction for his restless spirit. For Blücher, social activity was a necessity. At Stargard and Stettin, he often came into contact with army officers. Such encounters always sharpened the pain and embarrassment he felt over being a civilian, an outsider no longer accepted in such circles. To avoid this anguish yet quench his thirst for human interaction, Blücher started attending Stargard's Augusta zur goldenen Krone Freemason Lodge, becoming a master on 6 February 1782.[70] Joining the Freemasons did not signal Blücher's interest in secret societies or speculative theories. In fact, he remained distant from the rationalist and humanist currents of the German Enlightenment that reigned at the lodge. To him, it served as a place to socialize with educated people, but the emphasis remained on socializing. For this reason, Blücher attended the local lodge wherever he took an extended stay. He especially liked to give speeches and talks on festive occasions. According to the German renaissance man Johann Wolfgang von Goethe, Blücher developed his superb oratory skills in the lodges of the Freemasons.[71]

Blücher continued to farm, but he made an attempt to clear his name on 15 January 1782. To erase the dishonorable discharge, he requested reinstatement as a major, upon which he would resign. "Because of my enthusiasm for Your Royal Majesty's supreme authority," he wrote to the king, "I left the Swedish army. By following this impulse, I moved my money from my Fatherland [Mecklenburg] and purchased the estate on which I reside here in

Pomerania. I count myself among Your Royal Highness's numerous happy subjects. Your Royal Highness, please grant me the opportunity to resign as a major."[72]

After receiving no response, Blücher again wrote on 2 May: "Merciful King, I realize and regret the mistake I made when I asked Your Highness for my retirement in 1773! Temper justice with mercy, graceful monarch! If I cannot have the good fortune of serving Your Highness, please let me resign as a major, so I am no longer deeply afflicted by the unfortunate thought that I have an unmerciful king."[73] This time he received a curt response from Frederick: "Why did you leave the service? It is your own fault."[74] Undaunted, Blücher responded by giving the cantankerous monarch a choice: either reinstate him in the army or repeal the dishonorable discharge with the promise that he could again serve in the event of war. In a memo dated 13 August 1783, Blücher wrote:

> Because of the bravery I displayed at every opportunity during the Seven Years War, I enjoyed the favor of my commanders, the confidence of the staff officers, and the affection of my comrades and subordinates. On every occasion, I showed my zeal for the service; I looked for opportunities and acted ambitiously—my regiment can testify to this. I served out of ambition and loyalty. None will surpass me in eagerness and bravery.
>
> In the company of two of my brothers, I, as a foreigner, devoted myself to Your Royal Highness's service—those two companions [Berthold and Burchard] lost their lives on the battlefield as able officers. I am the unfortunate survivor of this little group. My fate has made me jealous of my brothers. . . . Allow me, Your Royal Majesty, to end my days the same way my brothers did: in the service. If it pleases Your Royal Majesty to have me serve only during a time of war, please bestow on me the rank of major . . . and allow me to wear the uniform of the cavalry.[75]

"That is nothing," snapped Frederick in response.[76] Two months later Blücher attempted another tactic: "Almightiest King: illness kept me away from the service, I never retired; my health has recovered and my eagerness to serve is most fiery."[77] The years passed, and still Blücher received no positive reply. It does not appear that Frederick disliked him personally, but he simply did not believe the future Prussian field marshal possessed the attributes of an officer. In fact, Frederick granted him a loan of 9,950 thaler at 1-percent interest for the improvement of Groß Raddow in 1783. Encouraged by the loan, Blücher again made his plea. "Merciful King," he wrote on 7 July," make me the happiest man alive; you have the evidence in front of you that I served well and that my character justifies the rank of major and allows me to wear the uniform of the cavalry so that when necessary, I can count myself among the group that proudly would guard the Fatherland. I fade away."[78] He finally received a response on 30 July: should Prussia find itself at war, or should new regiments be raised, the king would reinstate him.[79]

Although a victory, Blücher pressed for more. "Merciful King!" he wrote that November, "the idleness in which I live is like martyrdom—I am respectfully requesting to either do something in the military or civil service. Teachable I am not, effort and honesty I pride myself with. As a foreigner, I served faithfully for eighteen years. During the Seven Years War, I exchanged health and fortune for shot up limbs. Through bravery, I gained the confidence of my superiors—bad luck for me that I did not serve directly under my King, who can pardon and reward, but not disown."[80] Blücher requested a position in the Pomeranian Forestry Department. Although this letter went unanswered, he became active in the Stargard Bureau of the Pomeranian Department of Agriculture, which his neighbor Philipp Carl von Borck presided over. Due to his "reliability and zeal," Borck appointed him to the honorary post of deputy to the department's board. Blücher gained a reputation for having a sharp eye and fast mind. Once during a general meeting of committees at Stettin with the king's representative, Großkanzler (Grand Chancellor) Johann Heinrich von Carmer, Blücher gave a verbal report noted for its circumspection and clarity.[81]

A letter to Frederick's nephew and heir, Crown Prince Frederick William, gained Blücher the future king's condolences. Yet he perceived an opportunity in the Netherlands when an opposition group called the Dutch Patriots challenged the power of their ruler, Stadtholder William V, Prince of Orange. Receiving considerable support from the Dutch middle class, the Patriots formed a militia called the Free Corps. In an effort to oust pro-government officials, the Patriots took military action in several cities. The Free Corps eventually became strong enough to challenge William's troops. Dynastic ties between Prussia and the Netherlands made service in the Dutch army attractive to Prussian officers. William was married to Wilhelmina of Prussia, Frederick's niece and the sister of

Crown Prince Frederick William. The strong-willed Wilhelmina provided the leadership for the pro-government faction. As violence escalated in the Netherlands, many Prussian officers left the service to join the Dutch army. Blücher attempted to use this to his advantage. In January 1785 he requested Frederick's permission to likewise enter the Dutch service. "Age and energy pressure me to serve," he wrote in his typical dramatic style, "the idleness in which I live is making me a martyr." He again asked to be allowed to resign from the Prussian army as a major so he could secure the same rank with the Dutch. He promised that if Frederick mobilized the Prussian army, he would leave the Dutch service and return.[82]

Ten days later Blücher again took up his quill, apparently to refute a response that has been lost but rejected his request to go to the Netherlands as a former Prussian major. Moreover, it appears Frederick told the former officer he had no one else to blame but himself. "Merciful Lord!" replied Blücher, "I would be the unhappiest man in the world had I left your service out of foolishness." Rather than his own rash actions, he again blamed illness for the events of 1772: "No, Merciful King, back then all of Pomerania knew about my poor health and I even had given up all hope of ever fully recovering." He explained that he wanted to join the Dutch army "to show at the first opportunity my bravery and then to beg at the feet of my King for readmission to the Army. All Merciful King, take this opportunity to restore my seniority!" Blücher pointed out that he had few options except foreign service if Frederick continued to reject him. "For a man of honor," he continued, "just the thought that there is nothing I can do for myself and my family is as much martyrdom as it is shameful. Not one of your native servants can or will ever serve with more eagerness than me, a foreigner. I am not driven by hardship or selfishness: true affection and reverence move me. I am dying."[83]

Later that year, 1785, Blücher learned that Frederick planned to expand the army. He immediately reminded the king of his earlier assertion to reinstate him if the army expanded: "As your servant, I request to be assigned according to this promise. I am dying."[84] Despite the theatrics, Blücher was very much alive. Karoline again conceived, giving birth to a daughter, Bernhardine Friederike—affectionately called Fritze by her father—on 4 March 1786. Blücher loved all of his children, but by his own admission, Fritze was his favorite.[85]

News of Frederick's illness brought Blücher no joy. He often lamented that his chance of being reinstated actually would dwindle after the great king passed. On learning that the childless Frederick had died on 17 August 1786, Blücher petitioned his nephew and successor, Frederick William II, "to end thirteen years of excruciating inactivity" by reinstating him at the rank of major. He also traveled to Berlin to speak with General Hans Rudolf von Bischoffwerder, who knew him well from his prior service, as well as Prince Frederick Auguste, duke of York and Albany.[86] A response that his petition would be considered did not satisfy Blücher. Instead, he decided on a bold gamble. With the new king planning to stop at nearby Stargard on his return trip from the royal coronation at Königsberg, Blücher planned to state his case in person. His friend, District Director Otto Friedrich Fürchtegott von Bonin, helped his cause by securing the advocacy of the district government.

On 25 September 1786 Blücher rode in front of the royal carriage on a beautiful horse. In green ceremonial attire with white collar and gold shoulder straps, he attracted Frederick William's attention. As the king pulled into his quarters in the suburb of Stargard, there stood Blücher waiting for him. He secured an audience with the new sovereign, made his request, and received the desired assurances.[87] Blücher immediately left Groß Raddow and rode to Berlin, but no post could be found for him. After 1786 gave way to the new year, a vacant position still could not be found. Spending a small fortune on living a posh lifestyle and still looking to impress anyone and everyone with his beautiful horses, Blücher passed the entire winter at Berlin without any positive result. For assistance, Blücher pressed his connections: Bischoffwerder and the duke of York. Finally, papers arrived on 23 March 1787 reinstating Blücher as a major and squadron commander in his old regiment, the 8th Hussars, now called the Red Hussars but still commanded by Schulenburg, now a general.

At forty-four, the age when most officers retired from the service if their financial assets permitted, Blücher received a second chance and returned to the army. "The King has fulfilled our wishes," wrote Blücher's wife, "my husband has regained his seniority." With the promotion backdated to 14 April 1779, Blücher now outranked Major Jägersfeld.[88] It is certainly a great irony that the officer who Frederick the Great did not consider worthy enough to be a major in his army would later attain the rank of Prussian field marshal and play such a decisive role in liberating Prussia from Napoleon's control.

Blücher's squadron contained 150 men and horses, one staff captain, two lieutenants, and one cornet. At that time, the squadron chief's name rather than a number designated the squadron. Indicative of the cosmopolitan characteristic of premodern European armies, Blücher Squadron consisted of sixty-three native Prussians and eighty-seven nonnatives, including eleven Saxons, six Mecklenburgers, five Poles, three soldiers each from Anhalt and Danzig (Gdansk), two Hungarians, and one man each from Hesse, Brunswick, Swabia, Alsace, Bohemia, Sweden, and Italy.[89] Mounts came from Ukraine; the long trek to Pomerania served to train the animals for extensive journeys.

Blücher took command right at the beginning of annual exercises in mid-April, when soldiers on furlough returned. The squadron assembled at the Pomeranian town of Rummelsburg (Miastko), eighty miles east of Groß Raddow. Morning work concentrated on individual training: riding, jumping, and swordplay, with emphasis on perfecting blows to the head. Riding by platoons and ranks in good order over long distances came next. In the afternoon the troopers practiced various maneuvers on foot. Maintenance of the horses and equipment filled the rest of the day and continued well into the night. The *Hussar Regulations*, dated 1743, was based largely on the drills used by the dragoons and cuirassiers. Since then, the Prussians had increased the size of their hussar squadrons to match the strength of dragoon and cuirassier squadrons, but that is where the similarities ended. The 1743 regulations also neglected the exercises performed during the regimental review, including volley firing, mounting and dismounting, individual riding, and unit maneuvers such as wheeling, charging, and reforming. After just two weeks of training, Blücher Squadron left Rummelsburg to join the rest of the regiment for review and exercises thirty-five miles north at Stolp.

With the squadrons widely dispersed in small garrisons for most of the year, the exercises provided an opportunity for the officers to bond. During his time away from the army, Blücher had maintained contact with some of his former comrades, especially because many passed through Groß Raddow to and from the annual review. At Stolp he reunited with seventeen other officers he had served with during the reign of Frederick the Great. After Schulenberg, only one colonel and one lieutenant colonel stood ahead of Blücher in seniority; the other squadron commanders (six majors, including Jägersfeld) followed. Indicative of the ossification that slowly froze the Prussian army in time, at forty-four years old, Blücher was the youngest of the squadron commanders. Following the controversy in Poland, the officers of the Red Hussars worked diligently to restore their regiment's reputation. In fact, in three consecutive years (1786, 1787, and 1788), three of its officers received promotion and command of other regiments in the army.

Illness prevented Schulenburg from participating in the 1787 exercises. Remaining on his estate near Stargard, he eventually died in June from edema (dropsy). Colonel Karl Friedrich von der Goltz, the former commander of the Light Blue Hussars, filled the vacancy. During the Seven Years War, Goltz served in the *Freikorps* (volunteer militia) commanded by Colonel Friedrich Wilhelm von Kleist, known as "the Green" because most of his cavalry and infantry units wore green coats. Goltz saw considerable action raiding Bohemia and gained a thorough understanding of the role of the hussars as well as partisan operations, known at that time as *der kleine Krieg* or *la petite guerre*.

At the end of May, the Red Hussars left Stolp and rode 150 miles in eleven days to Stargard, where they united with the other Pomeranian regiments for a royal review. Frederick William II maintained his uncle's tradition of holding the annual Pomeranian review from 2 to 5 June. Following this event, Blücher Squadron returned to Rummelsburg. Most of the native Prussian soldiers went on furlough, reducing the unit to seventy-seven sabers. During this quiet time, Blücher moved his wife and three children (Franz, Georg, and Fritze) to join the other 1,300 inhabitants of Rummelsburg. With Karoline again pregnant, unrest in the Netherlands shortened their time together.

After the Dutch Patriots engineered a general revolution, Wilhelmina requested military support from her brother, Frederick William II. Prussian forces—twenty-five battalions and twenty-five squadrons commanded by Field Marshal Duke Charles William of Brunswick—entered the Netherlands in September 1787. In addition, one battalion of the Red Hussars, commanded by Colonel Friedrich Eberhard von Göckingk, likewise went west. Blücher received orders to have his squadron ready to move out in twelve days as part of Göckingk's battalion. His duties included recalling his furloughed troopers and obtaining horses for the chuck wagons, pack horses for the officers and the squadron's equipment, nags for the surgeons and farriers, and replacements for retired mounts.

On 10 August 1787 Blücher Squadron departed Rummelsburg to embark on a 540-mile journey through Schwedt, Berlin, Magdeburg, and Minden to Lingen on the Dutch frontier. The troopers averaged eighteen miles per day to cover the stretch in thirty-seven days, including five for rest. On 18 September the battalion crossed the Dutch frontier. Meanwhile, Brunswick's army had crossed the border seventy-five miles to the southwest at Emmerich on the thirteenth. From there, the Prussians advanced along a broad front toward Amsterdam. Together with a small British force, Brunswick drove through the outnumbered rebels to reach Amsterdam on 1 October. After pacifying that city, the Prussians restored William to his throne at The Hague.

Meanwhile, Göckingk's battalion occupied Upper-Ijssel Province with instructions to observe suspected rebels in the Dutch cities of Kampen, Zwolle, and Deventer as well as to secure Brunswick's line of communication. Commanding two squadrons, Blücher first went to subdue Deventer, the scene of much antigovernment violence.[90] In particular, he was to monitor one of the suspected ringleaders of the Patriot movement. With his calm and humor, he executed this order purportedly by drinking a glass of beer and coolly smoking his clay pipe with the suspect at one of Deventer's inns. Believing the man to be relatively harmless, Blücher gained his trust as well as his pledge to end the violence. After a few days of these meetings, the two purportedly raised their glasses as friends.[91] Throughout the city, small hussar patrols disarmed the people.

From Deventer, Blücher moved north to Zwolle, but the Prussian police action ended in October. All of Brunswick's troops, including Göckingk's battalion, withdrew to Kleve; only one hundred hussars remained in the Netherlands at Hertogenbosch for the winter. In the beginning of December 1787, the rest of the battalion marched home, celebrating Christmas between Hildesheim and Brunswick. Blücher's troopers averaged only twenty miles per day, taking forty-three days, including eighteen for rest, to reach Pomerania. Although four horses came up lame, his squadron did not lose a single man in the operation.[92]

A grateful William insisted that the Dutch government pay the traditional winter bonus: every company and squadron commander received five hundred thaler, junior officers fifty, noncommissioned officers ten, and every soldier three. All generals and staff officers received a medal embossed with the image of the Duke of Brunswick. Frederick William presented these on orange ribbons during a celebration. The financial gains of the campaign did not satisfy Blücher's deep pockets, nor did policing rebels quench his thirst for combat. Yet the journey west brought him to new lands, thus broadening and enlightening his perspective.

Blücher returned to Rummelsburg on 1 February 1788. Karoline greeted him with their third son, born on 15 December 1787 and baptized Gebhard Leberecht. Unfortunately, the birth had been difficult, and she remained sick and weak for more than a year. Her condition worsened in the summer of 1788, when their eight-year-old son, Georg, fell ill and died on 14 June. Despite this tragedy, the Blüchers enjoyed their years at Rummelsburg. They established friendships with the town's bourgeoisie, becoming especially close to the mayor, Wittcke, and his family. Blücher gambled at card games, speculated on land, and loved to hunt. In 1789 he sold Groß Raddow for 24,000 thaler. In the following year he sold the rest of his land, making Rummelsburg his permanent home.[93]

Per tradition, the regiment conducted its annual exercise at Stolp in May, followed by the royal review at Stargard in early June. According to new regulations for the event, the regiment approached the king in a line of three ranks. Dismounting, the troopers then walked forward in four platoons two lines deep; officers and noncommissioned officers continued a few steps farther on the right. After the king walked along the front observing the men, his adjutant shouted the command "recruits present arms." This applied to all those who had joined the service after the last review or had been promoted to noncommissioned officer. Native Prussians stood to the right, foreigners to the left. At this time also occurred the discharge of soldiers considered invalids. After all of this took place, food was served. While the new soldiers ate, the king inspected the "veteran" troopers and finally the horses. During the following days, the Red Hussars joined two dragoon regiments and one of cuirassiers to form a cavalry wing and conduct maneuvers with the infantry against an invisible enemy.

Blücher's performance earned him promotion to lieutenant colonel on 3 June 1788 as well as an invitation to observe the great annual fall maneuvers at Berlin. Taking place on 17–18 September, the revue featured the fifteen battalions, eleven and one-half squadrons, and six horse batteries of the Berlin garrison, commanded by General Wichard Joachim von Möllendorf. On the first day Frederick William reviewed the troops. On the second day Möllendorf divided his units for a mock battle. After returning to Rummelsburg, Blücher spent the winter of 1788–89 complying with a general directive to recruit native Prussians to form a reserve pool for the squadron. He also devoted much time to the training of his unit's young horses.

Blücher's efforts appeared to pay off. As a result of his performance in the Pomeranian review of 1789, Frederick William awarded him the Pour le Mérite, Prussia's highest military order, and invited him to the annual fall maneuvers at Potsdam. Held on 21–23 September, the exercises featured the Potsdam garrison, reinforced by other troops, conducting rehearsed maneuvers under the king and Möllendorf before a large crowd. In the evening most of the officers received free tickets to attend a comedy at the Potsdam theater. On the last evening, all officers received invitations to the elegant New Palace. The magnificence of the palace overwhelmed some of the guests from poor noble families. Blücher probably numbered among them.[94] Promotion to full colonel came on 20 August 1790 as well as the appointment to command the regiment's 2nd Battalion, but his duties essentially remained the same as those of a squadron commander.[95]

Meanwhile, war had erupted in the east between the Ottoman Empire and an alliance of Austria and Russia. After the 1780 death of the Austrian ruler, Maria Theresa, her son and successor, Holy Roman Emperor and Archduke of Austria Joseph II, sought to make common cause with the Russians concerning both states' mutual interest in expanding at the expense of the Ottomans. At the court of Tsarina Catherine II, a pro-Austrian party eclipsed the pro-Prussian faction, leading to a shift in international partners. Consequently, Catherine and Joseph signed agreements in May and June 1781 to create an Austro-Russian alliance. Although Prussia officially remained Russia's nominal ally until 1788, the signing of the Austro-Russian accords left the Prussians isolated.

Joseph struck first, initiating the Austro-Turkish War of 1787–91. In 1788, following Catherine's visit to the Crimea, the Ottomans declared against Russia, thus starting the Russo-Turkish War of 1787–92. Initially successful on the Austrian front, reverses at the hands of the Russians sent Sultan Selim III scrambling for allies. After turning to Frederick William for support, Prussian and Turkish officials signed an alliance on 31 January 1790. This came right as Austria suffered internal unrest as opposition to Habsburg rule flared across Hungary and Belgium. The Prussians threatened to support rebels in the latter, known at that time as the Austrian Netherlands. According to the diplomatic practice of the period, when one major power expanded, the others sought and received compensation. In this case, with Russian and Austrian forces making substantial gains at Ottoman expense, the Prussians demanded a piece of the action.

Frederick William did not intend to fight Austria and Russia but instead hoped to capitalize on their distraction by forcing the former to make humiliating concessions and by adding more Polish territory to Prussia, ostensibly as compensation for the latter's recent gains in Moldavia and the Crimea.[96] On 29 March Frederick William forced a mutual defensive alliance—the Polish-Prussian Pact of 1790—on King Stanislaw II Augustus of Poland that awarded Prussia control of the fortified town of Thorn (Toruń) on the Vistula (Wisła) River and the great port city of Danzig on the Baltic Sea.[97] To force the Austrians and Russians to accept this new arrangement, Frederick William mobilized the Prussian army. He personally commanded three "corps" in Silesia along the Austrian frontier, while a fourth assembled at Königsberg (Kaliningrad) in East Prussia and a fifth in West Prussia.[98] The Red Hussars received orders to join the king's army in the Silesian county of Glatz (Kłodzko). In July the regiment proceeded southeast along the northern face of the Silesian Mountains separating Prussia from Austrian-controlled Bohemia.

Meanwhile, Austrian and Prussian diplomats met at Reichenbach (Dzierżoniów) to reach a settlement. After Leopold II succeeded his brother, Joseph II, in February 1790, Austrian foreign affairs took a turn. Beset by problems in Belgium and Hungary as well as the threat posed to his sister, Queen Marie Antoinette, after the outbreak of the French Revolution, Leopold sought a peaceful solution to Austria's latest row with Prussia. On 27 July he pulled a coup by securing Frederick William's signature on the Convention of Reichenbach. Although the agreement compelled the Austrians to return the vast majority of the gains they made in their war with the Ottomans and to renounce their support of Russia, the adroit Leopold gained the time he needed to restore Austrian control over his domains. In turn, Reichenbach precipitated the Treaty of Sistova (4 August 1791) ending the Austro-Turkish War. Less than six months later, the Russians ended their war with the Ottomans by signing the Treaty of Jassy (9 January 1792).

Although consenting to Reichenbach, Frederick William found the wind taken from his sails. Agreeing not to support the rebels in Belgium and renouncing his intentions to expand eastward, his bold attempt to capitalize on Austria's distractions flopped, leaving the king looking foolish. Moreover, Leopold actually turned the tables and secured Frederick William as his ally when the two jointly issued the Declaration of Pillnitz on 27 August 1791, warning the French revolutionaries to respect the authority of King Louis XVI. Many observers noted the degree to which Leopold II outmaneuvered the Prussian king.

As for Blücher's regiment, after the Convention of Reichenbach defused the situation with Austria, the unit moved north along the Polish frontier in anticipation of confronting the Russians. The hussars passed the winter of 1790–91 quartered at Hohensalza (Inowrocław), some 110 miles southeast of Blücher's home at Rummelsburg. In the spring of 1791, he led his cavalry battalion to Danzig, while the other battalion moved to Königsberg in East Prussia. At his quarters in Schönsee (Jeziernik), Blücher learned that Karoline died on 17 June at age thirty-five, purportedly due to complications from Gebhard's birth.

We know little of his reaction, other than Friedrich Wigger's assertion that the news devastated Blücher. Franz, Gebhard, and Fritze lived with the Wittckes until the fall, when the lieutenant colonel returned home. Karoline had named Blücher her heir, but he renounced the inheritance himself in favor of his children. After their maternal grandparents, the Mehlings, died, Franz, Fritze, and Gebhard received considerable assets. By the end of 1791, Blücher was already looking for a new wife to raise his children. He courted his much sought-after niece, the daughter of his brother Gustav, but she did not return his feelings. Unable to find a wife to maintain his household, he decided to separate the children. He took his oldest son, Franz, with him to serve as a cornet in the Red Hussars, but Gebhard and Fritze went to live with the Mehlings on their estate of Schönwalde.[99]

In the following year, 1792, Prussia and Austria officially declared their support for King Louis XVI of France. Besieged by revolution since 1789, Louis made an attempt to flee to his eastern-frontier fortresses in June 1791 to unite with an Austrian army that would be provided by his wife's brother, Leopold II. The failed flight unraveled what little trust the people had in their king. Saber rattling ensued between Vienna and Paris as the plight of the French monarchs worsened. Curiously, the various political factions in the new parliament that assembled in Paris in the fall of 1791 all reached the same conclusion: each could achieve its agenda through war. Consequently, France declared war on Austria in April 1792. Frederick William immediately sided with Austria's new ruler, Francis II, who had succeeded his late father, Leopold II. The German powers agreed to invade France.

Much to Blücher's dissatisfaction, his regiment did not receive marching orders. As with Frederick the Great, he did not hesitate to write direct to Frederick William:

> Right from the beginning of Your Royal Majesty's glorious reign, I threw myself at your mercy and requested reinstatement in the army. Your Royal Majesty listened to me. Should, however, the Goltz Hussar Regiment, in which I currently serve, not receive marching orders, I shall embrace your royal knees one more time and full of gratitude I will request that I not be excluded from the troops going on campaign. I am healthy, Merciful King, but the thought of sitting idle while others sacrifice themselves for their King might kill me. First of all, no one shows more zeal and loyalty for the sacred person of my King. I am dying in the deepest submission. Your Royal Majesty's most obedient servant.[100]

This letter did nothing to change the situation. Blücher remained behind as Prussian forces mobilized. In the summer of 1792, the Duke of Brunswick again led the army west, crossing the Rhine River at Koblenz. Encountering little resistance, the Prussians drove through northeastern France, taking the fortresses of Longwy on 23 August and Verdun on 2 September. Nothing stood between Brunswick and Paris. Yet on 19 September two French armies united behind him. With his lifeline to Germany thus cut, Brunswick turned his command of 34,000 men and fifty-four guns around and marched east. The next day he encountered the French at Valmy. Aside from the bad weather, many of Brunswick's troops suffered from dysentery as a result of gorging themselves on unripe apples in the Argonne Forest. Mainly through a long-range artillery duel, the French kept their adversary at bay for most of the ensuing Battle of Valmy. After a half-hearted Prussian advance faltered, the whole French line moved forward. This convinced Brunswick to concede the field after losing only 200 men. Giving the French a wide birth, he did not halt until his army moved across the Rhine. The French had saved their revolution.

Known as the War of the First Coalition, the conflict expanded when Great Britain, the Netherlands, Spain, Naples, Portugal, the Holy Roman Empire, and most of the Italian states joined the war against France either voluntarily or as a result of Paris declaring war on them. After gaining much success in 1793, the Allies suffered numerous setbacks in 1794, including the loss of Belgium and the left bank of the Rhine. French success can be attributed to the *levée en masse*, which conscripted hundreds of thousands of men to form an army of unprecedented size. While the French deserve credit for their miraculous turnaround, the Allies shoulder much blame for their own failures. Although military cooperation between the various national forces remained adequate, the explanation for defeat lies in their inability to sacrifice goals of national self-interest in favor of the common objective of defeating France. No other state best exemplified this than Prussia.

CHAPTER 2

THE RED KING

In the fall of 1792, the Prussians prepared to reinforce their army for another invasion of France. Several regiments received marching orders, the Red Hussars among them. Blücher left Rummelsburg on 28 November, reaching Berlin on 18 December. There, Goltz received orders from now Field Marshal Möllendorf to send his own 1st Battalion to the Netherlands, while Blücher's 2nd Battalion would join Brunswick, the king, and the main army for the campaign in France.[1] Because Blücher was second in command of the regiment, the colonel needed to remain with General Goltz and the regimental staff to provide for a smooth transition if necessary. Consequently, Goltz had to transfer Blücher and his squadron to the 1st Battalion for the campaign in the Netherlands. Again missing an opportunity to fight in the presence of his king, and thus viewing it as an affront to his honor, Blücher again grabbed his quill.

> All Merciful King! Already now for four years Your Royal Majesty has entrusted to me the command of the 2nd Battalion of the Goltz Hussar Regiment and I have always pleased you. At this moment, when the battalion marches to a campaign, I have lost [the command]. Nothing else in this world, Merciful King, has made me more disheartened than Your Royal Majesty's disgrace; I am anxious and can find no rest. Life is a burden. With God as my witness, I served Your Royal Majesty with keen diligence. All Merciful King, don't destroy an innocent man. Everyone here looks at me like I am a royal outcast. . . . Deeply afflicted with sorrow, I request on behalf of myself and my battalion, that Your Royal Majesty extend your mercy upon me. I pray to God that I will have the opportunity in the forthcoming campaign to show His Royal Majesty that I am not unworthy. I am dying in deepest servitude to be your Royal Majesty's most obedient servant.[2]

As with Blücher's epistles to Frederick, this letter to Frederick William II did not change his situation. After spending the holidays in the capital, 1st Battalion departed for the Rhine on 12

January 1793. Blücher proceeded through Magdeburg, Wolfenbüttel, Hildesheim, and Wesel to cross the Dutch frontier at Venlo.[3] He kept a journal throughout the war, which friends helped him publish in January 1796 under the title *Blücher's Kampagne Journal der Jahre 1793 und 1794*. Received with acclaim, a second printing took place in Schleswig before year's end. In 1797 the work was added to the official list of officer reading material issued by Berlin.[4]

At the end of February 1793, 1st Battalion joined a small corps commanded by Brunswick's younger brother, Duke Frederick Augustus.[5] The Prussians moved west to support Duke Frederick Josias of Saxe-Coburg's Austrian army of 77,000 men. In the wake of their victory at Valmy, the French had not only overrun the Rhineland and captured Mainz but had taken Belgium as well. For the campaign of 1793, Saxe-Coburg received the task of driving French forces—estimated to be 100,000 strong—from Belgium in conjunction with British, Hanoverian, German, and Dutch troops (altogether 32,000 men) as well as Duke Frederick's small Prussian contingent of 8,000 men.[6] On the Rhine front, Brunswick's army of 99,000 men presumably would retake Mainz and push the enemy out of the Rhineland and into France proper. As for the French, on 16 February General Charles François Dumouriez, the conqueror of Belgium, led his Army of the North out of Antwerp to invade the Netherlands. After crossing the Dutch frontier and taking Breda, his offensive stalled thanks to a series of Austrian victories. Failure often meant the arrest and execution of the defeated French general by the national razor in Paris—the guillotine—but Dumouriez managed to keep both his head and his command.

Personal animosity and disagreements over strategy with Saxe-Coburg prompted Duke Frederick to resign his command on the pretext of ill health.[7] To replace him, Frederick William appointed seventy-year-old General Alexander Friedrich von Knobelsdorf, a Prussian officer since 1741. Until Knobelsdorf arrived, the Prussians remained in the Netherlands. Consequently, they missed Saxe-Coburg's victory over Dumouriez at the 18 March 1793 battle of Neerwinden, which forced the French to withdraw from Belgium. While in the Netherlands, Blücher led several raids on enemy posts, demonstrating his fitness for command. After Knobelsdorf arrived, the Prussians marched to join Coalition forces in Flanders.

Fearing the guillotine, Dumouriez defected to the Allies in early April. General Augustin-Marie Picot de Dampierre then received command of French forces in the Flanders theater: the Army of the North and the Army of the Ardennes. Although the Allies could have smashed through Dampierre's demoralized and ill-supplied troops, Saxe-Coburg opted to advance along the Scheldt River and take the French border fortresses of Condé and Valenciennes as the prelude to an operation against Dunkirk demanded by the British.[8] Spurred on by the radical revolutionary government in Paris, Dampierre attempted a counterstroke eight miles west of Condé at Saint-Amand on 19 April, but the Allies managed to fill the gap between their forces and repulse the French. Following this engagement, Saxe-Coburg ordered Knobelsdorf's 8,000 men to occupy a thirty-mile line extending northwest to southeast from Menen to Saint-Amand, with the French fortress of Lille in the center.[9]

Although Blücher did not participate in a general battle, he engaged in almost daily outpost skirmishes, taking advantage of the opportunity to train his junior officers. On 6 May the French conducted demonstrations along the length of the Prussian line. On the seventh they attacked Saint-Amand; Blücher camped with three squadrons in a village just southwest of the town. To slow the enemy advance, he received orders to strike the French left flank with one infantry battalion, two hussar squadrons, and two guns. Blücher succeeded in driving off the French, but they returned the next day in even greater numbers to relieve Condé. Fortunately for the Prussians, the Duke of York arrived with some British battalions to support Knobelsdorf's line. During the day's fighting, Dampierre received a mortal wound; General François Joseph Lamarche assumed command. On the ninth the French attacked again, and Blücher repeated the same maneuver as on the seventh. With troops broken and demoralized by the loss of Dampierre, Lamarche withdrew into the fortress of Valenciennes and the fortified camp of Famars some four miles to the south.

After no further attacks occurred, Saxe-Coburg struck Famars as the prelude to a siege of Valenciennes. While the twenty-six-year-old Duke of York spearheaded the assault on Famars with his fresh British and Hanoverian troops, the Prussians crossed the Scarpe River to attack a French position at Hasnon, twelve miles northwest of Famars and a few miles south of Saint-Amand. The first attempt to dislodge the French from Hasnon's strong abbey misfired on 23 May. Reinforced by Dutch howitzers, Knobelsdorf resumed the attack the following day, but the defenders had abandoned the position during the night. Knobelsdorf immediately commenced a pursuit with the troops on hand but soon found himself preempted by Blücher, whose hussars already had ridden six miles west to reach and occupy Marchiennes. There, the colonel received command of the Prussian advance guard, while Knobelsdorf remained at Hasnon with the main body. Meanwhile, Saxe-Coburg's attack on the twenty-third misfired after the Duke of York delayed his assault on the French center, thus allowing the enemy to escape in the night. Instead of pursuing, Saxe-Coburg continued his plan to invest Valenciennes. This allowed the enemy to regroup at the entrenched position known as Caesar's Camp near Bouchain, eleven miles downriver from the fortress.[10]

Although the French received General Adam Custine, the conqueror of the Rhineland in 1792, as their new commander, stalemate ensued. Eventually, Saxe-Coburg decided to pull back almost to the line from which he commenced the counteroffensive. Blücher received the task of observing the French posts north of Douai and Lille. With the enemy close at hand, several sharp skirmishes occurred, particularly that of 4 June 1793. On that day the Prussians captured fifteen officers and twenty-six soldiers. Shortly after, one of the officers, a Colonel Monjout, died of his wounds at Goltz's headquarters. The Prussians brought the corpse to the nearest village and hired a carpenter to make a coffin. After burying Monjout with military honors, Blücher berated the carpenter in front of the French inhabitants for a poorly crafted coffin.[11]

On the request of William of Orange, who operated in the Tourcoing sector northwest of the Prussians, the entire Allied army shifted west on 7 June to better guard northern Flanders. Knobelsdorf's Prussians moved into a camp at Bouvines, eight miles southwest of Lille. Blücher continued his tasks of outpost skirmishing, patrolling, and raiding. After Goltz received a mortal wound on 4 July, Knobelsdorf placed all Prussian outposts under Blücher's command.[12] To avenge the general, who died on 13 August, Blücher led a raid involving 300 troopers and 660 infantry on 25 July.[13] At the town of Sainghin-en-Mélantois near the current Franco-Belgium border, the Prussians netted forty horses and one hundred prisoners. The raids continued through the first half of August.[14]

Both Condé and Valenciennes held out until July, surrendering on the tenth and twenty-eighth respectively. Paris looked darkly on this turn of events, rejecting Custine's excuses and summoning him to the capital for a national shave. With the fall of the two fortresses, the road to Paris lay open to the Allies. Custine's successor as commander of the 30,000 demoralized and disorganized soldiers of the Army of the North, the Scottish-born general Charles Edward Jennings de Kilmaine, failed to rally his forces. On 7 and 8 August, Allied pressure forced him to abandon Caesar's Camp. Saxe-Coburg could not have wished for a better situation. A concerted drive on Paris could have ended the war. At this moment, which proved nearly as fateful as Valmy did eleven months earlier, the members of the Coalition succumbed to pursuing their own national objectives as opposed to the general goal of defeating the French. London instructed the Duke of York to separate from Saxe-Coburg and commence the operation to take Dunkirk. The Prussians withdrew from the theater altogether after Knobelsdorf received orders to move his troops southeast to join Brunswick's main army in the Rhineland.[15] In view of the reduction of his forces, Saxe-Coburg settled on besieging Le Quesnoy, which finally surrendered in mid-September.

The Prussians moved out of their place in the line on 23 August 1793, replaced by the Hanoverians. After spending three days at Saint-Amand, they passed Valenciennes on 26 August and on 10 September Arlon, where the Prussians met a small Austrian corps commanded by General Johann Gottfried von Schröder. While marching through Luxembourg on 12 September, they learned that from their position at Rodemack, the French attacked the Austrian outpost chain some seven miles south of the city of Luxembourg. Blücher received the task of relieving the Austrians. With three squadrons already exhausted from the day's march, he and his troopers rode another ninety minutes. Attacking the main body of the French infantry at Frisange, the Prussians and Austrians drove off the enemy. According to Blücher's account, they inflicted 500 casualties on the French and captured five officers, 110 men, and forty-two horses. The colonel received a flattering letter from Saxe-Coburg thanking him.[16]

Continuing their march eastward, Knobelsdorf's troops passed Grevenmacher on 18 September and crossed the Moselle River. Four days later they united with the right wing of Brunswick's army under General Friedrich Adolf von Kalckreuth at St. Wendel on 22 September. Knobelsdorf's troops moved ten miles farther south in hilly, wooded terrain to the region of Neunkirchen. Once again Blücher commanded the outpost chain.[17]

For seven weeks, Brunswick's right wing remained idle behind the Saar River facing the French Army of the Moselle, commanded by General Lazare Hoche. In the meantime, the Prussian commander sought to pressure the left flank of the French Army of the Rhine with his own left wing of ten battalions, fifteen squadrons, and one and one-half horse batteries. After the Austrians drove the Army of the Rhine back onto Strasbourg, Brunswick advanced southwest through the narrow valleys of the Haardt hill chain at the northern end of the Vosges Mountains, detaching forces under Crown Prince Frederick William to invest and bombard Landau. Conversely, Hoche crossed the Saar River on 17 November, resolving to attack Kalckreuth and Knobelsdorf. But Brunswick already decided to winter his army along a sixty-mile stretch extending from Lauterecken in the north through Kaiserslautern to Wissembourg, which required his right wing to fall back some thirty miles westward. Brunswick ordered Kalckreuth and Knobelsdorf to commence their marches during the night of 16–17 November.

Initially, Knobelsdorf's retreat to the region of St. Ingbert progressed smoothly. But during the course of the 17 November, a strong French detachment from Hoche's left wing likewise advanced on St. Ingbert, forcing Knobelsdorf's column to retreat fifteen miles northeast across the Blies rivulet to Waldmohr during the night of 17–18 November. Blücher himself accompanied General Franz Otto von Pirch's column, which withdrew through the valley of the Sulzbach stream. After French cavalry harassed Blücher's posts, the colonel himself struck out and personally captured an enemy trooper. From him he learned that the French intended to continue their advance. Pirch and Knobelsdorf united at Waldmohr, with Blücher commanding the rear guard. After crossing the Blies, he established his posts near Bexbach on the hills east of the rivulet and secured communication with Kalckreuth's column at Homburg, six miles to the southeast.[18] Eight miles south of Homburg, Brunswick reached the Zweibrücken–Pirmasens region with his army's left wing. He intended to hold this position for several days before continuing the retrograde movement to his winter quarters.

The French followed as far as the line of the Blies. On the nineteenth they drove two Red Hussar squadrons from Ottweiler and pushed south to Neunkirchen, less than four miles west of Blücher's outposts near Bexbach. Upon hearing gunfire from the direction of Ottweiler, the colonel hurried there, ordering the retreating squadrons to move east instead of south and thus remain a threat to the advancing enemy's left. This led to a surprise attack near St. Wendel, where the Prussians captured twelve prisoners and fourteen horses without losing a single man. Based on information provided by these captives, Blücher reported to Knobelsdorf and Kalckreuth that a French force of approximately 10,000 men camped in the valley of the upper Blies. On 20 November a combined-arms detachment attacked Blücher's position; he withdrew from the hills to open terrain where his cavalry could operate, but the French did not follow. Supported by units of Kalckreuth's cavalry, Blücher held his position during the night of 20–21 November.[19]

At this point in his advance, Hoche ordered a halt, thus allowing the Prussians to withdraw and unite at Kaiserslautern on 25 November. During the march, Blücher commanded Knobelsdorf's rear guard. After arriving in town, he received the task of providing right-flank coverage from Altenglan, eighteen miles to the northwest. On the twenty-fifth Brunswick ordered him to conduct a small diversion against the left of the enemy forces steadily approaching Kaiserslautern. From Altenglan, Blücher led his cavalry battalion three miles west through Kusel and then rode eleven miles south to Schönenberg. There, the Prussians encountered and dispersed a French patrol, netting eight prisoners, including the commanding sergeant, who Blücher claimed to have captured personally.[20]

After passing the night of 25–26 November at Schönenberg, Blücher continued three miles southwest to Waldmohr, where he spotted a French force preparing to ambush him. Striking before the French expected, the hussars took some prisoners, including a staff officer. But before Blucher could escape with his prizes, the French attacked from every direction, purportedly. Misunderstanding the colonel's orders, the commander of the Prussian advance-guard platoon charged the enemy. Fortunately for that unit, the French hesitated, giving Blücher enough time to redress the situation and commence the retreat to Waldmohr. At a point where the road narrowed and curved, he turned his cavalry to face the pursuing French. Unable to use their superior numbers because of the slight width of the road, the enemy withdrew from Waldmohr, leaving seven troopers and twenty horses in Prussian hands.

Despite this success, Blücher recognized that the odds did not favor him. Outnumbered and far from any support, he formed his battalion into two lines and slowly withdrew toward Schönenberg.

After clearing this village, the Prussian rear guard came under attack by the pursuing French. Blücher claims that having anticipated this move, he concealed a few platoons behind the outlaying houses where the terrain most suited cavalry action. With this support in place, he charged the enemy, taking more prisoners and forcing the French to fall back. Halfway to Kusel, Blücher's hussars repulsed one last French attack, convincing the enemy that these horsemen were not worth the trouble. Without losing a single trooper, the battalion returned to Altenglan with sixteen prisoners and forty-eight horses.[21]

After Blücher reported the presence of strong French forces at Waldmohr, Brunswick became concerned over his supply depot at Lauterecken, eleven miles northeast of Altenglan. To ensure its safety, he directed not only Blücher's cavalry battalion but also two infantry regiments, the Leib Cuirassier Regiment, and one battery—all commanded by General Ernst Christian von Kospoth—to Lauterecken on 27 November. Had Blücher remained in contact with the enemy south of Kusel, he would have observed that Hoche did not order his left to continue northeast toward the depot but instead turned it directly eastward. Nevertheless, Blücher's raid did have a positive influence on the upcoming battle at Kaiserslautern, causing Hoche's left-wing commander, General Jean-Jacques Ambert, to have concern over the army's left flank.[22] Therefore, instead of enveloping Brunswick's right, Ambert remained close to Hoche and the French center. At Lauterecken Blücher missed participating in Brunswick's 28–30 November 1793 victory nineteen miles to the south at Kaiserslautern. Still, he provided useful service, securing the evacuation of supplies by pushing his squadrons into the valleys of the Lauter and the Glan.

Hoche planned a three-pronged assault on Brunswick's position around Kaiserslautern. With the left wing, Ambert would attack from the north, while Hoche with the center approached from the northwest, and the right wing, under General Alexandre-Camille Taponier, closed from the west. On 28 November Ambert advanced to Otterbach, where his division crossed the Lauter and attacked Brunswick's right under Kalckreuth. After the French made initial progress, the Prussians drove them back across the Lauter. Meanwhile, Hoche led his men through the thick woods west of Kaiserslautern but failed to cross the stream. Taponier's men did not arrive in time to affect the battle.

Alarmed on the twenty-eighth by reports of French forces (Ambert's division) advancing between Lauterecken and Brunswick's main position, Blücher led two squadrons up (south) the Lauter halfway to Kaiserslautern. After posting these units, the colonel himself rushed back to Lauterecken to convince Kospoth that remaining in his current position served no purpose. Agreeing, the general authorized Blücher to assemble his battalion at Schallodenbach, ten miles north of Kaiserslautern, that same night. Kospoth and the remaining troops joined him on the twenty-ninth.[23]

On that day Hoche managed to get across the Lauter, but Ambert failed to move his division into a position to envelop Brunswick's right. Consequently, Hoche's attack degenerated into a frontal assault that the Prussians repulsed. Taponier again did little with the army's right wing. Hoche's position completely separated Blücher and Kospoth from Brunswick's army, but they had the advantage of being behind the French army. At dawn on 30 November, the French resumed the battle with a fierce cannonade. From their post, Blücher and Kospoth observed the assault unfold. Both Ambert and Hoche moved across the Lauter for a joint attack on Brunswick's position west of Kaiserslautern. To assist the main army, Blücher led his four squadrons through the woods north of Kaiserslautern against Ambert's division; Kospoth followed with his ad-hoc brigade. Before either could engage, Kalckreuth repulsed Ambert, and withering artillery fire forced Hoche to retreat. On his right Taponier encountered the fresh troops of Brunswick's left and likewise withdrew.

Seeing Ambert's retreat, Blücher requested that Kospoth reinforce him with two cuirassier squadrons. Before they could arrive, though, he observed a larger French cavalry force at Sambach, less than five miles north of Kaiserslautern. With enemy batteries lining the hills on the opposite bank of the Lauter, Blücher wanted to engage the French troopers before they came under the protection of their guns. In his journal he claims that he knew he could not expect to succeed against such a large mass of cavalry but hoped to attack and then retreat, thus enticing the French to pursue. By the time this occurred, support would arrive to increase his numbers. Placing himself at the head of a squadron commanded by Lieutenant Friedrich von Katzler, the colonel led the charge. The Prussians soon found themselves hopelessly outnumbered; Blücher signaled the retreat. By this time the two cuirassier squadrons as well as Blücher's fifth hussar squadron had arrived to take them in. With the French pursuing in a disorderly mass, the colonel ordered his troopers to turn around, and all seven squadrons charged. Slicing through the French, the Prussians broke the little cohesion the enemy officers managed to restore. During the course of the engagement, Blücher rode into a ravine. A French officer moved behind him with pistol cocked. One of the colonel's junior officers shouted a warning. Blücher quickly turned his horse to the side to evade the onrushing ball; the beast heaved upward and out of the ravine. Locked in a fierce melee, both sides approached the Lauter when suddenly the French guns on the opposite bank opened fire. To spare his troopers, Blücher had the buglers sound the retreat and moved his units out of the artillery's range, bringing with them several prisoners. With the French holding the line of the Lauter, Blücher broke off the combat after losing two killed and thirty-seven wounded.[24]

Satisfied with extracting 3,000 casualties from the Army of the Moselle, Brunswick had no interest in conducting a general pursuit. Driven by the whips of the revolutionary commissars, French generals often proved to be an unpredictable lot. For this reason, the duke prepared to be attacked and ordered only his light horse to follow the enemy. Blücher crossed the Lauter on 1 December, striking the highway to Ramstein. He reported to Brunswick that "the enemy does not retreat, he flies! I follow him to Homburg." Southwest of Ramstein at Spesbach, he caught up with Ambert's rear guard, taking forty prisoners and inflicting an estimated seventy casualties. His pursuit continued the next day, with the Red Hussars pushing through Waldmohr and turning south on the road to Homburg. Before reaching the latter, a large French force compelled them to return to Waldmohr.[25]

On 5 December Blücher received orders from Brunswick at Kaiserslautern to conduct a reconnaissance toward the Blies, where Hoche's main body camped. The commander offered him all the infantry and guns he deemed necessary, but Blücher responded that his own cavalry battalion would suffice. Early on the sixth he led his main body toward Homburg, sending officer-led patrols toward Neunkirchen and St. Ingbert. Despite these efforts, he could not obtain enough information to determine Hoche's next move and so returned to his headquarters at Ramstein.[26] In fact, after quickly reorganizing his army, Hoche decided to march south from Lorraine to Alsace and support General Jean-Charles Pichegru's Army of the Rhine against Austrian general Dagobert Sigmund von Wurmser's Army of the Upper Rhine operating against Strasbourg. After Hoche defeated the Austrians at Froeschwiller (18–22 December) and Wissembourg (26 December), Wurmser withdrew across the Rhine on 30 December. Wurmser's retreat, combined with Brunswick's failure to exploit his success at Kaiserslautern, forced the Prussians to raise the siege of Landau and likewise fall back to—but not across—the Rhine. The Prussians commenced this retreat on 30 December to winter quarters in the triangle formed by Bad Kreuznach, Worms, and Mainz, this last city having been liberated from the French earlier that year (23 July). The light troops held an outpost line curving from the Rhine just downstream of Mainz to just upstream of Worms. Blücher's battalion held the stretch north-west of the town of Alzey.

To Blücher's satisfaction, Prussian headquarters attached the Red Hussar Regiment to a brigade commanded by the aggressive General Ernst von Rüchel, who he described as a "friend of all offensives."[27] Although twelve years younger than the colonel, the two kindred spirits quickly developed a friendship, demonstrating Blücher's ability to take orders from officers younger in age but senior in rank. Although the lack of Allied unity during the campaign of 1793 caused disgruntlement among many high-ranking Prussian officers, neither Blücher nor Rüchel allowed this to dampen their enthusiasm.[28]

On 9 January 1794 Blücher spearheaded an attack to the northwest of the Prussian line that drove a large combined-arms French detachment from Bad Kreuznach.[29] A few days later the French attacked Blücher's positions from Morschheim to the southwest. Aggravated by the daily harassment along this sector of his line, the colonel requested permission to surprise the French forces at Morschheim. Rüchel agreed, adding one fusilier battalion, sixty Jäger, and two horse guns to Blücher's cavalry for the operation. Around midnight on 12 January, Blücher assembled his forces in thick fog at Offenheim, less than three miles north of Morschheim, forming five columns. The first, consisting of two hussar squadrons, moved west through Bechenheim to approach Morschheim from the northwest. His second column—100 infantry and sixty Jäger under a Captain von Trütschler—crept south through the right (western) side of a wood that rose halfway between Offenheim and Morschheim. The 200 infantry of the third column proceeded through the wood to the left (east) of the Offenheim–Morschheim road, while the fourth column—100 infantry—marched south through the wood along the right (western) side of the road. Blücher and his three remaining hussar squadrons formed the fifth column, which struck the Offenheim–Morschheim road. Trütschler's assault would be the signal for the general attack.

Blücher's subordinates executed his plan to perfection, sealing off the French on three sides. After a sharp struggle, the enemy retreated three miles south to Kirchheimbolanden. But fog and poor roads prevented Blücher from restoring order in time to achieve decisive results. He returned to Alzey with 190 prisoners, including three officers, as well as thirty horses. His troops lost three killed and several wounded. Blücher noted in his journal that the French would think twice before occupying Morschheim again.[30]

A few days after the surprise attack, the Red Hussar Regiment reunited on 16 January 1794 after Blücher's battalion exchanged its place in the line with the neighboring battalion of the Light Blue Hussars. The colonel noted that the officers of the regiment greeted each other with true warmth after being separated for one year. In addition, the new regimental commander, Colonel Joachim Ehrenreich von Dehrmann, went to Mainz on sick leave, meaning Blücher temporarily commanded both battalions.[31] He also had at his disposal one fusilier battalion, commanded by Lieutenant Colonel Johann Friedrich Wilhelm von Müffling; the Schmettau Dragoon Regiment; three Jäger companies; three squadrons of Palatine light cavalry; and one battery of horse artillery.[32] By changing places in the line, the Red Hussars fell under the orders of Prince Frederick Louis of Hohenlohe-Ingelfingen. As the prince likewise believed the war needed to be conducted with more energy, he got on well with Blücher.[33] Not only did Blücher change commanders, but the entire army did as well. Disagreements with Frederick William II led to Brunswick's resignation and replacement by Möllendorf, now a field marshal.

Blücher established his outpost chain along an eight-mile stretch from Westhofen to Alzey. According to his calculations, a French advance corps camped at the foot of the Haardt hill chain between Bad Dürkheim and Neustadt—some ten miles west of his sector—and strongly occupying Wachenheim and Forst in between. He did not allow the cold of winter to quench his burning thirst for action. In his journal he described as his first concern the need to obtain good scouts possessing a thorough knowledge of the terrain. Two hunters from Leiningen who knew every footpath and valley along the middle Rhine met his requirements. He brokered an arrangement with them: each time they served as scouts in an operation led by Prussian officers, Blücher would pay them one karolin for every enemy cavalry trooper captured and one dukaten for each infantryman.[34] Blücher explained in his journal that in this way, the hunters had a vested interest in Prussian success.[35]

After Hoche demanded the surrender of Mannheim some forty miles up the Rhine from Mainz, Möllendorf arranged a demonstration by the left wing of the Prussian army. Blücher's hussars along with two dragoon regiments received the task of harassing the French. Blücher put his two scouts to good use, leading a hussar detachment of sixty troopers commanded by Lt. Hans Joachim von Sydow in a surprise flank attack at dawn against a patrol moving through Bad Dürkheim that resulted in the capture of twenty prisoners.[36]

Although Möllendorf expanded the mission's scope from a demonstration to a joint operation with the Austrians to drive the French from Mannheim, Blücher went on leave for two weeks in early March 1794. Dehrmann's return from sick leave may have prompted him to take the respite—Dehrmann purportedly had no appetite for enterprising raids or continuous engagements with the French. Regardless of the reason, Blücher took the opportunity to show his head in Prussian headquarters at Mainz and indulge in the delights of metropolitan Frankfurt.

While away, Blücher received a cabinet order naming him commander of the Red Hussar Regiment in place of Dehrmann, who already had requested retirement. The notice hardly satisfied Blücher, for it did not name a new *Chef* (proprietor) of the regiment. In fact, the name of the regiment remained the "Goltz" Hussars, even though Blücher now officially commanded the unit. Regardless, he returned from leave on 20 March to find that the French had not remained idle during his absence. On 8 March they had plundered a village northeast of Bad Dürkheim. On the twentieth they moved even closer, plundering Grünstadt, eleven miles southwest of the Prussian extreme right at Worms. Blücher only waited for better weather to resume his raids.[37]

On 4 April Blücher learned of a French operation to build two large redoubts on a prominent hill near the village of Herxheim-am-

Berg, some fourteen miles southwest of Worms.[38] A large enemy detachment from the camp at Leistadt (two miles southwest of Herxheim) occupied the hill while an estimated five hundred workers labored on the entrenchments. Blücher notes in his journal that the presence of redoubts there would have provided the French a formidable position; much Prussian blood would be spilled evicting them. To prevent them from completing the entrenchments, the colonel resolved to attack immediately. He hastily gathered all the cavalry he could as well as nearby dragoon and cuirassier pickets and summoned the rearward squadrons of his regiment. After sending an adjunct to find two squadrons of the Brown Hussar Regiment that were patrolling toward Freinsheim just east of Herxheim, Blücher advanced. At Herxheim he found only one enemy battalion, which retreated, leaving the workers behind. Wildly firing as they withdrew, the French inflicted only two casualties on the Prussians. After taking possession of the Herxheim hill, Blücher ordered the workers to demolish the half-finished redoubts. He noted in his journal:

> Prince Hohenlohe himself came up. Happy to see the enemy's intentions thwarted, he rode over to the redoubts. Because he was in musket range of the enemy's skirmishers, who had crept through the vineyards and were now firing steadily, I asked the prince not to expose himself, but instead this excellent, bold leader always had the habit of providing an example of cold-bloodedness and decisiveness, and therefore did not move. Our workers, busy with demolishing the redoubts, were not as calm under this constant fire; they began to complain miserably and to beg that they be spared the risk of being shot dead. It seemed to me that scaring the skirmishers might be the best remedy. I placed several buglers and hussars behind a hill, and had the former sound the attack while the latter sprang from behind the hill and charged the enemy. The enemy, who had never heard the signal for the attack without an attack following, thus hastily retreated. The peasants completed their work cheerfully.[39]

This success did not satisfy Blücher. Knowing that the skirmishers would appear as soon as he departed, the colonel decided to set a trap. He hid troopers who possessed forty of his fastest mounts behind a large building near Herxheim, while the remainder started the ride back to the outpost line. Just as he suspected,

French skirmishers ran out of the vineyards and into the open to begin trailing the Prussians. Blücher sprang his trap: the forty troopers charged, cutting down many of the enemy soldiers. According to his journal, this took place in full view of several French battalions camped at Leistadt. Infantry soon emerged from there in a vain attempt to save their comrades from the Prussian sabers. At that moment Blücher unveiled his last surprise. His section of horse guns, which he had concealed, now emerged to greet the advancing infantry with canister. The French conceded the hill to Blücher. He returned to his camp, leaving a post on the hill to observe Leistadt.[40]

On 5 April 1794 Blücher attempted to ambush the French at Herxheim, but despite having a good plan according to Möllendorf's statement, the attack misfired. Some of his hussars rode four miles south to raid Bad Dürkheim, where the French kept much of the cattle they had requisitioned from the surrounding region. Another ambush conducted on the night of 9–10 April with fifty hussars wiped out an enemy patrol at Ungstein, two miles north of Bad Dürkheim. As a result of this pressure, Hohenlohe-Ingelfingen reported that the French had evacuated the hills around Herxheim and Bad Dürkheim.[41] Blücher noted in his journal that "through the persistent capture of patrols, I kept the enemy at bay."[42]

Regardless, the French responded to the constant harassment. Blücher claims that on one occasion, three of his hussars pursued some fleeing enemy troopers into Bad Dürkheim. After apprehending two of the *chasseurs-à-cheval* (mounted infantry), the Prussians turned to exit the town. As they approached its gates, they saw French infantry forming. Leaving behind the two prisoners, the Prussians charged through the enemy foot soldiers and burst out of Bad Dürkheim. As they rode away, one hussar received a ball in the back. They spurred the exhausted horses to go faster but again found the road blocked by French infantry. The wounded man fell to the ground, while the horses of both his companions staggered from wounds. "Thus, all three finally fell into the hands of the volunteers, who massacred them in an inhuman manner," recorded Blücher.[43]

The tale of these atrocities affected Blücher the same as the murder of his men in Poland more than twenty years earlier. "I learned of these shameful events from prisoners and deserted troopers, who themselves had a bad opinion of the volunteers. I resolved to take bloody revenge and two days later when we again attacked their outposts, I approached the enemy flankers with my adjutant,

Count Goltz, and told them that I would make reprisals. They shouted back to me that for their part they had treated the prisoners well, but that the rabble running away from us—pointing to the volunteers—could not be stopped." Deciding to bide his time, Blücher soon found an opportunity to "punish" the offending troops. "From the camp of Leistadt, they came one morning in fairly large numbers through the vineyards and fired incessantly at the hussars. I placed myself with 40 horses behind a wall near Herxheim and instructed the hussars, upon whom the [enemy] infantry fired, to pretend to retreat: now they [the French] became still bolder. I suddenly charged them with the 40 horses[,] and the volunteers, despite their heavy fire, were all cut down. This example worked and our prisoners, who always remained few in number, were treated more humanely in the future."[44]

Another ambush of an enemy patrol on the night of 19–20 April west of Leistadt near Kallstadt earned a mention in Hohenlohe-Ingelfingen's report to Field Marshal Möllendorf, who responded with gratitude. Aside from expressing his appreciation for Blücher's boldness, the Prussian commander in chief wrote: "The affair with the patrol has pleased me immensely, because it completely conforms with my wishes and my idea that we gradually begin to stir and seek to reinstate the proper respect. I express to Colonel Blücher as well as the officers who led the patrols my satisfaction and respect, and I shall not fail to send with the next outgoing courier Colonel Blücher's report in its original to His Majesty the King and the [names of the] officers who deserve to be commended."[45]

Blücher took a few days' leave again to enjoy the pleasures of Frankfurt. Returning to duty on 29 April, he immediately prepared a response to a raid on Kirchheim, six miles north of Bad Dürkheim. Early on 1 May, a large French detachment marched north from Bad Durkheim. They encountered Blücher's patrols on the Herxheim hill and pursued the Prussians north through Kirchheim to Grünstadt. The colonel summoned his rearward squadrons from their quarters to Grünstadt and rode toward the action. Upon approach, he estimated 400 French cavalry were at Grünstadt, with infantry moving north from Kirchheim. Blücher attacked before the enemy foot could arrive, killing and wounding more than 100 French troopers and capturing seven officers, thirty-two men, and ninety horses. After the French unlimbered artillery on the Herxheim hill, the Prussians broke off the attack. But on seeing the approach of the remaining squadrons of the Red Hussar Regiment, the French withdrew south through Kallstadt and Bad Dürkheim to Wachenheim. Blücher's losses amounted to seven troopers killed and some wounded. Möllendorf again praised his subordinate, promising to recommend the colonel and his officers to Frederick William. He also expressed his hope that "after a few such lessons, the enemy would finally lose his lust for plunder."[46]

In early May Möllendorf constricted his front. Blücher's outposts now extended five miles from Neuleiningen to Freinsheim, with the colonel quartering at Grünstadt. To his right, Rüchel's outposts stretched to Kirchheimbolanden, while those of General Erich Magnus von Wolffradt spread south on his left. Impressed by Blücher's constant activity and hoping for bolder strikes, Möllendorf placed at his disposal three grenadier battalions posted at Bockenheim and commanded by Colonel Leopold Alexander von Wartensleben. The fiery Blücher now considered his force "strong enough to take on an entire enemy army."[47] With these reinforcements, he conducted numerous raids on French positions from Leistadt to Wachenheim until Möllendorf commenced his 1794 campaign.

Although Saxe-Coburg struggled to secure Belgium, he still hoped to launch an operation against Paris. For this he wanted to assemble as large an Allied force as possible in the Netherlands. But Möllendorf refused his request to shift his army to the northwest, knowing that by uncovering the middle Rhine he would expose Mainz, Frankfurt, and the heart of Germany. Yet the French diverted a large portion of the Army of the Moselle to the Ardennes along the Belgian frontier, leaving only a weak masking force to face Möllendorf's 40,000 Prussians. In fact, the Army of the Moselle—at most 25,000 men commanded by General Jean-René Moreaux—extended almost 105 miles from Kaiserslautern to Longwy in a thin cordon. Its troops at the eastern end faced the center and right of Möllendorf's army as well as Austrian forces at Luxembourg and Trier. East of Moreaux, the 35,000 men of General Claude-Ignace Michaud's Army of the Rhine held a fifteen-mile line along the Speyerbach from Speyer to Neustadt. Opposite Michaud's right wing stood Hohenlohe-Ingelfingen with the left of Möllendorf's army. At Mannheim, the Austrian, Palatine, Hessian, and Bavarian units of the Austrian Army of the Upper Rhine, now commanded by Prince Frederick William of Hohenlohe-Kirchberg, immediately faced the center and left of Michaud's army.[48]

A determined offensive by the Allies could have crushed the Army of the Moselle, but Möllendorf limited his objectives.[49]

On Saxe-Coburg's repeated pleas, the Prussian field marshal sent a large detachment northwest to Trier. As further proof of his good will, he decided in mid-May to push out some 5,000 troops from Ambert's division of the Army of the Moselle from Kaiserslautern, shattering their communications where possible and driving them across the Lauter. To dislodge the Army of the Rhine, Möllendorf called on the assistance of the Austrians at Mannheim. Consequently, on 22 and 23 May, Möllendorf converged on Kaiserslautern with the right wing of the Prussian army in four columns. Meanwhile, Hohenlohe-Ingelfingen advanced through Bad Dürkheim with the army's left wing to attack the French Army of the Rhine along the Haardt hill chain in conjunction with the Austrians.

Blücher received the task of maintaining contact between Möllendorf and Hohenlohe-Ingelfingen through the rugged, wooded hills of Haardt. Moreover, he had to prevent French reinforcements marching west from Bad Dürkheim and northwest from Neustadt from reaching Hochspeyer, seven miles east of Kaiserslautern. For this assignment, the colonel commanded the five squadrons of his 1st Battalion, three infantry battalions, three Jäger companies, and two battalion guns.[50] The general Allied advance began on 22 May; Möllendorf expected to assault the French at Kaiserslautern on the following day as Hohenlohe-Ingelfingen likewise attacked the enemy in his sector. To sever the Kaiserslautern–Neustadt road, Blücher led two-thirds of his force west from Bad Dürkheim to the hills east of Frankenstein on 23 May. There, he encountered a strong French infantry post, which the Prussians drove off. Resisting his desire to pursue, Blücher continued south along the Kaiserslautern–Neustadt road. Marching through a thick forest belt, the Prussians encountered numerous enemy forces en route to Hochspeyer. Blücher soon found himself surrounded. After holding his ground, two Prussian infantry battalions came up, allowing him to push the French through the woods and into Weidenthal, from where they retreated a further four miles along the Kaiserslautern–Neustadt road to Neidenfels.

Blücher remained at a clearing in the wood near Weidenthal, only two miles south of Frankenstein. After two hours he received the report of an enemy force estimated to be two battalions, two guns, and one hundred cavalry advancing south through

Frankenstein. Although uncertain of the outcome of Möllendorf's operation at Kaiserslautern, Blücher rode north to intercept the enemy: a detachment from Ambert's division commanded by General Jean-Baptiste de Bresolles de Siscé. On making contact with the French, he informed them that they were surrounded and so demanded their surrender. Bresolles de Siscé responded with a general volley. Shortly after, Blücher learned that the French force at Neidenfels had turned around and was closing on his rear. The colonel deployed his troops as best he could. He turned one battalion to face south, ordering it to prevent the Neidenfels column from gaining any ground. With Müffling's fusilier battalion, he took a position on a hill facing Bresolles de Siscé. Blücher posted his two cannon next to each other, one facing south and the other north. Bresolles de Siscé attempted to envelop the small Prussian force. Driving the detached Prussian Jäger and skirmishers before him, the French general ordered his soldiers to storm the hill and re-form to face the Prussian infantry. Blücher hastily instructed Müffling to have his men fix bayonets and charge. For the hussar squadrons, which stood to his right at the base of the hill, he sent orders to charge any French forces that emerged from the woods on his right. Regardless of the enemy's strength, Blücher demanded that his troopers attack and cut down everyone.

Joining Müffling's advancing infantry, Blücher observed the impact of the first French volley: four officers and several men fell. With bayonets fixed, the Prussian fusiliers closed the holes in their ranks and continued. At thirty paces they accelerated. Seized by both fear and excitement, the men surrendered to their emotions and bellowed war cries. Slamming into the French line, the Prussians drove their adversaries down the hill. Blücher claims the enemy left many dead and wounded on the hilltop. The Prussians captured both enemy guns and took several prisoners. Bresolles de Siscé remained behind with a small reserve. Observing his attack fail, the French general boldly attempted to drive through the disorganized Prussian infantry to regain the Neustadt–Kaiserslautern road. According to Blücher, however, the gunners of his sole cannon facing in this direction aimed well enough to break the French column, which fled northeast, dragging Bresolles de Siscé along with it.[51]

Blücher does not offer details concerning the French force coming from Neidenfels, but we can assume they did not affect the Prussians because he states, "I remained master of the terrain and the goal of my mission was completely achieved."[52] Known as the combat of Weidenthal, the engagement earned Blücher Möllendorf's recommendation on 24 May 1794 for promotion to general. "With just a few men he cut down two battalions and captured two guns," wrote the field marshal to the king, "he is the most senior colonel. During my time as the commander in chief, he has truly distinguished himself many times and I hope this will further encourage him."[53]

Meanwhile, darkness set in without Blücher receiving any news from Möllendorf or Hohenlohe-Ingelfingen. He assumed the French remained at Neustadt because a post still held Neidenfels. An uneasy night passed, with the Prussians bivouacking behind a rock wall at the edge of the forest. They placed the prisoners in the middle of the infantry's camp, with the hussars forming the outer ring. In his journal Blücher relates a very moving story of an encounter with a wounded French prisoner whose upper femur had been smashed. The Prussians placed him next to a campfire, offering him bread and brandy. Not only did he decline these and refuse to be bandaged but also repeatedly demanded that the Prussians shoot him dead. Blücher could hear his men say to themselves that "this is quite a stubborn, obstinate Frenchman!"

Blücher and Müffling approached the group. After his demands went unheeded, the wounded Frenchman fell so completely silent and withdrawn that he appeared to no longer notice what went on around him. Believing the man to be in shock, Blücher sent for several blankets and covered him. The soldier suddenly looked up at the colonel questioningly, then lowered his eyes. Blücher took the opportunity to tell the man that he had to allow himself to be bandaged and to eat something to maintain his strength. His adjutant, Lieutenant Goltz, repeated Blücher's statement in French. The Frenchman offered no response. Through Goltz, Blücher continued, stating that he considered a man who surrendered so easily to his fate to be weak; in the least, he found it unseemly for a soldier to find refuge in despair. Besides, the man should not give up hope for his recovery. Blücher assured him that he was among compassionate people who would do everything to help him.

> Now I looked at the suffering man again; a stream of tears fell from his eyes and he reached for my hand. I gave him wine and he drank, and he no longer objected to having the regimental surgeon bandage him. Such a rapid change in the behavior of this

man struck me. I asked him for the reason of his previous stubborn behavior. His answer: "I was forced to serve the Republic; my father was guillotined; I lost my brothers in the war; my wife and children live in the most miserable conditions. Therefore, I believed that death would put an end to my suffering and therefore wished for it. Your kind reminder has brought me to a more mature reflection; I thank you for it and I am now determined to receive my fate with dignity."

Blücher claims that this story touched all those who heard it. It pleased him to see his soldiers so willing to help this fellow warrior. After the Prussians bandaged all the wounded, the colonel had them transported to the nearest village—Weidenthal—where they were handed over to the mayor for further care.[54]

After this episode Blücher sent Goltz east toward Bad Dürkheim in the hopes of finding Hohenlohe-Ingelfingen. He also sent a patrol west to Hochspeyer. Goltz returned late in the night with the news that Hohenlohe-Ingelfingen attacked and drove back the French from Bad Dürkheim on the twenty-third but then withdrew northward after learning the Austrians had been stopped at Schifferstadt and thrown back upon Mannheim with considerable loss. Although the French returned to Landau, Hohenlohe-Ingelfingen remained north of Bad Dürkheim. The next morning, 24 May, Blücher's patrol returned from Hochspeyer with the news that Prussian troops held both that town and Frankenstein. More importantly, Möllendorf completely defeated the French at Kaiserslautern on the previous day.[55] Soon after, Blücher received a letter from the field marshal that confirmed this news and summoned him to a meeting at Hochspeyer. Turning command over to Müffling, the colonel rode hard to Hochspeyer, where Möllendorf greeted him with "exquisite favor," telling him to express to his troops the field marshal's "gratitude and complete satisfaction."[56] Thus, only the Prussians' vanguard had engaged the enemy's rear guard. Currently, the continued French presence at Neustadt troubled Möllendorf, and he feared they would drive back Hohenlohe-Ingelfingen.[57] Consequently, he ordered Blücher to hold his position and patrol toward Neustadt.

Blücher's return ride gave him ample time to think. He concluded that despite the difficulties, he would attempt to drive the French from Neustadt with his own small force. As the trip to and from Hochspeyer consumed the entire day of the twenty-fourth,

Blücher did not return until after nightfall. The French had pressured Müffling throughout the day. At dawn on 25 May, the colonel commenced his operation. Concealed by a thick fog, his patrol reconnoitered Neidenfels and found the French in the process of withdrawing. While attempting to catch the enemy's rear guard, he sent his adjutant, Captain Bonin, with thirty hussars on a mission to seek Hohenlohe-Ingelfingen and deliver the news that Blücher would soon be at Neustadt. After summoning the rest of his troops, the colonel scrawled a short report to Möllendorf and then rushed forward to join his advance guard. On receiving the dispatch, Möllendorf ordered Hohenlohe-Ingelfingen to Neustadt to exploit the enemy's retreat if possible.[58] During the course of the day, Blücher reached Neustadt, where Bonin delivered the news that Hohenlohe-Ingelfingen planned to move south from Bad Dürkheim and join him there. Thus, on the twenty-sixth the prince reached Neustadt and reinforced Blücher with another fusilier battalion, the 2nd Red Hussar Battalion, and half of a horse battery.[59]

Hohenlohe-Ingelfingen's target, the four divisions of Michaud's Army of the Rhine, stood slightly north of Landau, with its right wing extending along the Queich River to Germersheim on the Rhine River, and the left wing to the edge of the Vosges. Michaud hoped to hold this position and await reinforcements and supplies. Yet on 28 May he sent one division to retake Neustadt. Early that morning Blücher's outposts alerted him on the approach of two large enemy columns. The colonel ordered the two infantry battalions posted at Neustadt to deploy, then rode ahead with the cavalry and two horse guns. After passing through Edenkoben, more than six miles south of Neustadt, the French left-wing (western) column deployed its artillery and sharply bombarded the Prussians. Soon after, the right-wing (eastern) column cleared Kirrweiler, which stood closer to Neustadt than did Edenkoben, and likewise unlimbered its artillery. At this time Hohenlohe-Ingelfingen rode up. Seeing Blücher already hard pressed by the French guns, he stated that a retreat to Neustadt would be acceptable. Declining, the colonel explained his plan to attack the right French column in its exposed position at Kirrweiler; two horse guns and two squadrons would keep the enemy in check at Edenkoben. Hohenlohe-Ingelfingen responded that such an attempt would result in high casualties. Regardless, the colonel intended to overwhelm his adversary through a surprise attack.[60]

Blücher based his chances for success on four hussar squadrons he concealed behind a hill on his left (east) near Kirrweiler. As soon as they saw their commander charge with the squadrons of the advance guard, they should likewise attack immediately. Blücher gave the signal for his vanguard to move toward Kirrweiler; the four flanking squadrons on his left likewise moved forward. Although the lead squadrons received considerable fire from the French at Edenkoben, they charged in conjunction with the four flanking units. The Prussians completely overwhelmed the French at Kirrweiler, taking four guns, several caissons, and inflicting more than 200 casualties on the tightly packed infantry. Support in the form of the Brown Hussars and Schmettau Dragoons arrived from Hohenlohe-Ingelfingen. South of Kirrweiler the French attempted to re-form at a defile north of Fischligen, but the Prussian cavalry broke them for good. Pursued by the Prussians, the survivors fled south to the village.

The sound of artillery to his right (west) prevented Blücher from enjoying the thrill of victory for long. Remembering the French column at Edenkoben, he directed fifty dragoons to Edesheim, less than two miles south of that town. With two squadrons, Blücher rode directly toward the smoke rising in the distance where he believed he would find the enemy guns. He encountered them at Edesheim along with a French cavalry regiment serving as rear guard of the column, which itself already had retreated south from Edenkoben. Noting Blücher's arrival, 400 carabiniers turned to meet the Prussians and gain time for the artillery to depart. Blücher charged, soon joined by the fifty dragoons, who likewise saw him arrive. He claims that the ensuing hand-to-hand melee raged back and forth. Finally, the two Prussian squadrons that had held the French at Edenkoben reached the field. With their numbers thus doubled, the Prussians drove the enemy cavalry into Edesheim, capturing the two guns. Blücher sets the scene: "The large number of those fleeing were stuffed in the narrow lanes of the village, where occurred a bloody massacre, and therefore the enemy's losses were very great before he could reach the exit of the village and escape under the protection of his artillery, which was situated on the Walsheim hill."[61]

According to Hohenlohe-Ingelfingen's after-action report, the Prussians captured two flags, five caissons, six guns, eleven officers, 350 men, and 200 horses and killed some 200 enemy soldiers.

Prussian losses amounted to twenty men.⁶² "Thus, the events of
that day ended," noted Blücher in his journal. "With mere cavalry,
we won a decisive victory over an entire enemy corps. . . . The battlefield at Kirrweiler, Fischlingen, and Edesheim was covered with
dead Frenchmen, while the loss on our side was slight."⁶³ Twenty-
four Prussian officers, including fifteen from the Red Hussars,
received commendations, while forty-one noncommissioned officers and soldiers received gold medals and fifty-nine others received
silver. Möllendorf described the engagement as "a truly beautiful
action." Fourteen days later, on 4 June 1794, Blücher received his
promotion to general major, and the king named him chef of the
regiment.⁶⁴ "My dreams have come true," wrote Blücher.⁶⁵

In the aftermath of the Second Battle of Kaiserslautern, both
French armies retreated: the Rhine Army to Landau and the line
of the Queich, and the Moselle Army to the Saar River.⁶⁶ Despite
Möllendorf's success, a stalemate in the Netherlands prompted the
Prussian field marshal to postpone further operations. Believing
nothing good could come from continued fighting, he urged his
king to make peace.⁶⁷ With such a mindset, Möllendorf made preparations for defensive positions. By 26 June Hohenlohe-Ingelfingen's
corps only had moved to Kirrweiler, with Blücher holding the outpost chain from his headquarters at Edenkoben.⁶⁸ His promotion
did not cause a change in his duties, and he continued to implement the tactics of the "small war" from his outposts for the rest
of the summer.

General Jean-Baptiste Jourdan's decisive victory over Saxe-
Coburg at Fleurus on 26 June signaled the beginning of the end of
the First Coalition's presence in the Low Countries. In the aftermath
the Austrians retreated east to a position behind the Maas River,
while the British and Dutch withdrew north into the Netherlands;
the French entered Brussels on 9 July. To support the Austrians,
Möllendorf agreed to move the bulk of the Prussian army northwest
from the middle Rhine to the lower Moselle, occupying the rugged
Hunsrück hill chain and covering Koblenz. Meanwhile, Hohenlohe-
Ingelfingen would mask Möllendorf's movement by driving on
Kaiserslautern. For this operation, he commanded an Allied force
of 35,000 men, half consisting of Prussians and the other half units
from Hohenlohe-Kirchberg's Austrian Army of the Upper Rhine.
Anticipating this move, Paris sought to drive the Prussians east and
against the Rhine. Michaud received orders to take the offensive

with the Armies of the Rhine and Moselle. His first attempt failed on 2 July, causing both armies to return to their original positions. With the political commissars sharpening the guillotine that now stood in the center of Landau, Michaud's headquarters, he and Moreaux devised a second offensive.[69] This time the French planned for the Army of the Rhine to fix the Prussians in its sector, while two of its divisions slipped around the Prussian right by hugging the eastern edge of the Haardt. Meanwhile, the Army of the Moselle would advance on Trippstadt and attempt to turn Kaiserslautern.[70]

Hohenlohe-Ingelfingen held a thirty-mile line that extended from Kaiserslautern through Trippstadt to Neustadt, with his main body to the east in the plain between the Rhine and the eastern edge of the Haardt. On 13 July Michaud began his offensive, but the Prussians repulsed him. The French resumed their operation the next day. Early that morning, Blücher's posts reported the advance of numerous cavalry units toward Edelsheim, just south of Edenkoben. Soon infantry and artillery could be seen. Turning northwest, the French passed to the left of Edelsheim and occupied Rhodt unter Rietburg and Weyher in der Pfalz, from where they deployed to take Edenkoben. Advancing east, the French attempted to drive back Blücher's infantry. Enemy reinforcements moved up, tripling their numbers, but Blücher maintained that Müffling and Major Karl Anton von Bila "took such appropriate measures" that the fusiliers repulsed each attack. He summoned the Manstein Grenadiers from Edenkoben and placed his half-battery of foot to enfilade the enemy's flank. Riding through the line of his infantry, whose muskets blazed away, Blücher shouted: "Children, today you will maintain Prussia's honor!" "O ja! Herr General! Just give us cartridges," they answered.[71] Three times during the course of the engagement, the general replenished their ammunition pouches.

Blücher posted his hussars in two waves, with the horse battery aligned with the first, the right wing leaning on Edenkoben. A French battery unlimbered south of the Edenkoben morass and directed its fire at the Prussian troopers. The horse guns responded, but more French artillery arrived. Shelled by twenty guns, Blücher ordered his artillery to fall back, but the Red Hussars stood their ground; the cannon fire claimed sixty horses. Soon after, he ordered the cavalry to retreat. After Blücher's guns departed, the French assumed his main body would follow. Hoping to turn this retreat into a route,

French cavalry escorted six horse guns from Edesheim onto the plain to the north, making for Edenkoben. Skirmishers also moved forward in pursuit. "It appeared to me that the time had come, where I could take cold revenge on my adversary," noted Blücher.

With the officers of his entourage already in hand-to-hand combat with the lead elements of the French vanguard, Blücher had his bugler blow the attack signal for the hussars. The foremost squadrons charged the French cavalry, which broke under the weight of the unexpected attack. French guns on the opposite side of the morass unloaded on the Prussian horse, but the hussars kept coming. Blücher's cavalry overran the enemy battery, taking three guns and sending the rest scurrying through Edesheim. The Prussians closed, but a volley into their right flank reminded them of the French infantry that had moved up. Blücher sounded the recall. He returned to Edenkoben with eighty prisoners, including the French cavalry commander, General Pierre Garnier Laboissière; over 100 horses; and the three guns. In his journal Blücher boasts, "Prince Hohenlohe and our entire corps watched the affair from the hills of Venningen" two miles east of Edenkoben. "The prince was so kind that he expressed to me his joy and gratitude, and lauded my regiment with such praise that it sparked in all of us the desire to earn more."[72]

Despite the success of Blücher's cavalry, his infantry remained engaged with the French infantry west of Edenkoben. Blücher rode there, dismounted, and ran toward a redoubt occupied by Bila and some of his fusiliers and one three-pounder field gun. From behind trees, French skirmishers sniped at him, but he reached the redoubt unscathed. After gaining Bila's assurance that he would hold the redoubt for as long as he lived, Blücher ran to Müffling's position. The fusiliers and grenadiers held their ground but sustained considerable casualties. By this time the hot summer day took its toll, and exhaustion set in. Blücher feared that his men's will to fight would give out before nightfall presumably ended the fighting. Around 4:00 in the afternoon, Hohenlohe-Ingelfingen finally sent reinforcements: two battalions commanded by Prince Louis Ferdinand of Prussia, cousin of Frederick William II.[73] After he and Blücher decided on an advance as their best option, "this young hero sprang from his horse, united his infantry with mine, and led the entire line toward the enemy, who fled in the greatest panic."[74]

To exploit the victory, Blücher sent 150 hussars on the road to Edesheim with orders to turn west there and strike the road to

Rhodt unter Rietburg, hoping to take the retreating French infantry in the flank. He maintained that his troopers cut down at least 100 Frenchmen near Rhodt.[75] "This beautiful act," states Hohenlohe-Ingelfingen's after-action report, "made such an impression on the enemy that for the rest of the day he did not dare attempt to move up artillery." According to Unger, "at that time, the French recognition of the dominating power of Blücher's cavalry found eloquent expression in the nickname they gave Blücher: 'le roi rouge' (the red king)."[76]

To better cover their retreat, the French set fire to the "beautiful" village of Edesheim, burning it to the ground. We do not know Blücher's losses, but they must have numbered a few hundred at least. Night fell, and the general's exhausted men dropped where they stood and camped under the open sky. Around 9:00 P.M. news arrived that threw the entire camp into disarray. Advancing from Hornbach and Pirmassens, the Army of the Moselle had overrun Prussian positions at Johanniskreuz and Trippstadt.[77] This compelled Hohenlohe-Ingelfingen to move his main body north to Neustadt. At midnight on 15 June, the Prussians commenced the retrograde march; Blücher's troops formed the rear guard.[78] Moreaux did not follow up his victory due to orders he received to take Trier, some sixty-six miles northwest of his position at Kaiserslautern.

By 17 July Hohenlohe-Ingelfingen's main body had retreated twenty-five miles north of Neustadt to Pfeddersheim; Blücher established his headquarters at Grünstadt. The Prussians passed two months in this position. Meanwhile, the Allies decided on a joint Austro-Prussian operation to recapture Trier, ninety miles to the west. To draw French attention as well as forces from that town, Hohenlohe-Ingelfingen received the task of retaking Kaiserslautern.[79] Shielded by Blücher's posts, he commenced his advance on 17 September by moving his main body sixteen miles west from Frankenthal to Göllheim at the edge of the Haardt. For the eighteenth, he planned to drive back the French posts. At Grünstadt southeast of Göllheim, Blücher received the task of clearing the front before the left wing and then advancing jointly with the main body.[80] He had his troops from various nations use the password "Deutsch!"[81] By nightfall the Prussians reached a line extending seven miles south from Winnweiler to Enkenbach-Alsenborn. Giving the soldiers a day off on the nineteenth, Hohenlohe-Ingelfingen ordered a general reconnaissance to the south for the following day. Conversely, the French decided to launch a counterattack that same day with three divisions.

On 20 September the main body of Hohenlohe-Ingelfingen's fifty battalions and fifty squadrons assembled along a short two-mile line between Sembach and Mehlingen, facing Kaiserslautern to the southwest.[82] One mile south of Mehlingen, Blücher commanded the vanguard of seven battalions, eighteen squadrons, and one and one-half batteries at Fröhnerhof. With Hohenlohe-Ingelfingen supervising, Wolffradt and Prince Louis Ferdinand conducted the actual reconnaissance; each led an infantry brigade and several cavalry squadrons due south to Hochspeyer and Fischbach. To facilitate their operation, Blücher received the task of keeping in check the French at Eselsfürth, two miles southwest of Fröhnerhof and four miles northeast of Kaiserslautern. Blücher maintained that Hohenloh-Ingelfingene instructed him several times not to attack. Yet should Hohenlohe-Ingelfingen find the French in an exposed position, the prince would notify Blücher immediately so the vanguard could gain Eselsfürth and its ford to cross the Eselsbach.[83]

A large wood separated Fröhnerhof and Eselsfürth. French skirmishers occupying its northeastern edge harassed Blücher's troops at Fröhnerhof with steady fire. He initially drove them off with a few bursts of case shot, but the persistent soldiers returned in greater number and "inconvenienced" his right wing. To put an end to the nuisance, he instructed Müffling to drive the enemy deep into the woods with his Jäger and marksmen. Müffling complied and quiet returned to Blücher's sector for some time. Suddenly, the roar of artillery and small-arms fire shattered the silence. Coming from the direction of Fischbach to the east, it signaled that Hohenlohe-Ingelfingen had found the enemy. Without waiting for word from the prince, Blücher decided to attack. He ordered Müffling to drive into the wood with the vanguard's two fusilier battalions. The infantry hardly entered the wood when Blücher "heard extraordinarily loud firing and shouting" coming from his right (west). "One had not been attentive enough on my right wing," he continued. "While we had been waiting, the French crept close to the forest's edge. Now, when the infantry entered the wood, they ambushed the right wing of the Palatine battalion." Blücher claimed that the battalion commander, Major von Bila, "did everything that could be expected from an intrepid officer, but the battalion was forced to retreat after losing many men. Muffling and Bila, these brave veterans, redressed the situation; they formed everything and now the Palatines took terrible vengeance, completely overwhelming the enemy. I had some sixty horses pass through the infantry and they inflicted a bloody defeat on the fugitives."[84]

Blücher then directed Colonel Prince Frederick Karl of Hohenlohe to advance south through the wood to take Eselsfürth with one Austrian battalion and two Red Hussar squadrons. He sent the rest of his Red Hussars, followed by all remaining troops, west to Morlautern, less than three miles north of Kaiserslautern. Shortly after, Blücher heard artillery from the direction of Eselsfürth. Fearing the French had sprung another ambush, the general immediately hurried toward the sound of the guns. He rode only a short way when he observed the Austrians approaching in retreat. Hohenlohe reported that three French battalions and two guns held Eselsfürth; one battalion would not suffice to gain the position. "I responded to him that it must absolutely be taken, and still committed only one battalion for this purpose. Now the brave prince advanced and drove back the enemy." The French withdrew toward Kaiserslautern. Blücher ordered his two squadrons and a detachment of Palatine light cavalry to pursue, but they failed to inflict any damage. "Then appeared the Brown Hussars and the Katte Dragoon Regiment on the left; the attack of these regiments overwhelmed the enemy; no man escaped."[85] In Hohenlohe-Ingelfingen's after-action report, the prince praised Blücher for his appearance at Edelsfürth: "A part of Blücher's regiment helped cut down three infantry battalions and contributed to the destruction of these troops. This haste proves how this outstanding unit is very much inspired by the noblest ambitions and how much they are influenced by the example of their worthy leader."[86]

After taking Eselsfürth, Blücher rode three miles west to join his troops at Morlautern. On arriving, he observed the retreat of French infantry from Kaiserslautern as well as from the hills southwest of the town. Scanning the horizon, he found the reason: Hohenlohe-Ingelfingen's troops were approaching from the east. At Fischbach, Louis Ferdinand's column encountered the French. After Wolffradt's column arrived to support, the Prussians drove the French toward Kaiserslautern. As a result, the Katte Dragoons caught up with the French forces that evacuated Eselsfürth.

Leaving the infantry and artillery on the hills of Morlautern, Blücher led his hussars, the Palatine light cavalry, and the Katte

Dragoons toward Hohenlohe's column. Seeing his approach, the Prussian commander rode to meet him. Purportedly smiling, he said to Blücher, "You already have attacked today without my orders." "Forgive me, my lord," replied the general, "but I heard it went well for you."[87] The prince responded with a handshake and orders for Blücher to sever the enemy's line of retreat by reaching Hohenecken, three miles southwest of Kaiserslautern. Although unsure of how to get there, Blücher promised he would. Hohenlohe placed Captain Bergen, a staff officer familiar with the region, at his disposal.

At a trot, cavalry detachments took various roads through the woods that surrounded Kaiserslautern's northern side while the infantry followed. Guided by Bergen, the general led the main body on the direct road to Hohenecken. With their horses running out of steam, Blücher nevertheless looked forward to the hunt, especially because the heavy rain that began to fall would prevent the French from firing their muskets. Despite his enthusiasm, the scouts could not locate the enemy. The idea dawned on Blücher that to better make their escape, the French probably abandoned the road in favor of marching through the thick undergrowth. He ordered a halt and instructed the cavalry "to search the forest in small groups, making noise when they encountered the enemy." Blücher himself remained on the main road with some platoons. To orient the detached units, he ordered the bugler to signal often. His account continues:

After I thus instructed all, a real battue took place. It was not long before we heard a great cry to our right, everything rushed there, and in a moment 300 infantry discovered there were cut down or taken captive. Now everything unfolded in quick succession: here and there, dense clusters of enemy infantry were attacked in the middle of the forest and overwhelmed. The noble Prince George of Hesse-Darmstadt had joined me and did not want to leave my side. Sometimes we came under fire from all directions, and I asked him to leave me so he would not expose himself unnecessarily. The worthy prince answered: "Dear General, please allow me to stay. I would not miss being witness to such a beautiful day for any price." Many a combat was fought, when I again heard an unusually loud noise; soon after I received the message that they'd discovered a few ordered battalions slowly withdrawing through the woods, and would probably offer vigorous resistance. We rushed to the area, and I soon heard the voice of my brave Captain Sydow, who called our people together and encouraged them. I galloped to him and saw the infantry, which consisted of at least 600 men that had moved behind a strong abatis. Noticing us, they started briskly firing at us. Captain Sydow was shot through the arm. . . . Anticipating losing a lot of men unless we maneuvered the infantry out of the abatis, I moved to my left. This had the desired effect. The enemy resumed his march and wanted to continue his retreat, but near Hohenecken had to pass through a small meadow some 500 paces long before he could return to the undergrowth. To me, this appeared to be the place where we could punish him. However, we were very weak because many of our men remained dispersed in the woods. I had the rally blown frequently and soon several hussars and dragoons came galloping to us. After I assembled eighty men, I ordered the advance at the very moment the enemy infantry started crossing the meadow. I called to our people to attack with good spirits because the French muskets had gotten wet and would not do much to us.[88]

Blücher praised the French commander for maintaining order, "but nothing scared our brave hussars and dragoons; we charged the enemy and although he stubbornly defended himself with the bayonet, we nevertheless drove through him." Somehow, one of Blücher's infantry battalions navigated through the wood in time to form and attack the enemy right. "And now the destruction of the French was complete. The bitterness of our men had reached its peak, and they cut down everyone. I had to use serious force to put an end to their fury, but I managed to save only 200 Frenchmen who were taken prisoner; the rest were sprawled on the ground dead." This final act marked the end of the Third Battle of Kaiserslautern. Blücher claims that the Prussians obliterated the 7,000 Frenchmen that they faced that day, killing and wounding 3,000 while taking 4,000 prisoners. The Red Hussars alone captured 1,500 enemy soldiers.[89] Blücher cited Prussian losses at a few hundred killed and wounded. Hohenlohe-Ingelfingen's official journal entry, based on the eyewitness report of the staff officer he placed at Blücher's disposal, describes the general as "always restlessly active as long as there was something else left to do."[90]

Like many previous occasions in the war, a Prussian retreat followed their victory. Continued French success in the Low Countries and along the lower Rhine prompted Möllendorf to return to his original position on the Primm River in late September. Meanwhile, under intense criticism for losing Belgium, Saxe-Coburg resigned as commander in chief of the Austrian main army. His successor, General Count François Sebastien of Clerfayt, could do little to stop the French. On 3 October Clerfayt evacuated the left bank of the Rhine. Köln and Koblenz fell to the French Army of the Sambre and Meuse later that month, posing a dangerous threat to Möllendorf's army. Consequently, the Prussian commander led his units across the Rhine at Mainz on 20 October, followed by Hohenlohe-Ingelfingen's corps. Blücher commanded the rear guard and covered the retreat of both commands. On 23 October he was one of the last Prussians to cross the Rhine. The French followed but never attacked.[91] Yet in the aftermath of the Prussian evacuation, the Army of the Moselle overran the left bank of the middle Rhine, entering Mannheim on Christmas Day.

The Red Hussars moved into quarters near Darmstadt in the angle formed by the confluence of the Main River with the Rhine. Blücher's journal describes the winter cold as so severe that the Rhine froze, thus removing this natural barrier between the Allies and the French. Instead of resting, his troopers manned "extraordinarily strong posts, where they constantly engaged the enemy."[92] With indignation, Blücher learned that attempts had been made to downplay the value of Hohenlohe-Ingelfingen's victory at Kaiserslautern. It is in this context that he made his famous quote about the prince that historians have misused over the years in an attempt to project Blücher's judgment over Hohenlohe-Ingelfingen's conduct in 1806:

> It would have been desirable if there had been less thinking and more fighting. Yet through this battle, the Prince of Hohenlohe gained unforgettable glory; with the loss of only a few hundred dead and wounded, he won a most brilliant victory. For this reason, all of his subordinates look at him with love and respect. It is most appropriate for Prussian troops to attack the enemy whenever he is close and I think that the general who does not destroy an enemy corps when he has the opportunity to do so while only sustaining minimal losses deserves to be criticized. The Prince of Hohenlohe doesn't need my praise, but I and all right-minded and impartial Brandenburgers agree that he is a general and a leader whom the Prussian army can be proud of![93]

By early 1795, the Prussian king as well as his army and his people no longer desired to continue the war against France. For the moment, he left the Prussian field army in winter quarters at Mainz astride the Rhine. Although Frederick William II could hardly bring himself to negotiate with the regicides of the French republic, by the end of February, talks had progressed to such a degree that the Prussian army started the march home. On 6 April the French and Prussian representatives, François de Barthélemy and Karl August von Hardenberg, signed the Treaty of Basel. Secretly the Prussians recognized French control of the left bank of the Rhine, while the French returned all Prussian territory they had taken on the right bank. Following Basel, Prussia embarked on a ten-year policy of official neutrality.

Due to events in the east, Frederick William II needed his army there. In a secret agreement Prussia and Russia each had taken another slice of Poland in 1793 during the Second Partition. This expansion required military resources that the Prussians simply did not have unless they limited their commitment against France. Afterward, the rump of Poland fell into anarchy. This fact, along with Austria's protests over being ignored in 1793, prompted the three eastern powers to finish the process in 1795 with the Third Partition. To take and digest this final bite of Poland, Frederick William recalled the manpower currently deployed against France. Thus, Prussia's membership in the First Coalition abruptly ended in 1795 just as French control of the left bank of the Rhine officially commenced. This region of Germany would remain under French rule until 1814.

Blücher blamed Allied disunity, particularly the mistakes of the British, for the failure of Möllendorf's 1794 campaign. Regarding the Duke of York's departure to take Dunkirk in the autumn of 1793 he attributed "the accumulated misfortunes that followed this and forced all German armies to retreat across the Rhine."[94] Moreover, he held Austrian weakness responsible for the overall poor results of the war. "The imperials have been completely defeated in the field and good old Frankfurt is in the hands of the Republicans after it surrendered," he concluded in 1796. "Hopefully, the imperials will retreat back into their hereditary lands; there's going to be peace and then the clean-up will start, and the Black Eagle [Prussia] will not be idle. Our King is at Pyrmont, probably to stay close."[95] In the end, Blücher did not believe the peace between France and Prussia would stick.[96]

Blücher gained valuable tactical experience by participating in several engagements, leading his troopers with distinction and gaining a reputation for boldness. His regiment alone captured 3,129 prisoners, including 144 officers and one general, 744 horses, eleven guns, twelve caissons, and six flags.[97] Over the course of two years, 29 officers and 130 noncommissioned officers and soldiers from the regiment received commendations.[98] Yet it is wrong to conclude that Blücher gained any real operational and strategic experience from his service in the War of the First Coalition. His opportunities to command combined-arms operations likewise remained limited. On such occasions he rarely led more than a few battalions and never commanded more than two batteries. For most of the campaigns, he simply organized and administered the outpost service, commanding his cavalry battalion (1793) or the entire regiment (1794), sometimes supported by an infantry battalion. Admittedly, he did so with all the daring and boldness associated with his name, and the operations that he did conduct pointed to a promising future for the Mecklenburger.

Laurent de Gouvion St.-Cyr, one of Michaud's divisional commanders in 1794, referred to Blücher's hussars as "the most intrepid" of all the Prussian regiments.[99] Moreover, the future French marshal adequately summarized Blücher's aggressiveness: while the Austrians were slow and cautious in attack, the Prussians were ardent in assault and pursuit. St.-Cyr claims the French had to seek the Austrians in their quarters but only show a detachment to get the Prussians to dash after it, which did make them susceptible to ambushes. Regardless, he acknowledged the superiority of the Prussian cavalry, describing it as "the best military cavalry in Europe, commanded by such officers as Blücher, Wolffradt, etc." Yet he does note that the French learned the art of la petite guerre from Blücher and his fellow officers so that by summer's end, the French believed they could match the Prussian horse.[100] Blücher had cemented an international reputation for audacity.

Away from the field, Blücher's vices continued to dominate him, especially drinking and gambling. Two years of hard campaigning and self-destructive living earned him a reputation befitting a hussar: unpredictable, energetic, and bold. In addition, a lengthy and mysterious illness struck shortly after the retreat into winter quarters. When Crown Prince Frederick William requested to join Blücher's staff, the fifty-two-year-old general refused in mid-February on the pretext of poor health. He expressed hopes of recovering but also revealed the darkness that had crept over his soul.

"Only the thought of still serving the King, my Lord, and all the royal house makes me hope that my health returns and my days are prolonged. Otherwise, I suffer from so many sorrows that I would happily look forward to their end."[101] This offers the first glimpse at an enemy that proved much stronger than any Blücher faced in the field: depression.

CHAPTER 3

FALSE SENSE OF SECURITY

French conquest of the Netherlands in early 1795 threatened the Prussian territory of Ostfriesland in northern Germany, Kleve on the lower Rhine, and the County of Mark on the middle Rhine in the region known as Westphalia. To safeguard these territories as well as all of North Germany, the Treaty of Basel permitted the Prussians to form and guard a line of demarcation. With headquarters based at Münster, Blücher led his regiment north to Ostfriesland, a Prussian territory since 1744 that bordered the far northeastern corner of the Netherlands. Its security had come into question after the British and Hanoverians withdrew from the Low Countries.

At the end of April 1795, a fully recovered Blücher moved into his new quarters at Emden, at the mouth of the Ems River. His remarks on the situation are worth notice: "In the town of Emden in Ostfriesland is a company from the Fusilier Battalion von Holzschuher. The very ungrateful city council of Emden went to the King and requested that the company not stay in the barracks. Emden made millions in profit because of this war; they need the garrison more than their bread. The city council should know that once the military leaves they will no longer be safe, and yet those devils don't want to provide quarters for 100 men? Blinded by their terrible prosperity, they look down on soldiers as if they are condemned creatures. As faithful as Ostfriesland is to the King, the rich Emdeners are beasts."[1]

Amid this transition from war to peacetime duties, Blücher became involved in an arranged marriage. Although the details are sketchy, the candidate, a Frau v. d. S., received an interesting letter from him written sometime in March 1795. The missive provides unique insight into Blücher the man and father:

> Madam! Full of gratitude and with reverence, I am acknowledging the disposition that Your Grace showed toward me. My silence is almost inexcusable; but madam, I am too honest and this is my

justification. I never beat around the bush and I will not be guilty of that now. Therefore, let's get to the point!

1. How can I offer you a relationship when my affairs are so disorganized and I am 5,000 thaler in debt? Of course I have a good future, also a good post that modestly supports me, but such things are never guaranteed.

2. I have three children whom I love. Their mother put me in charge of her inheritance; because of the love for my children, I rejected the inheritance. Therefore, my children are properly provided for; but I received nothing.

3. I am not an odd fellow. To live with my officers, to stand besides my subordinates if they need me, that is what makes me happy; but I am not getting rich by doing that.

4. I am unable to enter into a relationship without considering my future as well as the welfare of my children.

Madam, don't misunderstand me! I am far from asking a woman who desires me to turn over her fortune to me while still alive! But your revenues should be added to mine so I would be able to maintain a woman according to her birth and character. Madame, I know you have considerable assets; I know you are fond of me; and I am grateful for your generosity. If you are determined to make me happy: my hand and heart are at your feet. If you survive me, and I hope you will, please don't expect that I will leave behind riches for you because I don't have any. But if destiny has me remain behind, Madame, I believe that you will make arrangements so that I and my children are provided for.

Madame! Here you have my honest and frank profession of faith; treat me in the same way! Tell me what you want to do for me. I will strive to earn your indefinite love and friendship, and I will make sure that you don't regret your decision to enter into a relationship with me.

I must mention one more issue that is important to me: I have a ten-year-old daughter who I love with all my heart. I will, Madame, place her into your arms and ask you to take over the education of this child because you, Madame, possess the perfection of a thousand of your kind to do so.

Madame, I hope I did not presumptuously offend you; this letter is based on the dignity and principles for which I am known and that are dear to my heart: I am open and frank, especially with those who I love and cherish. I believe it is necessary to tell you my circumstances and I request that you do the same so I can judge the mettle and esteem of the future Mrs. General Blücher. I don't need to cause a stir; but my wife has to, wherever she appears, be noted and admired. Grant me the honor of your answer soon! Turn it over to destiny! Always count on my limitless admiration, yours lovingly and respectfully: Blücher. PS. Today I received notification that I will march to Westphalia; we are getting closer—I was sick for two and one-half months with a bad cold but I am better now.[2]

Later realizing that this woman was not his soul mate, Blücher backed out on 1 April 1795:

Madam! With awe-inspiring appreciation I recognize your nobleness. I would be happy to spend my remaining days with such a friend who thinks so nobly. But, Madame, my last correspondence revealed my situation and my shattered finances; I am unable to offer you anything in return for your noble sacrifice. I would never be free of criticism for having moved you from quiet, pleasing conditions to a dissatisfactory situation. Furthermore, when we are at war, only God knows where my job and duty will bring me. All this leads me to important considerations; rational thinking tells me to carry my destiny on my own. Please allow me once again, Madame, to thank you from the bottom of my heart for the generosity and I am grateful and ensure you that my respect for you is unlimited and will last a lifetime. I remain your totally obedient, faithful servant.[3]

Aside from fighting off the ladies, Blücher apparently had only one occasion when an "overweening" French general crossed the line of demarcation and forced him to "harshly" drive the intruder from Prussian territory. Other than this affair, he had much time on his hands. The general passed many hours at Emden's Freemason lodge, where he took advantage of its newspapers and journals to follow international events, though more often than not played cards. Blücher differentiated between persons and occasions. He spoke the language of the common man among his soldiers. In the circle of his officers, he displayed camaraderie without much regard to rank. Frank among friends, he was usually very careful in his conversations: "silence betrays no one" was his motto.[4]

Sometime after reaching Ostfriesland, Blücher attended a banquet hosted by the Prussian governor of Ostfriesland, Peter von Colomb. He found himself sitting next to Colomb's beautiful daughter, the twenty-two-year-old Katharina Amalie. Smitten by her, the fifty-three-year-old Blücher, father of the seventeen-year-old

Franz, wasted no time courting her. At first she played coy, purportedly even "provokingly" so. Although not very tall, the general presented "a fine figure of a man and looked extremely good in
uniform."[5] After two months he asked Colomb for his daughter's
hand. Initially concerned by their age difference, the father eventually agreed. On 17 July 1795 the couple married at the small estate
of Sanhorst. Colomb provided a handsome dowry. Amalie has
been described as "a beautiful woman with an unrivalled expression of kind-heartedness and friendly goodwill in her blue eyes. By
her unending engaging smile, immaculate white teeth, and petite
hands, she made many younger women envious."[6]

Blücher's true and unending love for her is best seen in the letters he wrote. "I am doing fine, dear Bonin," he reported on 4 April
1796. "On the domestic front, I am very happy because of my wife.
My finances redeemed themselves because of my position, and the
King treats me with graciousness. My wife sends her regards, I kiss
your wife's hand and I am eternally your loyal Blücher."[7] Later that
year he explained to one of his squadron commanders, "my wife is
well and sends greetings; her service is that she has turned me into
a calm and proper man."[8]

Just prior to the marriage, Blücher jumped across a stretch of
water "in youthful exuberance" and thus strained his foot. He
went to the spa at Pyrmont for treatment but found no immediate
relief. "Many" advised him to return through Hamburg and con-
sult a *Hofrat* (privy councilor) by the name of Schulz, who informed
Blücher that he had received the wrong treatment. Schulz prescribed keeping the foot bandaged, resting, and not riding for six
weeks. "I don't like this treatment," complained the general. "Yet I
will endure it to be able to serve."[9] Ever afterward, Blücher walked
with a slight limp; no longer able to maintain straight posture, he
slouched somewhat to the left.[10]

Being barred from the horse proved just as much a consequence
of his promotions as it was his injury. The hussar discovered that
the higher he climbed in rank, the less exciting became his job. In
addition, finances forced the Prussians to reduce the forces observing the line of demarcation; Blücher's 2nd Battalion received orders
to return to Pomerania. "Now, let me tell you about my affliction," he wrote the king's adjutant, Colonel Friedrich Wilhelm von
Zastrow, on 19 September 1795. "My whole regiment is so dispersed that I don't know where it is. The right wing is at the North

Sea, the left far across the Wesel; the 2nd Battalion marches home and the 1st must form the entire cordon; the squadrons number less than ten men. Everywhere we are surrounded by foreign solicitors, and the common man is not under my supervision but on his own, I must expect desertion. Admired friend, I wrote the King and asked him to pull me out of my dilemma. If you have an opportunity, please support my request."[11]

The dilemma Blücher refers to was being passed over by General Hans Karl von Strantz for the post of inspector general of the Pomeranian cavalry.[12] As with his attempts to be reinstated by Frederick the Great, Blücher demanded that his service in the recent war receive due consideration. His letter to Zastrow provides insight of how Blücher perceived the role of field-grade officer at war:

> Tell me, friend, what have I done, that General Strantz was appointed inspector? I am far from it to acknowledge the merit of this man! On the contrary, I know that he is capable and am very much his friend.
>
> Nevertheless, they used me during the war for all kinds of positions; on the decisive day, they entrusted me with 10,000 men. I was assigned all of the difficult operations; the Duke of Brunswick, the field marshal [Möllendorff], General Knobelsdorff, and Prince Hohenlohe—I served under all these generals—will attest that I completed my tasks successfully; that I never made a mistake when I attacked the enemy, fought him, and vice-versa; that under my command, no noncommissioned officer ever robbed, no officer ended up in an enemy prison, although thirteen received severe wounds; that I can prove that in order to maintain the regiment at full strength during the campaign, I added eighty-four of my own horses to the regiment; that there were never complaints about the regiment, so therefore I believe I can preside over an inspection.
>
> But I have no luck, and we hussars suffer during a war. We are never promoted to distinguished positions during peacetime and how we compare to the [heavy] cavalry, well, our budget shows. But by God, I swear, I never want to learn my craft with the [heavy] cavalry, not even as much as riding or learning any kind of system—satisfied that the best King is my Master, and the army is happy with me, the whole world can't deny me my credentials, I am an honest man in faithful duty to my Master. I lay at the feet of the King my own duty record as well as that of the regiment entrusted to me and enclose a copy as well. If we did not do more, it was not because of a lack of zeal, but opportunity.

Although 550 miles away, Blücher also complained that the army's Oberkriegskollegium (supreme military council) transferred the regiment's Pomeranian base sixty miles west from Stolp to Belgard (Białogard). "After completing exhausting campaigns as a faithful servant of His Majesty the King, I am not even allowed to pick the garrison of the regiment entrusted to me?" he asked. "The Russians and Turks don't proceed any harsher." Apparently, the Oberkriegskollegium already had rejected his request to keep the regiment and its headquarters at Stolp. According to Blücher, the council believed that, first, the issue of importing fodder for the horses during regimental exercises would be better served at Belgard. Second, that town had an enclosed hippodrome, but Stolp did not. "I have a few [small] estates near Stolp; my own house is in the town," explained Blücher. "If I go to Belgard, all of these benefits will be gone. The Leib squadron of my regiment has been in this garrison since its creation; the foreigners are almost all married and live here. Is the happiness of the common man not worth regarding? Concerning the hippodrome, I am not such an old fool of my trade to break and train young Polish horses in a small enclosed environment. . . . A hussar must break his horse in open fields and not hide in a box during bad weather."[13]

Zastrow intervened on Blücher's behalf, and the king decided to allow the regiment's headquarters to remain at Stolp. As for Strantz, Blücher had to accept the situation. "It takes a lot to restore my calmness after it disappears," he wrote Zastrow on 2 November, "although I cannot shake off the thought that no matter what I do, I will never earn the confidence and satisfaction of my Master, otherwise General Strantz would not be the inspector of my regiment. I am from the bottom of my heart the friend of this man, but in my truthful opinion I did more service for the King and I did more for the reputation of Prussian troops than Strantz—although I must admit that I had more opportunities than he and I am convinced that Strantz did the best he could. Nevertheless, I will be quiet, that's the way it is."[14]

Another slight occurred that made the general fume and probably attribute the woes of his career to being a foreigner. After the drawdown, five cavalry battalions, including Blücher's, served as an advance guard observing the demarcation line. "I am the only general among these troops," he explained, "but General Lieutenant Romberg has to stay to command them. Am I not capable of commanding in peacetime? I also attribute this to my benefactors on the Oberkriegskollegium."[15] Zastrow again came through: Berlin recalled Romberg, and Blücher received command of the advance guard, though he had to transfer his headquarters to Münster. He did not much care for this small city, where he would reside for most of the next ten years.[16]

As Blücher relocated south, the French withdrew across the Ems River to Bentheim, where they decided to demolish the local Schloß with more than a ton of powder. Before they could finish their destruction, news arrived of Blücher's march up the opposite bank of the Ems, and they decided to leave the Schloß if he crossed the river. Although it is not clear how they got there, the French had thirteen mostly large metal cannon and howitzers with them that lacked draft horses. They hoped their new Dutch "countrymen" soon would arrive with teams to pull them away. Hearing of this, the general received permission from Möllendorf to cross the Ems one night with 300 troopers and all the teams of his supply wagons. As the Prussians approached the Schloß, the French withdrew. That same night his men unearthed all the powder barrels and tossed them into the wet moat. "In record time," noted Blücher, "I had the gunpowder thrown into the water." He hitched the guns to his teams and recrossed the Ems. "When the next day came, the French were surprised how we made all this possible. The field marshal praised my zeal and promised that he would make it possible for my regiment to receive gratitude for the cannons. To make sure the cannon were safe from other claims, I had my teams bring them to Lingen, on Prussian soil." Blücher received a request from the Protestant church for a few of the cannon to be donated and melted into bells; other requests came in for the metal to be used for nails. To ensure that his troops received a reward, he solicited Zastrow for advice:

> I beg you, my dear friend, in the event that the request of the people of Lingen is granted, please try to get a commitment to pay something to the regiment. Tell me if you think it is wise for me to discuss this with the King? I am far from it to request the whole price for the guns; if only we could get fifty thaler per piece! Attached to the regiment we have in each garrison a little school to educate the children of our hussars in writing and math. To add to this, we have saved a small sum in the campaign chest and I would like to use the money from the guns to employ a teacher for

each garrison. This will benefit the regiment because in the future it will have a lot of educated noncommissioned officers and we can also educate the young cantonists and especially the sons of the foreign hussars.[17]

Unfortunately, we do not know the fate of the captured cannon. On learning that the army soon would be expanded, Blücher also beseeched the king's adjutant to lobby on behalf of his regiment's officers. Here, as with the schools for the children, Blücher demonstrated his paternal care for his men. Moreover, he recognized the importance of earning the respect of both officer and soldier.

> The regiment is fortunate to have a proficient, experienced officer corps and my senior lieutenants are people who have [served] for forty years; the senior captain, Goltz, is fifty years old. Oh, my dear friend, it is a blessing to be surrounded by people who serve happy and are content; and by what do we measure the confidence of our subordinates, when they believe that we have their well-being in mind and make our own secondary. In this war, I have experienced that one can accomplish much with the subordinates when one has their trust. My adjutant general, Captain Bonin, has now been in this position under four different generals. My dearest friend, consider that those who served in the same capacity under Prince Hohenlohe, Count Kalckreuth, and General Rüchel have all advanced—none of my companions have made headway. Admittedly, I did not accomplish great things, but in my little sphere I did not miss anything.[18]

Blücher's official duties required him to be the steward of the Prussian forces that sprawled from the North Sea to the Ruhr River. He had to ensure they received the necessary lodging, food, equipment, and fodder for their horses. The general earned the respect of his soldiers by demonstrating concern over their welfare. Münster especially proved to be a very expensive city for the pay of an average soldier. Thus, he insisted that his men cultivate their own potatoes to become self-sufficient. "The whole commissariat can go to hell, and I will feed the corps myself if I have to," he assured Bonin.[19]

The hussar found the monotony of independent command in peacetime overbearing. "Our situation is unchanged," he wrote in July 1796. "The Duke of Brunswick has his headquarters at

Minden, the troops are quartered near Minden; I am stationed with the advance guard near the Ems and the Ruhr, my left wing is near Duisburg, the right near the North Sea. I am fed up; I have a regiment, but I don't see it. My job is writing. I doubt I will stay healthy doing this. . . . [A] soldier looks forward to rest, but in his grave."[20] "I am stuck at the desk," he explained in October 1799. "You know how active I am and how I hate to sit still. My circumstances are fatal; for almost four years, I have not conducted military business. Heaven must end this."[21] Almost two years later he declared: "I wish I would be put out of my misery and get out of this land of holiness, where people are much poorer in common sense than in wealth, where forty-two carefree clerics squander the sweat of the poor. The middle and lower classes bless us, but the aristocratic thieves curse us."[22]

Blücher found a pleasant distraction in becoming a landowner again. In 1796 the king granted him the estate of Duninow (Duninów Duży) on the Vistula River in South Prussia. The forest itself contained more than one hundred square miles of timber. "From the revenues of the last three years," he wrote his chief foreman, Häse, "I already expended 8,000 thaler in cash and paid 2,100 thaler for the survey." In Pomerania Blücher owned Grumbkow and a small estate near Stolp named Ripnow. Not far from Berlin, in the Havelland, the estate of Groß Zieten, valued at 110,000 thaler according to Blücher, likewise belonged to him. "Sure, sometimes things will go too far," he wrote on 17 October 1799, "but I am certain my servants and tenants will not suck me dry; this is a pleasant reassurance. If I could just get there and see it all! It would be ungrateful of me to retire now because I don't have too much longer to serve. But I am getting old and I owe it to my children to conserve what I have left."[23] Concern for his children remained paramount, as a letter to Bonin demonstrates:

> Who else can I have a deeper trust in than you, my best friend? But let's get to the point. All of this uncertainty over whether I will stay here or march and to where bothers me and especially concerning my two children [Gebhard and Fritze], who I love without limit. Your brother told me that his wife possibly will come to me; this would be a great opportunity to bring my daughter as well if the little woman is nice enough to fulfill my request. Of course, I will pay half of all travel expenses. But if the little woman is not

coming, perhaps you can come, my friend, to Pyrmont and bring my child with you; she is still little and must be entrusted to you.

Do me a favor, send a wagon posthaste to Schönwalde and pick up my daughter. I wrote my former in-laws that you would pick up Fritze from there. I hope you understand, dear Bonin, that the time has come for me to take charge of the education of my children. Should it be the case that neither you nor your sister-in-law can come to the spa [at Pyrmont], best and dearest friend, then I ask you to keep my child with you until I come or make other arrangements. Splurge on her education, nothing is too good, and I will pay over 300 thaler. I kiss the hands of your adorable wife and adjure her at the ashes of her friend to be a mother to the orphaned child. I will be thankful, but God will reward you, and you can be sure of both. I will say nothing more now; my most important matters are always in your good hands.

I wrote the mademoiselle who is now with my child that I will pay her a year's salary and a gift of forty thaler; money for that is at Schönwalde. My little son goes to Neustettin to the gymnasium and to a boarding house. Major Breetz, who is my friend, will chaperone, and also my cousin, Lieutenant Blücher, a solid man, will look out for him. If my daughter's hair is already curly, for God's sake comb it out.[24]

To Breetz he wrote: "Thank you for the kind disposition that you have toward my little son. I already got an earful from my former in-laws that when I get home, the little one should be with you at Neustettin."[25] During these years, the Blücher family continued to grow. Franz's wife, Bernhardine, gave birth to Gebhard Bernhard Carl von Blücher at Münster on 14 July 1799. "Häse, just think about it," reflected the general, "I am already a grandfather; I have a superb daughter-in law who loves me dearly and my son is calming down too. My properties are worth 300,000 [thaler] and, thank God, I don't owe a heller to anyone.[26] If I can get all of my money together and 10,000 in bonds, I would stay at Grumbkow and get rid of all the rest."[27]

Blücher eventually discovered that his Grumbkow estate manager, "a covetous, unscrupulous human being," was cheating him. "You labeled Herr Rempert a do-no-good loser; he deceived and duped us all and I am glad I got rid of him," he wrote to an attorney named Kutscher, who previously served as quartermaster of Blücher's regiment. "I am sending you the requested power of attorney for the sale of Grumbkow; you know how much it cost me;

I don't want to take a loss; I will not sell below 46,000 thaler. Payment is to be made in the same currency that I used to purchase it. I was certain that I had made a good deal with Grumbkow, but my constant absence did not help."

Always willing to help a veteran, Blücher hired a retired non-commissioned officer named Rudroff. "I told you in yesterday's letter about him," continues his missive to Kutscher; "but do not let this stop you from selling—I can use Rudroff on my other estates. Should the sale not go through, we will give the estate to old Rudroff to run; just make sure that a competent estate manager or farmhand is there who understands how to plow and harrow, how the sequences on a farm follow each other, and believe me, things will be better than under Herr Rempert. He certainly is a God-damn administrator; I have to get my estate back from him by court order. Just at this moment, Rudroff arrived here and he would love to take over the estate. I will give the old man 100 thaler in cash and him and his wife plenty of free hands. I am sure that the old man will not cheat me and will do his best regarding the estate."[28]

Hoping to add to his holdings, Blücher wrote the king's adjutant general: "The Prebendary of Fürstenberg died, he had a prebend at Halberstadt.[29] I will ask His Majesty to award it to me. I don't want to become Catholic, but I would like to have this Catholic morsel; anyway, the King will just give it away, and I have three children, all of whom cost me a lot of money and, unfortunately, I myself cost the most. From the dead King, I received an estate [Duninow], but I am not able to get back on my feet," he lamented. "I don't belong to those who get good things, and Minister von Voß made sure that I would not get rich from that gift. The Halberstadt prebendary could bring me up to 5,000 thaler."[30] Although Blücher heard that the king planned to grant such positions to his officers, he did not receive this "Catholic morsel."

With his private resources becoming stretched, Blücher decided to request a promotion to general lieutenant. "I cannot survive in these countries as the commanding general; I have expenses that a normal general does not incur," he explained to the quartermaster general at Emden.[31] That same year, 1801, the promotion came on 20 May. Yet the money went just as fast and sometimes faster. "I see that you have no money in my accounts," he wrote his accountant on 29 July 1802, "and yet I was careless and sent you bills with the request to pay for me and my women [wife and daughter].

Pardon me. In the future, there cannot and will not be a shortage of money. See the attached note for how payments will be made. . . . I also transferred 9,000 thaler from Pomerania to [your account in] Berlin."[32]

The dead king Blücher referred to was Frederick William II, who passed on 16 November 1797; his pious twenty-six-year-old son succeeded him as Frederick William III. Frederick William II had shown Blücher great favor, and in him the general saw not merely his king but also his greatest benefactor, praising the monarch all of his life. The late king had a well-earned reputation for debauchery, which Blücher no doubt approved. Young Frederick William III, however, was of a different stamp. With his "sincere and honest sense, purity of morals, and penetrating natural intelligence," the new king "in general raised the highest hopes. Blücher was drawn to him and became absolutely devoted to him." For his part, young Frederick William knew Blücher from the Rhine campaigns and held the general in esteem. His wife, the beautiful Queen Louise, soon "viewed the general in a heroic sense. She found pleasure in his exuberant, cheerful nature, his conversation, and his uninhibited, striking, often witty remarks. She saw him with pleasure at her table."[33] A gentle, kindhearted man who loved his wife and children, Frederick William III would find himself engaged in a life-or-death struggle with a ruler one year younger than him—Napoleon Bonaparte. His fate as well as Frederick William's became bound with that of the native Mecklenburger who Colonel Belling had convinced to enter the Prussian service in 1760.

CHAPTER 4

THE COLLAPSE

In 1798 the War of the Second Coalition ensued between France on the one hand and Great Britain, Austria, Russia, Naples, and the Ottoman Empire on the other. Prussian foreign minister Christian von Haugwitz urged Frederick William III to join the Coalition in an attempt to safeguard his kingdom's remaining possessions on the left bank of the Rhine, including Kleve. Nevertheless, the young monarch wanted to see how far neutrality would get him with Herr Bonaparte. We have nothing from Blücher's own hand regarding his thoughts over this war or Prussia's neutrality in it.[1] Instead, Berlin agreed to join Russia, Denmark, and Sweden in the League of Armed Neutrality to protect neutral shipping against the British navy's wartime policy of unlimited search of all vessels for French contraband.

As a result of the Treaty of Lunéville, which ended the War of the Second Coalition on 9 February 1801, the Prussians no longer needed to guard the line of demarcation. In March Blücher took quarters at Emmerich in Kleve, but his troops moved northeast to guard the coast of Ostfriesland. He joined them in April, establishing his headquarters at Emden, from where his hussars patrolled a one-hundred-mile stretch of North Sea coast to Cuxhaven. The collapse of the league shortly after the assassination of Tsar Paul on 23 March 1801 eventually brought a new assignment for the general. In November of that year, he received orders to transfer his headquarters to Lingen along with a portion of his troops. At that time of year, poor roads and weather made it difficult for the dependents of his soldiers to follow on foot.[2] The quandary in which he found himself offers a unique look into the world of the soldier.

> The squadrons and companies each have fifteen to twenty sick, the usual fall fevers. But this is the least of our problems: the women folk and the children are especially annoying. Each company and each squadron has at least thirty *Weiber* [broads] and daily the enlisted soldiers are getting married because the girls in this region have money and His Majesty gave orders to issue

wedding licenses. We cannot prevent these Weiber from following their husbands from the garrisons because a young person who
is married before and during a deployment can expect to return
home and find that his young wife has grown old. We have been
gone for nine years and there are fusiliers and hussars who have
fathered five children, with the oldest not more than five years
old. Where should these helpless creatures now go? The commissariat will not pay for their transportation [by wagon].

Blücher claimed that he wrote to Brunswick over this matter
three years earlier. With the troops preparing to depart, the general again voiced his concern. He received a response to have the
children transported by the best means possible, which meant by
wagon, but the commissariat refused to pay. "If we don't make
arrangements," warned Blücher, "the consequences can be great for
the interests of the King and, considering the loss of fathers, moth-
ers, and children, certainly for the state. If I start marching and leave
the wives and children behind in a country where it is so expensive,
the father might desert; when we catch him and question him, he
will explain: 'I will run away ten more times because I don't want
to see my wife and child in ruins.'" Blücher insisted that while he
did everything possible to prevent desertion, he could not "guarantee anything if moving the children is not made secure. The Weiber
can, if they have to, walk beside the wagons, but the children must
to be transported."[3] Blücher lost this battle; unfortunately, we have
no details of the consequences.

Meanwhile, Napoleon's steady reorganization of Germany benefitted the Prussians. Diplomatic relations between France and
Prussia remained strong, with Napoleon insinuating that he supported Berlin's goal of organizing North Germany into a Prussian-
dominated confederation. The death of Archduke Maximilian
Francis of Austria, prince-bishop of Münster and youngest child of
Maria Theresa, on 26 July 1801 opened the door for the Prussians to
occupy the large bishopric. The Franco-Prussian Treaty of Paris (23
May 1802) confirmed Berlin's acquisition of much of the secularized
Bishopric of Münster, which Frederick William III transformed into
the Fürstentum (Principality) of Münster, naming himself hereditary prince. As part of the same treaty, Napoleon granted to Prussia
the city of Mühlhausen as well as much of Erfurt and its surrounding countryside. During the 1803 Reichsdeputationshauptschluss
(Imperial Recess), Napoleon awarded Prussia generous territory

as compensation for districts on the left bank of the Rhine lost to French expansion during the War of the First Coalition.

Blücher's troops paraded into Münster on 3 August 1802. A few months later, Frederick William appointed Heinrich Friedrich Karl vom und zum Stein to the post of president of Münster to coadminister this newest Prussian state along with its military governor: Blücher. The official appointment is dated 10 February 1803. Blücher's oldest son, Franz, served as his father's adjutant and secretary. His other son, Gebhard, served with the Red Hussars and likewise quartered at Münster. His daughter, Fritze, engaged to be married to Major Count Ludwig von der Schulenburg, likewise lived in the vicinity.[4] Despite this favorable situation, or perhaps because of this favorable situation, Blücher again thought of retirement at the end of the year. "I have to think about a reasonable fallback. I will retire and live a quiet life. I hope I can arrange a vacation; if war does not come, then I will not return to Münster. I own a very nice estate near Berlin and I will spend my days there. I sold the South Prussian estates, which frees my hands. My daughter is getting married on 1 February and then I will be alone with my wife."[5]

The possibility of war stemmed from the occupation of Hanover in May 1803 by 30,000 French troops commanded by General Adolphe-Edouard Mortier. Situated between Westphalia and Brandenburg, the French presence there posed a threat to Prussia. Even with the thought of war, Blücher remained melancholy, but the fact that Berlin did nothing to prevent the occupation aggravated him. He apparently tried to intervene in some way by appearing at French headquarters on 1 June to express his desire to participate in the operation. He received an interview with Mortier, but neither their conversation nor the purpose of Blücher's efforts is known.[6] After the Hanoverians surrendered and signed the Convention of Sulingen on 3 June 1803 recognizing their state as French territory, a dejected Blücher returned to Münster.[7]

By the end of the year, his mood had improved, but he still found no comfort at Münster. "I am moving in a few days to the [bishop's] palace and can live there in comfort. In the other wing of the palace lives President Stein; he is an honest man and we get on well." The king also allocated the profits from the estate's agricultural production to Blücher and Stein as well as the surrounding woods so they could hunt. "I now could be satisfied," he continued, "but I am not. I don't like Münster and the people here, and that the regiment is not with me is unbearable. If I serve the King any longer, then he will have to give me a governorship closer to my regiment; this is the only requirement for me to continue being a soldier. Otherwise, I will return to the plow; agriculture now has more advantages than the service; everything changes."[8]

Blücher spent 1804 seriously engaged in speculation over the value of his assets like a high-stakes gambler. On 10 January he wrote Kutscher:

> The geese that old Herr Rudroff sent arrived well and we liked them a lot. Please tell the old guy that the necessary construction at Grumbkow must be started right away. I have to tell you that I am doing some wild thinking here. I sold the estates in South Prussia, received a whole lot of money for them, but I still can't let go. So, if I sell Grumbkow and the house, I cannot do so for less than 50,000 thaler. I realize that Grumbkow requires a lot of investment, but now that I have a free hand I can do it. Nothing can come up short at Grumbkow, my dear Kutscher; the acreage is too large for this, and old Herr von Zitzewitz from Dumröse told me six years ago that Grumbkow can't lose because it is big, the soil is good, the majority is still fallow, and I manage the forest so well that it increases in value every year. In case we decide 50,000 thaler is too much, then, my dearest friend, I will invest 12,000 thaler in Grumbkow. Just remember: if I sell, I have to buy something else, and nowhere else will I find an estate as reasonable.[9]

A French presence at Münster kept Blücher alert. "God knows," he wrote on 9 June, "the French give me lots of work to do and nothing else gets done; the city is not one day empty of them. If we stay on good terms with the French, I will come to Pomerania this fall."[10] One month later he added: "As long as the French don't cross me, I will go to the fall maneuvers at Potsdam and from there straight to Pomerania. For now, we have a better understanding with them."[11] But after they violated international law by seizing the British chargé d'affaires at Hamburg, George Rumbold, in October 1804, Blücher hoped his government would take action. "For four weeks I have stood with my foot in the stirrup but cannot mount," he wrote on 27 November. "We must be determined to give a pounding! The French must learn that in the north there are still Germans who will punish them."[12] On Frederick William's request, Napoleon freed Rumbold.

After taking the waters at Pyrmont, the general went to Potsdam for the fall maneuvers. There, his complaints to Frederick William III over the treatment of the hussars apparently received sympathy. "I hope the hussars are no longer considered step-children; it appears the King is open-minded. I spoke very forcefully about our neglect."[13] The general situation of the Prussian military establishment, especially the canton system, so concerned Blücher that in early January 1805 he wrote a treatise titled "Thoughts over the Formation of a Prussian National Army." In it the general called for compulsory military service, shortening the required length of service, an increase of pay, and better treatment of soldiers. By circulating this essay, Blücher joined many Prussian officers who sought to restructure the kingdom's military, partly in view of the success of French arms and partly because they believed in evolutionary reform. In fact, an entire society of officers, known as the Militärische Gesellschaft, formed at Berlin in 1801 under the direction of Major Gerhard Johann David von Scharnhorst to discuss military change. Reform ensued, though at a pace too slow to prevent an approaching disaster.[14]

Unfortunately for Blücher, the French presence at Hanover compelled the king to deny his request to take leave in Pomerania.[15] At his headquarters, the general contended with boats of serious illness. Debilitating and persistent pain in his head and both ears forced him to take leave from 6 July to 6 August 1804. "Now, my friend," he revealed to Kutscher, "I must tell you that my health is not getting better but worse. I am afflicted with gruesome and constant pain in my head, especially in both ears. This is probably the consequences of old age and fatigue, but also not-always-correct-clean-living. The doctors recommended a treatment."[16] Blücher took the waters at the Pyrmont spa, but this did little for his condition. Frederick William promised a transfer from Münster as soon as the French withdrew from Hanover.[17]

On 2 December 1804, Napoleon crowned himself emperor of the French. Restoring the rank of marshal, he raised eighteen generals to this exalted status. Names like Louis-Nicolas Davout, Nicolas Soult, Jean Lannes, Joachim Murat, Jean-Baptiste Bernadotte, Michel Ney, Pierre Augereau, and André Massena caught the attention of the international press. These developments did not appear to alarm Blücher, however. Three days after Napoleon's coronation, he noted, "It seems to be quiet here; I believe we stand in a good relationship with the new Emperor."[18] Regardless, he kept a close eye on the French. "I cannot report any news from here [Münster]," he explained on 2 February 1805, "only that I still have a lot of contact with the French. Sitting around idle is a life I hate."[19] Even when hostilities erupted in Europe—the 1805 War of the Third Coalition, which pitted France and Spain against Great Britain, Austria, Russia, and Sweden—Blücher doubted his government would act. If it did, he preferred a war with France but did not rule out conflict with the Coalition. "If at all possible, I will visit my regiment this fall," he wrote on 21 May 1805, "because we will not know until the fall if we will get along with Russia and Sweden. I don't believe General Zastrow [Prussian ambassador to Russia] will do everything we are hoping for, because we can't just leave France; the friendship is already too close."[20]

To guarantee Prussia's neutrality, Frederick William III decided to mobilize. Regardless, both the French and Russians soon violated Prussian territory. In response, the king ordered the formation of armies in Silesia, Franconia and Thuringia, and Westphalia, appointing Brunswick as commander in chief. Moved by a personal meeting with Tsar Alexander I at Potsdam in November 1805, Frederick William agreed to join the Coalition. He pledged to first issue an ultimatum to Napoleon demanding a French withdrawal behind the Rhine among other stipulations. Should the emperor refuse, Prussia would join the Third Coalition. Haugwitz, as the king's plenipotentiary, received the task of delivering the ultimatum to Napoleon's headquarters in Bohemia. On his own accord, he dithered for four weeks, hoping to buy time for Brunswick's lethargic mobilization as well as for the military situation to show some sign of change in favor of the Coalition. Upon his reaching French headquarters, however, the emperor refused an interview.

In the meantime, Blücher received command of the vanguard belonging to the Westphalian army then assembling between Münster and Hamm and led by Elector William I of Hesse. On 10 November 1805 he reported to William's headquarters that intelligence from "all corners and places" indicated the march of imperial troops, particularly from Belgium and Holland, down the Rhine. "I don't trust this business completely, but there might be some truth to it. But, Your Highness, I must say that if the news is correct, I believe our troops are needed here and at the Lippe [River] more than in the Paderborn area. Yet we can only leave Münster in the greatest emergency, otherwise the Hagken Infantry Regiment and the fusiliers, which is comprised entirely of natives, will desert because they'll believe their fatherland is in danger. I for one cannot stay away from this region for long because the circumstances change by the hour and require a quick decision.[21]

The 2nd Battalion rejoined the Red Hussars from Pomerania on 17 November 1805. On 2 December Blücher received orders to report to Brunswick's headquarters at Göttingen to command the advance forces of the army assembling in Franconia and Thuringia.[22] To ease the cost of the mobilization, Frederick William III gave Blücher 1,000 thaler to purchase horses for himself and his adjutant, Goltz. After traveling over 300 miles from Münster through Göttingen, the general caught up with the vanguard at Bayreuth on 20 December. "I arrived here exhausted and took over a nice body of troops that is not yet too tired. All the troops that I met during my ride were in great spirits; we all could use some of this happiness. I miss having the King with the Army; he alone is missed; headquarters is now at Gotha. . . . I have the Thuringian Forest behind me. Herr Augereau, who is supposed to be my opponent, is near Ulm." The Bavarian city of Ulm stood 146 miles southwest of Blücher's position at Bayreuth, itself some 90 miles south of Gotha. According to reports, Marshal Augereau moved northeast toward Donauworth. "I don't care," remarked Blücher, "I hope he comes closer so that when it starts we don't have to waste time looking for him. According to reports, he has 40,000 men, but it could be less."

The Prussians knew that Napoleon had pursued the Austrians and Russians deep into Moravia and that the two armies now faced each other, the French at Brünn (Brna) and the Austro-Russians at Austerlitz (Slavkov u Brna). Rumors circulated of a great battle at Austerlitz on 2 December. "We receive nothing but French reports," which Blücher found to be contradictory. "The Russians suffered a lot on the 2nd, but were able to make good on the 4th and 5th." Regardless, an armistice between Austria and France appeared imminent. "It may be that we are alone, but our confidence will be all the more stronger." Blücher complained that his superiors did not display more urgency: "Everything goes too slow for me. Of course the troops need rest after the [long] march, but our needs [supply] mean that we can't stay long in one place."[23] To many, Brunswick's slow mobilization appeared deliberate.[24]

Sketchy reports over a great battle fought in early December and followed by an armistice kept Blücher on edge. From Bayreuth, he requested instructions. "Armistice, peace—these collide with each other hourly. I believe that nothing will come out of the latter and the former will be suspended. Soon we have to hear from Berlin concerning what will happen in this matter." The arrival of Grand Duke Constatine, Tsar Alexander's brother, at Berlin excited him. "Yes, Constantine is in our capital city, and what I heard, he presented further to the King over the arrangements of the Russian army in the name of his brother. If we get them closer to us, then we can eat the boogie man with all his men and mice." From media reports, Blücher learned of French forces marching west to Würzburg and Bamberg, apparently returning home. He believed they would continue to the Rhine. "Something uncomfortable must have happened to Herr Napoleon," he wrote. Referring to the British admiral whose fleet trapped General Bonaparte's army in Egypt in 1799, Blücher quipped:

> Either Sydney Smith inconvenienced him, or in his mind he sees faces that he does not like; quick, he is in a terrible situation, and watch out: he will make noble a peace to get his head out of the noose. It would be inexcusable if this does not become a game of life or death with him; is it possible for the gods to spare him? I am predicting that they [the French] will all die as a consequence. Here, we know with certainty that few of his Guard are left; only the stupidity of the Russians gave him an advantage at the end. The bravery of the Russians and their Tsar shocked him. He hardly will ask for another fight with them. Davout is dead; Murat is crippled, all his adjutants died or are badly maimed. Displeased with Austria, Alexander moved away; yet he will be back soon, if there is no peace. Thank God! Good night, now, I must sleep.[25]

Thus the general described the greatest victory of Napoleon's career: the 2 December 1805 battle of Austerlitz. Despite the news Blücher heard, the Russians did not "make good" on 4 and 5 December. In fact, after Tsar Alexander was found crying under a tree on the second, the Russian army limped home. Kaiser Francis of Austria did indeed request an armistice, which Napoleon granted on 4 December. Three weeks later, on 26 December, the French and Austrians signed the Treaty of Pressburg (Bratislava), ending the Third Coalition and opening the door for such sweeping changes as the dissolution of the Holy Roman Empire.

While negotiating with the Austrians, Napoleon finally summoned Haugwitz to French headquarters at the beautiful palace of Schönbrunn in Vienna. Rather than present his ultimatum, Haugwitz found himself forced to sign the Treaty of Schönbrunn on 15 December. This humiliating document created a Franco-Prussian alliance, signaling Napoleon's desire to harness Prussia for his own use. As his reward for ratifying the treaty, Frederick William III would receive Hanover. Always ready to give that which did not belong to him, Napoleon knew well that the Prussians would earn the enmity of the British crown as long as they held Hanover, the personal possession of King George III. In return, Berlin would cede the territories of Ansbach, Wesel, Kleve, Berg, and the Swiss city of Neuchâtel—a Prussian possession at that time—to France and its allies.

Although the Prussians recognized the trap, Napoleon's offer proved tempting. Possession of Hanover long had been a national-security objective. Although Tsar Alexander promised to place an army of 65,000 men at Frederick William's disposal, Brunswick's preference for peace convinced the king to accept Hardenberg's advice to pursue Napoleon's "offer." According to the diplomat, Frederick William would agree to provisionally annex Hanover while the Prussian foreign office sought to secure Great Britain's approval. Caught between France and Great Britain, and with the victorious Grande Armée taking winter quarters in southern Germany, the cost of keeping his forces on a war footing nevertheless prompted Frederick William to demobilize his army.

In an attempt to buy time to lobby the British, Haugwitz journeyed to Paris in the hope of securing some favorable concessions to the Schönbrunn terms. An enraged Napoleon accused Frederick William of ingratitude and issued harsher demands in the proposed Treaty of Paris that Haugwitz signed on 15 February 1806. Not only would the Prussians occupy Hanover but they also would close all North German ports and rivers to British commerce and commence the seizure of all British goods. In addition, Napoleon demanded Hardenberg's dismissal. Having to choose between an alliance with Napoleon or war with him, Frederick William ratified the treaty on 3 March 1806. Haugwitz replaced Hardenberg as foreign minister, and General Rüchel led Prussian troops into Hanover. The closure of the North German coast forced the British to declare war on Prussia in April 1806. The whole affair had blown up in Frederick's face: never had Prussia been so isolated and humiliated.

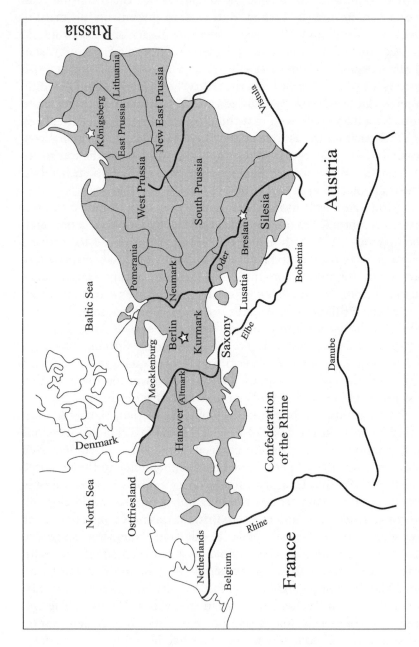

Prussia in 1806. Map drawn by Alex Mendoza. Copyright © 2014 by the University of Oklahoma Press.

As Rüchel's advance-guard commander, Blücher observed the French border with Prussian Westphalia. In addition, his troops had to guard the coast against a British landing in Friesland, the north-west corner of Dutch territory. Blücher returned to his headquarters at Münster. Napoleon's sister, Caroline, and her husband, Marshal Murat, took possession of the emperor's gift to them: the Grand Duchy of Berg. Less than seventy miles west of Münster, the new state consisted of the Duchies of Kleve and Berg on the right bank of the Rhine. On 29 March 1806 Blücher learned that Murat's troops occupied Essen and Werden, some one hundred miles up the Rhine from Kleve and Elten, between Berg and Kleve, which Napoleon had awarded to Prussia during the 1803 Imperial Recess. According to the reports the general received, the French forcefully escorted Essen's small Prussian garrison to the frontier.[26]

Probably unaware of just how precarious the international situation was for Prussia, Blücher decided to reinsert his troops, writing from Münster on 31 March: "I will be very restless until I again hold Essen and Werden. If the French don't want to leave in good faith, I will issue orders for the troops to take no notice of them, but the inhabitants will be sternly advised . . . to not give out bread or food to the French; should they use force, then I will reply with force, because one has to remain master of his own house."[27] He sent seven battalions, five squadrons, and six guns to reoccupy the three districts, which occurred without the Prussians meeting any resistance. Blücher then sent his son Gebhard to Berlin for further instructions.

The general took some heat for his actions, not from his king, but from the French media, as he explained to Frederick William on 2 July 1806: "Your Mighty, Powerful Highness, the King! Graceful King and Master! I was abused by the French *Moniteur* as well as by the German Wesel newspaper. Because I serve for only one reward, and that is the satisfaction of my king, such a thing does not displease me. The accolades of the French do dishonor me, yet their criticism also gives me an unlimited reassurance."[28] Ten days later he reported rumors claiming that Napoleon planned to make Murat king of all Westphalia. Labeling such an event highly probable, he warned the Prussian monarch that "more and more French troops move into the already haggard and looted Duchy of Westphalia. My military circumstances would not be so awkward, if we were not on such friendly terms with France."[29]

In the meantime, Murat had ordered his commandants to avoid trouble with Blücher's troops. Napoleon, however, refused to suffer the insult but was not ready to wage war with Prussia. Nevertheless, the affair took a turn that aggravated Blücher. According to a July 1806 agreement, all Prussian troops would evacuate Essen, Werden, and Elten on 20 July, while all French troops would move out on the twenty-first, with the two powers establishing a joint interim administration in August.[30] Blücher's vigilance certainly did not abate following this development with "friendly" France, as illustrated by his report to the king's adjutant, Friedrich Emil von Kleist: "If the French violate our territory, I will not hesitate, and they will violate it, because they know nothing about borders and always want to go the most direct way." He assured Kleist that the tense situation along the border did not allow him to rotate his units: "From now on I will not rest the troops, because the commotion will be too strong if I pull back." He also viewed the situation with Great Britain as a waste of valuable manpower that otherwise would guard the frontier against the true enemy. "Should the relationship between us and England get better, please let me know I can recall the troops from Ostfriesland." In addition to the units posted there, he had to keep detachments in the Ahrenberg hills along the right bank of the Ems at Meppen, Aschendorf, and Papenburg to maintain communication with Ostfriesland. Should the French attempt an invasion of North Germany through the Ahrenberg, Blücher planned to move troops north from Osnabrück to fill the gap between Münster and Ostfriesland. "God in Heaven, why was I not born fifty years earlier or fifty years later? Farewell and come here; it is better to discuss these circumstances than write about them."[31]

This letter to Kleist marks the opening salvo of another of Blücher's written bombardments. As with Frederick II and Frederick William II, Blücher had absolutely no reservations about writing candidly direct to the king or to someone who made sure his letter would be read by the monarch. In late July 1806 the general did everything he could to convince Frederick William III to go to war. Unlike the hawks of the court—Queen Louise, Prince Louis Ferdinand, Rüchel, and others—Blücher based his demanded for war on what he saw at the front rather than Napoleon's continued diplomatic slights. On the very next day, 23 July, he again wrote to Kleist, assuring the royal adjutant that he would "proceed exactly according to my instructions; my troops will certainly avoid all trouble. It is the will of my master and to follow this is enough for me." Yet he declared that he would "respond to violence with violence." According to spies, 2,000 imperial troops would fortify the powerful fortress of Wesel before the end of July. "If this happens, then we will also see other developments," he assured Kleist.

Blücher also insisted that Murat intended to add territory to his grand duchy. His wife, Caroline, was rumored to be planning a trip to the spa at Pyrmont, where Queen Louise happened to be taking the waters as well. Not wanting his queen scandalized by the upstart Bonaparte, Blücher confided to Kleist that he would warn her: "I cannot possibly believe that it would be acceptable for our beloved queen to be in the same spa at the same time. My travels through Paderborn and Herford brought me one day to Pyrmont and I found the queen in good health and spirits; she told me that the trip and the spa are good for her well-being."

After providing the supporting evidence, the general stated his case:

> I beseech you, my dearest friend, to tell His Majesty in my name, that I believe the French have dishonest intentions against us. The King is the only righteous power who can swim against the currents; through friendship wrapped in deceit or force, whatever the circumstances offer, this dike will rupture. We are still full of strength and it would be faint-heartedness if we believe that we could not stand up to these windbags. Our army is good and there is a good mood among it, and even if we have a few who are pigheaded the same had happened under Frederick II. This, however, should not stop us from looking the enemy in his face and beating him. The latter will happen as sure as I am alive. But it is now urgent that we make up our mind for this vendetta. United with Saxony and Hesse, the French cannot conquer us. If we need money, England will give it to us, and they will do this. If the war does not occur, then in a few years the case can arise that it would be very hard for us to face this colossus. I would be very happy to start the dance.

Blücher could not hide his displeasure with Brunswick. "But now a word in confidence: tell me, what is going on? The Duke of Brunswick has his headquarters at Hildesheim, but he is at Brunswick; Scharnhorst, his quartermaster general, is mainly in

Westphalia; while the first adjutant general is at Magdeburg. Truly a laudable separation."[32]

Two days after writing Kleist, Blücher targeted Frederick William himself. The theatrics of his prose certainly make us envy those who heard the man make a speech. More importantly, the letter captures the heart of a true patriot, a warrior who believed that national honor had been sullied, and a nobleman who sought to defend his personal honor:

> Highest Almighty King, gracious King and Master! Summoned by loyal and honest attachment to His Highness, prompted by lively participation in the glory, the honor, and the wellness of Your Royal Majesty's States and Army, and finally compelled by the daily, critical situation and the increasingly dangerous steps regarding the military that France allows itself to take against Your Royal Majesty, I finally must lay my heart at the feet of the King, my master; as a loyal servant of your noble house I lay my opinion regarding France for the first and last time at Your Majesty's feet.
>
> France does not have good intentions, especially toward Your Royal Majesty, the only power that stands between her conquering and enslaving Germany. They do not even hide their intentions; although they are making sweet pretense, all the actions against your Royal Majesty attest to this. The invasion of Hanover, the forced march through the Ansbach, and the recent heist and occupation of Essen and Werden, as well as the completely arrogant tone that the French monarch uses [toward you], shows Your Royal Majesty more than enough than what I have to say. All loyal servants of Your Royal Majesty, all true Prussians, and especially the Army deeply felt the loss of dignity caused by these French actions and still feel them now, and all wish that the offended national honor is soon—very soon—avenged in blood.
>
> Whoever describes the behavior and demeanor of Your Royal Majesty from another viewpoint—whoever advices Your Royal Majesty to give in, to make peace with this nation, is either very, very passive, very short-sighted, or was bought with French gold. Your Royal Majesty, just ask your most enlightened, your most talented, your most loyal, your most energetic servants—State Minister Hardenberg, General Lieutenant Rüchel, General of Cavalry Count von der Schulenburg, State Minister Stein—and I swear on my life that all of these men will tell Your Royal Majesty that what I am presenting to you here is in the utmost devotion.
>
> Each day that we declare war on France before she [declares war] on us is a huge victory for Your Royal Majesty, because

with every hour the French emperor strengthens and monopo-
lizes his position, his influence, and better organizes his armies,
establishes tributary kings and princes, [and] blackmails for more
resources. If Your Royal Majesty would now personally lead our
brave Army, which burns with this thought, to fight the French
and to take humanity's revenge on these looters[,] . . . then victory will be assured. The Army's hatred and disdain against the
French is more unbelievable and bigger than Your Royal Majesty
can imagine; it has only one wish: soon—very soon—bloody war
against this nation.

Only one victorious battle and we [will] have allies, money, and
resources from all places and corners of Europe: Russia, England,
Sweden, the majority of the German empire, and even Austria will
attach themselves to our glorious flags, share the honor with us
of defeating the French. And what glory for Your Majesty! What
glory for our brave Army, to humble these hordes of looters, who
until now gained more through deceit and through the miserable
actions of their opponents than through courage. They will never
conquer a Prussian army and they will never conquer us.

Your Royal Majesty, please just come to the center of your brave
Army, lead us to honor and victory, listen to the advice and ideas
of the veteran generals who have proven themselves in the field
to be concerned for Your glory[,] . . . and we will always be victorious, we will resurrect the most beautiful and honorable times of
Frederick the Great and the Great Elector, we will resurrect our
Fatherland, we will cover the name of Prussia with honor again,
our Army will again be feared and glorified. God the Almighty,
who under the guidance of Your Royal Majesty we strongly
believe, with this wish I will live and die as Your Royal Majesty's
humble servant devoted to Your Royal Majesty.[33]

Blücher followed up this letter on the very same day with
another situation report to Kleist, which he requested be shown
immediately to the king.[34] Numbering among the several letters
that Frederick William III received on the subject, Blücher's missive
did not move him to a sudden decision for war. Instead, Napoleon's
constant diplomatic maneuvering did more for the patriot perspective than any letter could from the commander of the outpost chain in Westphalia. During the summer of 1806, Napoleon
continued to expand French influence. In particular, his creation
of the Confederation of the Rhine jolted Berlin. As its official
"Protector," the emperor harnessed the resources of all of Germany

except Austria and Prussia in a military and political alliance with the French Empire. In addition to these momentous changes in Germany, Napoleon altered the situation in southern Italy, where French forces drove the Bourbons from their Kingdom of Naples in 1805 and Napoleon installed his brother, Joseph, as monarch. Fleeing to Sicily, King Ferdinand IV established a government in exile under British protection. From there, the British supported a revolt in Calabria to destabilize Joseph's regime. To ease the pressure on his brother, Napoleon commenced secret negotiations with London in the summer of 1806: if the British withdrew their support for the Neapolitan Bourbons, Napoleon would return Hanover.

Napoleon's duplicity proved to be the final straw for the Prussian king. On 8 August 1806 he decided on war. Frederick William issued an ultimatum to Napoleon, summoned help from Russia, and healed the rift with Great Britain, thus forming the Fourth Coalition. Following the decision for war against France, the Prussians conducted a disorderly and incomplete mobilization. Large detachments and garrisons remained in Silesia and East Prussia, where they would be absolutely useless in the upcoming struggle. Instead of assembling over 200,000 soldiers to confront the new god of war, Frederick William managed to field only 130,000 Prussians and 20,000 Saxons under Brunswick's overall command. Wishing to spare their own lands the horrors of war, the Prussians decided to confront Napoleon in central Germany. This required the army to march west before the arrival of their Russian allies. A calculated risk, Frederick William simply hoped to bloody Napoleon's nose and gain time for the Russians to reach the theater.

As for Blücher, the general hoped Brunswick would move faster than he did in 1805. As early as 16 August, he attempted to impress on the duke the need to take the offensive sooner than later.[35] To another general he wrote: "And I will repeat my advice to you: if at all possible never be attacked by the French, always be the attacker even if you command the smaller force. If you follow this, then you never need to fear an enemy who is double your strength and you don't have to lose ground even if [he] has superiority. I know the French from experience. If the first action is bloody, determined, and successful, you will intimidate them for the entire campaign."[36]

On 13 September Blücher left Münster with orders to march east toward Göttingen and Paderborn to unite with Rüchel's troops; he arrived at the latter the following day.[37] Although the hussar had hoped to march west to attack Murat's troops, news that the Hessians would join the Prussians pleased him. He assured Rüchel that "it is not that bad if the French poke around a little in Ostfriesland and in the Münster region because from now on it is important that we proceed and defeat them with the united strength of the people; then we can detach and cleanse our provinces."[38] On 18 September he advised Rüchel "to avoid all serious engagements until I arrive because I can see from your deployment that you are not very strong. The first strike must be decisive; therefore, you must start it with all forces [possible]. As soon as I unite my troops with yours, I believe we can measure ourselves with one of their marshals, and if one gets a beating [in battle] then he will tell the others and word will spread. By the way, believe me my dearest friend, the French are as certain that they will be beat, as we are certain that we will beat them; I know that their smart generals tell this to each other."[39]

Brunswick botched the initial deployment by spreading his army across a front of 190 miles north and northeast of the Thuringian Forest. This prompted Blücher to ask: "God, what happened to us? But all is not lost yet because soon we will see the King in our midst."[40] The actual plan of operations Brunswick issued pleased Blücher. "Rest assured that the war is coming," he wrote from Göttingen on 6 October. "If our plan of operations gets implemented the way it is written, its success will bring joy in general."[41] Brunswick planned to assume offensive operations with ten divisions divided into three armies. Commanding the main Prussian force of 40,000 infantry (fifty-two battalions organized in five divisions), 10,000 cavalry (eighty squadrons), and 230 guns, Brunswick would concentrate at Naumburg, 170 miles southwest of Berlin. The second group, 40,000 men commanded by Prince Hohenlohe-Ingelfingen, would cover Dresden, the capital of Prussia's reluctant ally Saxony. With 20,000 men, Rüchel would launch an offensive toward the Main River to cut off from the Rhine and France itself the imperial army that Brunswick believed would advance to Saxony. After getting behind the French army, Rüchel would operate against its rear and flanks. Blücher would serve as Rüchel's advance-guard commander. Brunswick figured a decisive battle would occur in Thuringia.[42]

On 8 October Blücher reached Creuzburg on the Werra River, some forty-five miles south of Göttingen. There, he learned that the Hessians ultimately decided against joining the Fourth Coalition. This news infuriated Blücher. "We should now immediately invade Hesse," he suggested to Rüchel, "burn the country, disarm the army, and get the rest of the loot out of Kassel."[43] The results of reconnaissance, which should have been conducted earlier and more frequently, did not reach Brunswick until that day. These belated reports revealed shocking news: after advancing from Bamberg, Napoleon would target Brunswick's overexposed left flank. The aging veterans of the Seven Years War who now advised Frederick William panicked, though not Blücher. "Dear friend!" he wrote with sheer joy. "War is declared. Napoleon is marching with his whole army toward Saxony; our army marches left [east] to attack the French during their rapid march. You will soon learn that important, very important events, have happened."[44]

Even after Blücher received orders to join the main army between Erfurt and Weimar, he still only thought of the offensive. Brunswick did not agree. With the opportunity for initiating the offensive lost, he decided to post the main army at Erfurt, 170 miles southwest of Berlin. Hohenlohe's group deployed twenty miles southeast of Erfurt, while Rüchel's troops now formed the reserve between Gotha and Erfurt, ostensibly as support for the main army. On 10 October Blücher reported to Brunswick's headquarters and received command of the main army's advance guard, consisting of his own regiment, one dragoon regiment, one light-infantry battalion, and one battery of horse artillery.[45]

Prussia's declaration of war had not found Napoleon unprepared. Intelligence reported the Prussian advance into Saxony as early as 13 September; five days later the emperor ordered the concentration of the Grande Armée. Arriving at Bamberg on 2 October, he took command of 167,000 veteran troops and 260 guns. Moving north through the Thuringian Forest, the French advanced on parallel roads in three massive columns forming the emperor's famed *bataillon carré*. With his six infantry corps, artillery and cavalry reserve, and Imperial Guard neatly packed along a front of only thirty-eight miles, the diamond-shaped bataillon carré provided equally effective strength in any direction. With the depth of the march likewise around forty miles, Napoleon needed just forty-eight hours to concentrate the entire army.[46] By re-fusing his left and sweeping around the Prussian army with his right, he planned to implement the strategic *manoeuvre sur les derrières*. This brilliant move would place

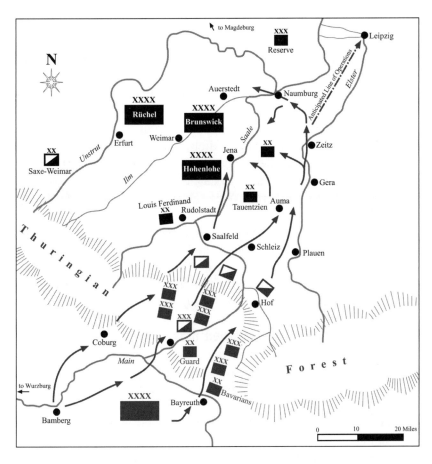

The Jena Campaign, 1806. Map drawn by Alex Mendoza. Copyright © 2014 by the University of Oklahoma Press.

his army behind the Prussians and between them and Berlin. By simultaneously threatening Brunswick's main line of communication as well as the Prussian capital, Napoleon would force the duke into a battle on terms that highly favored the French. Secrecy and speed provided the keys to success. After emerging from the Thuringian Forest, Napoleon used the Saale River to mask his army's advance. Brunswick never expected the French would move north along the *eastern* bank of the Saale. By the time he realized this monumental oversight, the French already were behind him.

Forming part of Hohenlohe's vanguard, General Bogislav Friedrich von Tauentzien's Saxon division made contact with the advance guard of Marshal Bernadotte's I Corps on 9 October at

Schleiz, twenty-five miles southeast of Jena. Tauentzien refused to withdraw, but the stronger French force eventually drove him back; neither side suffered considerable casualties. The same could not be said of the following day's engagement at Saalfeld. That morning, 10 October, French skirmishers from Marshal Lannes's V Corps harried Prussian outposts near Rudolstadt, where Prince Louis Ferdinand of Prussia commanded another portion of Hohenlohe's vanguard. With orders to hold the Saalfeld road, the king's fiery second cousin could not resist the temptation to attack. Shifting his troops from their defensive positions to engage the French, he soon found himself fatally outnumbered. While skirmishers held the Prussians in check, Lannes's main body moved up the road to Saalfeld. The marshal wasted no time charging the Prussian lines, overwhelming Louis Ferdinand's 8,000 men. In desperation the prince led a cavalry charge to stem the advance and met his fate at the hands of a French sergeant. As the French stripped the uniform from his lifeless body, Louis Ferdinand's terrified soldiers fled, leaving behind seventy-two guns and carrying off as many of their 3,000 casualties as possible. Small bands of survivors staggered back to Hohenlohe's position, spreading panic and consternation. Louis Ferdinand's death had a tremendous psychological effect on the Prussians. On his own initiative and without notifying Brunswick, Hohenlohe retreated to Jena.

The sound of artillery coming from the southeast finally revealed to Brunswick the great danger that faced his army. Realizing Napoleon sought to outflank his left, the duke wanted to concentrate his army and move east to confront the French head on. During a contentious council of war that same day, 13 October, the Prussians decided that Brunswick and Rüchel would withdraw northeast toward Leipzig—itself ninety miles south of Berlin—to head off the French advance. Hohenlohe would mask their departure by holding the line of the Saale.

Napoleon anticipated Brunswick's decision to protect his line of communication by assembling the Prussian army between Erfurt and Weimar, then withdrawing along it. To intercept it, he ordered Marshal Davout's III corps to Naumburg. On the morning of the thirteenth, the main Prussian army evacuated Weimar and marched toward the lower Unstrut River, hoping to unite with a reserve corps under Duke Eugene Frederick of Württemberg. Reports of French forward troops reaching Weimar later in the day prompted Frederick William to order a retreat to the Elbe River by way of Auerstedt. Later that evening, in a breakdown of Prussian leadership, only a few cavalry patrols reconnoitered the Weimar–Naumburg road. Although having prior knowledge of French troops at Naumburg, the Prussians failed to send a sufficient cavalry force to clear the road or to make an initial advance in strength on the enemy position. Forewarned of this move, Davout concentrated his corps. Frequent confusion resulted in delays that forced Brunswick's army to pass the night camped around Auerstedt.

Early on 14 October, a thick autumn mist lay over the countryside. Six battalions and ten guns from the French 3rd Division, commanded by General Charles-Étienne Gudin, deployed against the approaching Prussian army. Their front faced west, while their left extended to the village of Hassenhausen. To protect their right flank from Prussian cavalry, the French infantry echeloned eastward. In the distance the two other divisions and the cavalry brigade of III Corps continued to move up, marching southwest from Naumburg. A few miles from the French, Brunswick's 60,000 soldiers marched east on the same road, making for Naumburg. Commanding the Prussian advance guard, the sixty-three-year-old Blücher watched the 8,500 soldiers of Gudin's division deploy. After receiving reinforcements from Brunswick, he gave in to his instincts. Blücher decided "not to allow the advantage that appeared to me to go unused. I gave the squadrons, which had formed with intervals, the signal for the attack to break through the enemy infantry's flank." He led the charge of ten squadrons. The rising sun started to burn through the fog, revealing the arrival of the 2nd Division under General Louis Friant. The French formed squares; Davout and his generals sought protection in them. Three times Blücher charged, and three times the French repulsed him. While regrouping after the third assault, his shaken cavalry received blasts of canister in the rear from their own horse artillery. With his adjutants wounded or dismounted, Blücher alone could not rally the men: "When I tried again to get the cavalry to go forward, my horse was shot. As I fell, everything was turned upside down."

Scrambling atop the horse of one of his buglers, Blücher barely escaped capture. "I hurried to the village behind me. To halt the fleeing cavalry, I grabbed a standard and placed myself on the dike in the village facing the fugitives; but all was in vain. To the left and to the right, all flew by me. Everyone shouted stop, but no one listened. I called to the officers to look around, there was nothing of the enemy

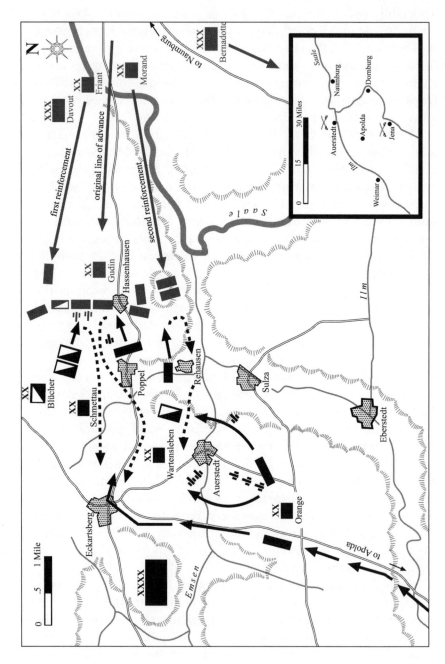

The Battle of Auerstedt, 14 October 1806. Map drawn by Alex Mendoza. Copyright © 2014 by the University of Oklahoma Press.

behind them; but the tide carried away everything and the cavalry fled to the woods not far from Eckartsberg." He rode to Frederick William, who stood on the hills by the town of Eckartsberg. "With a bleeding heart," the general reported to the king "that his cavalry had not done its duty." Till the end of his days, Blücher remained convinced that three infantry battalions and one horse battery with some additional cavalry would have enabled him "to completely roll up" the right wing of Davout's corps. Regardless, Blücher had attacked too soon, wasting the Prussian horsemen. A hussar of the light cavalry, Blücher simply did not understand the shock tactics of heavy cavalry. His future subordinate, Colonel Hans David von Yorck, said at the time: "Blücher is no Seydlitz. A hussar general with independent command may charge recklessly. If the charge fails, he waits all the more eager for the next charge. However, the cavalry shock in battle must be unleashed when the time is right; then it must crush all before it."[47]

During Blücher's cavalry action, General Friedrich Wilhelm von Schmettau's 3rd Division deployed west of Hassenhausen, north of the Weimar–Naumburg road, and advanced to the attack; shortly after, General Leopold Alexander von Wartensleben's 2nd Division deployed south of the road. While Brunswick led a regiment of grenadiers to take Hassenhausen around 10:00 A.M., a musket ball sliced through both of his eyes, mortally wounding the duke.[48] His chief of staff, Colonel Scharnhorst, had left Brunswick's command post to direct the deployment of troops elsewhere on the field. With Scharnhorst absent, Prussian leadership completely collapsed after General Schmettau suffered a serious wound soon afterward. Frederick William neither appointed a successor to Brunswick nor assumed command of the army himself. Regardless, the Prussians made progress in the struggle around Hassenhausen until Davout's 1st Division under General Charles Antoine Morand arrived at 11:00, allowing the intrepid marshal to launch a counterattack. By now Prussian morale began to wane in the confusion and disorganization that accompanied the breakdown of command and control. Davout timed his counterpunch perfectly. Around noon, the king ordered a retreat seventeen miles southwest to Weimar.

Frederick William himself rode forward with a few squadrons to establish communication with Hohenlohe. At dusk he reached the hills north of Apolda, the halfway point to Weimar, where the monarch could see masses camping south of the town. Moving closer and expecting to be hailed by Prussian sentries, he soon realized that he faced a huge French bivouac. The king thus assumed that Hohenlohe, from whom he had not received any news, had retreated to Weimar. Continuing the ride southwest, he encountered fugitives and wounded men from Hohenlohe's army who told of a crushing defeat. At Weimar an officer from the prince's command confirmed the news: Napoleon and the main French army had routed Hohenlohe's forces at Jena.

While Davout had marched southwest toward Brunswick on the thirteenth, Lannes pursued Hohenlohe's retreating forces northwest. Napoleon hurried to join his advance guard, thinking it had found the enemy's main army. He directed all other corps in the vicinity to hasten to Jena, having at his immediate disposal only the 25,000 men of V Corps and his Guard. But by 10:00 A.M. the next morning, Napoleon could count on a force of 55,000 men, nearly 80,000 by noon, and 96,000 by 1:00 P.M.

Hohenlohe foolishly scattered his 38,000 men around the Jena–Weimar road in isolated packets. Considering Lannes's force a mere advance guard, he remained convinced that the French would not attempt a frontal assault. Tauentzien received orders to contain Lannes with 8,000 men and prevent the French from further advancing. Throughout the evening, the enemy fortified their position on the Landgrafenberg heights and moved closer to Tauentzien's units; the Prussians did nothing. At 6:00 A.M. on the fourteenth, Tauentzien's artillery opened fire as his infantry surged forward. A fierce volley of French musketry and artillery stopped the Prussians and Saxons in their tracks. Napoleon gave the signal to commence the attack, with V Corps in the center, VII Corps on the right, and IV Corps to the left. After watching the French completely overwhelm his first line, Tauentzien dispatched several messages to Hohenlohe describing the severity of the onslaught and pleading for reinforcements. At 8:30 A.M. Hohenlohe finally responded by ordering him to fall back. With Marshal Michel Ney's VI Corps starting to arrive, the French advance continued with renewed vigor.

Hohenlohe ultimately realized the perilous condition of his center and ordered his widely dispersed forces to converge. An attempt to turn the French right flank failed, resulting in Hohenlohe's left being separated from his center for the entire battle. After two hours of suffering brutal losses, the Prussians started to waver. With their left already turned, their right buckled, and Hohenlohe exhausted his center in many futile attempts to take the village of Vierzehnheiligen. Despite occasional heroics, the Prussians fell back. They maintained order until 2:00 P.M., when the center broke, causing widespread chaos.

Observing the Prussian collapse, Napoleon unleashed the fury of Marshal Murat's Cavalry Reserve. A relentless pursuit covered two bloody miles, filling the plain with carnage. French infantry quickly overwhelmed Rüchel's 15,000 men as they came up. Hohenlohe's army became nothing more than a mass of helpless fugitives: all resistance ended by 4:00 P.M.

During the Battle of Jena, the 54,000 French soldiers who actually engaged the enemy suffered 6,500 casualties. Prussian losses are unknown but are believed to be around 25,000 killed, wounded, and captured. At Auerstedt Davout's 24,000 infantry, 1,400 cavalry, and 44 guns repulsed the attacks of Brunswick's 50,000 men and 230 guns. The fact that most of the Prussian infantry did not see action takes nothing away from Davout's heroic yet costly victory. Prussian losses at Auerstedt amounted to 10,000 casualties, 3,000 prisoners, and 115 guns. According to Davout, III Corps sustained 7,000 casualties, 25 percent of his entire force. Combined, the Battles of Jena and Auerstedt cost the Prussians 25,000 prisoners, 200 guns, sixty regimental standards, and perhaps as many as 30,000 killed and wounded.

Blücher commanded the rear guard as the wreck of Brunswick's army followed Hohenlohe's battered divisions northwest to Nordhausen, the gateway to the Harz Mountains. Of Brunswick's army, only 10,000 soldiers could be collected at Sömmerda, eighteen miles northwest of Weimar, on the night of the fifteenth. At daybreak Brunswick's successor, General Kalckreuth, commenced the thirty-five-mile march to Nordhausen, where the army turned northeast and headed toward Magdeburg on the Elbe to reunite with Hohenlohe's survivors. With the French pressing, Blücher and his men barely escaped through Nordhausen on the seventeenth. During that day's action, the general made the acquaintance of Scharnhorst. These two men from very different backgrounds thus started a personal and professional relationship that would characterize the Prussian army of the nineteenth century: the military marriage of brains and brawn.

Admittedly, this union did nothing to save the Prussian army in 1806. Just two days after Jena-Auerstedt, the humiliating

capitulations that marked the end of Frederician Prussia commenced with the surrender of 12,000 demoralized soldiers at Erfurt
on 16 October. On the seventeenth Bernadotte's I Corps smashed
the 16,000 fresh Prussians of the Duke of Württemberg's reserve
at Halle. After stopping for a few days at Magdeburg, Hohenlohe
continued the retreat northeast in the hope of reaching the fortress at Stettin, on the Oder River. En route, Kalckreuth's "army"
reunited with Hohenlohe, who assumed command of all Prussian
forces. Murat, whose cavalry proved to be the bane of the Prussian
army during the pursuit after Jena-Auerstedt, caught Hohenlohe at
Prenzlau, only thirty-five miles west of Stettin's 281 cannon. Fooled
by Murat into thinking the French surrounded him, Hohenlohe
ordered his 10,000 men and 64 guns to surrender during the 28
October battle there. Another 4,000 Prussians surrendered the following day at Pasewalk to two light-cavalry brigades. That night,
29–30 October, Stettin, with its 5,300-man garrison and formidable
array of artillery, capitulated to a single brigade of light cavalry. On
1 November the 2,400 men and 92 guns of the fortress of Küstrin
(Kostrzyn) surrendered to one of Davout's brigades. One week later
Magdeburg's garrison of 25,000 soldiers surrendered to Ney's VI
Corps. In the meantime, Napoleon entered Berlin on 27 October
after a two-week campaign that cost the Prussians upward of 40,000
casualties, 165,000 prisoners, 4,000 cannon, and 100,000 muskets.
Fighting continued in East Prussia and Silesia, but the Prussian
state lay prostrate at the feet of the new Caesar.

On Scharnhorst's suggestion, Blücher and his command parted
ways with Kalckreuth, who did not care for the Mecklenburger, and
hugged the feet of the Harz while escorting the Prussian heavy artillery. He crossed the Elbe at Sandau on 24 October and linked with
Hohenlohe, who assigned him command of the rearguard corps, consisting of eighteen battalions, thirty squadrons, and twenty guns—
10,500 men. With Scharnhorst as his chief of staff, Blücher covered
the further retreat of the remnant army from Magdeburg to Stettin.
As noted, Hohenlohe never made it there, capitulating at Prenzlau.
On that day, 28 October, French forces came between Hohenlohe's
main body and Blücher's corps. With the road to the Oder blocked,
he and Scharnhorst turned west, passing north of Berlin to reach
Neustrelitz, forty miles from Prenzlau, on 30 October. At Waren
the following day, Blücher took command of a division formerly led
by General Karl August, Grand Duke of Saxe-Weimar, consisting

of sixteen battalions, forty-four squadrons, and twenty-eight guns—more than 10,000 men, most of whom had seen action. The division's rearguard commander, Colonel Yorck, had provided strong and successful leadership in repulsing the charge of Soult's IV Corps. Scharnhorst reorganized Blücher's 21,000 men into two small army corps, each composed of three combined-arms divisions.

Time did not favor Blücher. While he hoped to tie up as many French units as possible, he lacked food, forage, and winter gear. More importantly, enemy forces closed on him from three directions. While the Prussians put three days between themselves and Murat's terrifying sabers pursuing west from Prenzlau, Bernadotte's I Corps remained only one march north of Blücher. Meanwhile to the south, IV Corps closed within two marches. Believing Bernadotte to be closer than he actually was, Blücher intended to deliver a battle "in which he hoped for victory through the superiority of his cavalry in numbers and quality," according to one of his staff officers. The general planned "to first distract the enemy a considerable distance from the Oder and not accept battle until necessity demanded it; even if the battle was lost, it would cost the enemy men and win time for the king."[49]

Blücher decided to march 100 miles west to Lübeck, where Sweden, Prussia's ally, had landed a brigade of 1,800 men. The column reached the Hanseatic city-state on the morning of 5 November after fighting several sharp rearguard actions with the French, who allocated nearly 50,000 soldiers for the chase. After forcing their way into the city, the Prussians rested after the grueling marches. Blücher appeared before the municipal government to demand food and drink for his men and promising he would not fight in the streets. Outside the city walls, the French closed in from the east and south while a Danish army approached from the north to enforce its country's neutrality.

Scharnhorst and Blücher did their best to turn Lübeck into a bastion, despite the general's promise, which he shrugged off when city fathers complained about the preparations. Regardless, a coordinated attack by Soult, Murat, and Bernadotte with approximately 35,000 soldiers overwhelmed the defenders on 6 November. Blücher and Müffling barely escaped, while Scharnhorst and the rest of the general staff became prisoners. Yorck received a serious wound during savage street fighting. Blücher led a cavalry charge in a vain attempt to save Scharnhorst but then had to cut his way out to escape across the Trave River. He launched one last counterattack, which failed with considerable losses. Afterward, the French sacked the city, committing horrible atrocities. Altogether, the Prussians sustained 2,000 casualties and lost 4,000 captured along with twenty-two guns. Blücher inspired his men to fight, and so they did: three entire regiments were wiped out fighting to the last man. French losses are estimated at 1,500 killed and wounded. Although a devastating defeat, Blücher's brave stand at Lübeck became legendary, earning him a prominent place among the few heroes of this disastrous war.

At daybreak on 7 November, the general mustered the remains of his two corps—less than 10,000 men—seven miles north of Lübeck at Ratekau. His situation appeared hopeless. South of him, French units from three army corps poured across the Trave at Lübeck; north and behind him, the Baltic lapped the North German coast; to his east, Bernadotte's I Corps guarded the Trave; and to his west, General Johann Ewald's Danes secured their frontier. Realizing that he had reached the end of his rope, Blücher sent his son Franz to ask for terms. Informing the marshals that only the lack of supply pushed him to take this step, he attempted to surrender solely to Bernadotte, who had offered him terms twice before. Murat and Soult objected, and so Blücher signed a document stating that he capitulated to all three marshals. Symbolizing his defiance of the French, which would make him a Prussian folk hero in the years to come, he added at the bottom of the document: "I capitulate, since I have neither bread nor ammunition." As for the Swedes, they surrendered to Bernadotte alone. His courteous treatment of them would pay dividends for the French marshal, whose descendants rule Sweden today.[50]

For Frederick William III, the War of the Fourth Coalition dragged on. General Levin August von Bennigsen's Russian army finally reached the province of East Prussia, where it met the advancing Grande Armée. Although the bloody stalemate at Eylau (Bagrationovsk) on 7–8 February 1807 prompted Napoleon to postpone operations until spring, only 20,000 Prussian troops remained in the theater. Spring brought no relief for the haggard king. On 26 May Kalckreuth surrendered the fortress of Danzig and its garrison of 11,000 soldiers, providing the French a strong base on the Vistula River. The capitulation also allowed the 27,000 men of Marshal François Joseph Lefebvre's X Corps to undertake field operations, thus increasing Napoleon's combat power. Nevertheless, Tsar Alexander remained determined to continue the war and summoned more Russian units to East Prussia. As for Frederick William, only a miracle could deliver his kingdom.

Many hoped the repatriated Blücher and a small force assembling in Swedish Pomerania would provide this miracle.[51] Although he surrendered at Ratekau, Blücher received lenient terms regarding his person. Permitted to keep his sword, he could go where he pleased as long as he did not to take up arms against France. Eventually, the French formally exchanged him for General Claude Victor-Perrin, Lannes's chief of staff and a future marshal. With the restrictions on his actions lifted, Blücher went to Stralsund, where Prussian units had been arriving since 6 May to reinforce the Swedish garrison on Rügen. Camping on the Baltic coast of Swedish Pomerania—territory he knew well from his younger years—the general worked to forge a cohesive fighting force from the stragglers who reached him. A British force of 10,000 men arrived to supplement these troops. With 16,000 men, Blücher planned to cross into Prussian Pomerania, unite with Colonel August von Gneisenau's garrison at Kolberg (Kołobrzeg), move against the Grande Armée's extensive line of operations, and "give Herr Napoleon a few sleepless nights."[52] The Allies hoped this operation, combined with a successful spring offensive by the Russians, would alter the course of the war.

Blücher and King Charles XIII of Sweden agreed to begin a joint operation on 13 July, although many recruits lacked equipment and their training still required much work.[53] Numerous shortages meant that it would be some time before these men could be considered battle ready.[54] Lieutenant Colonel Karl Leopold von Borstell commanded the cavalry, while Colonel Friedrich Wilhelm von Bülow led the infantry. Both men diligently worked with Blücher to prepare their units. Numerous obstacles impeded organization and training, though. The multinational composition of the corps and the blurred lines of authority only complicated matters. For example, Bülow suffered through disagreements with the Swedes, who questioned his right to command. Despite these hindrances, Blücher considered the corps combat ready in early July. The general maintained a constant state of readiness, and all anxiously awaited the order to march. But this order never came. Instead, disturbing news arrived of a Russian defeat at Friedland (Pravdinsk) on

14 June and the subsequent armistice concluded at Tilsit (Sovietsk) on the Niemen (Neman) River eleven days later. In consequence of the peace negotiations, the British and Swedes departed. All preparations halted after news reached Blücher that Napoleon and Alexander had concluded a peace agreement on 7 July. He also learned that Frederick William III had accepted Napoleon's treaty two days later on 9 July. Consequently, he received orders to cease hostilities and return to Prussia. Blücher left Swedish Pomerania with a burning hatred for Napoleon, a personal vendetta the likes of which the emperor might have encountered on his native Corsica.

CHAPTER 5

THE AGONY OF DEFEAT

H err Kalckreuth and his peace can go to the devil! It's a disgrace,"
howled Blücher in a letter to Foreign Minister Hardenberg
shortly after learning the details of the Treaty of Tilsit. "Your letter brought me to tears."[1] The draconian terms of the agreement
reduced Prussia to a listless rump: Frederick William III lost half of
his kingdom. Although Tsar Alexander intervened to save Silesia
and Pomerania, Prussia could barely be considered a second-rate
power. Less than five million subjects remained from the kingdom's prewar population of 9,752,731 inhabitants, while its territory shrunk from 5,570 square miles to 2,877. Napoleon awarded
the provinces of New East Prussia and South Prussia to his newly
created Grand Duchy of Warsaw; Danzig became a free city under
French authority. Most of Prussia's western possessions, including
the Universities of Duisberg, Erlangen, and Halle, wen t to Jerome
Bonaparte's new Kingdom of Westphalia or Murat's Grand Duchy of
Berg. Other conditions stipulated that French troops would occupy
several Prussian fortresses, including the great bastions on the Oder
River: Glogau, Küstrin, and Stettin.[2] After refusing to treat with
Hardenberg at Tilsit, Napoleon ensured that one of the treaty's
stipulations required his dismissal as foreign minister. As a result,
Kalkreuth, now a field marshal, mainly represented the Prussians
during the negotiations, prompting Blücher to refer to the treaty as
"Kalckreuth's peace."

Blücher's troops remained in Pomerania awaiting orders; the
general did not know what to do next. Instructions soon arrived for
him to lead the men to Brandenburg as soon as the French evacuated the province, yet the French showed no sign of moving. To
avoid attracting their attention and to save limited funds, Blücher
sent the majority of his troops home. He remained the nominal
commander of the Pomeranian units and established temporary
headquarters at Kolberg.[3]

Blücher's correspondence at the end of the war reveals a natural blend of anger, hope, insecurity, and weariness that would

typically accompany a defeat. "If I was not so optimistic, I would resign immediately," continues Blücher's July letter to Hardenberg. "Yet, my dearest friend, I have to tell you that I have not lost heart. Certainly different and unexpected things will happen. German courage is only asleep: awaken it, and it will be devastating. In any case, the situation certainly will not continue like this."[4] In congratulating Gneisenau for his heroic defense of Kolberg ("you leave the scene invincible and with honors"), Blücher added that he remained "uncertain how the peace will be," that "only time will tell." More telling of the stress of the war and the toll it took on him is the comment: "I am longing for quiet and rest; in these enlightened times a soldier's life is the most wretched of all."[5]

The general took interest in the work of resurrecting the army, which Frederick William initiated at Memel (Klaipėda) in far East Prussia. He provided Gneisenau with erudite advice that demonstrates his understanding of how the French changed warfare: "Say hello to my friend Scharnhorst and tell him that I urge him to form a national army. This is not as difficult as one thinks; no one must be excused from the service, no one in the world must be exempt, and it should be a disgrace for those who do not serve for reasons other than physical affliction." He continued by explaining to Gneisenau how to form a system of trained reserves to maximize manpower without damaging the nation's economy by conscripting the productive elements of society: "After the soldiers have been well trained, they would go home for two years and only return to service in the third year; thus the burden on the state will be eased, and there will not be a shortage of people. It is also a mistake to believe that a trained soldier will forget in two years all that he has learned, and that in eight days he cannot again be combat ready. The French proved this and many other things to us." Commenting on the Frederician military system that the French overwhelmed at Jena-Auerstedt, Blücher concluded: "The soldier can completely forget our useless pedantry. The army has to be formed into divisions: the divisions must be composed of all arms that maneuver with one another in the autumn." He understood the importance of learning the art of war through field exercises, where combat could be simulated to provide both commanders and troops the experience of battlefield conditions more accurately than sterile parade-ground drill.[6] "There: you have my creed!" the general finished. "Give it to Scharnhorst and tell me of your opinions."[7]

Blücher played no direct role in the reform process that spanned 1807–1812. Considering that the Prussian Reform Movement required the contributions of scores of officers and civilian officials, his omission offers insight into the general's standing in the postwar era. His appointment to command first the Pomeranian expeditionary force at the end of the war and then the Pomeranian Brigade afterward suggests that he managed to retain the confidence of his superiors despite the surrender at Ratekau. In addition, he established a close relationship with Scharnhorst based on mutual respect and admiration. Blücher's inclusion on the Military Reorganization Commission would have provided a loud voice of support from an experienced commander. Yet the king did not summon him to Memel. Two reasons may account for this. First, the incompetency displayed by senior commanders during the war traumatized Frederick William. Although the king could not risk further conflict with Napoleon, he wanted his remaining generals to be firm with the French, loyal to the state, and obedient to him. Blücher met all the requirements. For this reason, he retained command over some of the few remaining units of the Prussian army.

Second, less likely but nonetheless intriguing while in complete contradiction to the above, was the possibility that Blücher soon could be relieved of his command and cashiered. On 14 November 1807 the Military Reorganization Commission presented the king with recommendations for the rigorous investigation of the activities of all senior commanders, the performance of every field unit, and the capitulation of each fortress.[8] Every operation and all of its aspects would be examined, including the commander's preparations, the enemy's strength, and the chances for success. Correspondence and orders would be sequestered, evaluated, and used to determine a commanding officer's responsibility. All guilty sentences would have to be reviewed and approved by the king. Thirteen days later Frederick William appointed a board of inquiry, the Immediat-Untersuchungskommission (Superior Investigating Commission), which held its first meeting at Königsberg on 10 December 1807.[9] Blücher's case joined several others on the docket for review. In 1808 the commission convened its hearings to examine the conduct of individual officers during the war. The body released its results in 1809: of the 142 generals who served in the war, 17 were cashiered, 86 received honorable discharges, and only 22, including Blücher, remained on active duty.

Through the multitude of emotions that besieged Blücher, one thought remained constant: his own personal salvation as well as that of the Prussian state remained in the hands of his friend and colleague from Münster, Baron vom und zum Stein. "Stein must return! I am certain that you [Hardenberg] will do everything to make this happen."[10] And happen it did. Napoleon's curious dislike of Hardenberg and his insistence that Frederick William dismiss him left the Prussian state without a strong personality to direct foreign affairs during these trying times. The king not only recalled Stein but appointed him principal minister of domestic and foreign affairs as well. Hardenberg wrote Stein on behalf of the monarch and included one of Blücher's letters in the packet.[11]

Stein assumed the task of breaking with the past and reforming the social, legal, and administrative fabric of Prussia. He took office convinced that the passive, somewhat apathetic Prussian subject had to be transformed into a responsible citizen imbued with collective spirit, civic sense, devotion to country, and national honor. The reform of municipal administration, education, contract law, taxation, and the justice system would help create a society of free citizens. Wasting no time, he took the crucial first step toward this transformation by issuing the Edict of Emancipation on 9 October 1807, which abolished serfdom as of 11 November 1810 and theoretically replaced a hierarchy based on birth with one based on wealth. The middle class and peasants received the right to purchase property from nobles, and nobles could engage in bourgeois occupations.[12] Emancipation provided the logical counterpart to the army reforms sought by Scharnhorst. His ability to create citizen-soldiers would be successful only if Stein managed to improve the status of the civilian. Although forced by Napoleon to resign and flee to Austria in late 1808, Stein's reforms successfully altered Prussian society by accelerating the evolutionary transformation of subject to citizen within an absolutist framework.

Blücher does not provide a definitive answer as to why he supported Stein's social reforms, leaving us to speculate. On the surface Blücher shared an important distinction with the main reformers. Like Scharnhorst and Hardenberg the Hanoverians, Gneisenau the Saxon, and Stein the Nassauer, Blücher did not fit the mold of a typical East Elbian Prussian Junker.[13] Not that any individual would risk a duel by questioning Blücher's loyalty to king and country, the fact remains that he was born a Mecklenburger and thus outside

Prussia's traditional circles of power. For these reasons, he could be more detached and less passionate about defending its old regime. He had not inherited East Elbian estates that had been awarded to his forefathers for service to the Great Elector. Like many other foreigners who joined the service, he did win acceptance into these circles as a blue-blooded Prussian, though not because of his pedigree. Instead, Blücher won respect professionally for his martial abilities while socially the management of his estates afforded him just enough wealth to intermingle with the Prussian elite, although he ever complained to the king of financial woes. Moreover, his career path precluded him from ever being a Berlin courtier. Thus, Blücher was never part of the "in crowd" that frequented court. The "conservative" members appointed to the Military Reorganization Commission—General Eberhard Friedrich von Massenbach and Lieutenant Colonels Count Carl Friedrich von Wylich und Lottum, Karl Ludwig von Oppeln-Bronikowski, and Borstell—did not number among the general's intimates. Finally, Blücher's compassion may provide one last reason for his support of social reform. Whether his own children, in-laws, soldiers, or the peasants living on his estates, he genuinely cared about people and always did what he could to help any and all.

Blücher's 1805 essay, "Thoughts over the Formation of a Prussian National Army," indicates his thoughts on the pressing need for military reform. After the war, his 3 August 1807 letter to Gneisenau contains the essential element of Scharnhorst's program: the creation of a national army though universal conscription. Moreover, he clearly understood the essence of Napoleonic operational success: the combined-arms division, which, thanks to Scharnhorst, he formed and utilized in the aftermath of Auerstedt. In his advice to Gneisenau, Blücher outlined the reserve system that Scharnhorst would implement with some modification in July 1810 as the *Krümper* (shrinking) system.[14] Experience in the French Wars certainly instilled these ideas in Blücher and demonstrated to him the need for change.

Although he probably had more in common with those officers who felt that the army's antiquated leadership deserved the blame for the defeat and that natural evolution would solve its problems, Blücher was neither blind nor stupid. He recognized that the French military system posed a stark contrast to the Prussian and that the latter needed change. Also, he greatly respected Scharnhorst and

Gneisenau, who in turn showered the general with admiration, respect, and friendship, demonstrating that they counted Blücher not only among their own in terms of favoring reform but also as their competent leader, as indicated by an 8 August 1807 letter from Scharnhorst to August Friedrich von der Goltz: "I am convinced that General Blücher is the only general (whom I have been with) who has the courage and determination to lead a corps or an army. He wrote me that he would not resign. I had asked him not to. I do not know whether he will stay in Pomerania or be sent elsewhere. In any case, it has been decided that the army will be divided into specific units of all arms that have a common commander."[15] One year later Scharnhorst showed his continuing support of Blücher during the general's illness: "All say it and all write it, and I see from your own letters that the spirit has not diminished. You are our leader and hero, even if you have to be carried to and fro on a stretcher; only with you will there be decisiveness and success."[16]

Following the peace, Blücher established his headquarters in the charming Pomeranian town of Treptow-am-Riga (Trzebiatów), approximately six and one-half miles south of the Baltic coast and some seventy miles northeast of Stettin. A small provincial town of 3,000 inhabitants, Treptow became the midpoint of the territory that the French had thus far evacuated. Couriers came and went, soldiers of all branches crowded the streets, and French officers occasionally strolled through the lush gardens watered by the Riga River. Blücher established his headquarters in the south wing of the Treptow Schloß with the idea of being able to escape quickly if the need arose. Nestled among a beautiful wooded garden on a terrace carved by the Riga, the manor afforded him the quiet and rest he needed. From its windows Blücher could survey a rich countryside of gardens, meadows, and cornfields. He could be seen walking in the garden and on the nearby paths clad in a white cardigan, colored pants, and a cap, which easily produced the picture of an old man contemplating retirement. More than ten years had passed since Blücher last lived in Pomerania. As a colonel of the hussars, he went to war in 1793 full of hopes of victory. Now he returned as a defeated general. Yet his thoughts were far from retirement. Among the faithful Pomeranians, he prepared for the day of reckoning.[17]

In mid-August 1807 the king appointed Blücher to be governor general of Pomerania and Neumark, a position that included authority over the civil administration. To assist him with this aspect of his duties, Hardenberg suggested Justus Gruner, whom Blücher appointed *Kammerdirektor* (chairman) to head the district council.[18] Stargard, the provincial seat of Pomerania, would serve as the governor general's headquarters. But Blücher decided to remain at Treptow until the end of September, when according to treaty stipulations, the French would withdraw from Pomerania. But this expectation proved premature. Not only did they delay their departure from Pomerania but also established a camp at the village of Sarow very close to Stargard. Consequently, Blücher remained at Treptow. "The king has named me commanding general in Pomerania and the Neumark, and likewise governor of Pomerania and Stettin," he informed his brother-in-law, "yet we still have guests and before they leave us, I will not see myself get hold of Stettin, and if they remain long, I will not assume the government."[19] In fact, Blücher separated his district from the judicial and governmental authorities at Stettin, the provincial capital, and vowed to keep this arrangement until the French garrison left the fortress.[20]

At times, laughter and mirth filled the Treptow Schloß. Blücher took great pleasure in the camaraderie he shared with the officers of his staff. When finances allowed, he assembled them all for lunch. Such days found the general in a good mood; nobody escaped the jabs of his wit. He especially liked to target the flamboyant Major Ferdinand Baptista von Schill, the commander of the 2nd Brandenburg Hussar Regiment, which distinguished itself in the defense of Kolberg to such an extent that he emerged from the war as another of Prussia's few heroes.[21] On one such occasion, Blücher went too far, offending the major with his version of a previous venture. Schill pushed himself away from the table, took a seat behind the general, declared that he had taken his rightful "position," and thus missed most of the meal. After eating, Blücher turned and instructed him to return to his place at the table: "Now listen to me, Schill, sit down and eat, or else you will starve here in the 'position.'" Allegedly, he put on an even bigger show for the civilians who also frequented his table.[22]

But his own "position" exposed Blücher to the full oppression of French occupation. "The French behaved disgracefully on their return march," he raged to Hardenberg, "today I wrote about this to the King. If he does not know how to stop this mischief the land will be ruined more by this than by the war. I have made myself clear to the French: they may make no further requisitions in the district that I hold; also, no military personnel can cross that line." Gruner displayed great insight in civil matters, providing invaluable assistance to Blücher, who even at this early stage of the occupation measured value in terms of thwarting the unwanted guests.[23] He informed Hardenberg that Gruner quickly gained his confidence: "he already has been very useful to me. On his account, I wrote to the King today and requested that he be placed in the government here; then at least the King will be informed of what goes on at Stettin. . . . [W]e accept nothing from the Stettin government that I consider to be authored by the French authorities." Regardless of his firm resistance, one month later the general lamented to the king's favorite *Kabinettsrat* (councilor), Karl Friedrich Beyme: "When I came here the province was still in a prosperous condition everywhere, but now it is completely ruined up to the district that I have occupied because of the marching [French] troops, who commit all kinds of debauchery and excesses. The generals want to maintain good order but cannot; the soldier receives no pay and so believes he is entitled to demand anything." Blücher could do nothing but helplessly watch as thousands of imperial troops ravaged Pomerania during their march home.

Despite his general aversion to the French, he initially got on well with certain commanders, employing a mixture of force and tact. "I have done everything to get the French out of Stargard; Marshal Soult is very accommodating toward me, but he has just received counterorders. I must commend the three Marshals: Brune, Soult, and Victor." Blücher also referred to General Jean-Jacques Liebert, the French governor of Swedish Pomerania and commandant of Stettin, as "a respectable man." Apparently, Soult related that he had orders to occupy all of Pomerania and confine Prussian troops to Kolberg. Blücher assured Beyme that the marshal would "refrain from this after I explained to him and made myself clear that I would not surrender any of what I now have."[24]

This confrontational attitude soon soured relations between Blücher and the new masters of Prussia, particularly after he refused Soult's request to evacuate the coastal town of Kammins so the French could establish fortifications to defend against the British. Although the general finally yielded after Frederick William explicitly instructed him to comply with the marshal's demands, only the intervention of his entourage prevented him from demanding a duel on account of a rude letter. Blücher had plenty of fears, but he shrank before no man and never concealed his displeasure. Even less did he understand politics and the precipice upon which his king teetered.[25] For these reasons, he attracted French attention; Napoleon himself did not lose sight of him. On 24 September 1807 the emperor ordered his chief of staff, Marshal Alexandre Berthier, "to have Victor inform Blücher, that if he makes any preparations for war and if he does not stop his ostentatious behavior, he [Victor] will send troops to arrest and imprison him at Kolberg, that this is the express command of the emperor, who is tired of the Prussian braggart, and that he is also to withdraw his posts and establish good order among his people."[26]

Blücher's anger slowly yielded to despair that became full-blown mental illness within one year. "Of my damned situation in which I was and still am, I have nothing to say," he wrote his brother-in-law. "My son, who delivers this letter to you, can explain it. It is most abject that I am always content with nothing and I must seemingly walk clumsily in the dark. God knows what will become of me; the King will do what he wants [with me]. . . . My health has suffered very much recently; the incessant worry has affected me more than all fatigue."[27] The volatile situation with the French precluded the companionship of his wife, Amalie, who remained in Saxony with his son Gebhard's in-laws, the Conrings: "As long as I do not have a free hand here, I will not allow her to come."[28]

The serious, chronically poor health of his son Franz multiplied his worries exponentially. During the war, death had claimed Franz's wife and daughter; eleven weeks passed before the grief-stricken major could climb out of bed and return to his father's side. Problems caused by personal finances and the plight of his relations likewise weighed heavily on the patriarch. That Blücher's expenditures far exceeded his revenues was nothing new, but Prussia's wrecked economy rendered loans almost impossible to secure, thus magnifying the general's debts. In addition, the decrees abolishing an officer's ability to profit from his command sharply affected Blücher as he no longer received stipends for the cost of supplying the squadrons of his Red Hussar Regiment. With the position of regimental chef now being purely honorary, the commander became completely dependent on the salary that accompanied his rank, and Blücher felt the pinch. At wit's end, he complained to his friend and former adjutant, Friedrich von Eisenhart, who accused the general's *Haushofmeister* (majordomo) of irresponsible economics and suggested his dismissal. Blücher initially balked at the idea, but his wife convinced him to appoint Eisenhart to take care of the household and eliminate the waste. In addition, creditors repossessed the china he had been forced to leave behind at his home in Münster and refused to surrender any piece without payment. Unable to pay, a disgusted Blücher washed his hands of the issue because all the legal papers that he received over the affair had the odious name of Jerome stamped on them.[29]

On another personal front, he waged a letter-writing campaign to secure positions for two of his brothers-in-law—Ludwig Christoph von Colomb, a former *Kriegsrat* (military councilor) at Kalisch in South Prussia, and Heinrich von Colomb, a former *Regierungsrat* (privy councilor) at Warsaw—both of whom lost their positions after Prussia ceded its Polish provinces to the Grand Duchy of Warsaw. A third brother, the youngest, Lieutenant Friedrich August Peter von Colomb, commanded a cavalry squadron in Blücher's corps. After writing the king in an attempt to secure new assignments for the other two, the general sought the support of Hardenberg, who still had much political clout in the Prussian government. "I have two brothers-in-law," explained Blücher, "both are upright people; both are dear to me; I hope and wish they can again be employed by us. Do your best for these people; I do not know who else to turn to."[30]

One month later he solicited aid from Beyme, claiming that the senior Colomb was "without means, and I am placed in a situation that I can no longer support or help [him] because I too have lost everything."[31] He suggested having Colomb assigned to his headquarters "to arbitrate all incoming judicial matters."[32] "Things occur here on a daily basis that must be dealt with by a lawyer, and I must admit that I have little to do with either the municipal court or the government at Stettin . . . because I consider them to be under French authority." Later in this letter he added: "You know that I have another brother-in-law. . . . [I]f you could do something for him I would be grateful. My unfortunate son-in-law, Count Schulenburg [Fritze's husband], must take his leave [from the army] or he will lose everything."[33]

Having to contend with many ups and downs, Blücher did his best to ignore the darkness that gradually crept over his mind and soul. His regiment, the Blücher or Red Hussars, dissolved at Ratekau but reformed in 1807. Although allowed to bear the name of its chef, the regiment received the official designation of the

Pomeranian Hussar Regiment. Blücher became more aggravated when the king changed the men's red uniforms to blue, which the general viewed as a deliberate insult. He refused to don the new garb and even attended court wearing the old red uniform.[34] The hussar fumed over this for an entire year. On 4 April 1809 he wrote his former adjutant, Karl Friedrich von der Goltz, who now served the king's brother, Prince William, in the same capacity: "The most annoying thing is that they took my regiment's name and uniform; I wrote the King over this and placed the regiment and my service at his mercy. The name was returned to the regiment; but the King informed me that he could not change back the uniform; he named the regiment the Pomeranian Blücher Hussar Regiment. I nominated Sydow to be commander of the regiment, but then his two brothers died and he received an inheritance of 150,000 thaler. He did not accept the position on the advice of his stupid wife so the regiment received a stranger; I resisted so much that the King finally accepted my nomination and named [Johann Wilhelm von] Czarnowski. The great joy for me is that I can help so many men earn a living."[35]

At times, however, his strong spirit did succumb, as a 7 September 1807 letter to his friend, Professor Anton Matthias Sprickmann, indicates: "My heart weeps over the misfortune that has befallen the state and my master, and the sad memory of so many lost friends, whose heartfelt devotion will be missed until the end of my days. Oh, if I could only see the entire world in fire and flames before I die and take delight in this spectacle once and for all in my life! Believe me, my dear friend, the world deserves nothing better than to burn; it is deplorable and for the most part people are monsters. Only a glimpse from this earth of a better life in the hereafter can bring some comfort, and it is in this hope that I commit my entire existence."[36]

Blücher managed to remain focused on his work, assuring Beyme that "one shall not accuse me of abandoning the King's service while he was in distress."[37] Nevertheless, his perception of loyalty, duty, and honor quickly became intertwined with a morbid, insatiable desire for revenge. "As long as I am still here, I will fulfill my duty with conviction; meanwhile, I am so deadened, that no steady impression can be made on me. I have suffered much and learned much, but by no means am I done; I see days before me, when all will be destroyed, or there will come a time, when human understanding, as in the past, can only see vengeance in the distance. Yes, Sprickmann, we will see each other again or all of our ideas about revenge are nothing but delusions settling in our bosoms in a pitiless way; God forbid! Shall the only thought that delights me be nothing else?"[38]

En route to Memel at the end of September 1807, Stein visited his biggest admirer. He noted to his wife that he found Blücher "as you know him: brave, guileless, devoted to king and country, loved by officers and soldiers, treated by the French with consideration and care, but older and not as cheerful as before."[39] Blücher used the occasion to speak with Stein, who left Treptow on the twenty-fifth, about the plight of his brother-in-law Ludwig. "Stein has assured me that you will be reassigned in an appropriate manner as soon as a little order is restored to the situation and we are free of the foreigners," he wrote. "Because I am also the temporary civil commissioner and have thus recommended you, I have the promise of getting you reassigned. Your older brother is already assigned by the king for the time being to me as *Regierungskommissarius* [district commissioner] in order to arbitrate all incoming judicial matters." As for getting rid of the French, the general commented, "we are now zealously bringing order to the issue of reparations because this is the only way to get rid of the foreigners." He saved a parting shot for Prussia's former subjects: "The Poles have received their freedom, like those who receive soap bubbles; they will remember the lenient Prussian government and the many good deeds of the King."[40]

As 1807 came to a close, the investigation of the officer corps began. In Pomerania the tribunal found the commander of Blücher's regiment guilty for not leading the 1st Battalion to the attack at Auerstedt and for quitting the regiment; one lieutenant was likewise dismissed for abandoning his unit. The proceedings did not sit well with Blücher, but his public demeanor and daily routine did not change. In fact, Ludwig von Vincke, a dear friend from Münster, called on his old mate while traveling to Königsberg. Vincke noted in his journal on 17 November 1807: "Three days of rest and joy at Treptow. . . . [A]t noon [meal], I was always with Blücher and in the afternoons I visited [friends]. In the evening I accompanied him to the nightclub, where a good time was never lacking."[41]

Soon, however, Blücher had to endure further outrage and aggravation that perhaps pushed him over the edge mentally and emotionally. With the new year, the *Berliner Zeitung*, the newspaper of the

Prussian capital, published an account of the war criticizing the army and lauding the French. According to Wolfgang von Unger: "With Prussia's external enemies stood the antagonists of army reform and the pro-French [party] in Prussia itself; they could not do enough to make known their malicious delight in the fall of the army and the state of Frederick the Great. They completely ignored the fact that the catastrophe was more the fault of politics than the army. In a shameless way, the Berlin newspaper wrote in jeering terms of the vanquished, and in terms that deified the victor."[42] While this assessment appears fanciful, it does capture the feeling of paranoia and chaotic insecurity that many Prussians felt following the defeat and occupation, the loss of half of the kingdom's territory and population, and the understanding that a handful of nonnative Prussians were about to turn what remained of the state upside down.

Blücher's role in the war did not go unnoticed. An anonymous article appeared in the *Berliner Zeitung* holding the general responsible for Hohenlohe-Ingelfingen's capitulation at Prenzlau. Specifically, the unknown accuser charged him with refusing Hohenlohe's 26 October 1806 order to immediately unite with him at Ruppin, making Blücher appear guilty. Blücher's demand that the writer reveal himself appeared in the newspaper on 26 January 1808. Hohenlohe's former chief of staff, Colonel Massenbach, came forward, providing a more detailed justification of his accusation that exceeded the truth. To make the matter worse, Massenbach tried to smother Blücher with self-loathing guilt, emphasizing how he could have been the savior of the Prussian army: "Had only you come, only you—you alone would have been a legion to us; you alone would have been a rescuing angel to us."[43] It is not known why Blücher or one of his intimates did not challenge his accuser to a duel. In view of his upcoming review by the Investigation Commission, Massenbach's allegations perhaps alarmed Blücher in his weakening emotional condition. Conversely, believing firmly in his innocence, he may have decided to await the findings of the commission. What is certain is that despite receiving Scharnhorst's unequivocal support, the affair extremely aggrieved the general.

As winter relinquished its icy grip on the Baltic coast to a pale spring, Blücher claimed on 14 March that his health had "seemingly recovered." Considering that emotional distress is often accompanied by physical ailments and vice-versa, we can assume that both mind and body improved. Yet "because unforeseen hazards occur," he requested permission to block the transfer of the regimental surgeon, Dr. Johann Karl von Horlacher: "I would pay anything to keep this first-rate doctor by my side."[44] Regarding ill health, Amalie and Gebhard's wife, Lisette von Conring, visited, but Frau Blücher, pregnant with their only child, was not well. Although she received treatment at Stargard, Lisette accompanied her to Berlin for further therapy. "I can only imagine with horror what she will get when she arrives there," Blücher informed Ludwig on 25 April, "may the heavens protect her from further harm to her already wretched health." He also informed his brother-in-law that the prospects of Ludwig's employment by the government had improved, but unfortunately nothing could be done for him until "our guests have evacuated the country."[45]

In the standoff with these unwanted guests, Blücher could do nothing overtly, but this did not prevent him from scheming. After word spread that a war party formed at the Austrian court to agitate for another confrontation with France, he wasted no time in dispatching Eisenhart to Mecklenburg to ascertain the mood of the people and to establish relations with partisans. After Eisenhart returned with encouraging news concerning the prospects of an anti-French insurrection in that region, Blücher immediately sent him to deliver war plans to the king at Königsberg. Eisenhart first went to Queen Louise's seventy-nine-year-old *Oberhofmeisterin* (lady in waiting), Countess Sophie Marie von Voss, who listened to these plans and then confidentially informed the queen of Eisenhart's mission. Louise then arranged for the captain to see the king, encouraging him "to call a spade a spade and to say everything that the one in Pomerania hopes for with great persuasion." With Louise watching, Eisenhart presented Blücher's ideas firmly but respectfully. He noted that the recent French invasions of Portugal and Spain caused numerous difficulties for Napoleon and that Austria possessed 400,000 combat-ready troops. He assured the king that 100,000 Prussians would answer a royal summons to take up arms against the oppressor and that all of Germany would join Austria and Prussia. Frederick William knew better: neither his army nor his finances were in a position to wage war. He ended the interview with a plea for Blücher to behave himself. "Give the General my regards and say to him that for the sake of everything sacred in the world he must remain completely calm; now is not the time to break loose unless we want to be completely destroyed.

Convey to him my heartfelt thanks and assure him that I will certainly write if any prospects for success arise."[46]

Of course, Blücher failed to see the wisdom and accuracy of the king's response. He was not the only patriot Frederick William disappointed. Despite their cries, nothing could convince the monarch to risk the remainder of his kingdom and the crown itself in another war with Napoleon. Blücher took the rejection of his proposals and the king's refusal to consider a war of revenge as a personal insult. Annoyed and bitter, he retaliated by mocking and refusing to comply with orders to curtail the activities of the underground nationalistic Tugendbund (League of Virtue), although the Prussian secret police suspected him of being one of the league's officers. This latest setback triggered severe depression combined with physical ailments, in this case an ulcerated urethra that caused tremendous pain and sleepless nights. On occasion, the sixty-five-year-old commander could not perform his duties. Moreover, the excruciating pain, depression, and sleep deprivation rendered his mind vulnerable to "the strangest hallucinations and apparitions. In the midst of this, however, he could drift back to his old banter."[47] Such behavior sparked the rumor that the general had lost his mind.

By June 1808 Blücher's condition deteriorated considerably. Frederick William decided that the old hussar needed a personal assistant to support him in all military capacities and functions. On 22 June Colonel Bülow received a transfer to Treptow. "Blücher's illness prompts me to assign you the task of going to Pomerania immediately to support him in all military business and arrangements," explained the king. "Should the illness increase and he can no longer exercise command, I authorize you to assume command." Should he be forced to relieve Blücher or if the general became incapacitated, Frederick William emphatically instructed Bülow to employ all means to sustain the Pomeranian Brigade. He wanted the troops fully provisioned and isolated from the imperial units that continuously moved through Prussia. Finally, the king demanded that Bülow sacrifice "the last drop of blood for the maintenance of the honor of my troops and the fortress of Kolberg."[48]

While in Swedish Pomerania in 1807, Blücher and Bülow developed a cordial relationship, agreeing on most issues and working well together. Varnhagen von Ense, who knew both men and wrote extensive biographies on each, claims that Bülow earned Blücher's confidence while serving the general in 1807. Unger adds that under

the circumstances of 1808, Bülow's "stiff nature and gruff character provided cause for all sorts of friction. Regardless, Blücher often
recognized Bülow's military talent with loud commendation."[49] On
assuming his new post at Treptow, the colonel found Blücher in fair
health. This eased his situation, for the prospect of seizing the reigns
of command from Blücher troubled him. For the fifty-two-year-old
colonel, relieving a mentally deteriorating sixty-five-year-old general lieutenant and possibly replacing him appeared a very difficult
task. The king attempted to ease the situation by writing Blücher on
24 August 1808: "I trust you to allow Colonel Bülow to direct the
formation of the regiments and all that concerns them."[50] On most
days Bülow's role remained that of a normal adjutant, and he rarely
found cause to intercede. Blücher performed his executive duties
with only sporadic relapses. During such times, however, he willingly conceded his authority to Bülow.

Although Prussia's appalling situation did nothing to facilitate Blücher's recovery, he wrote on 19 August 1808 that "the condition of my health improves daily." Yet the very next line of his
letter suggests that emotional recovery remained elusive: "I live
inexpressibly and truly confess that in this situation my existence
is abhorrent." Frederick William's rejection of his war plans still
stung: "I can only assure you temporarily that the measures being
taken here are completely appropriate for the present state of affairs
because I doubt very much that they will be directed against France
as Königsberg does not inform me of our political situation." The
situation with the French did not improve. Aside from occupying
Stettin, they dispersed their troops throughout Pomerania to ease
supply problems. The country's inability to provide enough provisions remained a constant source of friction between the Prussians
and their masters. In addition, French repression increased throughout the empire as a result of the Spanish insurrection.

To tighten his chokehold on the kingdom at a time when
imperial units stationed east of the Rhine had to be transferred to
Spain, Napoleon forced the Prussians to accept the Treaty of Paris
on 8 September 1808. The main points of the new accords established the size of the Prussian army. Effective 1 January 1809, the
army could not exceed 42,000 men for a period of ten years. Other
terms prohibited any measure to increase the size of the military
through conscription, a militia, or a national guard. Few patriots
could be optimistic about this latest humiliation, particularly after

Napoleon forced Stein to resign and flee to Austria in late 1808. Frederick William wanted to appoint Hardenberg as Stein's successor, but Napoleon refused. But after the Altenstein-Dohna ministry defaulted on reparations payments, the door again opened for Hardenberg to return to office; this time the emperor did not interfere. Frederick William not only recalled Hardenberg but also handed him full control of the government under the new title of *Staatskanzler* (state chancellor). Despite conservative resistance, he continued the work started by Stein.

During this time, Blücher suffered personal tragedy. Amalie gave birth to a boy on 27 July 1810; unfortunately, the infant died on 18 November. After a full year of mental and physical deterioration, these personal and professional heartbreaks combined to send Blücher over the edge. He clearly walked the dark corridors of depression. Becoming obsessed that his death was close at hand, he gave his staff detailed instructions of how he should be buried and chose a grave under the tall trees next to the Wischower Church in Treptow.[51] He lost so much weight that he later confessed to having looked like a skeleton.[52] Images of his infant son staring at him with outstretched arms tormented Blücher. At times, he startled the household by shouting and smashing furniture as he engaged an invisible foe. Insisting that his head was made of stone, he frequently begged his servants to smite it with a hammer. In another incident, he claimed to be pregnant and became very fierce when Eisenhart nervously laughed at him. One night a deceased officer supposedly appeared, threatened the general, and gave him the finger.[53] Scharnhorst's close intimate, Hermann von Boyen, attests that Blücher "actually believed he was pregnant with an elephant. . . . [H]e imagined that his servants, bribed by France, had heated the floor of his room to burn his feet. Therefore, when sitting, he kept his legs raised above the floor or he would walk on the tips of his toes."[54]

As his condition worsened, Doctor Horlacher's concern for the general's life increased considerably. Alcoholism, the ulcerated urethra, perhaps venereal disease, and what appears to be schizophrenia produced bizarre behavior. According to one biographer, Blücher's staff "prepared for the worst because the ill man frightened them with the strangest talk. The patience of his entourage was harshly tried, but their attachment to the old hero helped them through the long hours when his irritability targeted them. Head-shaking friends listened to him complain over this and that peculiar ailment. Outsiders said that certainly he had lost his mind." On good days he affectionately joked with his attendants, who were never quite sure which General Blücher would greet them. One day he unexpectedly welcomed the officers of his staff to lunch in his nightgown. As Eisenhart walked past, he struck the captain with his cane so hard that the officer loudly cried out, to the general's great amusement.[55]

Autumn passed into winter with no change in Blücher's health, prompting the king to act again. Franz Blücher, himself fully recovered, received Frederick William's decree appointing him to be his father's adjutant to better take care of him.[56] On 21 November 1808 the king promoted Bülow to general major and brigadier of the Pomeranian infantry, further clarifying the relationship between him and Blücher in regard to the chain of command in the Pomeranian Brigade. He received authority to assume the functions of civil governor as well if Blücher's health worsened. Although it appeared that nothing changed in their relationship and Bülow still remained Blücher's personal assistant, the army recognized Bülow as the actual commander of the brigade, as evidenced by the correspondence between him and Scharnhorst.[57] Personally, Bülow regarded Blücher as an insane hypochondriac whose excesses brought on his poor health.

At the end of November 1808, the French regiment that occupied Pomerania withdrew, allowing Blücher to finally move to Stargard. But exchanging the Treptow Schloß, which he had grown sick off in his forlorn frame of mind, for the small rooms of a house that he shared in downtown Stargard did not help his situation. On 30 November he complained to the municipal officials that the three rooms assigned to him hardly suited a provincial governor. He could not host dinners nor meet with people in such cramped quarters. In response, the magistrate saw to it that Blücher received use of the entire house, where he resided until he left Stargard.[58] Although we have no correspondence from Blücher during this period, the fall of Stein, which occurred in late 1808, must have been a tremendous blow to him. The general's illness returned in greater strength with the new year, and by February 1809, Bülow assumed the functions of civil governor of Pomerania.

Fearing the end was near, Blücher's wife and children rallied to him. Ever the loving patriarch, he drew strength from their presence. After months passed with little change, the spring of 1809 finally

brought improvement. "I have recovered so well from my unfortunate illness that I am far healthier now than I ever have been," the
general wrote on 4 April. "I have such an appetite that I am con-
tinually upsetting my stomach. . . . I have put on so much weight
that I am stronger than ever before." He boasted over how well his
sons had evolved into Junker estate owners. After leaving the service, Gebhard had married Lisette and assumed his maternal grandparents' large ancestral manor of Schönwalde under opportune
conditions. "Gebhard is a farmer with heart and soul, has an ami-
able wife, and is flourishing. Regarding my good Franz, his situation has changed very much for the better and he has become a
total businessman; I gave my beautiful estate of Zieten to him." Not
only did Blücher appear to have recovered physically but mentally
and emotionally as well. "Goltz," he professed, "I live here in indescribable happiness. The Pomeranians treat me with every consideration, daily I receive new proof of their friendliness and affection.
Everything is back to normal: in the mornings, I take care of business and then I enjoy life playing cards just like old times."

Blücher suffered from numerous ailments over the previous
year, but amnesia did not number among them. He keenly felt the
pangs of humiliation, choosing to view Bülow's special position as
a sign that friends and superiors had given up on him. "I am in a
feud with the gentlemen at Königsberg. After my unfortunate illness, these gentlemen consider me to be a semi-invalid. I now say
to them that if my service is no longer needed then give me my discharge; I have written to the King as much. I can support myself
and ask for nothing, yet the monarch treats me as of old but the
others [curses], I will show them. The old Surgeon General, Goerke,
told the King that there is no general as healthy as me. You know as
well as I that they told the King that I lost my mind, but the King
has been instructed otherwise and now treats me with complete
confidence like old times." Referring to his hope that Prussia would
side with the Austrians in what many believed to be an imminent Franco-Austrian conflict, he concluded: "Now my friend[,]
. . . I expect the arrival of the enemy in my vicinity any day now.
I keep myself ready to greet them wherever they are and will proceed according to my own views because I am completely without
instructions."[59] On 9 April 1809, five days after Blücher wrote this
letter, war erupted between France and Austria.

CHAPTER 6

THE FIFTH COALITION

U nfortunately for Prussian patriots, the passage of one year did little to change Frederick William's mind. Regardless, Blücher lobbied hard for war. Had he known that the king absolutely refused to join the Austrians, the general still would have done everything in his power to convince him otherwise. At the end of April 1809, he hurried to Berlin for a meeting with Vincke. They drafted a petition asking the king to leave Königsberg and return to his capital. Reports of Austrian success excited Blücher, but for unknown reasons they never sent the petition.[1] Upon returning to Stargard, the general learned that on 28 April 1809, Major Schill led his 2nd Brandenburg Hussar Regiment out of Berlin supposedly for maneuvers. "By now," wrote Blücher, "Schill has probably crossed the Elbe to unite with the disgruntled [inhabitants] of the kingdom of Westphalia in a joint enterprise to support the long prepared and now unavoidable insurrection."[2]

The year before, Stein himself targeted Jerome Bonaparte's kingdom of Westphalia, with its Hessian, Prussian, Hanoverian, and Brunswicker populations, as ripe for insurrection. Now in 1809, the former Prussian subject and now Westphalian officer Captain Friedrich von Katte led 300 mainly Westphalian rebels from Prussian territory into Jerome's kingdom on 2 April in an attempt to instigate a rebellion. Although Katte failed, Schill likewise invaded Westphalia with around 2,000 followers in the hope of uniting with Colonel Wilhelm Casper von Dörnberg's Westphalian rebels and starting a war of German liberation. Just across the Silesian frontier in Bohemia, the deposed Duke Frederick William of Brunswick, the son of the former Prussian commander in chief and known as the "Black Duke," recruited a Freikorps that included Prussian officers and soldiers.[3] Finally, in the extreme southern reaches of Germany, the brave Tyroleans raised the standard of revolt and defeated their French-backed Bavarian overlords at Bergisel near Innsbruck on 12 April.[4]

Schill, one of Prussia's few heroes from the recent war, enjoyed great popularity in Brandenburg and especially at Berlin. Blücher wasted no time explaining the implication of the major's actions to the king: "From this step alone, Your Majesty can infer the mood of the nation and your troops; by uniting with Austria to wage war, they want to free themselves from the onerous yoke that has been placed on them as a result of the last unfortunate conflict. The right wing of the Austrian army supposedly has advanced in force into Franconia and gained some advantages." He stressed that throughout Germany, the people would respond to the opportunity to end the occupation. Blücher assured the king that "the example of the Tyrol appears to have produced a powerful effect on the former [Prussian] provinces on the other side of the Elbe and already at Kassel [capital of Westphalia] and other places it has produced significant resistance."

Then, like a card player holding a great hand, the general placed all of his chips on the table. Perhaps he always sensed that Frederick William was the weaker man, or perhaps it was out of desperation to save Prussia, but regardless of the cause, Blücher designed his next paragraph to intimidate the king, and it could have landed him in jail. "With all of this, Your Majesty can correctly recognize and rightly fear Major Schill's great influence on the people of Berlin and in the Mark, and that if decisive measures are not taken very soon the people may ignore all authority. Indeed, especially the troops in the Mark may partially disband to follow Major Schill. According to confirmed reports . . . an even more dangerous mood reigns in Silesia. If not used for your interests or powerfully countered within a very short time, its secession to join with the Austrians is guaranteed and the partition of your states will rock Your Royal Majesty's throne as the unavoidable consequence."

Blücher continued by urging the king to "take such energetic measures to secure your authority, to obviate all further compromise, and to safeguard your troops so that they do not become a part of the overexcited rabble." He promised Frederick William that chaos would be avoided "if Your Majesty places yourself at the head of your people, taking advantage of the present mood." After the fire and brimstone diatribe, Blücher assured the king that this "respectful and urgent request" arose purely from the "honest concern over your inherent welfare. Only through the faithful devotion to Your Majesty and to your house can I bring myself to suggest this step." He concluded with one last plea and final warning: "The desired moment has arrived to restore the extent of your states and regain the rights of your royal house, but if this moment is not seized, a general disintegration is to be feared."[5]

Frederick William III did not appreciate this letter. As Blücher's chief biographer, Wolfgang von Unger, states: "Through his skill, Blücher sought to personally influence Frederick William. But the king only sought to silence Blücher."[6] The outspoken general completely discounted or simply did not understand the situation's complexity. His words and actions placed him amid a crisis of loyalty, trust, and confidence between the king and his army as well as some of the most important figures of the reform movement. Of course, hindsight allows us to paint a clear picture of how Blücher fit into this web, yet at the time the king had enough details to suspect the general's involvement. What was the evidence? First, Blücher had a direct connection with Schill, serving with the now-proscribed major during both war and peace. Also, he knew many of the officers who had joined Schill. His blunt support of the rebellion and the assurance that it would spread in the army served to strengthen the rumors of Blücher's collaboration. Second, the general had indirect links to the revolt that made him suspect. French agents had spotted his sons talking to the major at a Berlin Christmas party in 1808. One of them, Franz, counted many of the officers riding with Schill as friends.

Moreover, French and Westphalian authorities presented evidence to Frederick William that the Tugendbund had sponsored Katte's rebellion in early April 1809. Embarrassed, the Prussian monarch issued a formal letter of apology to Jerome. Scharnhorst and Gneisenau—both leaders of the league—earned their king's wrath for involving his administration in such a clumsy and risky undertaking.[7] Obviously, the Tugendbund likewise supported Schill's rebellion. Although Blücher was not a member of the league, the involvement of his allies may have rendered him guilty by association to royal eyes.[8] In the least, he was not looking out for his master's interests when, after Schill met his fate on 31 May, Blücher wrote to Gneisenau: "I will have Schill's briefcase in my hands before anyone learns of the contents of the letters it contains. This much I can say in advance: nothing exists that will compromise anyone, which had me worried."[9]

Amid Schill's ride, the Westphalian ambassador at Berlin informed Jerome that Blücher would attack Magdeburg. Bonaparte's panic started a chain reaction that extended all the way to Paris until Napoleon himself firmly declared that the general would do nothing.[10] Blücher did make plans to mobilize his brigade, just as he had informed Goltz one month earlier. He considered launching a surprise attack, though on Stettin rather than Magdeburg. Without authorization, he purchased several draft horses to make his artillery mobile.[11] "General Blücher . . . purchased some horses to complete the team of a battery and received a reprimand for this," explained Gneisenau in a letter to Götzen, the governor of Silesia. "Anything that has even the slightest appearance of a mobilization is highly disapproved of and I must warn you to be cautious in this respect."[12]

Blücher, of course, vehemently denied any wrongdoing. He complained that the equipment of his Pomeranian troops lagged behind that of the Brandenburg and Silesian Brigades. "I cannot purchase the necessary horses without providing evidence that will make the king suspicious of me," he complained. The general blamed his political opponents at Königsberg, assuring Gneisenau: "I fully believe they told the King that like Schill, I wanted to cross the Elbe with my troops. But woe to those wretches! If I find the one who speaks so disgracefully of me, I swear on the high altar that his life will not be safe from my punishment. I can provide the King proof of how I rejected all proposals for unauthorized action, but it would humiliate me if I had to defend myself."[13]

Regardless, coming on the heels of Stein's debacle, the embarrassment caused by Blücher's imprudence, which did not go unnoticed by French spies, pushed Frederick William too far, causing him to harshly rebuke the senior commander in a cover letter that accompanied a proclamation to the army dated 8 May 1809. The declaration expressed the king's disgust over Schill's actions, proscribing the major and his followers as deserters and promising courts-martial for all the outlaws. Above all, he reminded the army of its duty to obey him.[14]

Based on the next letter Blücher wrote to the king, Frederick William's reprimand must have been severe. Unfortunately, the monarch's epistle has been lost, but Blücher's conciliatory and dutiful reply provides many clues regarding the tone of the royal dispatch. "The succession of years during which I loyally served Your Royal Majesty and the State must convince you that your orders will always be sacred to me. I impressed most sharply on the troops under my command Your Royal Majesty's orders from Königsberg dated 8 May, and I promise my head that they will punctually obey them. If not, I will punish the guilty . . . with the loss of life as an example: a procedure that Your Majesty will certainly endorse, because in certain . . . cases, decisive measures provide the most salutary means." Concerning his comment that Schill's insubordination would provide an example for other units in the army to revolt, the general quickly backtracked: "the demeanor of the local brigade . . . enables me to assure Your Royal Majesty that an over-excited step like that of Major Schill will never occur and my own example of punctually fulfilling Your Royal Majesty's orders shall and will always serve as the guiding principle of my subordinates."

Blücher then changed tactics. He assumed the role of the injured, but intense pride and resentment are also evident. Aside from being debilitating and nearly fatal, his recent illness had emasculated him. While a successful estate owner when he had to be and always a caring patriarch, he measured the value of his existence in his martial ability to lead men. This provided the source of his strength and his will to live. By all means macho and egotistical, he had to live up to the image of the brazen hussar. During the previous year, however, he had been anything but that, and a humiliated Blücher fought to regain respect, dignity, and his image. He feared having lost the king's favor and confidence, complaining that several officers junior to him received honorable assignments, "which hurts me very deeply."

In particular, Blücher complained that the king appointed General Ludwig August von Stutterheim as the new military governor of Berlin, a position that included jurisdiction over Blücher's brigade. Stutterheim's assignment represented Frederick William's growing concern over the loyalty of his army and the increasing anti-French mood of Berlin in the wake of Schill's actions. The king likewise replaced General Ludwig August von Chasot with General Friedrich Heinrich von Kleist as commander of the Berlin garrison. He resolved to prevent his army, his people, or both from thrusting him into a war he could not win. We can only speculate how much of this Blücher knew or understood. Yet it is clear that he believed the king had lost all confidence in him. This feeling, along with the fierce desire to regain his reputation after an embarrassing and debilitating illness, drove Blücher to confront Frederick William despite the political crisis.

"If I may speak freely," the general continued, "as a loyal servant who has rendered the State significant service and as one of the most senior officers in Your Majesty's army, I can certainly complete the assignment that he [Stutterheim] received just as well because I have the confidence of the nation and the love of the military (both of which General Stutterheim must earn)." He pledged his head as his guarantee that he could still satisfy the sovereign. Again speculating that political opponents informed the king that the general's recent illness had sapped his physical strength so that he could no longer perform duties that required "vitality and energy," he requested an audience with Frederick William at Königsberg to disprove the malicious rumors. "Perhaps then I will be fortunate enough to convince Your Majesty that I can carry out your orders just as good as General Stutterheim." Reference to his displeasure over Bülow's special assignment followed this request. He vowed that while he met with the king, the Pomeranian government would be "properly supervised by General Major Bülow, who during my long illness filled this post to Your Majesty's satisfaction."

Yet if the king indeed lacked faith in him and found him unworthy of the type of assignments that Stutterheim received, then Blücher desired a "speedy discharge without pension, although I will be poor and will have to seek my bread in a foreign service." Should that be the case, he would leave Prussia "with the most sad feeling" of being unable to participate through "restless effort and my own sacrifice" in the restoration of the state. Regardless, he promised Frederick William that he would always be a loyal supporter of Prussia. Ever the gambler, Blücher attempted one last roll of the dice. In his concluding paragraph, he combined his request for a war to save Prussia with his desire to resign if the king no longer found him acceptable. Thus, if Frederick William did not accept his view of the war, he should send Blücher on his way. We will never know if this tactic was merely theatrics or if Blücher was attempting to strong arm the monarch, but his boldness is certainly admirable. As to the nation's salvation and his departure, he wrote: "I and the majority of Your Majesty's loyal servants beseech God the Almighty, who perhaps will only hear these multiple prayers when Your Majesty decides to take part in this latest struggle: an opportunity which for Prussia will certainly never recur. This is the confession of faith of a servant who has grown gray with honor in Your

Majesty's service. [Accept my loyalty], but in the opposite case, I again humbly request my discharge without pension because I no longer want to be a burden to the state in any way."[15] To his friend, Bonin, Blücher claimed to have told Frederick William that after losing the king's confidence, serving him no longer held any meaning.

Although Blücher requested his dismissal without a pension, the king responded by promoting him to general of cavalry effective 20 May 1809. "He knows how very much I am attached to his person and that I have and always will have had his confidence," Blücher explained to Bonin. "Now, I have again written to his entourage that I am content, but the king must not believe that the General of Cavalry will act or think any different than the general lieutenant."[16]

Blücher would have preferred to receive notification of a declaration of war and still hoped to convince or even force Frederick William to change his mind. In a 14 June letter to Götzen, Blücher boasted that he assured the king that the promotion meant nothing if he did not enjoy the monarch's confidence. Again he associated this confidence with the king's acceptance of his advice to wage war against Napoleon. He planned to give Frederick William an ultimatum. "If war is not ordered, if we do not reach a decision, then I will go and utilize my remaining strength for the sake of my beleaguered German Fatherland. Go in chains if you want—I will not."[17]

News of Austrian setbacks and an ensuing retreat to the Danube reached Prussia, but this did not shake Blücher's confidence in the least. Informed of events by the Austrian envoy at Berlin, he optimistically judged the situation to be favorable for that kingdom. After witnessing the collapse of the Prussian army after Jena-Auerstedt, Blücher viewed the Austrian army's orderly retreat after successive defeats as an achievement in itself. That the commander, Archduke Charles, managed to put the Danube between him and Napoleon appeared encouraging. "The French are now very evasive," commented Blücher. "They can say what they want, but by going to Vienna, Herr Napoleon will march into a mousetrap. First, he has to completely defeat Archduke Charles; then he will need time to get to Vienna. Before he can do this, he will experience the 'Pultawaschen Zug,'" referring to the decisive defeat of Sweden's Charles XII by Peter the Great of Russia at the Battle of Poltava on 27 June 1709. Regarding the other theaters, Blücher wrote: "In Italy, the gentlemen are unevenly matched and in Galicia, Herr Dabrowski was completely destroyed; he himself should be dead.[18]

And by all of this one is forced to say: Borussia [Prussia], you sleep!"[19] Traveling through Stargard en route to Königsberg, Queen Louise's brother, Prince Carl of Mecklenburg-Strelitz, met with Blücher and agreed to deliver a request to the king. The general sought permission to cross the Elbe with 30,000 men and operate against the weak French forces in North Germany.[20] But fear of Napoleon, mistrust of the Austrians, and the lack of confidence in his own army prevented Frederick William from accepting Blücher's proposal.

Reports that the Austrians stopped Napoleon at the Battle of Aspern-Essling on 21–22 May quickly spread north. Although no Poltava, Aspern-Essling was a French defeat—Napoleon's first. "Over the past several days I have received good news to send you," Blücher scrawled in excitement, "it appears that the light is shining on us and the fear among us of Herr Napoleon and his northern companions has diminished. Herr Napoleon is in a fix and will have difficulty working his way out of it."[21]

Rumors of French reverses prompted the king to issue a new warning against insubordination. Blücher immediately sent his adjutant, Lt. Magnus von Brünneck, to Königsberg to reiterate the request for a corps of 30,000 men. Blücher demanded a decision. According to a letter to Gneisenau, he claimed to have told the king, "I will no longer serve if indecision continues on our part."[22] Confident that his ultimatum would be accepted, Blücher prepared for Prussia's declaration of war with feverish activity.[23] Others knew better, though. Gneisenau explained the mood at Königsberg following the news of Aspern-Essling: "One should no longer expect war on our part. The Austrian victory cannot minimize this pacific attitude. One of the ministers said to me: when the Austrians win a second, third, and fourth battle, and we can then be convinced of the integrity of their dispositions, then it will be time for Prussia to get involved, and Austria must gratefully understand this. So spoke a man whose own integrity stands in good reputation. What can we expect from the others?"[24]

Not all the news was good. Schill's ride ended with his death on 31 May after being driven northward by imperial forces and entrenching himself at Stralsund. Although several ship captains offered to take him to Great Britain, Sweden, or Pomerania, where he could seek Blücher's protection, the major resolved to turn Stralsund into a fortress. Commanding between 1,200 to 1,500 men, Schill faced a combined Dutch and Danish force of 5,000 men commanded by French general Pierre-Guillaume Gratien. While attempting to cross through Stralsund to rally his men on the other side, Schill rode into an enemy detachment. He received the fatal wound shortly before 2:00 P.M. Falling from his horse, the Dutch stabbed him in the side to make sure the Prussian was dead. That night, hoping to collect the 10,000-franc bounty that King Jerome placed on Schill, the general had four doctors remove the major's head. Preserving it in a cask of wine, Gratien intended to present it to Jerome.[25]

The news of Schill's death saddened Blücher but did not devastate him: "Schill's expedition has come to an end; he fell as a brave chap, but his head was dearly bought."[26] Of the major's followers, the Schill'schen, Gratien sent 550 as prisoners to France, where they suffered in prison hulks until the First Peace of Paris in 1814. Some of the rebels managed to escape Stralsund, while others had not been with Schill for the final act. Left behind for various reasons, they now scurried around the Baltic coast as fugitives. Proscribed by Frederick William, many turned to the only individual in North Germany who might help: Blücher.[27] By 6 June, 900 men had made their way to Kolberg and Stargard. Schill's companions "are under my care," wrote Blücher. Again challenging Frederick William's authority, the general refused to disarm them, explaining to the king that they had acted only on the major's orders. According to Prussian regulations, he argued, they had to obey him and thus could not be held accountable.[28]

Despite the king's earlier decision to court-martial the Schill'schen, Blücher suggested organizing the infantry into a light battalion and the cavalry into a hussar regiment.[29] Frederick William, under pressure from French and Westphalian authorities—not to mention Napoleon himself—refused to budge. A 5 June cabinet order instructed Blücher to arrest the Schill'schen, prompting the general to declare one week later that the affair caused him "miserable frustration."[30] Regardless, he did not comply with the directive. As late as 16 July, he assured Gneisenau that if he received an order to incarcerate the Schill'schen at Kolberg, he would see to it that they all ran away.[31] Frederick William did not want to court-martial the rank and file but had to take a strong stand to placate the French and to send a firm message to his army. He managed to evade Napoleon's demands for justice and eventually pardoned most of the Schill'schen. For the moment, though, he did not show the same mercy toward the fifty-three officers who participated in Schill's ride, half of whom returned to Prussia. Of these men, twenty-two were locked away at Kolberg awaiting courts-martial.[32]

The king's rejection of Blücher's request to dispose of the Schill'schen as he saw fit appears to have aggravated the general more than Schill's death. He again connected this negative response with the loss of royal confidence. Blücher did not blame the monarch directly but instead claimed that "miserable people succeeded in ambiguously describing my conduct to the monarch." Moreover, in Blücher's mind, the controversy over the Schill'schen became part of the struggle to get Frederick William to comply with his wishes for war against Napoleon, which would indicate he had regained his master's confidence. Weeks passed as the tension mounted. In mid-July Blücher again lamented that the king had lost confidence in him. For the first time in his service to Frederick William III, he "received undeserved reprimands."

To Blücher, the king's confidence meant his respect, almost to the point of royal subservience. Frederick William's ploy to placate him failed as the promotion meant little to Blücher. Only the acceptance of his suggestions, plans, and demands would provide the general sufficient proof that the king respected him, did not believe the stories of his insanity, and still regarded him as a man. Upon receiving this recognition, Blücher could assure himself that he had defeated the illness that had robbed him of his manly dignity. This, in turn, would allow him to deal with the man who had robbed him of his martial dignity: Napoleon. After 1806 Blücher became obsessed with vengeance on the emperor. While he went through the motions of respect, honor, and fealty to his king, such dutiful expressions could and would be dropped if he got in the way of the general's pursuit of vengeance.

At times, Blücher's emotions bled like a true patriot; on other occasions, his rants resembled those of an individual who unjustifiably demands respect and receives none. Some of his letters contain both traits, such as one penned to Gneisenau on 16 July. Referring to the royal reprimand, he was confident that "as a man of true German emotion," Gneisenau could easily judge his mood. Blücher viewed a royal rejection as not merely the dismissal of his proposal but also the refutation of his recovery. If he failed to convince the king that he had recovered, then Blücher would not be able to seek his revenge on Napoleon. Consequently, he believed that he had no choice but to leave the Prussian army. "What should occur must happen soon or else all will be lost because too much time has been wasted," he wrote Gneisenau. "As long as I serve the King, I cannot begin nor do anything, but I have firmly decided to leave this service in time to be able to do what I intend without delay." In short, as long as he served a king who no longer had confidence in him, he could never fully recover, and if he could not recover, he could not seek vengeance on Napoleon.

Before taking this ultimate step, he hoped to make one last appeal to Frederick William and so returned to the idea of going to Königsberg. He asked Gneisenau and Scharnhorst to arrange a meeting between him and the king. "If you could both succeed in having me summoned to Königsberg much would be accomplished. I will speak with the Master respectfully, but also openly and candidly and the unfavorable, the weak, and the stubborn shall be silent while I am there. . . . God knows with what sadness I leave a state and an army in which I spent fifty years. My heart is sick over being forced to desert a Master who I love, for whom I have sacrificed a thousand times over. But all the same and by God in heaven—I will suffer no more insults." Again he brought up the king's decision to change the name of his regiment: "Think of my vexation! Not only did they take my name from my regiment, they replaced its honorable [red] coat." He went on to reference how, in his opinion, the king viewed him: "Invalid-commandant will I be no more; younger men shall not be placed ahead of me, do not inform me of their inflated, extended authority." He assured Gneisenau that for a long time he had refused offers from other states, but he would now seek service elsewhere. "I will not pass my time in idleness while other virtuous German men fight for the liberation of their German Fatherland." He asked Gneisenau to ensure that Scharnhorst processed his request for a discharge as quickly as possible when it arrived. He planned to go to London and seek service with the British. "Never will I completely separate myself from the interests of this state, but since I cannot work for its betterment in my current situation, I must labor in another way."[33]

Certainly, Gneisenau and Blücher were implicated in the Schill affair, perhaps Scharnhorst as well, but the documentary evidence is sketchy. But Gneisenau's connections with the British evolved into a scheme that involved Blücher. As early as 15 February 1809, Gneisenau proposed that "under certain circumstances" (a Franco-Austrian war), he would leave Prussia and take refuge with Stein in Austria. He then asked Stein to comment on the idea of forming a Prussian legion at Prague consisting of the best of the officers who had been placed on half-pay; soldiers would be recruited along the border between Saxony and Bohemia. He explained that should Frederick William "be paralyzed by the Russian influence" and not support the Austrians, "such a legion could be a refuge for the last remnant of the Prussian spirit to assemble with honor. Because of my many connections, I am well suited to form such a legion and England will probably be more than willing to provide equipment and pay."[34]

Thus was born the idea of a British-sponsored Prussian legion. Blücher strongly supported it and, with no mention of first seeking royal approval, proposed that he himself would raise an entire corps, whose nucleus would be formed by this legion. Gneisenau immediately informed Archduke Charles of Blücher's plans. To influence popular opinion, Blücher maintained his contacts in Mecklenburg and Brandenburg despite increased French and Prussian vigilance. He remained in close communication with the Austrian envoy at Berlin and with Götzen in Silesia to be quickly informed of events in Austria. In short, Blücher prepared to rush headlong into the struggle with or without Frederick William, waiting only for the word from Gneisenau.[35]

Throughout the following months, Gneisenau utilized his contacts to lay the groundwork for the legion. In April he forwarded the draft of an extensive plan to Count Ernst von Hardenberg, the Hanoverian envoy at Vienna, based on the assumption that Hardenberg was serving as the diplomatic liaison between the Habsburg court and the British cabinet. Gneisenau explained to him how British foreign secretary George Canning had made supreme efforts to successfully provide arms and ammunition for the defense of Kolberg in 1807. While London's actions impressed him then, he could not say the same of his own government in 1809. He complained to the count about Frederick William's lack of resolve: "I've had to struggle with indecision, timidity, languor, venality, and treachery. The warped views of numerous important people are major obstacles that oppose my efforts. I fear nothing, and told my monarch and master verbally and in memoranda using the strongest but respectful language what to do for his salvation, and what will be his fate if he continues to wait." Sounding very much like Blücher, he declared: "I will take part in indecision no longer and I wish to serve one of the armies fighting France."

Gneisenau explained that as a member of the Superior Investigating Commission, he was in perfect position to select "the most capable of the officers of our army. I have many friends in the Prussian states and it will not be difficult for me to raise a Prussian legion against France, which under the right conditions can be increased." According to his plan, the British would pay the cost of equipping the unit, while the Austrians would purchase its arms at "factory cost." The legion would fight under the Austrian flag until Prussia entered the war, at which time it would "return to the service of its former master." If Prussia did not enter the war, then it would serve anywhere in Europe at the pleasure of Great Britain or Austria. Gneisenau declared that the legion would link with the right wing of the Austrian army in Germany and "undertake the most dangerous of missions." He requested that Hardenberg do everything in his power to work out the details of the plan and to send his response to either Gneisenau or Götzen only.[36]

By July, Gneisenau had accomplished everything he could from Königsberg: to achieve his goal, he had to go to London. He was already contemplating British service, as he had hinted to Hardenberg in April, and Blücher likewise thought of donning the red coat of King George's army. It is not known when Gneisenau informed Blücher of these ideas; much communication passed between the two by way of oral messages delivered by Franz. Regardless, Blücher urged his colleague to quickly reach an agreement with Great Britain. By 16 July, the general knew that Gneisenau, accompanied by Franz, would soon leave for London to discuss both the legion and service in the British army. Effective on 1 July, Frederick William released Gneisenau from the Prussian army to embark on a year-long, state-sponsored diplomatic mission to Great Britain, Sweden, and Russia. "As soon as I have news from you or my son I will act," wrote Blücher, "take the [British] service—at the very least it is a better position, and I will hurry there myself. Live well, may the heavens bless your endeavors. No time is to be lost, do what you can where you are! I only say to you that I will not twiddle my thumbs."[37]

Essentially, as soon as Gneisenau reached an agreement with the British, Blücher would submit his resignation—thus his request that Scharnhorst effect its rapid execution. As a token of his

sincerity, he sent Franz, whom the king permitted to go on the pretext that it was in the interest of improving the major's health.[38]
Despite their efforts, nothing came of the Prussian legion owing to
the British desire to use their resources to liberate Holland, open
the mouth of the Scheldt, and combine the Netherlands with northwestern Germany to create a large Guelph state. After receiving a
taste of parliamentary politics, Gneisenau left London in disgust
but continued his diplomatic work on behalf of the Prussian crown.
He did not return to the army until 1811.

As for Blücher, inaccurate reports from Austria and the North
Sea coast drove his enthusiasm. On 14 July an Austrian courier passed through Stargard en route to London claiming another
Austrian victory. The next day the general received "private letters"
(from Götzen) stating that Charles again defeated Napoleon on 27
June. News of this second Austrian victory accompanied rumors
that a British expeditionary force of 30,000 men had landed near
Cuxhaven at the mouth of the Elbe.[39] Like a coiled spring ready to
release its energy, Blücher tensely awaited the king's decision. "The
return of my adjutant, Lt. Brünneck, will harden my resolve completely. If the King takes no part, if we take no steps to break our fet-
ters, then whoever wants may wear them, but not I! I have sacrificed
everything for the State and will abandon it as one divorces himself
from the world: poor, naked, and bare, but my courage is unbound.
Wherever I go, a soothing conscious and plenty of honest people will
accompany me."[40] Not trusting the perseverance of the Austrians,
the king still refused to take the ultimate step. Despite the maligned
reputation that has followed him into posterity, Frederick William
III understood war. He correctly believed that Charles poorly
exploited the victory at Aspern-Essling. Consequently, the Prussian
monarch preferred to await the outcome of a second, more decisive
battle. This finally occurred on 5–6 July at Wagram. After crossing the Danube, Napoleon forced Charles to yield after noteworthy
Austrian resistance.

News that Frederick William still refused to take a decisive step
along with reports of Napoleon's victory at Wagram, which Blücher
received sometime on 17 or 18 July, did not daunt him, nor did it
induce him to submit his letter of resignation. Write he did, but
once again he aimed to regain the monarch's "confidence" on the
eighteenth. "All of the reports that reach me attest to the difficult
situation of the French army," he declared in either desperation or

complete disrespect for Frederick William's common sense. "Albeit the Emperor Napoleon seemingly has achieved success by crossing the Danube, his army has entered a land where it will encounter ill will and where, on the contrary, its adversary will receive all possible support." Rather than dwell on Wagram, he urged the king to consider the mounting evidence that pointed to Austria's imminent success. He explained that "insurgents" flooded Bavaria, that the Austrians "maneuver with success" in the Tyrol, that an Austrian corps of 8,000 men invaded Saxony, that Duke William of Brunswick defeated Jerome, that 30,000 British troops landed on the coast, and finally that Napoleon's allies "are lukewarm and the first French defeat will bring to fruition their decision to abandon the emperor. All of this paints a ruinous picture of the French army," he assured the king. The general begged his king for permission to cross the Elbe with one corps of 16,000 men.[41]

Considering Prussia's devastated finances, Blücher predicted that he could make war pay for war within four weeks of crossing the Elbe and could accomplish this without overburdening the inhabitants. "Most Gracious King," he submissively asked, "grant the request of one who has grown gray in your service, who is as honest as he is devoted to you, who is ready to sacrifice himself for you, and whose burning wish is to devote the last days of his life for the benefit of you and your glory." Again pledging his head, he vowed to regain Prussia's lost western provinces. "Please do not consider my views to be exaggerated! They are not. I know what I have promised on the other side of the Elbe and in Westphalia. Imagine the gratitude that you will reap from the entire German nation when it learns that you have decided to liberate it from the unbearable yoke!" He promised that the Hanoverians and the Hessians would "sacrifice with their life and possessions. Time, Most Gracious King, cannot be lost, or the enemy will exhaust our provinces and make it difficult to ever receive anything from them again." Concluding in a less confrontational tone than his previous letters, he simply expressed his self-loathing for "having to bear these foreign chains. I was born free and so must die free."[42]

Further reports only strengthened Blücher's convictions. By the twentieth, he believed that the British had penetrated deep into North Germany, passing through Celle en route to the Weser River.[43] His impatience and excitement spiraled; he even considered entering the Austrian service if the king refused him.[44] We do not know Frederick William's response to Blücher's 18 July letter. Regardless, the situation changed completely after news arrived of the 12 July 1809 Armistice of Znaim between Charles and Napoleon. Ironically, this news aided Blücher's cause on the eve of army maneuvers. Charles's request for a ceasefire caused the Prussian peace party to consider Napoleon's next step. What if the king's apparent inability to control the Tugendbund as well as his army and the members of his own administration prompted the emperor to turn north after he concluded his business with the Habsburgs? Based on this consideration, Frederick William finally appeared ready to enter the war if Austria resumed the struggle. To be better prepared for conflict, he extended the time of maneuvers so the army could be quickly concentrated.[45] After months of disappointment, Blücher finally could taste success. "I made a serious proposal to the King," he later explained to Götzen, "and requested that he allow me to cross the Elbe with a corps of his troops. I thought I would receive a negative answer, but from the enclosed you will see the opposite. The unfortunate armistice provided the King reason to treat with me. Should the fight be renewed, I will have greater cause to be even more pressing."[46]

A tense month of waiting followed. Stress brought on various ailments such as colic in July and then a fever that lasted for several days in September, but with the prospect of war, Blücher's mind remained healthy, thus allowing him to overcome the physical afflictions. He found some relief from his anxiety in the August exercises of the Pomeranian Brigade around Stargard. On the eve of the maneuvers, the general issued an order of the day that captured his mood as well as his direct manner: "If the officers have to report to me or I require such, I thus request that they strive to do so in the shortest possible terms and that they spare me from French expressions since it is well known that my French is not good. I wish that anybody who writes me will write as if he is speaking to me and omit all grace and submissiveness and I will then respond in the same fashion. Also, the officers' enormous sideburns must be completely cut off since I find these suitable only for coachmen."[47]

The troops, who he described as "brilliant," performed well.[48] Amid the maneuvers, Blücher received reports that the Austrians ceased negotiating with the French and renounced the armistice. "This has sparked much hope in me," he expressed to Bonin on

9 August. "Kaiser Francis has assumed command of the army and surrounds himself with bold generals."[49] As August passed into September, the Pomeranian Brigade remained assembled at Stargard, Frederick William still vacillated, and Kaiser Francis did nothing. Blücher became skeptical of the king. "I still do not despair that our German Fatherland can be saved," he confessed on 12 September, "but it must be assailed with fire. I do my share loyally and the King will receive no rest from my side until he decides [for war] or dismisses me; I am ready for either. If I am dismissed, then I can dispose of myself as a free man."[50]

As September passed into October, Blücher faced yet another problem: debt. Ever the salubrious host, Blücher, however, did not like to foot the bill associated with his rank. He quarreled with the General War Department regarding payment of "the fees for my commission as General of Cavalry." Blücher refused to pay, believing that the war ministry should absorb the costs. He complained over the bill to the department, which informed him that he alone bore the responsibility for the payment of his debts, advising him to seek assistance from the king. Perturbed, he issued a very acrimonious reply: "By no means have I found the refusal of the payment, as determined by the General War Department, to be good. I cannot understand how a royal department can conceive an idea that claims the mistake . . . was made on my part. To my knowledge, I have not requested the dispensation of the fees for the commission, and likewise I have not complained to the War Department, nor turned to the King to correct this problem. Nevertheless, for the time being, I will not pay the commission for General of Cavalry until my budget has been set by the King."[51]

Although we do not know the details, Frederick William agreed with Blücher and later dismissed the fees.[52] In addition, he sought to ease the general's financial woes by awarding him, on 10 October 1809, a church benefice in Brandenburg that he allowed Blücher to either sell or retain for income; Blücher chose the latter. Frederick William also increased his salary from 6,400 thaler to 8,400. After these measures failed to cover the debts, the pressure of his creditors forced the general to have 200 thaler garnished from his monthly salary. Despite the deduction of his wages, Blücher could not reconcile his debts, prompting the king to comment that Blücher was "a bad landlord" who made poor "calculations at every opportunity" that allowed his outstanding debts to grow exponentially.[53]

By October 1809, fighting had not resumed between the French and Austrians, yet Blücher still hoped, schemed, and speculated: "French forces are always considerable, but the Austrians are not inconsiderable. If only Kaiser Francis remembers and trusts in the old German saying: 'fortune smiles on the bold.' The mood in Westphalia is terrible; daily I receive letters of invitation. I have explained all of this to the King without holding anything back." On 2 October he informed Götzen that he received good news "from the world and from Gneisenau himself at London. If we only make the right decision we will receive help from all sides." He dismissed the Pomeranian Brigade yet kept the battalions close enough to be concentrated rapidly. Although he claimed to be "fit as a fiddle," the end of maneuvers left him idle and with nothing to do but dwell on the international situation: "the lovely boredom, the desk, and the perpetual monotony are poison for me."[54] One week later the situation changed for the last time.

Although the Franco-Austrian Treaty of Schönbrunn that ended the War of the Fifth Coalition bears the official date of 14 October 1809, Blücher received the details of its terms on the ninth. Draconian and punitive, the treaty stunned him because of its implications of how Napoleon might treat Prussia in the future. "So, we will now earn the reward for our hesitation," he replied to Götzen.[55] Blücher immediately dispatched a very blunt letter to the king that contained the news of Schönbrunn. "With the most profound pain, I must report to Your Royal Majesty the news of the conclusion of peace, which for Austria is disastrous. The fate in store for us is horrible, because Napoleon himself has stated his intention to collect the contributions that are in arrears. Only a few months earlier, a bold decision by Your Royal Majesty could have provided the proper turn to what is the common cause of all nations. It pains me excessively that you, Most Gracious Master, refused my urgent, respectful request, which I dared to make out of true, unbounded devotion."

Blücher continued by assuring Frederick William that the French would undoubtedly reoccupy the majority of Prussia. He employed the plural to describe Napoleon's intentions for Prussia: "We will suffer the fate of the Hessians and fall through a mere stroke of Napoleon's pen." To Götzen, however, the general expressed the true meaning of this statement, which the king most likely understood: "Without holding back, I said to him [Frederick William] that his fate will be that of the Elector of Hesse."[56]

Based on the assumption that Napoleon planned to disenfranchise Frederick William III as he had William I of Hesse, Blücher urged the king to act out of desperation. "We have nothing more to lose because an honorable death is better than going through the world with a branded life. Your Royal Majesty can still save the royal family and the country if you place the weapons in our hands." He maintained that with fewer resources, the king's great-uncle, Frederick II, resisted subjugation during the Seven Years War. Blücher insisted that Frederick William could count "on an army of 60,000 men, on just as many men who are partially trained and partially combat ready, and on the entire country, which will certainly fight for its beloved King and sacrifice itself rather than bear a foreign yoke. All of Germany, whose last thread of freedom Your Majesty holds, can and will make common cause with us. What we can do, what we want to do, does not mean anything if our king does not accept us, does not fight by our side, and does not prefer death to disgrace! I will remain faithful to my King until death and guarantee that it will go well if only we seize the right means."

As a first step, Blücher proposed a surprise attack on Stettin. He maintained that the imperial garrison of mostly sick German troops numbered only 1,900 men. "Does your Royal Majesty have the matchless mercy to hear my humble request and to accept it as I candidly lay it at your feet as a German man? Does Your Majesty have the mercy to grant me permission?" He then requested instructions on how to proceed if imperial forces occupied Berlin and moved into Pomerania, which he believed would occur shortly. He also wanted permission to prevent imperial reinforcements from reaching Stettin and Küstrin.[57] "If I know Your Majesty's intentions we can avoid being surprised. Why should we act any less than the Spanish and the Tyroleans! We have greater resources than them."

Blücher saved his best for last: "Not by false ambition, not by a preposterous view, not by the idea of a possibility will my King and Master fall into the abyss through the pernicious advice provided by so many miserable councilors who seek to deter the natural courage and decisiveness of my boundless beloved monarch. . . . [O]nly the most fervent desire to maintain the royal house on the throne and to not see our poor country tread underfoot leads me to make this humble request." He concluded by reminding Frederick William that Napoleon created Westphalia from Prussian territory and to consider the territorial concessions Austria now had to make. Adding to this his doubt that the emperor would not excuse the Prussians from the contributions that were in arrears, Blücher reiterated his concern that Napoleon would partition the kingdom. "This conviction has persuaded me to lay this proposal at Your Majesty's feet. If you deign to give me just a glimmer of hope, I will calm down."[58]

After writing the king, Blücher fired a missive to Götzen, instructing him to prepare Silesia for "the Poles to commit an act of roguery." Concerning Napoleon and the French, he told him what the Prussians needed to do: "My advice is to call to arms our Nation and the entire German Nation to defend the native soil, to not surrender to a people who want to subjugate us. Any German who takes up arms against us will receive death. I don't know why we don't act like the Tyroleans and the Spanish. I must wait to see how my candid summons will be received and whether the King will finally awaken from his slumber and send his advisors, who surround him like sluggards, to the devil. For me, my decision is made: I will stop at nothing to convince the King to bind himself to his army and his people and to prefer an honorable death to slavery. If nothing works, then I will go over land and sea." Ever hopeful that the situation could change, the general requested that he notify him as soon as the Austrians signed the peace.[59]

Götzen answered with great empathy but feared that nothing would result from Blücher's efforts. He told the general that it was their "duty to leave behind a glorious legacy and a good example for our descendants; I at least hope to be able to act." Shortly afterward, Francis signed the Treaty of Schönbrunn, and the war officially ended. With the conclusion of the War of the Fifth Coalition, Frederick William prepared for the worst, but Napoleon simply demanded—albeit firmly—the payment of the reparations. Of course, the emperor fumed that after he reduced the size of the indemnity, the ungrateful Prussians contemplated joining the Austrians. He ordered Frederick William to transfer the government and royal residence back to Berlin as a sign of the king's good faith; the royals returned on 23 December. In reality Napoleon wanted Frederick William amid the imperial garrisons that still occupied Stettin, Küstrin, and Magdeburg not only to intimidate him but also to better supervise a king who had difficulty controlling his own army and administration. As a result of Napoleon's pressure, Frederick William ordered the dissolution of the Tugendbund.

Although the secret societies continued to operate underground, the league lost its royal approval and thus protection. More demands and humiliations would come in the following year, but the Prussian monarchy survived the scandals and turbulence of 1809.

On 1 November the king answered Blücher's 9 October letter: he could send him no new orders in regards to the general's conduct toward the French, but "thank you for the true devotion that you show me anew."[60] In December the court traveled through Stargard en route to Berlin. Meeting with the queen and king on the twenty-first, Blücher received their deep appreciation for his service. Supposedly, "assurances of loyalty flowed from Blücher's mouth."[61] Despite his bluster, the general neither rebelled nor resigned. Conversely, a very patient Frederick William forgave the fiery, impetuous, brazen commander who on the one hand promised genuine devotion, but on the other continued to add to the king's headaches. Of course, Napoleon's spies informed the emperor of the efforts by Blücher and Götzen to organize frantic resistance against him. Upon receiving Prussia's envoy in Paris, he angrily asked who really ruled that kingdom: "Is it that man in Silesia [Götzen] or Schill or 'Blüquaire'?"[62]

Disillusionment and outright disgust over royal inaction was not confined to Blücher.[63] Frederick William's instructions "not to prepare a rising against France, but to secure Prussia a more tolerable existence under French hegemony" considerably undermined his credibility among the war party.[64] No member of this group came as close as Blücher to disregarding the king and taking action against the French. Unger firmly believes that the general assured Götzen of his cooperation if the French moved into Silesia. In such a crisis Blücher would have acted without awaiting royal authorization.[65] Once again, documentary evidence is sketchy and, as noted, his envoys not only delivered his letters but also conveyed his thoughts orally. Despite the lack of documentation, it is very likely that Blücher would have disregarded his remaining scruples and led the Pomeranian Brigade to its destruction in Silesia. Perhaps never before in the history of the Prussian army had a general placed himself in such glaring and deliberate contrast to his king as Blücher did in 1809.

We are left wondering why Blücher never followed through with his threats and plans to rebel or resign. First and foremost, he pledged his honor several times that he would "do nothing before I am released from my local obligation."[66] Blücher took seriously his word of honor as well as his oath of loyalty to the king. For these reasons, he did not attempt an unauthorized military operation like Schill. To the very end, he always hoped the king would accept his plans and join him. Second, Blücher loved Prussia more than he hated Napoleon. He ultimately reached the conclusion that he could do more for his state by remaining in Prussia and preparing for the eventual day of retribution than by taking service in a foreign army. After Napoleon respected what remained of the kingdom's territorial integrity and the immediate fear of a humiliating partition and dethronement passed, this perception of his role increased. Third, the field maneuvers around Stargard in August did much to improve Blücher's mental image of himself. Commanding troops in the field replaced the humiliating vision of an old dotard begging his servants to smite his head with a hammer. Fourth, and admittedly the least likely but still worthy of mention, was Blücher's financial situation. As a man of honor, he had to pay his debts. Receiving a Brandenburg domain certainly brought him closer to debt relief than seeking service in a foreign army.

By the end of the Franco-Austrian war in October, Blücher had overcome his psychological need to be reaccepted as a man by the king, thus his rants about losing the king's "confidence" diminished. Instead, he now perceived Frederick William to be the weaker man and thus no longer needed his affirmation. While Blücher feared no man, he clearly sensed the king's fear of Napoleon and sought to exploit it to motivate him throughout 1809. He certainly did not understand the arguments of the peace party and, as his letters indicate, could not accept that they too worked for Prussia's salvation, though advocating a different course of action. To Blücher, these individuals were the same weak, "miserable sluggards" who had caused the king to lose confidence in his abilities. But who was weaker, the men giving the impotent advice, or the man accepting the advice and rejecting the sword? In Blücher's mind of simple cause and effect, Frederick William became the weaker man. Instead of finding affirmation of himself in his king, he looked at the real cause of his own as well as his state's emasculation: Bonaparte. Only Blücher's active contribution to Napoleon's destruction could erase the embarrassing memories of 1806, 1807, and 1808. Although the king never accepted his war plans, Blücher's personal honor prevented him from sullying his own name. After the Franco-Austrian war, his devotion to the royal family, albeit to a king who was a weaker man, overcame his frustration and anguish.

CHAPTER 7

HOPE AND DESPAIR

P russia survived the consequences of Austria's attempt to spark a war of German liberation, but it could not escape French demands for the payment of reparations. Frederick William III requested postponement, but on 8 January 1810 Napoleon threatened to detach part of Silesia if the king continued to default. Certain that the stipulations of Schönbrunn would prevent Austria from posing any threat in the immediate future, the emperor disregarded the terms of his 1808 treaty that required Prussia to provide an auxiliary division in the event of a Franco-Austrian war. To economize and make the necessary payments, he suggested that Frederick William dissolve the entire Prussian army except the Royal Guard.[1]

Payment of the indemnity practically consumed all Prussian revenues. Consequently, Napoleon's pressure on the kingdom's wrecked finances destroyed the reformers' hope of expanding the army through universal conscription.[2] In the spring of 1810, Scharnhorst made one last attempt to secure royal approval for universal conscription, but his days in office were numbered. As a result of his opposition to the emperor's suggestion to dissolve the army as well as French suspicion of his military reforms, Napoleon forced Frederick William to relieve him of all duties. Scharnhorst "retired" on 6 June but maintained secret communication with the government and especially the war ministry, which continued the work of reform. The main consequence of his removal was the end of the campaign for universal conscription.

Meanwhile, Hardenberg assumed the office of chancellor, a position especially created for him that contained more power than any Prussian minister ever wielded. Starting on the same date that Scharnhorst resigned, he first sought to repair Prussia's finances through strict economizing to prevent Napoleon from detaching any further territory. Instead of the army receiving increased funding per Scharnhorst's requests, the 1809–10 military budget dropped from 7,038,976 thaler to 6,402,500 thaler, with the shortfall mainly covered by extensive furloughing.³ Knowing that the emperor had refused to deal with him in 1807, and with Stein's fall providing a severe lesson to be heeded, Hardenberg maintained a favorable disposition toward the French and their interests in all of his actions.

In late June 1810 Gneisenau secretly returned to Berlin from his mission to London via St. Petersburg. For this reason, he did not stop at Stargard while en route to the Prussian capital nor did he write Blücher. In fact, his presence at Berlin was supposed to be kept secret, "but thanks to the idleness of various people, and the cautious affection of my exalted friends in the capital of H[errn] F[eld] M[arshall] K[alkreuth] and others, this failed." He finally explained himself in a letter to Franz on 22 October 1810: "On my return from Russia, I avoided the road to Stargard. Because of that, I missed the pleasure of giving my deep adoration to our venerable hero, your father, and greeting you, my dear friend. Please don't resent me for this, but instead understand the importance of the reasons that prevented me from fulfilling such a pleasurable duty. It was hard for me to not be able to do this; but wisdom demanded it, and by returning to private life may I never again attract public attention on myself nor embarrass my patrons and friends through my corrupting presence."

Returning empty handed from London and St. Petersburg took the fight out of him. He painted a grim picture for Blücher's son: "Our beautiful hopes are now destroyed. I will not hide it from you that the desperation of our affairs has overcome me. Nothing more will happen, nothing more can happen, at least not with the hope of some success. A bit more sovereignty is lost and so one gradually chokes us until we suffocate. If you have hopes please share them with me; I will gladly believe in them, as long as you give some hope for a new life. But I fear that a stupor has overcome all of us." The future chief of the General Staff of the Prussian Army planned to become a farmer but left the door open for getting involved when the day of retribution arrived.⁴

As for Blücher, we know little of his activities during the first six months of 1810. Napoleon's oppression weighed heavily on him, as Wolfgang von Unger notes: "The cloud that now hung over Prussia distressed Blücher deeply."⁵ "I am now all alone," the general wrote in early June. "My wife is in Berlin, Franz is [back] on his estate. I will be happy when the first hunt takes place."⁶ Hunting indeed provided him an escape from a life that he described as "boring and mundane."[7] While hunting fox at Pützerlin, Storkow, or Ludwigsfrei, Blücher would interject his hatred of Napoleon into the chase. After the hounds cornered the animal, the general would shout that just once he wished to have Bonaparte trapped in such a manner. He often visited the theater, where he so loudly cursed Napoleon as an oppressor that the peace-loving citizens shuffled away from his proximity. During the day, Blücher could be found holding forth at the Gieseschen Tavern next to the post office or before the post itself, sitting and comfortably chatting with the people who came there. He particularly liked to be on hand the days mail arrived so he could meet the people coming from abroad. In the afternoons he frequented a beer garden at a tavern in the market square. His servant brought his pipe and lit it for him. The general attracted a large gathering and soon a social club emerged. If the conversation lagged, they happily moved indoors to gamble. Rumors spread that the stakes could be extremely high and that a chap named "Blüchern" sometimes lost a good bit of money.[8] The old hussar also assisted in times of crisis. In October a fire would have destroyed the home of a tanner had not Blücher "intervened right away with all seriousness."[9] During another fire near a granary on 29 December 1809, he arrived quickly and directed the fire-fighting effort, thus saving the structure.[10]

Rumors of Hardenberg's return had excited the general: "Tell me," he wrote Eisenhart on 6 June 1810, "what post will Hardenberg take? One told me that he has been reappointed, but I do not know the capacity; I think as prime minister. He is a brave man and has the experience that is necessary for such a post; he also has knowledge of our internal situation."[11] Four days after Frederick William named Hardenberg chancellor, the general expressed his satisfaction: "Hardenberg's appointment pleases me."[12] An energized Blücher even thought Prussia might take up the sword: "Be ready, war can still come."[13] But in mid-July 1810, he informed Eisenhart that "from 'P' nothing reasonable or at least nothing advantageous will come."[14] It is not known whether he is referring to Paris, to where Frederick William had dispatched Field Marshal Kalckreuth, or to Gneisenau's return from Great Britain through St. Petersburg.

Regardless of who Blücher meant, the prospect of Prussia willingly seeking war with France in 1810 did not appear very good. Yet this did not mean that the reformers, with Scharnhorst always in the mix, stopped preparing for war. By August 1810, the Prussian

army consisted of 33,857 active soldiers, 10,781 reserves on furlough, 1,300 garrison troops, 3,300 invalids, and 11,218 soldiers from
disbanded regiments still capable of service. Normal regimental
reserve training made available an additional 9,883 men as replacements for the sick and wounded. In addition, the Krümper system
provided an extra 3,488 *Beurlaubten* (available trained men), or
additional troops not required for a regiment's normal replacement
needs.[15] Successfully evading Napoleon's restrictions, this system
allowed Prussia to build a reserve of trained soldiers so that approximately 35,600 Krümper reserves doubled the size of the field army
in 1813.[16]

Aside from the Krümper system, the constraints Hardenberg
encountered in his attempts to maintain good relations with
Napoleon while resuscitating the Prussian economy gave the appearance that Berlin's policy of compliance had not changed. In particular, Prussia felt the consequences of France's economic war with
Great Britain. Napoleon's 4 August 1810 Trianon Tariff imposed a
50-percent import tax on all colonial goods such as cotton, sugar,
coffee, and spices. Enforced duties and the seizure of supplies in
Prussian storehouses followed its passage. Selfish and misguided
conduct by Prussian merchants along with French enforcement of
the tariff aggravated Blücher: "The incident of exhausting the ware-
house and the granary [at Stettin] by the French is a consequence
of the insatiableness and imprudence of our merchants. I have seen
this situation coming and have stated my opinion over it, but the
merchants believed they had the assurances of the [French] Consul.
My opinion regarding our tariff and excise administration should
also have received more attention, because the seizures and the
confiscations could have occurred for the good of the King and his
interests. . . . I think it would be good if the authorities at Stettin
received information that I have made these statements; because I
have a good relationship with General Liebert [governor of Stettin],
many similar issues can be resolved."[17]

On Napoleon's demand, Prussian troops fortified the Baltic
coast to prevent the smuggling of British goods. This led to con-
frontations with the Royal Navy, which safeguarded British trade.
At times Blücher seriously enforced his orders to treat the British
as the enemy. On other occasions, though, either he or his staff
sought to redress the situation. His vacillating attitude toward
being placed in the middle between the official British enemy and

the hated French overlord is interesting. "The English gentlemen appear to want to amuse us because they are daily in view and come very close to land, but only with sloops," he wrote on 15 July 1810. With Kolberg weakly garrisoned, Blücher noted that the troops there "must always be ready to skedaddle."[18] A few months later he assured Eisenhart that although "the British tease me all day, I will soon rap them on the knuckles." Yet in this same letter, dated 10 September 1810, he also reacted to French troop movements in Saxony: "Soon, soon the general fire that I have been expecting for so long will start. The French are again in Saxony—this is a sign! Always nearer it approaches! Only when it begins to burn the skin, does it teach the need to act."[19] On 10 March 1811 Blücher wrote to Bonin over the failure of the third French invasion of Portugal: "A lovely letter from my gracious wife brought me so much pleasant news: to his horror, Herr Massena was stopped" at Torres Vedras by the British.[20]

A few months later the commandant of Kolberg, Lieutenant Colonel August Ernst von Kamptz, informed the general that on 3 June 1811 a British frigate anchored in the harbor and sent a small boat toward shore. After the Prussians fired two warning shots, the boat returned to the ship, which sailed off. Although in March he had raved over British success in Portugal, Blücher's response again demonstrates not only his fickle attitude toward the British but also, more importantly, his demand that orders and military regulations be followed in the strictest manner: "It is very unsatisfactory to infer from your report how the fire from the fortress against an enemy ship that was approaching was not directed as desired. In the future, you will send to the bottom any enemy vessel that approaches the harbor and comes within range."[21] On the following day Kamptz sent a letter delivered to Kolberg by a British *"Parlamentärboot"* expressing an admiral's complaints over the incident. In fact, the British insisted that the boat had raised a flag to request negotiations. In his response Blücher expressed his regret over this violation of international law but stated that he had clear orders from his king to avoid any communication with Great Britain and to consider that power as an enemy. "The orders of the King, my master," he concluded, "are always sacred to me and I will seek to comply with them upon the strictest."[22]

Three months later a small British naval boat ran aground near Kolberg. Prussian fishermen seized it along with the captain and six sailors. Blücher had the vessel towed to Kolberg and reported the incident to the king. To comply with French regulations, Frederick William instructed him to have the ship publically auctioned. The implications of such a move troubled the general, who immediately wrote Hardenberg: "I will give myself some time regarding this; our transport of grain is now en route to Kolberg by sea; the English must allow it to pass. Should they learn that we have auctioned their ship here, we can expect them to place obstacles in the way of this grain shipment. Thus, I believe the auction can wait for the time being."[23]

A trend toward conciliation with the British is certainly apparent on Blücher's part.[24] Although he does not tell us why his attitude softened, Unger offers a logical explanation: "Later, when he counted on war against France and on British support, he was of another mind-set."[25] While certainly plausible, Gneisenau poses a deeper and more intriguing question. In May 1811 he wrote: "What news do you have from Blücher's headquarters? It is important to maintain a good mood there because one is not impervious to foreign intrigue and selfish purposes—not to change the mind of the virtuous general, because this is impossible—but instead paralyze the execution of bolder things. You know that Blücher's headquarters is ever a seat of intrigue and that one never can be sure what the result will be of the factional strife."[26] Blücher's future chief of staff attributed the general's dithering to the influence of the personalities that surrounded him.

In the meantime, while trying to cope with being a conquered people, the Prussians suffered another blow: the unexpected loss of their queen on 19 July 1810. The illness, presumably lung cancer, struck quickly. Dying in Frederick William's arms, the thirty-four-year-old Louise left behind seven children, ranging in age from fourteen years to eight months, including the future King Frederick William IV (fourteen) and Kaiser Wilhelm I (twelve). Her premature death devastated the king; all of her subjects mourned her passing, none more than Blücher: "It is as if I have been struck by lightning," he wailed to Eisenhart. "The pride of womanhood has departed from the Earth. God in Heaven, she must have been too good for us. Write me, old friend; I need encouragement and support. How is it possible for a state to suffer a succession of so many misfortunes? In my current mood, I would like nothing more than to learn that the four-corners of the world are burning."[27]

Following Scharnhorst's dismissal, Blücher became more vocal in his criticisms of a few of the innovations being introduced in the army. His complaints sounded very much like the arguments made by traditionalists who favored leadership changes and evolutionary reform. "I feel sorry for this small, but really good army if the cursed writing mania and lust for innovation is not limited; we will soon have many professors, but no soldiers," he explained to Boyen, who now served as the king's adjutant general. Blücher did not base his criticism on ideology but on what he thought best for the army. His correspondence provides a glimpse of some of his complaints. For example, he maintained that as a result of "new orders that have made so many regulations," the soldier received only three nights per week without guard duty instead of the six that the king himself mandated. He asked Boyen to bring this to the attention of Frederick William "so that by all means he can deal with this." The physical demands placed on the troops during exercises also concerned him: "we do not want to exhaust the strength of the young men with maneuvers because their strength has yet to be fully developed; instead, this is the time to learn rather than become lost in the multitude."[28]

A more serious case involved Lieutenant Colonel Borstell, an opponent of Scharnhorst's reforms and the author of new cavalry regulations that earned Blücher's ire. "Herr Borstell's instructions for the training of the young troopers," he complained to Eisenhart, "involves so many dumb things and contradictions that I am convinced the truth will be obvious to the King; I have yet to say a word to him. Herr Borstell already knows my opinion. He came before me like some hero, who upon returning from a crusade attacked a windmill with his lance and was completely surprised that his cold-blooded opponent would not yield."[29] To the former commander of the Blücher Hussars and current commander of the 1st Uhlan Regiment, Major Katzler, he wrote: "What do you think about all our changes? I am in a feud with Colonel Borstell over the instructions for exercises that he drafted and I have turned the matter over to the King. One has been a little irresolute over this; but it serves nothing, I give in to nothing; Borstell must knuckle under, for he has put his foot in it, [and] admitted so, but this is not enough. I have responded to his instructions point by point and given them to him. The entire business is a mockery of clarity. Now we will see what becomes of it."[30] With maneuvers approaching, Blücher again vented on 15 July. "I await an answer from the King: I have responded to every point of these exercise instructions and threw out several. . . . I have attacked Herr Borstell over this. . . . [H]ow can such a fool give the regiments regulations that still have not been approved? I will not allow him to get away with this; he shall soon learn that he has come too close to an old Prussian."[31]

Nothing came of the issue, meaning that the army implemented Borstell's cavalry regulations in the 1810 maneuvers, which financial concerns curtailed to tactical exercises on the parade ground. "We are in a real quandary here because of the cavalry exercises," Blücher angrily notified Boyen on 20 October 1810. "I will disregard Herr Borstell's art of fencing until the King commands us to use it but, because everyone is so scatterbrained, for goodness sake stop this buffoonery!"[32] Scharnhorst intervened; given Boyen's close relationship with Scharnhorst as well as the latter's esteem for Blücher, we can assume that the general's complaints received due consideration. In January 1811 the king finally rejected the proposed regulations. "They will make Herr Borstell either a general or an envoy to Kassel [capital of Westphalia]," joked Blücher. "Good luck! Sending him on his way for such unimaginative handicraft is the best thing."[33] Still running the army from behind the scenes, Scharnhorst formed a commission that eventually issued new cavalry regulations on 15 January 1812.[34]

In more routine matters, Blücher found that some of the noble ensigns attending the army's military school at Stargard "have made a stupid, juvenile mistake and dueled." Although he upheld martial law in his brigade, he "ventured to make an intercession with the monarch on behalf of the young men," suggesting punishment and "rough incarceration" as necessary. Requesting Boyen's support in the matter, the general explained that he wished "to prevent their discharge and misfortune. When so many young people are assembled, such events are bound to happen at least once."[35] Although a civil offense, Blücher believed that he could handle the issue within the parameters of military law.

In 1809 Minister of the Interior Count Friedrich Ferdinand Alexander zu Dohna-Schlobitten had ended the dual system of military and civil courts. Prior to this change, all civil suits involving military personnel were tried in military courts. Starting that same year, all such cases would be tried in civil courts.[36] Blücher objected to the increased police powers, which according to him only served to harass his soldiers rather than protect the people. "Today," he notified Boyen on 20 October 1810, "I sent the King a grievance from the commandant of Kolberg against the police chief of that city: what his people are doing there is not permitted. This is a result of the minister of the interior [Dohna] failing to provide the police officials with proper instructions on how far they can go. The police must be supported, but they cannot be allowed to torment the public: this only results in disgruntlement and a baleful mood. Good God, everything was fine before our new police arrived; now everywhere things are stolen and we even have secret societies."[37]

Fed up, Blücher sent the king a pro memoria (plenary memo) on 15 November 1810 concerning "the frequent insults and innovations that military personnel encounter every day. I do not know if the Master will reflect on this, but I am content having fulfilled my duty as, so to speak, the most senior officer and to refrain from being silent, which would compromise me in our profession." He noted that "the field marshal in Berlin [Kalckreuth] is silent all the time," which strengthened Blücher's opinion that the army's senior leadership had a responsibility to question changes it found impractical. Indicative of how important he felt this duty to be, he sent copies to Hardenberg and Boyen.[38] To Eisenhart he wrote: "Today, I sent the King and the Chancellor a lengthy memo concerning the injustice that is permitted against the military, especially regarding the law. Please keep your ears open as to what kind of a sensation this causes."[39]

By the end of 1810, Blücher's prediction that "soon, soon the inferno will erupt" appeared to be more than just another one of the general's apocryphal rants. As relations between France and Russia steadily soured, Prussia again found itself at risk. Throughout the winter of 1810–11 and into the spring, this danger became more apparent. According to one contemporary, "the political heavens increasingly began to cloud; the outbreak of war appeared unavoidable. [French] troop movements continued."[40] Indeed, imperial troops continuously marched through Prussian territory without providing the required notification. Technically a violation of Prussian sovereignty, the offense did more than wound national pride. Yet any step taken by Berlin that could be interpreted as hostile would cost Prussians more than they could afford. Thus, they resorted to secrecy, deception, and passive-aggressive resistance. Blücher led the charge.

On 21 January 1811 Blücher received reports indicating that the French planned to occupy the Baltic port of Swinemünde (Świnoujście), just across the lagoon from the fortress of Stettin. According to his intelligence, the French planned to replace the Prussian customs officials with imperial administrators to better enforce the Continental System.[41] He immediately took action to eliminate this excuse by reinforcing the Prussian garrison, having the confiscated vessels and colonial merchandise carefully guarded, and arranging for strict supervision of the many foreigners residing at the port. Frederick William expressed his approval, noting that the general's actions were "completely commensurate with the political situation."[42]

In March Blücher concentrated the reinforced Pomeranian Brigade under the pretext of defending the coast against a British landing. In the tense atmosphere, squabbles with the local French authorities, even General Liebert at Stettin, could not be avoided. In April Liebert sought to reroute the French line of communication between Küstrin and Danzig. Blücher refused and once again received Frederick William's support. But after a formal protest, Liebert scored a victory, thus cooling his relationship with Blücher.[43] A few weeks later Blücher learned that a French "general" would inspect the coast by Swinemünde. He doubted that the individual was actually a general, claiming that he would have received notification from Liebert if a high-ranking officer was scheduled to tour the Prussian coastal defenses. Believing that the individual was some sort of spy, Blücher informed his subordinates to treat him with courtesy, though as a civilian traveler. Until the king offered some direction on the matter, he assured Boyen that "the French can expect the greatest courtesy from me, but not compliance with their unmeasured demands. I must say, their demeanor has been very different for some time. Only General Rapp [at Danzig] acts orderly and well behaved. It is difficult always having to be compliant."[44]

Blücher stewed over Prussia's situation, writing to Yorck that "one can crush us any day now, but we can only blame ourselves for this." Many, including Blücher, Scharnhorst, and numerous reformers, believed that their nation's salvation lay in an alliance with Russia. "If only Russia would finally make a bold strike and overrun Poland," continues Blücher's letter to Yorck. "This would stabilize the situation very much."[45] Not everyone agreed. Some of the king's closest advisors questioned if the state could withstand another Russian defeat. With the obvious answer being negative, a pro-French party formed based on the idea that the kingdom's salvation lay in a firm union with France. Blücher referred to the individuals of the antiwar, pro-French party—Field Marshal Kalckreuth, General Karl Leopold von Köckritz, Foreign Minister August Friedrich von der Goltz, and the royal advisor Johann Peter Friedrich Ancillon, to name a few—as the *Sicherheitskommissare* (security commissioners).[46] After the passing of his strong-willed, anti-French queen, Frederick William's resistance to their arguments weakened. Rumors soon circulated in Berlin of the projects Napoleon planned to implement based on a Franco-Prussian alliance.

For the present, the king sought to demonstrate Prussia's value as a French ally and to train additional reserves. Thus, he complied with Napoleon's demands to form a coastal-defense force to guard against a British landing, presumably while the emperor led the Grande Armée into Russia. On 7 April 1811 the East and West Prussian, Pomeranian, Brandenburg, and part of the Lower Silesian Brigades as well as the Brandenburg and Prussian Artillery Brigades received instructions to partially mobilize and occupy the coast.[47] To Blücher, complying with Napoleon's wishes and seeking an alliance with France seemed utterly baffling, but he admitted that "strange things occur in our times that defy reason."[48] Despite the confusing politics, the deployment of the Pomeranian Brigade excited him. "His Majesty the King, our exalted Sovereign, has delighted me with the confidence of commanding a corps; I will justify this in the strongest sense of the word."[49]

Prussian strategy in occupying the coast focused on taking positions that obviously allowed them to guard the shore but, more importantly, to observe the French and quickly react to their movements. As a result, Blücher received orders to concentrate the Pomeranian Brigade around Kolberg and to transfer his headquarters back to Treptow, thus moving it away from the region near the imperial highway between Stettin and Danzig.[50] In an order dated 1 May 1811, the general formally reasserted his command over all troops in Pomerania. Writing in the 1880s, Blasendorff had access to Blücher's journal, which extended from 1 May to 14 October 1811. According to Blasendorff, the journal contained 109 mostly detailed orders of the day. The entry for 1 May captures Blücher's frame of mind in regard to his command, authority, and relationship with

Bülow: "In special and general regards to the situation, today I begin as commanding general and will [proceed] accordingly."[51]

As the official Pomeranian Infantry's brigadier, Bülow, who resided at Treptow, commanded all of the troops guarding the coast with the exception of the Kolberg garrison. Outranked by Blücher, the Pomeranian Brigade commander, Bülow had no choice but to assume the subordinate role. Moreover, with both officers now at Treptow, their proximity accentuated their enmity, and Blücher immediately attacked a fellow officer now perceived as a rival. In an order of the day issued on 1 May, he repeatedly praised Bülow for the good training of the infantry and the expedient measures he took for the occupation of the coast. Then he urged him not to express his opinion in public over political matters, calling it "political hot air, which could lead to nothing more than the compromising of the state."

This reprimand proved embarrassing enough, though nothing compared to what came next. After instructing the junior general to hold his tongue, he then castigated Bülow for reporting directly to the War Department instead of to Blücher himself. From that day on, Bülow not only had to report to him daily, but he also had to first submit to Blücher all reports and suggestions he intended to send to the king or the War Department. "On the contrary," Blücher wrote, "I believe that everything must be brought into a simple routine and that as commanding general I must know everything that concerns the troops." To add insult to injury, he stated that this process would relieve Bülow of the burden of having to report to Berlin. "Until other instructions arrive, my order of the day is to be followed verbatim," he declared in a statement to Boyen over the affair.[52] The personal relationship between Bülow and Blücher remained tense, with no foreseeable rapprochement.

In addition to admonishing Bülow, Blücher also used this order of the day to express his indignation over the attempt of another officer to seek support for a petition that criticized his patronage of Franz, who returned to serve as one of his father's adjutants. Blücher's fierce rebuttal of the allegation that he allowed his son to influence him indicates that the protest deeply aggrieved the general. By chance he learned that an officer who received an assignment from him had turned to Franz for help in getting the assignment changed.[53] Moreover, his assault on Bülow along with the diatribe against the petitioning officers suggests that Blücher again saw the rumors of his madness in 1808 at work. Wanting to reassert himself as a man and erase those memories not only from his own mind but also from the thoughts of any who doubted him, he took the offensive against these nasty reminders of his weakness: Bülow, his special assistant since 1808, and the officers who asserted that Franz, likewise charged by the king with taking care of his father's special needs, took advantage of his unique position. Blücher wrote: "My adjutants have absolutely no influence over me other than to deliver my verbal commands. As they decipher my specific orders, I have realized that some of them tried to improve them; this then is certainly the criticism of the petitioner. But any man of tact and any man who understands his job will certainly avoid such a move, and only those who love crooked ways will follow them. I thus advise everyone to walk a straight line, because you are dealing with a straight man."[54]

In the meantime, Blücher and his staff returned to the Treptow Schloß at the beginning of May. Like a vigorous young officer, he sprang from his coach, shouting to his hosts, the Brummer family, "With gratitude I departed, with gratitude I have returned!" While his friend, Friedrich Wilhelm Ribbentrop, represented him in the provincial government, the general went to work preparing the troops. Although a trained cavalry officer, he became well versed in issues concerning all branches of the service: he mustered and reviewed the troops, inspected the coastal fortifications, and subjected the fortress of Kolberg and the adjacent works to diligent scrutiny. From all troops, the general demanded silence during the exercises. He insisted on having the officers parade daily but warned against seeing powder and pigtails—the use of both having been abolished. Blücher forbade the misuse of orderlies and declared that all officers arriving at Treptow had to report to him and Bülow. He also issued strict orders to prevent the exasperation of the local population that would provide lodging for the soldiers: "I most urgently recommend good behavior in the quarters. The poor farmer, who is already so oppressed by the necessity of the present measures, must not see the soldiers as his daily plague. They will make efforts, through friendly behavior, to assist their hosts and because the soldier will be fed well, which I guarantee, I thus expect no complaints over them."[55]

In early May 1811 Blücher warned the garrison of Kolberg to expect a British attack; he recommended strict discipline but did not want tension and insecurity to reign in the fortress. He observed exercises there, praising the commandants and commending the troops; his only objection came when he spotted a sentry wearing an overcoat in the hot sun. In mid-May Blücher inspected the individual battalions, squadrons, and batteries at their posts. At the beginning of June, he reviewed the Brandenburg Dragoon Regiment exercise on foot and then mounted. Although a few individuals needed additional training, Blücher departed satisfied with "the rider becoming accustomed to being master of his horse." The progress of the infantry particularly pleased him. Prince August of Prussia, the king's cousin and inspector general of artillery of the Prussian army, praised the work not only of the Pomeranian artillery but also of all components of the brigade. Blücher exhorted the troops to prepare for fall maneuvers and especially instructed the cavalry to utilize sentry duty to become completely familiar with field service.[56]

Life at Treptow itself could be monotonous, accentuated by the bothersome reports that had to be completed every time a British ship appeared off the coast. Blücher did his best to pass the time in a manner suitable to his tastes. Finding the extra 200 thaler vital to his monthly budget, he already instructed Boyen to issue his full salary. "I cannot suffer the deduction from my salary because I must support the lifestyle of my position," he explained in April. As for his debts, he stated: "Both me and my creditors are patiently awaiting the arrival of the time when everyone can dispose of their property. Pay I can and will gladly, but my hands are tied and I have not received what I rightfully demand from the state," thus indicating that the discrepancy over the commission fees had yet to conclude. Not wanting to embarrass himself any further, he emphasized to Boyen that "under the current circumstances, it would be unacceptable to have to bother the King with my problems."[57] "Since the Rhine campaign," he wrote in May 1811, "I have been constantly on the move. Although my colleagues enjoy peace and comfort; I do not envy them, because I do not love the former and can gladly do without the latter as long as I am healthy. I desire nothing more than to be active again for the general good; but my wallet becomes lighter with each new incident."[58]

Secretly, Blücher did what he could to support former officers who had been cashiered by the Superior Investigating Commission but, in case of war, would be recruited as veterans. He also maintained an extensive spy network. Both endeavors took a toll on his financial resources. "Think about the throng I have around me and come to me daily," he wrote in August. "My house is like a pantry so to speak, for if I do not keep these people close to me, I will not learn much, and I will lose the trust of these people."[59] In Prussia's poor economy, the church benefice in Brandenburg bestowed upon him by the king in 1809 generated little income. Occasional allocations and salary increments also failed to satisfy his needs.[60]

Not able to fall back on his private funds and with his salary six months in arrears, Blücher again solicited assistance. "I can't continue to live like this," he wrote Boyen's assistant, Captain Ludwig Gustav von Thile. "Will the King not consider this and grant me a monthly stipend that will allow me to live respectably? Do I not deserve to receive from him my outstanding pay for the last six months? Am I a servant, who is not worth his salary, who is of no use to him and the State? I have completely ruined myself in his service and am now so pressed by my debts that I must subtract half of my salary. If I was a civilian, I would have long since been paid, but we treat old soldiers with contempt and even forget them." Blücher expressed the pain and embarrassment of having to beg. In the end, he threatened that anger would be the only result of being "treated like a pack animal and not even given fodder." "It will be interesting to see if the King will accept this argument," concluded Blücher, "or if he will forget the one who will now serve him best."[61] The king did not forget.

Meanwhile, to guard the coast, Blücher extended his eight battalions, fourteen squadrons, and two batteries in a cordon from Swinemünde to the Leba River. In addition, he had at his disposal twelve Krümper "work brigades," the manpower attached to the depots, and the cavalry troopers who still lacked mounts.[62] The 7 April 1811 cabinet order to create the coastal-defense force allowed the Prussians to increase the army's trained reserves while complying with Napoleon's demands. Approximately 11,740 Krümper joined units mobilized along the coast as well as those that remained in the interior.[63] "The local corps already has increased to 16,000 men and it appears that it will only continue to grow," Blücher excitedly noted during this time.[64] He paid particular attention to the uniforms and the military training of his Krümper, appointing a special inspector to oversee their progress. He demanded that when not working on the fortifications as laborers, these men "should be thoroughly trained and prepared to such an extent that they will need only the musket."[65]

The War Department decided to employ the work brigades to build or repair fortifications as part of their military training. But Colonel Georg Ernst von Hake, Scharnhorst's successor as head of the War Department, suggested to Privy Councilor Johann August Sack, the president of Pomerania, to utilize Krümper for the improvement of the military highway from Stettin to Danzig. In return, the workers would receive additional pay for their labor. Sack accepted the suggestion, asking the Pomeranian government at Stargard to estimate how many men would be needed and where as well as the reimbursement they should expect to receive. The Pomeranian government went a step further. As if the matter already had received approval, they requested that Blücher place the necessary Krümper at the disposal of the magistrates in the rural districts. These men would receive one groschen (penny) for seven hours of work a day. In addition, they had to supply their own spades, hoes, and other equipment if they wanted to be paid.[66]

The Pomeranian government took this proposal to the wrong man. Blücher unloaded on them on 20 May, demonstrating a concern for his men that far surpasses a mere turf war regarding jurisdictional authority.

> Up to this moment, I have yet to be notified by the War Department regarding the use of Krümper to repair the road, and I must honestly admit that it is repugnant to me to think that this proposal has been suggested by a military man. First of all, you want to send soldiers, who are actually employed building redoubts, to God only knows how far from the coast and pay them one groschen for one day of work? In France, if the soldiers actually work, they are paid according to the current daily wage. Meanwhile, this groschen can hardly be expected to quench the thirst in this heat. Second, a large portion of the Krümper lack footgear. Third, you must consider how this measure affects the esprit de corps of the soldiers because in France and many other states, slaves [convicts] are used for this work. If you want to employ the soldiers for this work, then pay them the daily wage and let them volunteer for this without coercion. Even if a Krümper himself had made this suggestion, this project never would have reached fruition because I would declare it as misanthropic. All the more, I note that the

vast majority of the Krümper do not possess hoes and spades, and it is not right to demand that only [men] with these tools will earn one groschen daily. If this beautiful project is actually executed . . . I will write the King that I cannot believe that he has allowed his soldiers to be placed in the same category as slaves [convicts]. If one needs soldiers, one pays them accordingly, if one needs day laborers, one should give them the current daily wage.[67]

Despite his vehement opposition, Blücher lost this battle. To circumvent the general, Hake and Sack secured authorization directly from the king. Although a defeat, Blücher had the satisfaction that at least the king decreed that the Krümper would receive two groschen per day of labor.[68]

By July, troubling rumors of imperial troop movements throughout north-central Europe reached Treptow. Blücher made good use of his intelligence network, in particular the reports from one of his former sergeants, whom the general had placed as a sentry in the French officer's district at Stettin. Thanks to his informants, Blücher separated fact from fiction. On 5 July he wrote to Adjutant General Boyen claiming that the "60,000 French who supposedly stand at Magdeburg and likewise the 100,000 who supposedly are to follow is a French story, which I can refute with certainty." In addition, he covertly dispatched one of his adjutants, a Lieutenant Horn, to Wesel. Horn reported that he found little sign of French troops on the Magdeburg–Wesel road. After leaving Wesel, which Horn reported to contain a garrison of 4,400 men, the lieutenant would travel to Holland to "comment on everything he sees and learns there." Blücher found concern only in the report of the movement of "much mobile artillery" on the Minden–Bückeburg highway.

While the general's intelligence allowed him to dispel many of the stories concerning military movements west of the Elbe, he could not do the same with the rumors that directly affected Prussia. "We can count on Stettin being reinforced," he informed Boyen. "All three Oder fortresses have very strong garrisons; Danzig's is more like an army than a garrison." Blücher also confirmed that the French planned to augment their regiments with a fourth battalion, altogether adding 10,000 men to their forces east of the Elbe. "The enormous transports of cannon and muskets are striking," continues his report to the king's adjutant, "yet all I can do is appear completely ignorant of this business and cause no concern to those in the know.[69] I request that you inform His Royal Majesty that the increase of Stettin's garrison will not please me." Perhaps bitter over his own financial troubles, he concluded his report by noting that "all revenues from the provinces on this side of the Rhine" had been allocated to Marshal Davout.[70]

Boyen shared Blücher's findings with Frederick William. Still hoping for a Franco-Prussian alliance, the king and Hardenberg dismissed the reports. "The behavior of the French government and the recent declarations of the French Emperor denote the good disposition of it and provide no cause to fear a sudden attack," explained the king. "Likewise reassuring is the course that the negotiations between the other Powers appears to have taken, while from this emerges the gratifying hope of the possibility that the occasional tensions can be settled in an amicable manner, thus preserving peace on the continent." Certainly, Frederick William wanted to impress this view on Blücher, but he also gave consideration to the morale of his troops. Perhaps recalling how fear and apathy had led to the pathetic capitulations in 1806, the king likewise did not want tension and fear to master his army. As a result, he had Blücher convey the official opinion to his troops.[71]

Frederick William's wishes did not deter the general. Like a bloodhound locked on a scent, it took less than three weeks for him to provide more alarming news. According to his informants, the French planned to build an entrenched camp between Damm and Moritzfelde on the right bank of the Oder facing Stettin. In such a position, imperial forces would sever communication between Blücher and the Prussian posts farther upriver. More importantly, the general feared being isolated and cut off from Berlin. He wrote the king on 25 July 1811 requesting instructions over how to proceed if troops actually moved into this camp. Of course, Blücher did not miss this opportunity for drama: "Your Royal Majesty's sacred person, the Fatherland, and my own honor are the greatest worth on earth to me; in the uncertainty and ultimate danger that I am in I cannot hide that I dread once again being placed in a situation like the one I found myself in Swedish Pomerania after the miserable peace of Tilsit."[72]

Two weeks later, on 9 August, Blücher again forwarded an ominous summary of his intelligence to the king. "Through various channels, the news has reached me that the 10,000 French troops at Mecklenburg are marching to Stettin and will move into a camp between Tantow and Garz." He warned that should this occur, he could no longer maintain his current position. "Due to the [French] numerical superiority, I will not be able to prevent the communication between my corps and the troops stationed on the Oder from being cut." Instead, he proposed concentrating his forces to prevent at least a portion from being cut off from Kolberg. Responding to the assurances the king provided in early July of Napoleon's good will, Blücher retorted: "I have not been instructed in the politics, but no guarantee in the world can convince me of the sincerity of the French cabinet. Hesse, Holland, Spain, and the Hanseatic cities have paid the unfortunate price for their gullibility." Similar to 1809, he demanded action: "Hiding from the French is now superfluous. They know and learn of all of our preparations and I believe that we must attract their attention as much as possible through our preparations." In concluding, Blücher finally took a swipe at the government's pro-French party: "As your old loyal servant, please believe me that all those who seek to better our situation by winning French magnanimity proceed from a secondary objective, idiocy, or plain evil."[73]

The fourteen days between Blücher's 25 July and 9 August letters to Frederick William proved to be the most exciting fortnight for the anti-French, prowar patriot party since the heady days of August 1806. In addition to Napoleon's disinterest in a Franco-Prussian alliance, all of the evidence produced by Blücher and many others finally persuaded the king that compliance with the emperor's demands brought no guarantee of preserving Prussia's independence. He ultimately agreed with the war party's preference for a desperate but honorable struggle for survival as opposed to voluntary subjugation. Certainly not a stupid man, Frederick William realized that "desperate but honorable" offered a slim chance of success, while "hopeless" probably would lead to the end of Hohenzollern Prussia. To stay on the side of desperate and honorable while avoiding hopeless, the king needed allies. To find some, he secretly dispatched Scharnhorst to St. Petersburg for the sole purpose of drafting war plans with the Russians: thus, not *if* the Russians would help, but *how* they would help. As for Blücher, he did not fear the outbreak of war but desired it. A line from a letter to Hardenberg in September 1811 captures his mood: "Because I am old, I live consumed by the sole thought of retaliating against our oppressor."[74]

CHAPTER 8

SCAPEGOAT

Scharnhorst's journey would take months. For the moment, the Prussians needed to take measures to prepare for the imminent French invasion. Around the same time that Scharnhorst departed, Hardenberg tasked the recently reinstated Gneisenau with drafting a plan of defense, which he submitted on 8 August 1811. While designing this plan, he established communication with Franz Blücher regarding the construction of an entrenched camp at Kolberg. To deceive French spies, the younger Blücher operated under the name of "Franz Poppe," while the conspirators referred to the general as "the old Poppe."[1] Works such as the Wolfsberg redoubt—initiated by royal decree in April of that year—mainly covered Kolberg's communications with the sea and created open fields that an enemy first had to master before commencing a siege. Yet these fortifications could do nothing for General Blücher if superior enemy forces drove his mobile units into Kolberg. Both Scharnhorst and Gneisenau expressed their ideas over the necessary fortifications to the Blüchers. Before departing for St. Petersburg, Scharnhorst accompanied the general on an inspection of Kolberg's works on 29 July 1811 and suggested the construction of two redoubts that could protect the main approach to the fortress.[2] Blücher, of course, would go further.[3] "My father is completely revived," wrote Franz to Gneisenau after the visit, "because he has the prospect of being able to live or die with honor, and he animates all of us."[4] Rejuvenated by Scharnhorst's visit and Gneisenau's communiqués with Franz, Blücher prepared for action.

On the same day that Gneisenau submitted the memo to Hardenberg, Blücher dispatched Franz to Kolberg with oral instructions for the engineer captain stationed there: "My adjutant, Major Blücher, will inform you of my views of our situation as well as my decisions. From this very hour I want everything to proceed with the greatest activity and to build the necessary entrenchments as quickly as possible. You will view what Major Blücher tells you as if I myself issued the orders. Do whatever it takes;

all responsibility comes from me and everything that I assign you is with the consent of your superior. Your upright character assures me that all of this will be done with great discretion; your relentless activity vouches that everything will be done as quickly as possible."[5] Ten days later he again pressed the captain for speed: "We don't have an hour to lose and I urge you to push ahead with all conceivable effort. Officers will come, as many as they can spare from Berlin. . . . Today I gave Ribbentrop the authority to procure all that is needed; the first part of our work must be completed in fourteen days."[6]

Surprisingly, Blücher did not personally correspond with Gneisenau until 19 August. His letter begins: "My son tells me, that you, my true friend, are at Berlin. This makes me uncommonly happy, for I know that wherever you are action reigns, and I do not need to tell you how necessary it is to not waste a single hour." After noting that the time for deliberations and conferences was over, he continued by informing Gneisenau that he had "sent many inquiries to Berlin and have brought many important issues to the attention of the authorities, but have received no direction; therefore, I have come to the conclusion that they want me to be independent and act. I take a good portion of responsibility on myself. My conscious tells me that I know best, and because no one gives me accurate and decisive instructions, I will think for my own self-assurance that they trust me to do what is right."[7] Based on this statement, it appears that Blücher had not received any official directives from the king or the War Department regarding the entrenched camp at Kolberg, nor had Gneisenau corresponded with him directly. Yet Franz went to Kolberg on 8 August equipped with his father's authority to commence work on the camp.

Blücher's letter provides an extensive look at the general's thoughts and plans amid the growing crisis. He began by making the case that Prussia had to be prepared for an immediate French attack: "I believe that you, my friend, are in agreement with me that if it is the intent of the great man [Napoleon] to destroy us or in the least to render us harmless to his plans; it would be unwise of him to proceed if he allows us time to mobilize our forces and to have them on the spot." To counter the threat, he advocated going "to work without losing time" to complete the camp at Kolberg. "I deem three weeks will be needed if heart and soul are employed and I hope they will say: old Prussia has risen again at Kolberg—this is completely feasible if they listen to my proposals." Concerning his initial steps, he had "seized" all timber stored at Kolberg when he inspected the fortress on 13 August. Work started that same day after the general "requisitioned all entrenching tools from the countryside. Thus 3,000 men are employed, and in four days' time I will have all that I need. If it becomes necessary, I will demand one man from every house from all of the villages situated around Kolberg. Work is in full progress on the two hilltops to the right and to the left of the road to Körlin [Karlino]."

The general then outlined six points that he viewed as vital for success. First, he cited his need for resources. He does not specify whether material, money, or manpower but simply insisted that "one must provide me everything that I cannot procure here myself." Second, the general inferred that some type of understanding had to be reached with the British. He did not state this requirement outright but simply discussed the need to clear the sea lanes of "obstacles" that could prevent "communication with [East] Prussia and the conveyance of supplies from there to Kolberg." Third, Blücher emphasized the need to dispense with secrecy and immediately mobilize: "Heaven forbid, we must not believe that we can conceal ourselves from France; they will know just as much as we do about all of our preparations, and the measures of caution we take based on common sense will only attract their attention more as we throw off our lowly submissiveness." Fourth, he estimated that 20,000 men would be necessary to defend the camp at Kolberg. This figure included a "solid reserve" that could "come to the aid of a threatened point in case of a serious attack and if such a moment did not occur, this reserve could take the offensive and hold the enemy in the distance for as long as possible and alarm him every night." In the fifth point Blücher stated his needs in terms of reaching a figure of 20,000 combatants. According to his estimates, he had between 5,000 and 6,000 Krümper, 3,000 "completely useable" muskets, and 2,000 other weapons that needed repairs, "which I am working on day and night." He needed an additional 4,500 men, which he assured Gneisenau "can be had in a minute," but lacked 4,000 muskets and uniforms for them. "If one authorizes me to turn to the Island [Great Britain], I would be able to procure both. The Prince Regent is my patron, and in a prior time I would have procured much at Stralsund had not the miserable peace of Tilsit thwarted everything." His sixth point concerned converting the Krümper work brigades into actual companies and battalions.

"I already asked the King to appoint the commanders of the battalions, and if he will not nominate the necessary officers [then I request] that he allow me to do so at least on paper, so that they can be called up at the hour when the masses of men can no longer remain in such disorder." Blücher's final point concerned acquiring horses from Pomerania before the French took them. "I already proposed that we obtain from the four districts of Stargard, Pyritz, Treptow, and Regenwalde, which have the best horses, the teams for a couple of batteries that lack them. . . . Horses for our light cavalry can also be found in this region. Yet I believe this decision will be put off until our adversary takes advantage of this for himself."[8]

Blücher's demand to throw caution to the wind in terms of secrecy proved too premature for Berlin. A few days earlier, on 14 August, the French consul at Stettin, Jean-Baptiste Gabriel Chaumette des Fossés, appeared at Kolberg and inspected the works without first obtaining the general's permission.[9] French protests quickly followed this surprise visit. Frederick William advised Blücher to be cautious, a warning that the general admitted "calmed" him. "Now I know the mind of the Monarch," continued Blücher, "and I completely recognize the necessity of proceeding with all caution; but I also know that we must observe a demeanor toward our neighbors that does not attract their attention; I will not lose sight of either. I know full well that one considers me a man who allows himself to be carried away in the heat of the moment. But I ask all persons who have been around me in critical situations, especially General Scharnhorst, if I ever allowed myself to be carried away in the heat of the moment. . . . I distance myself from all the useless anxiety that reduces a general in the eyes of his subordinates. The King can be assured that I will not begin any hostilities. But treat me and my troops violently, then honor and duty demands tit for tat." He also assured himself that French forces had little chance of surprising him: nothing could move at Stettin without him knowing it, and his spies would inform him of any threat coming from Mecklenburg and Magdeburg.[10] "Our neighbor will not surprise me. I will not be the one attacking, but I will treat any bad behavior sternly."[11]

Remembering the horrible start to the 1806 campaign and how the war progressed from bad to worse, Blücher understood "how important it is not to begin with a defeat and lose everything at once." He planned to remain in Pomerania for as long as possible without exposing himself "to any disadvantage by lingering too long." In the end, he did not think the French would start an offensive against Pomerania, citing that the imperial garrison at Stettin possessed only a single cavalry regiment, "and I am superior to this arm in number and quality." He noted that only one-third of the garrison consisted of native Frenchmen. "They cannot occupy Stettin with less than 5,000 men and the majority of these must be French; beginning an offensive against us with only German troops would appear too dangerous to them. Because a large number of French troops have not arrived, I feel I still have time to finish my measures at Kolberg; and when they are finished, I will fear nothing! Also, I will use everything to stir the Germans and agitate an uprising."

Blücher's confidence in his "measures" soared: "there is unbelievable work being done at Kolberg. When I finish the redoubts, I will build an entrenched camp for the entire corps. I have instructed Captain von Kleist to draft a plan utilizing the most appropriate earthworks for both infantry and cavalry. I will change my mind if I am shown that straw works and abatis are better, cheaper, and faster to procure. I have requested the opinion of the experts based on their precise examination of this issue, but I will decide how it should be."[12] Blücher found the terrain around Kolberg to be very favorable. "The positions where the redoubts and fleches will be built were all chosen by me based on my little wit but keen eye."[13] Aside from the existing fortifications and the Wolfsberg, Blücher planned to build no less than three large, seven regular, and five small redoubts as well as two "works" and to dam waters to flood a portion of the terrain.[14] He exhorted the Krümper to be diligent so that they would not have to be called up again that year. The general often personally inspected the progress of their work; loafers were rendered second-class soldiers. He started forming a Streifkorps (flying column), appointing Major Wilhelm Ernst von Zastrow as its commander and instructing him "to dash here and there, harass the enemy everywhere, and obtain all possible news for me." After learning that a general mobilization would not be decreed, Blücher decided that he would increase the Kolberg garrison by raising as many recruits "in an inconspicuous manner and under the pretext of work" as he had muskets.[15]

According to his plans, the Pomeranian Brigade, which by now reached the size of an actual corps, could concentrate at Kolberg in two days. Should imperial forces attack the entrenched camp,

which would be built southeast of the fortress, Blücher planned to
form three reserves. He would position the first between Sellnow
(Zieleniewo) and Bork (Borek), somewhat behind the redoubt at
Sellnow; the second by the redoubts alongside the road to Körlin;
and the third between the Wolfsberg and Binnenfeld hills. As soon
as he received approval from Berlin, he planned to transfer ten cannon from Swinemünde, Stolpemünde (Ustka), and Rügenwalde
(Darłowo) to Kolberg itself. Three light-infantry companies from
the battalion stationed at Swinemünde moved to Wollin (Wòlin).[16]
Blücher hoped to increase the garrison to 20,000 men or more: "We
can easily produce this number of combatants if they listen to my
proposal." He lectured Kleist that "a fortress must do everything
possible, as long as it is possible, to keep the enemy from its walls
and to dull his ardor before he can open the trenches."[17] He expected
all work on the fortifications to be completed by mid-September
1811. "Yesterday," boasted the general on the twenty-second, "I was
at Kolberg. I brought everything into activity with such force that
the most important [measures] will be ready in fourteen days, the
whole project in three weeks."[18]

Along with the enthusiasm and optimism came cause for
concern from many directions. In matters close to home, Kleist
encountered difficulties obtaining lumber. On 20 August Blücher
responded to the captain's concerns: "I hope that unnecessary
obstacles will not be encountered and the timber will be provided
as requested. The palisade and redoubt work has not started; it
must all be completed shortly and the timekeeper shall and will
be there on time."[19] Outside of Prussia, the Saxons took a threatening position, with two divisions apparently aimed at Berlin and
a third poised to enter Silesia; the garrison of Mainz and all depots
on the Strasburg–Wesel line received orders to march.[20] News from
Berlin indicated that Frederick William's ardor had cooled; Blücher
feared that Scharnhorst's absence would expose the monarch to the
influence of the pro-French party. "Do what you can to drive away
the security commissars and *Faultiere* [fomenters] from the King,"
he urged Gneisenau. "Shrugs and sighs nearly always give away a
scoundrel! Write me when our Scharnhorst returns."[21]

As fall approached, Blücher became desperate. Biographer
Unger mentions another bout of illness but offers no specifics as to
whether it was mental or physical. A complaint in early September
suggests that depression could have been at work again: "I live here

in my accursed Schloß, which is just not pleasing, and decay over the endless paperwork."[22] He again spoke of unauthorized action: "my decision to act is firm and nothing in the world can change or delay it."[23] Yet he lamented to Gneisenau over the king's refusal to mobilize: "But what good is it [the entrenched camp] if I am not strong enough to occupy it? Is Scharnhorst with you?" No longer able to contain himself, he fired off a missive to the king reminiscent of the forceful letters he wrote during the Franco-Austrian War of 1809. He summarized the content for Gneisenau: "Today, I have written my last word to the King. If he does not take it to heart he will go to his doom, and his fate as well as that of his house will be that of the Bourbons, which I explained to him a year ago. With his full confidence, not with half, must I be equipped, then all will see what I can and will achieve. Believe me, my friend, it is completely mean-spirited to give me the reputation of Schill: I will not act without authorization. I laugh at the twaddle, but it does hinder my plans." To be able to proceed with authorization, he asked Gneisenau to secure for him a cabinet order, such as the one that had authorized him to proceed according to his own conviction in Swedish Pomerania during the 1807 campaign. He justified this request by stating: "No one has need to worry that I will act prematurely; the importance of the situation does not escape my consideration."[24]

Not every officer supported Blücher's decisions. In fact, Bülow held strong convictions regarding the entrenched camp at Kolberg. In a 14 August memo to the king, he described this plan as "ruinous in several regards." Due to its locality and the cold autumn wind that swept in from the Baltic, he believed that disease would claim the men and horses, thus weakening the corps and allowing the French to force the position. With only a narrow dam serving as the line of retreat to the fortress, Bülow predicted the complete destruction of the mobile troops. He informed Frederick William that Kolberg lacked space for the secure accommodation of magazines and the sick.[25] Along with Blücher's letters, Bülow's memo joined many other opinions that the king received at this time. Such diverse views prevented him from taking a strong stand on this or any other issue.[26] Illustrating the difference of opinion in the army as well as the difference between the reform party and the evolutionists, Boyen commented: "in the means to be taken, Bülow could not separate himself from the former views of large field operations, which did not suit our current situation."²⁷ Scharnhorst favored basing the army on entrenched camps as well as Prussia's remaining fortresses, while others like Gneisenau lobbied for an immediate guerilla war similar to the Spanish example.

Disagreement over Kolberg only added to the problems between Blücher and Bülow, which their unclear professional relationship exacerbated. Bülow and the evolutionists did not support the idea of a national uprising, instead wanting to rebuild the Prussian army for a confrontation with the French. They sought to keep the military situation free from foreign control so that Prussia would maintain a degree of independence in the next war. Above all, they believed that Prussia's regeneration would eventually allow the state to stand as an independent power rather than as a Russian or French client state. For these reasons, Bülow had advocated patience in 1809. In his opinion, Blücher's plans in 1811 appeared disastrous for the state. As a result, the discord increased between the two generals. Now that the two men again resided in the same town, their malignity reached new heights. The general wished to demonstrate his authority over Bülow in all possible ways.

One evening Bülow took a stroll before the Treptow gate, where he met two officers who had recently arrived but had not reported to him. One of the officers, Captain von Kardell, was one of Blücher's spies. Bülow knew him to be a zealous member of the outlawed Tugendbund and suspected he might attempt to recruit his men and establish a chapter at Treptow. He reproached the officers for failing to report. The two claimed that they had reported to Blücher, who forbade them from reporting to Bülow. An argument ensued, and Bülow had the men arrested. He hardly returned to his quarters when Blücher himself appeared. A fierce altercation resulted, in which each contested the other's authority in this matter. Blücher allegedly shouted: "Herr General, you are well to order, but bad to obey." He left Bülow's quarters, sealing the final break between them.²⁸

Bülow had become accustomed to Blücher's fits. Despite sharing irreconcilable political differences since 1809, the two generals could cooperate professionally, despite the awkwardness of Bülow's position as Blücher's special assistant. Past arguments had been followed by periods of calm that enabled the two men to tolerate each other. While en route to Russia, Scharnhorst had stopped at Treptow on 29 July in the hopes of reconciling their differences and cultivating a balance, but he found that Bülow was not the right man to be at Blücher's side.[29] His opinion provides a vivid example of the struggle between the various factions that existed in the officer corps during the reform period. "When I went to Pomerania," explained Scharnhorst to Yorck, "my plan was to cause a rapprochement and to propose to General Blücher that he make Bülow his general quartermaster. The reconciliation proved only partially successful; I gave up the other plan because the ideas that I heard from Bülow over the war were much too systematic and did not fit into our situation, and ultimately because Bülow had a bad opinion of Kolberg. In my opinion, Blücher's views and the spirit in which he spoke conform to our current ideas, while those of Bülow reflect our former conditions."[30]

Following the incident over Captain Kardell, Blücher became implacable.[31] "Meanwhile," he wrote Gneisenau shortly after the encounter with Bülow, "all of this causes me no sorrow; I know that I am the commander here and must answer for everything; all must and shall obey; good advice I take from each, but advice it shall remain."[32] According to all accounts, Franz urged his father to remain irreconcilable, and the general saw in his disagreement with Bülow a threat to the execution of a strong defense.[33] As the situation grew more unbearable, it became obvious that the two officers had to separate. Bülow's sister-in-law, Friederike von Auer, recorded in her journal that "the tension that existed between Blücher and Bülow for a long time was now well nourished by the general's oldest son, Major Blücher, and erupted into a feud. As a result, Bülow suddenly left his position and went to Berlin in order to personally report his situation to the king." Bülow resigned his command of the Pomeranian Brigade and requested a new assignment; Blücher hoped to replace him with Gneisenau. With nothing available at the moment, the king permitted Bülow to take leave on 19 August and await a new position.[34] Later in the year it appeared he would assume a lateral transfer as the infantry brigadier of the East Prussian Brigade, but on 29 November 1811, he received a promotion to command the entire West Prussian Brigade.[35]

After the squabbling with Bülow, a letter from Scharnhorst that arrived on 23 August 1811 cheered Blücher. Scharnhorst suggested some modifications and additions to the works at Kolberg; Blücher forwarded the letter to Kleist, instructing him to follow it verbatim. "You understand that the situation is urgent because Scharnhorst himself advises haste," states his cover letter. "You must not allow any of the people who are in and around Kolberg and who are close to you to make any objection, to cause any difficulties; you only need to say that I have ordered everything. I will be with you soon and you can count on my support. Send Scharnhorst's piece back to me, only you read it."[36]

By early September, Blücher still remained hopeful that his deadlines for the completion of the fortifications would be met and that his position at Kolberg would be unassailable. "I and my neighbors [the French]," he informed Bonin, "work against each other; I hope the gentlemen will drop in on me. I will so secure Kolberg that any attempt will be foiled. Regardless, I hold any attempt as unlikely: the stakes are too great on both sides."[37] Ten days later he boasted to Hardenberg: "I at least am not worried about Kolberg, and when I am at the strength that I wish to be and that I can reach, I would dare hold fast there with an army for such a long time that it could not be affected by other areas." His available manpower increased by 7,000 soldiers and 20,000 Krümper. He hoped to secure enough supplies to sustain 40,000 men for six months, but finances limited him to four months of provisions for 20,000 soldiers.[38] Thus, in the same letter to Hardenberg, he went on to bitterly complain of a desperate need of money, supplies, muskets, and uniforms, particularly in response to the chancellor's 9 September request that the general reduce his cash expenditures. Blücher lamented that he could not turn to the "Island" (Great Britain); "if I could," he vowed, "I would swim back from there with much." The general had his son deliver the letter to Hardenberg, requesting that the chancellor "be so kind to tell my son as much as I am allowed to know; I vouch for him with my head." Conscious of the fact that Schill's insubordination still hung over the army and that some considered him to be prone to commencing his own "ride," he bluntly told Hardenberg, "I do not possess the trust of my comrades and the respect of the inhabitants; malice and envy are active to portray me as unpredictable and to label me a second Schill; but I scorn these miserable people."[39]

The tone of Blücher's letter offended Hardenberg, who communicated his feelings to Gneisenau. He too objected to the general's insensitivity. Writing to Franz, he explained that while Berlin allocated all possible resources to Kolberg, the other fortresses, which were just as important if not more so, received nothing. "Here [Berlin], we have proceeded on the work for Kolberg with a certain partiality for the simple reason that your father stands at the head.

The King himself seems to be less cautious in the measures that concern Kolberg. From this [letter] as well as what I will tell you here, you will be able to understand the effect that the bitter tone of the letter has made. Hardenberg is aware of everything that is situated within the bounds of his power and indeed will do everything out of friendship for your father, who is the soul of our present movement and without whom everything would go cold."[40]

At Berlin, the government's resolve to prepare for war stiffened. On 22 August 1811 Hardenberg received the latest report from his special envoy to Paris, Colonel Friedrich Wilhelm von Krusemarck. During a 15 August reception at the Tuileries to celebrate Napoleon's forty-second birthday, the emperor berated the Russian ambassador, Aleksandr Kurakin, and severely criticized Tsar Alexander's policies.[41] In addition, Krusemarck reported that Napoleon again rejected the king's request for the return of Glogau to Prussian control. The public humiliation of Kurakin—a calculated provocation on Napoleon's part—and the retention of Glogau indicated to Hardenberg that the outbreak of war between Russia and France could no longer be doubted.

Although Scharnhorst had yet to step foot on Russian soil, the king had to act fast. In response to Krusemarck's report, Frederick William appointed a committee, chaired by Hardenberg and consisting of Sack, Hake, Gneisenau, and Boyen, to oversee a rapid expansion of the army, which already had increased to 74,553 men. The king wanted to mobilize 120,000 men. A few days later he decreed that companies be increased to full combat strength and that forty reserve as well as eleven depot battalions be formed from surplus Krümper. On 24 August he expressed to Blücher his approval of the work at Kolberg, encouraging him to zealously pursue the construction of the entrenched camp. If necessitated by a French invasion, Frederick William advised the general to retreat into the position. Gneisenau and Hardenberg initiated negotiations with London to obtain weapons.[42] In addition, Colonel Dörnberg, who had fled to England in 1809 with the "Black Duke" of Brunswick after the abortive revolt in North Germany, secretly arrived at Kolberg on a diplomatic mission for the British government to evaluate the Prussian mood. Although Dörnberg had been instructed not to discuss the possibility of subsidies, Gneisenau used the opportunity to raise the issue of forming a Prusso-German legion. He communicated with Dörnberg through Franz "von Poppe," and Ribbentrop arrived from Stargard to assist.[43] According to the colonel, a British convoy carrying 10,000 muskets, 2,000,000 cartridges, and 3,000 barrels of powder would soon reach the Baltic.[44] All Blücher needed to make his Krümper combat ready appeared to be within his grasp—if only Berlin would take the plunge.[45]

Blücher encouraged the work and pressured Hardenberg for the army's full mobilization, writing on 12 September 1811: "Please allow me to remark that our secrecy is no longer of any value. Our neighbors are informed of everything we do. Regardless, they cannot blame us if we take security measures—which are advisable just as much from common sense as from necessity—as a result of their blatant measures. I believe that their actions must be made to benefit us. If they see that we are determined to prevent ourselves from being subjugated and we can win time [to mobilize], then they must indulge the idea that armed masses will prevent them from executing their malicious task. Stand by me, my true friend and patron, and our neighbors shall be roused to consider our current situation." Hinting at the need for an alliance with Russia, he implored Hardenberg not to surrender to fear and mistrust: "If we have time, if we carefully utilize it, if we do not allow ourselves to waste the time in unfounded fear and in too little trust, then I believe the danger will not be so great."[46]

Frederick William ran out of time before Scharnhorst could even meet with the Russians. Of course, Prussia's military preparations did not escape French vigilance. On 20 September the French ambassador, Italian-born Antoine Marie de Saint-Marsan, presented an ultimatum: Prussia had three days to disarm, reduce the army to the limit stipulated by the 1808 treaty, discharge all recruits and workers, cease all work on the fortifications, and immediately inform the Russians of these steps. Under the condition of this disarmament, the emperor declared himself favorable to concluding a Franco-Prussian alliance. If Frederick William refused, Marshal Davout would invade the kingdom with all of the imperial forces stationed along the Elbe. On the following day, Hardenberg informed the ambassador of the king's decision to completely comply with the wishes of the emperor. Frederick William immediately issued orders to halt the mobilization.[47]

In Pomerania Blücher refused to obey the order to demobilize, viewing it as French blackmail, yet his tone had changed in a 4 October 1811 letter to Frederick William. He began by informing the king of the latest intelligence. No change could be detected in the demeanor of the imperial garrisons at Danzig and Stettin. Yet the emperor had left Paris, presumably en route to Germany, while Davout had arrived at a French camp at Rostock. "All of this leads us to believe that an explosion will result." While the general assured the king not to fear for Kolberg, "because by this time, the sacred place shall be in a defensible condition that will place me in a similar situation as the English General Wellington at Lisbon," he expressed his profound fear for the safety of the monarch. Claiming that he already had suffered through several sleepless nights over the issue, he begged Frederick William to leave Berlin. "To know that Your Royal Majesty's sacred person is so exposed in the currents state of affairs is a sad perspective for any devoted servant, for me the saddest; and I thus humbly request that Your Royal Majesty . . . leave Berlin."

Although Blücher truly did not believe it, he assured Frederick William that no one regarded the monarch as a timid man. To the general, the safety of the king as a symbol of Prussia was more important than the safety of Frederick William the man. He could not bear to see his beloved state suffer another humiliating blow if the French apprehended the monarch. "Only a sense of duty from one of the most senior officers of Your Royal Majesty's army prompts me to write this," continues his 4 October letter, "and should you not agree . . . , heed the fact that with the loss of our sovereign, the name of Prussia also ceases to exist. This is a terrible thought, which certainly will make Your Royal Majesty more alarmed. With this loss, an entire brave nation will be thrown into a long bondage, and any loyal servant of Your Royal Majesty will painfully cry out: 'if only the person of our good King had been secured sooner.'"[48] Eight days later he raged to Hardenberg: "Allow me to say that the King's continued stay at Berlin is inconceivable to me. Can the monarchy survive in this city? I know full well that he does not want to decide. I have presented the danger to him, but he has not answered me. He who has no confidence in himself has none in anyone else; the King has none in his nation, and in this thought he is reinforced by miserable people, who depict to him the danger as great and our strength as entirely insufficient. You, my friend, I trust with all of my heart; with your honest intent, with all efforts you will attain the goal; indecisiveness stands contrary to you."[49] On the same day, 12 October, he wrote the following to

Gneisenau: "Our indecisiveness beats us to the ground. The King has no confidence in himself, therefore he has none in others and the nation. For Heaven's sake, what is he doing in Berlin? I have clearly presented the danger that threatens him. Typical of his old habit, he still has not answered."[50]

Gneisenau, Dörnberg, Hardenberg, and Blücher agreed to retaliate if the French abducted the king either through ruse or force. Yet time ran out for the king and was running out for Blücher. To fully comply with Napoleon's ultimatum, Frederick William's cabinet order of 26 September 1811 discharged the workers at Kolberg. Instead of immediately terminating their service contracts and rendering thousands unemployed, the men would be used for improving the roads and other public works. On 4 October French authorities again complained, insisting that work on the fortifications continued and that more men appeared to be working. To end this scrutiny, Frederick William decided to discharge all civilian workers on 5 October and furlough all Krümper on the eighth.

Whether Blücher received the cabinet orders of 26 September and 5 October, received verbal instructions to deviate from them, or simply refused to comply with them is not clear. In all likelihood he received the orders but chose to ignore them. Regardless, the French consul at Stettin, Chaumette des Fossés, made another surprise visit to Kolberg on 7 October. Finding an estimated 9,000 workers busily employed on the fortifications, he wrote his report to St. Marsan on the spot. The ambassador immediately complained to Hardenberg, declaring Chaumette des Fossés's discovery to be a violation of the Prussian government's promise. He also demanded Blücher's recall.

On 8 October Captain Thile appeared at Treptow with Hardenberg's verbal and written instructions for Blücher as well as letters from Gneisenau to Franz von Poppe and Ribbentrop. Although Hardenberg still hoped Scharnhorst would return with good news, the chancellor revealed to Blücher the seriousness of Prussia's position, claiming it to be the worst in the state's history. Apparently, the French knew all of the details of the country's military preparations. Thus, the state had to employ everything to please the imperial authorities, which meant immediately stopping all preparations for war. "As we are surrounded on all sides by troops," explained Hardenberg, "we still do not know whether a treaty between Russia and France will restore the status quo or whether it will come to war. As difficult as it is, it is absolutely necessary to proceed according to the circumstances. On the one hand, we have to use everything to fulfill the desires of the French authorities seemingly to the utmost, to give their numerous emissaries and spies no reason to submit negative reports, and to assume the friendliest and most trusting face toward them. On the other hand, we must not, as much as possible, neglect our precautions. Of course this is a very difficult problem, but one that we still must seek to solve." Gneisenau likewise expressed hope to Franz. Referring to Scharnhorst, he wrote: "I see a bright spot on the dark horizon. Perhaps it will become clearer in a few days and then we may expect salvation. Admittedly, we cannot do what is best, what is possible, but we will do the next best thing that is possible . . . : console your worthy father."[51]

Quite possibly, Blücher needed four days to accept the gravity of the situation. According to Unger, who like Blassendorf had access to Blücher's journal, the entry for 10 October 1811 contains the first mention of the order of 26 September: "Because the redoubt work at Kolberg will cease, the poor roads in the local region will be repaired." The entry for the eleventh contains a more definitive explanation, stating that "due to imminently approaching bad weather and other conditions," the king ordered that "the dispensable men living six miles around Kolberg be placed on leave." On the twelfth the journal reveals the extension of furloughs for 2,500 men and that the discharge of the redoubt workers had been ordered "because the total certainty of the existence of peaceful conditions has occurred."[52]

On that same day Blücher made desperate pleas for Hardenberg and Gneisenau to come to their senses. He still questioned the king's continued presence at Berlin, which he attributed to indecisiveness rather than an assessment of the military situation. In terms of the latter, Blücher attempted to convince his friends that Prussia still had time. Although Napoleon had approximately 130,000 men available for operations in North Germany in addition to the 70,000 Poles, Saxons, and Westphalians that surrounded Prussia's borders, Blücher scoffed at the threat to have Davout invade in three days: "So, the threat to visit us in three days actually fulfilled its purpose, but by devil, who will invade us?"[53] And to Hardenberg: "Our adversary's entry into our provinces in three days is a Gasconade. Who will invade us? Not the garrison at Stettin.

Liebert has more fear of me than I of him. Only 6,000 French are at Stettin; they must remain in the fortress because they do not trust the imperial troops and already have them locked up in Stettin. The 11,000 men they have at Mecklenburg are conscripts; those at Hamburg and Lübeck must remain there. . . . Thus, what shall beat us must first cross the Rhine." Moreover, the first British convoy of arms and ammunition appeared in the protected anchorage off the coast of Kolberg on 9 October, confirming Dörnberg's statements and increasing Blücher's angst.[54]

Being on the verge of renouncing all of his work at Kolberg incensed Blücher. He simply could not accept seeing his efforts and hopes vanish like the autumn mist. In response to Hardenberg's instructions, he bluntly wrote that he could not furlough his men; he had to have 20,000 men or he could not be held responsible for Kolberg. "If I cannot occupy the redoubts that were so laboriously built at such a great cost they will be more dangerous to me than useful," he explained. Blücher assured the chancellor that he would maintain the utmost secrecy. "But I must say to you," he warned, "if I let the men leave here now and our adversary invades our country, we will not be able to get hold of these men again." Perhaps sensing that time had run out for him, the sixty-nine year-old concluded: "My lot would be better if I found an honorable death before Kolberg."[55]

Blücher wrote this on 12 October 1811, not knowing that his fate already had been decided two days earlier. Gneisenau did what he could to defend his friend, including securing the intervention of the Hanoverian-born British agent Ludwig Karl von Ompteda (the younger brother of Christian), who convinced Hardenberg that dismissing Blücher outright would make a very negative impression in London, St. Petersburg, and Vienna. Yet the chancellor sought to convince Ompteda that Blücher's recall did not signify a change in the king's opinion of the general: Blücher only would appear to be stripped of his responsibility; if Prussia went to war, command would be returned to him. As a result of the agent's intervention, Hardenberg granted Blücher an opportunity to refute in person a fourteen-point indictment.[56] On 10 October the king issued a cabinet order stating, "The French legation has complained that the work on the entrenchments at Kolberg continues after I declared such to be forbidden." He summoned Blücher to "immediately come to Berlin after the arrival of General Tauentzien, who will replace you as commanding general, in order to explain the absolute inaccuracy of this rumor and defend yourself sufficiently through an oral deposition."[57]

As his letters to Gneisenau and Hardenberg on the twelfth make no reference to this cabinet order, Blücher apparently received it on the thirteenth or fourteenth. Thus, the first mention of the order in his journal comes on 14 October: "His Royal Majesty has summoned me to Berlin. General Tauentzien will assume command of the local corps during my absence." How Blücher accepted this news is not known. Eisenhart maintained that the general admitted that the summons took him completely by surprise. Yet Franz insisted that his father had never been stronger in the face of adversity.[58] Gneisenau hoped for the best and sent a letter to Franz that accompanied the king's order. "Indeed the venerable hero will be angry over the new message that comes to him from here," he warned. Nevertheless, Gneisenau expected a "smooth change of command" to occur in Pomerania. Afterward, the general would go to Berlin and employ his "talent of speech, which he possesses in such a high degree, and through his cordiality possibly move the disposition of the King and deter him from making feeble decisions. If this was not my hope and if a star was not shining in the distance [Scharnhorst], I would advise you to seek another country."[59]

The details of what followed are sketchy. Sometime over the next few days, Blücher went to Berlin and explained himself. Hardenberg claimed that the general kept his cool throughout the proceedings and completely justified his actions. If necessary, he offered to accept royal censure for the sake of the state. He also submitted a written defense drafted by Ribbentrop. Despite being hastily written, the document conclusively refuted all fourteen points of the indictment. After reading the document on 24 October, Frederick William refused to allow it to be submitted to St. Marsan. Deeming it to be inappropriate, verbose, and poorly written, he first wanted considerable editing completed before forwarding it to the French legation. Nothing ever came of this because the emperor eventually decided the issue.[60]

On 29 October St. Marsan informed Hardenberg that the emperor had accepted the idea of an alliance with Prussia. Frederick William believed that an alliance with Napoleon could best guarantee the survival of his state. Yet the emperor refused to tolerate Blücher's continued presence in the Prussian army. After accusing the general of disobedience, the French could not reverse their stand and tolerate having him placed at the head of their new ally's army.[61] On 3 November Napoleon instructed his foreign minister to insist on Blücher's dismissal.[62] Eight days later the general received his discharge. Thus, Blücher had to take the fall in order to conclude a Franco-Prussian alliance.

On 11 November Frederick William informed Blücher that "the current circumstances" did not allow the king to grant him a command. Moreover, he desired that the general select a residency outside of Berlin "where you want to live completely free until further notice." A second letter from the king but in Hardenberg's hand accompanied the official communiqué: "As a result of orders from the current day, you will cease for the moment your activity and distance yourself from here, and you must attribute this only to the pressure of the circumstances that demand this measure. Based on your patriotism and the assurances you have given me, I trust you will obey. I have considered with absolute fairness your meritorious service and the zeal to serve that you have so often demonstrated and have thus instructed the state chancellor to reimburse you with the sum of 2,000 thaler for your stay here and for your journey to a locality to be selected by you. You understand that this as well as the contents of the present letter must be kept secret. In the meantime, I cannot wait until I again see you active—as soon as the circumstances allow it."[63]

Blücher ultimately went to Breslau (Wrocław), the provincial capital of Silesia, to spend his exile far from the troubles of Berlin. Not only did he suffer the personal indignity of being cashiered, but he also watched as Frederick William accepted a treaty of alliance with Napoleon. Scharnhorst's mission to Russia came to naught, except that it cemented his esteem in the eyes of Alexander and several high-ranking Russian officers. This eventually proved indispensable for Prussia in early 1813, when Scharnhorst and the Russians negotiated a plan to fight the French. But before that could occur, Prussian patriots like Blücher had to stomach the painful spectacle of watching their troops depart as French allies for the invasion of Russia in 1812.

CHAPTER 9

THE SIXTH COALITION

Thirty minutes from the gates of Breslau stood the Scheitnig Schloß, which belonged to Prince Hohenlohe-Ingelfingen. There, overlooking a spacious park, Blücher resided. Many of his friends likewise made their way to Breslau. "Gneisenau, Chasot, Justus Grüner, [Ernst] Moritz Arndt, and afterward Blücher, appeared at Breslau," recounts Heinrich Steffens, a professor at the University of Breslau. "In the agitated state of the people, these arrivals occasioned great astonishment. The police watched their movements, suspiciously, but without interference." A disgusted Scharnhorst received the task of supervising the fortresses, military schools, and munitions factories at Potsdam and throughout Silesia, the regions of Prussia that the French could not transit according to the latest treaty with Napoleon. Consequently, Scharnhorst, and his adjutant, Carl von Clausewitz, went to Breslau. Frederick William's adjutant general, Boyen, likewise received orders to go to Silesia. Because Boyen numbered among the anti-French party, the king wanted to distance him from his entourage to avoid Napoleon's suspicion.

"I was brought into immediate connection for the first time with those men whose position and principles marked them as the hope of Germany," continues Steffens. "They passed much time at my house, when I took every precaution to exclude all other visitors. Sometimes we met at a tavern, and remained in close conference till midnight; a small room behind the public saloon was reserved for us. It is easy to suppose that these arrivals at Breslau were the subject of intense interest, and that I appeared in a new character by my connection with them. The police president once said to me that he knew I had assembled a little Koblenz, referring to the noble émigrés who had made themselves extravagantly conspicuous in that city at the beginning of the [French] Revolution. I felt the remark to be a warning, but did not acknowledge the comparison."[1] Blücher's old nemesis, the pro-French Field Marshal

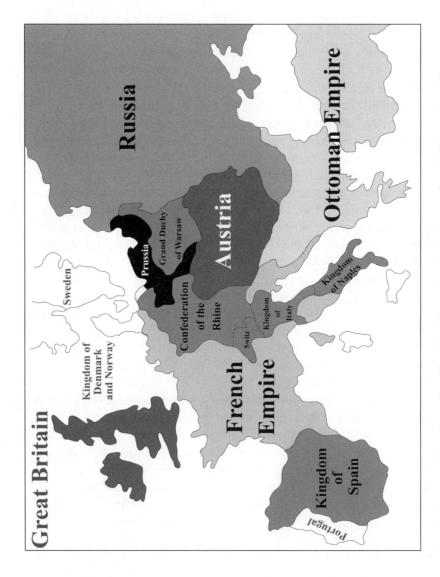

Europe in 1812. Map drawn by Alex Mendoza. Copyright © 2014 by the University of Oklahoma Press.

Kalckreuth, now governor of Breslau, reported the supposed intrigue at Scheitnig and how it undermined the state. But the patriots still had friends in high places. The king's cousin, Prince August, who had led the reform of Prussian artillery from his head-quarters at Breslau, boldly intervened to silence Kalckreuth and his supporters.[2]

Arndt described Blücher's youthful physique, despite his seventy years: he appeared nimble and strong, his attitude merry but dignified, yet he was weighed down by the seriousness of the times.[3] Unfortunately, we have very little from Blücher himself during this period. His massive private correspondence, which has been published in various works, contains nothing from the general's own hand between February and November 1812. The little that we know comes from bits and pieces provided by contemporaries, which German historians assembled for their biographies of Blücher. Accordingly, the Scheitnig Schloß naturally became a gathering place for Prussian patriots. Wine loosened tongues during the daily card games. All lamented the state's misfortune, yet the time together helped cement their bonds of friendship as well as their commitment to the "sacred cause." "The misfortune of the Fatherland has reached its climax," wrote Clausewitz about this period, "for its princes are slaves, who upon the command of their master would take up the sword against each other. Actually, we now have nothing more to fear and everything to hope." Scharnhorst expressed his opinion that Napoleon could very well meet his fate on the Russian Steppes.[4]

Gradually, the daily crowd at the Scheitnig Schloß dwindled, and soon Blücher became very lonely. Similar to 1809, Gneisenau resigned his commission but undertook a secret diplomatic mission through Vienna, St. Petersburg, and Stockholm to London.[5] Boyen went to Russia to maintain communication with the tsar; Clausewitz and many others resigned and accepted commissions in the Russian army. Scharnhorst remained busy with his studies and limited official duties; only Hardenberg's personal request prevented him from resigning as well. According to Wolfgang Unger, Blücher despaired over ending his days with Prussia still in a state of slavery, but it does not appear that he experienced a relapse of disease, physical or mental.[6]

On the evening of 22 June 1812, the Grande Armée commenced the invasion of Russia. A Prussian corps of 20,000 men commanded by Hans David von Yorck marched toward Riga with the rest of Marshal Étienne Macdonald's army group. Napoleon led the main body of the Grande Armée in pursuit of the Russians, who implemented a defensive strategic withdrawal. After the war started, news of a Russian retreat and unfavorable reports regarding the disposition at Russian headquarters reached Breslau. In Blücher's loneliness and uselessness, such information increased his anxiety. From his perspective as well as many others, it simply did not appear that the war would have a favorable outcome for tsar. Yet news then arrived that the Russians made a stand and stopped retreating. Rumors that the war turned against Napoleon reached Prussia in November. In the middle of that month, Blücher learned of the burning of Moscow and Alexander's rejection of peace proposals. Soon came word of the French retreat and the Russian pursuit.

Tales of Napoleon's retreat prompted Blücher to write Frederick William on 17 November. Believing Napoleon would take further measures to secure his rear, Blücher feared for the safety of the king and begged him to come to Breslau. "My true devotion to Your Royal Highness's sacred person and concern for the future welfare of the nation moves me to make the most humble request for Your Royal Majesty to take the security of your person and that of the crown prince in the highest attention in these dangerous times." Noting how Napoleon had dethroned the Spanish Bourbons in 1808, Blücher added: "Spain provides an example that demands caution. Do not leave the arms of your loyal nation! Delight us with your presence."[7]

By all accounts the king "gruffly" and "ungraciously" rejected this request. Aside from rumors, nothing official reached Berlin from the depths of Russia indicating the emperor's setback. At such a critical time, the king feared any step that could be perceived as treacherous, and he particularly wanted to prevent his generals from interfering in state affairs. His response to Blücher, dated 28 November 1812, recognized the caring intent of the request but instructed the old man to mind his business. Perhaps hoping to discourage Blücher from following his normal practice of bombarding him with a series of letters that steadily grew more forceful, the king explained that the general's limited perspective did not allow Blücher to fully grasp the state of affairs. Instead of instructing the king, his duty would be fulfilled if he left the decision making to the monarch.[8] The tactic worked: Blücher remained silent for the rest of 1812.

Nevertheless, Frederick William's determination to keep a firm grasp on the situation received a potentially fatal blow on 30 December when Yorck agreed to the Convention of Tauroggen (Tauragė) with the Russians under the command of the Prussian-born general Johann von Diebitsch. Accordingly, Yorck's corps immediately separated from Macdonald's command and became neutral, thus opening the East Prussian frontier to the approaching Russians.[9] Regardless of whether Yorck acted with or without royal authorization, he started a chain reaction that led to Prussia's official alliance with Russia and declaration of war against France. As an immediate result, the wreck of the Grande Armée continued the retreat, evacuating the lower Vistula and abandoning a large garrison at Danzig. Without Yorck's relatively fresh 20,000 men, the French could not hold the Russians at the Prussian frontier.[10]

Stories that Napoleon fled through Silesia traveling day and night set Breslau on fire with excitement. "At Breslau," recalled Steffens, "all household chores and affairs were forgotten, everybody assembled in the streets, and all looked for the leader who would order them to arm."[11] Confirmed reports of the Grande Armée's destruction had old Blücher chomping at the bit, and he could hardly contain himself. Although news of Tauroggen had yet to reach him, he wrote Scharnhorst on 5 January 1813: "Each of my fingers itch to grasp the sword. If His Majesty our King and all other German princes and the entire nation remain content and do not rise up and sweep from German soil all of the rascally French brood together with Bonaparte and his entire entourage, then it appears to me that no German man is worthy of the name. Now is the time to act and to do what I suggested in 1809, mainly to call the entire nation to arms and drive out those princes who refuse and who oppose us just like Bonaparte. For it is not a question of Prussia alone, but of reuniting the entire German Fatherland, of reconstructing the nation."[12]

Blücher's impatience increased to the extreme; to any who would listen, he emphatically stated that the French could not be allowed to breathe: "everything should stand up and fall on the French like a holy thunderstorm." He believed that only 30,000 men would be needed to drive them from German soil.[13] Learning that Stein, now in Russian service, reached Königsberg, he wrote his friend on 25 January: "I will not refrain from saying to you that I am in complete agreement with your opinion that in the current situation Prussia must help the entire German Fatherland and hunt Bonaparte in such a virtuous form and manner. . . . [T]he King and Prussia can maintain their existence and power only in unison with the German Fatherland."[14] Despite these strong opinions, after being told to mind his business, Blücher did: not one letter went to Frederick William during the hectic months of January and February 1813.

Although Blücher remained muzzled, Scharnhorst and Hardenberg informed him of developments as best they could, but anxiety and excitement gnawed at him. Boyen arrived at Breslau, and he learned that Gneisenau reached Kolberg on 25 February en route from Great Britain. "Stein is here," he wrote Franz on the twenty-sixth. "On Monday, he and Hardenberg, also Scharnhorst and the Russian Anstedt, were with me. Stein is the same old sincere friend."[15] He eagerly listened as Stein explained Alexander's plans to continue the war.[16] "The cause must now go forward. No one tells me what is being said; in the meantime, my fate is sealed and I quietly await everything," he assured Franz.[17] Perhaps the controversy surrounding the seventy-year-old general was the reason that his informants suddenly went silent.

Scharnhorst's departure for Russian headquarters signaled Frederick William's decision for war. This now required him to appoint field commanders. Scharnhorst lobbied for Blücher to be named commander in chief of the Prussian army, firmly believing that only he harbored no fear of Napoleon. Scharnhorst encountered opposition, especially from the king's adjutant general, Colonel Karl Friedrich von dem Knesebeck, who pushed for General Tauentzien to receive command.[18] Enjoying what the nineteenth-century Russian general and historian Mikhail Bogdanovich calls "the special good disposition of the tsar," Tauentzien "made strong claims on the main command of the troops."[19] Opponents of Blücher employed terms such as "old," "sick," and "reckless" to describe him: recent history confirmed such labels.[20] Opposition to his appointment could even be found in Scharnhorst's own camp. Boyen objected based on Blücher's history of mental illness, insisting that the general even claimed to have been pregnant with an elephant. Scharnhorst retorted: "Even if he has a thousand elephants in his belly, he must lead the army."[21] With difficulty, Scharnhorst persuaded the king to at least appoint Blücher commander of the Prussian troops in Silesia.[22]

On 28 February Blücher received a handwritten letter from Frederick William that reinstated him in the army: "I have decided to assign you command of the troops that will be the first to move into the field. I thus task you with making them mobile as soon as possible. The General War Department will inform you of your campaign budget as well as the troops that you will command. The important task that you have received will convince you of the trust I have in your military experience and in your patriotism, and I am certain that you will comply with this trust and give me and the Fatherland reason to show you our special gratitude."[23]

In the meantime, all waited breathlessly for news from Scharnhorst over negotiations with the Russians at Kalisch, seventy-five miles northeast of Breslau. "Scharnhorst, who is expected back from Russian headquarters any day now, will bring back the latest decision—and then we will roam," wrote Blücher on 5 March. "I am, thank God, still healthy and have enough to do."[24] The same could not be said for the general's son-in-law, Count Schulenburg, who suffered a mental breakdown at Berlin and would soon require charity. For this reason, Blücher's daughter, Frederike, joined him and Amalie at Breslau after officials cautioned her against going to Schulenburg in his current condition. Despite the preparations and apprehension caused by the imminence of war, Blücher, as always, demonstrated concern for his family. Claiming that the inactive life would not be fitting at such a time for a young man, he summoned his younger son, Gebhard, to Breslau.[25]

Although the king had yet to issue orders to form army corps, Blücher suspected he would receive command of one of the two corps Prussia probably would field for the upcoming campaign. He believed Yorck should command the other but admitted that the king, still fuming over Tauroggen, "does not at all agree with this." Stein assured him that the Russians would provide "a good portion of Cossacks" for use in his own corps. Even at this early stage, the mobilization bit deep into Blücher's wallet, costing him 1,500 thaler for horses alone. In early March he summoned the officers he wanted at his side. While Franz returned to his regiment, Blücher secured the appointment of Captains Brünneck and Count Friedrich von Moltke as his adjutants. As of yet, nothing had been decided concerning his staff. He did receive many requests for assignments to his headquarters, many of which he had to reject because of the financial burden he had to bear. "You will not believe how I am tortured—all want to go with me; but I have rejected all of them because they would devour me." Blücher described the response to mobilization as "great." He expected Tsar Alexander himself to soon reach Breslau. "The Russians have crossed the Oder with an entire corps," he informed Franz. "At Berlin, the French will be *Schmiere gekriegt* [crushed]."[26]

After Scharnhorst departed Breslau on 26 February, the measures to expand the army slowed. Frederick William's inactivity did little to sooth Blücher's increasing impatience. "As for me, everything moves too slowly," he complained to Franz. Wanting to keep Napoleon guessing for as long as possible, the king recognized that the creation of a dozen new regiments could not be concealed from the French. He also questioned where the officers to command the new units would be found. Consequently, he not only refrained from issuing a declaration of war but also refused to take further steps to expand the army until Scharnhorst identified a sufficient number of commanders. Blücher and the patriot party hoped the king would summon the nation to war, but the conservative monarch preferred to wage a conventional campaign rather than place the fate of his monarchy in the hands of commoners. His alliance agreements with Russia stipulated that Prussia would double its combat strength through the creation of a Landwehr (militia), but as of yet no steps were taken for this expedient outside of East Prussia. Blücher keenly understood the detriments of this delay and impatiently awaited Scharnhorst's return.[27] "As soon as Scharnhorst returns," he assured Franz, "I will proceed with force."[28]

As for other friendly forces, Bülow and Borstell completed the mobilization of the Pomeranian, East Prussian, and West Prussian Brigades. The Russian main army escorted the headquarters of the tsar and Field Marshal Prince Mikhail Kutuzov, supreme commander of all Russian troops, to Kalisch. The Hessian-born General Ferdinand von Wintzingerode's advance corps reached Rawitsch (Rawicz), some sixty miles west of Kalisch and forty miles north of Breslau. The need to besiege or at least blockade the numerous French-held fortresses on the Vistula and throughout the Grand Duchy of Warsaw reduced the Russian main army to approximately 45,000 extremely tired soldiers. In fact, General Alexander Tormasov's "main army" consisted only of the Russian Guard and Reserve after General Mikhail Miloradovich's 15,000-man corps besieged Glogau. General Ludwig Adolph Peter zu Wittgenstein, the commander of the Russian right wing, reached the Oder north of Küstrin with his corps of 20,000 men.[29]

Wittgenstein unleashed three large Streifkorps totaling 5,000 men under Alexander Chernishev, Alexander Benckendorff, and a native Badener, Friedrich Karl von Tettenborn, all of which wreaked havoc among the French along the left bank of the Oder. Chernishev and Tettenborn briefly occupied Berlin on 20 February until French infantry and artillery drove them off. Despite orders to hold the Oder, the commander of French forces, Napoleon's stepson Eugene, withdrew to Berlin. Convinced that his troops could not retain the Prussian capital for long, he evacuated the city on 4 March; Chernishev's Cossacks entered that same day. Eugene's forces retreated to the Elbe in two columns, the first turned to Wittenberg, the other to Magdeburg. Chernishev and Benckendorff hurried after them while Tettenborn proceeded to Hamburg.[30] French garrisons still held the key Oder fortresses of Stettin, Küstrin, and Glogau, but the Prussian heartland was free: a vital prerequisite for mobilization.

For operations, the Russians adopted Scharnhorst's plan, which called for Wittgenstein's northern army to advance on Berlin while a southern army under Blücher marched on the Saxon capital of Dresden. With Tormasov's army, Kutuzov, now Allied commander in chief, would follow three marches behind on a front broad enough to support either Wittgenstein or Blücher. Wittgenstein's army totaled 48,000 men; of this the number, the Prussians provided the majority, Yorck's I Corps of 13,200 men, Bülow's 11,300 soldiers, and Borstell's 5,300 troops. Wittgenstein's Russian troops included a corps of 12,650 men under General Gregor von Berg and the 5,000 men divided among Tettenborn, Chernishev, and Dörnberg. Blücher's southern army consisted of approximately 26,000 Prussians and Wintzingerode's 10,500 Russians.

These two forward armies had to determine the march direction of the enemy's main force, jointly advance against it, and avoid being destroyed individually. Upon reaching Berlin, Wittgenstein would immediately turn south if the French remained at the Elbe "to bring the enemy between him and Blücher's corps and attack the enemy jointly from two sides." If the main French force advanced through Dresden and Torgau in the direction of Warsaw, Wittgenstein and Blücher would unite and operate against it jointly or in unison with Tormasov's army. Conversely, should the French attempt to drive through Saxony between Lusatia and the Bohemian frontier, Blücher would take a defensive position to fix the enemy's front while Wittgenstein attempted a strategic envelopment of the French left and rear. "Concerning operations on the other side of the Elbe," states the campaign plan, "nothing can be decided beforehand; it is highly probable that we will soon encounter considerable enemy forces. Operations will be conducted in accordance with the disposition or movements of these forces."[31]

On 9 March 1813 Blücher received the royal order appointing him commander of the Prussian II Corps: 645 officers and 26,510 men of the 71,382 soldiers who constituted the Prussian field army.[32] As of the eleventh, he still had no idea which regiments would be assigned to him. The troops mobilizing in Silesia did not all converge on Breslau. Instead, Scharnhorst spread them along the left bank of the Oder. A few cavalry units reported to depots situated on the right bank northeast of Breslau. Garrison battalions occupied the fortresses of Glatz, Neiße, Kosel, and Silberberg. Dissatisfied with what appeared to be a lack of organization, Blücher complained to Scharnhorst's office: "It has been two days since the royal orders arrived allowing me to introduce myself to the troops. But I do not know where they stand and which [units] will be placed under my orders. I request that you the send me these details."[33] Blücher's grousing mattered little to Scharnhorst: speed counted most. The units designated for II Corps assembled between Breslau, Jauer (Jawor), Löwenberg (Lwówek Śląski), and Liegnitz (Legnica).[34]

On 17 March the king issued eighteen "Articles of War" concerning the punishment for crimes against the security of the army. According to the monarch, he issued such harsh decrees "not because he believed there could be a traitor to the cause of the country among his people, or in Germany, but for the weak, especially among the civil servants, who are inclined to give in to threats and who are much more likely of misdeeds." Hardenberg received a copy with instructions to make the decree a public statute.[35] The king's message was clear: in this war of survival, there could be no repeats of the shameful capitulations, dereliction of duty, and desertion that crowned Prussia's humiliation in 1806.

On 16 March, the day Frederick William issued his declaration of war, Blücher's lead units struck the road to Dresden; the remaining troops followed on the seventeenth.[36] Excitement, nerves, drink, and sleepless nights took their toll on Blücher's immune system.

The good health about which he had boasted to Franz temporarily abandoned him, and he succumbed to a debilitating fever that limited his activities for almost two weeks. Instead of leading his troops, the sick general followed them on the eighteenth.

Relations between Blücher and Kutuzov started on a friendly note. "The King has entrusted the corps to me and to my sincere joy has subordinated me to Your Highness," wrote Blücher on 17 March. "I have the double honor of fighting in unison with the victorious Russian army and to be under the orders of a commander who has earned the admiration and gratitude of the peoples. I await your command."[37] Kutuzov answered two days later: "With great appreciation, I received your letter of 17 March in which you express your feelings toward me. I consider it a special honor to begin the campaign with a general who has long attracted the attention of all of Europe and upon whom the Fatherland places so many hopes. Let's hope that the struggle upon which we now embark will end successfully since undertaking it is a righteous cause and continuing it is a sacred responsibility."[38]

Because of Scharnhorst's frequent absences from Blücher's headquarters, Gneisenau—reinstated by the king on 11 March at the rank of general major—received the post of assistant quartermaster general, technically assistant chief of staff. Majors Karl Wilhelm von Grolman, Johann Wilhelm von Krauseneck, and Johann Jacob Rühle von Lilienstern, joined later by Friedrich Karl von Müffling—all future chiefs of the General Staff of the Prussian army—as well as many other majors, captains, and lieutenants rounded out Blücher's staff.[39] Upon the general's request, Count Goltz, the Prussian envoy at Munich, hurried to Silesia to be Blücher's first adjutant; Blücher's old assistant and friend, Ribbentrop, served as the army's Kriegsrat. Frederick William granted Professor Steffen's request for a sabbatical from the University of Breslau so he could serve on Blücher's staff as a propaganda specialist.[40] Clausewitz, who remained in the tsar's service, accompanied the staff as the Russian liaison. After Scharnhorst returned, this circle of friends and colleagues represented the very pinnacle of Prussian military thinking and indeed may have been the greatest staff of all time in terms of intellect, acumen, and collective experience. It certainly helped that friendship formed the basis of their professional relationship. "I am very cheerful," Clausewitz later wrote to his wife, Marie, "and the moment is almost perfect. I'm in my previous situation, with my old general who is again chief of his staff, only the circumstances have somewhat changed and increased in importance. Blücher, Scharnhorst, and Gneisenau treat me with superb kindness and friendship. I can think of no better situation. One will long seek in vain to achieve this unity, this mutual trust, respect, and camaraderie."[41]

In addition, the number of royal mouths sitting at Blücher's table justified his endless concern over money. Prince August, the king's cousin, accompanied headquarters as general inspector of the artillery.[42] In addition, the seventeen-year-old crown prince, affectionately called "Fritz"; the king's brother, Prince William; the king's nephew, Prince Frederick (son of Frederick William's brother, Louis); and the king's brother-in-law, Prince Carl von Mecklenburg-Strelitz, all joined Blücher to earn their spurs. Frederick William III, however, neither complimented Blücher's headquarters nor trailed behind the army. Instead, when the tsar departed Breslau on the nineteenth, the king likewise left, exchanging the provincial capital for his palace at Potsdam, where he arrived on 22 March. After returning to the theater, though, he remained with the tsar throughout the war.[43]

On 19 March Blücher's headquarters reached Liegnitz, 120 miles east of Dresden. Reports indicated that Davout held the Saxon capital with 5,000–6,000 men and that Eugene stood another 70 miles to the west at Leipzig with a corps of 20,000 men. Intelligence gleaned from informants in Liegnitz claimed 80,000 imperial soldiers were marching from Mainz toward Erfurt. On the eighteenth Eugene had started to concentrate his forces at Magdeburg in compliance with Napoleon's directives. Ignoring a desperate plea from the king of Saxony, Davout blew two of the arches of Dresden's bridge—purportedly the most beautiful bridge in Europe—and led his troops toward Wittenberg, from where he proceeded to Hamburg to secure the lower Elbe.[44] As the French moved down that river, Russian Cossacks from Blücher's army established posts along the right bank, from the Bohemian frontier to Wittenberg. On the twenty-fourth Wintzingerode reached Dresden's Neustadt (New City) on the right bank.

The pressure of Cossack raiding parties and Streifkorps drove the French, Bavarians, and Saxons from Dresden and other crossing points along the Elbe. A Saxon force of less than 2,000 troops under General Karl von Lecoq withdrew into Torgau on the twenty-seventh, while the French and Bavarians evacuated the capital.[45]

To escape the Cossacks, the Saxon king, Frederick Augustus I, fled ninety-five miles southwest to Plauen with his treasury and two cavalry regiments. He remained in communication with Napoleon, proclaimed his continued adherence to the French alliance, and told his people he would return with reinforcements but closed the fortresses of Torgau to all belligerents.[46] According to Gneisenau, the commandant of Torgau, General Johann von Thielmann, refused to admit French soldiers into the fortress "and because of his behavior arouses the hope that he has changed sides." Regardless, the Prussians did not think Napoleon would respect any decision made by Frederick Augustus short of absolute compliance with French demands.[47]

After passing through Bautzen on 28 March, Blücher's headquarters covered the next thirty-five miles to reach Dresden's Neustadt on the thirtieth. "I am at Dresden," he wrote Hardenberg, "and with God's help will go farther. The disgraceful destruction of the bridge is very adverse for Saxony, but the move will not stop me."[48] The other units of the corps remained echeloned eastward to Silesia until Wintzingerode could continue his march. This occurred on the thirty-first, when the Russians completed a pontoon bridge and Wintzingerode led the rest of his corps across the Elbe; Blücher moved into Dresden's Altstadt (Old City) on the left bank of the Elbe. Thus far, the Saxons received Blücher with courtesy. "I have been nearly overwhelmed with compliments here," he wrote to Amalie, "but it appears that these are all that the Saxons are willing to give."[49] To Hardenberg he was more explicit and frank: "Of my reception in Saxony, I am very pleased in regards to the nation; but . . . the distinguished gentlemen . . . find it especially [odious] that we requested some necessities from them; I notified them that we come to them with our allies, as they [the Saxons] had gone [to Russia] with theirs [the French], and that we have to provide ours with the necessary food."[50]

After receiving Kutuzov's order to advance farther west to Leipzig, Blücher assured Hardenberg that "if this does not force them [the French] to move away from Leipzig, they will run the risk that I and Wittgenstein will drive them into the sea. I will now cross the Elbe and advance to facilitate the operation of Wittgenstein's corps; I will offer him my hand and we will see what can be done together." Blücher spent five days at Dresden. He remained in high spirits and appreciated any effort by the Saxons to advance the Allied cause despite their king. On 1 April a young Saxon whom Blücher had given permission to copy a collection of war songs sought entry to Prussian headquarters so he could thank the general. Finding him at breakfast, the Saxon waited quietly while Blücher reviewed the latest reports. Finally presented to Blücher, the civilian thanked him, but the Prussian stood up and placed his hand on the man's shoulder, saying: "People love to sing; it lights the fire under them. Now, everyone has to sing what they feel in their hearts, some with their mouths, and others with their sabers." "But Your Excellency, I do not want to stay with the people who sing with their mouths," responded the youth, "I await the Lützow Corps so I can join it." "That is wonderful," bellowed Blücher, "let's toast good camaraderie."[51]

Blücher's army reached the Mulde River on 5 April. He sent his Streifkorps across the Saale toward Halberstadt, Nordhausen, Naumburg, and Jena to threaten Eugene's communications and force him to evacuate the stretch between the Elbe and the Weser.[52] His patrols formed an eighty-mile screen west of the Saale River, extending from Halle to Saalfeld, to monitor the imperial forces assembling at Bayreuth, Erfurt, and Würzburg. The Allies did not know whether Napoleon would advance through Hof and Plauen or through Würzburg and Erfurt and whether he intended to gain time or to take Berlin.[53] This uncertainty held them in check on the Mulde between Dresden and Leipzig, and on the Elbe between Leipzig and Berlin until the end of April.

Beautiful spring weather accompanied the march from Dresden to the Mulde. Clausewitz commented on the feisty mood of the army: "The troops are cheerful and sing 'Auf, auf, Kameraden' and similar songs, others yodel in perfect tone."[54] All of this served to increase Blücher's confidence. "Already I am here," he wrote from Borna on the fifth, "and in two days I will be at Leipzig. I think I will soon try my strength against my adversary." Extremely over-confident, the general offered Amalie the prospect of a June vacation that would culminate with a visit to their old home at Münster.[55] Although the Russians and Prussians cleared all of Saxony as far as the line of the Mulde in just two weeks, his thought of reaching Münster by June certainly indicates his heightened assurance as well as a touch of naïve optimism.

Blücher fell sick sometime after 12 April, but the days passed quietly while he recouped. The affection that the inhabitants of Altenburg and the surrounding lands showered on the general and his entourage helped him cope with his impatience and illness. Visitors and well-wishers came from Weimar; kind messages and heartfelt encouragements flowed into Prussian headquarters. On the fifteenth the Masonic lodge of Altenburg held a celebration to honor him. Despite his malady, he took the opportunity to inspire the participants with a speech stressing fortitude and the hope of a better future. No doubt alcohol loosened the general's already uncensored tongue. "Blücher was quartered at the Hotel Stadt Gotha," relays Steffens. "When I first joined the table there [on the fifteenth] he was absent, with many of his officers. The Freemasons held a great meeting at Altenburg, and Blücher was the grand-master. His love for speech-making made the society attractive to him, and it is said that he obtained his remarkable facility in speaking at the Freemasons' lodge. He came to the hotel before the dinner ended, and the conversation seemed to indicate that the war was about to begin in earnest, and that an engagement was expected."[56] A letter arrived addressed to Blücher lacking a signature, but the general immediately recognized the author: Duke Karl August of Weimar. The letter concluded with the meaningful words: "Always move forward! Do you want to relive the year 1806?"[57]

In this vein, pressure mounted in Blücher's headquarters, fueled by aggravation with Kutuzov's slow march westward. The Prussians felt that the army's inactivity damaged morale on the home front. "Malchen!" Blücher wrote Amalie on the twenty-second, "I have not written you for some time because of my many duties and a damned fever; thank God I am now better; my old Horlacher has freed me of it. I am completely healthy again. The damn fever indeed bothered me, but my old doctor knew what to do." Responding to Amalie's remark that she was surprised to read so little in the newspapers of Blücher's corps, he retorted: "I cannot proceed as I wish because of my illness and because of the Russians who still remain in the background. Nevertheless, seven cannon and over 1,000 men already have fallen into my hands." The general did not allow his optimism to be curbed by Kutuzov's lethargy, informing his wife that soon he would be at Münster to settle their personal affairs. "I stand five [German] miles away from the Prince of Elchingen [Ney], who commands the French army, and will soon move closer."[58]

Alexander and Kutuzov reached Bunzlau (Bolesławiec) in Silesia on 18 April. There they parted ways. Too ill to follow the tsar, the

Allied commander in chief remained at Bunzlau after Alexander departed on the twenty-first. Two days later Alexander held a council of war to discuss taking the offensive. A unanimous vote in favor of not merely accepting battle between the Saale and Elbe, but seeking it, indicates the change of attitude at Russian headquarters.[59] Escorted by Tormasov's corps-sized "army," Alexander and Frederick William established Allied headquarters at Dresden on the twenty-fourth.[60]

The decline of Kutuzov's health forced the monarchs to discuss the issue of his successor.[61] According to Pertz and Delbrück, the names of Wittgenstein and Blücher repeatedly surfaced. But Blücher withdrew his name, thus making it easier to secure the agreement of the Russian generals for the appointment of a Russian to the overall command.[62] To succeed Kutuzov, Alexander appointed the forty-four-year-old Wittgenstein, whose campaign the previous year on the Dvina River had earned him fame as the savior of St. Petersburg.[63] Compared to Kutuzov's lethargy, Wittgenstein's vigor, recently demonstrated by his liberation of Prussia, appeared absolutely necessary for the crucial responsibilities of this post. Moreover, his fluency in French and German enabled him to easily communicate with his allies. His concern for Berlin and defending the Prussian heartland also made him popular among the Prussians.[64]

Blücher repeatedly stated that he did not have the slightest reservation about serving under a younger man, and it is relatively safe to assume that he would not have objected out of principle to being subordinated to a Russian. Nevertheless, for the sake of establishing unity of command, Frederick William specifically requested on 28 April 1813 that he make a formal statement of his agreement to serve under Wittgenstein.[65] The following day Blücher responded that when the king decided for war, he resolutely declared his willingness to sacrifice all personal considerations for the interests of "Your Royal Majesty, the Fatherland, and the general cause"; his actions would prove that he remained true to these "sacred principles." He then sent Wittgenstein an explicit declaration that he would obey his orders and follow them verbatim. "Today, I have repeated the assurance to General Wittgenstein that I place myself under his orders and will follow these punctually," he informed the king. "This is only a small proof of the feeling of true devotion and the deepest reverence with which I would die for you."[66]

Blücher certainly had come a long way since his utter contempt for Frederick William's weakness, but the king's decision for war had done much to reorient the warrior's thinking.

After Napoleon miraculously fielded the Army of the Main, his imperial legions marched east to the Saale River at the end of April. As the French advanced across the river valley and through Naumburg, small engagements flared across Blücher's front beginning on 28 April. The general could not have been more ready to grapple with Napoleon. "My son was lightly wounded after maintaining himself against an enemy ten-times stronger," he wrote Boyen. "I have wished for some time that the enemy would cross the Saale and come in the open field."[67] We can "assume that the enemy will advance with his force from Naumburg toward Leipzig," he informed a subordinate on the morning of the twenty-eighth. "We are now ready for this case. Count Wittgenstein has moved to Leipzig and Wintzingerode toward me. It would be very desirable if we could deliver a battle on the plain of Leipzig, somewhere near Lützen. The last part of the Russian main army crosses the Elbe today; its advance guard stands at Zwickau. If we are attacked, the Russians will move closer to us."[68] Blücher knew the French faced him along the Saale from Saalfeld through Halle and correctly assumed that Napoleon only awaited the arrival of his most rearward troops before crossing the river. Confidence in the Allied army could not have been higher. "We have daily combats, which turn out well," Blücher wrote his wife on 29 April. "Franz fights every day. The great blow is close at hand."[69]

Reports of French movements indicated that the emperor would converge on Leipzig in two columns: Eugene's Army of the Elbe from Magdeburg and Napoleon's Army of the Main from Weißenfels. Wittgenstein resolved to attack. With battle approaching, Blücher thanked the troops for demonstrating good military discipline, especially toward the inhabitants:

> Soldiers of my Army! Your exemplary conduct has undergone no change whatsoever since you left your native provinces and entered the territory of Saxony. You have hitherto made no distinction between the two countries, but have held yourselves bound in duty to observe the same excellent discipline. I thank you for this proof of your noble forbearance. Such conduct evinces the true spirit of warriors, and is best fitting for us, since we fight for the noblest good: our Fatherland and our freedom.

The moderation of your demands and the mildness of your treatment proved to the inhabitants of the German provinces that we have come not as their oppressors, but as their brethren and saviors. Continue to act with this excellent spirit of subordination, and should the fame of your exalted behavior proceed you far and near, you will be received with blessings and open arms wherever you show yourselves and wherever fate may lead you.[70]

Blücher had been vindicated. His triumphal return to command an army provided him the opportunity to erase the humiliating memories of the twin disasters that had emasculated him professionally and privately in 1806 and 1808, surrender and insanity. That others had not forgotten mattered little to Blücher, who feared nothing except the horrifying prospect of going to the grave before regaining his masculinity and securing the salvation of his state. Surrounded by some of the best and brightest military minds ever produced by the Prusso-German military establishment, the seventy-year-old commander planned to wage a war of retribution to destroy the one individual responsible for the dishonor that had ravaged him and his country for seven years: Napoleon. For the next fifteen months, he would experience no recurrence of insanity—physical illness yes, but not mental. Blücher remained fixated on the only recourse available to him that could heal the scars of his painful professional and personal embarrassment: destroying Bonaparte. During this crusade, he would not stop until he reached the very gates of Paris, and he would listen to no one, including his king, who did not speak the language of revenge. But to be a good leader, Blücher first had to learn to be a good follower. For the present, that meant following the lead of his political masters and senior Russian partners—a task that became increasingly difficult not only throughout the month of May, but throughout the war itself.

The capture of Swedish cornet Gebhard von Blücher. DEUTSCHES
HISTORISCHES MUSEUM, BERLIN.

The Belling Hussars. Anne S. K. Brown Military Collection, Brown University.

Total Death Hussar. Lithograph after Richard Caton Woodville II.

Colonel Wilhelm Sebastian von Belling in the uniform of the
Black Hussars. Engraved plate by Jakob Adam.

Frederick the Great returning to Sans-Souci after the Potsdam Maneuvers, 1789. By Edward Francis Cunningham. ANNE S. K. BROWN MILITARY COLLECTION, BROWN UNIVERSITY.

The Red King, 1794. Hand-colored aquatint, full-length portrait of General Major Gebhard von Blücher in hussar uniform as commander of the Red Hussar Regiment. ANNE S. K. BROWN MILITARY COLLECTION, BROWN UNIVERSITY.

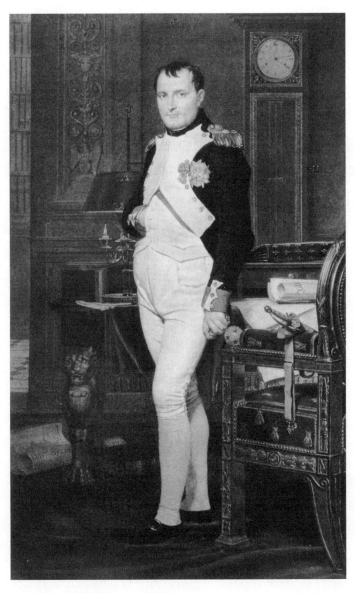

Emperor Napoleon I (1769–1821). Anne S. K. Brown Military
Collection, Brown University.

King Frederick William III (1770–1840), 1814. Portrait by François
Gérard. ANNE S. K. BROWN MILITARY COLLECTION, BROWN UNIVERSITY.

Blücher at the Battle of the Katzbach, 26 August 1813. This rolling battle
scene depicts Blücher on a white horse leading a cavalry charge. The original artist is Georg Bleibtreu, and the plate is a lithograph by Ferdinand
Chevalier. ANNE S. K. BROWN MILITARY COLLECTION, BROWN UNIVERSITY.

Blücher dueling with Napoleon, 1814. Napoleon and Blücher are shown
dueling in the foreground, watched by German peasants, a Russian
Cossack, a British sailor, and caricatures of French generals. Original ink-
and-watercolor illustration by Johann Gottfried Schadow.
ANNE S. K. BROWN MILITARY COLLECTION, BROWN UNIVERSITY.

"The Two Veterans." This satiric etching depicts Blücher in uniform carousing with the prince regent at a small supper table in July 1814. A very alert Blücher proposes a toast; behind him is a large pile of empty bottles. The tipsy regent tilts his chair, kicking the table so that it slants, upsetting the large bowl of punch. Lord Yarmouth leans over him and dips his ladle into the punch to fill the regent's extended glass, not noticing the pending catastrophe. Above Blücher's head hangs a battle-piece: the pursuit of the terrified Napoleon by himself on a galloping horse. Above the regent is a picture of Punch and his wife, Judy, fighting. COURTESY THE BRITISH MUSEUM, NO. 1868,0808.12800. © TRUSTEES OF THE BRITISH MUSEUM.

Blücher and the prince regent of Great Britain at Hyde Park. The prince regent, tsar of Russia, and king of Prussia ride in Hyde Park after the review on the 20 June 1814. Blücher is to their left. An 1815 painting by Aleksander Zauerveid. Anne S. K. Brown Military Collection, Brown University.

Blücher's fall at the Battle of Ligny, 16 June 1815. Prussian cavalry rescuing the general as French cavalry retreat (right background). An 1818 illustration by Charles Turner Warren. ANNE S. K. BROWN MILITARY COLLECTION, BROWN UNIVERSITY.

Blücher and Wellington at Belle-Alliance, 18 June 1815. Painting by
Thomas. J. Barker; engraved by Charles. G. Lewis. ANNE S. K. BROWN
MILITARY COLLECTION, BROWN UNIVERSITY.

Le déjeuner à la fourchette

Le déjeuner à la fourchette, 1815. Blücher having Napoleon as a midday snack. ANNE S. K. BROWN MILITARY COLLECTION, BROWN UNIVERSITY.

A Delicate Finish to a Corsican Usurper, 1814. Caricature of the defeat of Napoleon, who is shown seated on a throne of skulls and bones, attended by his conquerors. Allied commanders look on at left while Blücher offers Napoleon an urn of water. The figure of Time hangs above Napoleon's head, about to cover him with an extinguisher, while three maidens dance with a plaque of Bourbon arms at right. In the distance a man is shown plowing. The original artist is John Nixon, the plate engraved by Thomas Rowlandson. ANNE S. K. BROWN MILITARY COLLECTION, BROWN UNIVERSITY.

Prussian pursuit of the French after Waterloo, 18 June 1815. This depicts a
night-battle scene of Prussian cavalry attacking from the right against fleeing French cavalry and infantry. Original 1818 watercolor, signed and dated
by artist Charles Turner Warren. Anne S. K. Brown Military Collection,
Brown University.

Blücher directing the attack on the Issy suburb of Paris, 3 July 1815.
ANNE S. K. BROWN MILITARY COLLECTION, BROWN UNIVERSITY.

Gebhard Leberecht von Blücher (1742–1819), 1816. From a lithograph after the painting by F. C. Gröger. ANNE S. K. BROWN MILITARY COLLECTION, BROWN UNIVERSITY.

Feldmarschall Blücher der Deutsche (Field Marshal Blücher the German), 1815. Engraving by Johann Carl Bock. Anne S. K. Brown Military Collection, Brown University.

Bust of Blücher by French sculptor François-Joseph Bosio, modeled at Paris. ANNE S. K. BROWN MILITARY COLLECTION, BROWN UNIVERSITY.

Blücher leading the charge, 1814. Illustration by Carl Wilhelm Kolbe;
engraved by Anton Wachsmann. ANNE S.K. BROWN MILITARY COLLECTION,
BROWN UNIVERSITY.

Portrait of Blücher wearing the Grand Cross of the Iron Cross of 1813
and the Star (Blücherstern) of the Grand Cross of the Iron Cross of 1813.
Artist unknown, copying Paul Ernst Gebauer, ca. 1815–19, oil on copper.
STIFTUNG STADTMUSEUM BERLIN.

THE SPRING CAMPAIGN

For the war's first major engagement, Wittgenstein marshaled approximately 88,000 men and 552 guns. Napoleon's army of 145,000 men and 372 guns outnumbered the Allies in infantry but faced a three-fold superiority in cavalry and nearly double the artillery. Although Napoleon possessed fewer total guns, he had more heavy batteries than the Allies, which granted the French artillery an advantage in range and effectiveness. On 2 May 1813 Wittgenstein decided to attack a supposed rear guard found in the villages northwest of his army at Großgörschen, Kleingörschen, Rahna, and Kaja. Blücher received orders to take the villages with one brigade; the salty Prussian replied that he would command the first wave himself. At 11:45 the old hussar "with hoary locks, but vigorous and fiery as a youth," galloped up to Wittgenstein, saluted, and with his sword drawn requested permission to open the struggle. "With God's help," responded the Russian commander in German.[1] Shortly before noon, Blücher led his 1st Brigade over the shallow ridge that to that point had concealed them and down the slope that led to Großgörschen. The Prussian attack took the French completely by surprise in part because the latter had not established a single forward post.[2] After fierce fighting, Blücher won Großgörschen, but the battle had just begun.

Had Wittgenstein ordered the rest of Blücher's corps to simultaneously advance, Kleingörschen and Rahna would have fallen into Prussian hands immediately after Großgörschen. But committing all of Blücher's corps did not appear prudent, particularly because the Allies did not know what enemy forces lay beyond the quadrilateral of villages. Until the rest of the Russian army arrived, Wittgenstein felt he could do little more than have Blücher continue the struggle for the four villages. Thus, around 1:00, Blücher's 2nd Brigade advanced on Kleingörschen—one mile northeast of Großgörschen. At the same time, Marshal Ney rallied his shocked III Corps. Soon, three French divisions slammed into the two Prussian brigades with an advantage in manpower of more than double. Blücher's soldiers

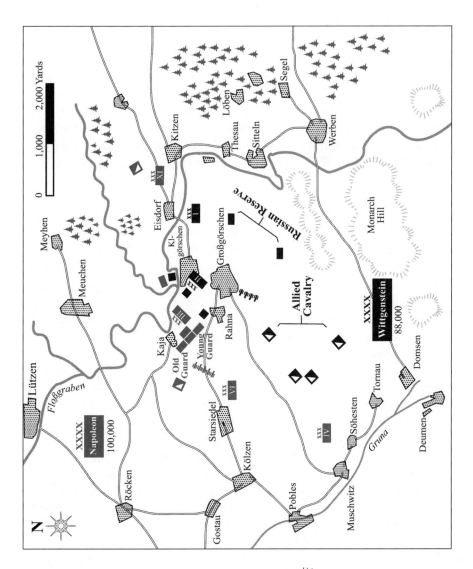

The Battle of
Lützen, 2 May
1813. Map drawn
by Alex Mendoza.
Copyright © 2014
by the University of
Oklahoma Press.

fought bravely, but Rahna and Kleingörschen fell to the French. From its position east and west of Großgörschen, Allied artillery managed to prevent the French from reaching that village.

Blücher now summoned all of his artillery—104 guns—and his 3rd Brigade for another attack. After brutal fighting, the Prussians drove the French from Kleingörschen toward Kaja, where Napoleon himself arrived around 2:30 with the Imperial Guard not far behind. For his immediate objective, Napoleon sought to prevent the Allies from advancing any farther north and reaching the plain of Lützen, where they could unleash their superior cavalry. He recognized that Wittgenstein certainly had considerable forces en route, otherwise a battle would not have been sought. Moreover, to achieve decisive results, the emperor needed time for his IV Corps to arrive on the Allied left and his XI Corps to envelop the Allied right. For the moment, he could only pour more men into the sausage grinder of the quadrilateral. Shortly before 3:00, Napoleon committed Ney's last reserve. As it surged forward, some one thousand individual soldiers from Ney's other divisions as well as numerous reorganized units joined the advance. Reinvigorated by the presence of the emperor, the French tide swept through Kleingörschen and Rahna, reaching the outlying structures of Großgörschen.

Gradually, Blücher's troops withdrew from the blood-soaked square; only Großgörschen, protected by the batteries south of the village, withstood the storm.[3] The general held his position with great difficulty. Scharnhorst, from the start very uncertain of the chances for victory, shed his usually calm demeanor. "I have never seen Scharnhorst as fiery as on this day," recalled his adjutant, Heinrich von Hüser. "Nothing appeared to escape him: he ordered, called Blücher's attention to many issues, and arranged several changes among the troops. Blücher mostly remained in the greatest calm in more or less the most dangerous places, indefatigably smoking his pipe. When the tobacco ran out, he put his hand up and called out: 'Schmidt,' whereupon his orderly handed him a fresh fill, and the old gentleman comfortably smoked further. For a long time we remained very close to a Russian battery; a shell exploded close to us. 'Your Excellency, a shell!,' someone shouted. 'Well, leave the hellish thing alone,' said Blücher very calmly, watching until it exploded and only then moving to a different position."[4]

As 3:00 rolled around, 18,000 Prussian foot soldiers faced some 36,000 French infantry. Wittgenstein finally released Yorck's corps to join the battle, and Blücher led a fresh column to storm Kaja. At Blücher's side, Prince Leopold of Hessen-Homburg fell mortally wounded by a ball that pierced his chest through the star of his house that he wore on his Silesian infantry uniform.[5] "That old Blücher was very brave you can just imagine," wrote Clausewitz.[6] The general had his horse shot out from under him.[7] One spent ball ricocheted off his belt, and a second grazed a finger, but a third penetrated his side and proved more serious. As he and Scharnhorst did everything possible to reform the battalions to hold Kaja until the Russian reserves could move up, the seventy-year-old reluctantly sought medical attention. Blücher sent his staff to Yorck, who now assumed command of all Prussian forces. With his side bleeding and accompanied only by a single orderly, he rode back at a trot to find a surgeon. Upon nearing a unit—the Prussian 1st Guard Regiment—that remained in reserve, he sought the divisional surgeon, Dr. Wasserfuhr. Believing the ball penetrated his abdomen, he despaired, shouting to the doctor: "The ball struck me in the stomach, I will collapse soon." "Children, bring me a general," he often called out with the greatest concern. Between these shouts, he lamented for the horse that had just been killed, "my poor mare."

While Wasserfuhr examined the wound, Crown Prince Fritz came up with his small entourage. Upon seeing Blücher, the future Frederick William IV also ordered his surgeon to attend to the wounded general. Despite the efforts of both doctors, the ball could not be found in the wound. As no exit wound existed, they figured a rib had stopped the ball's journey through his body. Actually, while Blücher was riding to seek medical attention, the ball had worked its way out; he eventually found it in his boot. After the doctors declared the wound to be non–life threatening, Blücher barely waited to be bandaged before mounting a fresh horse. Johann Christan Friedrich Nauck, an orderly at Blücher's headquarters, recounted, "when old Blücher was wounded in the tumult of battle, he swallowed his pain, allowed himself be to bandaged, lifted at first on a wooden stool, and then on his white horse, and returned to the battlefield."[8] At the same moment that Blücher mounted his horse, a cannonball struck a drummer between the feet, shattering both of his legs. "Stay with that poor devil," Blücher shouted to the doctors as he sped toward the enemy.[9]

Meanwhile, Napoleon calmly watched the Prussians gain a foothold in Kaja after two failed attempts. Around 5:00 P.M., the artillery of his XI Corps—sixty cannon and howitzers—opened fire. Thirty minutes later, one brigade of the Young Guard advanced to retake Kaja. The effect on Allied morale had to be crushing. Napoleon recognized that the time to deliver the coup de grâce had arrived. With the sun sinking, he snapped a simple command: "eighty guns." The entire Guard Artillery—fifty-eight guns—unlimbered next to the powerful French batteries southwest of Kaja. Together, the artillery hurled their round shot and grape into the Allied line for thirty minutes. While the cannon pounded, sixteen battalions of Young Guard formed around 6:30 between the great battery and Kaja. Behind them, six battalions of Old Guard followed by the Guard Cavalry formed the last reserve. As the emperor rode past the Guards' position, he issued his orders in classic form: "*La garde au feu!*"[10]

Blücher was on the scene. He and Scharnhorst assembled a dozen Prussian squadrons and charged the bearskins. As Gneisenau's fifteen-year-old son, August, fought at his side, Scharnhorst received the leg wound—inflicted by a musket ball—that would eventually take his life on 28 June.[11] August likewise took a ball to the meaty part of the upper calf, a flesh wound that his proud father later referred to as "a sign of honor."[12] Scharnhorst had to be evacuated to Pegau, his wound described by Clausewitz on 3 May as not serious.[13] After Rahna and Kaja fell, the Prussian defenders of Kleingörschen could not resist the Guard. Only when the French approached Großgörschen did the Allied artillery have a devastating effect on the dense columns. Yet the fall of Rahna and Kleingörschen forced the Prussians to all but abandon that village too—only a small garrison held on to the town center. After reorganizing the troops, a final counterattack drove the French from Großgörschen, where the bloodbath had started.

After 7:00, darkness blanketed the field and brought an end to the fighting. A deep silence, interrupted only by the groans of the dying, replaced the thunder of the guns. The French did not attempt to emerge from the quadrilateral. Lacking sufficient cavalry, Napoleon could not reap the full reward of his infantry's efforts. Allied commanders began the arduous process of reorganizing their units. Under the protection of the famed Kolberg Regiment, Blücher's corps regrouped southwest of Großgörschen. In the darkness, notes the Russian historian Modest Bogdanovich, a French column ran into Blücher's infantry, which already had stacked its muskets in pyramids. The unexpected encounter disordered the Prussians.

After gaining their composure, they repulsed the enemy. Raddled by the audacity of the French, Blücher wanted to make them pay for it through a night attack.[14] Summoned to attend a council of war, the old hussar stormed off in a fury.

Around 9:00, Wittgenstein assembled the corps commanders to discuss retreating or remaining to renew the struggle on the third. During the ensuing debate, a strong voice shouted in the dark: "What! All the blood that has been shed here will be for nothing? Never at any time will I retreat, instead I will cut the French to pieces this very night; all of you who have said the word retreat should be ashamed of yourselves." Not recognizing the voice, the tsar's adjutant, General Ludwig von Volzogen, responded: "Who is that talking?" "Blücher," responded the general, with his arm in a sling.[15] Before departing, Wittgenstein gave an indignant Blücher permission to launch a night cavalry assault with the Prussian squadrons immediately at hand.[16]

Nine squadrons consisting of the Garde du Corps, the Brandenburg and East Prussian Cuirassier Regiments, and two squadrons of Brandenburg hussars advanced in two waves. Despite his throbbing wound, Blücher placed himself at their head; Gneisenau joined him. Without the aid of moonlight, the burning hulks of the villages provided the only light; the Prussians made for the flames of Rahna.[17] The charge routed one infantry regiment and came very close to another square, behind which stood the emperor himself. After regaining their composure, the French repulsed the horsemen. The Prussian charge proved to the French that the battle had not broken the Allies and that they could continue the fight. On a more practical note, the attack kept the imperial camp in a state of alarm throughout the night, denying the soldiers much-needed rest and facilitating the withdrawal of the Allied army.[18] During the charge, Gneisenau became separated from Blücher, who could not keep up with his troopers. Afterward, Blücher went to Pegau to have his painful wound treated, but Gneisenau "searched in vain for him on the battlefield." Unable to find his general, he joined the Kolberg Regiment just as the order to retreat arrived.[19]

The Allies marched from the battlefield refusing to believe they had been defeated. "The battle was pretty much a draw," wrote Clausewitz on 3 May, "and it is still not certain whether we have done well to withdraw."[20] They held Großgörschen against all French attacks. Despite criticism of the officer corps, the new Prussian army proved to be a worthy opponent in terms of combat effectiveness: the infantry sustained crippling losses but continued to press the imperials throughout the day; the artillery covered their attacks in a selfless manner; and the brigade cavalry exploited opportunities to support the infantry. An explanation for this performance can be found in Blücher. His personal influence, especially his ability to motivate both officer and soldier, is clearly apparent. On this day he richly repaid the confidence and trust that Frederick William, Hardenberg, Scharnhorst, Gneisenau, and the Prussian nation placed in him. His disposition, which alternated freely between emotional theatrics and stoic composure, combined with his defiance of death to strongly influence the troops.[21]

"Blücher was an actual troop commander in the best sense," judges the German General Staff historian Rudolf von Caemmerer, "a man of sharp mind and great human nature, who actually enjoyed taking risks. That he, in his burning hatred of Napoleon, opposed the superman without any fear was of infinitely more value in that difficult time."[22] In the saddle since 2:00 A.M., the stamina of the graybeard astonished his subordinates, driving them to emulation. He navigated the tumult of battle, participated in the hand-to-hand combat, lost considerable amounts of blood to a flesh wound that certainly weakened the seventy-year-old warrior, and continued to lead the troops from the front until dark. Throughout the battle of 2 May, he never relinquished the thought of achieving victory. In stark contrast to Wittgenstein's lack of fortitude, he again mounted in an attempt to seize victory in the eleventh hour through a nighttime cavalry attack. As one biographer notes, his performance bordered on the superhuman.[23]

A morose Blücher passed the night at a post house in Pegau, where he received medical treatment. He refused to accept that the situation demanded a retreat. For a short while, the memory of Auerstedt overwhelmed him. Gneisenau arrived around 2:00 A.M. After spending several hours at the general's side, he managed to convince the old man that no choice had been left to the Allies but to retreat. With Napoleon poised to double envelop the army, Gneisenau recognized the likely outcome of renewing the struggle on the third. He explained to Blücher that all the zeal and confidence with which the troops had fought would be squandered along with the hope of ultimate victory unless the Allies extracted themselves from this perilous position. Blücher understood as well but could not bring himself to accept retreat. Eventually, he grew calm, and "with that easiness with which Blücher in different circumstances knew how to find himself, he soon gave in to necessity."[24]

On the third Prince William delivered to Blücher the king's own handwritten praises for the performance of his troops at Großgörschen. "I instruct you to express my complete satisfaction and my thanks to the army for the great bravery and exertions with which it fought yesterday. Without exception, it achieved all that boldness and discipline are capable of achieving and brought the highest honor to the Prussian name. If the army persists in this spirit, it will overcome any adversity and certainly achieve the goal of its efforts. The greatest zeal will be employed toward increasing our forces to quickly replace yesterday's losses, which cost the enemy far more than us."[25] The following morning the general wrote a few lines to his wife, hoping to beat the media's coverage of the battle, which no doubt would include some information on his wound. "Despite any news you receive remain calm because although I received three balls and had a horse shot out from under me, I am not in any danger and remain in complete activity. I have gained sufficient satisfaction from attacking Napoleon twice and throwing him back both times. The battle was so murderous that both sides were exhausted and both had shortages of ammunition; the enemy lost double compared to us. But it has also taken many brave comrades from this world. Franz is again completely recovered. Before today I could not write anything since I had to march. I was shot in the rear, which hurts me very much; I will bring you the ball."[26]

Later that same morning, 4 May, Blücher ignored his throbbing wound and rode from Borna to the troops assembled on both sides of the road leading to Colditz. According to Nauck:

> At his approach, the order was given: "present arms!" Blücher shouted from afar: "Oh put down your muskets!" "Therefore: stack arms!" A general silence reigned. Blücher rode up and with a mighty voice addressed them: "Good morning, children. This time everything went very well. The French must have noticed with whom they now have to fight. The King himself thanks you." With these words he removed his field cap and waved it over his head. "No powder is left. For this reason, we will go back behind the Elbe. There, more comrades will arrive who will bring us more powder and shot, and then we will again take on the French, damn

their eyes! Whoever now says that we are retreating is a cur, a wretched chap! Good morning, children!" These words strengthened the soldiers, animated the officers, and stifled any backbiters. With a general shout of joy, the hero was greeted and the army followed him in retreat across the Elbe with absolute joy.[27]

Professor Steffens, who joined Blücher on the third, recounted:

For the first days, the retreat was continued over a sandy plain. Blücher was in the midst of the troops as they proceeded leisurely. The army was in such perfect order that many considered the retreat an unnecessary disgrace, and as this opinion was rather boldly expressed, it came to Blücher's ears, who thought it necessary to address the troops about it. This was my first opportunity of admiring his astonishing eloquence. The substance of the speech is generally known, for it was published to appease the whole army, as well as to tranquillize the people. "You are right," I heard him say, "you are not beaten—you maintained the field, and the enemy withdrew; his loss was greater than yours"; and then he explained to them all his reasons for not continuing the battle as well as those for retiring. I heard him repeat the same to various divisions as they came up; and while I praise the facility and noble simplicity of his expression, as well as the power of giving the same meaning in so many various forms, as often as he had to repeat it, I must confess that there was something besides the words that gave such effect to the address, and that much was owing to the appearance and the manner of the aged but powerful-looking man.[28]

Although accepting the situation, the circumstances behind the retreat did not sit well with the Prussians. Muted for the sake of unity, their anger and resentment festered over Russian leadership. The Prussians departed the battlefield believing the Allies had won the struggle; Frederick William's messages of congratulations to his corps commanders described the day of Großgörschen as a victory.[29] Blücher's adjutant, Ferdinand von Nostitz, provides poignant insight of the general's thoughts:

Since the beginning of the campaign, Blücher had no favorable opinion of Count Wittgenstein's talents as a commander, but he, the senior general, was placed under his orders. The battle of Lützen, in which the Prussian army did everything that courage and perseverance allowed to achieve a victory, had been lost and of course, as the general maintained, only because of the poor dispositions of the commander in chief and the inconsiderate inactivity on this day of entire units of the Russian army, namely the great majority of the cavalry. The general himself had been wounded, likewise his friend General Scharnhorst, who saw himself forced to leave the army. The beautiful hopes to baptize the War of Liberation with a glorious deed were frustrated, and the Fatherland had to again pay the price of all the horrors and devastations that are the inseparable companion of every theater of war.

All of this filled the general with anger and vexation, and the conviction that better leadership and a better utilization of the available combat power would make the defeat of the enemy unavoidable, had led to even more bitterness in his relationship with General Wittgenstein. Under his [the Russian's] leadership, he saw no salvation for the Allied cause and would have loudly expressed this conviction had he not been restrained by the concern of maintaining internal harmony at such a critical moment. Colonel von Both of the Prussian General Staff was assigned to Wittgenstein's headquarters—an officer who had neither the confidence nor the favor of the general and thus had no influence. The situation continued, as well as the circumstances that could cause the rupture that all painstakingly sought to avoid.[30]

Alexander's praise helped mitigate the ill feelings at Prussian headquarters, especially after Blücher received the tsar's 5 May commendation: "The bravery that you displayed in the battle on 2 May, your service, your devotion, your enthusiasm, and the brilliant manner in which you always placed yourself where the danger was the greatest, your steadfastness in not leaving the field although wounded, in a word, your complete demeanor during the battle leaves me with admiration and gratitude. As proof of my sincerity, I award you the insignia of the Order of St. George, Second Class. You have won this in a battle, through the conduct of the brave troops who you commanded and who so distinguished themselves. . . . [M]ay it also serve as proof to them of my personal affection."[31] On 6 May arrived a second extremely flattering letter with 300 St. George Crosses for Blücher's officers and men as well as a request for names of officers to be further recognized.

Despite his wound, Scharnhorst undertook an assignment to Vienna in the hope of goading the Austrians to declare war. Blücher would never again see his dear friend. Improper care of the wound led to Scharnhorst's death in June. Gneisenau replaced him as chief of the General Staff of the Prussian Army. In turn, Lieutenant Colonel Müffling assumed Gneisenau's position. Although more akin to Blücher in attitude, aggressiveness, and temperament than was Scharnhorst, Gneisenau never filled the shoes of his predecessor. Much has been written about the military marriage of Blücher, the seasoned, hard-hitting field commander, and Gneisenau, the erudite, conscientious chief of staff. But such descriptions are not accurate. In the case of Blücher and Gneisenau, the relationship more resembled the military marriage of two aggressive field commanders bereft of the system of checks and balances that Scharnhorst envisioned would be created by the relationship of commander and staff chief. Indeed, the relationship—famously and accurately depicted as a friendship based on devotion, mutual respect, understanding, support, patriotism, and a hatred of Bonaparte—thrived because the two evaluated success only on battlefield results, similar to their great adversary.

On 9 May Blücher's wound so pained and weakened him that the seventy-year-old needed rest. "After the battle, I remained on horseback for another six days," he explained to Amalie, "but this made my wound so bad that I was finally overcome, and had to submit to the King's demand to take it easy."[32] "The health of General Blücher becomes more doubtful with each day," reported the king's aide-de-camp, Major Oldwig von Natzmer, on the tenth. "Since yesterday, he has been suffering so much from his wound and from the return of an old ailment that he can travel only with great difficult lying down in a wagon."[33] On the ninth and tenth, Blücher had to be transported in a carriage.

By 14 May, he felt well enough to mount his horse. Overexertion sent him right back to the bed, which is where his old friend, Nostitz, found him later in the day "suffering from the wound he received at Lützen."[34] Yet after resting under Horlacher's care, the general's aged body responded. His first writings of May were in a letter to his wife on the fifteenth. "I write a few lines to calm you and Fritze. Because I had the good fortune of again meeting my old doctor, I feel so much better that yesterday and today I was able to ride my horse and no longer have any particular discomfort. It will be fourteen days to three weeks before my wound is completely healed, otherwise I am very well." Despite the "old ailment" that afflicted the general along with the wound, his frame of mind appeared sound. "We again stand with the enemy in sight and look forward to a second battle; I think it shall go no better for Napoleon than the first. We have completely recovered and are battle ready; our brave people are full of courage. Franz is in the rear of the enemy army, so is your brother; I believe they will do well. I have 1,000 thaler with me and I will send it to you. Franz has received the Iron Cross and your brother [command of] the squadron. Kiss Fritze and Amalie [Fritze's daughter] a thousand times. Don't be concerned, God stands by the good cause and you will receive good news. The French may bluster as much as they want, but they will not soon forget the 2nd of May."[35]

After Lützen, Wittgenstein decided against holding the Elbe and continued the retreat to the Spree River, where he took a commanding position just east of the river and the town of Bautzen. The imperials followed slowly and cautiously, engaging in almost daily combats with Wittgenstein's rear guard as both armies marched east. Unable to quench his thirst for battle, Blücher quenched his thirst for alcohol at Bautzen's Masonic lodge on the fifteenth. As usual, the spirits unfettered his tongue: "Since the days of my youth," roared the general, "I have been under arms for the Fatherland and have grown gray in the process: I have seen death in its most horrible forms and I have it in sight daily: I have seen homes burned and their inhabitants driven off naked and destitute and I could do nothing to help. Thus emerges the actions and rage of human beings in their impassioned state. Yet, gladly would I see the better person emerge from that wild throng; and gladly will I bless the hour, when I can draw my last breath with good, true brothers in a higher place, where a pure bright light shines upon us."[36] Blücher's optimism aside, his headquarters felt the gravity of the situation. "The fate of Silesia," recalled Nostitz, "perhaps of the entire Prussian state depended on the outcome of the battle about to be delivered here. The importance was felt by everyone, thus a serious, solemn mood generally reigned. The last encounter had not shaken the courage of the troops and they loudly expressed their strong desire to meet the expectations of the Fatherland as a whole."[37]

After spending two weeks at Dresden, Napoleon rejoined his army on 19 May, issuing orders to attack the Allied left wing and center on the twentieth. This would fix the Allies as Ney circled around their right wing to deliver the coup de grâce the following day. Napoleon needed twenty-four hours for Ney to be at full strength so he could slam the Allies like a hammer on an anvil. Remembering his experiences in Russia, the emperor could not allow his adversaries to slip away during the night.[38] Thus, he had to fix Wittgenstein without entangling himself in a full frontal assault on the formidable position east of the Spree. He spent the morning of the twentieth moving his pieces around the board to increase Wittgenstein's concern over his left wing. Although the general did not fall for the ruse, Alexander did. Ignoring his army commander's objections, the tsar transferred his few reserves to the left wing. Having had enough of being ignored, Wittgenstein napped under a tree.[39]

Around noon on 20 May, French artillery blasted the Allied positions while four infantry and one cavalry corps advanced toward the Spree. According to Crown Prince Fritz, no one believed the shelling indicated the opening of a battle; Blücher and his entourage calmly rode back to his headquarters for a quick lunch. En route, they learned that Allied headquarters was moving to a better location to observe the battle, but still the Prussians did not think the French would launch a general assault.[40] As Blücher and his staff sat down for a frugal meal, "the report arrived that Kleist's Russo-Prussian corps was very hard pressed and that our corps should thus advance to take him in. The meal was discarded, we mounted our horses. Blücher sent me . . . the order to immediately depart with the cavalry to support Kleist. The infantry followed and soon all stood in the designated battle order. Blücher rode with his entourage onto the Kreckwitz Heights from where the surrounding region could be surveyed."[41]

After observing the battle from the center of the Allied position somewhat northeast of Baschütz, the monarchs and Wittgenstein visited Blücher's command post for a short time. "The hill that he occupied," recollected Steffens, "and on which he was closely surrounded by his staff, is strongly impressed upon my memory, for we kept our post there the whole of that day and the following day. A bare rock of granite crowned the hill, and it commanded an extensive view, including the widespread field of battle. Every part of the field was clearly visible in the dazzling noonday."[42] Although the tsar again snatched the leadership of the battle from Wittgenstein's hands, the commander purportedly attempted to "meddle in Blücher's arrangements."[43] "After he had spoken much about the advantages of the position and the preparations that had been made,

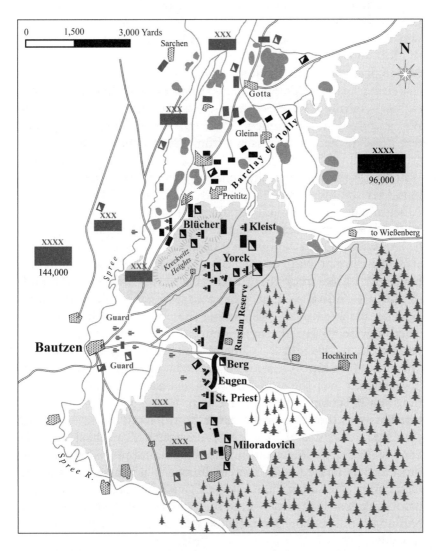

The Battle of Bautzen, 20–21 May 1813. Map drawn by Alex Mendoza.
Copyright © 2014 by the University of Oklahoma Press.

Wittgenstein turned to the General with the following words: 'If today you hold this position, tomorrow's battle will be won for us.' The general responded with some fierceness: 'I will hold the position today—this I give my word of honor—but tomorrow you must win the battle.' An enemy grenade, which exploded at the foot of the hill and shattered Captain Hüser's leg, brought an end to the conference."[44] Blücher and his staff remained in the maelstrom.

Firing ceased along Blücher's front around 8:30 that night; eighteen burning villages illuminated the sky.[45] Altogether, the Allies lost some 2,000 men: 800 from Miloradovich's corps and 600 Russians and 500 Prussians from Kleist's corps. French losses are not known.[46] The day's action won Napoleon the keys to Wittgenstein's forward position: the town of Bautzen and the crossings over the Spree north and south of the town. By pinning the Allies and deceiving them over the point of his attack, the emperor attained basic objectives through the simplest of means.

At dawn on the twenty-first, Marshal Nicholas Charles Oudinot attacked the left wing of the Allied position.[47] Blücher addressed his troops as they took their places: his fiery words evoked rounds of spirited "hurrahs" that echoed in the hills. He called for a defense to the extreme, designating the position as the "Prussian Thermopylae."[48] His II Corps occupied the numerous hilltops of the Kreckwitz Heights.[49] "General Blücher," recalled Gneisenau, "having before him the wood on the side of the Spree, could form no judgment over the strength of his adversary, and only some trifling affairs between the Jäger and light troops occurred in the valley. This was the state of the battle [until] about noon."[50] Around 9:30 A.M., Ney's divisions drove off General Michael Andreas Barclay de Tolly's forces on Blücher's right and moved south, taking Preititz, immediately east of Blücher's position.[51] "This village," adds Gneisenau, "lay between General Blücher and General Barclay, . . . consequently behind the right wing of General Blücher. Nothing could be more important to this general than possession of this village."[52]

Hard fighting enabled the Prussians to chase the enemy from Preititz around 1:00. After sustaining considerable losses, the French withdrew to Ney's position at Gleina's windmill hill.[53] Blücher now requested that the Russian general resume his former position, but to no avail.[54] Barclay refused to move up, although Kleist suggested that they jointly retake the Gleina hill.[55] After regrouping, Ney personally led three divisions against Preititz, forcing the Prussians to abandon the village around 3:00 and fall back on Belgern. With 32,000 men, the marshal turned west to storm the Kreckwitz Heights. Around this same time, two massive Guard batteries under Napoleon's personal supervision opened fire from the hills of Burk west of Blücher's position, spewing ruin on the Kreckwitz.[56]

Fighting on three fronts, Blücher requested reinforcements from Yorck, who held a position in the Allied center. Headquarters finally released Yorck to support Blücher, but time had run out.[57] As imperial forces closed on his position from the west, north, and east, Blücher became convinced that the heights could no longer be held. Even Blücher, one of the most intrepid characters in an epic filled with audacious warriors, concluded that further resistance there would lead to certain destruction.[58] Thus, sometime between 3:00 and 4:00, he chose "a well-ordered retreat over the danger of being completely destroyed by continuing the struggle against such superior numbers."[59] Knesebeck, who the tsar looked to for advice rather than Wittgenstein, suggested breaking off the battle.[60] Alexander refused; the Allied left and center held firm.[61] Around 4:00, as reports of Blücher's retreat on the right arrived, he reluctantly turned to Wittgenstein and said, "Commandez la retraite, je ne veux pas être le témoin de ce désordre" (Order the retreat, I don't want to watch this mess).[62] Although not an easy task, the Allied army executed its retreat in a noteworthy manner.

In the hilly terrain, Blücher's withdrawal went unnoticed by the French for some time. Yorck executed a brief counterattack to keep them off balance, but the imperials easily repulsed it. Regardless, the action provided just enough time for Blücher to slip away. Bursting upon the Kreckwitz hills from three sides, the imperials came face to face with each other: Blücher had escaped. Now jammed together in a narrow space, their columns crossed, and their tired men became less responsive to orders. Time was needed to reorganize before they could pursue the Allies over the broken terrain. To end the day, the skies opened and let lose a "hurricanelike" downpour to cleanse the soil of man's sad barbarity.

Blücher was not done. He fully expected to receive orders to continue the struggle. Ney's presence at Preitwitz made such ideas ludicrous, and the monarchs had no intention of lingering west of Weißenberg any longer than necessary. East of Purschwitz, the general awaited the order of the monarchs; their decision crushed him. "It was truly a sad sight," noted one of Yorck's staff officers, "when we found Blücher, dismounted from his horse, sitting on a rock in despondency."[63] By that evening, the emperor had 144,000 combatants on the battlefield facing 96,000 Allied soldiers. Wittgenstein's losses on the second day of Bautzen are estimated to be 10,850 men, including 2,790 casualties from Blücher's corps.[64] Bogdanovich cites 6,400 Russian and 5,600 Prussian casualties. One gun that had been shot to pieces was all the Prussians left on the battlefield. By comparison, French losses reached 22,500 men, including 3,700 missing. Napoleon could not interpret the Battle of Bautzen as anything but a disappointment.[65]

Moral victory aside, a second defeat worked against the shaky unity of the Russo-Prussian high command. Blücher became more forceful. Many times during the battle he had informed headquarters of the threat to his position. From his command post at Jenkwitz, Alexander remained obsessed with the threat he perceived to the Allied left. Wittgenstein begged the tsar to listen to reason. As the French advanced, Frederick William suggested that the left wing move up to support Blücher's position on Kreckwitz. By the time Alexander agreed, the situation had become untenable.

"Had I a free hand and had I not stood under the orders of a Russian general, our situation would be much better," Blücher later declared.[66] Nevertheless, the old Prussian warrior received as good as he gave. Some blamed him for the events on the twenty-first. His detractors pointed to the slight number of casualties in his corps among field-grade officers and none among the general officers. Worst of all, Blücher retreated. Starting at the top with him, the Prussian leadership came under fire. Soon, the searing comment could be heard: Blücher was a brave man, but no general. Extremely dissatisfied over the evacuation of the Kreckwitz hills, Alexander shared the discontent felt by his generals.[67] Blücher's supporters, led by Gneisenau and those who spent the second day with the general, steadfastly rejected the accusations. Nostitz described the effect of this controversy on Blücher:

> The loss of this second battle of course deeply and powerfully affected the disposition of the general, but the grit with which the troops fought and the confidence with which they evacuated the battlefield animated in him the anticipation of future victories and would have calmed him completely had not Colonel Both stated

his opinion at Allied headquarters that the premature retreat of the Prussian corps had caused the loss of the battle. Both's statement was communicated to Blücher by the staff officer Major Oppen.

This allegation angered the general even more because he was convinced that the corps was saved for the King only by using the favorable moment to retreat. He always spoke with the greatest bitterness over this accusation directed against him and at every opportunity conveyed his displeasure to its author.

As unjust as the accusation of breaking off the Battle of Bautzen too early was and how this cost us the engagement, it nevertheless had extremely disadvantageous consequences. Regrettably, this accusation aroused in the general's heart the suspicion that one was working to remove him from the command of the army. With pleasure, Count Wittgenstein heard from the mouth of a Prussian officer that not he [the count] and not the Russian army, but Blücher and his corps bore the guilt for the loss of the battle. The tsar felt likewise. The general's enemies and the large number of those who did not know how to appreciate his worth and his characteristics said that it was necessary to place the command staff in better hands. Even General Yorck expressed this sentiment: that he would harbor no misgivings obeying orders from the much more junior General Kleist and through this comment he designated the one who he felt to be most worthy to command the army. Blücher heard and knew all of this; it increased his anger, but it did not worry him; he did not think it possible to lose command.[68]

Like Lützen, Napoleon could not exploit the victory at Bautzen without cavalry. Despite how fast his men marched, infantry simply could not replace cavalry. For his part, Wittgenstein had no appetite for a general engagement and so did not utilize the favorable positions at Reichenbach or on the Landskrone in eastern Saxony. Instead, he continued the retreat to Görlitz, seeking to use the four bridges that spanned the Neiße in its vicinity to slip into Silesia. Departing Görlitz on 23 May, the Allies divided their army into two columns. Barclay led the northern wing, which consisted of his own corps as well as those of Kleist, Yorck, and Blücher. The southern wing, under Wittgenstein's direct command, contained the main body of the Russian army. Throughout the retreat, the tenacious Russian rear guard maintained steady contact with the imperials. Systematically destroying bridges as they crossed them, they forced Napoleon's soldiers to fight for each yard they gained.[69]

On 24 May the Allied army reached Bunzlau and Löwenberg on the Bober (Bobr) River, with Blücher's headquarters at the former. It continued the eastward trek a further sixteen miles on the following day to Haynau (Chojnów) and Goldberg (Złotoryja). Despite the retreat, Blücher maintained his sense of humor. Outside of Haynau, the brigade commander of his right wing reported that an enemy column had enveloped him and, with Napoleon at its head, was already in the rear of the Prussians. Of course, Blücher's entourage closed around the adjutant who delivered the report to hear the news. According to Müffling, Blücher asked the officer: "in whose rear, your commander's or mine." "In Your Excellency's," he responded. "Now say this to your commander," snapped Blücher, "I am extraordinarily pleased over this news, because now the chap will be in the right position for me to give him a special honor which can only come from my behind." The general's entire suite roared with laughter.[70]

Following Bautzen, Wittgenstein's position as commander in chief became completely untenable.[71] Per the count's request, the tsar decided that a change was needed. Alexander summoned Barclay de Tolly to Jauer for an interview on 25 May. The general advocated having the Russian army exit the theater for six weeks, returning only after it had recovered and received reinforcements and supplies in Poland.[72] By appointing Barclay the new Allied commander in chief on the twenty-sixth, Alexander endorsed his proposal to withdraw from the German theater.[73] Wittgenstein retained command of the left wing, while Blücher assumed leadership of all the troops of the right wing (the Prussian I and II Corps as well as Barclay's corps, now led by General Langeron); Kleist succeeded Blücher as commander of II Corps.

While Barclay met with Alexander at Jauer, Blücher took advantage of his absence to launch a bold cavalry strike against the pursuing French at Haynau on 26 August. Perturbed by the continuous retreat, which brought back the evil memory of the lesson he learned at Lübeck, Blücher wanted to attack simply to reinvigorate the troops. One British observer, Charles Stewart, described it as "one of the most distinguished cavalry attacks against solid squares of infantry that has been recorded during this war."[74] French losses amounted to 1,363 men, one-third of the division that Blücher victimized. Prussian losses totaled 226 men, including nineteen officers and 205 horses. Fifteen of the nineteen officer casualties were fatal, and 70 of the 226 men likewise died from their wounds.[75] Thanks to Blücher, fear of Allied cavalry increased French caution substantially.[76] The king later remarked to him: "You had a very favorable combat at Haynau, but it also caused great losses in my Guard." Blücher answered: "Your Majesty, I sincerely regret the loss of so many brave lads, but on such an occasion the head of the Guardsman is worth no more than that of the militiaman."[77]

Before the advance could resume, on the morning of the twenty-sixth, Marshal Macdonald dispatched numerous detachments to round up hundreds and perhaps thousands of marauders and stragglers.[78] These ugly indicators—marauding and straggling—of an army pushed beyond exhaustion could be found in every imperial corps. Although not the ultimate factor in Napoleon's decision to accept an Austrian proposal for an armistice, this development as well as the realization that he simply could not substitute infantry for cavalry and expect to win a decisive victory, led the emperor that day to authorize Armand de Caulaincourt to begin negotiations at the small village of Neudorf just south of Liegnitz, with Kleist representing the Prussians and General Paul Shuvalov the Russians. Meanwhile, French foreign minister Hughes Maret held talks with the Austrian Ferdinand von Bubna behind the Grande Armée. Napoleon instructed Caulaincourt to negotiate an armistice that would last at least two and one-half months so that he would have sufficient time to rebuild his cavalry. In addition, he warned him not to agree to a peace congress while hostilities continued. As the line of demarcation, Napoleon proposed the Oder.[79]

Unsure if the tsar would follow Barclay's suggestion to withdraw from the theater, Frederick William took steps to reestablish a Prussian field army separate from that of the Russians. In a letter from Breslau dated 28 May, he appointed Blücher commander of the Army of Silesia: Yorck's I Corps, Kleist's II Corps, and the Silesian Landwehr Corps. Blücher also received command of Bülow's corps, which eventually became III Corps.

Despite the armistice negotiations, Barclay's retreat continued on the twenty-ninth. Blücher's headquarters moved through Jauer, halting seven miles north of Schweidnitz (Świdnica). He gave the troops some rest that day while patrols reestablished contact with the imperials to monitor their movements. By nightfall, the 90,000 men of the Grande Armée stood on a southwest–northeast axis extending twenty-three miles from Jauer through Eisendorf

(Snowidza) to Neumarkt (Środa Śląska). Gneisenau felt certain Barclay would turn and fight.[80] Yet as Blücher predicted, the new commander in chief refused to exploit the situation. Plans for a third battle fizzled under Barclay's concern for the debilitated condition of the Russian commands.[81] On 31 May the army moved into a position southeast of Schweidnitz to engage in unit reorganization. Barclay transferred all Russian troops assigned to Yorck and Kleist to Russian units, while the Prussian Guard left II Corps to be part of Grand Duke Constantine's Russian Guard Corps.[82]

East of Jauer, at the tiny village of Gäbersdorf (Grzegorzów), the French, Russian, and Prussian envoys agreed to halt operations and hostilities for thirty-six hours at 3:00 P.M. on 1 June. The representatives believed this preliminary measure would provide time to reach a more comprehensive agreement. While the French maintained their positions, the Allies continued the retreat on 3 June. Barclay intended to withdraw across the Oder with or without the Prussians. He already decided to have the army reach the left bank of the river by the fifth. Unless Alexander intervened, Frederick William would be faced with a decision of profound importance and unfathomable difficulty. News that an Austrian proposal to extend the armistice to 20 July had been accepted at Pläswitz (Poischwitz) on 4 June spared the king from having to choose between following the Russians or facing Napoleon alone.

CHAPTER II

THE ARMISTICE

We know little of Blücher's activities during the nine-week
armistice, which he passed recuperating at Strehlen (Strzelin).
Stubbornness and bravado had denied his body the opportunity
to heal from the wound sustained at Großgörschen. In the quiet
Silesian town, he finally allowed his body and mind to rest. In mid-
June, when Stein paid a visit, Blücher still had not fully recovered.
His old friend found him "in the process of healing, but otherwise
the General is healthy, he speaks of nothing but battles and fighting."[1] One week later Blücher wrote: "With God's help it resumes
in four weeks. We will go forward with even greater strength than
we did when we started the war and it will go very well."[2] Nostitz
recalled that after the wound finally healed, Blücher "flourished in
the best health. . . . The conviction that Prussia would put a glorious end to the imminent struggle had mastered his soul to such a
degree that he spoke of it with a confidence that removed all doubts
and concerns. Offered an opportunity to address the troops, he did
it with his unique power of speaking, animating in the hearts of his
subordinates the faith that they soon would be victorious and liberate the Fatherland."[3]

The Sixth Coalition's decision to accept Austria's suggestion to
hold a peace congress at Prague alarmed the general. "Once more,"
he stressed to Hardenberg's assistant and author of the king's
famous "An Mein Volk" proclamation, Staatsrat (Privy Councilor)
Theodor Gottlieb von Hippel, "tell the State Chancellor: for heav-
en's sake no peace!"[4] Müffling explained that those who opposed
the armistice feared "it could be the prelude to a dishonorable
peace, which Napoleon, with his well-known cunning, would talk
us into if we negotiated with him." Thus, the belief became widespread that whoever supported the armistice also desired a harm-
ful peace.[5] Steffens captured the mood of Blücher's entourage: "[G]
reat anxiety was caused by the truce. . . . It was feared that he
[Napoleon] would use the time to influence the Austrian court,
and there were fears that many in the Russian and Prussian courts

were still secretly attached to his interests. There were rumors of a proposal from Napoleon that the Elbe should be the boundary of his territory. At Blücher's headquarters the determination was fixed and strong that he should be treated with only on the other side of the Rhine."[6] As the armistice dragged on, Blücher grew impatient. Arguments in favor of the armistice buying time for the Austrians to complete their mobilization had little influence on him. "I am starting to lose faith in the Austrians," he confided to Gneisenau.[7]

Despite Blücher's zeal, word soon reached him that his detractors pressed the king to remove him as commander of the Army of Silesia. "The cabal has drawn their daggers," he warned Gneisenau. "They will not get me to retire before I see whether we will fight again or not—whether we will remain together with our allies or we will detach ourselves from them." In addition, the fact that the promotion board passed over Franz for lieutenant colonel aggravated him, but he managed his outrage. Blücher attributed this slight to royal displeasure: "Once again the king has labeled my own son a total agitator."

News about Scharnhorst's health did not appear optimistic. For some time, reports indicated an unfavorable turn for him. During the journey to Vienna, he neglected to properly care for his wound even after gangrene set in. "It does not go well with our brave Scharnhorst," Blücher informed Gneisenau on 29 June. "I'd rather lose a battle than lose Scharnhorst!"[8] Little did he know that his fifty-seven-year-old friend was already dead, having passed the day before at Prague. Although Blücher took the death very hard, he weathered the crisis without a return of his debilitating psychological problems. By mid-July, he appears to have accepted the hand that fate had dealt. A letter to Gneisenau on 24 July captures his melancholy thoughts over Scharnhorst's death: "Now come to me soon, my friend; our friend is dead, thus it is necessary that we proceed together, hand in hand, then I will not fear any cabal defying us. I have a great desire to start a subscription to build a statue of our Scharnhorst in the garrison church at Breslau; Minister Stein has requested that I do this. Write me your thoughts over this if you cannot come here directly."[9]

On 12 July Frederick William issued an order titled "Formation of the Army." Accordingly, it established three corps under Yorck, Kleist, and Bülow. Many units were swapped, but eight days later the king finalized the organization that the army maintained until the end of the war. Aside from confirming the three corps designated for field operations, he decreed the formation of a fourth. Commanded by Tauentzien and consisting primarily of Landwehr, it would conduct the sieges of enemy-held Prussian fortresses. Frederick William likewise made official the formation of the Royal Guard, which had been divided between I and II Corps, into a special brigade separate from the army corps.[10]

Like Scharnhorst, Gneisenau believed only Blücher could command this Prussian army. Thanks to the great confidence that Hardenberg placed in Gneisenau, Blücher's interests received effective representation in the king's councils. In addition, Stein, who probably placed considerably more faith in Blücher than did Hardenberg, diligently lobbied Alexander to trust the Prussian general. Yet neither Blücher nor Gneisenau attended the campaign-plan negotiations that took place at Reichenbach (Dzierżoniów), Gitschin (Jičín), and Trachenberg (Żmigród). Gneisenau's many responsibilities with the Landwehr precluded him from participating, while Blücher's absence does support the claim that his contemporaries attributed little to his understanding of the operational art of war. Rather than either the nation's foremost soldier, Blücher, or Scharnhorst's heir-apparent, Gneisenau, the king's adjutant general, Knesebeck, led the Prussian delegation at the talks. According to Müffling, Knesebeck served as Frederick William's "strategist," and Alexander also held his military opinions in high esteem.[11]

As July slowly crawled by, Blücher's recurring financial problems brought headaches, especially as he came to grips with his own mortality. "My dearest and worthy friend," he wrote Hippel. "In the enclosed is a letter that I urgently request that you give to our patron [Hardenberg]. Please support my plea; you will find it reasonable. If I do not settle my affairs before the expiration of the armistice, I cannot distress over the estates further; just think, if I am shot dead or overcome by ailments, what misanthropic advice from Wilken will help my wife and children manage? Really, I am so irritated with this Jewish fellow that I would like to put him to work on the redoubts at Schweidnitz."[12]

Nevertheless, news from Spain kept Blücher going. Arthur Wellesley, the future duke of Wellington, defeated a French army commanded by Joseph Bonaparte and Marshal Jourdan at the 21 June 1813 battle of Vitoria. "Long live Wellington," he raved to Gneisenau, "we must fight the French the same way; we can do this if we use all our strength."[13] Thus began his deep respect and admiration for Wellington, a general who in Blücher's eyes measured victory by the same criteria as he: results on the battlefield. Over the next few years and across the miles, this perceived kinship with Wellington increased and would contribute mightily to Blücher's decisive actions in 1815.

Around the same time Blücher learned of Wellington's victory, instructions arrived from Barclay de Tolly on 23 July to have the army ready to march at one hour's notice. As noted, the belligerents agreed to extend the armistice, yet Barclay had not received official confirmation. Blücher gushed with excitement over this order and Russian assurances over the quality of their troops. "The Grand Duke Constantine . . . requested that I go with him to Grottkau [Grodków] to inspect the cavalry, but I said that at the moment I would not dare be absent for one day." He expected the king, who had been held up by the Oder's high waters, to arrive at any time.[14] "Thank God I have completely recovered and look forward with longing to the resumption of the feud," he wrote a friend. "Our army, 90,000 men strong, is in good condition. All are armed and the men play their part well. Gneisenau has earned great fame for the organization. The speed with which they were brought into readiness surpassed all human expectation. I do not believe the armistice will last. The armies are very formidable."[15] "I hope in three weeks to again be like thunder and lightning," he declared to Hippel.[16] Unfortunately for the old war warrior, confirmation reached Silesia on 26 July that the armistice had been extended to 10 August. All troops returned to their quarters, but few believed peace would be attained.

Frederick William and Alexander decided that the Prussian and Russian armies would not fight as separate entities, but instead their various corps again would be integrated in multinational armies. This decision, made before the Austrians joined the Coalition, did not sit well with Blücher, who continued to harangue Hardenberg through Hippel. "Can't it be arranged," he queried, "so that our troops play their own part and the Russians play theirs? If so, I will comfortably wager my head on a good outcome; but together it will not go well. Our allies demand too much from us; we have done the most possible, but the Russian Guard and their heavy cavalry are conserved like ammunition chests while all else is spent."[17]

After Austria declared in favor of the Coalition, the Allies finalized their plans to field three multinational armies. Austria's foreign minister, the cunning Klemens Wenzel von Metternich, insisted that an Austrian be named Allied commander in chief. Consequently, Field Marshal Karl Philipp, Prince of Schwarzenberg received command of the Coalition's main force, the Army of Bohemia. Its 254,404 men included 127,345 Austrians, 80,879 Russians, and the 43,301 Prussians of II Corps and the Guard Brigade.[18] The Army of North Germany, commanded by the former French marshal and current crown prince of Sweden, Jean-Baptiste Bernadotte, consisted of the 73,648 Prussians of III and IV Corps as well as 29,357 Russians and 23,449 Swedes. In addition, Bernadotte held nominal command over Russian general Ludwig George von Walmoden's 28,000-man corps, which consisted of various contingents (the Russo-German Legion, Lützow's Freikorps, Mecklenburgers, Swedes, Hanoverians, and Hanseatic Germans) and stood in Mecklenburg to observe Davout at Hamburg and the Danes in Holstein. The Army of Silesia received the Prussian (I Corps) and Russian forces that remained in that province: 104,974 soldiers and 339 guns.[19]

On 8 August, two days before the official expiration of the armistice, the Allies made the final decision to award Blücher command of the Silesian Army. "For the next campaign," recalled Nostitz, "the monarchs assigned a command to the General that exceeded his boldest expectations: at the head of three army corps, he could and would achieve the results that he thought would justify the trust and shame the doubters; he spoke of nothing else."[20] Gneisenau also received orders to assume his post of chief of the General Staff of the Prussian Army at Blücher's headquarters, where he would likewise serve as staff chief of the Silesian Army.

Many suspected Blücher would receive command of that army, but the "cabal" had not been silent. Yorck briefly held pride of place but lost out to Blücher because of his tactlessness and the likelihood that his sour mood would poison relations with the Russians.[21] "With almost unqualified disapproval," many senior Russian and Prussian officers labeled Blücher a poor choice.[22] His previous health problems and old age caused concern, not to mention the general's infamous love of gambling and drink. His detractors doubted that he could handle the demands and responsibilities of commanding an army. Many raised the issue of "whether Napoleon could ever be defeated by generals who were strangers to his method of warfare."[23]

Blücher's reputation fell prey to the argument that his military experience belonged to a time long passed. Not only had the

general learned an art of war that Napoleon had rendered obso-
lete, but he also earned his spurs in relatively subordinate positions. He never received a formal military education, which many
believed to be indispensable for the leadership of a large army,
and his rough exterior did not lead anyone to believe he possessed
even a general education: he could not write a decent report or even
spell correctly.[24] In a long career that spanned six decades, he never
commanded a large combined-arms army. The nineteenth-century
Russian General Staff historian Bogdanovich adds that "Blücher's
most glorious success came in a period when he commanded only
detachments of a few thousand men."[25] Few believed that he really
understood strategy or tactics.[26] Specifically, his critics questioned
if the general, the brazen hussar, had any understanding of the use
of infantry and artillery.[27] German historian Gustav Droysen claims
that Yorck, Blücher's own countryman, saw in him "only the
'Hussar General,' who an eccentric party had managed to build up
to a popularity that extended far beyond his abilities. Since the time
of the retreat to Lübeck, Yorck had the opinion that Blücher was
completely dependent on his entourage."[28] "The staff appointed to
keep him straight," judges Maude, "Gneisenau, Müffling, Rühle
von Lilienstern, and Scharnhorst, were all held to be interlopers or
reformers by the classic old survivors of the Frederician period, of
whom Yorck was the most typical."[29]

Regardless, Alexander wanted the Army of Silesia commanded
by a Prussian general; Frederick William designated Blücher for the
post, and the tsar agreed. As to why Alexander wanted a Prussian
to command an army that contained twice as many Russians,
Bogdanovich only states, "since Prussia's existence depended on
the Silesian Army, command over this army was conferred to the
Prussian field-commander Blücher." The Russian staff officer and
future military historian Alexander Mikhailovsky-Danilevsky
wrote: "The Allies proposed that the Silesian Army be given to
General Barclay de Tolly rather than General Blücher, but the tsar
did not agree. Through this he proved that in the impending war
he did not seek fame for Russian arms, but only dependable support for the general peace."[30] Despite Blücher's retreat at Bautzen,
his bravery at Lützen and Haynau had made a considerable impression on Alexander. He possessed attributes that compensated for
his lack of formal schooling and experience. His indomitable will
and unfailing courage inspired men. Blücher provided an example

that motivated the soldiers to accomplish incredible feats. He had tremendous presence of mind and the ability to make quick decisions based on the information available. If he despised planning and looking at maps, at least he had the good sense to allow his staff to handle such matters. Above all, he hated Napoleon and wished for nothing more than to live long enough to see his overthrow.[31]

According to the Coalition's blueprint for operations—the Trachenberg-Reichenbach Plan—the three Allied armies would form a wide arc around the imperial forces occupying Saxony. The main tenet of the plan called for avoiding battles with Napoleon by retreating before the emperor's onslaught. As Napoleon could personally command only one army at a time and thus could directly challenge only one Allied force at a time, the other two armies would attack his flanks and lines of communication while the threatened army refused battle but induced the emperor to pursue it.[32] The Allies assumed he would evacuate Silesia, unite all his forces on the left bank of the Elbe, and turn against either Schwarzenberg or Bernadotte. Based on this supposition, Coalition strategists assigned the Army of Silesia a secondary role based on the conviction that Napoleon would withdraw his forces from Silesia for a general advance to either Bohemia or Brandenburg. As enemy forces presumably retreated from his region, Blücher would delay and continuously harass them with his light troops but always avoid a battle with superior forces. At the same time, his army would protect Silesia and, in unison with General Levin August von Bennigsen's Army of Poland, guard Russian communications. The Allies concluded their meetings with the understanding that upon commencement of hostilities, Schwarzenberg's Army of Bohemia would advance into Saxony along the left bank of the Elbe, while Bernadotte immediately crossed that river between Magdeburg and Torgau to march on Leipzig.[33]

Barclay de Tolly, the former Allied commander in chief and now the ranking commander in Silesia, summoned Blücher and his staff to Reichenbach on 10 August for the verbal conveyance of the ultra-secret Trachenberg-Reichenbach Plan. Barclay described three general principles that should guide the Army of Silesia. First, Blücher would move toward the enemy. Second, he could never lose sight of his adversary; if the imperial army in Silesia advanced against Schwarzenberg, he had to arrive to support the Bohemian Army at the same time. Third, Blücher had to avoid all decisive actions and not engage a superior enemy force: only the Bohemian and North German Armies could take the offensive and "proceed decisively."[34] The reason for the cautious role assigned to the Army of Silesia can be found in the decision to augment the Austrian army with a large contingent of Russians and Prussians as well as the fact that the Silesian Army did not come together until the eve of the campaign. At the time the Allies made this decision, they expected that the Russian and Prussian troops remaining in that area would number no more than 50,000 men. Although the actual strength of the Silesian Army doubled this figure, the fast pace of events provided no time to officially modify the army's task.[35]

Specifically, should Napoleon advance toward him, Blücher would withdraw his main body toward the Neiße River and his respective wings along the Silesian mountains and the Oder. His task would be to draw the French deep into Silesia. Should the general thus facilitate Schwarzenberg's advance, he had to pursue the imperial army in Silesia as soon as it broke off the chase and turned around to confront the Bohemian Army. If Napoleon allocated his main force to operations in Saxony or Brandenburg, Blücher would advance. If Napoleon directed his main strength against the Army of North Germany, which was rumored to be likely, the Bohemian Army would pursue along the left bank of the Elbe while the Silesian Army moved down its right bank. Thus, according to Müffling's account, Barclay informed the Prussians that only Schwarzenberg's army would take the offensive by advancing from Bohemia to Saxony by way of Teplitz (Teplice). "Consequently," Müffling states, "the main goal was to avoid being defeated and to arrive at the right moment to participate in a general battle on the Elbe."[36] Blücher also received instructions to dispatch Streifkorps to disrupt imperial communications. Interestingly, Unger claims that Barclay authorized Blücher to occupy the neutral zone that separated his forces from the imperials in Silesia before the expiration of the armistice.[37]

The general listened quietly, shaking his head doubtfully. Rumors already had reached him regarding the supposed role of his army. According to one of the king's adjutants, the army would remain in Silesia to serve as an observation corps. This immediately affected morale: "We actually envied," commented one of Yorck's staff officers over the departure of Kleist's corps, "our comrades who were marching to the great army in Bohemia as well as to the Army of North Germany because we believed that these strong armies would deliver the main blows."[38] Barclay de Tolly's lecture appeared to confirm the Silesian Army's passive task. When he finished, Blücher stood up and offered his resignation. Explaining to a shocked Barclay that he had no choice but to decline such an assignment, the general refused to be limited to a strict defensive. Urging him to find an officer better suited for this strategy, Blücher declared that he had no understanding of the art of Fabius, that all he knew was to rush straightforward, and that he did not fear a numerically superior enemy. As a cavalryman, he knew the difficulties of determining the size of an enemy force before an encounter, even in his own country with exceptional cavalry. Barclay maintained that Blücher misunderstood the instructions and that the Prussian could take the offensive under favorable circumstances: "An officer in command of an army of 100,000 men can never be tied down absolutely to the defensive; thus, if a good opportunity arose, he could attack and defeat his enemy."[39]

Countering, Blücher demanded a written addendum or at least a statement from the monarchs approving this modification. If they did not agree with this condition, then they could find another assignment for him. Uncomfortable with the idea of amending instructions he had received from the monarchs, Barclay deferred signing any document himself. Blücher responded by saying that he thus accepted command of the Silesian Army based on this modification of his instructions and urged his commander to notify Alexander and Frederick William. "It is probable that General Barclay de Tolly did inform the sovereigns of this conversation," notes Müffling, "but nothing more ever transpired on this subject, either verbally or in writing. As Blücher received no other assignment from the sovereigns, he took it as a sign of their approval of his views, and considered himself authorized to act quite independently, according to circumstances. This result gives considerable importance to this conference at Reichenbach."[40] In his mind, Blücher had unfettered himself from both a Fabian strategy as well as any reproach of having overstepped his bounds should he suffer a setback. This marks the beginning—before the campaign even opened—of Blücher's refusal to submit to Allied headquarters. Like Napoleon, he would settle for nothing less than complete freedom of action, especially the independence to seize the initiative.

Totaling 104,974 men on paper, Blücher's army consisted of Yorck's I Corps (38,484 men), Langeron's Russian army corps (34,551 men), General Fabian Gotlieb von der Osten-Sacken's Russian army corps (18,353 men), and General Guillaume-Guignard St. Priest's Russian army corps of 13,586 men, temporarily commanded by General Petr Pahlen.[41] In round figures, the Army of Silesia neared 74,000 infantry and 24,000 cavalry, with Yorck's corps containing 31,000 infantry and 6,000 cavalry; Langeron's 25,000 infantry and 7,000 cavalry; Sacken's 9,000 infantry and 8,000 cavalry; and St. Priest's 9,000 infantry and 3,000 cavalry.[42] Not utilizing the successful model provided by Napoleon, the Silesian Army contained no artillery or cavalry reserves at the army level for the commander's immediate use. Blücher eventually worked around this shortcoming after much trial and error.[43]

On 9 August the general moved his headquarters to Schwentnig (Świątniki Górne). Forming the right wing of the Silesian Army, Sacken's corps stood just east of Breslau on the right bank of the Oder. Between Breslau and Schweidnitz, Yorck's corps formed the center. As the left wing, Langeron's corps camped north of Schweidnitz at Jauernick (Stary Jaworów). On the extreme left wing, Pahlen's corps took post in the mountains by Landeshut (Kamienna Góra), having the task of maintaining communication with Bubna's Austrian 2nd Light Division of 6,000 men on the opposite side of the Riesengebirge.[44]

On the eleventh Blücher reviewed Yorck's corps.[45] That night bonfires illuminated the skies from Prague to Reichenbach, signaling the end of peace negotiations. Hardenberg gave Blücher and Gneisenau a farewell dinner at Breslau before the two officers left to join Yorck's corps at the foot of the Zobtenberg (Mt. Ślęża, Sobótka)—a lone mountain jettisoned north from the foothills of the Riesengebirge—overlooking Zobten. Blücher dispatched Steffens to Landeshut with the task of reconnoitering the French on the upper Bober with Pahlen's advance guard. Steffens claimed that Blücher believed the right wing of the French army would advance east from the Bober to Schmiedeberg (Kowary), only thirty-five miles west of Schweidnitz.[46]

To better cover his communication with Dresden, maintain his mastery of the Elbe, and capitalize on Allied mistakes, Napoleon initially chose to start the fall campaign on the defensive. He assembled the Guard, three cavalry corps, and I, II, VI, and XIV Corps between Bautzen and Görlitz, while in Silesia he planned for III, V, XI Corps and II Cavalry Corps to withdraw to Bunzlau after the expiration of the armistice. This would allow him to concentrate almost 270,000 infantry and 30,000 cavalry between Görlitz and Bunzlau to oppose what he believed to be the main Allied army: 200,000 Russians and Prussians in Silesia.[47] Based on the actions of the Allies in May, Napoleon counted on them accepting battle in Silesia, where he planned to decisively defeat them before the Austrians could launch a serious operation against Dresden.[48] While his larger left wing assumed the defensive, he entrusted his right wing to Marshal Oudinot, who would conduct an offensive against Berlin with IV, VII, XII Corps and III Cavalry Corps supported by Davout's XIII Corps coming from Hamburg. After defeating the Army of North Germany, this French "Army of Berlin" would liberate the Oder garrisons and advance to the Vistula, wheeling behind the Allied main army, which would be reeling eastward after being defeated by the emperor. Should Bernadotte somehow check the Army of Berlin, Napoleon could easily dispatch forces from the Silesian theater to Brandenburg to finish the job.[49]

In Silesia, III, V, and XI Corps and II Cavalry Corps formed a strong advance guard to oppose Allied forces there.[50] The foremost troops held the western edge of the neutral zone from Liegnitz to Goldberg along the Katzbach (Kaczawa) River and on the upper Bober at Löwenberg. West of this army group stood Napoleon's main body—the 150,000 men of the Guard; I, II, and VIII Corps; and I, IV, and V Cavalry Corps—between Bautzen, Görlitz, and Zittau. South of Dresden, the 26,000 men of XIV Corps guarded the Elbe from Königstein to the Saxon capital. In Lower Lusatia, the majority of Oudinot's 70,000-man Army of Berlin assembled at Luckau to advance against the Prussian capital in unison with Davout's 30,000 men as well as 15,000 men from the garrisons of Wittenberg and Magdeburg. As we will see, the Coalition's decision to form its main army in Bohemia as opposed to Silesia caught Napoleon by surprise. Regardless, it was Blücher's pressure that opened the door for the Bohemian Army to reach Dresden.

Four rivers and their major points of passage would dictate the course of operations in the Silesian theater. From east to west, the Katzbach, Bober, Queis (Kwisa), and Neiße Rivers—all part of the western watershed of the Oder—presented impassable barriers that required bridges for all arms to cross. The fifty-seven-mile stretch of the great east–west highway between Liegnitz on the Katzbach and Görlitz on the Neiße represented the extent of the theater's width.

Major population centers naturally provided the best means for the contending armies to get across the rivers. Blücher's crossing of the neutral zone on 14 August prompted the retreat of the imperial units posted along the Katzbach and the Bober.

The hallmark of Blücher's operations in August and September would be the seriousness with which he maintained constant contact with imperial forces in Silesia. In a 12 August note to Sacken, he emphasized the importance of the Cossacks following hard on the heels of the enemy, "whereby I assume, that if no other means for the crossing are available, they will swim across the Oder." Four days later Gneisenau stressed in his instructions to Yorck's advance-guard commander, Lieutenant Colonel Friedrich Ludwig von Lobenthal, "if possible, half of your cavalry must reach the enemy today and send the news it obtains back to you through stationed orderlies. Tomorrow, the cavalry will remain close to the enemy and follow him step by step."[51] Blücher and Gneisenau recognized the gravity of their task: they had to be able to reach the Elbe at the same time as their immediate adversaries to prevent Napoleon from achieving overwhelming mass against one of the other Allied armies.

Like Napoleon, French commanders in Silesia believed that they faced the Coalition's main army, having not yet learned of the departure of 100,000 Russians and Prussians for Bohemia.[52] Their initial movements occurred haphazardly because the emperor had yet to name a commander in chief. He remedied this situation on 15 August by assigning Ney command of III, V, VI, and XI Corps and II Cavalry Corps. His instructions called for the marshal to withdraw west to Bunzlau if the enemy's main force advanced through Liegnitz on the great east–west highway. Should Blücher drive from Jauer through Goldberg, Napoleon directed him to retreat to Löwenberg.[53] On the sixteenth and seventeenth, Ney concentrated the divisions of his III Corps as well as II Cavalry Corps at Liegnitz. All departed west for Haynau as part of the general movement across the Katzbach on 17 August.

Napoleon initially expected that the Russo-Prussian army he pursued to the Oder in May would advance west from Silesia toward Saxony, while the Austrian army in Bohemia invaded Saxony either along the right bank of the Elbe or through Zittau.[54] He knew of the Trachenberg-Reichenbach Plan but did not think the Coalition would dare leave Silesia only weakly guarded by sending considerable forces to Bohemia.[55] Due to the fortifications around Dresden, he had little concern over an Allied operation along the left bank of the Elbe. Napoleon reached Bautzen at 2:00 A.M. on the sixteenth. Later that day he received intelligence from spies that Barclay de Tolly and Wittgenstein led the Russian army from Silesia to Bohemia. There, it would join Schwarzenberg's army, which had moved to the left bank of the Elbe. In addition, Blücher's army—a mere 50,000 men, according to the emperor's estimate—started driving west from Breslau.[56] Blücher's violation of the six-day suspension of hostilities following the expiration of the armistice irked Napoleon, who referred to it as "la conduit infâme des Prussiens (the infamous conduct of the Prussians)."[57] The support of the Russian and Prussian commissioners at Neumarkt did little to console him.[58]

Although the emperor wanted confirmation that the Russians had left Silesia, the news of Barclay de Tolly's departure allowed him to tighten his plans and take the offensive. To threaten Prague and occupy Schwarzenberg, he would have 100,000 men advance to the Bohemian frontier, with II and VIII Corps actually moving onto Austrian soil.[59] Napoleon planned to personally lead II and VI Corps as well as I Cavalry Corps to Silesia to commence the campaign by destroying Blücher's *small* army, thus removing the threat it posed to the rear of both his Grande Armée in Saxony and Oudinot's Army of Berlin. "Je marcherai en force pour enlever Blücher (I march in force to wipe out Blücher)," he assured Marshal Macdonald.[60]

Although opting for the offensive, Napoleon still remained determined to follow his plan to move his headquarters to Görlitz, where he would unite I, III, V, VI, and XI Corps, while I and II Cavalry Corps held a forward position at Bunzlau. According to his estimates, this would produce an army of 130,000 to 140,000 men that, combined with the five divisions of his Guard, would total 180,000 men at the Görlitz–Bunzlau line.[61] From there, he sought to "debouch on Blücher and Sacken . . . who, it appears, are marching on my troops today and after I have destroyed or routed these corps the balance will be restored." Upon destroying the Coalition's army in Silesia, he planned to either march on Berlin, depending on Oudinot's success, or drive through Bohemia to reach the rear of the Austro-Russian army if it invaded Bavaria.[62] He left Bautzen on the evening of the seventeenth, making for Reichenbach en route to Görlitz on the great east–west highway.

At 7:00 on the morning of the nineteenth, Napoleon dispatched a letter to Ney explaining that "according to all available news, the Russian army has entered Bohemia; it is certain that Barclay de Tolly himself arrived there on the fifteenth and every indication is that Wittgenstein, with a corps of 40,000 men, was at Bohemian-Leipa on the seventeenth. All of this suggests that while there are few Russians in Silesia, there is the Prussian army, which seems to maneuver in the direction along the mountains, intending to win Zittau to establish communication with the Austrian army through this great pass."[63] That night he received Ney's report over the determined advance of the Silesian Army.[64] Although he did not know exactly where Schwarzenberg would lead the Army of Bohemia, Napoleon decided to continue his plan to march against Blücher, defeat him, and then rush back to Dresden.[65]

CHAPTER 12

SILESIA

On 18 and 19 August, III and V Corps as well as II Cavalry Corps of Ney's army completed their march *west* by reaching Bunzlau and Löwenberg on the Bober. Baffling Allied spies, VI Corps concluded its march *east* by reaching Bunzlau. Upriver, XI Corps crossed the Bober and continued *west* toward the Queis. From Görlitz on the afternoon of the twentieth, Napoleon wrote his marshals: "At 5:00 [P.M.], I will be at Lauban. The main business at this moment is to unite and march against the enemy."[1] He then led the Old Guard and I Cavalry Corps to Lauban, where he passed the night planning his offensive against Blücher, whose army the emperor accurately reassessed to be 80,000–90,000 strong and posted along the Queis.[2] He intended to attack Blücher on the following day, the twenty-first: "I plan to fight tomorrow, from noon to 6:00 P.M."[3] French intelligence still incorrectly placed Kleist with Blücher's army, and the emperor did not know the exact location of Ney's army nor if imperial forces still held Bunzlau.[4] Nevertheless, it is difficult to believe one contemporary's claim that Napoleon "was extremely uneasy on being informed that he had to deal with three generals full of energy and experience: Blücher, Kleist, and Langeron, who possibly might prevent his junction with his marshals."[5] As of 4:00 on the afternoon of the twentieth, he felt confident, writing his foreign minister, Hughes Maret, at Dresden that the upcoming battle "probably would be a very successful event."[6]

At midnight, headquarters issued the attack disposition for the twenty-first. Ney received instructions to cross the Bober at Bunzlau at 10:00 A.M. If he found less than 30,000 men before him, Napoleon instructed him to pursue briskly and then cut sharply south to Giersdorf (Żeliszów) to form the army's left wing. Napoleon's belief that the mass of Blücher's army stood on the upper Bober is stated as the reason for Ney's march southeast rather than due east.[7] Marshal August Frédéric Marmont's VI Corps would advance between Ney and Löwenberg on Napoleon's left. General Jacques Alexandre Lauriston's V Corps followed by Macdonald's

XI Corps would cross at Löwenberg to form his right. Napoleon expected VI Corps and the Old Guard to reach Löwenberg at noon.[8] The arrival of the news that during the previous afternoon, Ney had ordered the evacuation of the Bober and a retreat to behind the Queis unsettled imperial headquarters during the predawn hours of the twenty-first.[9]

As for Blücher, during 15–20 August, he chased Ney westward from the banks of the Katzbach River to the Bober. He chomped at the bit to smash the French forces at Bunzlau and Löwenberg through a rapid offensive across the Bober. By nightfall on the twentieth, he expected all of the Army of Silesia to reach the right bank of that river: on the left Pahlen at Hirschberg (Jelenia Góra), on the right Sacken east of Bunzlau, and Langeron and Yorck in the center facing Löwenberg.[10] He personally reconnoitered the French position at Löwenberg from the Luftenberg Height on the right bank of the Bober around sunset on the twentieth. Eager to rush forward, a trace of uncertainty seized him as Barclay de Tolly's instructions echoed in his ears. His report to Frederick William that day states: "In accordance with my instructions, I follow the enemy army with caution so I can avoid becoming entangled in an uneven contest before the Bohemian Army can begin its operations."[11] Langeron subsequently reported that spies and deserters claimed that Napoleon had reached Löwenberg on the afternoon of the nineteenth. Blücher refused to fall for a French ruse. In addition, word from his forward patrols confirmed his belief that Ney would continue the retreat but defend the Bober to conceal his movements. His assumption that the advance of the Bohemian Army on the left bank of the Elbe would soon affect imperial forces in Silesia fed this supposition. Moreover, a message from Sacken that arrived in the evening confirmed the evacuation of Bunzlau by enemy forces.[12]

At 7:00 on the morning of 21 August, infantry could be seen massing at Löwenberg. The French apparently received considerable reinforcements. Around 9:00 the Prussians clearly heard the shout go up in the imperial camp, "Vive l'Empereur!"—Napoleon had arrived. Blücher returned to the Luftenberg to see for himself. From their strong position, the Prussians believed that only a flanking maneuver posed a threat to their army. Should Ney cross the Bober at Bunzlau to attack Sacken, or cross farther south to drive between Sacken and Yorck, Blücher and Gneisenau planned a general retreat to avoid "a battle under unfavorable circumstances." If the

French launched a general offensive, the Silesian Army would retreat behind the Katzbach to "provide time for the Bohemian Army as well as the North [German] Army to . . . begin their main drives." If the French withdrew, they intended to "follow with caution," though also with enough boldness to slow their retreat. Silesian-army headquarters assumed that by detaining imperial forces in Silesia, "the operation of the Bohemian Army on the left bank of the Elbe, designated for the 25th, can begin in earnest."[13]

The imperial camp remained quiet, but in the distance the Old Guard could be seen marching up from Lauban. Regardless, Blücher returned to his headquarters. The 1:00 hour struck. With it came the roar of artillery as the French launched their assault from Löwenberg. It appeared Napoleon planned to fix Blücher's center and turn his right.[14] In accordance with his plan, Blücher ordered a general retreat. The loss of fifty-one officers and 2,095 men reflected the difficulty of conducting a fighting withdrawal before the emperor.[15] Retreat never sat well with the man who eventually earned the epithet "Marshal Forward," but at least Blücher understood the circumstances. The same could not be said of the average soldier. Concern over morale prompted the general to take action. That night he issued an order of the day that explained his decision to the troops: "The enemy wants to force us into a decisive battle, but to maintain our advantage we must avoid it. Therefore, we will go back in a manner that causes him to lose time so the combined Russian, Austrian, and Prussian army gains time to break out of Bohemia and cross the Elbe in his rear, while the Crown Prince of Sweden advances from the Mark and also attacks him in the rear. Thus, the Allied army entrusted to me will view itself as not being forced to retreat, but as voluntarily retreating to lead him [the enemy] to his doom."[16]

The Prussians knew Napoleon could not pursue them indefinitely and overextend himself from Dresden. As long as the Bohemian Army advanced toward the Saxon capital, French operations in Silesia would be limited. Blücher believed that as soon as Napoleon sensed the Silesian Army would not accept battle, he would depart for Saxony to attack Schwarzenberg. To provide time for the latter's massive army to advance, Blücher needed to distract the emperor for as long as possible. He suspected that Napoleon would mask his eventual departure for Dresden through a tactical offensive by his marshals.[17] Thus, the dilemma: because the

situation could change at any hour as a result of Napoleon's departure, the Silesian Army had to maintain constant contact with the
French to be able to immediately react to the emperor's absence.
Yet this meant executing a methodical, fighting withdrawal in the
presence of the master of operations, of the *manoeuvre sur les derrières*, and of the *manoeuvre sur position centrale*. Blücher simply
could not flee before advance guards but had to find a way to force
the imperials to deploy for battle, determine if the energy they displayed indicated the emperor's presence, and then react accordingly
by either continuing the retreat or assuming the offensive.

The complexity of this task cannot be underestimated, particularly considering Blücher's penchant to attack. With no choice but
to surrender the initiative, his opponent's actions would dictate his
own. If the French advanced, he had to retreat. If the French withdrew, he had to follow. If they stood still, he had to determine the
reason for their halt: was it temporary or was it the prelude to an
extensive operation? For this reason, the cavalry of his advance
guards traversed the area between the Katzbach and the Bober three
times within twenty-four hours. To accurately assess the adversary's
intent, Blücher's army had to remain in close contact at all points
along its front. This required exhausting marches and countermarches regardless of the time of day, with apparent indifference to
the needs of man or horse. Although well provided with intelligence,
errors in judgment could be made just as easily while on patrol as at
army headquarters. At times Blücher's orders appeared haphazard or
contradictory to his corps commanders, who never appreciated the
difficulty of a mission he never felt inclined to explain.

Blücher passed his first major test. Overcoming his instinct to
attack the French army, especially one commanded by Napoleon
himself, he complied with the tenets of the Trachenberg-
Reichenbach Plan. According to Gneisenau, headquarters proceeded
according to a very basic principle: as soon as the French threatened one flank, the army broke off the engagement and retreated.[18]
Moreover, Blücher accepted the principles of Allied strategy, fixing Napoleon's attention on himself to provide Schwarzenberg and
Bernadotte time to cross the Elbe and reach Saxony from Bohemia
and Brandenburg respectively. Indeed, he accomplished much by
boldly advancing. Not only did he throw Ney's army into disarray but he also brought the emperor to Silesia with his Guard, VI
Infantry Corps, and I Cavalry Corps. The general certainly cannot be

faulted for the inability of the Bohemian Army to exploit Napoleon's absence from Saxony.

Blücher never lost sight of the best way to liberate Silesia: by crushing the French army in a decisive battle, which could be sought as soon as the emperor departed. Retribution for Jena-Auerstedt remained ever present in his mind. For now, though, he conducted a slow, fighting withdrawal. Not for one moment did the general believe the retreat would be indefinite, again because he understood how the operations of the two other Allied armies would facilitate those of his own according to the Trachenberg-Reichenbach Plan. Six weeks later the lethargy and blatant inactivity of Schwarzenberg and Bernadotte would change his mind. Fortunately for the Allied war effort, he did, for it made possible the Battle of Leipzig.

The tenets of the Trachenberg-Reichenbach Plan called for all three Allied armies to converge on Leipzig. However, Allied headquarters, convening at Prague, learned that Napoleon had left Dresden on the fifteenth and proceeded to Bautzen, presumably to continue through Görlitz to Silesia. Preliminary thoughts focused on the Bohemian Army taking a position to threaten French communications running west from Dresden through Leipzig, but the news that Napoleon had gone to Silesia made it imperative to undertake a more immediate demonstration to relieve some of the pressure on Blücher. Thus, a drive on Dresden surfaced as an afterthought to assist the Silesian Army. On 22 August the Allied "Grand Army" crossed the Saxon frontier in four columns. Yet nothing significant occurred in this theater for three days.[19]

As for French forces in Silesia, Napoleon continued his quest to destroy Blücher or at least engage and defeat the salty Prussian. Word reached imperial headquarters that the general had been wounded the previous day.[20] With the Guard, VI Corps, and I Cavalry Corps resting at Löwenberg, III, V, and XI Corps as well as II Cavalry Corps pursued the Army of Silesia eastward between the Bober and the Katzbach on 22 August.[21] Napoleon followed V Corps toward Goldberg. On receiving news of Blücher's retreat across the Katzbach, the emperor returned to Löwenberg, "his mind being rendered easy with respect to the success of his arms, which had made him gain ground on that side."[22] Statements from prisoners allowed the emperor to draw a conclusive picture of Blücher's army. It consisted of three corps, with Langeron commanding five divisions and Sacken three. In a letter to Maret, he did not recognize

Blücher as the commander in chief, stating only that Blücher and York commanded one corps of four divisions. The entire Army of Silesia amounted to twelve divisions, which Napoleon estimated to total 80,000–90,000 men. "What is good is that their infantry is extremely poor," he judged. Yet something had to be afoot to account for the army's retreat. Instead of attributing Blücher's withdrawal to Allied strategy, he chalked it up to ineptitude and fear. "It seems that their Army of Silesia advanced with more speed than the Allied plan called for and under the belief that we would retreat across the Elbe. They believed that all they had to do was pursue because as soon as they saw our lead columns resume the offensive, terror took them, and we are convinced that their leaders want to avoid a serious engagement. The whole Allied plan was based on assurances from Metternich that we would retreat across the Elbe, and they are very confused to see otherwise." The only negative aspect of the campaign thus far proved to be his subordinates' lack of confidence in their abilities. Left on their own, his marshals and generals seemed to always exaggerate their difficulties.[23]

With Blücher running, Napoleon's attention immediately switched to Bohemia. Contrary to most histories of the campaign, he had not received cries for help from Marshal Laurent de Gouvion St.-Cyr at Dresden. On the night of 22–23 August, Chief of Staff Marshal Alexandre Berthier issued orders for the Guard, VI Corps, and I Cavalry Corps to return to Görlitz.[24] Leaving behind III, V, and XI Corps and II Cavalry Corps—100,000 men according to Napoleon's calculation—the master formed the Army of the Bober, naming the forty-eight-year-old Macdonald its commander.[25] He then summoned Ney to join the imperial entourage, thus transferring command of III Corps to General Joseph Souham; General Maurice-Etienne Gérard took the helm of XI Corps in place of Macdonald.[26]

Although Macdonald would prove an utter failure as an independent commander, the instructions he received from the emperor and Berthier cannot be considered either difficult or complicated with one important exception. Napoleon did not want Blücher to exploit the gap between Macdonald's left and the Oder to threaten the Army of Berlin or hug the Reisengebirge and squeeze past his right to reach Lusatia and Saxony. Should Blücher take the offensive, Macdonald received the authority to reciprocate. Napoleon encouraged the marshal: if he posted the army in accordance with these instructions, he could explode from Löwenberg or another point and beat back any enemy offensive. Basically, the Army of the Bober would shield operations against the Bohemian Army in Saxony. Equally important, it had to protect the rear of Oudinot's Army of Berlin as it drove on the Prussian capital. Macdonald simply had to hold Blücher at the Bober River long enough for Napoleon to dispose of the Army of Bohemia and return to Silesia with overwhelming forces. But his instructions, confirmed by a second letter from Berthier, referred to the position on the Bober as a defensive one. Should Macdonald lose a battle on that river, he would retreat to the Queis, which had to be held at all cost.

On the twenty-third Napoleon initiated tactical strikes across the Katzbach to drive Blücher beyond the Wütende (Raging) Neiße and to keep the old Prussian guessing. Although the emperor prescribed the building of numerous fortifications on both the Bober and the Queis, he wanted the Army of the Bober to remain mobile and ready to march. All corps would receive rations for eight to ten days. As Macdonald's main supply depot, Lauban had to be entrenched and defended by redoubts on the surrounding hills.[27] For its first assignment, the army received the task of driving across the Katzbach.[28] But Macdonald was unsure of his next move. Neither Napoleon's letter nor Berthier's dispatch made it clear whether Macdonald should continue to drive the enemy beyond Jauer and then return to the Bober or if he should first build the entrenchments to fortify the Bober position and then meet Blücher on a prepared battlefield. Napoleon's oversight in this matter led to the failure of his plan—a failure that ultimately would cost him Germany.

Commenting on the refusal of the Army of Silesia to accept battle, Napoleon informed Maret that nothing would be more fortunate than "an enemy march on Dresden, because a battle would then occur."[29] Upon reaching Görlitz late in the afternoon of 23 August, he finally received such news. Writing at 11:00 P.M. on the twenty-second, St.-Cyr explained that a Russian corps (Wittgenstein) had debouched through the Peterswalde Pass with what appeared to be the entire Austrian army following. Always looking to deliver a knockout blow, Napoleon welcomed Schwarzenberg's advance on Dresden as an opportunity rather than a setback. He and Berthier made the arrangements. Napoleon promised St.-Cyr that he would soon be at Dresden with 200,000 men.[30]

Little did Napoleon know that as he made these plans, the Prussians of the Army of North Germany were successfully defending Berlin. As dawn broke on 23 August, the Army of Berlin converged on the Prussian capital. Tauentzien's IV Corps held General Henri-Gatien Bertrand's IV Corps at Blankenfelde, while Bülow's III Corps engaged General Jean-Louis Reynier's VII Corps at Großbeeren, a quaint village eleven miles south of Berlin. Prussian losses numbered 159 dead, 662 wounded, 228 missing, and six destroyed guns. Bülow's troops captured fourteen guns and fifty-two caissons. Reynier's two Saxon divisions lost twenty officers and 1,918 soldiers, while the French 32nd Division sustained 1,138 casualties.[31] Bernadotte claimed that Bülow's soldiers fought with the greatest courage.[32] Despite the low body count, Oudinot ordered a headlong retreat that did not stop until his army reached the safety of Wittenberg on the Elbe. The victory at Großbeeren saved Berlin and provided much-needed confidence for the Prussians.

Early on 23 August Blücher's headquarters made preparations both to defend Goldberg and hold the line of the Katzbach.[33] Later in the day French columns seemed to appear out of nowhere.[34] "All of these circumstances indicated that by executing my disposition I could not avoid a battle," wrote the general, "and since under the current circumstances I did not know the true strength of my adversary, I decided to remain at the Katzbach and await the deployment of the enemy's forces."[35] By 10:00, three separate engagements raged in the Goldberg area. With French columns reportedly marching against his right, Blücher recognized that retaking Goldberg did not warrant the risk of becoming embroiled in a general battle. Moreover, prisoners claimed that Napoleon remained with the army.[36] Although it tore at every fiber of his being, he ordered the army to retreat in the general direction of Jauer. Fortunately for the Allies, an intense pursuit ended at Prausnitz (Prusice). Altogether, the Silesian Army sustained over 4,000 casualties during these engagements.

Instead of pursuing the Silesian Army on the twenty-fourth, the Army of the Bober remained on the banks of the Katzbach. The fact that Macdonald's army simply did not do much that day excited the Prussian commander. To Blücher, the energy displayed by the imperials in Napoleon's presence at Löwenberg had fizzled out. No appreciable French movements could lead to only one conclusion: the emperor had departed, presumably in response to the Bohemian

Army's advance on Dresden, the push at Goldberg serving to mask his exit, just as Blücher predicted. Some members of his suite speculated that Napoleon would not have ended the pursuit after attaining such paltry results.[37] Blücher shook his head. Around 7:00 on the evening of 24 August, army headquarters issued orders for the next day. If contact with the imperial army could not be made, Blücher wanted to know where it went. Regardless of whether the French marched south to utilize the mountain passes into Bohemia or marched west toward Lusatia and Saxony, the Army of Silesia would follow.[38]

Blücher's 25 August letter to Amalie is worth citing in full because it perfectly captures the general's understanding of his role and that of his army:

> The tide has turned! For three days the Emperor Napoleon attacked me with all his forces and tried everything to bring me to battle; I successfully thwarted all of his plans. He retreated yesterday evening; I will follow him immediately and I hope Silesia is now safe. I have saved Berlin by drawing the Emperor of France here and delaying him for seven days, during which the Grand Army [of Bohemia] invaded Saxony from Bohemia. The Crown Prince of Sweden is marching from Berlin to likewise invade Saxony. Both large armies advance in the rear of the enemy, while I now follow close on his heels and will attack him wherever I find him. They will bless us in Berlin. I am well and very pleased that I have led the great man around by the nose; he will be very angry that he could not force me to fight. Both sides have suffered casualties; the enemy has lost three times as many as us. We have already captured 1,500 men; the enemy has taken less than 100 from us.[39]

By 9:00 A.M. on the twenty-fifth, the information at Blücher's disposal appeared very persuasive. On his right, the French apparently had marched west to Bunzlau. In his center, the enemy remained at Goldberg, while nothing of the imperials could be found on his left. Blücher ordered the army to cross the Katzbach and from there planned to lead it to the Bober. "Two different plans of the enemy are already ruined," he assured his corps commanders. "He has lost time that is precious to him. If we quickly follow him and act with energy, this latest plan will be foiled as well."[40] Three hours into the advance, new reports arrived from the forward cavalry patrols. Large imperial forces remained at Goldberg

and several columns—Souham's III Corps—could be seen marching *east* from Haynau to Liegnitz.[41] By 1:00, Blücher had heard
enough and ordered an immediate halt due to the threat posed by
Souham to the army's right. All advance-guard infantry posts held
their positions along the Katzbach, while headquarters remained at
Jauer. Blücher and Gneisenau concluded that the imperials would
maintain a defensive position north of the river. Having no idea
that Macdonald intended to take the offensive, they proceeded
with their own.[42] Some accounts mistakenly claim that Blücher
convened a council of war. Per his tradition, the general did speak
openly with Gneisenau in the presence of his staff officers, especially those charged with writing and delivering orders. But in 1817
Blücher himself refuted this claim of a council of war, telling an
associate "that a dumb chap had just written a book" on the history
of the Katzbach "in which he said that before the battle he [Blücher]
had held a council of war. This was not true—never in his life had
he [Blücher] held one."[43]

Macdonald eagerly prepared to move against Blücher's suspected position north of Jauer on the twenty-sixth. From Goldberg
he issued lengthy, complicated, and partially unclear instructions at
11:00 on the night of the twenty-fifth. For the next day, Gérard's XI
Corps would form the center of the army and proceed from its positions around Goldberg to Jauer. On the right wing, V Corps would
take the military highway southeast from Goldberg to Jauer. On the
left wing, Macdonald wanted III Corps marching by 7:00 "to pursue the enemy in the supposition that he is retreating on Jauer."
General Horace François Sébastiani's II Cavalry Corps would depart
at 7:00 A.M. to move on the town, using the Bunzlau–Jauer road.[44]

Consequently, Macdonald directed his army to descend on Jauer
in two groups separated by the Katzbach and Wütende Neiße (hereafter referred to as the Neiße). For good reason the locals referred
to the latter watercourse as raging. With the water level constantly
increasing thanks to the summer rains, the Neiße could become an
impassable obstacle in a matter of hours. The few bridges found in
the tiny villages along its banks hardly provided the opportunity for
mutual support between Macdonald's right and center. No doubt
to the marshal's horror, the situation that unfolded led to the iso-
lation of the 27,000 men of II Cavalry Corps and elements of XI
Corps on the plateau east of the river. There, they faced 55,000 men
under Yorck and Sacken. On the other side of the Neiße, Lauriston's

corps—reduced to 17,000 thanks to the detachment of one division—confronted Langeron's 24,000 Russians.

To be fair to Macdonald, his operation complied with Napoleon's instructions, and although advancing, he did not seek battle. Perhaps being better acquainted with Blücher would have triggered the idea that the impetuous Prussian might launch his own offensive. Such a consideration can be made only with the benefit of hindsight. As of August 1813, Blücher remained noted as the man who had recklessly squandered the Prussian cavalry at Auerstedt, the man who had surrendered at Lübeck, and the septuagenarian loudmouth who the emperor had cashiered. If the Russians doubted his abilities, how could the French not? Indeed, he had followed the French when they retreated west but fled before the emperor. If the Prussian commander's marches and countermarches infuriated and dumbfounded his subordinates, they must have looked just as erratic to the French as those of Brunswick in 1806. Although Langeron and Sacken remained in contact with Macdonald's wings, what reason did the marshal have to assume they would not follow Blücher's center and retreat deeper into Silesia?

Heavy downpours on 26 August limited visibility to a few hundred yards.[45] Both armies moved toward each other without knowing it, but the similarities end there. Preparing for battle, Blücher concentrated his army. Preparing for envelopment and pursuit, Macdonald extended his. By 1:00 P.M., the lead elements of II Cavalry Corps, followed by 2nd Brigade from 36th Division of XI Corps, drove Yorck's advance guard across both the Katzbach and the Neiße. This much the Prussians knew: having met gutsy yet brief resistance, the imperials pursued what they perceived to be Yorck's rear guard without having any idea of the proximity of the entire Silesian Army. With no intention of retreating, Blücher planned to allow the enemy to ascend the plateau and then drive them over the cliffs. He and Prince William rode before the front of each battalion, inciting the men and demanding that they attack with cold steel rather than try to fire their muskets in the rain.[46] "My brave lads," shouted Blücher, "this day decides it! Prove to your king and to your country that your courage is equal to your devotion. Prove it, I say, at the point of your bayonets. Look yonder, there's the enemy. Now march and prove yourselves to be gallant Prussians."[47]

On the plateau Yorck and Sacken faced 2nd Brigade, 36th Division, XI Corps; 8th Division, III Corps; and two of Sébastiani's

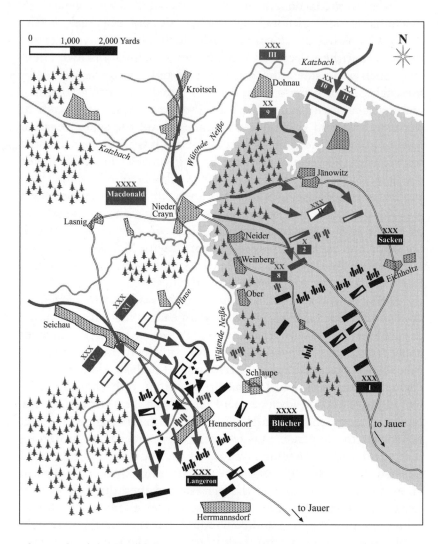

The Battle of the Katzbach, 26 August 1813. Map drawn by Alex Mendoza. Copyright © 2014 by the University of Oklahoma Press.

cavalry divisions as well as thirty-six guns (Sébastiani's horse batteries and the heavy battery from 36th Division). There, the contest quickly ended thanks to a massive Russo-Prussian cavalry
attack. "A great cavalry combat began with alternating results,"
described Gneisenau, "mostly occurring in one long line. The venture hung in the balance for a moment."[48] From three directions,
the Russo-Prussian cavalry fell on Sébastiani's troopers.[49] Blücher
then gave the order for the general advance; with sword drawn, he
placed himself at the head of Yorck's Reserve Cavalry. Behind the
horsemen, Yorck led the thick attack columns of infantry. As this
corps moved north, Sacken's infantry likewise advanced. While
additional artillery unlimbered, the Russian cavalry linked with
the right of the Prussian horse. Around 6:30 P.M., II Cavalry Corps,
8th Division, and 2nd Brigade collapsed. Only a few imperial battalions, aided by the onset of darkness, managed to descend the
plateau in order. On the height's northern edge, Yorck and Sacken
combined to drive the late-arriving divisions of III Corps—9th,
10th, and 11th—across the Katzbach at the end of the battle.

While French sources contest the notion of a rout on the plateau
itself, Macdonald's units certainly disintegrated in the defiles and
valleys. Infantry, cavalry, guns, and caissons rushed down the steep
gorges leading from the plateau to the Neiße valley and from there
to the Katzbach. In the chaos, wagons and guns overturned, horses
lost their footing and crashed down the slopes, and men crawled
over each other seeking to escape. In a short time wreckage blocked
the defiles. Leaving behind their weapons and equipment, survivors
struggled to reach the bridges and fords of the Neiße and Katzbach.
Many soldiers and horses tumbled down the slopes to the valley
floor. Dazed and injured, they now found themselves trapped as ruin
fell from the sky in the form of enemy shells. Even the elements
appeared to conspire against the French. Within a matter of hours,
the constant, streaming rains transformed the shallow mountain
streams into raging rivers; the swollen Neiße and Katzbach became
ferocious tempests. Their maelstrom swept away the men who
attempted to wade across. The bridges in the neighboring villages
could not be crossed safely by the masses that attempted to push
across. Hundreds fell into the water and drowned in their panic-
stricken attempts to swim. Thousands wandered along the banks of
both rivers seeking a way to cross, with many men and horses eventually finding death beneath the torrents.

Meanwhile on Blücher's left wing, Lauriston's V Corps actually overwhelmed Langeron's Russians. From the plateau, the weather prevented Blücher and his staff from gaining a complete overview of the situation, but the Russians apparently could not hold their position. Blücher and Gneisenau became indignant: Langeron appeared to abandon one good position after another.[50] Around 6:00, Blücher ordered Yorck's 1st Brigade to cross the Neiße and operate against Lauriston's rear and flank. Informed of the Prussian success on the plateau, Langeron ordered a general counterattack. Despite the Allied pressure, Lauriston retained a good portion of the field. Combat continued until around 11:00 P.M.; imperial forces remained on the field until as late as 4:00 A.M French reports claim that no one left this sector of the battlefield with a sense of defeat. In fact, in his report written two days after the battle, Lauriston maintained that his "position at the close of the day was beautiful; we were masters of the heights and could have remained there."[51]

The exhausted Russians and Prussians remained where they stood when night fell and the battle ended. Blücher's losses as a result of combat are not known, but they were slight in consideration of the victory. Two days later on the twenty-eighth, he reported that "perhaps never before has a victory been purchased with so little blood; for although I still have no report over the losses, at most they amount to 1,000 men." The account to the king stated that battlefield trophies amounted to thirty-six guns, 110 caissons, two medicine wagons, four field forges, and 1,200–1,400 prisoners, including numerous officers.[52]

To avoid a second battle, Blücher and Gneisenau wanted to finish Macdonald's army before it escaped from Silesia. This was not to be. Although command and control in the Army of the Bober teetered on the brink of collapse, the French managed to outdistance Blücher in part due to the flooding of Silesia's rivers. The euphoria of the victory quickly turned to disgust. "Regarding our cavalry," complained Gneisenau privately, "only few could be assembled. They did not pursue because they no longer understood their craft . . . ; in part the commanders could not be found, others were not in the mood."[53] Writing Blücher's official report to the king on 28 August, the staff chief retracted his claws: "The darkness of night and the obstruction of all defiles by cannon and powder wagons hindered the execution of this order [to pursue]. . . . The Wütende Neiße and the Katzbach rose so much that the former was very difficult to cross and the latter thoroughly impossible. Despite all of the Army's efforts, it could not pass the Katzbach at Goldberg and Liegnitz on the 27th because of the continuous rains."[54]

Macdonald hoped to outrun the Allies and reach Lusatia, where he could reorganize his army close to Napoleon's legions in Saxony. Resorting to a survival-of-the-fittest mentality, he accepted the harsh reality that thousands would be lost to straggling and desertion.[55] Yet if he could save the core of his army, he stood the chance of escaping the emperor's fury. Allied detachments led prisoners away by the hundreds as Macdonald's army started to disintegrate.[56]

Believing that Schwarzenberg's offensive into Saxony would prompt Napoleon to abandon Dresden and fall back to Torgau, Blücher directed the Army of Silesia to Görlitz. He wanted to drive on Dresden, finishing off the Army of the Bober in the process. During the night of 28–29 August, the rains of the past three days finally ended, and beautiful weather returned. Gneisenau proudly tallied the results of the hunt: "Some 80 guns, 300 caissons, mobile forges, etc., 11,000–12,000 prisoners are the trophies that we have ripped from the enemy. The swollen waters halted our pursuit, but we followed as best we could. The consequences of the terror that seized the enemy are visible everywhere on the roads from the Katzbach to the Bober: corpses stuck in the mud, overturned wagons, and heaps of prisoners. I hope to completely destroy Macdonald's army. Long live the King! His throne is now safe and we will leave national independence to our children. Now I go to sleep happy."[57]

Early on the morning of 31 August, Sacken's corps led the crossing of the Bober at Bunzlau. By nightfall, only the Queis separated the main bodies of the two armies.[58] As for Blücher, that day found him feeling "very sick." Nostitz tells us that normally the general's "health left nothing to be desired. His strong, powerful body endured with ease all the fatigues of war and although seventy-years-old his spirit maintained a juvenile cheerfulness. He accompanied all marches on horseback."[59] Learning about the loss of one of his staff may have contributed to his condition. "But all luck is accompanied by misfortune: my good Count Moltke is no more. I sent him to the King with news of the victory, where he certainly would have received a considerable reward. On the way, he drowned in high water [the Elbe] and here we grieve his loss."[60]

That same day, 31 August, rumors reached Blücher of a great French victory over the Allies at Dresden. A captured Westphalian officer confirmed the news. As noted, the Bohemian Army moved across the Saxon frontier on 22 August; Wittgenstein stormed the imperial camp at Pirna on the twenty-third. As the Silesian Army engaged the Army of the Bober on the twenty-sixth, Schwarzenberg assailed Dresden. Amid the fighting, Napoleon unexpectedly arrived with the Guard to repel the assault. During the night, II and VI Corps came up, increasing imperial combatants to 135,000 men against 215,000 Allied soldiers. Continuing the battle on the twenty-seventh, Napoleon enveloped Schwarzenberg's left, crushing two Austrian corps. With the French also steadily working around his right, Schwarzenberg ordered a retreat. The Army of Bohemia withdrew after losing 38,000 killed, wounded, and captured along with forty guns. Although the imperials sustained far fewer casualties in comparison (10,000), decisive victory again evaded Napoleon. Despite having adequate cavalry, illness forced him to leave the field rather than personally direct the pursuit.

Blücher and Gneisenau immediately recognized the gravity of the situation: Napoleon would leave the pursuit of Schwarzenberg to his marshals and return to Silesia with reinforcements. So much for the emperor's retreat to Torgau. Still on the thirty-first, Blücher instructed his corps commanders to have their light cavalry maintain constant contact with the enemy. Their advance guards would remain within supporting distance of the forward cavalry, but their main bodies would not cross the Queis until further notice. Recognizing the need to again proceed with caution, Blücher wanted his advance guards to continue to pressure and unsettle Macdonald's forces. At the same time, he halted the main body of the army and concentrated his corps. In this way, he planned to be battle ready when Napoleon arrived with superior forces.

On the morning of 1 September, Blücher repeated the order for the cavalry to maintain contact with the enemy and for the infantry of the advance guard to follow at a suitable distance. "The army has a day of rest," concludes the order. "At 6:00 this evening will be a religious service, both by the corps as well as by the advance guards. Following it, a victory volley will be fired from large and small cannon to celebrate the victory on the Katzbach and the liberation of Silesia."[61] With his advance guard in Upper Lusatia, Blücher's first campaign as an independent army commander ended with clearing Silesia of imperial forces in just fourteen days. To celebrate, the jaunty commander issued a general order, courtesy of Gneisenau's quill:

> Silesia is now liberated from the enemy. To your courage, brave soldiers of the Russian and Prussian army under my orders, your exertions and perseverance, your patience in the endurance of hardships and shortages, I owe the good fortune of having ripped a beautiful province from the hands of a greedy foe.
>
> During the battle at the Katzbach, you defiantly opposed the enemy. Courageously and with the speed of lightning you broke forth from behind the hills. You spurned attacking him with musket fire; without hesitating, you advanced, your bayonets drove him over the steep valley edges of the Wütende Neiße and the Katzbach.
>
> Since then you have waded through rivers and swollen streams. Some of you have suffered from the shortage of provisions because washed-out roads and lack of wagons prevented their transport. You have struggled with cold, wet, and privations, and some of you lack sufficient clothing; nevertheless, you did not grumble and you pursued your defeated enemy with effort. I thank you for such praiseworthy conduct. Only he who combines such characteristics is a natural-born soldier.
>
> In our hands are 103 cannon, 250 caissons, the enemy's hospital equipment, his field forges, his flour wagons, one general of division, two generals of brigade, a large number of colonels as well as staff and other officers, 18,000 prisoners, two eagles, and other trophies. The remainder of those who faced you in the battle at the Katzbach have been so seized by the terror of your arms that they can no longer bear to see your bayonets. You have seen the roads and fields between the Katzbach and the Bober: they bear the signs of the terror and confusion of your enemy.
>
> Let us sing praises to the Lord of Hosts, through whose help you have defeated the enemy and in a religious service let us publically thank Him for the glorious victory. A three-fold salvo of artillery will conclude the hour that you consecrate to prayer. Then, after your enemy anew![62]

Feeling better than the previous day, Blücher boasted to Amalie: "Yesterday I chased the last Frenchman across the Saxon frontier. This evening around 6:00 P.M. will be a general religious service and early tomorrow morning the bridges over the Queis, which the enemy burned and destroyed, will be repaired and I will pursue."[63]

Blücher ordered the army to cross the Queis and proceed to Görlitz the next day. The triumphant proclamation Blücher issued to the troops on 1 September masked the anxiety at army head-quarters, which only increased on the second. On this day Major Wenzel von Liechtenstein delivered a 30 August request from Schwarzenberg. Defeated at Dresden and intensely pursued by I Corps during his retreat to the Eger River, the Allied commander in chief feared Napoleon would invade Bohemia along the left bank of the Elbe with vastly superior forces. Planning to take a position on the right bank of the Eger, Schwarzenberg sought substantial rein-forcements to stop Napoleon. Thus, he petitioned Blücher to per-sonally aid him by leading the majority of the Army of Silesia, at least 50,000 men, to Bohemia.[64] The general refused, maintaining that he would accept direct orders only from Tsar Alexander.[65]

General Dominique Vandamme's I Corps, followed by XIV and VI Corps, led the pursuit of Schwarzenberg's beleaguered army. On 29 August Vandamme caught Wittgenstein's corps at Kulm (Chlumec), thirty-five miles south of Dresden and just inside the Bohemian frontier. Neither side gained an advantage despite sav-age fighting. With the battle continuing the next day, Kleist's II Corps marched east to Nollendorf (Nakléřov), directly north of Vandamme's position. While the Prussians attacked Vandamme's rear, the Russians pushed against his front, and an Austrian corps enveloped his left. With XIV and VI Corps too distant to support, Vandamme attempted but failed to drive through the Prussians. Imperial losses on 29 and 30 August amounted to 25,000 killed, wounded, and captured along with eighty-two guns; Allied casual-ties numbered 11,000 men. Fortunately for Blücher, the unexpected victory at Kulm rendered Schwarzenberg's request for massive rein-forcements superfluous.

Following the defeats at Großbeeren, the Katzbach, and Kulm, Napoleon considered either an offensive against Prague or another march on Berlin as his next step. Both projects sacrificed the prin-ciple of annihilating the main enemy army, which would have pro-vided the most direct means of achieving total victory. Rather than a decisive battle with one of the three Allied armies, geographic objectives dominated the emperor's planning. Rejecting the Prague offensive, Napoleon returned to the capture of Berlin. A victory over the Army of North Germany and the timid Bernadotte appeared certain. An offensive in this direction would allow him to remain in central position and close to his magazines. He deemed that the fall of Berlin would produce a moral victory that would erase the memory of the defeats and make a huge impression on the German princes of the Confederation of the Rhine. The Oder fortresses could be relieved, and Davout's XIII Corps could clear the way to Danzig. Furthermore, by taking Berlin and driving to the Vistula, the emperor envisioned the ultimate dissolution of the Bohemian Army. After the loss of their capital, he thought the Prussian contingent of Schwarzenberg's army would depart Bohemia and make for Brandenburg. As for the Russians, they would fall back on their lines of communication as soon as a French army threatened Poland. Should Allied resolve proved stronger and should Schwarzenberg hold his army together to lead a new offensive against Dresden, Napoleon would have a force of four corps commanded by his brother-in-law, Joachim Murat, to slow their advance.

Consequently, the emperor decided to allow the Army of Bohemia to recover after its recent drubbing while he personally commanded the march on Berlin. He planned to lead 30,000 men from Dresden, unite with the Army of Berlin, and resume the operation against the Prussian capital.[66] As for the Army of Silesia, Napoleon underestimated the dissolution of Macdonald's Army of the Bober after its defeat on the Katzbach and so hoped the marshal could hold the line of the Neiße. Should his lieutenants succeed, he predicted that fourteen days would suffice for him to take Berlin, resupply Stettin, and return to the Saxon theater to confront either Blücher or Schwarzenberg.

Blücher's steady pressure on Macdonald forced Napoleon to forgo these plans. Instead, he decided to reinforce the Army of the Bober, quickly demolish the Silesian Army, and then "march in great haste on Berlin."[67] Ney, who replaced Oudinot as commander of the Army of Berlin on 3 September, never received word of the change of plans. Therefore, when he began his operation on the fourth, he ordered the Army of Berlin to march eastward to unite with Napoleon, who, according to Ney's information, would reach Luckau two days later. Instead of his emperor, the marshal found the Prussian III and IV Corps of the Army of North Germany at Dennewitz. French losses amounted to 21,500 dead, wounded, and captured along with fifty-three guns. Prussian casualties numbered 9,700 killed and wounded. After this victory, the Army of North Germany pursued the wreck of the Army of Berlin to Wittenberg and Torgau.[68]

Meanwhile, Napoleon rode toward Bautzen on the morning of 4 September. At noon, three massive columns commenced the advance toward Görlitz. Meanwhile, the main body of the Silesian Army continued west toward the Wurschen–Hochkirch line. Around 3:00 P.M. the imperials surged eastward, blasting through Blücher's vanguard.[69] Again, the general demonstrated that going backward could be just as valuable as going forward. Without hesitating, he ordered the army to retreat east. Allowing Napoleon no opportunity to envelop him, Blücher continued the retreat of his main body for the next two days. The three corps of the Silesian Army withdrew across the Neiße and marched to the Queis.

By now, Napoleon began to suspect that Blücher's retrograde movements conformed to an Allied plan that sought to avoid battle with him personally. As at Löwenberg, Blücher slipped away. Unlike at Löwenberg, Napoleon no longer attributed his refusal to accept battle to ineptitude and fear.[70] Not wanting to waste any more time on Blücher—or Macdonald—he hoped to finally participate in the offensive to capture Berlin. Reports from St.-Cyr concerning the movement of Schwarzenberg's army again forced him to at least postpone these aspirations. Napoleon and the Guard returned to Dresden on the night of 6 September.

That day Blücher received numerous reports that the imperials did not appear inclined to continue the pursuit across the Neiße. Intelligence confirmed his hunch that such idleness again marked Napoleon's departure. After granting his soldiers a day of rest on the seventh, Blücher seized the offensive the next day. Gneisenau issued orders for a two-day operation that Blücher hoped would either force Macdonald back on Bautzen or accept a battle at the Neiße.[71] Although the general failed to pin the marshal at the river for a second engagement, his operations on 8 and 9 September succeeded in forcing the Army of the Bober to retreat toward Bautzen.[72] Taking stock of the situation, Gneisenau considered a further pursuit pointless and even detrimental to the overall strategic situation. Favorable results would drive Macdonald's army across the Elbe and into Napoleon's arms, allowing the emperor to again fall on the Bohemian Army with superior forces before the Silesian Army could come to its support.[73] Consequently, Blücher gave his troops a day of rest on the tenth; only the advance guards remained in contact with the imperials by pursuing them toward Bautzen. Continuing through Hochkirch and Weißenberg that day, the majority of Macdonald's army halted on the hills east of Bautzen.[74]

As noted, the second French operation against Berlin met with defeat at the Battle of Dennewitz on 6 September. Thus, detaining Napoleon in Saxony from 31 August to 6 September must be counted as one of Blücher's great achievements during the fall campaign. Had Napoleon and the Guard united with the Army of Berlin, it is difficult to imagine that such a force would have been stopped. Warned of the emperor's approach, Bernadotte probably would have retreated.[75] The campaign in Brandenburg then would have depended on how well Napoleon could maneuver in conjunction with Davout, who likewise mortally terrified Bernadotte, and how well the prince-royal could counter their movements. While the Swedes and Russians followed the crown prince, Bülow and Tauentzien would have made a stand somewhere to bravely sacrifice their troops rather than continue a shameful retreat. If imperial forces held up against Schwarzenberg and Blücher, Bernadotte eventually would be forced to fight or risk being driven across Swedish Pomerania and into the Baltic. By maintaining constant pressure on Macdonald and then going backward at the right moment, the future Marshal Forward prevented this scenario altogether. Instead of triumphantly entering Berlin as he did in 1806, Napoleon returned to Dresden having achieved nothing.

CHAPTER 13

LEIPZIG

L ate on the morning on 11 September, Silesian Army headquarters received news that Napoleon had launched another
offensive against Schwarzenberg.[1] With the Grande Armée apparently advancing south to Bohemia, Blücher resumed the pressure on Macdonald, with the goal of cutting off the marshal from
Dresden.[2] For the next three days, the Silesian Army sought to
pivot on Bautzen with its right wing (Sacken), while its left wing
(St. Priest and Langeron) executed a sweeping envelopment to the
west. Despite excessive marches, the Russians and Prussians again
failed to catch and destroy the Army of the Bober.

More decisive for the overall course of the war, Blücher dodged
more calls from Allied headquarters to transfer 50,000 men to the
Bohemian theater. Rather than events in Bohemia, the Prussians
pondered the situation in northern Saxony along the right bank of
the Elbe. Upon reaching the river after the victory at Dennewitz,
the Swedish crown prince halted operations and tasked Bülow
with laying siege to Wittenberg. Blücher suspected that Bernadotte
would remain idle if the majority of the Silesian Army marched to
Bohemia. He believed the time had come for Bernadotte to cross the
Elbe and enter the main theater of war. A 9 September letter from
the crown prince raised his hope that the Army of North Germany
would cross the river without much goading.[3] Responding to
Schwarzenberg's call for reinforcements, Blücher insisted that considerable advantages could be gained if the Army of North Germany
crossed the Elbe and his army marched northwest to link with it.[4]

Major Rühle von Lilienstern received the task of delivering
Blücher's answer to Allied headquarters. Rühle reached Teplitz on
the evening of 14 September and immediately met with the Russian
and Prussian monarchs. His persuasive argument convinced
Alexander and Frederick William to discard for good the plan to
transfer the Silesian Army to Bohemia. Instead, General Bennigsen
received orders to lead the Army of Poland to Bohemia. As soon as
Bennigsen exited Silesia, Blücher could pursue his plan of leading

both the Silesian and North German Armies across the Elbe and advancing on Leipzig. For these reasons, the decision to accept the general's proposal proved to be one of the most profound and consequential resolutions of the fall campaign. Rühle rejoined Blücher on the evening of 18 September and reiterated the great news: as soon as the Army of Poland reached Bohemia, the Prussian commander could march north to cross the Elbe at an appropriate point.[5]

Meanwhile, on Blücher's front, the imperials retreated from Bautzen toward Bischofswerda during the night of 11–12 September. Around 5:00 A.M. on the twelfth, the rear guard evacuated Bautzen, with Yorck's advance guard following hard on its heels. After receiving reports indicating that Macdonald had retreated across the Elbe, Blücher followed cautiously on the thirteenth and fourteenth.[6] A message from Streifkorps commander Major Falkenhausen noted the departure of large forces from Dresden north toward Großenhain; confirmation of this report by several sources came later in the day. Early on 15 September, news arrived from Teplitz of the rapid withdrawal north toward Dresden of the considerable forces holding the passes of the Erzgebirge. Blücher and his staff immediately interpreted all of this news as the opening moves of Napoleon's renewed offensive against the Silesian Army. Reports from the forward troops concerning imperial movements along their front likewise reinforced the idea of an enemy offensive. That evening Sacken confirmed that Murat had reached Großenhain with 50,000 men on the fourteenth. As for the Army of North Germany, not only did Bülow's III Corps arrive before Wittenberg on the fourteenth but his engineers also started bridging the Elbe at Elster, ten miles upstream of the city made famous by Martin Luther. Northwest of Bülow's Prussians, the remainder of the Army of North Germany moved west to Roßlau and Zerbst, while 2,000 Cossacks crossed the Elbe. Blücher received Tauentzien's request to drive through Kamenz toward Großenhain and secure communication with Bernadotte. Bennigsen indicated that General Pavel Stroganov's advanced division of the Army of Poland would reach Görlitz on the sixteenth, while General Dmitry Sergeyevich Dokhturov's corps would reach the Queis.[7] As soon as the Russians cleared Silesia, Blücher planned to march northwest and away from Napoleon.

As for Bonaparte, he busied himself with preparing a strike against the Army of North Germany. But events of the fourteenth turned the emperor's gaze back to Bohemia: Schwarzenberg concentrated his army and stood his ground. For the next three days, from 16 to 18 September, Napoleon launched tactical strikes across the Bohemian frontier to test the Austrian's mettle. During the course of the sixteenth, imperial cavalry dispersed a mass of Allied horse at Peterswalde (Petrovice u Chabařovic) and Nollendorf. A wounded Lieutenant Colonel Franz von Blücher numbered among the prisoners taken by the Polish lancers. Commander of the 1st Silesian Hussar Regiment attached to Kleist's II Corps, Franz received a nasty gash to the head. With bravery to match that of his father, he attacked superior Polish cavalry to cover the Prussian retreat to Nollendorf. Napoleon addressed a few kind words to the younger Blücher, placing him under the medical care of his suite.[8] Nevertheless, he could not refrain from boasting that Blücher's son had been taken prisoner.[9]

Word of Franz's wounding and capture reached his father on 19 September. He wrote Amalie on the twentieth:

> Yesterday, I received bad news from the Grand [Bohemian] Army that my good Franz was again wounded and taken prisoner; his wound should not be dangerous and consists of a sword laceration to the head. The tsar of Russia immediately sent a messenger to the enemy to inquire about him. Napoleon wished to see Franz and did so; he talked to him quite nicely and sent him a doctor. He is looked after well and I hope he will be exchanged soon; he is probably at Dresden. Poor Franz is very unlucky and his fever is very great. I know nothing of your brother except that he is well. What concerns me is that I have no letters from you. None of you are to worry about Franz because I just received confirmation from [Adjutant] General Knesebeck that he is only lightly wounded and is looked after well; this will certainly be the case because I have captured so many generals and can retaliate against all of them.

Blücher also learned that his son-in-law, Count Schulenburg, died from illness. "This is the best for him and for Fritze," he assured Amalie.[10] A few days later he received a letter from Franz dated 17 September:

> In a heated cavalry combat at Peterswalde, I had the misfortune of being captured after receiving many blows and stabs. Prince Berthier has taken me in his quarters and overwhelmed me with kindness; I am being cared for by his doctor who assures me that my wounds are not serious. A stab wound in my back inconveniences me very much, but the slash on my head does not appear

to be dangerous. Please, if possible, expedite my exchange. I cannot praise enough the excellent manner with which they have treated me and I request that you treat any French officer with the same kindness, which certainly is inherent in your character. My captivity brings me no disgrace because I sacrificed myself to save several others.[11]

Despite Franz's favorable treatment at the hands of the French, the elder Blücher remained anxious. "As good as everything goes for me," he wrote Bonin on the twenty-second, "I have had some misfortune because my son was wounded for a third time and also taken prisoner. The Emperor himself has spoken with him. He has had much misfortune from his wound; he is also very feverish. By allowing himself to be captured, he saved some batteries that the enemy wanted to take. Of your son, I know nothing more than that he is with General Zieten and is healthy. I will do everything to get back my son; I only fear that he already is on the way to France."[12]

With his son suffering, Blücher became incensed when the promotion board passed over Franz. "He is my son," he wrote to Knesebeck, "and so I cannot say anything. As long as the struggle continues, the King can reduce me to a captain and him to corporal and we will still win. When the war is over, then I will speak." Franz's injury and the respect shown him by the emperor made Blücher even angrier over the snub from the promotion board. "He will make the old proverb come true: squeeze the lemon, one throws out the peel," the general predicted. "He can comfort himself with the fact that he handled himself well in the face of the enemy and that the Blücher name is irreproachable. I remain true to my intention: as long as the struggle continues, I will use my last breath not to seek rewards, no, if peace is made tomorrow, I will leave the service and the state with a white cane [the sign of a beggar]. The overall worthwhile knowledge of having fulfilled my duty faithfully rests in my bosom, and indeed is more than any mortal can give me." In conclusion, he vowed vengeance on the cowards who punished the son because they lacked the manliness to challenge Blücher himself: "If Providence allows me to live through this war, I shall place Germany in a position to correctly judge everything that has been hidden until now."[13]

Blücher's movements, which caused panic at Macdonald's headquarters as early as 18 September, finally caught Napoleon's attention.[14] The advance on Kamenz brought the Silesian Army "so close to the central position of the French army that the whole strategical [sic] edifice was shaken."[15] Consequently, Napoleon ordered two divisions of Young Guard as well as the Guard Cavalry to cross the new bridge at Pirna and move east. Masked by the Poles of VIII Corps and IV Cavalry Corps a few miles east at Stolpen, the master instructed his shock troops to take positions in a triangle formed by the villages of Lohmen, Röhrsdorf (Dürrröhrsdorf-Dittersbach), and Stürza. The northern point of the triangle—Röhrsdorf—lay seven miles south of the Großharthau–Arnsdorf line, which Macdonald occupied that same day. "If the weather is less terrible tomorrow," wrote Napoleon at 11:00 A.M., "I am inclined to march on the enemy and push him beyond Bautzen." He gave the Poles strict orders to ensure that Blücher remained completely ignorant of the approach of the Imperial Guard.[16]

Napoleon passed the night of 19–20 September at Pirna. Adverse weather on the twentieth prompted him to postpone operations.[17] The following day the Poles informed him of Blücher's advance toward Stolpen. The emperor insisted that Macdonald support the Poles "so that under no circumstances would they be obliged to evacuate Stolpen."[18] His letter to Berthier provides an interesting snapshot of the extent to which Blücher's movements bedeviled Macdonald and by extension himself. "The situation of the enemy between the Spree and Bischofswerda appears uncertain," wrote the emperor. "The Duke of Tarente [Macdonald] indicated in his letter of the 14th that the corps of Langeron and Saint-Priest . . . maneuvered to the right [south], and that he decided to concentrate on his position. Since then, he claimed in his letter of the 19th that he feared taking a position at Weißig because the enemy, after operating on his right, now maneuvered on his left and threatened to reach Dresden before him. Finally, according to yesterday's report, the Duke of Tarente's spies announced that 15,000 men from Yorck's corps are on the far left [north], and that another Russian or Prussian corps is following, always in the direction of the Elbe."

Revealing his frustration with Macdonald, Napoleon put down the imperial foot: "In this situation, the Emperor orders the Duke of Tarente to attack between 11:00 A.M. and 1:00 P.M. on the 22nd with his left, center, and right, approaching all of the enemy's positions and carrying everything before him until he finds himself facing an army ready for battle and in strength equal to or greater than his.

He will try to take prisoners; he will interview the inhabitants to gather as much information as possible about enemy movements." He hinted that he would probably follow Macdonald, ready to unite with the marshal according to circumstances and to attack Blücher the next day "if we find the enemy line." As usual, Napoleon wrote these instructions to Berthier, who then generated a second letter to Macdonald. But per the original letter, the major general included the admonition: "Today's attack, a great reconnaissance, is ordered by the Emperor as part of the general affairs of the whole, and should not be postponed on any pretext whatsoever, unless the weather is as bad as it was on the 20th; but, if the weather is like it was on the day of 21st, the attack should take place."[19]

Macdonald received these orders at 9:30 on the morning of the twenty-second. Not expecting to be called on to launch an offensive, he had earlier dispatched large detachments to procure food supplies. Responding with a request to postpone the operation until the following day, the marshal learned that his imperial master would reach the vanguard "between 12:00 and 1:00 P.M. Between noon and 2:00, we will make a sudden attack and take some prisoners."[20] Consequently, after orders for its dissolution already had been issued, the Army of the Bober marched one last time.

According to the reports that reached Blücher's headquarters, the intensity of the imperial advance clearly signaled Napoleon's presence. Not knowing the number of reinforcements the emperor brought with him and expecting he would continue the offensive, Blücher ordered a limited but general retreat to Bautzen for the twenty-third. For the moment, he planned to halt there before determining his next move. "If our Grand [Bohemian] Army does not operate soon," Blücher wrote to Knesebeck, "I will be paralyzed here and winter will come before we have achieved anything considerable with 500,000 men under arms."[21]

Napoleon spent the entire afternoon of the twenty-second collecting reports before retiring to Großharthau for the night. He obtained the desired information.[22] Around 11:00 on the twenty-third, the Army of the Bober resumed its advance in three huge columns. Yet as on previous occasions, the drive now lacked urgency and intensity—Napoleon already had departed. Passing the night of 22–23 September at Großharthau, he received word from Ney that Bernadotte's troops completed a bridge across the Elbe at the mouth of the Black Elster.[23] Napoleon spent most of 23 September at Großharthau, purportedly in a fit of indecision. Frustrated by the Trachenberg-Reichenbach Plan in general but specifically by Blücher's refusal to accept battle, the master decided to evacuate the right bank of the Elbe.[24] In his mind, he offered the right bank as bait, particularly to attract Blücher. Moreover, he dispensed with detaching independent army groups to operate far from his support. He would concentrate and let the Allies come to him, using the Elbe to first lure them into his lair, then as a trap for a strategic envelopment. The imperial withdrawal across the river commenced on 24 October. Napoleon himself again rode east almost to Bischofswerda before returning to Dresden during the night of 24–25 September. As unlikely as it seems, he ignored Blücher for the next several days thanks to Schwarzenberg's decision to advance on Leipzig.

So confident became Blücher that he spoke of peace and retirement: "The situation now goes well," he informed Bonin. "We will certainly reach the Rhine before winter and then there will be peace. If I live to see this, I will say farewell to the service and live a few days for myself. I would be happy to spend a few days with you. When peace comes, I will again settle down in Pomerania; I want to die in this brave land." Expecting further rewards for his service, the old hussar boasted cynically: "One has hung so many orders and crosses on me that I can hardly wear them. From the Russian tsar came the Orders of St. Andrew and St. George, from Austria the Commander's Cross of the Order of Maria Theresa and from the King the Great Cross of the Iron Cross. I only hope these people will remember that in the least a considerable estate should go along with this so that my life will be commensurate with all these signs of honor. Promises are sufficient; I think, in the end a grant (dotation), like the French marshals received, would suffice. After all, my daughter is now a widow."[25]

On 23 September Blücher and his staff correctly assumed that Napoleon no longer accompanied the Army of the Bober, implying that Macdonald no longer sought battle. They hoped to exploit this transition of command with a surprise attack on Macdonald's left.[26] Yet the staff's recurring problem of cutting orders late in the day rendered this operation impracticable on the twenty-third. Joining Yorck's advance guard, Blücher prudently watched and waited throughout the next morning, but the imperials could not be found in strength: Napoleon had ordered the retreat to the Elbe, Macdonald's forces apparently withdrawing during the night of 24–25 September. Consequently, the Silesian Army resumed the advance around noon. By 8:00 on the morning of 25 September, Blücher's staff still remained unclear over the meaning of these movements. Although reports had yet to arrive, the Prussians believed that Napoleon finally had relinquished the offensive against the Silesian Army. They correctly speculated that the emperor decided to completely evacuate the right bank of the Elbe.[27] Furthermore, the last troops of Bennigsen's army presumably would clear Zittau on the twenty-fifth. By focusing on Blücher, Napoleon's short two-day offensive had allowed the Army of Poland to reach Bohemia unnoticed and unmolested. Based on these circumstances, the situation appeared ideal for the Silesian Army's march down the Elbe.

Gneisenau lost no time dispatching Rühle to find a suitable point to cross the river. Reports that Bülow's men built a pontoon bridge at Elster made this locale the initial target, but Gneisenau wanted confirmation of its utility for an entire army. As soon as Rühle completed the reconnaissance, he would hurry to find Tauentzien and Bülow. Gneisenau tasked the major with pointedly asking the two corps commanders if they would follow the Army of Silesia across the Elbe without the crown prince's approval.[28]

On 26 September 1813, the army commenced the march from Bautzen to Elsterwerda, from where it would continue to the village of Elster. From the crown prince of Sweden came a surprise: a vow to cooperate with Blücher. If the Silesian Army crossed the Elbe, the Army of North Germany would do so within three or four days.[29] Blücher informed Bernadotte that he intended to cross the Elbe at Elster on 3 October and attack Ney's Army of Berlin at Kemberg on the fourth. After defeating Ney, the Army of Silesia would be ready to unite with the Army of North Germany at Bad Düben on the Mulde River.[30]

While at Elsterwerda on 1 October, Blücher received a long letter from Bernadotte communicating reports of an enemy advance toward Wittenberg, apparently to attack Bülow. His letter requested that Blücher cross the Elbe as quickly as possible either at Elster or Mühlberg. "If your disposition can conform to my wishes," the crown prince concluded, "together we would form a mass of 120,000 men which can quickly move on Leipzig and venture a battle against the majority of the Emperor Napoleon's forces."[31]

Sunday, 3 October 1813, broke with foggy, cold, wet weather. Around 5:00 A.M., Yorck's corps marched northwest to Elster in two columns. After crossing the Elbe, he soon found his corps engaged in a bloody contest with the 13,000 men and thirty-two guns of Bertrand's IV Corps around Wartenburg. At the end of the day, the imperials retreated, thus opening the road for the entire Silesian Army to cross the Elbe. Yorck's casualties amounted to sixty-seven officers and 1,548 men. The Prussians claim to have taken 1,000 prisoners, seventy wagons, and eleven guns. Not numerical superiority but the bravery of the Prussian troops combined with the prudence and calmness of their leadership produced the success of this difficult day.[32] Blücher clearly recognized the implications this victory would have on Allied strategy and operations. "The trophies are not as considerable as at the Katzbach, but the consequences of the victory are much greater because now everything will cross the Elbe and the Bohemian Army can advance from Bohemia. The great man [Napoleon] will be at Leipzig and I expect him in a few days."[33]

By crossing the Elbe, Blücher executed the most crucial and consequential operation of the entire fall campaign. By marching downriver and crossing, he set the stage for the monumental struggle at Leipzig less than two weeks later. Well planned and conducted, the bold move represents one of the best examples of operational planning to that point in military history. For his part, Schwarzenberg decided to advance on Leipzig rather than another attempt at Dresden: the Army of Bohemia began the march north on 1 October. During the night of 3–4 October, Blücher received a letter from Bülow stating that the crown prince would cross the Elbe with the entire Army of North Germany.[34] Through this joint operation, Blücher hoped to entice Napoleon to turn against the Silesian and North German Armies. By baiting the emperor, he wanted to buy time for the Bohemian Army to reach the Saxon plain.

Accepting battle with the master meant accepting the possibility of defeat. Thus, the next question to be addressed concerned escaping Napoleon's blow. Upon his approach, both the North German and Silesian Armies would be forced to fall back either across the Elbe or behind the Saale. As Napoleon most likely would give chase, the limited number of crossings over both rivers meant the losses incurred in rearguard engagements could be high. Moreover, a separation of the two armies could allow Napoleon to isolate and defeat each in turn. Based on these considerations, a temporary halt of the Army of Silesia at the Mulde River to unite with the Army of North Germany appeared prudent. Should Napoleon move north to the Mulde, Schwarzenberg would gain plenty of time to herd the Army of Bohemia into Saxony. Moreover, if the emperor remained at Dresden and turned directly against Schwarzenberg, the Prussians felt confident that they would learn of this movement early enough to rush through Leipzig and Altenburg to support the commander in chief.[35]

As Blücher pushed west, Ney found his Army of Berlin caught between the two Allied armies. Not known as a gifted strategist, the marshal nevertheless recognized the implications of the operations unfolding around him and retreated to the Mulde River. Pursuing, the Silesian Army reached the Mulde by nightfall on 5 October; Langeron's corps reached Bad Düben, where Blücher and army headquarters likewise passed the night. West of the general's position, the Army of North Germany had started crossing the Elbe at Roßlau on 4 October, led by Bülow's corps; the Swedes and Russians followed on the fifth. Bernadotte concentrated his army in the square formed by the towns of Aken, Köthen, Jeßnitz, and Dessau.

Reports that reached Blücher's headquarters on the fifth placed Napoleon and the Old Guard at Dresden as late as 3 October. The general also learned of Ney's withdrawal south from Dessau toward Leipzig and of his union with Bertrand. Nothing arrived from Schwarzenberg: the Prussians assumed the Bohemian Army would complete the crossing of the Erzgebirge around 5 October and thus be vulnerable to an attack by Napoleon until then. Not certain of the next step to take, Blücher decided to drop his plan to force the passage of the Mulde on the sixth. Instead, he awaited the emperor's next move.

To be prepared to counter Napoleon, Blücher wanted to be certain that Bernadotte remained true to his word. In a letter dated 5 October, he reminded the crown prince that "your army and the Silesian [Army] have Leipzig as the objective of their operations" based on the tsar's instructions of 25 September.[36] On 6 October Bernadotte responded: "I received your letter from yesterday. The memo that it contains is in complete agreement with my ideas . . . but due to the circumstances, which are so crucial, we cannot do enough to guard against [unforeseen] events. This consideration, as well as the longing to renew an old acquaintance with you, stirs in me the wish for us to meet if possible at Mühlbeck, where we can speak with each other and through a discussion cut short what takes so long to write." He notified Blücher of his intention to transfer his headquarters to Zehbitz, twenty-five miles west of Bad Düben, on 7 October. With Mühlbeck roughly halfway between their respective command posts, the crown prince proposed a meeting there for the evening of the seventh.[37]

A report from Sacken turned Blücher's attention eastward. On the morning of 6 October, Russian patrols found endless troop columns marching down the left bank of the Elbe for forty miles from Dresden through Meißen to Strehla. Numerous bivouac fires—those of III Corps en route to Torgau—dotted the environs of Strehla during the previous night (5–6 October). Per Müffling's cautious advice, Blücher chose to remain at the Mulde and await the Bohemian Army's drive on Leipzig. Later that day news finally arrived concerning Schwarzenberg. A letter from Bennigsen dated 4 October indicated that 60,000 men of the Bohemian Army commenced the advance toward Chemnitz on that day and that Allied headquarters would depart Teplitz on the fifth to follow the army.[38]

Consequently, on 7 October "a complete change in the judgment of the strategic situation appears to have taken place, which was probably due to Blücher himself. The prolonged standstill at the Mulde hardly corresponded to his nature. His bold way of thinking obviously favored a continuation of the advance, making him master of Leipzig, and from there striving to unite with the Bohemian Army and, once united, delivering a decisive battle wherever Napoleon was found."[39] Thus wrote General Friederich in 1904. In the century that has passed since the Historical Section of Germany's Great General Staff published its official history of the Befreiungskriege, nothing of note has surfaced to counter the assertion of this erudite analyst. Not a soul at Blücher's headquarters knew where Schwarzenberg's army stood on 7 October, but that mattered little. All had to assume that the Austrian, Russian, and Prussian legions of the Allied main army were beating the plains of Saxony. To comply with basic strategy, the needs of coalition warfare, the spirit of the Trachenberg-Reichenbach Plan, and honor itself, Blücher wanted to do his utmost to move his army closer to Schwarzenberg's.

Conversely, Bernadotte warned Blücher to be prepared for Napoleon to strike the left wing of the Silesian Army.[40] Bowing to caution and perhaps Bernadotte's warning, he reinforced Sacken. In the end, the reports that reached Blücher on the seventh did not offer a clue regarding Napoleon's intentions. Yet they provided no reason for the general to renounce his drive across the Mulde and toward Leipzig. Of the troops that remained on the right bank of the Elbe, Falkenhausen's Streifkorps severed communication between Meißen and Dresden. Learning of the march of a French column between these two points, he commenced the hunt. His horsemen took many prisoners, horses, an empty supply train, and some boats. More importantly, his post opposite Meißen clearly recognized Napoleon. This enabled Falkenhausen to report the emperor's movement as well as the continued march of large columns through Meißen in the direction of Leipzig.[41]

During the afternoon of 7 October, Blücher rode eleven miles west from Bad Düben to Mühlbeck for his meeting with Bernadotte, who traveled fourteen miles east from Zehbitz. Believing that Napoleon remained at Dresden, both commanders assumed their armies could reach Leipzig before his. Thus, they decided to begin the advance toward Saxony's second city on the very next day, the eighth.[42] As preparatory movements, Blücher agreed to push his three corps in the direction of Mühlbeck, Bad Düben, and Eilenburg, while the North German Army advanced on the road to Delitzsch, sending cavalry to Eilenburg to cover Blücher's flank. The march on Leipzig would continue jointly on the ninth.

Four days earlier, on 3 October, Napoleon received enough information from spies to confirm the departure of the Silesian Army from the Bautzen area, apparently marching in the direction of Elsterwerda.[43] Owing to Schwarzenberg's advance on Chemnitz, Napoleon believed Blücher either would make for Dresden or likewise drive on Leipzig. Belated reports concerning Prussian activity at Meißen and Mühlberg unsettled the emperor but reinforced his assumption that the general would attempt to pass the Elbe between Meißen and Torgau.[44] He wrote Macdonald, with a hint of desperation: "I attach great importance to knowing exactly what became of Langeron, Sacken, and Yorck. Therefore, tomorrow, I want you to reconnoiter with 7,000 to 8,000 infantry, cavalry, and artillery toward Großenhain [Sacken was there], and that you send patrols in other directions so that you know positively what has become of the enemy army from Silesia."[45]

Napoleon knew of the Allied bridge work at Elster but attributed it to the Army of North Germany. To put an end to the nuisance caused by Bernadotte, he authorized Marmont to assemble VI Corps and I Cavalry Corps at Bad Düben and "march against the enemy.

Eliminate his bridges at Wartenburg, Dessau, and Aken; then he will have none."[46] A vague report from Marmont over the engagement at Wartenburg—written at 11:00 on the morning of 4 October—reached Napoleon at Dresden sometime before 3:00 A.M. on the fifth. Although uncertain over who attacked Bertrand, the emperor's response suggests that he did not think the Silesian Army had crossed the Elbe at Wartenburg.[47] Still suspecting Blücher to be in the Meißen region, he prepared to go there himself, leaving Murat to face the Bohemian Army as it rumbled toward Leipzig.[48]

Sometime before 3:00 A.M. on the sixth, Napoleon received shocking news. Not only did Bernadotte's army cross the Elbe but the entire Silesian Army did so as well.[49] The advance of the Allies in two large masses from opposite directions completely changed the situation by bringing the decisive conclusion within reach. Although on the verge of being strategically enveloped, Napoleon's position improved drastically. Having moved out of the positions protected by river lines and mountains, the Allies became accessible to him. He could focus his attention on two directions, enhancing his personal command and control. By utilizing central position and interior lines, he could defeat Blücher and Bernadotte before they could unite with Schwarzenberg. He finally would wage the decisive battle that he long sought, but which the Allies had evaded with great skill. With some 150,000 men, he hoped to defeat Blücher and Bernadotte. Napoleon initially planned to cross the Elbe at Torgau, march downriver along the right bank, and destroy all of the enemy's bridges. In so doing, he would severe the rearward communications of both Allied armies, thus making their retreat across the Elbe, as well as their avoidance of a battle, impossible. Napoleon then planned to return to the left bank of the river via Wittenberg to force Bernadotte and Blücher into a battle. A decisive defeat of at least one of them would force the other to retreat across the Elbe. Then, he could concentrate all of his forces to contend with Schwarzenberg.[50]

At 1:00 A.M. on the night of 6–7 October, Napoleon assessed the situation that confronted him. Further reports indicated that Blücher would drive on Leipzig while Bernadotte led his army to Halle. Consequently, he changed plans and decided to concentrate the Grande Armée at Wurzen: eighteen miles east of Leipzig, forty miles south of Wittenberg, twenty miles southwest of Torgau, and sixty miles northeast of Dresden. He remained uncertain of his next step, but the Wurzen concentration offered several options. "As the result of this movement," Napoleon concluded, "I shall be master to do what I want: from Wurzen I can move on Torgau and on the enemy, debouching from Wittenberg, or move my whole army on Leipzig and have a general battle, or cross the Saale. On the 8th, the army under my personal command will be at Wurzen."[51]

With Blücher having at his disposal only the sole bridge at Wartenburg and Bernadotte the bridges at Aken and Roßlau, Napoleon could expect decisive results if he drove them against the river. By crossing the Elbe, the Allies crossed their Rubicon: they could only retrace their steps in defeat. They finally exposed themselves and offered the master a target he could hit. "The whole army of Silesia debouched through Wartenburg," he wrote to Murat, "and there's nobody from Dresden to Gorlitz, or Dresden to Berlin. St.-Cyr remains at Dresden. Hold back the Austrians as much as possible so I can defeat Blücher and the Swedes before their union with Schwarzenberg's army."[52] His plan should have worked. That it failed can be attributed only to Blücher.

At 9:00 on the morning of the eighth, Napoleon went to Wurzen. By nightfall, his position appeared formidable. Some 150,000 men grouped in twenty-two infantry and twelve cavalry divisions held a front that stretched a mere twenty-two miles from Taucha to Schildau.[53] A report from Ney provided Blücher's whereabouts. According to the marshal, the Silesian Army no longer appeared to be marching on Leipzig nor seeking to unite with the North German Army. Instead, Blücher seemed to be isolated at Bad Düben with 60,000 men, while Bernadotte remained thirty miles north-northwest at Dessau with 40,000. Based on this information, Napoleon again altered his plans. With the Army of Silesia extended along the Mulde, he sought to engage Blücher at Bad Düben on 9 October. Success seemed certain if the Prussian stood firm and accepted battle. Napoleon could also count on Bernadotte retreating across the Elbe to the right bank as soon as the Grande Armée crushed Blücher. Thus, on 10 October he planned to raise the siege of Wittenberg, cross to the right bank of the Elbe, eliminate the bridges at Dessau and Wartenburg, and destroy the Army of North Germany.[54]

Blücher returned to Bad Düben after his meeting with Bernadotte on 7 October. For the eighth, he instructed his Army "to seek the enemy in the region of Leipzig." With headquarters remaining at Bad Düben, he directed Yorck and Langeron to the Mulde, sending their advance guards across the river.[55] Despite the agreements made during their meeting, Bernadotte maintained his positions at Radegast and Jeßnitz that day; only Tauentzien's IV Corps moved up from Dessau to Hinsdorf, four miles north of Zehbitz.[56]

Although confusing reports over the enemy's operations continued to filter in throughout the night of 7–8 October, the Silesian Army marched early on the eighth in accordance with these orders. At army headquarters, Falkenhausen's dispatch arrived around noon reporting Napoleon's presence at Meißen, from where the emperor struck the road west to Leipzig.[57] Other reports indicated the concentration of large imperial forces at Wurzen. Consequently, Blücher and his staff finally gained a clear picture of the situation, which had changed considerably in just twenty-four hours. Regardless, some important questions still needed to be answered. Did Napoleon intend—just as Bernadotte warned—to launch an offensive against Blücher's left? Alternatively, would the emperor seek to gain Leipzig and then proceed north against Bernadotte or move south against Schwarzenberg? Regardless of Napoleon's plan, if Blücher continued his advance on Leipzig, he risked an encounter with the enemy. Certainly the old Prussian did not shirk from the thought of such a confrontation, but the extenuating circumstances demanded prudence.

A major impediment to decisive action remained the sobering realization that Blücher had to defer the initiative to both Bernadotte and Napoleon. As for the latter, if the emperor turned against the Army of Bohemia, then Blücher and Bernadotte had to follow and be in position to fall on his rear and flanks as soon as he engaged Schwarzenberg. As for Bernadotte, preexisting agreements with Blücher would dictate their responses to a French offensive. If Napoleon attacked the Army of Silesia between the Mulde and the Elbe, Blücher would retreat to the entrenched camp at Wartenburg, sending the majority of his cavalry to unite with the Army of North Germany. Thus reinforced, Bernadotte would operate against Napoleon's flank and rear if he pursued Blücher. But if he commenced an offensive against Bernadotte between the Saale and the Elbe, the Army of North Germany would withdraw to the bridgehead at Roßlau while Blücher operated against the emperor's flank and rear.

Under the circumstances, an immediate retreat to Wartenburg hardly appealed to Blücher. Yet without Bernadotte's full support, he could not face Napoleon. Only the combined Armies of Silesia and North Germany would be strong enough to meet the Grande Armée. He dispatched Rühle to Bernadotte's headquarters on the evening of the eighth to work out the details. Instead of engaging Napoleon, the crown prince preferred to escape across the Elbe at Aken. Rühle responded that Blücher preferred to move across the Saale, where he could operate against Napoleon's communications and cooperate with Schwarzenberg. Bernadotte accepted the idea and proposed a joint crossing of the Saale. Then, if Napoleon pursued, both armies would march north, bypassing Magdeburg and crossing the Elbe at Ferchland. Rühle countered that instead, Blücher would march south, thus up the Saale, and unite with the Bohemian Army. Aghast, the crown prince retorted that such a movement violated all the rules of war because Blücher would completely sacrifice his line communication and cut off the army from its ammunition transports, supply convoys, and reinforcements. Gradually, Bernadotte became receptive to the idea of retreating across the Saale but still insisted on withdrawing north and across the Elbe if Napoleon pursued. His conditional acceptance of the Saale option required Blücher to position the Silesian Army south of the North German Army and cross the river at Wettin, where the crown prince promised to strike a bridge.[58]

By convincing Bernadotte to remain on the left bank of the Elbe, Rühle achieved his purpose. Still, he failed to attain the crown prince's complete agreement with Blücher's plans. The Prussians regarded a movement across the Saale as a means to seek the union with the Bohemian Army, while Bernadotte viewed it as the prelude to a further retreat across the Elbe at Ferchland to preserve his communications. Thus, the Army of North Germany did little on 9 October.

Rühle returned to Bad Düben that morning. Although sacrificing all of his rearward communication, Blücher turned his command toward Napoleon's communications.[59] As it turned out, the Silesian Army would not see its baggage, which remained on the right bank of the Elbe, until the trains caught up with it at the Rhine in mid-November.[60] "Convinced," he wrote Bernadotte, "that at this moment a movement to the right [west] in order to reach the left bank of the Saale is preferable to any other, I will immediately order my army to march in this direction. Demonstrations against Leipzig appear necessary to mask our movements. Thus, I will attack Eilenburg today."[61]

Preliminary reports on the ninth indicated Leipzig to be the French objective. Having no idea of the emperor's approach, Silesian Army headquarters did not make haste. Around noon, unbelievable news reached Blücher: enemy troops were marching down both banks of the Mulde toward Bad Düben. He wanted to wait for Sacken to arrive before he departed with Langeron's corps, but Sacken never showed, and anxiety mounted. Headquarters did not know that the Russian corps commander received Blücher's orders three hours later than expected.[62] Finally, Blücher's posts reported the approach of a column marching on the right bank of the Mulde. Believing it to be Sacken's corps, the commander delayed his departure even longer and ordered Langeron's rear guard to remain at Bad Düben. Soon, columns could be seen marching down both banks of the river, but they did not belong to Sacken's corps. With imperial troops closing on Bad Düben, Blücher finally took the road to Pouch at 2:00 in the afternoon. Less than sixty minutes after he departed, French cavalry entered the town; Gneisenau barely avoided capture. Although Langeron's rear guard escaped, Napoleon succeeded in cutting off Sacken's corps.[63]

Sacken then executed a brilliant march northwest, circumvented Bad Düben, and cut through the large forest north of that town to reach Jeßnitz.[64] By late morning on the tenth, the entire Army of Silesia had escaped across the Mulde. By renouncing his intended march to Leipzig on 9 October, Blücher again escaped the emperor's attack through a timely retreat. After delivering the army from the brink of chaos, he addressed a detailed letter to Bernadotte describing the enemy's operation. He explained that the movement along the right bank of the Mulde appeared too serious to be a mere reconnaissance. Consequently, the Prussians judged that the Army of North Germany could march to Halle unmolested.

Never happy with retreating, Blücher proposed making a stand.[65] With imperial forces moving east from Leipzig to the Mulde to join the large columns advancing north and west on Bad Düben, he offered to shield Bernadotte while his army slid southwest to a position between Halle and Leipzig. Meanwhile, Blücher would assess the situation from Zörbig, with crossings over the Saale available twenty-three miles northwest at Bernburg and eighteen miles due west at Rothenburg. The intent and genius of this plan should not be overlooked. Blücher and his staff ultimately believed that both armies would be compelled to cross the Saale. Upon doing so, the Prussians wanted these forces to march south along its left bank to unite with the Army of Bohemia. Yet they feared that Bernadotte would attempt to move north, slip across the Elbe, and fall back into Brandenburg under the pretext of guarding Berlin. By offering to shield the Army of North Germany as it marched southwest to a point between Halle and Leipzig, Blücher created the façade of sacrificing his army for Bernadotte's. He thus hoped that, blinded by this magnanimous offer, the crown prince would accept, thus placing the Army of Silesia between his army and its bridges to escape across the Elbe. With Blücher driving him from behind, Bernadotte would have no choice but to march south and seek the union with Schwarzenberg.

Although a cunning ploy, Bernadotte was no fool. He rejected Blücher's suggestion to cross the Saale at Halle and place his forces south of and next to the Silesian Army. To protect his army, he preferred that Blücher remain at Zörbig—halfway between the Mulde and the Saale—on the tenth while the North German Army took a position north of and next to the Silesian Army, bridging the lower Saale at Alsleben and Bernburg. The crown prince appeared explicitly concerned with securing his line of retreat to the Elbe bridges rather than cooperating with the approaching Bohemian Army.[66]

While Bernadotte's proposal appeared to concur with Blücher's bid to make a stand between the Saale and the Mulde, the specific details proved too suspect for the Prussians. The crown prince's penultimate statement appeared the most dubious of all. Assuming Blücher dismantled his bridge at Wartenburg, Bernadotte advised him to "immediately transport the pontoons to Aken or Roßlau."[67] Thus, the Prussians believed he wanted to maintain the liberty to either take part in a great battle with Napoleon or fly across the Elbe.[68] Despite Blücher's "selfless" offer to shield the Army of North Germany as it marched southwest to Bruckdorf, Bernadotte refused to post the Silesian army between him and his Elbe bridges. This placed the Prussians in a difficult situation by jeopardizing the entire purpose of crossing the Elbe at Wartenburg.[69] For the moment, they accepted this check in their chess match with Bernadotte. Rather than attempt another move, Blücher wanted to convince him that the roads to the Saale remained open.[70]

Passing through Zehbitz on the road to Zörbig, Blücher met with the crown prince.[71] The general abandoned the idea of placing his army on the left wing—between Bernadotte and the Elbe—and driving the North German Army south toward Schwarzenberg. Instead, he consented to posting the Silesian Army on the right wing and crossing the Saale at Wettin, thus leaving Bernadotte with a clear path to his bridges across the Elbe. According to the Prussians, the crown prince promised to immediately strike a bridge at Wettin and to extend his left wing only as far as Alsleben. At this point, Blücher lost all faith in Bernadotte.[72]

During the course of 10 October, Bülow's corps reached Zörbig, while his advance guard extended three miles farther south to Quetzdölsdorf, approximately five miles northwest of Yorck's vanguard at Brehna. Bernadotte instructed Bülow to cooperate with the Silesian Army by supporting it at Jeßnitz if necessary.[73] Upon learning that the Prussian III Corps had arrived at Zörbig, Blücher sent Müffling to inform its commander of the result of the Zehbitz meeting, tasking Müffling with convincing Bülow to unite his corps with the army if Bernadotte refused to participate in a battle with Napoleon. Although he had little love for Blücher, Bülow not only promised to cooperate but also expressed his conviction that Wintzingerode would proceed in the spirit of Tsar Alexander and do the same. Blücher's personal visit to the corps commander sealed their secret agreement.

Blücher also contacted the Prussian, Russian, Austrian, and British envoys attached to Bernadotte's headquarters. Of this group, the assistance of British general Charles Stewart proved invaluable. A good friend of Gneisenau, Stewart monitored Bernadotte's actions to determine if the crown prince conformed with the stipulations of the subsidy agreement between Great Britain and Sweden. He also held the purse strings, having the authority to apportion the funds or refuse payment. Stewart did not fail to threaten Bernadotte that he would exercise his power should the crown prince proceed in a manner contrary to the general cause.[74]

Such a promising start to the day of 9 October ended in failure for Napoleon. This time, blame could not be placed on a hapless subordinate. Blücher escaped because of quick thinking and cooperation with Bernadotte. But where had the Prussian gone?[75] Napoleon's disappointment would have been much greater had he learned that Blücher did not retreat north to the Elbe but instead abandoned all his rearward communication and withdrew west to the Saale. For the moment, this movement remained hidden from the emperor, who assumed that on the ninth the Silesian Army retreated northwest to Dessau, while Sacken's corps marched east to Wartenburg.[76] He planned to pursue Blücher north, trusting Marmont to alert him to any Allied movement toward Delitzsch or Leipzig. Always seeking to boost the confidence of his subordinates, he wrote Marmont: "It appears that our offensive movement was totally unexpected and that the enemy believed we were one-hundred leagues away."[77]

Around noon on 10 October, Napoleon rode to Bad Düben, where he received crucial information. He learned of the Army of Bohemia's advance on Leipzig. Yet several sources confirmed Blücher's retreat northwest to Dessau.[78] Reports also placed the Army of North Germany at the Saale: a move the emperor attributed to Schwarzenberg's approach.[79] Regardless, he hoped to wage a battle on the next day, the eleventh, with at least Blücher.[80] Thus, the master felt certain that he could maneuver Blücher into an engagement in the Dessau-Roßlau region. If the Prussian evaded a confrontation, Napoleon still planned to cross the Elbe at Wittenberg, destroying the bridges at Roßlau, Aken, and Wartenburg from the right bank. He hoped that by threatening these bridges, both Blücher and Bernadotte would accept battle to protect their points of passage. He figured that the defeat of these two adversaries would prompt Schwarzenberg to fly behind the Erzgebirge without risking battle. If the Allied commander held his ground, Napoleon would return to Dresden and commence an operation to drive the Bohemian Army out of Saxony.[81] As soon as he accomplished this, he would return to his pet project of taking Berlin.[82]

Shortly before 1:00 A.M. on the eleventh, Napoleon received confirmation that Sacken's corps had reached Dessau. Based on this verification, he concluded that the rest of the Silesian Army as well as the North German Army would concentrate at Dessau. He intended to cross the Elbe and proceed along the right bank to Roßlau, thus north of Blücher and Bernadotte.[83] If their armies escaped and withdrew across the Saale, Napoleon considered a coup de théâtre, transferring his base of operations to Magdeburg. Completely abandoning Saxony, he planned to have Murat withdraw through Torgau and Wittenberg to reunite with him. Communication with France would be reconstituted along the Magdeburg–Wesel road.

By thus shattering the rearward communication of both Blücher and Bernadotte, he would place them in a highly disadvantageous position. In turn, he could maneuver along the entire right bank of the Elbe, debouching at will through Magdeburg, Wittenberg, Torgau, and Dresden.[84] After issuing a flurry of orders, all Napoleon could do was wait and wonder if he would catch Blücher.

Around 5:00 that same morning, the Silesian Army commenced its march west to Wettin. Coming from Jeßnitz, the pontoon train would not reach Wettin until the afternoon, which Blücher learned en route to Wettin. This meant that his army would be limited to the sole bridge that the Prussians thought Bernadotte promised to have ready at daybreak.[85] About four miles northwest of this town, Lieutenant Scharnhorst, who had been sent forward to check on the progress of the crown prince's bridge, returned with the news that no bridge existed at Wettin and no preparations ensued to build one.[86] Naturally, Blücher interpreted this as Bernadotte's insidious attempt to force the Silesian Army to remain with the North German Army on the lower Saale.[87] "For the sake of keeping himself in the good graces of both Paris and Stockholm, the crown prince will not sacrifice any Swedes or do anything to make the French suffer," vented Blücher.[88] To be sure the crown prince learned a lesson, he ordered the army to immediately swing south and take the road to Halle. Describing the result of this apparent breach of faith, Müffling noted: "Here, the commanding general appears to have resolved to no longer proceed in concert with the crown prince and to rely only on his own forces; to make decisions in the future without consulting the crown prince, and communicating to him only his decision."[89]

For the eleventh, Bernadotte planned to have his troops marching by 4:00 A.M. He informed Blücher that the Army of North Germany would cross the Saale in accordance with their agreement, while Bülow's corps would accompany the Army of Silesia to Wettin.[90] The Swedes crossed at Alsleben, the Russians at Rothenburg. Upon learning of Blücher's march to Halle, Bülow led his corps to Rothenburg. Yet Wintzingerode's troops took so long to cross the river that Bülow's men passed the night on the right bank. Tauentzien's IV Corps remained at Dessau astride both banks of the Mulde, with forward troops pushed to Wörlitz and Oranienbaum.[91]

That evening Blücher reported his progress to Tsar Alexander: "Tomorrow, I will occupy Merseburg with St. Priest's corps. After this secures communication with the Bohemian Army, I will await your orders. The three armies now stand so close to each other that a simultaneous attack can occur on any point where the enemy concentrates his forces."[92] To Bernadotte he wrote: "Upon arriving at Wettin, I found that the bridges still had not been built; I thus decided to march to Halle and unite the army there. According to the reports that the courier will give you, I assume that you will push your corps toward Leipzig to be able to attack the enemy in unison with the Bohemian Army. I request that you give me your decision over this."[93] "My dear General Blücher!" responded the crown prince, "I heard you encountered many obstacles in striking a bridge at Wettin and so decided to go to Halle. The position you have taken at Halle implicitly places you in the front line."[94] While he did not reject the idea of accepting battle, the crown prince offered no response to Blücher's request for him to move closer to Halle—classic Bernadotte!

News from the Bohemian Army reached Blücher's headquarters during the afternoon of the twelfth. On the previous day, General Ignaz Gyulay's Austrian corps reached Lützen, less than thirteen miles southwest of Leipzig. Twenty miles southeast of Gyulay, Kleist and Wittgenstein took Borna. Farther south, Allied headquarters and the monarchs halted at Altenburg. Moreover, after posting one corps to blockade Dresden, Bennigsen likewise led the Army of Poland toward Leipzig.[95] During the evening of the twelfth and the night of 12–13 October, the only significant news that reached Blücher concerned St. Priest's establishment of communication with the Bohemian Army at Weißenfels.

Napoleon, at Bad Düben on 11 October,, expected 66,000 men (VII, IV, and XI Corps; 27th Division; I and II Cavalry Corps) to cross the Elbe at Wittenberg, drive off the Prussian blockade corps, and move downstream to the bridge at Roßlau. This westward movement would be covered by III and VI Corps. At Kemberg the Guard would remain ready to engage in any direction. By the end of the day's toils, the disposition of the Grande Armée hardly corresponded to these plans. Of all the troops ordered to cross the Elbe, only 27th Division and VII Corps as well as two light-cavalry divisions reached Wittenberg, though considerably later than the emperor expected.[96]

While his army slowly moved north, Napoleon had no idea that Blücher and Bernadotte already had escaped west. Cavalry sweeps found few enemy troops around Mühlberg or Jeßnitz.[97] Further reports indicated that the two Allied armies no longer stood at Dessau, but where they went remained unknown. Rumors claimed that the Army of North Germany withdrew across the Elbe, while the Army of Silesia turned toward Halle.[98] Yet good news from the south helped ease the emperor's mind: Murat reported that he repulsed Wittgenstein at Borna on the tenth.[99]

Napoleon notified Maret that the reports he received during the night of 11–12 October indicated that the majority of the Allied forces marched in the direction of Halle and the lower Saale.[100] Still, he remained convinced that at least some Allied units remained at Dessau.[101] Between 4:00 and 4:30 A.M. on 12 October, he issued orders to attack these forces, to take Dessau and Roßlau, and to observe the Allies at Halle, keeping them in check should they advance on Leipzig.[102] With only Tauentzien's Landwehr standing in his way, Ney smashed through the positions at Wörlitz, while III Corps advanced in several columns toward Dessau and Wörlitz later in the day. Ney reported that his men netted over 1,500 Allied prisoners. This strengthened Napoleon's conviction that Ney found Bernadotte's entire army rather than a mere corps.[103] Meanwhile, VII Corps marched from Wittenberg along the right bank, reaching Roßlau that night after capturing 400 Prussians from Bülow's 4th Brigade.[104]

At Bad Düben Napoleon waited impatiently for news that would clarify the situation. Late in the morning he received news, but not the sort he wanted. Around 9:30 arrived Murat's report from the previous day, stating that rather than retreat, Schwarzenberg had launched another offensive on Leipzig. Murat already fell back to the outer suburbs of the city; his further retreat to the Mulde appeared likely. These tidings moved Napoleon to consider concentrating the entire army for a showdown with the Allies at Taucha, six miles northeast of Leipzig.[105] Yet indecision seized him. Unable to abandon his operations on the Elbe, he delayed issuing orders for this concentration; only VI Corps marched southwest toward Leipzig.

Another report from Murat arrived at 8:00 P.M. that night. This time he stated that he could hold his position south of Leipzig on the thirteenth.[106] Based on Murat's confidence, Napoleon decided to make one more attempt to find Allied forces south of the Elbe before marching south. Reynier and Ney would continue their movements toward Aken and Dessau. But by 5:00 A.M. on 13 October, Napoleon received confirmed reports that both the Army of North Germany and the Army of Silesia had retreated across the Saale. Unless he truly intended to execute his coup de théâtre, continuing the operation on the Elbe no longer served any purpose. A concentration against the Bohemian Army appeared imperative. The emperor ordered the army to Leipzig, expecting a battle to occur "on the 15th or 16th."[107]

Meanwhile, rumors that claimed Napoleon would proceed through Wittenberg against Berlin, Magdeburg, or even Stralsund pushed Bernadotte over the edge. Deciding to fly across the Elbe, the crown prince ordered Blücher to follow. Furious, the general refused, demanding that Bernadotte hold his ground and await the approach of Schwarzenberg's army. This pointed refusal and the news of Napoleon's march to Leipzig changed Bernadotte's mind. On the fifteenth he informed Blücher that the Army of North Germany would unite with the Army of Silesia. At Halle Blücher's headquarters celebrated its victory: the Silesian Army had dragged the crown prince across the Elbe and kept him in the theater.

On 13 October a letter from Blücher dated two days earlier reached Allied headquarters at Altenburg. The communique confirmed that the Silesian Army did not retreat across the Elbe as feared. Instead, it had reached Halle, the Army of North Germany likewise stood on the right bank of the Saale, and Napoleon pursued both armies with his main force. Blücher requested orders for a general advance. His letter concludes with the words: "The three armies are now so close that a simultaneous attack against the point where the enemy has concentrated his forces can take place." Blücher's proximity breathed life into Allied headquarters. "The advantage of our present position allows us to consider the destruction of the enemy army," responded Schwarzenberg that same day.[108] The Allied commander in chief's instructions for the next three days called for a concentric advance on Leipzig to suffocate the French.

Despite more disagreements with Bernadotte, Blücher methodically closed on Leipzig from the northwest. On the sixteenth he ordered Yorck and Langeron to attack Marmont's VI Corps at Möckern, just north of the city. The murderous artillery and savage fighting reduced Yorck's corps from 16,000 men to 9,000; Langeron sustained over 2,000 casualties. Marmont's corps suffered the loss

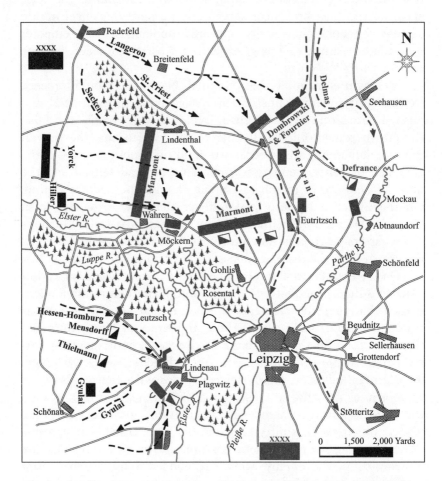

The Battle of Leipzig, Engagements of Möckern and Lindenau, 16 October 1813. Map drawn by Alex Mendoza. Copyright © 2014 by the University of Oklahoma Press.

of 7,000 soldiers in addition to 2,500 prisoners. Hearing the sound of Blücher's guns, Bernadotte nevertheless did nothing to support the Silesian Army. Blücher should have committed his reserve—Sacken's corps—earlier in the battle. Fearing that Napoleon would disengage from the Bohemian Army and strike the Silesian Army as soon as he saw his line of communication to the west seriously threatened, Blücher withheld the Russians for too long.

Although Blücher resolved to resume the attack on the seventeenth, Schwarzenberg postponed the Bohemian Army's operations until the eighteenth. Consequently, Blücher granted his men a much needed day of rest. Early the following day, Schwarzenberg's guns thundered on Blücher's right. After reluctantly agreeing to cede Langeron's corps to Bernadotte in return for the Army of North Germany's participation in the battle on the eighteenth, Blücher attempted to advance with Sacken's corps. Despite several attempts, the Russians could not move forward and even needed Yorck's support to hold Gohlis. Nightfall and exhaustion ended the fighting on 18 October. News that Napoleon had commenced the retreat from Leipzig toward Merseburg prompted Blücher to dispatch Yorck's survivors to Halle that night.

For the nineteenth, Blücher planned to storm Leipzig with the infantry of his two Russian corps. With Langeron's arrival delayed, he ordered Sacken to attack Leipzig's Halle suburb at 11:00 A.M. Although Langeron came up, the Russians failed to dislodge the imperials. After one hour of fighting, the defenders withdrew thanks to Bülow's soldiers, who penetrated Leipzig and threatened to cut off the troops holding the suburb. The Russians drove through the position with Blücher at their head shouting "Forward! Forward!" Upon reaching the inner city, they heard a loud blast from the west. A unit of Sacken's corps had penetrated close to the Elster Bridge, where thousands of imperial soldiers waited to commence the retreat west. After the Russians opened fire, a French soldier detonated the bridge. The ghastly shower of body parts that fell on the inner city did nothing to stop the fighting. By now, troops from the North German, Silesian, and Bohemian Armies had breached the defenses. All pressed toward the marketplace in the city's center. Imperial resistance crumbled. Blücher reached the marketplace, where the troops greeted him with hurrahs. After some time Bernadotte arrived, then Alexander and Frederick William, and finally Kaiser Francis.[109]

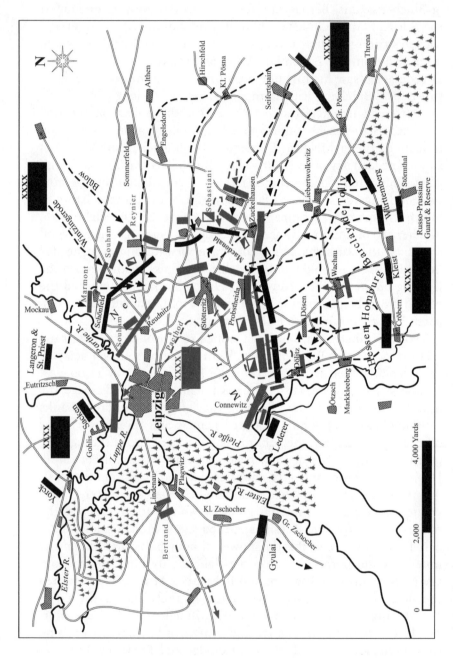

The Battle of Leipzig, 18 October 1813. Map drawn by Alex Mendoza. Copyright © 2014 by the University of Oklahoma Press.

On 20 October Blücher described the scene to Amalie:

Yesterday, I could not write. I was too tired, but my friend
Gneisenau wrote and told you I am well. On the 18th and 19th
occurred the greatest battle that the earth has ever seen: 600,000
men struggled with each other. Around 2:00 P.M., I took Leipzig
by storm, the King of Saxony and many generals were captured,
the Polish Prince Poniatowski drowned; 170 cannon were captured and around 40,000 men are prisoners. Napoleon escaped, but
he is not safe. This moment my cavalry has brought in another
2,000 prisoners; his entire army is lost. The Tsar of Russia kissed
me in public in the marketplace and called me the "Liberator of
Germany." The Austrian Kaiser heaped praises on me, and my
King thanked me with tears in his eyes. Because the Tsar cannot give me any more decorations, I received from him a golden
sword beset with gems; it is quite valuable. I will go with my army
through Thuringia to Westphalia and my troops shall soon be at
Münster.[110]

To Bonin he exclaimed:

We just had two great, beautiful days; during the 18th and 19th,
the Great Colossus fell like an oak tree in a storm. He, the
Great Tyrant, saved himself, but his henchmen are in our hands.
Poniatowski was wounded and drowned; we believe Augereau
was as well. Reynier and Lauriston have been captured; the former is wounded. On the 19th, at the end of the battle, Leipzig was
stormed with great bravery. The Russian infantry first entered the
city on my side, on the other side it was the brave Pomeranians. It
was an incomparable fight; 100 cannon were captured in Leipzig.
Our monarchs, the Austrian and Russian Emperors and our King,
thanked me on the marketplace. Alexander embraced me.[111]

On the twentieth Frederick William promoted Blücher to the
rank of field marshal. "Through numerous victories," wrote the
king, "you increase your worth to the state more than I can follow with signs of my gratitude. Accept a new proof of this through
the appointment to *General-Feldmarschall*, and long may you grace
this position to the joy of the Fatherland and as a model to the army,
which you have so often led to fame and victory."[112] Five days later
Blücher informed Amalie of his promotion: "Now, as Mrs. Field
Marshal, you must conduct yourself very properly; do not be greedy

and lose some weight. I will now receive a respectable salary, yet none of us have received any pay for the last two months because nothing could get through to us from Berlin. Write me soon. I have four beautiful white horses for you and two mules—if only I could get them to you. Everyone here is fine and sends their best regards. PS. I just do not know what to with all of these decorations. I'm covered in them like an old coach-horse, but my greatest reward is the thought that I was the one who humbled the arrogant tyrant."[113]

With a fury, Blücher pursued the wreck of Napoleon's army as it retreated to the Rhine. He encountered all sorts of obstacles: bad weather, mountains, insubordinate corps commanders, and Schwarzenberg's typical lethargy. On 30 October he gave up hope on catching Napoleon, as his letter to Amalie suggests: "I don't know what else to write you. On my chest I have every decoration conceivable. Daily, I hunt the Emperor Napoleon. Serious engagements will no longer occur on this side of the Rhine, and in seven days I will be at Frankfurt or Koblenz according to the direction the enemy turns. I and my entire entourage are healthy. I have received no further news from Franz other than his healing goes well and he is out of danger. I hope that Dresden, where he is, will soon surrender and then he will be free. Your brother, I hear, is well. Enclosed is a letter from the Austrian Kaiser. At Vienna, they will make a monument of me. You must send my portrait to Prague."[114] Finally, on 3 November, he wrote:

> The great operations have now come to an end; the French have been driven completely across the Rhine. For eight consecutive nights I occupied the quarters vacated by Napoleon and slept where he slept. He has lost the majority of his army, especially his artillery, and if we had not made a great mistake, he and all of his army would have been captured. He will not soon return to Germany. . . . The day after tomorrow I go to Wetzlar and will then move to the Rhine, and perhaps cross. The joy with which I am greeted is great everywhere. It will not be my lot to go to Münster, but another part of the army will soon appear there and so your dear homeland soon will be liberated. One will return to us or compensate us for all the property we left behind. I think only of the beautiful tea set and my wine. Very soon I will send you 3,000–4,000 thaler . . . take care of it, but have a good time.[115]

Blücher, Gneisenau, and Müffling devised a bold plan for the Army of Silesia to cross the middle Rhine and advance through Aachen and Liège toward Brussels, while the Army of Bohemia crossed the Rhine between Mannheim and Mainz. Paris would be the general goal of all operations. The Prussians hoped to surprise the French and capture several key fortresses during the initial confusion. Blücher believed he would be ready to cross the Rhine on 15 November and estimated reaching Brussels ten days later. "You ask what I will do now that I am on the Rhine?" he wrote Bonin. "And I say to you, we will cross it, we will conquer Holland and Brabant, and we will rout him [Napoleon] so that he must make peace. The discontent of the nation is active and Napoleon's reign will end. This is my belief."[116] Without authorization, Blücher led his army northwest toward Köln on 7 November. Four days later at Altenkirchen, some thirty-five miles southeast of Köln, he received explicit orders from Tsar Alexander to turn around and assume the siege of Mainz. The following day the Silesian Army reversed its march. From a height on the Taunus Mountains, the Prussians caught a glimpse of the flashing Rhine and greeted it with a loud cheer. According to a sergeant major of the Black Hussars, whose Jäger squadron reconnoitered the riverbank: "We rode cross-country at full speed, down wooded slopes, through vineyards, and greeted the German—or soon to be freed from the foreign yoke—Rhine with endless cheers. We dismounted and with our hands scooped up the holy water or else lay full length and drank it."[117] Blücher had reached the Rhine, but he would have to wait until the new year before crossing the historic river.

CHAPTER 14

FRANCE

For the Austrians, the spirit of cooperation that produced the Battle of Leipzig ended when the Allies reached the Rhine. Since Austria joined the Sixth Coalition in August 1813, Metternich actively sought to undermine the war objectives forged by the Russians, Prussians, and British. At Frankfurt both Metternich and Schwarzenberg hoped to mold the Allied campaign plan to fit the needs of Austrian grand strategy. On the one hand, the foreign minister wanted to create a balance between the great powers by using France as a counterweight to Russia. On the other, he wanted to establish an equilibrium of power among all European states: the powerful and the weak, the victors and the vanquished. Metternich's brilliant comprehension of the political landscape earned him considerable advantages not only in laying the groundwork for a postwar Europe that served Austrian grand strategy but also in the perpetual struggle to restrain and counter Austria's allies.

After the invasion of France began, Schwarzenberg continued to allow his strategy to be dictated by Metternich and allowed his own fears to master his operations. The field marshal viewed an advance on Paris as imprudent both militarily and politically. In his opinion, taking the city would not necessarily end the war and could prove to be just as much a disaster for the Allies as Moscow had been for Napoleon. Yet as Carl von Clausewitz points out in his history of the campaign, his actual operations exposed the main Allied army to a crippling defeat that would have had profound consequences for the Coalition. Schwarzenberg's "200,000-man army began its assault on France along four eccentric radii," explains Clausewitz, "not counting the detachment sent to Lyon, and extended itself 150 miles between Strasbourg and Dijon. Its reserves were in the middle of this immense circle, so the main force, by which the commanding general was found, was not stronger than 30,000 men. . . . Indeed, if [Marshal Claude Perrin] Victor with 14,000 men at Strasbourg and [Marshal] Mortier, who was on the march with 12,000 men from

Reims to Langres, had been in position, this 200,000-man army would have been in peril."[1]

Unlike Metternich, Schwarzenberg never understood that by accelerating his march, he could end the war much faster. He unquestioningly accepted the minister's guidance and advice, delaying his operations at the moment when an energetic offensive could have achieved decisive results. Consisting solely of Austrian troops (1st and 2nd Light Divisions; I, II, and III Corps; and the Austrian Reserve), Schwarzenberg's left wing conducted a lengthy, excessive wheeling movement through Switzerland, Franche-Comté, and southern Champagne that wasted three weeks. After chaining II Corps to Besançon and directing 1st Light Division to Lyon, the field marshal squandered more time by uselessly maneuvering 2nd Light Division, I Corps, and the Austrian Reserve between Dijon and Besançon; only III Corps lumbered toward Langres. Finally realizing that he had denuded his center to such an extent that it was weaker than his flanks, Schwarzenberg ordered 2nd Light Division, I Corps, and the Austrian Reserve to force march to Langres. He then spent 13–24 January advancing through Langres and Chaumont to Bar-sur-Aube, inconceivably leaving behind the Austrian Reserve at Dijon, II Corps at Besançon, and a considerable siege corps at Belfort. At Bourgogne on the army's left wing, I Corps echeloned along the road from St. Seine to Châtillon-sur-Seine, while 2nd Light Division marched toward Auxerre. In the center, the Russo-Prussian Guard and Reserve loitered around Langres, thirty-five miles south of the head of the army (III and IV Corps), which reached Bar-sur-Aube. Far to the south, 1st Light Division retreated all the way to Geneva after having failed to secure the surrender of Lyon's weak garrison. In addition, the prospect of destroying the French forces that faced Schwarzenberg's right wing and defended Alsace and Lorraine did not entice the Austrian to conduct an operation to dislodge them. Instead, he summoned Blücher to cross the Rhine on New Years Day.

In mid-January 1814 Marshals Victor and Marmont completed a retreat from the Rhine to Nancy and Metz, respectively, in order to prepare a defense of the Moselle. Although joined by Marshal Ney and one division of Young Guard, their forces totaled no more than 30,000 men. Aside from Mortier's Old Guard divisions, totaling 10,000 men, at Langres and Marshal Macdonald's 10,000 men at Maastricht, these 30,000 men represented all that remained of Napoleon's combat-ready forces in France proper. With Blücher in hot pursuit of the marshals, Schwarzenberg could have chosen one of three military options. First, he could have rapidly advanced through Langres to firmly establish his army on the Seine to threaten the French capital before Napoleon completed the organization of his new army. Second, he could have masked enemy forces at Langres and closed on the marshals as they retreated from the Moselle to the Meuse and then to the Marne. In conjunction with the Army of Silesia coming from the east, Schwarzenberg could have delivered a decisive pocket battle that would have eliminated the majority of Napoleon's available combat power. His third option, to simply allow IV and V Corps to support the Silesian Army, would have led to the same result. Rather than allow his right wing to cooperate with Blücher's army to envelop and eliminate this French force, Schwarzenberg purposefully weakened his right wing by summoning IV and V Corps to support his center at Langres, which faced no more than 10,000 men of Mortier's Old Guard. All that remained of the Bohemian Army's right wing was VI Corps, which lingered so long between Haguenau and Strasbourg that it remained several marches behind and provided no support for Blücher. The orders for IV and V Corps to march west came at a time when the bulk of Schwarzenberg's left wing remained idle between Dole and Lyon.

For his part, Metternich feared a decisive Allied victory in December 1813 or January 1814 more than a French victory. During the two months of the invasion, a French collapse and total Allied victory had to be avoided. Schwarzenberg's own fears and loyalty to Metternich assured this outcome. His cautious leadership, "which decided nothing and risked nothing," corresponded perfectly to the minister's view of how the war should be conducted in Austria's interests. As the Bohemian Army advanced, Schwarzenberg stripped his center of any sizeable forces in order to strengthen his left wing, which was first used to establish Austrian influence in Switzerland, then to drive into southern France with no clear objective other than to destabilize Napoleonic control over the region bordering French-controlled Italy. After Schwarzenberg perceived enemy forces in Alsace, he summoned Blücher to cross the Rhine. Although the French withdrew from Alsace, new rumors of a concentration of 80,000 men at Langres troubled the Allied commander in chief. Recognizing the weakness of his center, he pulled his rightmost units away from Blücher and closer to his center to reinforce his units crawling toward the domineering plateau. He made few changes to the operations of the corps, light divisions, and reserves operating on his left wing. Rather than direct his IV, V, and VI Corps to cooperate with Blücher to destroy Victor, Marmont, and Ney, he summoned them to Langres. Not until peace negotiations with Napoleon failed in February would Metternich allow Schwarzenberg to heed Tsar Alexander's wishes to conduct the war with more vigor.

As noted, Blücher led the Silesian Army across the middle Rhine on New Years' Day 1814 in response to the commander in chief's call. During the course of January, the two Allied armies gradually approached each other as Schwarzenberg moved west from Basel toward Langres, and Blücher advanced southwest, eventually crossing the Marne River and reaching Brienne, the place where Napoleon attended military school as a youth. In his rapid drive across the Marne, the new field marshal did not engage the emperor. In fact, to oversee the mobilization of France, Napoleon remained at Paris during the initial phase of the Allied invasion. On 25 January he departed to join his marshals; Victor, Macdonald, Marmont, and Ney had traded land for time, thus doing much damage to the emperor's attempts to mobilize an army of 400,000 men. Napoleon's operations in February mainly sought to stall the Allied advance and gain time for this mobilization to reach fruition.

After spending one week in the region of Langres, the Army of Bohemia started moving northwest between the Marne and the Aube Rivers in the direction of Paris. As Schwarzenberg's troops lumbered forward, the Allied commander received the surprising news that the Silesian Army stood on the same road only one march north of him. After leaving Langeron's 34,000 men to besiege Mainz and Yorck's 21,500 men among the fortresses on the Moselle River, Blücher had continued his advance with the 27,000 men of Sacken's corps. The Prussian field marshal turned south to seek a union with Schwarzenberg and propel the Bohemian Army into either a battle with Napoleon or an accelerated march on Paris. The emperor made his first appearance in the field just in time to strike the rear of Sacken's corps as it followed the course of the Aube northward on 29 January. Blücher accepted battle at Brienne, engaging the French as they assaulted from the northeast. Napoleon did not have all his forces at hand, so the combat essentially pitted 30,000 French against a similar number of Russians—Schwarzenberg's main body remained too distant to support. Both sides sustained approximately 3,000 casualties, and both claimed victory. Although he conceded the field by withdrawing seven miles south to Trannes, Blücher considered the battle a personal victory over Napoleon. "Yesterday the great man himself attacked me at Brienne," he wrote Hardenberg. "I repulsed him. Eight cannon are my prizes."[2]

The two armies remained in this position on 30 and 31 January. To appease the tsar and the Prussians, Schwarzenberg finally authorized Blücher to deliver a battle on 1 February at La Rothière, halfway between Trannes and Brienne. He placed III and IV Corps under Blücher's direct command. Furthermore, the 34,000 men of Barclay's Russo-Prussian Guard and Reserve would support at Trannes and Bar-sur-Aube, but Blücher received no direct authority over these units.[3] In addition, Schwarzenberg ordered the 26,000 men of his V Corps to advance west toward Brienne. Not only did he make approximately 85,000 men available to support Blücher's own 27,000 troops, but Schwarzenberg relinquished command of the upcoming battle in favor of the Prussian. He also rejected the notion of a battle of annihilation that would interfere with Austrian politics. To avoid the suspicion of his allies, he transferred command to Blücher but did not place all of the troops committed to the engagement at his disposal. Because the Austrians did not desire a decisive victory, Schwarzenberg provided Blücher only enough manpower to drive Napoleon from his position, not to destroy him. Should the operation fail, the corps of the Bohemian Army not participating in the battle would take an *Aufnahmestellung* (receiving position) to cover the retreat.[4]

In the meantime, Napoleon mustered all the forces he could: 45,100 men and 128 guns. Fortunately for the French, the terrain forced Blücher to make a narrow approach that prevented him from deploying his superior numbers. Combat lasted deep into the night. Napoleon vigorously led his troops in several counterattacks. Late in the evening, Allied cavalry advanced through gaping holes in the enemy's center and left, forcing the emperor to commence a general retreat. French losses amounted to 6,000 men, including 2,400 prisoners, and fifty-four guns, while the Allies claimed to have captured 3,000–4,000 men and seventy-three guns.[5] Berthier issued the disposition for the army's general retreat to Troyes via Lesmont, which the emperor scheduled to begin at 2:00 A.M. on 2 February.[6]

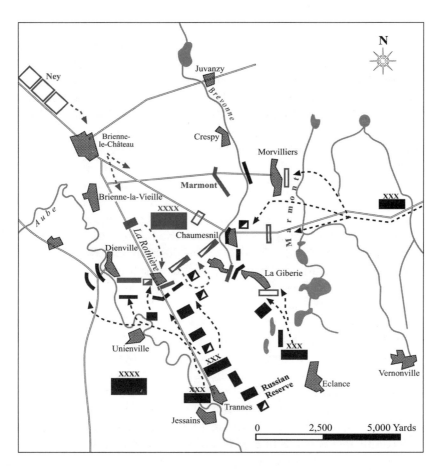

The Battle of La Rothière, 1 February 1814. Map drawn by Alex Mendoza.
Copyright © 2014 by the University of Oklahoma Press.

A general pursuit could have ended the war, but Blücher lacked fresh reserves after a snafu at headquarters sent half of the Russian grenadiers and all of the cuirassiers in the wrong direction.[7] Schwarzenberg's rearward units remained too distant to participate. His I Corps could have demolished Napoleon's disorganized units had the commander in chief directed it to the bridge over the Aube at Lesmont, the crossing point of the retreating army.[8] The battle cost the Allies approximately 6,000 men—over half being Russian—mainly due to the effectiveness of enemy artillery. Although a victory, the outstanding feature of the Battle of La Rothière is that the Allies achieved no deceive results. Blücher scored a tactical victory over Napoleon on French soil, routed a majority of his forces, inflicted more casualties proportionately although not numerically, and captured a considerable portion of French artillery, but much more could have been achieved. Several reasons contributed to the squandering of the opportunity presented at La Rothière, and blame falls on Allied headquarters. Approximately 125,000 soldiers could have been committed to the battle, but only 80,000 actually saw action on 1 February. Rather than destroy the enemy, Schwarzenberg limited the objective to driving him from Brienne.

That Napoleon escaped did not dampen the enthusiasm at Silesian Army headquarters. "The great blow has been delivered," Blücher boasted to Bonin. "Yesterday, I decisively defeated Napoleon; he is in full retreat on Paris. We predict a fast peace because he can no longer defy us. Sixteen cannon and many prisoners are in my hands. The number of dead was very large because the Russians are very embittered. The Tsar and our King were spectators; they turned everything over to me. I had only five Prussian squadrons with me, the rest were Russians, Austrians, and Württembergers. The Emperor Napoleon had 30,000 men, I almost 60,000. Alexander squeezed my hand and said: 'Blücher, today you have crowned all of your victories, humanity will bless you.'" The soldiers also felt that they had accomplished a great deal. "When I showed myself to the troops at daybreak today," continued Blücher, "they greeted me with a Hurrah, bringing tears to my eyes. I owe much thanks to my loyal assistant, Gneisenau."[9]

Napoleon's stand at La Rothière should have been a monumental defeat for the emperor. Unless the two Allied armies separated, another confrontation could result in a French disaster. Fortunately for Napoleon, Schwarzenberg decided to separate the two armies.

This step appeared logical to the Prussians of the Silesian Army, who welcomed the decision. Although the forces just achieved their union, a separation made sense in terms of operations. During the November 1813 meetings at Frankfurt, the Allies decided to continue the Trachenberg Plan, which required separate operations by the Coalition's main armies. Logistics likewise demanded the parting. Nevertheless, the Allies remained keenly aware of Napoleon's ability to exploit a central position and utilize interior lines. To counter this advantage, commanders agreed on a concentric operation in which Schwarzenberg and Blücher would mutually advance, though always remaining in position to support the other within twenty-four hours. Blücher agreed to Schwarzenberg's suggestion that the BohemianArmy pursue Napoleon while the Silesian Army marched north and then west to strike the highway to Paris. His first task would be to direct Sacken to Châlons to reunite with Yorck as well as Kleist's corps, which had been transferred to the Silesian Army. From Châlons, the Silesian Army would proceed along the Marne through Meaux to Paris, while the Bohemian Army moved through Troyes to drive along both banks of the Seine to Paris.

Of the dangers entailed, the march objectives of Troyes and Châlons contradicted the idea of both armies advancing in mutual supporting distance. Instead, the two forces would be separated by almost forty miles, which amounted to a march of three days. Schwarzenberg and Blücher did not view this as problematic, for the two highways that led west to Paris would gradually bring the Allied armies closer together as they converged on the capital. In addition, Schwarzenberg assigned the task of maintaining communication between the two armies to Wittgenstein's VI Corps, which reached St.-Dizier on 1 February, and to General Alexander Seslavin's Cossack corps.[10] Yet for the plan to achieve complete success, *both* Allied commands had to march on Paris, while contact with Napoleon's army had to be maintained on a daily, if not hourly, basis.

Early on the morning of 3 February, the French army reached Troyes on the Seine. Estimating Schwarzenberg's army to number 150,000 men, Napoleon assumed the commander in chief would lead his masses to Troyes in direct pursuit of his own defeated army. As for the Silesian Army, he deemed where it would go next. "It is possible," he wrote on 2 February, "that Blücher's army will move between the Marne and the Aube, toward Vitry and Châlons."

By utilizing the highway that ran through Sézanne, the emperor planned to operate against any Allied column that targeted Paris. If the city did not appear threatened, he would "maneuver against Blücher and delay his march."[11] Aware of the Prussians move to Fère-Champenoise on the road to Châlons, he led his army thirty-two miles northwest from Troyes to Nogent-sur-Seine on the night of 6–7 February.[12]

Although considering an attack on Schwarzenberg's left wing at Bar-sur-Seine, the need to defend Paris kept Napoleon's attention focused on Blücher.[13] In response to Macdonald's evacuation of Châlons, he decided to move the army twenty-two miles north-northeast to Sézanne and from there fifteen miles north-northwest to Montmirail. He planned to unite with Marmont and Macdonald, then maneuver the army to a position to block Blücher's advance. Napoleon acknowledged the possibility that Schwarzenberg could conduct an offensive against Paris or Nogent but counted on the Austrian's notorious lethargy. In any event, the master would be close at hand should the Army of Bohemia advance.[14] He believed that he would make short work of Blücher and then be able to turn against Schwarzenberg with all his forces.[15] Two days later, on 9 February, he clearly explained his view of the situation to his brother Joseph. Assuming Blücher commanded no more than 45,000 men, he hoped to "*écraser* (crush)" the Army of Silesia within "two or three days" with his force of 80,000 men. Believing this would put Blücher out of action for several days, the emperor then could deal with Schwarzenberg. Even if he lacked sufficient numbers to attack the Bohemian Army, he hoped to paralyze its commander for anywhere between fourteen and twenty days. This would provide crucial time for further mobilization.[16] Leaving 14,000 men under Victor to hold the bridge at Nogent-sur-Seine, Napoleon departed on the evening of 9 February to conduct his defensive strategy by executing offensive tactical strikes.[17] After advancing north from Nogent through Sézanne, he struck like lightening in the ensuing Six Days Campaign.

Meanwhile, to reach the Seine, Schwarzenberg's III, IV, and V Corps marched west to Lesmont and crossed the Aube on 2 February.[18] After the French evacuated Troyes during the night of 6–7 February, his I Corps occupied the town while the rest of the army moved into billets in the surrounding region. With his army in need of rest, Schwarzenberg halted operations until 10 February.

Tragically for Blücher's soldiers, the Allied commander in chief summoned Wittgenstein's VI Corps to Troyes rather than Arcis-sur-Aube. Seslavin, whose Cossacks should have maintained communication between Wittgenstein and Blücher, received orders to raid as far as possible westward toward the Loire River. Thus, communication between the Bohemian and Silesian Armies no longer existed. Only one hundred Cossacks from the small Vlasov Regiment roamed the wide space between the Seine and the Marne.

As for the Prussian field marshal, his headquarters reached Soudron, twelve miles southwest of Châlons, on 5 February. With Macdonald retreating, Blücher hoped to at least finish the business he started six months earlier at the Katzbach. He directed Yorck to advance from Châlons to Château-Thierry along the Great Paris Highway. Instructing Sacken to proceed along the Little Paris Highway, Blücher wanted the Russians to reach Montmirail on the eighth. He tasked Sacken's cavalry with patrolling south toward the Aube and the Seine. Escorted by Langeron's IX Infantry Corps, commanded by General Nikolay Olsufiev, Silesian Army headquarters would follow one day behind Sacken, reaching Montmirail on the ninth, according to Blücher's timetable. He ordered Kleist to force march so his corps could reach Montmirail by 10 February.[19] In addition, General Petre Kaptsevich's X Infantry Corps, likewise from Langeron's command, would also leg it to Montmirail. Despite being reinforced by Kleist's II Corps, Blücher's army totaled only 50,000 men.[20]

The Prussians felt confident that Napoleon did not have the numbers to mask Schwarzenberg, protect Paris, and conduct an offensive against the Silesian Army. In addition, Sacken's cavalry and Seslavin's Cossacks would monitor the gap between the two armies, which Schwarzenberg had promised to plug with Wittgenstein's corps. Assuming the commander in chief honored his commitment, Blücher felt confident of success. "The enemy withdraws toward Paris," he wrote Amalie. "We are now fifteen [German] miles from Paris and will reach this capital in eight days. In all likelihood, Napoleon will lose his crown. The Count d'Artois [Louis XVIII] already arrived from England; the Allied powers intend to set him on the throne and the French nation, I believe, will gladly accept. Here, winter holds on; today it is mild and rainy. I am in the region that makes the best champagne in all of France. I am sick of war and desire my rest; with God's help, peace will soon come. Now, on to Paris. I do not believe Napoleon will deliver another battle."[21]

Patrolling from Sézanne, General Akim Karpov's Cossacks from Sacken's corps found French troops at Montmirail and La Ferté-sous-Jouarre on the morning of the seventh. But they reported that the soldiers appeared to be disbanding: troopers traded their horses for peasant garments. Blücher and his staff interpreted this to mean the dissolution of Macdonald's corps. Yet on the evening of the eighth, the French forced Karpov to evacuate Sézanne. In fact, Polish lancers proceeded north, crossed the unoccupied bridge over the Petit Morin at St. Prix, and attempted a surprise night attack on Olsufiev's troops at Baye, some six miles southwest of Blücher's headquarters at Étoges. The Russians detected their bitter foes before the Poles could attack.[22]

That evening Blücher had sat down to dine with his staff at the château in Étoges when a breathless Russian officer burst in to report that Polish cavalry had surprised his comrades at Baye. From his excited and barely understandable words they concluded that the enemy followed close behind. According to Nostitz, "The report made during dinner at Étoges by the Russian artillery officer of the sudden appearance of the enemy was like a flash of lightening from the heavens: everyone was amazed and had trouble explaining the cause of this strange phenomenon."[23]

Because Olsufiev's infantry corps lacked cavalry, Blücher dispatched a portion of his staff guard to conduct reconnaissance. Uncertain of the situation, he decided to withdraw his headquarters to Vertus later that night. Opinions over the meaning of this raid remained divided. Müffling claimed that he advised caution and urged Blücher to have Sacken remain at Montmirail. But Gneisenau, who saw the attack as a mere reconnaissance, sent verbal instructions to Sacken. If the French presence at Sézanne did not appear threatening, then he should continue the march to La Ferté-sous-Jouarre and cut off Macdonald from the west while Yorck pursued the marshal from the east.[24]

On 9 February Blücher received letters from Tsar Alexander and Schwarzenberg requesting that Kleist's corps veer southwest toward Arcis-sur-Aube and Nogent-sur-Seine to cover Wittgenstein's VI Corps, which should have been securing Blücher's left flank.[25] A second letter from Schwarzenberg, dated the seventh, informed Blücher of Napoleon's retreat to Nogent-sur-Seine. With

Wittgenstein pursuing the French on the road from Arcis-sur-Aube, Alexander and Schwarzenberg requested flank coverage for the Russian corps.[26] On this occasion, Blücher did not refuse the call for assistance. As Kleist's II Corps numbered a mere 8,000 men, prudence compelled him to reinforce it with the 11,000 bayonets of the Russian IX and X Infantry Corps.[27] Yorck and Sacken would finish off Macdonald while Kleist, Kaptsevich, Silesian Army headquarters, and Olsufiev marched toward Sézanne on the tenth.[28]

Gneisenau immediately issued orders to comply with Blücher's pledge. That same afternoon, 9 February, Kleist's advance guard trooped eleven miles south from Vertus to Fère-Champenoise. The next day his main body, followed by Kaptsevich, would march to Sézanne, while Kleist's advance guard proceeded to Barbonne-Fayel; Olsufiev would remain ready to follow from Champaubert. Yorck received orders to move closer to Sacken by crossing the Marne at Château-Thierry and marching to Montmirail. The old curmudgeon disagreed with Gneisenau's assessment of the situation and so refused to fully execute his orders. On the tenth Yorck sent his advance guard across the Marne but directed it to proceed only five miles along the right bank to Chézy-sur-Marne, while the head of the main body barely cleared Château-Thierry.[29]

Hoping to receive more-detailed reports over the French as well as the position of the Bohemian Army, Blücher and his staff joined Kleist on the march to Fère-Champenoise during the afternoon of the tenth. While en route, a Russian orderly delivered dreadful news: Napoleon had crushed Olsufiev at Champaubert earlier that afternoon. The Russians managed to cut their way out, though not before Olsufiev and nine guns fell into French hands. Russian casualties amounted to more than 2,000 dead and captured; only 1,600 men and fifteen guns escaped to rejoin army. On the following day, Napoleon turned against Sacken, who was attempting to reach the army's assembly point at Vertus. Marching southeast from La Ferté-sous-Jouarre, the Russians encountered the emperor's main force at Montmirail, twenty-two miles west of Blücher's position. Yorck, who urged Sacken to flee across the Marne with him, committed his 7th and 2nd Brigades to cover the Russian retreat. Around 7:30 P.M., all firing ceased, and the French did not pursue. Russian casualties reached 2,800 men as well as six flags and thirteen guns; the Prussians lost thirty-one officers and 860 men. French losses are estimated to have been 2,000 men. Sacken quartered at Château-Thierry, Yorck at Viffort. That night one of Yorck's staff officers returned from headquarters with Blücher's verbal order for him and Sacken to immediately withdraw north across the Marne and march to Reims, the new general-assembly point of the Silesian Army.

Early on the twelfth, Napoleon led the army north in pursuit of Sacken and Yorck. He caught them at Château-Thierry. Although hard pressed, both the Russian and Prussian rear guards bravely held until the two corps crossed the Marne. Compared to only 600 French casualties, Yorck lost twenty-two officers, 1,229 men, three guns, and part of his baggage; the Russians lost 1,500 men, five guns, and much of their baggage. The destruction of the bridge at Château-Thierry prevented the French from pursuing Yorck and Sacken the next day. Consequently, around 4:00 A.M. on 14 February, Napoleon rode east to attack an enemy force reportedly moving west on the Little Paris Highway.

Blücher remained optimistic on the evening of the thirteenth. "I have had three bitter days," he explained to Amalie. "Napoleon attacked me three times in three days with his entire force and all of his Guard, but he has achieved no purpose and today he is on the retreat to Paris. I will follow him tomorrow and unite our army; a main battle before Paris will decide everything. Fear not that we have been defeated. Without an unexpected mistake, this would not have been possible."[30] To relieve the pressure on Yorck and Sacken, he resolved to advance west with Kleist and Kaptsevich. Reaching Vauchamps around 9:30 on the morning of the fourteenth, the Allies ran into Marmont's VI Corps. Soon after, the emperor arrived. Around 2:00 that afternoon, he launched his main attack, involving an estimated 12,000 cavalry troopers. Upon viewing the mass of French horse, Blücher quickly concluded that they faced Napoleon himself. A captured officer not only confirmed his presence but also claimed that on the day before, Yorck and Sacken had retreated across the Marne. Based on this news, Gneisenau advised that the retreat begin without delay; Blücher concurred. A harrowing flight ensued from Vauchamps through Champaubert to Étoges. The French cavalry, commanded by General Emmanuel Grouchy, hounded the Allies. Despite brave resistance, Prussian losses amounted to eighty officers, 3,908 men, and seven guns, while the Russians lost 2,000 men and nine guns; French casualties numbered a mere 600 men. Nostitz picks up the story:

We came to a battalion of the 7th Reserve Regiment, which at the moment formed a square against enemy cavalry. Individuals in the battalion started firing and the General always remained a short distance before its front. The firing increased; the onset of darkness made it so that no one could clearly recognize the General. . . . An orderly who joined us by chance was wounded, but the General remained rigid in the same spot. Then the suspicion mounted in me that he was determined not to survive a day he considered to be the grave of all the results achieved for the Fatherland and the laurels he acquired. The question of what he intended to achieve by his presence at such a dangerous place went unanswered, whereupon I said to him with all the excitement that such a moment could justify: "If Your Excellency wants to be shot dead here, while only you alone are in the position to wrest the corps from an otherwise unavoidable destruction, then history will have little to say of you some day."

This worked. "To where shall I ride," asked the Field Marshal? I led him to the right wing of the battalion, almost at the same moment that the French cavalry attacked but was repulsed. We now rode along the highway and soon reunited with the surviving persons of headquarters. Unable to find the Field Marshal, they turned around to look for him. After we continued the retreat together for quite a stretch, the General dismounted from his horse to attend to a need (urinate) and said: "My dear Gneisenau, since I was not shot dead today, which I gladly wanted, I am convinced anew and stronger than before that everything will end fortunately and good." General Gneisenau asked me the meaning of these words, and I explained to him what had happened, but requested that it be kept a secret. This occurred; only a sketchy rumor over this affair later spread and the Field Marshal always recognized our silence with appreciation.[31]

Blücher ordered the remains of his army to retreat eighteen miles east to Châlons, where ample supplies awaited the exhausted survivors. Protected by the Marne, the army could reunite and reorganize. His main body rested a few hours at Bergères-lès-Vertus before night marching across the plain to Châlons; the French routed the Russian rear guard at Étoges but broke off the pursuit. Arriving at the Marne around 9:00 on the morning of the fifteenth, the field marshal immediately dispatched couriers to Yorck at Reims and Sacken at Jonchery-sur-Vesle with orders for them to reach Châlons by noon on the sixteenth.[32] While another commander may have sat idle for a prolonged period, Blücher would have his army marching in just two days to answer Schwarzenberg's call for help.

As scheduled, Yorck and Sacken reached Châlons, though with gaping holes in their ranks. Many of Blücher's units had lost half of their effectives and had to be combined. Kleist's corps shrunk from thirty-one battalions to thirteen, Yorck's from thirty-seven battalions to sixteen. As for numbers, Yorck's corps mustered 13,679 combatants, while Kleist's barely fielded 3,500. The Russians fared no better as Sacken reported that his corps numbered 13,653 men, Kaptsevich 7,936, and Olsufiev 1,700. Morale plunged after the soldiers realized that they stood just as far from Paris as they did after La Rothière two weeks earlier. The depots at Châlons helped heal the spirit of the army by providing footgear and ammunition and repairing damaged equipment; even the horses could be freshly shod. Just at the right time reinforcements arrived. Besides replacements and heavy artillery, the last units from the Prussian I and II Corps that remained before the Moselle and Meuse fortresses finally moved up after being relieved. Fresh Russian troops also arrived: 6,000 infantry and 2,000 cavalry reached Vitry on the eighteenth. Moreover, Langeron received orders to turn over the siege of Mainz to the German V Corps and rejoin the Silesian Army with his corps less St. Priest, who remained at Mainz with one cavalry and three infantry regiments.[33]

With the arrival of reinforcements, Blücher's spirit soared. "The Emperor Napoleon was superior to me in cavalry," states his letter to Hardenberg, "but tomorrow and the day after tomorrow I will unite the four corps of Yorck, Sacken, Kleist, and Wintzingerode, and the situation will change. On the 19th, I will march straight toward my adversary. If he stands, I will defeat him—this you can count on as certain—but the Bohemian Army must now move forward or the situation can become unfavorable. Please use all of your influence to make this happen so we can settle the affair; all of the nation will be supportive if we defeat the Emperor, but he wins if we delay."[34]

On 16 February Schwarzenberg continued his drive on Paris, which commenced with a general crossing of the Seine. He sent another request to Blücher for the Silesian Army to move closer to his own.[35] The very next day Napoleon stopped the commander in chief's advance at Mormant, some thirty miles southeast of Paris. Concentrating the corps of Victor, Macdonald, Oudinot, and Ney as well as the Guard and reinforcements that arrived from Spain, Bonaparte commanded some 55,000 men, including 20,000 cavalry. A council of war at Schwarzenberg's headquarters decided on a general retreat to Troyes, where the two Allied armies could unite and accept battle. Pursuing the Army of Bohemia in three columns on the eighteenth, the French closed on Schwarzenberg's IV Corps at the crossing over the Seine at Montereau, inflicting some 6,000 casualties.[36]

Meanwhile, Blücher received Schwarzenberg's letter on the seventeenth. In compliance, he ordered Kleist and Yorck to cross the Marne at noon on the eighteenth. Early on 19 February arrived a letter from Schwarzenberg, dated the morning of the eighteenth, stating that the Bohemian Army would be ready for battle at Troyes on 21 February. On that day he wanted the Silesian Army at Arcis-sur-Aube. From there, Blücher would begin the offensive on the twenty-second and support Schwarzenberg.[37] Despite increasing concerns over feeding the Allied masses in the dead of winter, Blücher decided to honor the Austrian's wishes. As a preliminary step, he assembled his army at Sommesous.[38] From there, it proceeded to Méry-sur-Seine, arriving on 21 February with 53,000 men and 300 guns.[39]

Napoleon's troops started crossing the Seine at Montereau on the morning of the nineteenth. During the next few days, the French army concentrated at Nogent-sur-Seine. Schwarzenberg assembled the Bohemian Army at Troyes, and Blücher reached Méry-sur-Seine. Just seven days after seeking death at Étoges, the field marshal had reorganized his army and marched forty miles from the Marne to the Seine. Thanks to Blücher's self-confidence, leadership, and ability to hold the army together, Napoleon failed to knock out the Silesian Army and freeze the Bohemian Army for "fourteen to twenty" days. Having intended to advance against Schwarzenberg, the emperor now had to forgo the offensive because of Blücher's flank position.[40]

At this point, even Schwarzenberg considered accepting a battle with Napoleon, expressing this intention to Blücher on the twenty-first.[41] He could not hope for better circumstances: over 180,000 Allied soldiers assembled on the eighteen-mile stretch between Méry-sur-Seine and Troyes facing the emperor with 60,000–70,000 troops. Nevertheless, uncertainty remained over Napoleon's next move. Schwarzenberg planned to conduct a general reconnaissance on the twenty-second, but the French moved first. On the afternoon of the twenty-first, the 9th Division of Oudinot's new VII Corps attempted to cross the Seine at Méry, seizing the portion of the village on the left bank of the river. Although Blücher's army moved up and forced the French to withdraw, the constant pressure applied by Napoleon caused the Allied commander in chief to question the wisdom of accepting battle.[42] As a result, he withdrew the Army of Bohemia east through Troyes and across the Seine; only III and V Corps remained on the left bank as rear guard.[43] Moreover, rumors of the march of Augereau's Army of Lyon against his rear prompted Schwarzenberg to dispatch I Corps south to Dijon. With Napoleon's army less than fifteen miles west of Troyes and Augereau's army moving north from Lyon, Allied headquarters opted to retreat across the Aube and return to Langres; Blücher's army would withdraw 117 miles to Nancy.[44] Although Alexander and Frederick William objected, an absurd report from Seslavins dated 10:00 A.M. on 21 February stated that Napoleon sought a major battle and commanded over 180,000 men, including eighty-two cavalry regiments. Schwarzenberg used this outrageous report as a virtual weapon to force the monarchs to approve the retreat.[45]

After receiving Schwarzenberg's 21 February letter, Blücher immediately commenced the march to Méry-sur-Seine.[46] But after learning of the decision to retreat, he feared the next step would be a withdrawal across the Rhine. To spare his army from having to withdraw, the Prussians dispatched Kleist's chief of staff, Grolman, to Allied headquarters with a suggestion for another separation of the armies. Mainly, the Silesian Army would march north through Sézanne to Meaux and cross the Marne. Blücher would unite with Wintzingerode and Bülow—both moving south from Belgium—and then advance on the right bank of the Marne against Paris. Agreeing, Schwarzenberg advised Blücher to first effect his union with Wintzingerode and Bülow. For the moment, the Bohemian Army would retreat to Bar-sur-Aube with hopes that the Silesian Army would cause a diversion to distract Napoleon's attention. Not mentioning Paris, the Austrian field marshal requested that Blücher operate against the emperor's rear and flank.[47]

In addition, both Alexander and Frederick William approved the Prussian's proposed operation. To reinforce the Silesian Army, they formally transferred Bülow's and Wintzingerode's corps from Bernadotte's command to Blücher's.[48] "I most humbly thank Your

Majesty for allowing me to launch an offensive," Blücher wrote the tsar. "I promise that everything bad will be made good again after Your Majesties order Generals Wintzingerode and Bülow to comply with my orders. United with them, I will advance on Paris, and will not at all be timid when Napoleon and his marshals move against me. At the head of my army, I will fulfill Your Majesties' wishes and orders."[49]

Schwarzenberg started his retreat on the twenty-third; Blücher's advance began the next day. On 25 February Blücher instructed Bülow to move his corps toward Paris via La Fère and Villers-Cotterêts. Wintzingerode likewise received directives to advance on the French capital by way of Reims and Meaux.[50] For his part, Blücher led the Silesian Army across the Aube River in the Anglure region on 24 February.[51] That day, reports arrived that Marmont stood at Sézanne. Without hesitating, Blücher decided to destroy the marshal. On 25 February the vanguard of the Silesian Army made contact with Marmont's VI Corps on the hills of Vindey, two miles south-southwest of Sézanne. Marmont executed a fighting withdrawal by skillfully employing his light artillery to repulse numerous cavalry charges. From Vindey, the marshal fell back twenty-one miles west to La Ferté-Gaucher. The next day, the twenty-sixth, his troops legged another sixteen miles northwest to La Ferté-sous-Jouarre on the banks of the Marne. There, he united with Mortier, who left Château-Thierry after being summoned by Marmont. On the twenty-seventh both marshals moved west to Meaux along the Great Paris Highway and took a position to intercept Blücher's columns.[52]

Blücher decided to turn his army northwest and continue the pursuit of Marmont—his tactical objective. With Paris as the strategic objective, he could not allow the marshal to remain on the banks of the Marne and threaten his flank and communications. Around 7:00 on the morning of 27 February, the Silesian Army advanced north in two columns to envelop the French. Marmont and Mortier retreated across the Marne at La Ferté-sous-Jouarre. Avoiding Blücher's trap, they raced to Meaux. Determined to hold the portion of the town on the right bank of the Marne, they repulsed Sacken's first attack and braced themselves for another onslaught, but it never came. Instead, Blücher opted to cross the Marne and proceed northwest to the Ourcq River and envelop the marshals at Meaux. Marmont guessed Blücher's plan and made for Lizy-sur-Ourcq on the twenty-eighth, driving Kleist's corps before him. During this combat, Blücher's Cossacks spotted a force of approximately 35,000 soldiers marching north toward the Marne—rumors claimed that Napoleon himself commanded this army. Regardless, Blücher prepared to cross the Ourcq, which now barred the road to Paris. On 1 March he launched a three-pronged attack to dislodge Marmont and Mortier from their positions along the river.[53] Although hard pressed, the marshals held their ground, due in part to the timely arrival of 6,000 National Guards from Paris. That same day Cossacks reported that the French force approaching from the southeast had moved through Sézanne.

As early as 24 February, Napoleon knew of Schwarzenberg's retreat toward Langres. He also learned that after arriving at Méry-sur-Seine, Blücher recrossed the Aube and marched on the road toward Sézanne. Refusing to believe that the latter had recovered from the drubbing of the Six Days Campaign, Napoleon estimated the Prussian to have a mere 10,000 men at his disposal. "As soon as I see what Blücher wants to do," he wrote Joseph, "I will try to fall on his rear and isolate him."[54] He issued orders for Ney to begin the pursuit and unite with Marmont.[55] At 2:30 on the afternoon of the twenty-sixth, Napoleon sent an urgent dispatch to Ney via Berthier's office: "inform the prince of the Moskova [Ney] that we heard a cannonade near Sézanne during the days of the 24th and 25th; that it is important for the prince of the Moskova to cross the Aube at Arcis to see what Blücher is doing and fall on his rear."[56]

Unable to communicate with Marmont because of the Cossacks, pressure mounted at imperial headquarters in Troyes. With Schwarzenberg before him and Marmont engaging Blücher to the north, Napoleon needed to make a decision. He wanted to strike Schwarzenberg, but his lack of materials prevented the French from crossing the Seine. "If I had the equipment for a bridge of ten pontoons the war would be over and the army of Prince Schwarzenberg would exist no more," he fumed.[57] Throughout the day, he eagerly awaited the news that Ney had crossed the Aube at Arcis and fell on the rear of the Silesian Army.[58] As more reports arrived confirming Blücher's offensive, the emperor emphatically demanded that under no circumstance could Ney allow the Prussian to take a position at Sézanne.[59] He ordered Victor to take Blücher's bridges on the Aube and move between the Silesian Army and Vitry-le-François. "It appears obvious that if Blücher no longer has bridges on the Aube and he sees that a corps stands between him and Vitry, he will renounce his operation, if it was anything other than returning to Châlons."[60]

After learning that Blücher drove Marmont to the Marne, Napoleon concluded that the Prussian commanded a much larger force than initially believed. At 7:00 on the morning of 27 February, he decided to march north with the Guard to finish Blücher for good. He believed that Ney's advance against Blücher's rear, Victor's march against his flank, and the loss of his crossings over the Aube would freeze the Silesian Army.[61] With Blücher thus halted, Napoleon would be able to fall on his rear while Marmont and Mortier fixed his front.[62] Leaving 33,000 men under Macdonald to mask Schwarzenberg, the emperor took painstaking measures to give the impression that he remained at the Seine facing the Bohemian Army. To dupe the Allies, he instructed Caulaincourt, his representative at the peace talks being conducted at Châtillon-sur-Seine, to address his correspondence to Bar-sur-Seine.[63] Departing Troyes at 11:00 A.M. on the twenty-seventh, he reached Arcis-sur-Aube six hours later. The chase was on!

CHAPTER 15

PARIS

Blücher wanted to renew the operation against Marmont and Mortier on 2 March 1814 but received confirmed reports that Napoleon had passed through La Ferté-Gaucher en route to the Marne. This news forced the field marshal to abandon his plans. Unsure if Napoleon planned to cross the Marne at Meaux, La Ferté-sous-Jouarre, or Château-Thierry, he decided to run for it. Prudence demanded that the Army of Silesia retreat north of the Ourcq to unite with Bülow and Wintzingerode.

Marching northwest from Sézanne, Napoleon arrived at La Ferté-sous-Jouarre on the left bank of the Marne at 2:00 P.M. on 1 March. His troops captured some of Blücher's baggage along with 300–400 prisoners—according to the emperor. Other than these unimpressive prizes, he found all of the opposing army already on the opposite bank, breaking the bridge behind them. Regardless, Blücher's campaign earned the emperor's scorn. "All conversations that are reported to me with officers from Blücher's army criticize his operation and call him a fool," he sneered to Joseph.[1] At La Ferté-sous-Jouarre, circumstances beyond Napoleon's control complicated his further pursuit of the Silesian Army. The lack of bridge equipment again ruined his plans. Stopped at the town and forced to build bridges, the loss of time allowed Blücher to escape across the Ourcq. Napoleon complained bitterly, claiming that if the pontoons had arrived from Paris in time, he would have caught the Silesian Army in full retreat on 2 March, and "the army of Blücher would be no more."[2] To further complicate matters, an early thaw turned the roads into quagmires that slowed the march of his main body, which did not reach La Ferté-sous-Jouarre until midnight; the rear did not catch up until after dawn on the second.

By the evening of 2 March, Napoleon found himself at a crossroads: did he need to continue the pursuit of Blücher or should he contend with Schwarzenberg?[3] His plan for defeating the Army of Bohemia entailed the operation the Austrian feared most. "I am prepared to transfer the war to Lorraine," he informed Joseph, "where I will rally my troops that are in my fortresses on the Meuse and the Rhine."[4] "Tomorrow," states his instructions to Berthier, "I will decide if I should move to Châlons and establish communication with Verdun and Metz, threatening the rear of the Austrian army and separating it from Blücher's army, which is currently moving on Soissons and Reims." Thus, he planned to operate against Schwarzenberg's rear and right flank. Macdonald and Oudinot received orders to prepare to commence this operation.[5]

Knowing that Allied headquarters dreaded such a move, it is easy to criticize Napoleon for postponing this plan. Nevertheless, knowing the Austrian commander as he did, the emperor should have implemented it immediately, for Schwarzenberg would have conducted a headlong retreat to the Rhine. The evidence to support this assumption speaks clearly. At Troyes, with Blücher merely eighteen miles to the north at Méry-sur-Seine, the Allied commander in chief convinced Tsar Alexander of the necessity to retreat to Langres. With Blücher now north of the Marne, an envelopment of the Bohemian Army's right wing and Napoleon's appearance on the Rhine would be viewed as a monumental disaster. It would take another three weeks of French dithering at the negotiating table, coupled with Blücher's victory at Laon, before this attitude changed. Instead of terrorizing Schwarzenberg, whose retreat eventually would have forced Blücher to abandon his own operations, Napoleon opted to continue the pursuit of the Silesian Army. He based this decision not on a personal hatred of the field marshal, but on his overwhelming concern for the safety of Paris. Not convinced that Marmont and Mortier could save the capital, Emperor Napoleon went against the better judgment of General Bonaparte. But Blücher's resolve to continue his operation after learning of Napoleon's approach drove the emperor to make this decision.

Just like the German campaign, Blücher did not plan on running for long. He intended to take a position north of the Ourcq and confront Napoleon. During staff meetings on the night of 1–2 March, Gneisenau reasoned that if Wintzingerode proceeded in accordance with Blücher's 25 February order to advance on Paris through Fismes, Oulchy-la-Ville, and Meaux, the Russian corps would arrive at Oulchy-la-Ville between 1 and 2 March. As for Bülow's corps, Gneisenau assumed it would cross the Aisne River on the way to Paris via Villers-Cotterêts around the same time Wintzingerode reached the area. If the junction with these two commanders could occur at Oulchy-la-Ville, Gneisenau estimated that Blücher would have a two-to-one numerical advantage over Napoleon and the marshals.[6] But the fact that they did not know the whereabouts of either Bülow or Wintzingerode tempered the excitement caused by this thought. Three days had passed since Blücher received Wintzingerode's 28 February report informing the field marshal that he and Bülow would march on Paris in accordance with their orders. If these two generals stood only one march from the Silesian Army, as Gneisenau assumed, why did Blücher have no news of them? Several staff officers dispatched to locate the two corps either fell into French hands or failed to find either commander.

Meanwhile, on 2 March Marmont and Mortier attacked Kleist near May-en-Multien. The Prussians slowly retreated, often turning to engage the invigorated French in hand-to-hand combat. During the night, Kleist cleared La Ferté-Milon, albeit hard pressed by Marmont, whose troops occupied the town around midnight. By dawn, the general's exhausted men reached Neuilly-Saint-Front, yet Marmont allowed them no rest. As his rear guard contested the marshals, Blücher proceeded to Oulchy-le-Château late on the night of 2–3 March, but without Bülow and Wintzingerode, he could not make a stand and risk another defeat. Having received no news from either general, the daunting question remained: where should the army go next? Blücher and his staff debated their options for most of the night. At 6:00 on the morning of 3 March, the field marshal dictated his orders to move the army to the Aisne along the shortest possible route, regardless of the French garrison at Soissons. According to the plan, Blücher would utilize his own pontoons to bridge the Aisne and continue his march farther north. He hoped to have the majority of his infantry across the river by the night of 4–5 March.

Not knowing the commandant of Soissons soon would make a critical error, Napoleon drove his men after Blücher. He planned to either turn his left if the Silesian Army remained fixed north of the Ourcq or sever its line of retreat should the army flee northeast to Reims or Berry-au-Bac.[7] After spending all of 2 March bridging the Marne at La Ferté-sous-Jouarre, the emperor himself crossed the river at 2:00 A.M. on the third. A smaller force under Victor already had passed at Château-Thierry.[8] Napoleon's tired but feisty conscripts rapidly closed the distance separating the two armies. That afternoon his main body came within nine miles of Oulchy-la-Ville before halting at Bézu-Saint-Germain. Napoleon's advance guard pushed all the way to La Croix-sur-Ourcq—only three miles south of Oulchy-la-Château.[9] Knowing that his troops occupied Soissons and its stone bridge across the Aisne, he did not think Blücher would continue his march to the southern bank of that river. Instead, he expected the Prussian to make a dash for Châlons, the Silesian Army's communication and supply hub. Based on this expectation, he assumed Blücher would march east from Oulchy to Fère-en-Tardenois and turn northeast to Fismes, from where he would continue up the Vesle River through Reims to Châlons. Near Fismes, some nineteen miles east of Soissons, he hoped to catch the flank or rear of the Silesian Army.[10]

Meanwhile, six miles south of Soissons, Blücher reached Buzancy shortly after 11:00 A.M. on 3 March. His engineers had yet to begin work on the pontoon bridges. Although this delay could have proved fatal, he received unbelievable news from Bülow: the commandant of Soissons, General Jean-Claude Moreau, had surrendered the city to the Allies earlier that same day. Shortly before noon, Bülow's pioneers commenced work on a pontoon bridge near the eastern suburbs of that city. The barges and boats moored to banks of the Aisne in the vicinity allowed the Prussians to complete another span across the river by the morning of the fourth. In addition to the large stone bridge at Soissons itself, the army would be able to cross the Aisne over three additional bridges: Bülow's own pontoons eleven miles east of town at Vailly-sur-Aisne; the pontoon bridge that Bülow's men built by Soissons's eastern suburb; and the boat bridge they completed on the morning of the fourth. Blücher immediately redirected his units to Soissons; he arrived there late in the afternoon of the third with Sacken's advance guard. The onset of darkness did not slow the Silesian Army's retreat, which continued throughout the fourth.

At Bézu-Saint-Germain on the morning of 4 March, Napoleon learned that Blücher moved west through Neuilly-Saint-Front to Oulchy-le-Château and Oulchy-la-Ville. Rather than continue northeast through Fère-en-Tardenois and Fismes to Reims, he believed Blücher would retreat ten miles north to Noyant-et-Aconin and then march thirty-five miles east to Reims. As late as 2:00 P.M. that day, he placed Bülow's corps at Avesnes-sur-Helpe, some sixty-five miles north of Soissons.[11] Consequently, Napoleon had no reason to believe that Blücher would cross the Aisne and move farther north, particularly because Soissons and its stone bridge remained under French control. He still planned to intercept the Silesian Army as it presumably marched to Reims en route to Châlons. "Blücher seems extremely confused and changes direction every moment," he boasted. "I hope this will lead us to a result. Then, I intend to make war from the side of my fortresses, maneuvering in the rear of Schwarzenberg, who will be forced to turn around when he sees his hospitals, magazines, parks and line of operations threatened by me and the Duke of Castiglione [Augereau]."[12]

During the course of the day, Napoleon directed his army northeast from Bézu-Saint-Germain to Fismes with the objective of enveloping Blücher. One cavalry brigade continued to Reims and cleared the Russians from that town during the night.[13] After arriving at Fismes, the emperor gleefully informed Joseph that Blücher "has been pushed in all directions; we have taken 2,000 prisoners and 400 or 500 baggage wagons and caissons. The Duke of Ragusa [Marmont] must be at Soissons, and my cavalry at Reims. The enemy appears to want to march on Laon and Avesnes. He is in the greatest disarray and has immense losses in men, horses, and wagons."[14] While the exaggeration of such numbers conformed to Napoleon's style, his lack of respect for Blücher made him view the Silesian Army's march to the Aisne as a disorderly flight. Not having heard from Marmont in days, the wish may have been the father of the thought.[15] More significant is Napoleon's casual mention that Blücher appeared intent on reaching Laon. Should this be the case, the master would be faced with the same predicament that he confronted on the evening of 2 March: should he continue the current pursuit or contend with Schwarzenberg. The next paragraph of his letter to Joseph insinuates that he intended to disengage from Blücher: "Send one of your officers to Troyes to inform the Dukes of Tarente [Macdonald] and Reggio [Oudinot] that it is possible that I will maneuver through Vitry, St.-Dizier, and Joinville against the rear of the enemy, which will make him move away and force him to quit the Seine to guard his rear in all diligence. This movement has the advantage of unblocking my fortresses, where I will find numerous garrisons and large reinforcements."[16]

Regarding the marshals, after pressing Kleist on 3 March, Marmont and Mortier crossed the Ourcq at Neuilly-Saint-Front around 6:30 A.M. on the fourth. Their cavalry thundered after Blücher's rear guard, pursuing to within five miles of Soissons. But on reaching Hartennes-et-Taux, Marmont learned of Soissons's surrender and canceled the pursuit; his cavalry merely observed the Silesian Army as it crossed the Aisne. The marshal informed Berthier that it appeared useless to continue to Soissons because its capitulation would change the emperor's plans. From his letter, which arrived at imperial headquarters during the night of 4–5 March, Napoleon learned that Blücher had escaped unmolested across the Aisne.[17]

By taking Soissons, Bülow and Wintzingerode accelerated Blücher's escape. On 4 March the marshals would have caught Blücher from the west and pinned the part of the Silesian Army that had yet to cross the Aisne. Considering that the Prussian had yet to start building his pontoon bridges as of noon on the third, a good portion of the army still would have stood on the southern bank when Marmont attacked Kleist at 6:30 on the morning of the fourth. On that day he and Mortier would have been obligated to face Blücher without the support of the emperor. It is doubtful Napoleon could have arrived that day with significant forces. First, the gap quickly widened between him and Blücher. At Bézu-Saint-Germain at dawn on the fourth, twenty-one miles separated Napoleon from the vicinity of the Aisne where Blücher planned to place his bridges. At Fismes that night, eighteen miles would have separated him from Blücher's crossings. Second, Napoleon would have needed a reason to change the direction of his march. By the afternoon, he still had not received a report from Marmont.[18] Moreover, he made no mention of hearing artillery fire in the distance, although Moreau heard Marmont's guns dueling with Kleist. Again, as in September 1813, Blücher used an unorthodox maneuver to outwit Napoleon. Instead of withdrawing east along his line of communication, he duped the emperor by retreating north and across the Aisne—a decision he and his staff made well before word reached them of Moreau's capitulation. Had the French detained Blücher for just twenty-four hours either by holding Soissons or contesting the crossing of the Aisne, Napoleon could have wheeled his army west and forced Blücher to accept battle on 5 March under extremely adverse conditions. After the Six Days Campaign, it is quite conceivable that the Prussian's haggard army might have disintegrated under Napoleon's onslaught.[19] As it stood, Moreau's treasonous conduct infuriated the emperor, but Blücher's escape probably did not come as a great surprise, considering his comment to Joseph on the fourth that the Prussian appeared to want to reach Laon.[20]

Wintzingerode's and Bülow's 40,000 men joined Blücher's four corps of approximately 63,000 troops. The unemotional reunion between Blücher and his two new subordinates occurred on 4 March.[21] Blücher remained angry that his orders for the advance on Paris had been ignored. He attributed his current predicament to this dereliction of duty. He made no mention of gratitude in reference to Soissons. Later that day the troops paraded through the city. Contemporaries unanimously agreed over the considerable impression that the disparate appearances of the troops made on both them and their commanders. Blücher's army was in appalling condition as a result of continuous forced marches, bloody combats, and deprivations. Persistent hardships had completely exhausted both man and horse. Starved and tattered, some soldiers marched without shoes, while others lacked weapons. According to Müffling: "When afterwards, in the town of Soissons, the Field Marshal made his corps march past, Bülow was standing at his side and I was present. 'Some rest will do these men some good,' said Bülow with great seriousness, regarding our tattered soldiers, but perhaps he meant in his heart: 'my men might soon look the same.' More was heard from his entourage."[22] One of Bülow's staff officers, Ludwig von Reiche, noted: "It was a beautiful and uplifting moment when we came together with our brothers. We welcomed and greeted each other with mutual sincerity. But not little astonishment and surprise was provoked on both sides at first sight. Due to continuous forced marches and mostly unsuccessful combats, they [Blücher's troops] suffered from strains and wants of all kind and some were without shoes. They were depraved and we could hardly believe what we saw. As certainly happens on such occasions, we attributed the blame for this to the army's leadership, which needlessly fatigued the troops with unnecessary marches."[23] But Müffling maintained that "our men looked remarkable with their thin faces blackened by bivouac smoke and long strangers to the luxury of a razor . . . [and] with tattered cloaks, badly patched trousers, unblackened leathers, and unpolished arms."[24]

Bülow's soldiers posed a striking contrast. Groomed, well nourished, and completely uniformed, the men of III Corps looked fresh from the parade ground. Reiche explained: "Our people [Bülow's troops] were in the best condition, well clothed and nourished;

we had conducted an easy, successful campaign and found ourselves in the best military condition. Yorck's corps granted an utterly pitiful sight."[25] None could question the fact that the relentless self-sacrifice of the Silesian Army provided the real driving force behind the War of the Sixth Coalition. Without Blücher's vigorous offensives and prudent retreats, Allied diplomats might have grown more conciliatory and a peace detrimental to Prussia might have been concluded much earlier. Regardless, the prevailing impression of Blücher's depraved men caused quite a reaction among Bülow and his officers. Müffling recalled:

> My eyes were constantly turning to Bülow and his entourage on whose faces I fancied I could easily read what was passing in their minds, as I had just met a portion of Bülow's corps in brilliant new uniforms, with pink and white cheeks, neatly curled locks and glittering arms. Gneisenau, who had known many of these persons from the time when the Tugendbund was a power and who had learned to esteem them as vigorous and honorable men, asked me if I had observed the impression our ragged troops had made and told me, laughing, that one of his old friends [Boyen] had given him a lecture on the means of sparing the troops. I too had been subject to such phrases, but I soon settled the matter by stating the fact that the spruce red-cheeked youths of Bülow's corps had still much to do before they could come up to our tattered soldiers of the Silesian Army.[26]

Likewise, the appearance of the soldiers of III Corps caused envy among the officers and men of the Silesian Army. Bülow also found Blücher's troops to be disheartened and miserable. He described he army as practically starved and lacking discipline: "to our disgrace, I must confess that it resembles a band of robbers."[27]

Blücher eventually treated Bülow with respect and congeniality, but Gneisenau and Müffling remained aloof. Bülow also met his old military colleagues Yorck and Kleist, imprudently questioning their loyalty to Blücher.[28] He expressed the general belief that Gneisenau and his staff actually controlled the army. "What are you, worthless servants?" he asked his fellow corps commanders. "How can you allow yourselves to be subordinated to headquarters, to that *verbrantes-Gehirn* (burnt brain) Gneisenau, to the views of Müffling and Grolman?" He wondered how corps commanders could allow themselves to be ordered by the staff adjutants of the Silesian Army. Bülow also questioned why they had allowed their troops to be expended. Even if Blücher could no longer command, either Yorck or Kleist, both senior to Gneisenau, should take the reins of the army. Initially, Yorck denied the accusations but soon agreed and became furious.[29] Bülow criticized the leadership of the army in a letter to his wife on 5 March: "This past period has been rich with events. I only wish that on the whole they would have been more beneficial for us and that one had not made so many dumb moves, whereby the corps of Yorck, Kleist, and Sacken were reduced by half and all, one after the other, were defeated en détaille. Since the Grand [Bohemian] Army withdrew from Troyes in order to unite with the advancing Austrian reserve army under Archduke Ferdinand, one had the idea to have Marshal Blücher advance with his army on Meaux around the enemy's left wing against Paris. The idea was good, but the execution poor. . . . Yorck, Kleist, and all from top to bottom are completely aggravated with the leadership of this fine army."[30]

Despite the differences between Bülow and Gneisenau, Boyen's first meeting with his close friend was cordial and intimate. Yet Boyen soon found that disagreements likewise came between him and Gneisenau. During a meeting with the army staff chief at Soissons, Boyen learned the full details of the army's operations in France. Schwarzenberg's inertia, which Gneisenau blamed for their misfortunes during the Six Days Campaign, affected Boyen. Two days later he explained in a letter to his friend that the Allies now had "to suffocate the enemy through simultaneous movements and well-chosen positions. . . . [T]he momentary glimmer of bold military exploits must be subordinated. . . . [A] needless, premature advance would place the whole conclusion of the campaign upon the uncertain goal of a battle and negate the advantages achieved thus far."

Either through the written or spoken word, Boyen influenced Gneisenau over the course of the next few weeks. He emphasized the political danger of sustaining large losses, imploring Gneisenau to look to Prussia's future and beyond the lust for vengeance that seemed to propel the Silesian Army deeper into France.[31] Boyen explained that with the victory at Leipzig, Austria achieved its political objective of driving the French from central Europe. Now, due to Metternich's influence, Schwarzenberg's operations slowed and appeared less committed. Boyen argued that Prussia should follow this example. He described the beginning of "a new epic in the history of the war in France. . . . [A] strategic preponderance over Napoleon has been obtained. . . . [H]is total destruction awaits and can be realized with slight tactical employment."[32] Boyen strove to persuade Gneisenau to refrain from active campaigning and urged his friend to allow the gradual effect of attrition to exhaust Napoleon rather than directly confront the French army.[33] Still smarting from the Six Days Campaign, Gneisenau ultimately agreed. Müffling provides further insight:

> Gneisenau's old friends [Boyen] claimed all of his time. After every conversation he had with them, I found him distant and gloomy. Some days later, he began to consider our situation as uneasy, critical, and dangerous. On seeing this . . . I mentioned the service we had rendered the Grand [Bohemian] Army by moving toward Paris. . . . Gneisenau answered that due to the weakness of our army, we would not be able to obtain good peace conditions at the Congress; and in doing this, he fell into the same thought pattern and almost used the same words I had heard from Bülow's entourage. To hear such opinions repeated by Gneisenau was the last thing I expected and it struck me forcibly . . . that Gneisenau wished to avoid admitting . . . that our allies had faithlessly deceived us.[34]

Faced with the choice of continuing the pursuit of Blücher or turning against Schwarzenberg, Napoleon chose the former. Again, he intended to envelop the Prussian's left wing, cut his lines of communication, and drive his army northward.[35] To achieve this goal, he needed the bridge at Berry-au-Bac. On 5 March his Guard Cavalry seized the town from Russian troops, and two French divisions moved onto the hills between it and Corbeny, twenty-seven miles east of Soissons. Napoleon arrived at 4:00 P.M., followed by the rest of the army.[36] To the west, Mortier and Marmont attacked Soissons and advanced through Braine and Fismes to Berry-au-Bac.[37] Through Berthier's office, Napoleon revealed to Macdonald his plan to drive Blücher from Laon, assuring the marshal that daily he caused the Silesian Army "much difficulty."

Napoleon expressed his hope that Macdonald still held Troyes, insisting that under no circumstances should the marshal quit the Seine before 12 March. From his fortresses in the Ardennes and on the Moselle, he would have "two strong divisions conduct sorties. The enemy does not invest them, and through St.-Dizier and

Joinville I intend to throw myself on the right flank of their main army at the same time that the Duke of Castiglione drives through Bourg and Lons-le-Saulnier against their left flank." To bolster Macdonald, he emphasized that "nowhere is the enemy as strong as they claim." Regarding Blücher's operation, he wrote: "it is a coup de main that he wanted to make on Paris and he has failed."[38]

Like most of his fellow marshals during the 1814 campaign, Macdonald failed his master. At noon on the sixth, Napoleon learned of Macdonald's retreat from Troyes. To Schwarzenberg's credit, the Army of Bohemia advanced as soon as Allied headquarters received confirmation that Napoleon pursued Blücher. On 27 February it took Bar-sur-Aube and commenced a general offensive, driving Macdonald from Troyes on 4 March. Two days later the marshal withdrew across the Seine at Méry-sur-Seine and did not stop until he reached Provins.[39] News of Macdonald's collapse stunned and outraged Napoleon. "I cannot believe this stupidity," he wrote to Joseph. "There is no better position than Troyes, where the enemy has to maneuver on both banks of the river. They cannot be any worse off than I am. At Troyes I left a fine army and a beautiful cavalry, but it lacks soul. In battle, this army is certainly stronger than anything Prince Schwarzenberg can oppose it with."[40] Although the Austrian now stood much closer to Paris than Blücher, Napoleon felt that the Silesian Army posed the greater threat to his capital. "This army is more dangerous to Paris than Schwarzenberg's," he later confessed to Joseph. "Schwarzenberg's army has been weakened by the detachments he has left in his rear, and he seems afraid of compromising himself by crossing the Seine. Nevertheless, I will move close to Soissons to be closer to Paris, but until I can engage this army [Silesian] in an affair that will compromise it anew, it is difficult for me to be elsewhere."[41]

The Silesian Army took extensive quarters around Soissons for some much needed rest. Blücher established his headquarters thirteen miles northeast at Chavignon. Cossack regiments remained south of Vailly-sur-Aisne on the left bank of that river to observe the terrain between it and the Vesle. On the sixth Blücher learned that the French crossed the Aisne at Berry-au-Bac. He instructed the staff to plan another battle. They chose the plateau between the Aisne and the Lette, north of and parallel to the former. That same day he moved east to strike the French marching from Reims to Laon. Russian infantry held Blücher's center on the heights of

Craonne, while Wintzingerode took a position at Filain with 10,000 cavalry and sixty horse guns. But the general failed to wheel around the French army's rear, and a bloody encounter resulted at Craonne on 7 March. Fighting a defensive action, the Russians suffered 5,000 casualties thanks to Wintzingerode's inactivity. The three Prussian corps could not arrive in time to support.[42]

After the useless bloodshed of the tactical defeat at Craonne, Blücher decided to concentrate his army in a defensive position at Laon. He did not wait long before the French arrived. Following his victory, Napoleon doubted that Blücher could assemble his entire army in time to confront him.[43] He therefore opened the assault on the evening of 8 March. Around 2:00 A.M. on the ninth, Ney pressed the attack, driving the Russians back at daybreak. A freeze occurred before sunrise, and snow blanketed the ground; a thick mist veiled the entire countryside. Several hours passed before, around 11:00, the mist burned off and objects became discernible. Estimates vary, but Napoleon probably commanded 48,000 men after sustaining 5,500 casualties at Craonne. Blücher surveyed the enemy positions and made adjustments. He learned of the approach of a French column of 9,000 men under Marmont on the highway from Reims.

Napoleon dispatched several officers with orders to accelerate Marmont's march against Blücher's left, but none escaped the Cossacks. Regardless, the emperor sensed the marshal's approach. Impatient, he ordered an attack on Blücher's right wing to induce the Prussian to divert men from his left. Napoleon hoped this diversion would enable Marmont to surprise and roll up Blücher's left wing. Two divisions attacked Clacy around 4:00 P.M., dislodging Wintzingerode's Russians after a heated engagement. Heavy artillery and musket fire ensued between the two lines until nightfall. Having learned nothing of Marmont, Napoleon ordered his infantry to bivouac on the battlefield.

Although Napoleon did not receive news from his marshal, the Allies observed Marmont's vanguard approaching and prepared a reception. That evening Blücher ordered a surprise assault. On this cold, dark night, the smoldering ruins of the village of Athies-sous-Laon provided the only light in this sector of the battlefield. The king's brother, William, silently advanced with six battalions followed by two brigades, while the cavalry of I and II Corps charged Marmont's right flank. Although caught by surprise, the French resisted with great courage. In the darkness an embittered

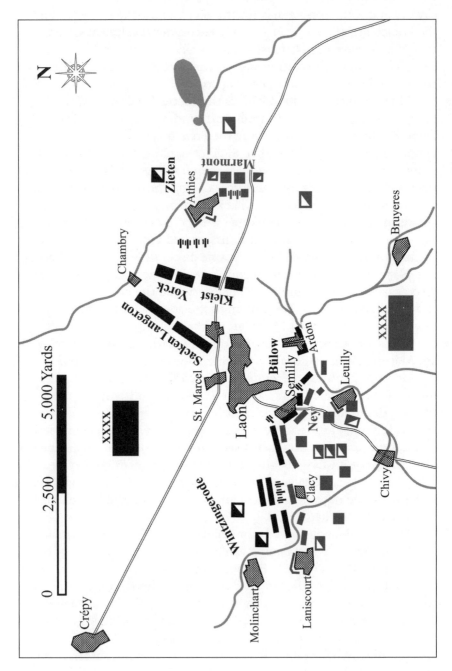

The Battle of Laon, 8–10 March 1814. Map drawn by Alex Mendoza. Copyright © 2014 by the University of Oklahoma Press.

hand-to-hand struggle ensued. After a confused melee, the French fled. The night attack produced decisive results: Marmont's corps dissolved. The Prussians captured forty-six guns and 130 caissons along with 2,000 men at a loss of 500 casualties.

On horseback throughout the ninth, Blücher's stamina gave out, and he retired to his bed around midnight after issuing the orders to continue the pursuit of Marmont's corps. Despite his worsening health, Blücher wrote several letters on the 10 March describing the destruction of Marmont's corps. "The attack from our side was made by Prussian troops under Yorck and Kleist;" he boasted to Bonin, "my troops are still in pursuit. It is more than possible that we will very quickly conclude a good peace. I have no news of our main army, whether it is now advancing on Paris or not."[44] Blücher assured the military governor of Berlin that "we draw close to concluding a speedy and good peace. Do me a favor and make this known to the brave Berliners in my name."[45] He also wrote Amalie early on the tenth. The end of this letter has been lost, so we do not know if he mentioned his illness:

> I have not written you for a long time because our communications were interrupted and still are not completely restored. I was close to Paris when the Emperor Napoleon turned his entire force against me. Although I withdrew a few marches, the maniac attacked me yesterday around 5:00 A.M.; combat lasted the entire day. I maintained my entire position; everything ceased after it became dark. But just now I attacked the enemy and within thirty minutes he was completely defeated. We have taken 40 guns, some 1,000 prisoners, and much ammunition. Napoleon is quickly falling back on Paris; my troops are still pursuing. Franz has distinguished himself, so has Katzler. My entire entourage is well. Yesterday, I stood under a windmill; a cannon ball went right through the mill. Count Chernishev, the Young Prince of Orange, and Nostitz were slightly injured by pieces of wood, but not me. This battle was unique because it lasted the entire day. My losses are not great, but the enemy has lost many men attempting to force my position.[46]

As noted, Blücher issued orders for the pursuit around midnight on 9–10 March. But sometime after the field marshal went to bed, Gneisenau cancelled the order. Aside from the measure itself, the fact that Gneisenau rather than Blücher signed the order provoked large misgivings among the corps commanders, especially Yorck. Both he and Kleist could have enveloped Napoleon's right and caused a French debacle. Some historians claim that Blücher's illness prompted Gneisenau to proceed cautiously. Yet as we see from his letters on 10 March, poor health did not completely incapacitate him or take the fight out of the old hussar.[47] In referring to an account of the battle published in 1843, Müffling notes:

> The sickness of the Field Marshal is portrayed to lead one to conclude that it was absence of mind amounting to incapacity. There is no doubt that at that time existed a party whose interest was to spread this opinion; but they did not dare express it openly, as the Field Marshal's physicians and constant attendants could prove the contrary. When this work appeared in 1843, the majority of the witnesses were dead. General Lieutenant Count Nostitz, who had been first adjutant to Blücher, undeceived the author, who expressed his willingness to be set right, and indeed printed the correction in the 11th edition of the *Militär Wochenblatt* for 16 March 1844. This correction affirms what was true: "that the Field Marshal was able from his room to conduct, as usual, the operations of the Silesian Army, but not a battle, where he was wont to be always in the hottest fight."[48]

Müffling attributes the counterorder to the chief of staff's new political awareness, caused by his daily discussions with Boyen.[49] Due to these talks, Gneisenau became concerned over the condition of the Prussian army. After reports over Marmont's route arrived, Müffling maintains that he urged an immediate advance to annihilate Napoleon's remaining forces, but Gneisenau found this suggestion too bold. He argued that at the peace table, Prussia's advantages would not be weighed according to the number of Blücher's victories, but according to the battle-ready army at the king's disposal.[50] Gneisenau heeded Boyen's message, though perhaps at the worst time in regards to the morale of the leaders of the Silesian Army.[51] We do not know the reason he gave Blücher for cancelling the pursuit order nor the latter's reaction. But the leaders of the army observed in astonishment on the morning of tenth that Napoleon not only maintained his position but also prepared to renew the struggle. Most likely, this provided Gneisenau enough evidence to make his case to Blücher, if he had to.

Due to the wind and sporadic firing that continued throughout the night, Napoleon's outposts did not hear the combat between the Prussians and Marmont. Consequently, Napoleon planned a general attack for the following morning.[52] Around 1:00 A.M., though, he learned of Marmont's destruction. Assuming Blücher would pursue the marshal's shattered corps, Napoleon decided to maintain his positions in an attempt to catch the Allied columns debouching from their positions around Laon. Throughout the day, he desperately pressed his attacks. Ney's failure to dislodge the Allies finally convinced the emperor that he could not break Blücher's formidable position without sustaining significant losses.[53] He withdrew during the night of 10–11 March in the direction of Soissons after losing 6,500 men and exacting 4,000 Allied casualties. Napoleon went to Chavignon that night and assembled his army at Soissons, which the French again occupied, throughout the eleventh. Upriver, Marmont reorganized his corps at Fismes. Remaining in these positions until the evening of 12 March, Bonaparte decided to attack Reims, where St. Priest arrived with the 8,000 men of his own VIII Infantry Corps as well as 5,000 Landwehr en route to rejoin Kleist's II Corps.[54]

With 20,000 men, Napoleon overwhelmed the Allies at Reims on 13 March, taking twelve guns and inflicting 1,500 casualties on the Russians. St. Priest, the native Frenchman, received a mortal wound. The Prussian Landwehr fared worse, losing 1,877 casualties and eleven guns. At 3:00 A.M. on 14 March, the French entered Reims after losing 800 men. Aside from exaggerating the extent of his victory for propaganda purposes, Napoleon believed that he succeeded in severing communication between Blücher and Schwarzenberg.[55] While a tactical victory that again demonstrated his endless energy and denied Blücher some reinforcements, Napoleon's success at Reims had no bearing on the strategic situation.[56] In the end, this victory, the emperor's penultimate on French soil, meant little.[57]

In the meantime, Blücher's illness worsened on the tenth. He remained indisposed—but not incapacitated—for most of the day, suffering from ague and ophthalmia. He even spoke of resigning.[58] His brother-in-law, Colomb, who came to care for him, wrote in his journal: "I found him feverish and he appeared quite uncomfortable, but completely informed of the upcoming battle."[59] After Napoleon departed, Gneisenau wanted to rest the army and reorganize its supply, but a crisis unfolded. Blücher's talk of resigning unsettled the Prussians because of recent changes in the command structure of the Silesian Army. With the arrival of Langeron, the most senior general in the army after Blücher, command would devolve to him rather than Gneisenau, Yorck, Kleist, or Bülow. Langeron's Prussian counterparts considered him completely unfit for such responsibility. Indeed, Langeron himself did not want the job. Although the French émigré makes no mention of Blücher's illness in his own memoirs, Müffling claims that Langeron "had the greatest dread of being obliged to assume command. This only increased after he visited him [Blücher] and found him quite exhausted. On exiting his room, he said to me: 'In the name of God, carry his corpse with us.'"[60] All the Prussian commanders feared that if the Silesian Army wavered under Langeron's leadership, a peace detrimental to their nation would be the result. Therefore, after Langeron returned, Gneisenau had to at least give the appearance that Blücher still commanded, despite the field marshal's worsening health. Nostitz relates the old man's agony:

> Confined to his room because of the inflammation of his eyes, robbed of his usual exercise, reduced to a strict diet, and with his heart full of anger over being doomed to inactivity right at the moment when the last decisive blow must be struck: all of this combined to not only shatter his health in general, but also to work extremely detrimentally on his mood, bringing forth the natural disposition which with him was the steady result of a physical ailment. To see him thus, constantly thinking of death with fear and anxiety, enduring each pain with faint-heartedness, always tormenting his imagination with the discovery of new symptoms and, only thinking of himself, indifferent toward everything, even the greatest and most important events; but then again, as soon as he recovered, surpassing all around him in strength of character, endurance of hardships, and heroic scorn of the greatest dangers, one could only be amazed at the great power his physical condition exercised over his mental faculties.[61]

Discontent increased in the army over this latest controversy. Yorck, most angered by the counterorder, would no longer obey an incompetent commander or a staff officer. He attempted to leave under the pretext of sickness. On 12 March the general sat in his carriage ready to depart. After several attempts to persuade him

failed, a frail Blücher finally emerged in his nightgown to personally request that Yorck stay. Kleist remained disgruntled, while the
Russian generals spoke among themselves of this bizarre conflict.
As for Bülow, after spending one week with the army, he believed
that a drastic step needed to be taken to prevent its dissolution.
To him, only one alternative remained open: to summon the one
odious personality whose skills could maintain the unity of the
Silesian Army. Therefore, he sent a courier to Bernadotte, who had
arrived in Liège at the beginning of March. Bülow requested that
the Swedish crown prince immediately leave Belgium and assume
command of the Silesian Army. Flattered by this, Bernadotte nevertheless declined. Some claimed that his aspirations for the French
crown prevented him from entering French territory as an enemy.[62]

St. Priest's debacle would not have been possible without the
inactivity of the Silesian Army. In response to Napoleon's coup de
main at Reims, Gneisenau concentrated the army between Laon and
Corbény.[63] Nevertheless, the inactivity continued until the seventeenth, when reports arrived that Napoleon had crossed the Marne
at Épernay with 20,000–25,000 troops to move south against the
Bohemian Army. The next day the Silesian Army marched to the
crossings over the Aisne at Pontavert, Berry-au-Bac, and Neufchâtel-
sur-Aisne. After the French destroyed the bridges and withdrew
westward from Reims to Fismes, Gneisenau ordered the mass of the
army to cross the Aisne by way of pontoon bridges thrown across
the river at Pontavert and Berry-au-Bac as well as the fords found
in these locales. Forming the left wing, Wintzingerode marched on
Reims. In the center, Yorck and Kleist pursued the French toward
Fismes, where Marmont and Mortier took up a strong position.
Sacken, Langeron, and army headquarters followed to Pontavert and
Berry-au-Bac. Blücher accompanied the march in a covered wagon.
The fifteen-mile ride from Laon to the Aisne so exhausted him that
he required a day of rest before continuing.[64]

On the right wing, Bülow advanced on the Laon highway to
Soissons. His corps would not join the Silesian Army for the latest operation. Instead, he received the task of besieging Soissons,
prompting Müffling to question Gneisenau: "What will Bülow say
to an assignment hardly fit for a brigade commander?" Gneisenau
remained adamant. Regardless, Müffling observed that "from the
day Bülow's corps was detached from the Silesian Army, General
Gneisenau was again himself: strong and vigorous in judgment, and

energetic in action. . . . I never . . . once mentioned the name of Soissons or Bülow's corps until we entered Paris."[65]

Not Blücher's incapacity but uncertainty over Napoleon's next move kept the Silesian Army in check. On 20 March only Sacken moved up the Aisne toward Bülow, who stood before Soissons. The next day word reached army headquarters that Napoleon had marched south, attacking Schwarzenberg at Arcis-sur Aube on the twentieth with 20,000 men. This news somewhat snapped Gneisenau out of his stupor, and he resolved to continue the march on Paris. In Blücher's name he informed Allied headquarters that the Silesian Army would first take Soissons and Compiègne to secure a base for the advance to the lower Marne. With 110,000 combatants, Gneisenau felt "no need to get out of the way if the enemy's entire force advances against me."[66] As Napoleon withdrew before Schwarzenberg's masses at Arcis-sur-Aube, the center of Blücher's army pursued Marmont and Mortier, who evacuated Fismes and marched west. Bülow invested Soissons, and Wintzingerode remained at Reims.

With great difficulty, Blücher's entourage convinced him to remain with army headquarters as it moved to Fismes on the twenty-first. "He would hear nothing of the business at hand," recalled Nostitz, "and showed little interest in the news from the various theaters of war." Then a report arrived stating that the marshals had destroyed the Château-Thierry bridge behind them and marched south toward Montmirail. Based on this information, the Prussians concluded that Napoleon sought to unite all of his forces for a general battle with the Bohemian Army. In fact, it appeared that he already delivered his blow and planned to exploit a victory. Cossacks intercepted a letter written by Napoleon to Marie Louise that reported his victory at Arcis-sur-Aube on the twentieth. According to its contents, he planned to go to St.-Dizier to distract the enemy armies from Paris and to move closer to his eastern fortresses.[67]

Nostitz asserted that "this news worked like a moral vesicant on the spirit and disposition of the Field Marshal. From this moment on there was no more thought of resigning his command, although the infection in his eyes still continued in its complete viciousness."[68] Explains Unger in his edition of Blücher's letters: "At the moment when the danger for the Bohemian Army was recognized, when Napoleon had turned against it with all of his forces, when forceful deeds by Blücher's army were urgent, the sick hero found his old energy again. He cast aside the doubts caused by the effects of the illness on him. His signature, which in the days after Laon looked like that of a blind man, now had no discernible difference from earlier in the campaign." The change in Blücher's health emerges in a brief letter to his wife, probably written on the twenty-second: "from the above you will gather that I am healthy. Admittedly, I have been through a lot, but I am without fever and in the saddle day and night [a lie so she would not worry about him]. We will soon deliver another battle. I have plenty of money, what do you need?"[69]

Displaying his loyalty to an ally, Blücher resolved to assist Schwarzenberg by attacking Napoleon's flank and rear. On 23 March the field marshal accompanied the Russians, though riding in a carriage with his eyes bandaged and wearing a green women's hat.[70] Additional intercepted letters revealed that Napoleon did not defeat Schwarzenberg at Arcis-sur-Aube. Regardless, the Prussians could not be sure of the Austrian's reaction to confronting the emperor. If Schwarzenberg froze as he did so many times previously, Napoleon would have the liberty to launch another campaign against Blücher. Continuing up the Marne, Wintzingerode's cavalry found the French rear guard on the road east to St.-Dizier. Consequently, Blücher learned that the emperor retreated *east* rather than *west* following the engagement at Arcis-sur-Aube.[71] "The enemy is in retreat, but not on Paris, instead on Moscow," reported the Cossacks.[72] In addition, Schwarzenberg cautiously followed the emperor and now stood west of Vitry-le-François. Not only were the two Allied armies on the verge of uniting for a third time but also they were closer to Paris than Napoleon.

Not all viewed these developments as advantageous. Should Napoleon unite the garrisons of his eastern frontier fortresses, he could devastate the Coalition's lines of communication, depriving them of supplies and reinforcements. With popular resistance following the Allied armies like a shadow, the difficulty of feeding the troops would increase daily. Already fragile diplomatic relations within the Coalition would be stressed to the breaking point. Although the Prussians could not predict Schwarzenberg's reaction to Napoleon's latest maneuver, they knew enough based on past experiences to predict his general preference: a retreat to the Rhine.[73] Again Nostitz tells us that Blücher expressed his belief that the only correct action would be an immediate march on Paris with all available units.[74] Gneisenau suggested that half of the Coalition's forces should pursue and destroy Napoleon while the other half sprinted to Paris.[75] But Allied headquarters settled the debate. Alexander believed that the Allies should not pursue Napoleon but instead march on Paris. Frederick William and Schwarzenberg agreed.[76] Only Wintzingerode's 10,000 cavalry would follow the emperor's forces. Blücher claimed credit for bringing about this decision: "After I decisively defeated Napoleon at Laon, I insisted, against the opinion of the monarchs' entourages, to march both armies straight to Paris. All of my opponents claimed that Napoleon would march in our rear and summon the troops in his fortresses and so march against Mainz and Frankfurt. I insisted that we should take Paris and let Napoleon do what he wanted because it would not matter as we would be in possession of the capital. Tsar Alexander took my side and we marched on the great city."[77] "This agreement with Allied headquarters," notes Nostitz, "which the Field Marshal held as the most expedient, made him very happy; all the more so because it was the first time during both campaigns that such harmony existed."[78]

Here the story of Napoleon and Blücher in 1814 concludes. After defeating Marmont and Mortier at Fère-Champenoise on 25 March, both Allied armies pursued the marshals to Paris. The following day Napoleon defeated Wintzingerode at St.-Dizier: the emperor's last victory before his abdication. Nevertheless, Wintzingerode achieved his purpose—Napoleon could not recover the lost time to reach Paris before Blücher and Schwarzenberg. Conversely, although Blücher loaned his two Prussian corps to Schwarzenberg, the Allies could not stop Marmont and Mortier from arriving at the city before them. An intense struggle for control of the French capital occurred on the thirtieth. Blücher again suffered so severely from ophthalmia that he remained confined to his yellow carriage with eyes bandaged for most of the battle. "The yellow carriage where he sat daydreaming was an important point upon which many gazes clung," wrote one contemporary. "All orderlies were to make a detour to the yellow carriage, but in the course of the affair it was often impossible to have it on hand to prevent bringing everything to a standstill. Then one heard numerous voices shouting: 'From where does the order come? From the Field Marshal, impossible, the yellow carriage is not here.'"[79] In the afternoon Blücher summoned enough strength to mount his horse and direct an attack on the Montmartre heights dominating Paris. Yet the pain proved too much for the old warrior. Before witnessing any combat, he dismounted at a large house in the La Vilette suburb.[80] The storming of Montmartre that day provided a fitting end to the Silesian Army's operations—and its existence.[81]

Around 5:00 P.M., news arrived that Tsar Alexander concluded a ceasefire with the marshals, who agreed to evacuate their positions. As negotiations for the surrender of Paris wore on, Blücher ordered all heavy cannon driven onto Montmartre and went there himself, determined to resume the struggle the next day. He found shelter in a house situated atop the heights. "Just like all the others," notes Nostitz, "it had been thoroughly plundered, in which the Russians occupied themselves with tireless activity for several hours. In a room robbed of all furniture, the Field Marshal's bed was set up; a somewhat large table was found and brought in." Blücher's exertions, as minimal as they were, exacerbated his eye infection and increased his pain. "The night of 30–31 March passed completely sleepless for me," explains Nostitz, "the mood of the Field Marshal was agitated in a high degree." In his agony the old hussar thought of Queen Louise, purportedly shouting, "She is revenged!"[82] Nostitz continues:

> After he rested in his bed for only a short while, he stood up. As best I could, I had prepared for myself a place on the above-noted table. The Field Marshal looked at it and thought it better than his own; I had to climb down and with much trouble help him onto it. Hardly was this difficult task completed when he realized his mistake and wanted to get down. The same process was repeated for the opposite purpose. Then the Field Marshal paced back and forth in the room, then lied down for a few minutes in his bed, in the meantime asking some questions to assure himself that I had not fallen asleep. Toward morning, the entire operation with the table was repeated, for which, naturally, many attendants had to be summoned to lend me a helping hand.[83]

On the following day, 31 March, the marshals surrendered Paris, and the ceremonial entry of the Allied sovereigns into the French capital occurred. With his eyes still burning, Blücher could not participate. "Under the gaze of their monarchs," continues Nostitz, "assembled almost all the troops that played such a glorious part in the Befreiungskrieg; by the conquest of the city, from which the misfortune of the world came from for so many years, the Field Marshal considered his work complete. 'From now on,' he said, 'there will be only talking and writing, not acting; I thus will have nothing to do, yet they can demand nothing of me.' He spent this lonely day with us, suffering very much in his room on Montmartre."[84]

The next day Blücher rode into Paris on horseback and went to the quarters prepared for him: the apartments of the former minister of police, Joseph Fouché, on Rue Seruti.[85] On 2 April his health worsened. His physician, Dr. Bieske, found the old man sitting on the floor in a corner brooding over his condition, fearing that he invariably suffered from dropsy, heart disease, tumors, and cancer. Begging Nostitz and Bieske to remain at his side, the field marshal insisted that death would claim him by morning.[86] "On this day," he later wrote to Bonin, "a deadly illness fell upon me and by the third day they feared for my eyesight and for my life. The King and the Tsar came to see me; I laid the command of the army at the King's feet and asked only to rest. He would not hear of it, but finally said, 'Well, in God's name rest and take care of yourself; you can live wherever you want.'"[87]

Frederick William and Alexander agreed to give Barclay de Tolly temporary command of the Silesian Army. Although the rest of the staff remained in place except for Nostitz, who stayed at Blücher's side, Gneisenau stepped down as chief of staff, taking an assignment with the royal suite. On 5 April Müffling informed Gneisenau that regarding the business at army headquarters, "everything remains as it was. . . . General Barclay wants everything to remain as if Field Marshal Blücher was present."[88]

"For six days," continued Blücher, "I lay blinded, but my nature rose above it all and I am completely recovered."[89] Despite Blücher's triumph over death, Napoleon's abdication brought the war to an end. Rushing west from St.-Dizier, the emperor learned of the surrender of his capital halfway between Fountainebleau and Paris. Three days later, on 3 April, a provisional French government deposed him, but Napoleon refused to relinquish power. Finally, after some of his marshals mutinied, he agreed to step aside in favor of his son on 6 April, signing the formal act of abdication at Fontainebleau on the eleventh. Regardless, the Allies restored the Bourbons under King Louis XVIII, and Napoleon went into exile on the tiny Mediterranean island of Elba. Blücher's view on the course of politics is clearly evident from a toast he made at a banquet in Paris: "May the fruits, which have been secured by the swords of the army, not again be destroyed by the quills of the ministers!"[90] "I have resigned the command of the army and will live my last days in peace," Blücher informed his cousin in May, "but I fear that the monarchs will ruin my intentions and I will again be harnessed."[91]

While preparing to leave Paris, Blücher wrote a final request to Frederick William:

> On the point of availing myself of Your Royal Majesty's graciously accorded permission and departing from an army whose bravery and unshakable courage alone has enabled me to lead it in a long succession of almost invariably victorious battles and combats from the banks of the Oder to the walls of Paris, which I have to thank for the happiest and brightest moments of my life, there is but one heartfelt wish I have at the end of my military career, the fulfillment of which will complete the happiness that Providence has so freely showered upon my gray head.
>
> Your Majesty will find this wish justifiable and natural, because at this moment of peace that was won by bloody sacrifice, it is only to see the proper reward bestowed on my brave comrades who earned the right to claim your exalted favor on so many glorious and decisive days.
>
> My great age and my health—ruined by the fatigues of war—will probably leave me little time to enjoy this period of glorious achievement. But I regard the army as my family and it would pain me to feel as if I left it forever without seeing it receive the rewards that I see as my sacred duty to obtain for it.[92]

Although we do not know the details of Blücher's requests, we know that the king could not satisfy them. Nevertheless, the moving appeal captures Blücher's love for his "children."

Amid his preparations, the field marshal received an invitation from the prince regent of England to journey to London. "You have long had my most dedicated esteem," the future King George IV wrote, "which through the events of recent times has only increased. Of course I cannot increase your well-deserved fame, which will live on in posterity, but I cannot deny myself the joy of stating my conviction that your exploits have done much to bring about the desired outcome of the long and difficult struggle. Much would this joy be increased by the pleasure of making your personal acquaintance, and I cannot suppress the wish that you decide to make a journey here, and through this I will have the opportunity to express to you my admiration, my gratitude, and to truly demonstrate my appreciation, in which I shall never cease to be your admirer."[93]

Wanting to return home, Blücher initially thought of declining. A discussion with Frederick William changed his mind. "Dearly beloved wife!" he wrote to Amalie on 22 April. "I am now, thank heaven, recovered to such an extent that I can travel and was in the process of leaving here when I unexpectedly received an urgent invitation from the Prince Regent of England to go to London to meet him. I showed the letter to the King and he thinks I cannot refuse. I will not stay there long, and will travel through Amsterdam, Münster, and Hanover to Berlin, where I hope to find you."

Blücher decided he would settle in Berlin, hoping to return to the Prussian capital by the end of June or the beginning of July.[94] "L'Estocq wrote me," he informed his wife, "have you already purchased a home there? If not, he will gladly obtain one; I only fear it will be too small. When I arrive, I will have every reason to be able to request a vacant home." As his popularity soared, he thought twice about permanently settling in Berlin. "You shall purchase a good home in Berlin," he instructed Amalie on 3 June, "preferably on Unter den Linden not far from the gate so that we can be close to the Tiergarten. I do not know at this moment where I will settle down, but in any case I will live in Berlin in the winter. I will sell the Kunzendörf estate because I will receive a new estate in Silesia; the Silesians very much wish that I come live among them, and the Pomeranians request the same; time will tell if I live in Berlin only."[95]

With his labors over, Blücher's thoughts dwelled on his wife and family. "Live well and when I return to you we will never again separate until death," he assured Amalie. "I will concern myself with nothing more; but because the King will not discharge me, I must remain in the service. Regardless, I will no longer look after any government."[96] His daughter, Fritze, had remarried to Major Maximilian von der Asseburg, a royal chamberlain, on 14 January 1814. "Fritze writes me very anxiously that I still have not given her my approval for the marriage. I have just written her that she should only marry likewise and I know not why the stupid chap waits for my approval; after all, he is a major."[97] "You know Fritze is at home," he wrote Amalie on 22 April. "I will speak with her during my trip through Magdeburg and invite her and her husband to Berlin; Gebhard shall also come with his wife. Your brother is now here and will accompany me to England along with Nostitz. I cannot write much because of my eyes, so I'll just say that I am looking forward so much to seeing you and holding you close to my heart."

As for Franz, after being released, he joined his father at Paris. "Franz is still here and says hello; he will go to a spa while on furlough and then come to Berlin. I want to see his children."[98] The field marshal could not help but be proud of his oldest son. "Franz says hello," he raved to his cousin, Conrad Daniel von Blücher-Altona, "he is a colonel and commander of a hussar regiment, and received military decorations from Austria and Russia as well as our own country. He served with much distinction, but has suffered much. He has been wounded seven times and was stabbed through the lungs and taken prisoner in an unconscious state; but he has completely recovered."[99]

Although excited about the trip to London, the extended time that it caused Blücher to remain at Paris vexed him. Initially believing that he would return to Berlin in June or July, he learned that the voyage to Great Britain would not occur until early June. "Paris as well as all of France pleases me not and I pine for German lands," he complained to Bonin on 30 April. "I am aggravated that I must remain here longer. Louis XVIII will make his entry here the day after tomorrow. Napoleon still has support here. I do not trust the French, especially after our army marches away."[100] On 16 May he complained to Amalie: "I am now completely healthy, but must still suffer here waiting until the King is ready to travel to London so I can accompany him there. This is annoying to me because I could already be in London and thinking about my return trip from there."[101] Still, his hatred of Paris did not keep him out of the casinos of the Palais Royal, where he indulged his two mistresses: alcohol and gambling. Daily he played for high stakes, purportedly leaving the French capital with 19,000 thaler in winnings alone.[102]

Like the rest of Europe, Blücher found French goods to be inferior to those manufactured by the British. "Perhaps I will bring you two beautiful carriage horses from England as well as a carriage," he wrote Amalie on 6 May. "I have bought nothing here, because I remember that everything in London is made better."[103] One month later he reiterated, "I wanted to buy many things in Paris, but one told me that everything made in England is better; the only bad thing is that I cannot bring much back."[104]

Still, the rewards and honors continued to roll in. "The city of London has awarded me a sword of honor that I will receive there," he boasted to his wife. "A local jeweler appraised the sword I received from Tsar Alexander to be worth 20,000 thaler; another saber like it is coming from St. Petersburg. What the devil shall I do with all these bejeweled weapons?"[105] To Bonin he wrote: "in Scotland, they have made me an honorary member of the learned society of Edinburgh. I must be careful not to make a fool of myself."[106] "The English kill me," he explained to Blücher-Altona, "they come from England in hordes just to make my acquaintance."[107] "More than 100 English have come here merely to see me and get to know me," he wrote on 6 May. "Yesterday, the famous Lord Wellington arrived here and I have been requested to spend three days with him, but I must watch my drinking! The new king of France is now here and has publically thanked me for being the prime reason he has been restored to his throne."[108] He reported to Amalie in early June: "The English flock here by the hundreds to see me; I have to shake hands with each and every one, and the ladies virtually make love to me; they are the craziest people I know. I am bringing along a sword and a saber on which are set 40,000 thaler worth of jewels. I have been admitted to the London societies without a vote. . . . It will be a wonder if I do not go mad. God only knows what will happen to me in Holland."[109]

Finally, the Allied entourage began to leave Paris en route to London in early June. "At last, at last, I am out of Paris and have reached the sea," declared a relieved Blücher, "but I still must wait two days until the King arrives so I can cross to England with him. Yesterday, I dined with the Duke of Clarence on a ship of the line, the *Impregnable*; I am deaf from all the thundering of the cannon and almost overwhelmed by all the events in my honor.[110] If this continues, I will go mad in England. At London, I will be forced like the devil to stay with the Prince Regent, but I will do my best to get out of it."[111]

Upon leaving French soil, Frederick William elevated Blücher to the noble rank of *Fürst* (prince). "You have blessedly and gloriously ended the struggle for the Fatherland," declares the king's letter of 3 June, "but the gratitude that the state owes you still continues. As proof of this, I hereby name you Prince Blücher of Wahlstatt and your heirs will be peers of the realm as Counts Blücher of Wahlstatt." Consequently, the title of prince would be for life only and not hereditary. Having pinched pennies as Gebhard von Blücher, he did not want to starve as Prince Blücher von Wahlstatt.[112] Thus, the king agreed that the title would be accompanied by a pension and an estate in Silesia. "What Wahlstatt means," he wrote Amalie, "is that after my death you will receive a lifetime pension that will allow you to live like a princess."[113] "Despite all of my objections," he explained to his cousin Blücher-Altona, "they have made me a prince. I was obliged to consent because they insisted that I do so for the sake of the nation. Yet it was as 'Blücher' that the nation shouted its acclaim for me. I refuse to join the army of starving German princes; without the money, I will refuse the title and tell the newspapers why I am doing so!"[114]

CHAPTER 16

THE SPOILS OF VICTORY

The *Impregnable* sailed to England with an esteemed passenger list highlighted by Tsar Alexander; King Frederick William; the Hohenzollern princes, including the future King William IV and Kaiser William I; Hardenberg; and Metternich, all of whom boarded according to honor and precedence. Blücher had to be coerced to board. After Frederick William warned him that his refusal would anger the tsar, he joined the others. With the Duke of Clarence's flag at the main, the Russian eagle at the fore, and the Prussian eagle at the mizzen, the *Impregnable* sailed from Boulogne on 3 June 1814.[1]

As the ship pulled into Dover two days later, cries of "Blücher forever" roared from an adoring crowd. The British media encouraged the public to give the field marshal a hero's welcome, and the people did not disappoint. After the greeting he received, Blücher reflected that he was lucky to be alive. "The people almost tore me apart," he explained to Amalie. "They seized me from my horse and carried me to London." People tore at his clothes in the hopes of taking away a memento. Women begged for a lock of his hair, but he pointed to his half-bald head and asked for mercy. The hugs and kisses continued throughout the day.[2]

After this rapturous reception, Blücher reached the British capital. He climbed the Monument to the Great Fire of London to survey the city. Upon seeing the filth, smoke, and fog, the Prussian muttered, "Was für plunder," which literally translates, "What rubbish." Bystanders misinterpreted the remark to mean: "What a place to plunder."[3] Blücher took quarters at St. James's Palace. At 6:00 on the evening of 7 June, the Royal Horse Guards escorted the field marshal, who rode in one of the prince regent's elegant open carriages, to Carlton House, the royal heir's palace. Upon arriving, a throng rushed the carriage to catch site of the Prussian, trampling the guards in the process. Blücher emerged. Kneeling, he kissed the prince regent's hand.

As at Paris, honors continued to be bestowed on the old hussar. On entering London's opera house on 9 June, the crowd rose and greeted him with thundering hurrahs. He joined the prince regent, Alexander, Frederick William, and several others for a visit to Oxford. By command of the prince regent, Blücher took quarters at Christ Church, where his great-great-grandson, Gustav, would one day become an undergraduate. The university conferred on him the honorary degree of doctor of laws. During the banquet at Radcliffe Library, the field marshal delivered the famous line: "If I am to be a doctor, they should at least make Gneisenau an apothecary, for we go together." Not to be outdone, Cambridge made Blücher a doctor of civil law, holding a magnificent dinner for him at Trinity College. Next, the mayor of London hosted a banquet for the field marshal at Guildhall. He reviewed the home fleet and the regiments near London. One night he dined privately with the prince regent at Windsor Castle. He appeared before Parliament to express his appreciation for £200,000 raised for poor relief around Leipzig. "Had I not a wife and children . . . I would never leave this blessed country. I cannot find words to express the true feelings of my grateful heart," he stated.

On one occasion, Blücher and Wellington emerged in public together; predictably, a crowd mobbed them. At a ball hosted by the prince regent, the usually stiff Wellington relaxed and danced a polonaise. Blücher joined in and did a German country dance. Many fascinating tales sprang up concerning the Prussian's doings. When he drove through London, the curious often climbed on the roof of his carriage to look inside through the windows. People, especially women, besieged the buildings at St. James's Palace where Blücher lived, demanding to be presented to him. Supposedly, the women would not leave until he kissed their hands. One morning the crowd grew so large that the door to Colomb's room suddenly burst open and four ladies charged in. Still in his nightgown, the major darted behind the curtains. Despite his demands for them to leave, the women could not get the door open. Forced to relieve himself behind the curtains, Colomb finished dressing and presented the ladies to the field marshal.[4] "In England," recalled Nostitz, "where I lived with Prince Blücher at the St. James Palace as the guest of the Prince of Wales, I was eyewitness to all of the so-often and described-in-detail homage that the Field Marshal (often in extravagant form) received. Blücher's popularity caused me to always climb into the wagon before him because the thick, pressing masses of people made climbing in after him impossible."[5]

"The French could not kill me," Blücher wrote his cousin on 30 June, "but the English and their regent will succeed through kindness."[6] Tired of being in the spotlight, he bade farewell to his hosts. From Harwich he set sail for the continent on Monday, 11 July. Landing at Ostend, he made small daytrips through North Germany en route to Berlin. At every stop the inhabitants celebrated. At Berlin he received a hero's welcome and much the same treatment as he did at London. Banquets, dinners, and fetes filled his days and nights. The University of Berlin conferred on him the honorary degree of doctor of philosophy. From the king he received the seventeenth-century schloß of Krieblowitz not far from Breslau in Silesia. There, he eased into semiretirement, for the king refused to discharge him. "The peace with France is now concluded," he wrote Amalie on 3 June, "and God willing it will last a long time for the good of mankind."[7]

Franz's severe health problems limited the extent that Blücher could enjoy the many celebrations that honored him in Prussia. While still at Paris the previous year, he summoned Dr. Bieske to care for his son, who complained of headaches and hemorrhoids. "The symptoms were easily removed by bloodletting and purgatives, and the patient returned to the amusements of Paris," notes Bieske's report, published in the *Berlin Gazette of Medicine* on 30 December 1835. Shortly after, Franz again complained of "tightness and pain about the head, with the impossibility of sleeping. The pulse was now quick and full; the skin warm and dry." Again Bieske cured the symptoms with "mild diaphoretics and a warm regimen," but "a little confusion in the ideas seemed to remain." Bieske attributed this to dementia, which the return of anxiety, insomnia, and "tightness of the head" accompanied, and hypochondria. He hoped, "both by acting on the abdominal cavity and by sulfurous baths, mineral waters, and relief of the patient's mind, to obtain a complete cure."

Bieske also examined the wounds Franz received during the skirmish with the Poles. Although healed, the scars "betrayed the extent and nature of each injury. One saber wound existed near the junction of the occipital and right parietal bones on the back of his head near the base of the skull. Excessively deep, Bieske figured the blow had penetrated the inner table of the skull. A second sabre cut, on the left parietal bone, appeared superficial, but a third near the junction of the right parietal bone with the frontal bone on the top right side of the head probably had penetrated the skull cavity. A scar on the neck signaled a lance wound and a second on the right side of the chest that Bieske assumed penetrated "the substance of the lungs, as was shown by the violent hemoptysis and other symptoms that accompanied and followed the wound."

After being treated by the famed French doctor Dominique-Jean Larrey, Franz appeared to recover fully. Exchanged for a captured French general, he had participated in the 1814 campaign. In May he left Paris with the intention of taking the mineral baths at a spa but never did. At this time he "conceived the strange idea that he was possessed of a secret that would save the kingdom of Prussia from all dangers and that its neighbors were constantly at work either to force this secret from him, or to deprive him of life and discover it in his entails. It was impossible to convince the patient, by any moral reasoning, of the folly of the ideas that possessed him." Using a compound tincture of bark with one of rhubarb and wine, the doctors thought they cured him. But "his irregular ideas soon returned."

Blücher remained extremely concerned about his son. "He is an extreme hypochondriac and has lost all sense of humor," the field marshal informed Gneisenau at the end of August. "I fear for him. The King has been very unfair toward my son. Not gladly will I challenge the monarch, but if he forces me, I'll write to him that my son and our name do not deserve insults."[8] At Berlin Blücher had the kingdom's best physicians examine Franz, but the results yielded no progress: his son regarded the doctors as "fiends and persecuting demons." Bieske, who Franz still trusted, hoped to find a cure through exercise "and acting on the intestinal canal." Unfortunately for the family, "it was impossible to overcome the morbid mistrust that constantly occupied his mind; in the intervals of lucidity, he often complained of confusion in the head, vertigo, and sparks crossing the eyes." Likewise unfortunate proved the misdiagnosis. Instead of attributing these symptoms to the brain, his medical attendants insisted on hypochondria. Rather than pursue antiphlogistic measures, his caretakers pursued "the opposite method with a fatal perseverance." One physician, a Dr. Bohne, advised him to drink champagne. Under the beverage's stimulating influence, Franz felt better, but within twenty-four hours "the patient became uneasy and agitated, and the attacks of vertigo were excessively violent; the pulse was now full and hard; the face and eyes much injected." Bieske wanted to draw blood from

the arm, yet Franz refused. He finally agreed to a bloodletting by twelve leaches and "a more cooling diet." Franz recovered momentarily and his appetite returned. Incorrectly attributing his recovery to Bohne, he made sure to drink one bottle of champagne daily.

"The baneful effects of such treatment were not long without manifesting themselves; the vertigo again appeared with excessive violence." Bohne again turned to bloodletting and sulfur treatments with a "cooling diet." Although this eased Franz, the change from champagne to cold water "inspired his mind with fresh distrust; he now refused every kind of medicament, determined to treat himself, and for this purpose made a journey on foot into Silesia, from which he returned in eleven days much more ill than when he set out." This worsening condition prompted the field marshal to summon another consultation with the Berlin doctors on 14 November. The physician general declared that no link existed between Franz's affliction and the wounds he received during the fall campaign. Instead, he "insisted on an aberration of the intelligence, which would best be treated by occupation and the effect of moral agents." Bieske noted that "these latter had no influence on the disease; the patient became so unruly and distrustful as to endanger his own life and that of others; he often walked about at night with loaded weapons, and once challenged a superior officer to a duel, who, he imagined, threw some shade on the glory of his father."

A third medical exam followed, resulting in Franz being declared mentally deranged and the duel being prevented. Not being allowed to defend his father's honor enraged Franz and worsened his condition. He vowed to kill the officer, but the inability to do so drove him insane. Amid hosting a breakfast for his friends, Franz pulled out a loaded pistol and fired it into the left side of his chest near the clavicle. Although not mortal, the wound was serious, and the ball remained lodged under the left scapula. Numerous other treatments followed but failed. "Confined at one time, at another allowed absolute liberty, the patient was at length sent under proper care on a journey to the Rhineland, but returned one year later without any benefit."

His physical symptoms seemed to abate with the exception of headaches. "The hand was constantly carried to the forehead or head, and at these times the patient expressed his suffering by crying out: 'O Gott, mein Kopf' (Oh God, my head)." Although the doctors failed to correctly diagnose Franz, Blücher immediately recognized the cause of his son's dementia: "His serious head wounds are the main reasons for his depression. In the hours when he is conscious, his condition brings him to despair. He attempted to shoot himself. It was not successful and he will recover, but the ball has not been removed and the doctor cannot find it. The doctor hopes for a complete recovery, but I am doubtful."[9]

Moreover, the resemblance to the behavior displayed by the elder Blücher in 1808 and 1809 is striking. Franz "not only believed that his food and drink were poisoned, but that a portion of his strength was lost each time his hair was cut, and hence he refused to be shaved or have his hair cut; he was also convinced that a part of his secret was contained in his excrement, and always satisfied nature in a remote and unfrequented place, after which he carefully buried the precious deposit." In this state Franz lived from 1814 until his death on 10 October 1829.[10]

While caring for his son, Blücher wrote Boyen, the new minister of war, on 17 February 1815 to firmly request his discharge so he could "live his last few days in peace and quiet."[11] His disgust with the First Peace of Paris and the Congress of Vienna contributed to his angst. Regarding the former, he wrote Bülow in the fall of 1814: "Whether or not the future holds another struggle for us only Heaven knows. I have no confidence in the situation. They neglected their opportunities at Paris. France's tone is growing too bold; they should have done more to clip her wings."[12] As for the latter, although ongoing, the Prussians learned that they would receive a portion of Saxony as well a stretch of the Rhineland that included Aachen and Köln. In return, Frederick William renounced his claims to Ansbach-Bayreuth and Ostfriesland.

Despite the blood that Prussia had poured into the conflict, these gains did not come easy. Ever conscious of the balance of power in central Europe, Metternich refused to allow Alexander to reconstitute a kingdom of Poland under Russian suzerainty. The tsar envisioned a Poland that included the territories taken by Prussia and Austria in the Second and Third Partitions. While Metternich rejected his ridiculous Alsace-Galicia proposal, in which Austria would receive Alsace as compensation for returning Galicia to Poland, the Prussians did not enjoy the same freedom. The plan for Prussia to exchange the Polish lands taken in 1793 and 1795 for all of Saxony formed the basis of the Russo-Prussian alliance treaties signed in February and March 1813. Not only did

Metternich hold firm against Alexander but he likewise refused to see Prussia annex all of Saxony. Great Britain's foreign minister, Robert Stewart, Viscount Castlereagh, likewise harbored concerns that Prussian expansion in the Rhineland and North Germany would seduce Berlin to set its sights on the Netherlands.

Thus, the Austrians and British went to Vienna committed to restraining Russo-Prussian expansion. France's foreign minister, the cunning Charles Maurice de Talleyrand, sensed and exploited the discord. In fact, Metternich, Castlereagh, and Talleyrand signed a "secret" treaty on 3 January 1815 pledging war to stop Russia and Prussia. Faced with a conflict against his former coalition partners now joined by France, the tsar conceded. He agreed to a smaller Poland, which forced Frederick William to receive only a portion of Saxony.

Sacrificing Ansbach-Bayreuth and Ostfriesland to keep Polish territory and gain Saxon land particularly irked Blücher. He wondered how exchanging Prussian states for "300,000 Poles and just as many Saxons, who hate us, could ever replace these faithful and self-sacrificing brothers? Oh ye politicians! Little do you know of humanity! The good Vienna Congress is like a fair in a small town to which each man drives his own cattle to sell or exchange. We drove in a fine bull and in return received a shabby ox, as the Berliners say. For my part, I have made my decision and have requested my discharge. I am daily awaiting the answer and then I will immediately go to Silesia, never to see Berlin or the court again. It is unheard of how they treat us soldiers."[13]

Before receiving a response from Boyen, Blücher learned that Napoleon had escaped from Elba with his personal guard of 1,000 men and four cannon in late February. Landing in France on 1 March, he entered Lyon on the tenth. After the forces sent to apprehend the emperor of Elba defected to Napoleon's cause, Louis XVIII fled to Belgium. Reaching Paris on 20 March, Napoleon restored the empire. To ease the public's increasing fear of an Allied response, he issued a statement claiming peace with Austria and a twenty-year truce with the other powers. He confidently declared to the French people that the Allies would not mobilize. Despite his attempts to secure peace, all diplomatic channels remained closed. The Allies branded him an "Enemy and Disturber of the Tranquility of the World." On 25 March Great Britain, Russia, Prussia, and Austria formed the Seventh Coalition against France. Each agreed to furnish an army of 150,000 men and to not lay down arms "until Bonaparte shall have been put absolutely beyond the possibility of exciting disturbances and of renewing his attempts to seize the supreme power in France."

Swift and obstinate Allied opposition forced Napoleon to create a new army. On his return, he found less than 200,000 men under arms.[14] With an unstable political position, he could not enact radical measures to increase his armed forces: a levée en masse remained out of the question. Instead, he relied on recalling thousands of furloughed men and deserters. Due to hopeless negotiations with the Coalition, French authorities did not post the summons until 9 April. Nevertheless, by the end of May, 224,000 men formed seven corps and armies of observation. Napoleon's Imperial Guard grew to three infantry divisions and two cavalry divisions totaling 30,000 men. The emperor's main force, the Armée du Nord (Army of the North), consisted of 120,000 men. He divided his remaining troops among the Armies of the Rhine, Loire, Alps, and Pyrenees. Should the Allies invade France, Paris and Lyon would serve as rallying points for these armies. The mobilization of 375,600 National Guards strengthened the frontier fortresses.

At the Congress of Vienna, the Allies altered their discussions of reshaping Europe to deploying five armies and invading France. Preliminary plans called for a Prussian army of 117,000 men led by Blücher and an Anglo-Dutch force of 93,000 men commanded by Wellington to operate in Belgium. With an Austrian army of 210,000 men, Schwarzenberg would take a position on the upper Rhine, while a Russian army of 150,000 men under Barclay de Tolly would deploy to the middle Rhine. From Italy, an Austro-Italian force of 75,000 men under General Johann Frimont would invade southeastern France.

Following Napoleon's first abdication, three Prussian corps and the Royal Saxon Army, totaling 40,000 men, remained in the field between Wesel and Koblenz under Kleist's overall command. On the middle Rhine stood I and III Corps, while II Corps, with the 14,000 Saxons, quartered near the Meuse.[15] With the formation of the Seventh Coalition, Frederick William authorized an immediate mobilization to increase their strengths to a war footing. A cabinet order of 18 March decreed the formation of four new corps: the IV would assemble between the Elbe and the Weser; the V on the Oder; and the VI and VII around Berlin. The king summoned Blücher to command the field army, christened the Army of the Lower Rhine. During the night of 8–9 March, Gneisenau approached Blücher's bed. Waking the field marshal, he informed him that Napoleon had escaped Elba and landed in France. Blücher purportedly exclaimed that "this is the greatest luck that Prussia could have! Now, the war begins anew and the army will make good all the mistakes made at Vienna!"[16] He later wrote that despite his desire to retire, he felt compelled to "obey the demands of the monarchs and the wish of the nation."[17]

A skilled staff of fifty officers, again led by Gneisenau, would coordinate the army's operations. The appointments to command I, II, and III Corps reflected Blücher's uncertain health and the army's chain of command. Should the field marshal again become incapacitated as he had at Laon in 1814, Frederick William wanted a smooth transition of command to Gneisenau. For this reason, Generals Hans Ernst von Zieten, Borstell, and the native Saxon Thielmann—all junior to the chief of staff—received command of corps. Although the king placed IV Corps in Bülow's hands, Gneisenau's original plan envisioned Blücher's army advancing to Paris in July, with IV Corps following as the reserve. Napoleon's unexpected June offensive negated these plans and brought Bülow's corps to frontline service.

On 16 April Blücher crossed the Rhine at Koblenz. Anxiety over Franz rendered the field marshal thoughtful and melancholy. "Now that I have crossed the Rhine, I am seated on its bank looking back at the past and thinking of the future; I cannot see much comfort," he lamented to Amalie. "My poor Franz is always before my eyes. On the night of the thirteenth, I had a vision while traveling that no one except I and Wilhelm saw because Brünneck and Nostitz were asleep. From that moment, I have not been able to fight off the thought that Franz is dead; give me some news." He then commented that he visited his new in-laws. "I found Asseburg, his wife, and the children well, but only stayed the night with them; I was very pleased to find Fritze so happy, and she has reason to be; she is living very agreeably, and her husband treats her with great affection. I talked him out of coming along. If I may advise you, go see Fritze, it will make you happy."

He informed Amalie that he planned to depart for Liège, where he would find army headquarters. As for the war, "no hostilities have occurred, but they cannot be far off." Referring to rumors that the Vendée area of western France opposed Napoleon, he commented that "in France the civil war has begun, they will finish themselves off and I do not believe we will have to do much. In the meantime, they are mobilizing a great mass of men and the lands will again be devastated and exhausted. Here, everything is in the most beautiful blossom and the weather is incomparable. I am received with joy everywhere and the troops rejoice to see me again; if I was free from worry, I would call myself lucky, but I enjoy no happy moments."[18]

Blücher penned another forlorn letter to his wife after reaching Liège: "I have arrived here by the army and the troops greeted me with joy. The army is full of courage and in the finest condition. I believe that if the war starts, we will finish it quickly. Franz is constantly before my eyes and I cannot get him out of my thoughts. I cannot escape the feeling that he is dead; all my pleasure on earth is destroyed by his fate. Please tell me how he is and what they have done with him. Now, dear child, I tell you that when the war is over I will not return to Berlin. Franz's misfortune and the unjust manner that he has been treated brought me to this firm decision. I cannot and will not have my sons murdered before my eyes day and night. What are Franz's boys doing?"[19]

On 30 March, I, II, and III Corps started moving into Belgium, although the mobilization continued. Many units, especially cavalry, never reached full strength. Like 1813, the combination of militia and line troops facilitated the army's rapid expansion. For the 1815 campaign, the infantry of I and II Corps consisted of one-third militia, that of III Corps one-half, and of IV Corps two-thirds. The arms, uniforms, and equipment of the army was rated satisfactory but very uneven—in the case of the Landwehr, barely serviceable. Missing equipment and dull boots did not unsettle Blücher. In 1813 and 1814 he led the most ragged of troops to victory. Morale and zeal mattered most to him, not buttons and caps. "We will soon see our adversary up close and he shall discover that we have not changed," wrote Blücher to the commander of his old hussar regiment.[20] To Hardenberg he declared: "Be assured, my esteemed friend, the French will again fight in the old manner. In our troops reigns a courage that becomes boldness."[21]

The Allies planned to defeat Napoleon through numerical superiority. Blücher, Wellington, and Schwarzenberg would then march directly on Paris, with Barclay's army in support; Frimont's force would advance on Lyon. All Allied armies would cross the French frontier between 27 June and 1 July. Aside from this strategy, Blücher and Wellington had yet to arrange a plan of operations. Regardless, the Prussian remained confident over the military situation. "My dear cousin!" he wrote to Blücher-Altona. "In your last letter you promised you would visit me, but how everything has changed! I stand here with 150,000 Prussians and await the order to beat the French again. At my side to the right at Brussels stands my friend Wellington. The French remain quiet and I do not believe Bonaparte will begin an offensive so soon." Instead, he thought the Allies should attack Napoleon "with the most possible haste. As long as the monarchs remain united the situation will go well. But it always will be difficult to keep a Bourbon on the throne if he cannot get on it himself and win over the nation." In fact, the field marshal expressed his belief that France should be reduced in size but allowed to form a republican government. "In this case, I do not believe they will be dangerous to their neighbors; but, as everything changes, I am certain that today's politics will be tomorrow's mistakes." Turning to the subject of Franz, Blücher informed his cousin: "You already know the unfortunate story of my oldest son. I cannot write about it, my heart bleeds, and all the joys of my life are in him. He was a man with the finest disposition and a distinguished officer."[22]

Fortunately for the old hussar, Gebhard, now a lieutenant colonel, delivered good news. "Gebhard has arrived," he informed Amalie in early May. "I am glad to know that you are well. Franz's situation is heavy on my heart; Gebhard calms me because he assures me that Franz is well looked after and treated, and that the boys are well provided for. I can do nothing more. Go wherever you want—to a spa—you can spend as much money as you want. Write me if you want more. Visit Fritze, it will do you good. I hope this war will not last long."[23] Two weeks later he wrote her: "I received your letter as well as one from Dr. Horn concerning my poor Franz. The doctor is hopeful that God will cure him."[24]

On 30 April Blücher received a cabinet order instructing him to divide the Saxons into two brigades: one consisting of soldiers living in the regions to be annexed by Prussia—thus, new Prussians— and the other consisting of those who would remain "Saxon," which would then join Wellington's army. Although the final agreement had yet to be signed at Vienna, Frederick William desired the separation to occur before hostilities with France commenced.

Uncertainty over the fate of their country already put the Saxon troops on edge. Knowing this, Blücher wanted to demonstrate his trust and confidence in them. As he did with the Russians during the previous war, the field marshal chose two Saxon regiments from Borstell's II Corps to escort his headquarters. Later he explained this decision to Hardenberg: "The King does me an injustice if he believes I exposed myself. When I arrived at Liège, I found no men other than Saxons at my headquarters. Had I distanced myself from them it would have conveyed mistrust; I thought I could win them over through good treatment. I would have succeeded had an officer not spurred on the men to insubordination."[25]

After reading the contents of this directive, Blücher expressed concern that its implementation could cause trouble, especially because the Saxon king, Frederick Augustus, had yet to release his soldiers from their oath of loyalty to him. Although the staff discussed the possibility of a revolt, Gneisenau insisted that the order be executed. On 2 May he addressed the Saxon commanders and explained the plan for separating their units. Reports of their soldiers toasting Napoleon's health placed him in a foul mood, vowing that opposition or interference of any sort would not be tolerated. Gneisenau explained that the "Prussian" contingent, which included the Saxon Guard Grenadier Battalion, would swear an oath of allegiance to Frederick William.[26] "Rather than permit a corps in our midst that plots in secret, I will see to it that the road to France be opened to you and let you share the fate of Bonaparte. I would prefer to see you arrayed against us as open enemies rather than having you among us as false friends."[27]

Before Gneisenau left the meeting, the Saxon Guard Grenadier Battalion gathered in front of Blücher's quarters at Liège. One source cites them as being in civilian dress. Whether in uniform or not, they protested with chants of "Long live Frederick Augustus!" and "We won't be separated!" The men pelted with rocks and insults General Anton Friedrich von Ryssel, a former Saxon officer who already had joined the Prussian army. Hurrying from their meeting with Gneisenau, the Saxon officers managed to temporarily diffuse the situation. Blücher later learned that an officer in the Saxon Guard had received word of the impending division. "The business was prepared by an officer of the Guard," he explained, "and this officer knew that the separation would occur before we did; therefore, they were warned from Vienna."[28]

At nightfall, the Saxon Guard Grenadiers returned to Blücher's house, many of them drunk. No officers could be seen. Warnings from Blücher's staff failed to convince them to stand down. With the field marshal watching through a window, the Saxons attempted to force their way inside; the Prussian officers slashed the foremost with their swords. Rocks came hurtling down on both the Prussians and the windows of the house, including those of Blücher's room. The commander flew into a rage and had to be restrained from taking up his saber. Besieged, the staff officers withdrew into the house, which the Saxons stormed. With his life in danger, the field marshal fled through the back door, much to his and the army's great embarrassment. "The Saxons mutinied last night at Liège," mocked Wellington, "and obliged poor old Blücher to quit the town."[29]

Blücher could suffer defeats in the field, but he could not suffer emasculation. After the rabble that commandeered his headquarters disbanded, he ordered the Saxon Guard to Namur. On the following day, 3 May, he wanted the remaining Saxon troops out of Liège and replaced by a Prussian brigade. Most of these units departed, but the 2nd and 3rd Grenadier Battalions rioted upon learning that they could not join the Guard Grenadier Battalion. After receiving permission from the ranking Saxon officer, General Joachim Friedrich Gotthelf von Zezschwitz, to follow the Guard, they marched out of Liège. Earlier in the day, Blücher and Gneisenau departed to meet with Wellington at Tirlemont and so did not witness the unrest that occurred. But on their ride back to headquarters, they passed the Saxon 2nd Light Regiment, whose men refused to salute the field marshal. With his pride wounded, Blücher demonstrated the same ruthlessness that he did forty-three years earlier in Poland.

"I shall surround them, disarm them, and then order them to hand over the ringleaders," he pledged to Frederick William. "If they do so, I shall have the latter shot. If they refuse, I shall take every tenth man and have several of them shot. I will then dismiss these battalions from the army as unworthy to fight."[30] Borstell, the commander of II Corps, received orders to disarm and separate the three grenadier battalions, shoot the ringleaders, and burn the Guard's standard, embroidered by the queen of Saxony herself. After promising the Saxons that he would not burn the flag, the general declared that he could not execute Blücher's orders. Despite Borstell's plea for Blücher to be lenient, the Prussians burned the standard in public. On 6 May four Saxons met their fate before a firing squad;

Blücher had three more executed before the affair ended.³¹ That same day he issued a proclamation to the Saxons, appealing to their courage and honor for the restoration of order.

Two days later, on the eighth, the field marshal relieved Borstell of his command and filed charges; General Georg Dubislav Ludwig von Pirch, known as Pirch I to distinguish him from his brother Otto Lorenz, took the helm of II Corps. "The affair with Borstell is likewise unpleasant," he confessed to Hardenberg, "but I must handle it in this manner if I don't want to lose my prestige in the army."³² Borstell sought a reconciliation, but the field marshal remained adamant. "Herr Borstell has expressed regret over his disobedience, but it is too late. The King has turned over the investigation to General Hirschfeld, and martial law will determine how long he remains at Magdeburg."³³ Later, in November, a court-martial found Borstell guilty of insubordination. Sentenced to six months of incarceration at Magdeburg, the general started serving his time in December. But on Blücher's request, the king pardoned Borstell in January 1816, appointing him commander of I Corps later that year.³⁴

"The news will soon reach Berlin that the Saxons wanted to murder me," Blücher explained to Amalie, "but pay no attention to this: you know well that I will not lose my head so easily. I am sorry that I have to execute four men as rebels tomorrow, but the Saxons must learn to respect my name with awe. With complete trust I surrendered myself to these people and did not keep even one Prussian guard. The beasts stormed my house; had I not acted resolutely and found safety, me and my entire entourage would have been sacrificed. But now I have them so completely under control that they cannot budge; the mistake was we should not have treated these people with kindness, but severity."³⁵

Blücher wrote a scathing missive to King Frederick Augustus over the incident. Although speculation exists over whether Hardenberg prevented it from actually being sent, the document provides great insight into Blücher's views of the situation. "By your earlier measures," he wrote, "Your Royal Majesty plunged your subjects, a respected German people, into the deepest misery. By your later measures, you have managed to cover them with shame." He accused the monarch of being directly responsible for the mutiny, maintaining that "the rebellion in the army was organized from Friedrichsfelde and Preßburg"—both being places where Frederick Augustus stayed after the Battle of Leipzig while en route to Berlin as a prisoner of war. Blücher lamented that the mutiny "broke out just as all of Germany is marching against the common enemy. The criminals have openly proclaimed Bonaparte as their protector and have forced me, who in my fifty-five years of service have been in the fortunate position of spilling the blood of only my enemy, to order executions in my own army for the first time." Including a copy of his 6 May proclamation, the field marshal warned: "From the enclosed, Your Majesty will see how I have sought up to this very moment to save the honor of the Saxon name, but it is the last attempt. If my words are not heeded, then without sorrow, but with the calm of a clear conscience and with the assurance of fulfilling my duty, I shall restore order through violence even if I should have to execute the entire Saxon army. As God is my judge the blood that is spilled will be that of the guilty—and before the All-Knowing will orders given and orders obeyed be considered one-and-the-same. Your Royal Majesty knows that an old man of seventy-three years can have no earthly objective other than for the voice of truth to be heard and for justice to take place."[36]

Later in the month Blücher explained his measures to Hardenberg:

> As for the Saxons, I have nothing good to say. To avoid the necessity of treating them with barbarity, I have separated all of them, sending the infantry, which certainly will defect at the first opportunity, across the Rhine, moving the artillery to Jülich, and keeping the cavalry, which appears good, with me. When the situation with Saxony is settled at Vienna everything will abate, but then they will say: 'Our king still has not dismissed us and we are not released from our oath.' I wanted Wellington to take the Saxons, but he did not want them. I prefer to see these people with Napoleon than with me. Just think how unlucky I could have been if the Saxon infantry learned that I replaced Herr General Borstell. I would have them all shot, because it is a dangerous situation when 8,000 men fail to obey. All the guilt was caused by the fact that these men were spoiled. We treated them like babies, and when they were to be split up, they believed I was the cause. But I finished with them before they found out that Herr Borstell wanted to be their legal advisor. I decided to carry out the business and to obediently execute the King's order and if necessary would have shot Herr Borstell as well. Now the chap realizes his mistake, but it is too late. My troops are so angry that I must use all of my prestige to protect the Saxons otherwise they will kill them.[37]

As late as 2 June, Blücher still fumed over the episode but took comfort that it was over. "I am pleased that I am free of the Saxons," he again wrote Hardenberg. "Here we have letters that serve as proof of their disgraceful mood. I only wish that Wellington would take them; he is extremely angry over this. The Saxons must not come around our Prussians; because of the offenses they committed against me, the bitterness of our people is so great that I would have to use all of my influence to prevent ugly incidents."[38] After the Berlin press broke the news in the capital, he wrote: "I saw that in Berlin one has portrayed the Saxon affair with much exaggeration. It was not as crazy, and afterward I had seven shot dead; the entire uproar was squashed and remorse replaced fury."[39]

Rumors of Napoleon's advance to the frontier produced the 3 May meeting at Tirlemont between Blücher and Wellington. As noted, the Allies had yet to establish a plan of operations. Earlier attempts had failed as Gneisenau and Wellington disagreed on the role to be taken by the Prussians. Gneisenau wanted to conduct the invasion just as he and Blücher had in 1814, with the objective of gaining Paris through a decisive offensive. Wellington, a general who always had a hand on the political pulse of his government, sought to continue the Anglo-Austrian attempts started at Vienna to contain Prussia. The last development this diplomatic struggle needed was Blücher in Paris at the head of a victorious Prussian army. To date, no official transcript of the discussion at Tirlemont has been found, and some of Blücher's biographers do not even mention the event. His trusted adjutant, Nostitz, recorded that the conversation mainly concerned the Saxons and the campaign plan, but he offered few details.[40] Wellington politely turned down Blücher's request to take the Saxons.[41] As for operations, the duke believed that should Napoleon launch an offensive, his army would be the target. He requested and secured support from the field marshal. That night Wellington wrote three letters, including one to Hardenberg, indicating his satisfaction that Blücher agreed to assist him in the event of a French offensive.[42]

Both commanders agreed to concentrate their armies on the Quatre-Bras–Sombreffe line, but Blücher most likely came away from the meeting convinced that Napoleon intended to attack the Anglo-Dutch army.[43] In the aftermath of this council, Blücher moved the army closer to the French frontier and transferred his headquarters to Namur. By the end of May, the army reached a position to support Wellington. Gneisenau posted the 32,692 men of Zieten's I Corps at Fleurus. Sixteen miles to the east at Namur stood the 32,704 men of II Corps. Eighteen miles southeast of Namur, the 26,421 men of Thielmann's III Corps camped at Ciney. Forty-two miles east of Namur, Bülow's IV Corps—32,239 men— moved up to Liège. This placed the Army of the Lower Rhine on a southwest–northeast axis, with fifty-five miles stretching between its extreme points of Fleurus and Liège. Ten miles southwest of Fleurus stands the town of Charleroi, itself less than twenty miles from the modern French border.

Blücher did not expect a rapid French offensive. For this reason, he has been accused of being careless and unprepared. His correspondence in May suggests otherwise. "Hostilities still have not occurred here," he wrote on 17 May, "but we stand close to each other and it can start any day; I hope it will not be so dangerous this time."[44] On the verge of leaving his headquarters to again meet with Wellington, his staff issued the necessary precautions: "On the 28th, I am traveling to Brussels and will return to Namur on the 30th. Should I Corps be forced to concentrate in consequence of an enemy assault, send the relevant reports to Brussels on the 28th. . . . If the enemy advances toward Mons and Charleroi, II Corps should assemble at Bossière and Onoz [both positions between Namur and Sombreffe and north of Moustier-sur-Sambre], III Corps at Ciney, and IV Corps at Hannut."[45]

Providing for the large army proved difficult as funds became scarce. Blücher and Gneisenau both pledged their personal credit of £50,000 to purchase supplies from British merchants. In addition, the field marshal secured a personal loan of 100,000 thaler to pay for necessities. "My journey here cost me 1,000 thaler," he complained to Amalie, "and here I have thirty people at my table every day. If we would only move into France."[46] As a result of Prussia's weak economic situation, Blücher could not adequately supply the army or pay to quarter the troops.[47] The Prussians advanced to the Sambre River assuming the Dutch government— the new master of Belgium—would completely supply the army. Due to Dutch inefficiency, they found no storage areas, depots, or system of supply.[48] On 27 May Blücher vented to Hardenberg: "For Heaven's sake, I and the army are completely combat-ready, please don't let us linger here any longer! The war must now occur, therefore let it begin as early as possible before the shortage of provisions here pressures us; the King of the Netherlands is a most unhelpful, secretive, and odd person. If I did not have the brave Wellington with me, I would immediately leave Belgium. . . . Tomorrow, I go to Brussels to speak with Wellington and to tell this monarch the plain truth."

Blücher also found that his budget fell far short of the needs of his headquarters. "Please believe me," continued his letter to Hardenberg, "that I do not complain without reason. Holck will tell you that every day I have forty to fifty people at my table. The English stream in, and from the Netherlands I also have a general and adjutants with me and none have food or drink. I cannot survive on my living allowance and by no means will I make any money from the estates given to me by the King."[49] "The King allotted me 333 thaler a month," he complained to Hardenberg a few days later, "truly this is not much, but I am content. If we win the war, all the great gentlemen will have thrived at my expense."[50]

Amid this, Blücher received a letter from a woman claiming she was his daughter. His reaction, found in a letter to his financial advisor, is worth reading in full because of the insight in sheds on his character:

From the enclosed letter you will see that a woman has turned to me for help. The person claims to be my daughter, but I doubt this. Yet it is possible that I had sex with her mother in 1764 at Wollin in Pomerania, where she served in my quarters. One year later, she wrote me that a child she gave birth to belonged to me. Afterward, the child grew up and married a bugler. On the intercession of General Borcke, I gave her a dowry of, I believe, 200 thaler, and her and her husband legally renounced all further claims on me. Since that time, I heard nothing from her except when I was at Berlin, where I received the enclosed letter from her. My intention was that when I went to Silesia, I would find out about the situation of this woman and, if possible, do something for her. Now, because I do not know when I will return, I request that you go to Meseritz and find out this woman's situation, especially her character. If her circumstances are bad and her character is irreproachable, I want the woman taken to Johanni, where we have assumed the Zauche estate in our management; if she is suitable, she can be used at Zauche or on one of its farms as manager; if this is the case, she will have a home and a good living. But if she has a cottage or a business at Meseritz and wants to remain there, you can give her 200 thaler for her best. But I believe it would be best for her to move to my estate. I leave it to your judgment how best to help this woman. Also, tell me if there are children; they should all be completely grown. In the meantime, this business must remain between us. I do not believe that she is my daughter, but her letter is humble and I am captivated by it. Tell the foreman that I will want to know that this woman is well taken care of and that if she is still active she can be used in the business; in the least, she must have a small flat, a garden, and food. I do hope that this war will not last long. If only it would begin. When it is over, I will go straight to Silesia and remain there. Write me soon, especially how it goes with the timber.[51]

Hostilities between Prussian and French outposts commenced as early as 25 April near Falmignoul, less than thirty miles south of Namur.[52] Contradictory reports over Napoleon's movements kept Blücher's headquarters in disarray. His scouting system also suffered in part due to the shortage of funds. Nevertheless, enough news reached Blücher to convince him that the time to strike had come. "I request that you arrange for operations to begin soon," he wrote Hardenberg. "Our delay only can have the greatest disadvantages. If all that our reports say is true regarding the great unrest that exists in the Vendée and that the French troops have to be brought there by wagon to quell the uproar, then it is inexcusable if we leave these well-intended people enslaved. If we cross the frontier, they will fight with more fury and it will benefit them."[53]

Blücher met with Wellington at Brussels from 28 to 30 May. Although the Prussian commander pressed for operations to commence as soon as possible to relieve his supply woes, Wellington refused to cross the frontier until Schwarzenberg's army reached the upper Rhine. Supplied directly (and copiously) from Great Britain, Wellington did not have the same headaches as Blücher, who depended on the inefficient Dutch to feed his men. He did agree to commence the invasion on 1 July, the timeframe that Schwarzenberg would be ready to cross the upper Rhine. In the event Napoleon attacked first, presumably to win Brussels, Blücher would concentrate the Army of the Lower Rhine at Sombreffe. From there he would either support Wellington's left flank, if Napoleon targeted the Anglo-Dutch army, or hold fast until Wellington arrived, should the emperor aim his blow at the Prussians. In this latter case, he would concentrate his army at Quatre-Bras and march to support Blücher's right.[54]

"I have met with Wellington," Blücher warned Hardenberg, "he is in complete agreement with me, and if the order to advance fails to materialize, [and] the unrest in France increases, I will do as I did in Silesia and march to battle. Wellington will accompany me. Old Wellington is goodwill himself and a very special man. We got on well together earlier. He showed me 6,000 of the most beautiful cavalry; they are almost too beautiful to use."[55] "War will again occur," he explained to his cousin. "Therefore, starting it as soon as possible is the smartest. Not long ago I was with my neighbor, Wellington, at Brussels; he agrees with me that we must not lose a day. We both write every day that they must allow us to begin the contest. But nothing will happen until the three great monarchs are together and the Russian army has entered the line; both are about to occur."[56]

Anxiety remained high at the headquarters of the Army of the Lower Rhine, and some members of Blücher's staff, including Gneisenau, believed Napoleon would not venture to the frontier. The endless waiting affected the commander's perception as well. "In ten days at most the flowers will bloom and we will invade France," he wrote Amalie on 3 June. "Bonaparte won't attack us. For that, we can wait another year; his affairs do not stand not so brilliantly."[57] He assured Hardenberg that the war would go well "because the great power that Bonaparte's security commissars dream of is a phantom; it fails him in everything and he especially loses confidence in himself and his destiny."[58]

Yet as mid-June approached, Blücher again spoke of being vigilant. Writing to Müffling, the Prussian liaison officer at the duke's headquarters, he instructed him on 11 June to communicate the following thoughts to Wellington: "I am not one who shuns an operation, but now, after we have delayed for so long, we must not take the situation too lightly. Our adversary has used the time that we gave him and will appear soon. Yesterday, Zieten received news from a spy that Napoleon arrived at Maubeuge. I cannot believe this; in my opinion, he has not assembled enough [forces] opposite us for him to arrive in person. I must say that I still consider myself very secure from his attack and if he advances against my neighbor [Wellington], I will not twiddle my thumbs."[59]

The news that reached Blücher's headquarters about Napoleon had the old Prussian shaking his head. After first betraying the emperor in 1814 by siding with the Allies, Murat, his brother-in-law and the king of Naples, attempted to reconcile. Berthier, who had not rallied to Napoleon but instead fled France, fell out of a window and died on 1 June at the German city of Bamberg. To this day, mystery surrounds his death as to whether he jumped or was pushed. Blücher's musing over the situation captures perfectly the personality of the old hussar: humorous but ever reflective. "Bonaparte may go crazy," he wrote his cousin on 9 June. "The Don Quixote–like journey of his brother-in-law, Murat, the departure from this world of his squire Berthier, the arrival of the entire Corsican family, which France must now support—all of this may completely unsettle him before going to bed. What if he followed Berthier? Then the war could be avoided and he would be in peace, if he is capable of finding peace. Here, I am surrounded by many Frenchmen, all of whom would die for Louis XVIII, but would not expose themselves [on the battlefield]. God, how deep has this nation sunk!"[60]

Blücher remained as confident as ever in what his soldiers could achieve. "I stand here with 130,000 Prussians who are in the most splendid condition and with whom I could dream of conquering Tunis, Tripoli, and Algiers if they weren't so far away and we did not have to cross water."[61] His trouble with supplying the army likewise appeared to be waning. While at Brussels, he made a point of seeing King William I of the Netherlands. He came away from that meeting believing that he made some progress: "The King of the Netherlands was very unobliging; then I showed him my favor, and now he appears to want to do more."[62]

Other issues weighed on his mind. The slow pace of the Allied juggernaut frustrated Blücher to no end, leading him to question the Coalition's resolve. "The courier who Schwarzenberg promised me would arrive in approximately two days to deliver the news of when the feud can begin has still not arrived today: six days late. It appears to me that the great ones hope Bonaparte . . . will follow Berthier and this will spare them from war. At Vienna, they most likely have not decided if they want to deal with this seriously."[63]

Concern over Franz continued to share equal time with the weighty issues of war. "The joys of life have all disappeared for me," he again wrote to his cousin. "Because of the unfortunate state of mind of my oldest son, I no longer live for myself, but instead act and live only still out of my duty and the wish of the Fatherland. The doctor in Berlin, where my poor Franz lies, gives me hope that he will recover because he is now completely at rest and conscious."[64] "With Franz's boys it goes well," he cautions Amalie, "but one must not deceive them.[65] I know they lack nothing, but they must not forget their great father."[66]

At 1:00 P.M. on 15 June, Blücher informed Amalie that "at this moment, I received the report that Bonaparte has attacked all of my outposts. I depart immediately and move to engage my adversary. With joy I will accept battle and will immediately inform you of the result. We are all well and I hope you and your entourage are also well. If you do not go to Pyrmont, have little Lisette [Gebhard's wife] come stay with you. The first part of this letter you can make known in Berlin. God be with you!"[67]

After months of waiting, the war began. Secretly, Napoleon concentrated 120,000 men on the Sambre River within a twelve-hour march of Charleroi. He wanted to seize the initiative and strike the Anglo-Dutch and Prussian armies in turn. Much like his 1796 campaign, he faced two armies that operated on different axes. Once separated, they would be forced to fall back in opposite directions. This meant Wellington would be forced to withdrew northwest through Brussels to the English Channel, while Blücher retreated northeast through Liège to the Rhine. To defeat each enemy army in turn, Napoleon had to pierce the center of the Allied front at Charleroi. From there, he had to *simultaneously* drive along both of his adversaries' lines of communication. Wellington's line, the Charleroi–Brussels road, ran north through Quatre-Bras, Genappe, Belle-Alliance, La Haye Saint, Mont St. Jean, and Waterloo; Blücher's ran northeast through Fleurus and Sombreffe to Liège. The east–west running Nivelles–Liège road, the main artery over which the two Allied armies could support each other, intersected Wellington's line at Quatre-Bras and Blücher's at Sombreffe. Should both armies be forced to retreat, they could still communicate with each other until passing the Nivelles–Quatre-Bras–Sombreffe–Liège road. Thus, after piercing the enemy's front, Napoleon's second objective had to be gaining Quatre-Bras and Sombreffe *simultaneously*.[68] His third step would be to mask one of the enemy armies, using economy of force, while overwhelming the other. Thus, Napoleon counted on both Allied armies falling back on their respective lines of communication to push them farther apart and eliminate their chances of mutual support. Like in 1813 and 1814, Blücher's refusal to conform to these wishes would thwart the emperor's plans.

CHAPTER 17

LIGNY

The Armée du Nord began its advance on 8 June with the Guard marching to Soissons.[1] Napoleon left Paris two days later. Joining the army at Laon, he reached Avenes on the thirteenth. On the following day Napoleon entered Beaumont, where he learned that Prussian posts held Thuin and Lobbes: twelve and eleven miles southwest of Charleroi respectively. That night the emperor issued extremely lengthy orders to commence the offensive. He directed his II Corps, supported by I Corps, to Marchienne-au-Pont with orders to drive the enemy out of Thuin and Lobbes and secure communication across the Sambre. Napoleon assigned the task of taking Charleroi to III Corps and I Cavalry Corps, followed by VI Corps and the Guard; IV Corps would advance north from Philippeville to Châtelet. By marching at 3:00 A.M. on the fifteenth, Napoleon wanted the army across the Sambre before noon.[2] "Tomorrow, the 15th," he wrote Joseph, "I will march on Charleroi, where the Prussian army is, the result will either be a battle or the enemy's retreat. My army is excellent, and the weather tolerably fine; the country is perfectly disposed."[3]

General Zieten's I Corps occupied Fontaine-l'Eveque, Fleurus, and Charleroi. Aside from the observation posts south of the Sambre at Thuin and Lobbes, his front extended twenty-seven miles. On the night of 13 June, he informed Blücher that his patrols observed French campfires at Beaumont and Solre-sur-Sambre, sixteen and twenty miles southwest of Charleroi respectively. In addition, deserters revealed Napoleon's approach with 120,000 men. Blücher instructed Zieten to delay the French advance for as long as possible before withdrawing to Fleurus. The field marshal intended to concentrate the army at Sombreffe—fifteen miles northeast of Charleroi and thirteen miles west of Namur—to attack Napoleon on the sixteenth. At noon on 14 June, Prussian headquarters received reports of the French movement. Blücher responded by issuing orders for the army's concentration at Sombreffe in two days.

At 4:30 A.M. on the fifteenth, Zieten heard the sound of enemy cannon and sent dispatches to Blücher at Namur and Wellington at Brussels. A continual skirmish lasted throughout the morning until superior French cavalry drove the Prussians from Charleroi toward Fleurus. As instructed, Napoleon's II Corps crossed the Sambre at Marchienne-au-Pont, while I Cavalry Corps advanced through Charleroi to the suburb of Gilly. After falling back, the Prussians occupied the heights behind that town and prepared to make a stand. After losing 1,200 casualties and six guns, Zieten retreated to Fleurus. Napoleon raved that his army destroyed four Prussian regiments and took 1,500 prisoners. The inhabitants of Charleroi purportedly greeted the emperor with enthusiasm. With the Prussians falling back along their line of communication, his offensive could not have started much better. "It is possible that an important affair will take place tomorrow," ends his letter to Joseph.[4]

Wellington, described as "always being inclined to accept a battle than to offer one," had done little to comply with the arrangement between him and Blücher.[5] The French assault at Charleroi did not convince the duke that Napoleon intended to drive a wedge between the two Allied armies. While Blücher concentrated his forces at Sombreffe, Wellington did nothing beyond ordering his troops to be ready to march from their cantonments. Apparently indifferent to Napoleon's advance, Wellington himself remained at Brussels to attend the Duchess of Richmond's ball on the fifteenth. Mastered by concerns over his line of communication, Wellington in fact changed his plan. Instead of concentrating at Quatre-Bras, where his army would be less than eight miles from the Prussians at Sombreffe, he decided to assemble at Nivelles, a further six miles west of Blücher. By increasing the distance between his and Blücher's army to some fourteen miles, the duke played right into Napoleon's hands. Wellington's dispositions for the sixteenth mention nothing in regards to supporting Sombreffe. Despite the plans made at Brussels on 28 and 29 May, Blücher would remain on his own.[6]

On the night of the fifteenth, Blücher inspected the troops of I Corps before transferring his headquarters to Sombreffe. The soldiers greeted the old field marshal with ringing hurrahs.[7] He also learned that Bülow's IV Corps probably would not arrive in time to participate in a battle on the sixteenth. Due to a misunderstanding of orders, Bülow's command remained twelve hours behind schedule. In his tribute to Blücher's life, Gneisenau maintains that the field marshal "still resolved to give battle in his position at Sombreffe although his IV Corps was not yet in line, and his army, in point of numbers, was much inferior to that of the French."[8] We can only speculate if Bülow's participation could have turned the tide of the battle that took place on 16 June, but the addition of 30,000 men doubtlessly would have helped. According to Blücher's report to Frederick William, he also had no news of Wellington at the time. "From Charleroi, it appeared that the French likewise advanced north on the Brussels highway as far as Frasnes. Tomorrow will see if the enemy turns against me or the Duke of Wellington. In any case, tomorrow is the decisive day." Blücher cited the strength of Napoleon's army at 120,000 men.[9]

Blücher based his decision to accept battle at Ligny in part on the promise of receiving support from Wellington. As noted, the duke attended a ball at Brussels the night before when he should have been gaining a precise overview of his disposition of forces. Consequently, the information he forwarded to Blücher proved extremely inaccurate. He informed the field marshal that units reached destinations they would not be able to attain for several hours. If Wellington's information about his own troops had been correct, he could have supported Blücher with more than 60,000 men by the afternoon of 16 June.

Around noon on the sixteenth, Wellington rode from Quatre-Bras to meet Blücher near the mill of Brye. The field marshal already had demonstrated his anticipation of support by moving his army southwest from Sombreffe to Ligny: Gneisenau positioned the army to firmly maintain communication with Wellington.[10] The meeting between the two legendary commanders lasted from 1:00 to 2:00. Much discussion about British aid occurred during their friendly conversation, but Wellington departed saying he would come only if the French did not attack him. At such a critical time in the war, it is unlikely that the duke intentionally misled the Prussians, even for political reasons. Nevertheless, Blücher expected at least 20,000 men from the Anglo-Dutch army. In view of this, the Prussians detached 6,000 men, mostly from III Corps, to guard the line of communication running east through Namur to the Rhine. More important, Blücher's right wing at Ligny remained "in the air," a sign that he expected support from the west.[11]

Meanwhile, assuming only one Prussian corps stood at Sombreffe, Napoleon ordered Marshal Grouchy to advance against it on the sixteenth with III and IV Infantry and I, II, and IV Cavalry Corps.[12] Ney, commanding I and II Infantry and III Cavalry Corps, received orders to drive through Quatre-Bras. With the Guard and VI Corps as the central reserve, Napoleon would follow, supporting either Ney or Grouchy as the situation demanded. If possible, Ney would swing northeast and behind the Prussians to isolate and destroy this single corps, estimated to be less than 40,000 men.[13]

During a very hot Friday morning, the French started filing through Fleurus at 10:00; the emperor arrived one hour later. Based on the incoming reports as well as his own reconnaissance, Napoleon gradually realized that he faced much more than a single Prussian corps. He ordered an observation platform built onto the Fleurus windmill so he could better survey Blücher's positions. The battlefield tilted on a northeast–southwest axis conforming to the portion of Blücher's line of operation running along the road from Fleurus to Gembloux. To Napoleon's experienced eye, the Prussians appeared to be waiting for Wellington to arrive on the Nivelles–Namur road and take a position on their right flank. Thus, he would attack Blücher's right, seeking to drive the Prussians down their line of operations and away from Wellington. He deployed III Corps and the 7th Division, II Corps on the left, while in the center IV Corps peeled northwest from the highway leading to Gembloux and deployed facing the village of Ligny. On the right, II and I Cavalry Corps and one division of IV Cavalry Corps formed east of the highway facing Tongrinelles, Boignée, and Balâtre.[14] Behind the first line, the Guard stood ready to support III Corps northwest of Fleurus, while VI Infantry and IV Cavalry Corps moved east of Fleurus to support the center and right wing. For the majority of the struggle, 60,000 Frenchmen would engage 61,000 Prussians in the numerous small villages nestled on undulating hills.[15]

At 2:30 on the afternoon of 16 June 1815, the French attacked Blücher's positions around the villages of Ligny and St.-Amand. On Napoleon's left, III Corps's assault sought to drive Zieten's 1st Brigade from St.-Amand, St.-Amand-la-Haye, and Wagnelée Brook. To the right, IV Corps confronted Zeiten's 3rd and 4th Brigades, stretching from St.-Amand to Ligny. On the far right, II and I Cavalry Corps faced Tongrinne, Tongrinelles, Boignée, and Balâtre, which 11th Brigade of Thielmann's III Corps occupied. Prussian artillery greeted the French as they advanced.

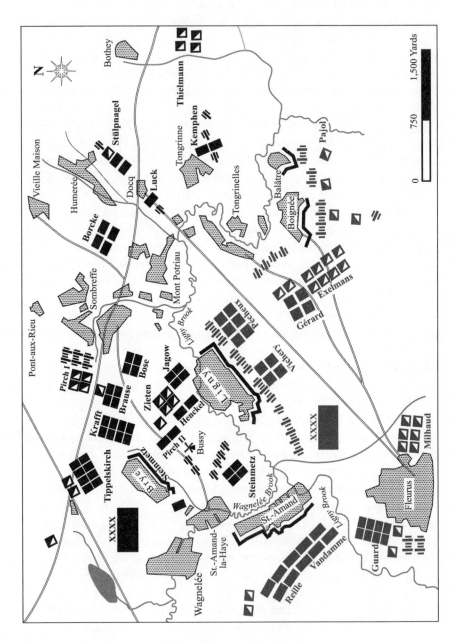

The Battle of Ligny, 16 June 1815. Map drawn by Alex Mendoza. Copyright © 2014 by the University of Oklahoma Press.

At St.-Amand, the three battalions of the 3rd Brigade's 29th Infantry Regiment prepared to receive the French 8th Division as it approached in three columns proceeded by skirmishers. After intense combat, the French ejected the 29th from the village. To support the regiment, Zieten moved forward the skirmishers from the 12th and 24th Regiments. This did little to slow the French, who prepared to debouch from St.-Amand. Zieten committed the rest of the 12th and 24th supported by Foot Battery No. 7, which poured canister into the French ranks. With tremendous effort, the 12th and 24th regained the now-burning village. More French troops moved up, inducing the Prussians to commit the final two battalions of 1st Brigade. To the northwest, the Prussians observed the 7th Division extend the French line to sweep around their right. Upon seeing Napoleon retake St.-Amand with an entire corps around 4:00, Blücher resolved to match him. He ordered the commander of 1st Brigade, Karl Friedrich von Steinmetz, to retake and hold the town until 2nd Brigade arrived to support him. Blücher also directed the 5th Brigade and Reserve Cavalry of II Corps to secure the debouches of Wagnelée on his extreme right and then proceed against the French 7th Division.

As the Prussians executed these orders, Steinmetz led all the battalions of 1st Brigade as well as the three of the 29th Regiment against St.-Amand. With bayonets fixed, the Prussians drove into the village. Making a stand at its walled cemetery, the French stopped the Prussian push. Both sides possessed a section of the village. This situation did not last long before 7th Division gained St.-Amand-la-Haye to threaten Steinmetz's right flank.

Blücher personally led Zieten's 2nd Brigade from the mill at Bussy to retake St.-Amand-la-Haye and relieve the pressure on 1st Brigade. Behind 2nd Brigade, 6th Brigade from II Corps moved up to Bussy. Brutal fire from the French 7th Division greeted these troops. Somehow they managed to reach the middle of the village, but the French held. Likewise, the Prussians could not eject the French from a massive, walled farmstead between St.-Amand and St.-Amand-la-Haye. At this time, 5th Brigade and the Reserve Cavalry of II Corps cleared Wagnelée and turned southeast to envelop the French left. Upon observing this movement, Blücher rode to the right wing to arrange the attack; his presence invigorated the soldiers. To his left, 2nd Brigade reformed and charged St.-Amand-la-Haye and the farm. The 28th Regiment completely overwhelmed and ejected the French from the farmstead, while the 1st West Prussian Infantry Regiment gained the entrances of the village. Meanwhile, 5th Brigade attacked from Wagnelée, but the first wave of mainly young recruits collapsed under fire and had to reform north of the village. This debacle forced 2nd Brigade to halt and be content with gaining St.-Amand-la-Haye. Because the village of St.-Amand stood south of the Wagnelée Brook, Blücher decided that the space north of town stretching toward St.-Amand-la-Haye would be defended by artillery alone. He recalled Steinmetz's 1st Brigade, which suffered a staggering loss of forty-six officers and 2,300 men—a casualty rate of 33 percent—to form the reserve at Brye. Battery No. 7 likewise had to be pulled from the line after exhausting its ordnance. To cover the remaining batteries, Blücher called up Zieten's cavalry brigade.

The performance of the French commander of III Corps, Vandamme, fell short of satisfying Napoleon: he wasted time and men without gaining results. To offset these losses, Napoleon sent an order to Ney at 3:45 to envelop Blücher's right and rear. Fortunately for the Prussians, by the time Ney received these instructions at 6:00 P.M., he could no longer execute them.

Meanwhile, the attack of IV Corps on Ligny commenced later than Vandamme's assault on St.-Amand. Zieten's 4th Brigade, commanded by Henckel von Donnersmark, made excellent use of the hedgerows and trenches. From these concealed positions, the Prussians unleashed a storm of lead on the three approaching columns. Three times the French attempted to storm Ligny, and three times they staggered back to their starting points. Napoleon decided to blast the Prussians with artillery, which Blücher's guns, well positioned to the left and right of town, answered. With the guns of both sides blazing, the French moved up sufficient troops to gain a foothold in Ligny's gardens and hedgerows. A final push against the Prussian left led to a hand-to-hand struggle that forced the Prussians to yield, reform, and counterattack. This succeeded in driving the French from Ligny and capturing two guns. Several fires burned in town, and its old chateau went up in flames.

General Friedrich Wilhelm von Jagow, the commander of Ziethen's 3rd Brigade, observed that 4th Brigade desperately needed reinforcements. On receiving his report, Blücher ordered 3rd Brigade to move up to Ligny, unite with 4th Brigade, and continue the struggle. The general's message arrived at the same time the field marshal issued orders for 2nd Brigade to counterattack

at St.-Amand-la-Haye, thus around 4:00. Jagow advanced toward
Ligny with four battalions, leaving the two fusilier battalions of
the 7th and 29th Regiments to cover Foot Batteries Nos. 3 and 8
to the right of the town. Two companies of Silesian marksmen
checked the French advance at the chateau. Two battalions of the
2nd West Prussian Regiment formed columns and drove through
Ligny, emerging on the opposite side, where they found the French
thickly bunched and unable to deploy. For thirty minutes, both
sides exchanged massed volleys. In Ligny itself, an isolated pocket
of French soldiers gained a foothold in the cemetery, opening fire
on the rear of the two battalions from the 2nd West Prussian, thus
unsettling the rank and file. In addition, the French moved up artillery. Thus beset, the two battalions withdrew, fiercely pursued.
Turning over the coverage of the 3rd and 8th Foot Batteries to the
Brandenburg Dragoons, Jagow summoned the two fusilier battalions
from the 7th and 29th Regiments. With these units, the Prussians
pushed into Ligny; again savage street fighting erupted.

With his left and center engaged in bloody stalemates, Napoleon
observed his right wing—II and I Cavalry Corps—advance toward
Tongrinelles, Boignée, and Balatre. Around 4:00 P.M., French infantry approached Tongrinne. Knowing that Napoleon would attempt
to drive him away from Wellington by attacking his right, Blücher
wanted to commit no more than two brigades to hold his left.
Thielmann's 11th and 10th Brigades received this task, but despite
the advantageous positioning of the guns, two brigades did not suffice to defend this stretch of the front. Initially, the struggle centered on possession of the village of Boignée as well as Tongrinne's
outlying houses.

About an hour later, Napoleon received a report that Ney had
engaged Wellington at Quatre-Bras and would not be able to envelop
Blücher. This news changed the situation significantly. Until that
point, Napoleon conducted a holding action to pin Blücher and
provide time for Ney to deliver the coup de grâce. Denied Ney's
flanking movement, he altered his plans. Instead of continuing
the struggle at St.-Amand against Blücher's right, he would blast
open the Prussian center at Ligny. Placing himself at the head of
the Guard Grenadiers, Napoleon commenced the attack. Preceded
by the Guard artillery and followed by the entire Guard cavalry,
the emperor marched toward Ligny. At that moment, 6:00 P.M.,
he received a frantic message from Vandamme. Claiming that an

enemy column of 20,000 men appeared to be closing on his left flank, the corps commander estimated it would arrive in one hour. This news prompted Napoleon to postpone the assault on Ligny until the situation on his left could be clarified.

Meanwhile, around 5:00, Blücher returned to the mill at Bussy. His entire line withstood Napoleon's first assault, and the 6th, 7th, and 8th Brigades as well as the artillery of II Corps remained in reserve. Similar to Wellington two days later, he hoped either his ally or darkness would arrive soon. He too eventually received reports of this mysterious column, but it remained quite far from his right wing. Moreover, the stretch of the Nivelles–Namur highway between Sombreffe and Quatre-Bras remained opened, enabling the field marshal to communicate with Wellington.

As noted, 6th Brigade moved up to the mill around 4:00, contributing four battalions to the struggle at St.-Armand-la-Haye and one to Ligny. At that time, 7th Brigade replaced 6th at the intersection of the old Roman road with the Nivelles–Namur highway just west of Sombreffe. Also in that area, 8th Brigade gradually followed 6th Brigade south, with 12th Brigade of III Corps taking its place. Seeing Napoleon's reserves at Fleurus, Blücher and his staff concluded that the emperor would employ them to take Ligny rather than continue the struggle at St.-Amand. Although that village provided a point to debouch in conjunction with Wellington's flank attack, they correctly deemed that the decision would be made at Ligny. Its loss, combined with a French pursuit, could be devastating. Therefore, Blücher resolved to maintain his center at any price. He ordered the remaining four battalions of 6th Brigade to support the fighting at Ligny and moved the six batteries of II Corps, including two heavy units, into the line, which stretched west along the hills from east of Ligny to St.-Amand. This expanded his fire and also relieved the batteries of I Corps as they depleted their ammunition.

On Blücher's right, Zieten still possessed fresh troops in the form of his cavalry supported by one brigade from III Corps. With 7th Brigade ready to support 2nd and 5th Brigades, he ordered a general advance against Vandamme's left wing south of St.-Amand. The struggle centered on a hamlet south of St.-Amand, which the Prussians mastered after bitter fighting. Zieten's situation became extremely favorable: 2nd Brigade held St.-Amand-la-Haye, and 5th Brigade now deployed in the open field south of St.-Amand, supported by one cavalry brigade, one horse battery, and two foot batteries; Blücher added another cavalry brigade. Vandamme's troops, shaken from the bloody combat in the villages and hearing rumors of the approach of a column of 20,000 redcoats, fell back in disorder. Observing this, Napoleon sent one division of Young Guard to join a light-cavalry brigade in bolstering III Corps. These reinforcements enabled Vandamme to halt Zieten's advance. Nevertheless, the Prussians held the entire plateau between Wagnelée Brook and St.-Armand. The four battalions from 6th Brigade moved up from St.-Amand-la-Haye followed by the lead elements of 7th Brigade. Blücher himself delivered the order for the 14th Regiment of 7th Brigade to enter the line and relieve some of the units at St.-Amand, St.-Amand-la-Haye, and the outlying hamlet between 6:00 and 7:00 P.M. The fresh troops arrived in time to meet and repulse the French counterattack. After expending its ammunition, most of 5th Brigade pulled out of the line to reassemble north of Wagnelée; casualties amounted to forty-three officers and 1,858 men.

Meanwhile, the other four battalions of 6th Brigade reached Ligny just as the French repulsed an attack by 3rd Brigade. The accompanying Foot Battery No. 5 assisted in halting the French pursuit, but the enemy returned in even greater numbers. Each of Ligny's houses became a small fortress. Both sides fought with extreme bravery and ferocity. After bitter house fighting, the French gained the advantage by securing the cemetery and moving two guns into the position. After collecting his battalions and all other troops he could find north of the town, the commander of 6th Brigade, General Karl August von Krafft, led a charge that reached the hedgerows on the south side. This advantageous terrain provided Krafft a few minutes of cover until a determined French attack drove his men back into Ligny. Fixing their bayonets, the Prussians turned the tables on their pursuers, driving then south through the narrow streets. More so than on the right wing, the street and house fighting as well as the hand-to-hand combat in Ligny's tight quarters formed a sausage grinder that claimed thousands. Krafft's 6th Brigade lost thirty-eight officers and 1,485 men. During the last few hours of combat, 8th Brigade's casualties amounted to nineteen officers and 1,268 men.

On Blücher's left, the battle continued to proceed at a slow pace, but the French gradually deployed more forces. At this time, Thielmann received the field marshal's order to have one of his brigades march west through Sombreffe to take the place of 8th Brigade, which itself would move up to Ligny. With 9th Brigade at Sombreffe, Thielmann possessed only the eleven battalions of 10th and 11th Brigades to hold the left wing. As 12th Brigade marched west, the French advanced against the line held by III Corps. Attempting to envelop Thielmann's right, they ran into 9th Brigade, advantageously posted slightly southeast of Sombreffe.

The Prussians held firm. Between 6:00 and 7:00 P.M., they maintained their center and left, while on the right Zieten gained ground. Had he been facing a commander other than Napoleon, Blücher probably could have counted on victory. Yet as with the majority of the battles he waged, Napoleon brilliantly managed his resources. While Blücher's fresh units consisted of 8th and 12th Brigades as well as six cavalry regiments, the emperor still possessed his regular reserve—VI Corps—as well as his Grand Reserve: sixteen fresh battalions of Guard as well as the Guard's heavy cavalry. The enemy column that caused him to postpone the Guard's attack proved to be his own I Corps, which spent the day crisscrossing the terrain between Quatre-Bras and Ligny, unsure of whose orders for support to heed, those from Ney or Napoleon.

Blücher still hoped that Wellington would arrive. Finally, he received a report from the duke that the French had attacked his forces at Quatre-Bras and he had no troops to spare. Around the same time, 7:00, Zieten reported from St.-Amand that the French appeared to be withdrawing. On the left wing, Thielmann likewise claimed to observe his adversary falling back. At the moment, only 8th Brigade could enter the line: 12th Brigade was marching through Sombreffe, while the survivors of 1st and 4th Brigades continued to reform. Regardless, Blücher resolved to exploit this favorable moment. He ordered Thielmann to immediately take advantage of the situation and to do as much as possible to support the fighting in the center at Ligny. Stretched too thin, the general's attack, mainly a cavalry and artillery affair, petered out with no results.

After issuing the orders for Thielmann, the field marshal rushed to the right wing, sending four battalions from 8th Brigade to Ligny and leaving one in reserve at Bussy. Blücher directed all remaining battalions of 8th Brigade as well as the fusiliers of the 23rd Regiment and two battalions from the 3rd Elbe Landwehr Regiment to advance to St.-Amand and St-Amand-la-Haye. He also ordered the fusilier battalions of the 12th and 24th Regiments from Brye to move to the right of St.-Amand-la-Haye, leaving one Landwehr battalion to hold the former. Every soldier he passed he directed to St.-Amand. With this large force, Blücher hoped to overwhelm Napoleon's left. Between 7:00 and 8:00, he rode into the struggle south of St.-Amand, driving Vandamme's men south of the hamlet and into the Young Guard.

In the meantime, while Blücher prepared his counterattack, Napoleon learned of the approach of I Corps, which then actually turned around and marched back to Quatre-Bras. No longer threated on his left, Napoleon resumed the Old Guard's attack on Ligny around 7:00. There, the bitter fighting had continued unabated. Two Prussian battalions from the 21st Regiment failed after six attempts to drive the French from Ligny. Reinforced by one line and one Landwehr battalion, they finally succeeded the seventh time. Nevertheless, at 7:45 P.M., the Guard smashed into the Prussian center. From Ligny, Krafft reported that he could barely hang on. With Blücher on the right wing, Gneisenau decided to hold the village for thirty minutes more. He sent all the manpower he could find to Ligny.

On the right wing, Blücher received a report that 2nd Brigade ran out of ammunition. He ordered its commander, General Otto von Pirch—known as Pirch II—not only to hold his post but to execute a bayonet attack. In the heat of battle, Blücher refused to believe that his weary men could fight no more. Officers and men nevertheless collapsed from exhaustion. Two fresh battalions from 12th Brigade moved into the firing line. Yet due to a mistake, 4th Brigade and part of 1st Brigade marched east to support III Corps. Night came accompanied by a violent summer storm.

By 8:30, the Prussian line still held, but Napoleon himself had reached Ligny. The Prussians stood their ground for more than Gneisenau's thirty minutes. Moving up the final eight battalions of the Guard—the 1st and 2nd Grenadier and Chasseur Regiments—Napoleon prepared to break through Blücher's center. The fighting raged, but the French artillery fell silent. Returning to the mill at Bussy, Blücher observed a retrograde movement by the French. Appearing to be a retreat, he reached the erroneous conclusion that his warriors had repulsed Napoleon's attack. With 12th Brigade still too far away to support, and 4th Brigade with part of 1st Brigade marching east to support the left wing, only three cavalry regiments from Zieten's Reserve Cavalry remained at his disposal. Blücher sent an aide to the Reserve Cavalry with orders to begin the pursuit. The 6th Uhlan Regiment, commanded by the famous partisan of the 1813 campaign, Ludwig Adolf von Lützow, now a lieutenant colonel, took the lead.

Actually, the retrograde movement Blücher saw was simply the withdrawal of the French artillery. Within a few moments, the situation became clear, helped by the fact that several French battalions broke through the northeast side of Ligny. Behind them followed five cuirassier regiments, one Guard dragoon regiment, and one mounted Guard grenadier regiment. Not knowing this, Blücher mounted his horse and drew his saber. He joined the left wing of the 6th Uhlans as they led the attack. He and Nostitz halted at the brook flowing through Ligny. The uhlans turned toward the first French infantry they saw and charged. Just before reaching the enemy, the Prussians suddenly found a sunken country road in front of them that the high corn concealed. Halted momentarily by this obstacle, they received a blast of French musketry at close range that killed, wounded, or dismounted eleven officers and seventy-four men—25 percent of their number. Lützow, wounded and trapped under his dead horse, became a prisoner of war. The next volley broke the uhlans. As they fled back to the Prussian line, the French cuirassier attacked their flank.

As Blücher joined his retreating cavalry, a ball struck his horse just below the field marshal's knee. After a few convulsive leaps, the beautiful animal, a gift from the prince regent, crumbled to the ground and rolled over on top of the Prussian commander. For a few seconds the poor beast lay on top of Blücher, with all four of its hoofs in the air. It its agony, the steed crashed to its side, crushing Blücher's right shoulder and leg. Nostitz quickly jumped from his own horse, which also received a wound to its neck, to defend the old man, who lay pinned under the dead animal. With enemy cuirassiers riding past in pursuit toward the Prussian line, Nostitz threw his cloak over Blücher to hide his medals. Blücher lay on the ground, dazed and unable to move. Fortunately for the Prussians, in the ensuing back and forth struggle between the French and Prussian cavalry, Blücher remained unnoticed. In addition, thick, dark storm clouds brought an early dusk that also helped conceal him. The uhlans reformed and charged again; the West Prussian Dragoons as well as the Kurmärk and Elbe Landwehr Regiments alternately joined the struggle. Finally, Nostitz recognized and hailed some Prussian uhlans and Landwehr troopers. Six soldiers lifted the dead horse and extracted Blücher, placing his limp body on a horse. Somehow, the Prussians managed to bring him back to their lines.[16]

Gneisenau, who likewise participated in the charge, found himself swept away by the torrent that streamed toward the Bussy windmill. Although the French followed, they could not overtake the Prussian mass. Pirch I organized resistance at the windmill. Unable to find Blücher, the staff feared he had been captured; Gneisenau assumed command. Despite the confusion, he organized an orderly retreat, protected by four cavalry regiments. Although the disorganized brigades could not attempt to throw back the French, they established a front along the Brye–Sombreffe stretch of the Nivelles–Namur road; 12th Brigade held Sombreffe. Most of the units on the left wing retreated there, but those on the right could not reach it because of the distance and the French forces deploying north of the Ligny stream. Fortunately for the Prussians, the pursuit did not amount to much, otherwise Jena would have been repeated on the fields of Belgium. Morale sank; rumors of Blücher's capture did not help.[17]

Nostitz asserts that prior to and during the battle, Blücher did not announce that the army would retreat north in the event of a defeat.[18] In fact, it appears that the issue of the direction of a possible withdrawal did not come up because a defeat appeared so unlikely. Yet on receiving Bülow's report at 11:30 P.M. on 15 June that IV Corps could not arrive in time for battle on the sixteenth, Blücher and Gneisenau instructed him to march to Gembloux and take the old Roman highway to the plateau of Ardenelle, three miles north of Sombreffe. That highland offered a strong position from where Blücher, if forced to fall back, could chose the direction he wanted to take for further operations.[19] For these further operations, Gneisenau knew that Blücher intended to remain in close communication with Wellington. Thus, an eastward retreat from Sombreffe to Namur along the Prussian line of communication would have the opposite effect. Moreover, Gneisenau's orders to Zieten on the night of the fifteenth tasked Steinmetz with "doing everything possible" to keep his right wing clear and communication with Wellington secure.[20] That same evening, the fifteenth, Blücher wrote to Schwarzenberg: "The French have commenced hostilities against me. Five army corps and the Guard face me.

At daybreak tomorrow my army will be concentrated in this region [Sombreffe]. Now, there is no doubt that the enemy's main force is united against the Netherlands, and that the armies on the Rhine can continue their operations with more security. . . . [T]he enemy intends to breakthrough between the army of the duke [Wellington] and mine."[21]

A student of Napoleon's wars, Gneisenau recognized the similarities between the current situation and that of the Austrians and Sardinians in 1796. By retreating eastward, he would create the conditions for Napoleon to defeat each army in turn. Even if the general disagreed with the decision to retreat north rather than east (as is famously depicted in both literature and film), he honored Blücher's wishes to continue cooperating with Wellington. Moreover, a retreat northeast to Gembloux to link with Bülow's fresh corps en route from Liège via Hannut to Sombreffe would have been more logical to sustain the army. Regardless, Gneisenau directed the retreat due north to maintain contact with the British; Bülow received orders to adjust his march. Sometime after 9:30 P.M., Gneisenau ordered the retreat to continue five miles northwest to Tilly.[22] As it turned out, Nostitz led the groaning field marshal through Tilly on the road to Wavre. Nostitz claims in his memoirs that *he* made the decision to retreat north toward Wavre. It is difficult to determine whether he actually did so himself or if Blücher expressed his wishes. In addition, Nostitz notes that groups of soldiers marched to his left and right. Thus, the trusted aide may simply have found himself caught in the throng.

Nostitz relates that on reaching the northern end of the deserted village of Mellery, two miles north of Tilly, Blücher could go no further, complaining of pain in his right side. He brought the field marshal to the only house in which a light burned. With much pain, the old hussar dismounted. He found wounded soldiers already inside. Refreshed by some milk, he took a short rest on a straw mattress thrown on the floor amid his wounded "children." Nostitz stepped outside, hailing some troopers to protect the field marshal while he rode south toward Tilly. Between the two villages, he found Steinmetz and requested infantry to guard Blücher. Returning to Mellery, he sent the cavalry that assembled at Blücher's quarters in every direction to quell rumors of his capture and to announce that the field marshal would pass the night in this village. He maintains that because of this, Gneisenau arrived before dawn.[23]

Blücher recovered, but he needed rest. On the seventeenth he ordered the march to Wavre to continue.[24] "Today, I have moved closer to Lord Wellington," he wrote Amalie, "and in a few days there probably will be another battle. Everyone is full of courage and if Napoleon still wants to deliver such a battle he and his army will be finished. In the affair yesterday, my beautiful English horse was shot out from under me; Gneisenau suffered the same fate; we both got tangled up with the horses in the fall. Otherwise me and my entourage are well, only my adjutant, Major Winterfeld, was seriously wounded. Gebhard is well and my worthy Nostitz did me a great service by helping me from under my horse."[25]

Napoleon's losses at Ligny are unclear, ranging from 8,000 to 12,000 men. As with Bülow's corps on the Prussian side, the arrival of the 15,000 men of the French I Corps certainly would have produced greater and perhaps decisive results. Nevertheless, Napoleon mauled Blücher's army, inflicting some 12,000 casualties, taking fifteen guns, and providing opportunity for 8,000 "new" Prussians from Berg, Westphalia, and the Rhineland to desert.[26] Blücher's 1st, 2nd, 3rd, 4th, and 6th Brigades suffered the heaviest losses. That few prisoners were taken by either side indicates the bitterness of the fighting. Yet the Army of the Lower Rhine rallied thanks to the durability of the corps system.

By the night of 17 June, the Prussian army camped in and around Wavre, establishing a strongly fortified position between Limal, Wavre, and the Dyle River. Zieten's I Corps and three brigades of III Corps occupied the left bank of the Dyle, with II and IV Corps on the right bank. Around 5:00 P.M. on the seventeenth, the munitions trains arrived, and the army prepared to fight again. Prussian patrols reported seeing few French units pursuing; it appeared Napoleon had pursued Wellington toward Brussels.

Wellington did not learn of the Prussian withdrawal until his reconnaissance returned from Ligny on the morning of the seventeenth. He calmly declared to his entourage: "Old Blücher has had a damn good licking and gone to Wavre. . . . As he has gone back, we must go too."[27] Wellington notified Blücher that he would make a stand if supported by two Prussian corps.[28] Reaching Wavre at 11:00 P.M. on the seventeenth, his aide informed the Prussians of the duke's preparations for a defensive battle at Waterloo. He positioned his Anglo-Dutch army on the road to Brussels, with its right wing at Braine-l'Alleud, the center near Mont-St.-Jean, and its left beyond

La Haye Sainte.[29] Blücher and Gneisenau debated for one hour in private while their staff officers waited outside. Over the general's objections, Blücher resolved to send three corps to aid Wellington. His response reached the duke around 2:00 A.M.: "I have arranged to dispose my troops as follows: Bülow's corps will march tomorrow at daybreak from Dion-le-Mont through Wavre towards St. Lambert to attack the enemy's right flank. The II Corps will immediately follow him, while I and III Corps will remain ready to follow this movement. The exhaustion of the troops, some of whom have yet to arrive, makes it impossible to move any earlier."[30]

At midnight on 17–18 June, Gneisenau issued orders for the morning's advance. He directed IV, II, and I Corps to march in two columns from Wavre toward Napoleon's right flank. Bülow and Pirch II would form the left column and proceed to Chapelle-Saint-Lambert, while Zieten led his corps on the right to Ohain. Gneisenau planned the advance so that the bulk of the army would move against Napoleon's right, while Zieten's units linked with Wellington's left. Being the freshest, Bülow's corps would lead the advance.

CHAPTER 18

AUERSTEDT AVENGED

While the Prussians beat a retreat early on 17 June, the French followed late. On the evening of the Battle of Ligny, Napoleon did not think it feasible to pursue the Army of the Lower Rhine any farther than the Brye–Sombreffe line. The orderly withdrawal of the Prussian right and left wings, their occupation of Brye and Sombreffe, and concerns that Blücher could receive reinforcements contributed to this conclusion. At dawn on the seventeenth, the emperor ordered I and II Cavalry Corps to pursue eastward on the road to Namur. Around 4:00 A.M., the commander of I Cavalry Corps, General Claude Pierre Pajol, reported from Balâtre that the enemy appeared to be in full retreat eastward toward Namur and Liège. Napoleon, having transferred his headquarters to Quatre-Bras, received this message at 7:00 A.M. One hour later he still remained uncertain but believed Blücher would withdraw in this direction and along his line of communication. Not long after commencing their hunt, the light horse of I Cavalry Corps captured a Prussian battery belonging to III Corps as it retreated toward Namur, despite being ordered to Gembloux. Pajol sent the thirty prisoners to headquarters, and his report strengthened Napoleon's conviction that Blücher would flee to the east. Soon, however, the reports of Pajol's forward units cast doubt on this. The cavalry general left the Nivelles–Namur highway and proceeded northeast to St.-Denis, where he found signs of the retreating Prussians.[1]

At imperial headquarters Napoleon tasked Grouchy with commanding the pursuit of Blücher. Having already conceived the idea of pursuing the Prussians toward Namur and the British toward Brussels, the emperor still needed to work out the details. Arriving at Quatre-Bras around 7:00 A.M., Grouchy sought orders but instead sat around waiting for an interview. Napoleon "conversed at some length with Grouchy, and several other generals . . . on the Legislative Assembly, Fouché, and the Jacobins. Some of those listening admired the freedom of mind which he preserved under such grave circumstances, but others were slightly disturbed at seeing him waste his time talking politics, allowing his thoughts to wander on irrelevant topics, instead of on those that should have completely absorbed him." At 9:00 A.M. Grouchy again requested orders, but Napoleon harshly rebuked him: "I will give them to you when I see fit."[2]

Around 11:00 A.M. he finally provided Grouchy verbal instructions: "Pursue the Prussians, complete their defeat by attacking them as soon as you catch up with them, and never let them out of your sight. I will unite the remainder of this portion of the army with Marshal Ney's corps, march against the English, and fight them should they hold their ground. You will communicate with me by the paved road that leads to Quatre-Bras."[3] Grouchy claims that Napoleon added: "All probability leads me to believe that Blücher means to effect his retreat to the Meuse [east]; therefore, proceed in that direction." By now, the emperor had convinced himself that Blücher would withdraw along his line of communication through Namur and Liège to occupy the line of the Meuse River, from where he could threaten the right of the French army as it advanced on Brussels.[4]

After receiving these orders, Grouchy departed sometime between 11:30 and 11:45 A.M. Shortly after, Napoleon decided to clarify in writing the verbal instructions. He directed his newest marshal to Gembloux with I and II Cavalry Corps, the light cavalry of IV Corps, 21st Division from VI Corps, and III and IV Corps. "You will send scouts in the direction of Namur and Maastricht, and you will pursue the enemy. Reconnoiter his march and tell me of his movements, so I can divine his intentions." With some 33,000 men and ninety-six guns—one-third of the Army of the North—Napoleon considered Grouchy's force sufficient to observe Blücher's movements, though not to accept battle with the Army of the Lower Rhine.[5]

Grouchy ordered III and IV Corps to move one mile east of Sombreffe to Docq (Point du Jour), the intersection of the Nivelles–Namur highway with the Charleroi–Gembloux road. After receiving intelligence that a large Prussian force moved through Gembloux, he directed III and IV Corps to continue there. Although only five miles northeast of Point du Jour, the troops, exhausted from their extreme efforts the previous day, marched less than one mile per hour. Slogging through streaming rain, III Corps arrived at 7:00 P.M., while IV did not pull in for another two hours. Grouchy ordered a halt, and the soldiers bivouacked around Gembloux, thirteen miles southeast of Wavre.

Starting around 6:00 P.M., Grouchy received contradictory reports. Some claimed that the Prussians marched through Perwez en route to either Liège or Maastricht. The 1st Brigade, 10th Cavalry Division reached Walhain, five miles north of Gembloux, while the 15th Dragoon Regiment of 10th Division halted at Perwez, eight miles northeast of Gembloux. Late in the evening, they both reported that the Prussians had retired on Wavre.[6] This led Grouchy to the erroneous conclusion that Blücher had divided his army, sending around 30,000 men to Wavre to link with Wellington, while the other part withdrew to Liège. In his report of 10:00 P.M., he vowed that if he found the Prussians to be headed to Wavre, he would continue pursuing and prevent them from linking with the British and Dutch.[7]

Grouchy's report reached Napoleon at 2:00 A.M. on the eighteenth, but the emperor refused to believe that the battered Prussians would abandon their line of communication and attempt to unite with Wellington. He remained convinced that he had achieved the separation of the Allied armies with the victory at Ligny and could now turn on Wellington. Napoleon responded to Grouchy's report by informing the marshal that a Prussian column passed through St.-Géry on its way toward Wavre. He specifically ordered Grouchy to march with all speed to Wavre:

> The Emperor has received your last report, written from Gembloux. You mention to His Majesty only two Prussian columns that passed at Sauvenière and Walhain. However, other reports state that a third column of some significance passed through Géry . . . making for Wavre. The Emperor bids me to warn you that at this very moment he is about to attack the English army, which has taken a position at Waterloo. . . . Accordingly, His Majesty desires that you direct your movements on Wavre to draw closer to us, so you can operate in concert with us, and preserve our line of communication, meanwhile driving before you any corps of the Prussian army that may have taken this direction and halted at Wavre, where you should arrive as soon as possible. You will pursue the enemy columns that have turned off to your right with a few light-infantry units so that you can observe their movements and capture the stragglers. Inform me of your arrangements and your line of march, as well as any news you may have

heard regarding the enemy, and do not neglect to maintain your communication with us. The Emperor wishes to hear from you frequently.[8]

Around 3:00 A.M. on 18 June, reports from Walhain increased Grouchy's confusion. During the seventeenth, three Prussian corps purportedly passed through there in the direction of Wavre. Locals claimed to know that these troops were headed to Brussels. Regardless, the marshal believed that the Prussians would halt at Wavre to reorganize after the drubbing at Ligny. He failed to recognize that Blücher maneuvered his army to unite with Wellington's on the other side of the Bois de Paris (Forest of Paris). From Wavre, one lateral march of ten miles separated the Prussians from the Anglo-Dutch position. To prevent the Allied armies from uniting, Grouchy needed to threaten Blücher by taking positions at St.-Géry and Mousty. Instead, he thought the Prussians would continue northwest to Brussels. To fulfill Napoleon's orders, the marshal planned to pursue them through Walhain. But it was too late. At Wavre the entire Prussian army already stood between Wellington and Grouchy; nothing could stop Blücher's advance. Facing Wellington, Napoleon desperately needed Grouchy to march parallel to the Prussians and arrive at Waterloo. Grouchy's decision to follow the Prussians proved a costly error and mightily contributed to Napoleon's impending defeat.[9]

Between 7:00 and 8:00 A.M. on 18 June, reports reached Blücher's headquarters telling of a strong French force at Gembloux. One dispatch estimated it at approximately 15,000 men.[10] Ten miles now separated the Prussians from the Anglo-Dutch army. Still committed to marching the entire army to aid Wellington, Blücher disagreed with Gneisenau and Grolman, who feared leaving the rear of the army vulnerable to attack. Grolman suggested sending only IV and II Corps. By noon, if the French at Gembloux did not threaten Wavre, then I and perhaps even III Corps could follow. After further debate, the field marshal's will held forth, aided by concerns over altering the march of the corps already in motion.

After the meeting, Blücher dictated a letter to Nostitz about 10:30 A.M. Addressed to Müffling, the Prussian liaison at Wellington's headquarters, Blücher stated: "I request that in my name you say to the Duke of Wellington that, ill as I am, I will put myself at the head of my troops and fall on the right wing of the enemy as soon as Napoleon begins the battle. Should the day pass without a French attack, I propose that we both attack him tomorrow." Gneisenau feared Wellington might retreat to Brussels without giving battle. In such a scenario, the Army of the Lower Rhine would be strung out on the march and highly vulnerable. Napoleon could smash its front while the force at Gembloux attacked its rear. In a postscript to Blücher's letter, Gneisenau expressed his apprehensions: "General Gneisenau is in complete agreement with the Field Marshal, but he requests that you divine the innermost thoughts of Wellington, and to ascertain whether he really entertains the firm resolution of fighting in the present position, or whether he intends to make a mere demonstration which may expose our army to the greatest peril."[11]

Blücher's movement to join Wellington posed logistical problems. His decision for IV Corps to lead the advance accounts for the army's late arrival on the battlefield. Bülow's corps, the most distant of Blücher's units in their current positions, had to cross the Dyle and march through Wavre. The concentration of the army around that town as well as the flooded terrain hindered progress. Rain fell from noon on the seventeenth to the morning of the eighteenth. Small field paths, wooded hillocks, and deep streams crisscrossed the region between Wavre, Lasne, and Ohain. After the heavy rain, the streams swelled and the paths became bogs of deep mud.

Earlier that morning at 4:00 A.M., IV Corps advanced from Dion-le-Mont but encountered a bottleneck at Wavre. Innumerable carts and artillery pieces, moved to the high ground during the rain, cluttered the roads. Crossing the bridge over the Dyle and moving through the town's narrow streets took longer than the Prussians expected. Bülow's advance guard passed through Wavre around 5:00 A.M. Shortly after, a mill near the Dyle caught fire. Spreading to the surrounding buildings, it soon threatened the nearby bridge and the numerous caissons parked in the town. Engulfing Wavre's main road, the inferno halted Bülow's march.[12] An entire battalion finally contained the blaze, though not before Bülow's columns lost precious time; IV Corps did not clear Wavre until long after sunrise.

The march to St. Lambert also proved to be extremely slow due to the poor condition of the road. Units became separated as the infantry waded through water for long distances. Moving the artillery required herculean efforts.[13] Reaching the narrow defile near St. Lambert, Bülow's advance guard finally passed and entered the village at 10:00 A.M. Around noon, 16th and 13th Brigades also arrived. The Reserve Artillery and Reserve Cavalry followed at 1:00 P.M.; the rear guard arrived two hours later.[14] In accordance with Blücher's orders, the brigades remained at St. Lambert until information on the French could be obtained.

Meanwhile, as Bülow's Reserve Cavalry followed the 13th Brigade through Wavre, French cavalry could be seen advancing between Vieux-Sart and a Prussian post at Mont-St.-Guibert. To determine if the French movement targeted his left flank, Bülow dispatched two cavalry regiments. The first, sent toward Maransart, found this point between St. Lambert and Genappe held by a French post. A second patrol reconnoitered to Mont-St.-Guibert, making contact with the Prussian post there. Patrols did not detect any French forces operating on the left bank of the Lasne River.[15]

After completing half of the march, IV Corps still had to cross the boggy valley and steep banks of the Lasne. On the stream's right bank sprawled the Bois de Paris, which would serve as the Prussian staging area. One hussar squadron patrolled the wood. At 11:30 A.M. the horsemen reported that the entire Lasne sector and pass into the forest remained clear. Blücher and Gneisenau, who reached St. Lambert around noon, viewed this report with skepticism. The general sent in a second patrol, accompanied by a staff officer for confirmation. After this second patrol confirmed the findings of the first, the 6th Silesian Hussars and two battalions moved forward to secure the forest.[16]

At 1:00 P.M. Blücher ordered the corps to cross the defile. Joining Bülow, the field marshal led the advance from St. Lambert at the head of the column. Movement on the road and across the Lasne taxed the troops. Any rise in elevation halted the gun carriages and caissons until the men dragged them through the mud. A steep hill where the columns crossed the river again delayed the artillery's advance. Although spurred on by their commanders, increasing numbers of men dropped from exhaustion.

Advance units of IV Corps reached the edge of the forest around 3:00 P.M. and continued through its 30,000 acres. Deep ravines often cut the narrow road. Dense wood flanked both sides ruling out chances of avoiding the road. At several points men could only march in single file. Columns again became stretched and sometimes even detached. By 4:00 P.M., the advance guard halted at the opposite edge of the forest and surveyed the soon-to-be battlefield.

Two battalions and two hussar regiments followed by 15th and 16th Brigades moved into a position covered by thick wood. The Reserve Artillery rolled through the forest; the Reserve Cavalry waited to follow at the opening of the wood. To the rear, 13th and 14th Brigades commenced the crossing of the Lasne.[17]

From the Reserve, Bülow attached two twelve-pound batteries and two additional cavalry regiments to the advance guard. Behind this screen, 15th Brigade formed to the right of the road exiting the forest and the 16th to the left. As they occupied the heights of Fichermont, the batteries viewed General Jean Domon's cavalry advancing in the distance. Two Prussian cavalry regiments sought to engage, but the French withdrew. The intensity of the struggle before him and the danger to Wellington's right flank induced Blücher to order the advance, although only half of IV Corps had arrived. "The remainder of the corps had yet to come up," recalled Müffling, "but he [Blücher] was apprehensive, lest the enemy, directing concentrated force against Wellington, should succeed in overwhelming him prior to his attack."[18] Blücher directed the advance guard along the ridge toward the farm of La Belle Alliance. Bülow arranged his two brigades in a line between the southern end of the Bois de Paris and the road west of Fichermont. At 4:30 the general's artillery began shelling the French to shield his infantry as it moved southwest.[19]

Due to the heavy rains and the condition of the battlefield, Napoleon delayed his attack on Wellington for five hours. As the Prussian IV Corps neared St. Lambert, he opened the battle. Shortly after 1:00 P.M., the emperor observed the Prussians marching on the hills near St. Lambert. At this time he interrogated a captured Prussian hussar who bore a letter informing Wellington of Bülow's arrival. The messenger claimed that the troops seen in the distance belonged to the general's advance guard. At 1:30 imperial headquarters dispatched orders for Grouchy to move closer to Napoleon's right flank and engage Bülow.[20] Receiving these orders around 5:00 P.M., the marshal still decided to commit his entire force to attack the Prussian rear guard at Wavre.[21]

The British also observed Blücher's approach. Hussey Vivian, a British major general and brigade commander, noted: "That the Prussians were seen advancing to our support long before their arrival on the field cannot be doubted. That it was understood between the Duke and Blücher that they would support us, and that

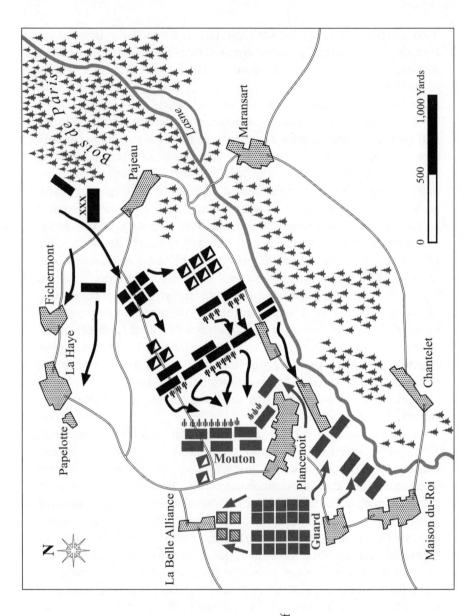

N

Bois de Paris

Lasne

Maransart

Pajeau

xxx

Fichermont

La Haye

Papelotte

Chantelet

Mouton

Plancenoit

Guard

La Belle Alliance

Maison du-Roi

0   500   1,000 Yards

The Battle of
Waterloo, Prussian
Intervention,
18 June 1815.
Map drawn by
Alex Mendoza.
Copyright © 2014
by the University of
Oklahoma Press.

such an understanding was a necessary part of our remaining in our position and risking battle is equally certain."[22] Horace Seymore, a British infantry captain, noted that after observing the Prussians debouch, "I was desired by the Duke of Wellington to tell General Bülow that the Duke wished that he would immediately send him Prussian infantry to fill up the loss that had taken place in his lines. On starting to deliver this message, my horse was killed, and I believe Colonel Freemantle delivered it to the Prussian general." J. Freemantle, Wellington's aide, concludes: "The Duke called upon me to go to the head of their column, and ask for the 3,000 men to supply our losses. Blücher had not arrived, but Generals Zieten and Bülow, at the head of the column, answered that the whole army was coming."[23]

Napoleon watched as the troops debauched from the Bois de Paris and realized they did not belong to Grouchy. Blücher's arrival provided tremendous assistance for Wellington. Instead of utilizing his entire force to break the duke's center, Napoleon detached 7,000 infantry from General Georges Mouton's VI Corps and 2,300 light cavalry to protect his flank and rear. He positioned VI Corps on either side of the road from Plancenoit to Fichermont, preparing to meet Bülow's advance.[24]

The two brigades of IV Corps emerged under the cover of two cavalry regiments and six batteries. After repulsing the French cavalry, the Prussians marched against VI Corps. Although outnumbered, Mouton held. Blücher ordered Bülow to drive into the right flank and rear of the French position. Bülow broadened his front by moving 13th Brigade between 15th and 16th.[25] As units of 14th Brigade arrived, he posted them behind 16th. His front gradually became an oblique line extending from Plancenoit to Fichermont. Blücher's front soon ran parallel to Napoleon's main line of operations, was well supported on both flanks, and commanded the French right and rear.

After Mouton fell back around 6:00 P.M., Bülow arranged a three-pronged assault on Plancenoit. Six battalions, including four Landwehr, assaulted the village walls on the right, center, and left. Outside the village wall, the Prussians captured a howitzer and two guns. After pressing through heavy fire, the right and center columns entered the village. "We remained long enough for me to see the French reserve and right form line *en potence* in order to meet the attack on Plancenoit," recalled a British soldier, "and I was surprised to see the tremendous fire the French were able to direct against the Prussians."[26] Street fighting erupted in the village, posing a serious challenge for the raw Landwehr. The Prussians gained possession of Plancenoit's cemetery, but the French fortified the surrounding houses and gardens. Elevated above most of the village and enclosed by a low stone wall strengthened by a steep outer bank, the cemetery became a Prussian fortress.[27] Skirmishing took place at distances of thirty paces. With Blücher in possession of Plancenoit and threatening his rear, Napoleon dispatched two divisions of Young Guard to retake the village. Eight Guard battalions aided by twenty-four guns soon ejected the Prussians. Mouton's cavalry pursued them until coming within range of Bülow's batteries.

Bülow then arranged his regiments for a frontal assault on Plancenoit. One line and three Landwehr battalions led the attack. Storming the village, the Prussians drove the French from their positions. Alarmed by this new assault, Napoleon dispatched two additional regiments of Old Guard. Led by General Charles Morand, the Guard fiercely swept the Prussians from the village again, driving them across the plain. A regiment of French lancers issued forth to rout the Prussian infantry. To save his regiments, Bülow ordered a charge by the 8th Hussar Regiment. After a brief clash, the French cavalry withdrew, leaving their own infantry exposed. Before the hussars could mount a serious assault, the French infantry retreated behind the walls of Plancenoit.

Bülow's two assaults had extended his front, causing a gap to widen between 15th and 16th Brigades. He filled it with the Reserve Cavalry. Led by the eighteen-year-old son of the king, Prince Wilhelm, the future German kaiser, the cavalry performed admirably, confining the French to the defensive and supporting the Prussian infantry. Around 6:00 P.M. the lead elements of II and I Corps began arriving. Blücher ordered Pirch I to secure the left flank of the army by sending 7th Brigade and one Landwehr cavalry regiment to Maransart. His 5th and 6th Brigades formed and moved left to support IV Corps. Zieten deployed his brigades at Ohain. Seeing the arrival of fresh Prussian units, Napoleon concluded that Blücher would attempt a third assault on Plancenoit. It became clear that the field marshal expected more troops to arrive. Sensing the threat to his line of retreat, Napoleon sought to accelerate the pace of the battle by finishing off Wellington. In one last gamble, he decided to launch a massive assault against the Anglo-Dutch center.[28]

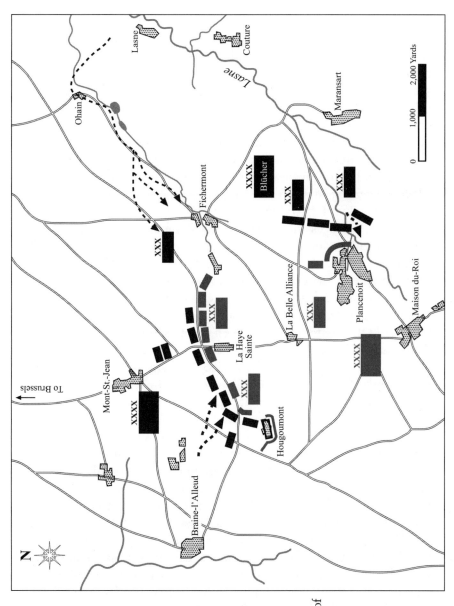

The Battle of
Waterloo,
18 June 1815.
Map drawn by
Alex Mendoza.
Copyright © 2014
by the University of
Oklahoma Press.

The advance of the Imperial Guard against Wellington necessitated the immediate renewal of the Prussian assault on Plancenoit and VI Corps. Observing that Bülow's IV Corps did not possess the strength to succeed, Blücher arranged a combined attack. Pirch's 5th Brigade joined 16th and 14th Brigades facing the village, 6th Brigade followed in support, while 7th Brigade, as noted, advanced on Maransart. To the right of IV Corps, 1st Brigade advanced against La Haye and Papelotte. Thus, Bülow's 14th and 16th Brigades combined with Pirch's 5th and 6th Brigades to attack Plancenoit, while the 15th and 13th Brigades supported by 1st Brigade simultaneously advanced against Mouton's VI Corps.

Eleven Guard battalions and units of Mouton's corps held Plancenoit.[29] Hedges and houses provided the defenders ample cover. The Prussian infantry formed multiple battalion columns for the advance. Bülow ordered two line regiments to lead the assault on the right side of Plancenoit. Two Landwehr battalions from II Corps advanced on the left side of the village. Bülow also directed two of Pirch I's line battalions against the walled cemetery, where two battalions of Old Guard held firm. A chain of skirmishers preceded the columns, while artillery supported from the heights in the rear.

In front of the village walls, 15,000 Prussians scattered Mouton's troops and entered Plancenoit. Bloody street fighting again erupted. One contemporary noted that "the fight raged on in gardens, orchards, streets, and houses; they slaughtered one another with a fury."[30] Although the Prussians decimated an entire Young Guard battalion that defended the cemetery, Pirch I's troops could not storm the town's walls. The troops defended their ground heroically, during which French hatred of the Prussians reached new heights; only General Jean-Jacques Pelet prevented the slaughter of prisoners.[31] After attempting several unsuccessful frontal assaults on the village, Blücher ordered a double envelopment. One fusilier battalion from II Corps crossed the brook passing through Plancenoit and attacked the Guard's reserve, which stood between the brook and the Lasne River. By 8:30 P.M., Bülow's men also flanked the village, taking possession of its right and assaulting the right wall of the cemetery. Around the same time, Pirch I's Landwehr flanked the houses and fences on the left side. Prussian troops crossed to the Lasne's right bank, completely encircling the village. Slowly advancing, they forced the French from house and hedge. Plancenoit became engulfed in flame; the cries of wounded men trapped in the

houses rose above the din of battle. Forced to abandon the cemetery, the French slowly retreated until the Prussians gained full control of the village.

As the final struggle for Plancenoit reached its climax, 13th and
15th Brigades assaulted VI Corps. Deployed in battalion columns,
15th Brigade led the advance, followed by four battalions from 13th
Brigade. To the right, one cavalry brigade and the 1st West Prussian
Uhlans covered the advance. Mouton effectively used the terrain
to sustain his resistance, driving back the Prussians several times.
Lacking sufficient cavalry support, the Prussian infantry became
paralyzed with fear. Mouton rallied his infantry and advanced. His
efforts became part of the general advance of the French right wing.
Also at this time, the Imperial Guard advanced between La Haye
Sainte and Hougomont against Wellington's center in Napoleon's
last great assault. French forces took Papelotte and La Haye, thus
posing a threat to Bülow's right. At the same time, 1st Brigade
reached Wellington's extreme left wing. Blücher ordered Steinmetz
to retake Papelotte and La Haye. After driving the French from
these positions in conjunction with four of Wellington's battalions,
Steinmetz advanced along the ridge toward Plancenoit. Zieten's
batteries, situated on the heights north of Smohain, opened fired
on Mouton's left wing. With the support of 1st Brigade on their
right, 15th and 13th Brigades advanced, pushing the French to La
Belle Alliance. As Mouton's units retreated up the far side of the
valley on Plancenoit's left, Prussian artillery blasted them from
the opposite hills. In the intervals, Prussian battalions descended
onto the plain and moved across the valley. French resistance gradually crumbled. Around 8:15 P.M., the Prussians punched through
Mouton's line. Broken on all fronts, the French evacuated the field
in a general retreat.

At 9:15 P.M., Blücher met Wellington at La Belle Alliance,
where he gave the reserved duke a bear hug. The field marshal
volunteered to execute the pursuit. His joy in seeing the rout of
Napoleon's army produced an intoxicating effect on the old hussar, who claimed to be "pregnant with an elephant" fathered by a
French grenadier. Fifteen minutes later he met with his corps commanders, ordering them to "pursue the enemy as long as they had a
man and horse able to stand." No quarter would be given.[32]

Following the capture of Plancenoit, elements of II and IV
Corps pursued the French toward Maison du-Roi. Reinforced by

5th Brigade, IV Corps moved south on the Brussels highway toward Genappe. Finding General Honoré Charles Reille's II Corps in retreat, the Prussians pressed the assault, killing or dispersing 5,000 Frenchmen. Bright moonlight aided the pursuers as panic ruled Napoleon's army. According to Gneisenau: "The causeway presented the appearance of an immense shipwreck, covered with an innumerable quantity of cannon, caissons, carriages, baggage, arms, and wrecks of every kind. Those of the enemy who had attempted to repose for a time . . . were driven from more than nine bivouacs. In some villages, they attempted to maintain themselves; but as they heard the beating of our drums or the sound of the trumpet, they either fled or threw themselves into the houses, where they were cut down or taken prisoner. . . . [T]he whole march was a continual chase, either in the cornfields or the houses."[33]

At Genappe, the French collected some artillery and entrenched themselves behind overturned carriages. At 11:00 P.M., musket fire halted the Prussian advance at the entrance of the village. Horse artillery blasted through the French barrier and the Prussians charged into Genappe, which fell after bitter fighting. Napoleon had abandoned his carriage there during the retreat to escape on horseback. The Prussians now took possession of the coach, which contained the emperor's hat, sword, baggage, and seal ring—all of which they presented to Blücher.

Blücher fought the greatest battle of his life, breaking Napoleon's right flank and sealing the Allied victory at Waterloo. The two armies completely defeated the emperor and routed his army. At Leipzig, Napoleon lost Germany but still retained France. At Waterloo, he lost everything. Like at Leipzig, Blücher appeared at the decisive moment. When Napoleon attempted to break Wellington's center, 10,000 of his men, including crack Imperial Guard units, were committed to stopping Blücher. It is difficult to imagine Wellington's army surviving 18 June if Blücher had not arrived. The day's bloody work amounted to 6,998 Prussian casualties, but Napoleon's power was broken for good.

On the morning of 19 June, Prussian cavalry continued the pursuit of the French army. By that evening, the Anglo-Dutch army, constituting the right wing of the advancing forces, reached Nivelles. On the left, Blücher's I Corps reached Charleroi, II Corps halted north of Mellery, IV Corps passed the night at Fontaine-l'Eveque, and the 5th Brigade of II Corps was at Anderlues. Unable to coordinate resistance on the Belgian side of the frontier, Napoleon proceeded to Philippeville, where he hoped to receive news of Grouchy. Remaining there for four hours, he directed his chief of staff, Marshal Soult, to send the remains of the Army of the North to Laon. In the meantime, the wreck of that army continued its retreat across the frontier. As coordination became difficult, units struggled to reach Philippeville. Many men simply disregarded their arms and returned to their homes. A few officers managed to collect some units and lead them to Laon. After leaving Philippeville at 2:00 P.M., Napoleon reached Laon later in the afternoon. His conviction to remain near the frontier to rally the army soon changed, and he departed for Paris.[34]

"What I promised, I have kept," raved Blücher to Amalie, "on 16 June, I was forced to retire; on the 18th, in conjunction with my friend Wellington, I have completed Napoleon's ruin. No one knows where he has gone. His army is completely routed, his artillery is in our hands. His decorations, which he himself wore, have just been brought to me; they were taken from one of his carriages."[35] In a letter to Knesebeck, he added a degree of drama: "My friend! The most beautiful battle has been fought. The most splendid victory has been won. Details will follow. I think Bonaparte's history is now over for good. I can write no more because all my limbs are shaking. The excitement is too great."[36]

On 20 June Blücher's army moved to secure the passage of the Sambre at Charleroi and cross the French frontier. French units continued the retreat to Laon as late as the twenty-second. There, Soult established headquarters and made efforts to resupply his troops. After a fierce battle at Wavre with Blücher's III Corps on the eighteenth, Grouchy withdrew to Reims. Napoleon hoped to unite the remains of his army with Grouchy to stop that Allied advance. At Paris, he went before the legislature to plead for a levée that would furnish the manpower he needed to destroy the invading armies.

After getting some rest, Blücher provided more details for Amalie:

> I have seemingly recovered from my fall, but another horse already has been wounded under me. I do not think there will be any more battles for a long time and perhaps never. Our victory is the most complete ever to be fought. Napoleon fled in the night without hat and sword; today I sent his hat and sword to the King; his magnificently embroidered seal and his carriage are in my hands, also

his field glass, through which he observed us on the day of battle. I will send you the carriage, it is a shame that it is damaged. His jewels and all his valuables are the booty of our troops, nothing of his equipment is left to him; many soldiers have taken booty worth 5,000–6,000 thaler. He was in the carriage trying to escape when it was overtaken by our troops; he jumped from it, threw himself onto a horse without his sword, whereby his hat fell off, and so he probably escaped safely in the night but only Heaven knows where.

Today, I enter France with the main body of the army. The results of this victory cannot be evaluated and I believe Napoleon's downfall must follow and the French nation will and must despise him; then I hope peace will come and with God's help I will be with you again before winter. Your brother is very well and on the day of battle fought as a first-rate officer with his new regiment. My entire entourage is healthy and well, and I expect to receive news from you. I am shaking so much that I was not able to write this myself, also I have no time. Good-bye and keep loving your most devoted friend.[37]

On the twenty-first the Army of the Lower Rhine reached France's northern fortress belt; Blücher ordered the investment of Maubeuge, Landrecy, Avesnes, and Rocroi. Pirch I's 5th and 7th Brigades blockaded Maubeuge, while 6th Brigade marched to Landrecy, and 8th Brigade moved to Philippeville. The next day the Prussians "bombarded the fortress of Avesnes; a powder magazine blew up in the fortress, causing the commandant to surrender." For the twenty-third, Blücher planned to shell Landrecy and Maubeuge.[38] "Had I more Cossacks and light cavalry with me," he informed Stein, "very few of the French would be left."[39] From Noyelles-sur-Sambre, he wrote Hardenberg on 22 June:

Are you now satisfied? In eight days, I delivered two battles and five large engagements and invested three fortresses. But how many brave officers have lost their lives for this? I lay a claim on your splendid heart, my true friend. Use everything so that the widow of the deserving officer is not ignored. Today, I received the news that our best officer in my opinion, Colonel Zastrow, has died; he leaves behind a wife and children, but no wealth.

I have only to thank the loyal support of Gneisenau and my own iron will for the beautiful outcome; the lamentations and the pleas to give the troops some rest have almost drove me crazy, but it does no good to explain to people who only think about their insignificant selves that I must first invest the fortresses behind me before I can think of rest!

Now I will see to the care of the troops and the day after tomorrow I will speak with Wellington. After this meeting and a day of rest for the troops, the journey will go forward.

Now, a word about myself. I have suffered very much this time and my strength is beginning to leave me. As soon as the end comes here, I will depart, otherwise I will perish; I wish nothing more than to be on my estate in Silesia. I will go straight there and live there. I no longer expect to have joy on this earth. The fate of my son weighs on me.

P.S. Napoleon has lost everything: his money, his jewels, and all of his equipment are now the property of my brave troops. The jewels have been sent to the King. His hat, sword, and seal are in my hands. He was so surprised that he had to jump from his carriage by which his hat fell off; he sprang on a horse and fled. I think he is finished. To my great joy, the inhabitants of the country greet us well; nothing is to be seen of his levée-en-masse.[40]

On 23 June both Wellington and Blücher ordered a general halt so their armies could rest and regroup. "One claims that Napoleon wants to assemble the wreck of his army at Laon," Blücher wrote to Amalie, "it will not trouble me much. If the Parisians do not kill the tyrant before I get to Paris, then I will kill the Parisians; they are a treacherous people."[41] The typical slow pace of his allies irked the field marshal: "If I am to remain healthy, then I think the war must soon end; if only the Austrians and Russians would do something!"[42]

Operations continued on the twenty-fourth. Blücher's army remained a full day's march in front of Wellington. Serving as the vanguard, Zieten's I Corps advanced to Guise, while III Corps reached Le Nouvion-en-Thiérache, and IV Corps made Aisonville-Bernoville. That night the Anglo-Dutch army camped around Cambrai, Le Cateau-Cambrésis, and Englefontaine. Soult remained at Laon and Grouchy reached Rethel.[43] That same day, 24 June, Blücher received a letter from the commissioners of the French government that revealed Napoleon's second and final abdication. They requested an armistice, but Blücher refused unless they surrendered Napoleon. He explained the situation to his cousin: "Bonaparte has been deposed by the Legislative Corps, and General

Morand has asked me to cease the hostilities. You can easily understand that I would not hear of this and answered that Bonaparte's
death or his delivery to me and the simultaneous surrender of all
fortresses on the Maas and Sambre were the only conditions that
would persuade me to cease hostilities. Without halting, my march
goes straight to Paris. If the Parisians do not kill or hand over Napoleon; as perjurers, they will feel my wrath: they best remember
Moscow. I depart toward Paris today; just now the keys to St. Quen-
tin were brought to me. Maubeuge and Landrecy will fall soon. Both
my army and Wellington's have lost much; the brave fell for the
great cause of mankind."[44]

Sharing Blücher's hatred of Napoleon, Gneisenau informed
Müffling that "Bonaparte has been declared an outlaw by the Allied
Powers. The Duke of Wellington may possibly (from parliamentary considerations) hesitate to fulfill the declaration of the Powers. Therefore, you will direct the negotiations to the effect that
Bonaparte may be handed over to us, with a view to his execution.
This is what eternal justice demands, and what the declaration of
13 March determined; and thus the blood of our soldiers killed and
mutilated on the 16th and 18th will be avenged."[45]

Reports claimed that after collecting the remains of the army,
Soult sought a union with Grouchy. But the provisional government at Paris relieved Soult; Grouchy received command of the
entire army.[46] The right wing of the French army stood at Reims,
with the left at Soissons. Viewing this force as a threat to the crossings over the Oise, Blücher ordered I and III Corps to hasten to Compiègne while IV Corps secured the bridges over the Oise at
Pont-Ste.-Maxence and Creil.[47] Blücher's rapid advance thwarted
Grouchy's attempt to secure the river passages and forced the marshal to retreat on Paris. French resistance was ebbing. Increased
desertions indicated the failing effort to reorganize the army. Realizing that his troops could not confront the Prussians, Grouchy
hoped to reach Paris by forced marches. Blücher's determined measures to destroy the French army misfired as the marshal skillfully
evaded his traps.[48] Regardless, the field marshal had Paris in his
sights. "Bonaparte has been deposed and wants to go to America,"
he informed Amalie. "Today, I sent Nostitz to Laon to tell Bonaparte's deputies that my condition to negotiate with them is either
Bonaparte's death or his extradition, and the surrender of all fortresses on the Sambre and the Maas. In spite of all of this, I march

straight to Paris today. I will strike while the iron is hot, then I will be home before autumn."[49]

On 27 June Blücher reached Compiègne. He could not allow the moment to pass without sharing his thoughts with Amalie. "Here I sit where Marie Louise spent her wedding night. One can find nothing more beautiful or more agreeable than Compiègne; it is a pity that I must leave here early tomorrow because in three days I must be at Paris. It is possible and highly probable that Bonaparte will surrender to me and Lord Wellington. I probably could not act any wiser than to have him shot: it would be a service to mankind. At Paris, all have abandoned him and he is hated and despised; I think the entire affair here will end shortly and then I will hurry home."[50] Incidentally, Wellington, shocked by the excesses committed by the Prussian troops, would have none of this. In no way did he support the idea of turning over Napoleon to Blücher.

By late evening on the twenty-eighth, the Prussian army succeeded in closing the French line of retreat along the main Soissons highway.[51] After crossing the Oise, Prussian forces captured 4,000 men and sixteen guns.[52] Blücher's outposts stood just five miles north of Paris, and the sound of his cannon could be heard in the city.[53] The remains of the French I and II Corps reached the Parisian suburbs; III and IV Corps retreated into the city, with the Guard and VI Corps following from Meaux.[54]

Blücher's old nemesis, Davout, the Iron Marshal, assembled 65,000 men and 300 guns to defend Paris.[55] Such a formidable host caused Blücher to reconsider his march route. To test the strength and will of the French troops, he ordered IV Corps to assault Aubervilliers, less than five miles north of Paris, on the night of 29 June. The Prussians routed a small force of 1,000 men, taking 200 prisoners. Pursuing to the St.-Denis canal, artillery and musket fire stopped them, indicating the presence of strong defending forces.[56] While contemplating his next move, Blücher learned that the French neglected to fortify the bridges over the Seine. He wasted no time taking advantage of this; Gneisenau shifted the army west and crossed the river. To mask the operation, the forward posts of I and IV Corps held their positions until relieved by Wellington's units.

On the thirtieth, I and IV Corps advanced toward St. Germain-en-Laye and then Versailles to assault Paris from the southwest, where the capital's defenses were weakest.[57] Blücher planned to take the heights of Meudon and Châtillon.[58] He described his situation to Amalie: "I stand before Paris. Wellington dined with me and we discussed how best to finish the whole affair. Last night, I sent your brother to Malmaison to capture Bonaparte. The bridge had been burned down otherwise the coup would have succeeded. Nevertheless, Colomb made a fine expedition and took the bridge at St. Germain, which the enemy was in the process of destroying. As soon as the King arrives and the business here is settled, I will leave the army. I am so very tired and will need to go to a spa; I will write you from where I go so you can join me. Tomorrow I will attack Paris and cross the bridge at St. Germain that your brother saved."[59]

Aware of the approaching Austrian and Russian armies, Davout viewed further resistance as pointless. Negotiations with Wellington opened on 2 July. After the duke declared that he would not agree to an armistice while Davout's army still occupied Paris, the French representatives withdrew from the talks. Blücher's determined advance to the capital on 2 July forced the marshal to plan a counterstrike the next day. At 3:00 A.M. on 3 July, two columns debouched from Vaugirard to assault Zieten's I Corps at Issy-les-Moulineaux. After both sides sustained heavy losses, the Prussians repulsed the French, pursuing them to Paris's outer wall. A ceasefire followed, and Davout opened negotiations with Blücher and Wellington.[60] "Around 8:00," wrote Blücher, "a French general came with the offer to surrender the city on conditions. I invited the Duke of Wellington to these negotiations. Yesterday and today I have lost around 3,000 men; I hope to God they will be the last in this war. I have had my fill of murder."[61] Later on the third, the Military Convention of Paris ended hostilities. The next day Davout led the French army out of Paris to the Loire River.

"Paris is mine," exclaimed Blücher to Amalie on 4 July. "The French army will retire behind the Loire and the city will surrender to me. I owe everything to the indescribable bravery of my troops, their unparalleled perseverance, and my iron will. There was no lack of complaints and lamentations over the exhaustion of the men; but I was deaf and knew from experience that the fruits of victory only could be exploited by a continuous pursuit. I cannot write more today, I am so very busy and I am so tired. Make the contents of this letter known in Berlin. Thank God the bloodshed is over."[62] After three weeks of combat, the two Allied armies entered Paris on 7 July 1815.[63] Blücher's 9 July letter to Amalie states:

Here I am at Paris, but I have taken temporary quarters; I will stay at St. Cloud in the beautiful château when the great gentlemen reach Paris. I am seemingly healthy, but annoyed to the highest degree because I am tormented: the French are loathsome and vile. Louis XVIII is back in Paris; but I am certain that when we leave, they will again drive him out within three days. As soon as our King arrives, I will begin work on my departure because I have had enough. But tell me why everyone receives letters from Berlin yet I receive nothing from you? Yesterday, Colonel Thile came back and brought 1,000 letters, but nothing for me; I hope you are well. Farewell and say hello to all your friends. I long for news of my poor, unfortunate Franz. Gebhard is well and says hello.[64]

Blücher urged his king to be more assertive at the peace table. "I respectfully request that you instruct the diplomats to not lose, again, what the soldier has won with his blood. This moment is the only and last to secure Germany against France. Your Majesty will he be revered as the founder of Germany's security and we will enjoy the fruits of our labors when we are no longer forced to always stand with our swords drawn."[65] He caused excitement by announcing his intention to destroy the Jena Bridge, built by Napoleon to commemorate the 1806 victory over the Prussians. On 6 July the Prussians mined the bridge. Many of Blücher's compatriots spoke against this irrational plan. They argued that Frederick William, scheduled to arrive at any time, would probably disapprove. Talleyrand claimed that the structure numbered among France's national treasures. This opposition only spurred the old man's zeal; he repeated his orders for the mining and detonation. "The bridge will be destroyed and I wish that Herr Talleyrand would place himself on it," Blücher wrote to Goltz, the Prussian ambassador to France. "How can this despicable man call the bridge a precious monument? Our national honor demands the destruction of this memorial that was erected to our shame."[66] Although the powder was detonated on the tenth, the awkward attempt caused little damage. After Louis XVIII promised to change the name, Blücher dropped the matter.

But an issue that the field marshal refused to drop concerned the troops: he sought new uniforms and a bonus of two months' pay for his soldiers. For this, he demanded 100 million francs from the French and wanted the support of his government to get it.[67] "I urgently request that you see to it that no one interferes with our plans," he beseeched Knesebeck. "Never again will we have such an opportunity. Our finances need some additional contributions and we must not leave France again under the reproach of having been outwitted by this depraved people. Talleyrand threatened us at Vienna; now he can pay at Paris. Concerning our army, I promised that when Paris fell, I would provide new uniforms and the men would receive two months of pay as a douceur; they deserve this and I must keep my word. I cannot wait to go to a spa. There probably will not be any more fighting. If the State Chancellor is there give him my regards. I remain here at St. Cloud because I despise Louis XVIII and all the French."[68]

After the Allied monarchs and diplomats reached Paris, Blücher experienced numerous setbacks. Wellington already had pulled a coup by ensuring that the battle on 18 June would be named "Waterloo" instead of Blücher's choice of "Belle Alliance." "Waterloo" threw the credit for the victory squarely on the side of the British, and Wellington would spend the rest of his life overtly and covertly eroding the role Blücher's army played in the battle. In addition, the "great ones" overruled his demands for reparations and the surrender of the fortresses. After local French officials refused his requisitions on the grounds that they required an order from Louis, Blücher arrested them. Frederick William ordered their release. "This is a signal to all other authorities," bellowed the field marshal, "and nobody will supply us with materials."[69]

On 25 July he angrily left St. Cloud and joined the troops moving farther west to occupy the region up to the Loire. In his place Gneisenau participated at the meetings of the diplomats. Grolman, who replaced Gneisenau on the staff, did nothing to calm Blücher's mood, especially after the king voided his arrangements to pay the army its bonus and give it new uniforms. Blücher claimed that he received both verbal and written assurances from the monarch in favor of these plans. Although Frederick William awarded him the "Blücherstern" of the Grand Cross of the Iron Cross, he demanded his discharge. "Now is not the time to justify my actions," he declared to Hardenberg. "But I will openly submit my conduct to the judgment of the King, the Army, the entire Nation, and the German Fatherland. I cannot and will not remain here; one believes that I have no say in the matter, and I believe that it is my duty to say something; because no one other than me will defend the Army. My convictions are completely different from the political views that now reign. My heart and my conscience tell me that I must now take my leave. Farewell; you remain my friend as I am yours and will remain so in all circumstances."[70]

He was blunt with Gneisenau: "You were present at the discussion between me and the Chancellor. Corresponding to the Chancellor's statements, I have received three cabinet orders that override all of the measures I have taken, although the King had approved them both in writing and verbally. I am now completely paralyzed and the Army is in the greatest trouble. We have not tapped all of the funds available to us. The money remains in the country and because of this our government securities suffer from inflation. Here we receive no funds and the army cannot make payroll, much less the douceur. According to the highest order, the issue of the Army's uniforms is to be dropped." He also urged Hardenberg to secure gains for the Prussian army at the peace table. Hardenberg firmly rejected the idea. His letter to Gneisenau continues:

> I must have the same rights as Schwarzenberg, Wellington, and Wrede, and I certainly do not intend to subject myself to the despotism of the diplomats. I cannot stay here for long otherwise things will emerge that will cause general harm and grant our adversaries malicious delight. I will not fight with my old friend [Hardenberg], which I will not be able to avoid if this continues. Through my pure intent to be useful to the State and to obtain for the Army the reward it deserves, I have been subjected to the hateful reproaches of the entire French nation and others who want to ingratiate themselves at my expense. How little I care for the greediness of the French is well known, but the manner that they acted toward me is insulting. I could become disparaging of the King, who has just given me a beautiful new proof of his satisfaction [the Blücherstern]; but because I am convinced that I can be of no more use here, I have done that [resign], which as you know, was already long in my plan.[71]

Blücher returned to Paris to make his case but soon became fed up. "Yesterday, they celebrated the birthday of our King," notes his letter of 4 August. "I was invited, but left after one hour." He informed his wife that because the Prussian cabinet opposed his every move, he resigned his command of the army. But Frederick William demanded that he maintain it until the signing of the peace. "To avoid embroiling myself with all foreign as well as our own ministers, I will completely avoid Paris and take my quarters in Caen, right on the coast," he declared. Stress began to take its toll on the seventy-three-year-old. "The war is over and I long to go home," he told Amalie.

Like the previous year, titles and trinkets had little real effect on Blücher. On 3 August the Order of the Bath arrived from England, "a distinction never yet awarded to a foreigner." The prince regent also invited him back to London, but he politely declined. After describing the Blücherstern to Amalie, he asked: "What good are all these decorations to me; it would be much better for me if we make a good peace that is advantageous for us. In the meantime, I am not at fault if we do not end the feud advantageously for ourselves."

Blücher assured his wife that he was not gambling: "I have enough now, why should I gamble. Gebhard has won a lot of money and went shopping diligently for Lisette. As I am now leaving this region, the gambling will end and he will be able to hold on to his money." Although he stayed away from the Palais Royal, Blücher spent handsomely. At Paris, he ordered a porcelain table setting for forty persons. In addition, he purchased life-sized portraits of the Bonaparte family, with Napoleon on horseback, all painted by the famous artist David. "Wilhelm writes me that Franz gets better every day; if God would give him back his mind I would leave this world in peace having done everything I could for my family," concludes his letter to Amalie. "Enjoy life; I will bring home a beautiful dog for you."[72]

On the verge of leaving for Prussia, he wrote a final letter to Gneisenau. "I cannot depart from this region without sending you my regards. I am happy to be leaving Paris. I am very annoyed because I am making no headway with the uniforms for the troops. I have ordered the commanding generals to remove the prefects, take them into custody, and transport them to one of our fortresses if they do not fill the requisitions. I must convince the King that he must either support me and sanction my measures or finally order me to relinquish my claims; then I can reconcile myself with the latter. If the great gentlemen do not leave Paris, we will live to see extraordinary things because the French know that one fears them. Farewell and remember your true friend."[73]

Blücher left the scene, traveling through Le Mans and Alençon, spending time at Caen in Normandy, and lastly passing a few weeks at Compiègne. At the beginning of November, the Allies began the march home; an international force under Wellington remained in northern France until 1818. Poor health brought on by stress and mental exhaustion delayed Blücher's journey home, however. Forced to remain at Frankfurt until the new year, he finally reached Berlin on 21 January 1816, though still sick. For the next three years, he enjoyed retirement in Silesia and received all the honors he deserved. Amalie recorded their last days together: "he had become very weak after the first six days of his illness and with each day his strength lessened so that on the whole he was too weak to do anything, but his head remained completely clear. Up until the moment of his passing he was completely conscious and said to me on the tenth day of his illness: 'I am happy to die, but wish to live only for your sake.'"[74] At Krieblowitz on Sunday, 12 September 1819, the heart and soul of Prussia stopped beating after seventy-seven years.

ASSESSMENT

On joining the Prussian army in 1760, Blücher served in the latter stages of the Seven Years War, fighting in the obscure Pomeranian theater against his former Swedish compatriots. Although transferred to the Saxon theater late in the war, the native Mecklenburger never received an opportunity to fight under the watchful and rewarding eye of his new king, Frederick the Great. This situation repeated itself during operations in Poland in the early 1770s. In addition to this disappointment, Blücher convinced himself that being a foreigner meant he had to go the extra mile to prove his worth to Old Fritz. Passed over for promotion by the Margrave of Brandenburg-Schwedt's illegitimate son, Blücher felt helpless, emasculated, and abandoned. In his mind, his sword had been rejected not because of alleged misconduct in Poland, but because he was a foreigner. Unable to change this fact, he took the problem head on. In his numerous entreaties to Frederick II, Blücher insisted that he served just as loyally as a native Prussian. While not a true Prussian blueblood, he emphatically stated that his blood ran bluer and truer than that of anyone. It is at this time that he developed his intense, almost fanatical loyalty and love for Prussia as a response to his own insecurities over being a foreigner. Also apparent here is his stubborn insistence to get his way with an opponent, even one as formidable as the great Frederick. Lastly, we see how Blücher's intense pride did not allow him to suffer humiliation. Being passed over for promotion followed by the discharge that stripped him of the honor of wearing the uniform cut him to the quick.

After his dishonorable discharge, Blücher spent fourteen long years as a civilian. Yet this time away from the army helped him grow as an individual and thus had a profound influence on his future. Rather than languish in peacetime garrison duty, where he certainly would have fallen prey to his own vices, he quickly recovered from the unexpected blow of his discharge and seized the initiative presented by his marriage to Mehling's daughter. Although he benefitted from his father-in-law's advice, Blücher's strength, drive, and attention to detail earned him success.[1] Moreover, separating from the army broadened his horizons by forcing him to move into very diverse circles. Feeling like a fish out of water, he nevertheless developed components of his personality that might otherwise have remained dormant. By conducting business at Stargard and Stettin, Blücher interacted with civic leaders; professionals such as bankers, lawyers, and merchants; and of course the Freemasons. Always competitive, he had to find ways to convince these people of his views or simply earn their friendship. He quickly recognized that his skill with the saber would get him nowhere. Therefore, to triumph in the civil arena, Blücher became a skilled orator, made himself accessible to people totally different from himself, and made a point of being open, honest, and genuine. Although no one has ever attempted to portray Blücher as a thinking man, exchanging the army's anti-intellectual environment for the erudite circles of the Freemasons; for interactions with Johann Heinrich von Carmer, one of Prussia's foremost legal minds; and for the opportunity to observe firsthand the inner workings of local and regional government certainly balanced his lack of formal education. In the end, nothing could change the fact that Blücher was a warrior, but he emerged from these years away from the military with a much broader perspective and confidence that his determination could overcome any obstacle.

At the head of his Red Hussars, Blücher made a name for himself as a bold advance-guard commander. In the 1793–94 campaigns, he bravely led from the front with saber in hand, demonstrating his confidence in the superiority of Prussian arms. Blücher's impressive martial figure, handsome features, fiery eyes, and silver-white hair inspired his soldiers. By knowing the thoughts, needs, and sensitivities of the common soldier, he pulled them through critical moments with his uncommon oratory skills. After the devastating defeat in the War of the Fourth Coalition, he believed that the Prussian army only needed bold leadership to defeat Napoleon. Out of touch with the nation's perilous political situation for most of the period between 1807 and 1812, he found that his king lacked the requisite leadership skills to restore the state. His own self-confidence, tremendous ego, and faith in Prussian arms made him one of the few Allied commanders who did not become paralyzed by the fear of Napoleon and his legions. From this fearlessness evolved one of the most essential characteristics of the field commander: freedom from self-consciousness. He never feared losing his reputation and the confidence of his subordinates because of a defeat or a retreat. At times, failure made him more cautious but did not diminish his eagerness for action. Blücher easily forgave mistakes made out of boldness but always reprimanded timidity. Like Napoleon, he stood as a powerful, driving influence who motivated his entourage, officers, and soldiers.[2]

Based on his actions during the spring campaign of 1813, we can identify some of Blücher's characteristics as a commanding general. First and foremost, we see restraint. According to the popular image of the "Hussar General," Blücher should have dashed across the Saale River in early April, not stopping until the French stopped him. Yet this was not the case. Restrained by Kutuzov's orders, Blücher limited himself to sending small Streifkorps across the Saale that did more reconnoitering than raiding. Second, we see a Blücher who can and did function within the constraints of a coalition, who can and did obey and execute orders from a superior, and who continued to subordinate himself under the extremely difficult conditions of defeat in battle followed by demoralizing retreats. He complained, but he obeyed.

In reflecting on the course of the fall campaign, we see the magnitude of Blücher's operations. On no less than four occasions, he opted to retreat rather than engage Napoleon. Each retreat can be completely justified as Napoleon—the master of central position, interior lines, mass, and speed—outnumbered Blücher on every occasion. Moreover, rather than merely conceding the field to the French, the first two retreats required rapid withdrawals under extremely adverse conditions that lasted for days. In the third retreat, a veritable coup de théâtre, Blücher led his Army of Silesia 120 miles down the Elbe to cross the river and link with the Army of North Germany. With both armies on the left bank of the Elbe, the emperor launched a secret offensive against Blücher. Just barely escaping Napoleon's trap, Blücher retreated a fourth time, dragging the Army of North Germany with him across the Saale. Bearing the stamp of the unorthodox, the significance of this maneuver cannot be overlooked: while the combined Allied armies advanced toward Napoleon's communications, they exposed their own and opened the roads to Brandenburg and Silesia. More importantly, the maneuver on the Saale created the conditions that encouraged Schwarzenberg to seek a decisive battle with Napoleon at Leipzig.

Blücher had much to be proud of: energy, controlled aggression, and a commitment to defeating the enemy army. After moving across the neutral zone in August 1813, his Silesian Army remained in constant contact with the imperials. Almost no day went by in which some part of his command engaged the enemy. While the need for the numerous combats, countermarches, and night marches can be debated, it is difficult to imagine how Blücher could have otherwise fulfilled his charge at a time when information, which was not always accurate, traveled only as fast as a horse could gallop. He often had to overcome the passive resistance, preconceived opinions, jealousies, and biases of his corps commanders, who habitually saw only difficulties in the task at hand.

Blücher's constant pressure prevented Macdonald from rallying his army at the Bober, the Queis, or the Neiße. By driving the marshal to Bautzen, Blücher completely disrupted Napoleon's timetable and planning, costing the emperor an entire week of indecision. From 31 August to 3 September, Napoleon sat at Dresden, uncertain if he should lead the offensive against Berlin or secure Macdonald in the face of Blücher's constant pressure. Forced to stop the Army of the Bober from retreating across the Spree, Napoleon transferred his VI Infantry and I Cavalry Corps from the Bohemian front to Bautzen, to where he also proceeded with his Guard on 4 September 1813. Hoping to quickly engage Blücher and destroy his army, the emperor lunged but missed. Again proving that going backward could be just as beneficial as going forward, Blücher retreated across the Neiße to the Queis.

Not only did Blücher comply precisely with the tenets of the Trachenberg Plan but his drive against Macdonald also helped reinvigorate Schwarzenberg. On 5 September the Allied commander in chief warned Blücher that Napoleon had moved imperial headquarters from Dresden to Bautzen.[3] Here we see the effect of Napoleon's decision to create a reserve (Guard, VI Infantry Corps, and I Cavalry Corps) at Dresden to take in Macdonald's beaten army. As Blücher predicted, instead of marching on Berlin, Napoleon went to Bautzen to personally restore the situation. Although an important victory, Kulm only managed to pull the imperials out of the passes of the Erzgebirge. While Schwarzenberg deserves credit for Napoleon's return to Dresden, the damage to the emperor's strategy already had been done. Owing to Blücher's pressure, Macdonald's retreat prevented Napoleon from taking personal command of the Berlin offensive from 31 August to 3 September. Then his pursuit of the Silesian Army cost the emperor another three days and culminated with his return to Dresden rather than marching on Berlin. Thus, Napoleon squandered an entire week contending with the difficulties caused by Blücher.

At the outset of the 1814 campaign, Blücher received an even less significant role than in the previous fall operations. Although unwilling to play second fiddle, he recognized that his plan to invade the Low Countries did not correspond to the tenets of modern war. To achieve decisive victory and bring peace to Europe, either Napoleon or Paris had to be the objective of Allied operations. Either goal would require close cooperation with the Bohemian Army. As Unger admits, "Much too boldly, he now assumed the role of the lead horse in the race, without considering the weakening of his own army by the investment of the fortresses in Lorraine."[4]

During the 1814 campaign, Blücher learned important lessons about coalition warfare that shaped his attitude in 1815. With insufficient forces, he collided with Napoleon at Brienne, between the Aube and Seine Rivers, in late January. Attacked by superior numbers, Blücher's combat leadership and the bravery of his Russians averted a defeat. Schwarzenberg's refusal to move north forced Blücher to retreat to the strong position at Trannes. Instead of attacking, Napoleon opted to wait for the arrival of his VI Corps. After Tsar Alexander demanded a counterattack, Schwarzenberg made his III and IV Corps available so that Blücher to take the offensive. In the tenacious contest around La Rothière on 1 February, the Prussian achieved a victory over his great adversary, thanks in part to the arrival of the Bohemian Army's V Corps, whose commander "marched to the sound of the guns."

Allied success at La Rothière healed longstanding rifts in the Coalition over strategy. In the aftermath of this victory, all factions agreed that Paris should be the principal objective. Blücher's army would concentrate at Châlons and advance along the Marne River, while Schwarzenberg's masses assembled at Troyes and proceeded to the French capital along both banks of the Seine River. This decision allowed Napoleon to demonstrate his superior generalship. Leaving a holding force to mask the slow-moving Schwarzenberg, the emperor launched his famous Six Days Campaign. Between 9 and 15 February, he defeated the Army of Silesia in four battles at Champaubert, Montmirail, Château-Thierry, and Vauchamps.

Blücher's headquarters issued several requests for assistance to Schwarzenberg, whose army crawled forward in the direction of Paris. A simple movement by the Austrian's closest corps—VI and V—against Napoleon's rear would have relieved the pressure on Blücher. Despite learning on 5 February that the emperor disengaged from the Bohemian Army at Troyes and was pursuing Blücher, Schwarzenberg waited an entire week before dispatching General Johann Karl Diebitsch with the Russian Light Guard Cavalry Division, one grenadier brigade, and six guns in the direction of Montmirail. On the fourteenth Diebitsch helplessly watched Blücher's defeat from the southern bank of the Petit Morin. Casualties during the Six Days amounted to 18,000 Allied soldiers to only 3,400 French. Of the 56,000 men who formed the Silesian Army on 8 February, barely 40,000 men returned to Châlons.

On 16 February the head of Schwarzenberg's overextended army came within seventy-five miles of Paris, causing Napoleon to disengage from Blücher and turn against the Bohemian Army. French forces surprised Schwarzenberg's forward troops, taking the Seine crossing at Montereau on the next day. In response, Schwarzenberg planned to concentrate his troops south of Troyes on the twenty-first and deliver battle. But at the last moment, he changed his mind, preferring to retreat and negotiate an armistice. Vowing to disobey any order to fall back, Blücher proposed another separation of the Allied armies, planning to resume the offensive by advancing as fast as possible on Paris. Schwarzenberg agreed in the hope that Napoleon would disengage from the Bohemian Army. Not only did Blücher receive approval, but the monarchs officially transferred to his command Wintzingerode's Russian corps and Bülow's Prussian corps.

During the night of 23–24 February, the Silesian Army crossed the Aube. Four days later, on the evening of the twenty-eighth, the Prussians learned that Napoleon was approaching through Sézanne much faster than Blücher expected. Fortunately for Blücher, Bülow and Wintzingerode negotiated the capitulation of Soissons on 3 March. The bulk of the Silesian Army escaped Napoleon's onslaught by crossing the Aisne at Soissons. Although Blücher now commanded six army corps—more troops than ever before in his career—a change occurred. A general feeling prevailed in his headquarters that the Silesian Army had done enough and it was time for Schwarzenberg's Army of Bohemia to bear the burden of waging war. Consequently, the strangest situation unfolded: Marshal

Vorwärts did not go forward. Instead, he positioned the Silesian Army behind the Aisne and waited for Napoleon to make the next move. Blücher engaged the French at Craonne on 7 March, but his decision to send half of the army to the defensive position at Laon strongly suggests that he was not seeking a decisive battle. After his defensive victory there on 10 March, Marshal Vorwärts still did not go forward. Only after receiving news that Schwarzenberg finally ordered the Bohemian Army to advance on Paris did the Silesian Army go forward on 25 March; six days later Paris fell to the Coalition.

According to the traditional interpretation, we see a more familiar Blücher in the 1814 campaign. Indeed, it appears that the "General Backward" of the 1813 fall campaign gave way to Marshal Forward, furiously driving his troops to Paris with reckless abandon. Contemporaries viewed it as such. On 29 January 1814 Schwarzenberg informed his wife that "Blücher and even more so Gneisenau . . . drive toward Paris with such a truly childish rage that they trample underfoot all the rules of war."[5] Following the victory at La Rothière, a powerful pursuit of Napoleon's army would have ended French resistance. After Schwarzenberg balked at the idea, Blücher conducted his first offensive against Paris, which ended with the near destruction of the Silesian Army.

A balanced assessment of Allied operations during the first two weeks of February allows us to determine the causes of Blücher's disaster during the Six Days Campaign. To begin, the plan agreed upon at the château of Brienne on 2 February called for the Silesian Army to advance along the Marne to Paris while the Bohemian Army followed the course of the Seine to the French capital. Schwarzenberg's inexcusable retreat to Bar-sur-Seine in the face of a suspected French offensive needlessly exhausted his troops and wasted precious time. In this sense Schwarzenberg never allowed himself to break free of the constraints of eighteenth-century warfare. Instead, he brooded over the fate of his eastward lines of supply and communication. Such concerns separated the generals of the Frederician school of warfare from those of the modern. Schwarzenberg should have recognized the opportunity presented by such an enemy offensive.[6] If Napoleon drove to the Rhine, he would expose Paris and separate his own army from its resources. During the fall campaign, when considering the operations Schwarzenberg could undertake, the master hypothetically wished the Austrian bon voyage should the Bohemian Army make for the Rhine and attempt to strand the Grande Armée in Saxony. Blücher also sacrificed his communications with Silesia after he commenced his march down the Elbe in late September.

Napoleon immediately exploited Schwarzenberg's timidity by escaping Troyes and marching to Nogent-sur-Seine, unnoticed and unmolested. Although occupying Troyes on 7 February, the Austrian allowed his army to rest until the tenth. No longer threatened by Schwarzenberg's masses, Napoleon seized the initiative, launching the Six Days Campaign. Meanwhile, instead of following the course of the Seine northwest toward Paris in accordance with the agreement of 2 February, the Allied commander in chief devised a new plan. Knowing the French emperor had gone to Nogent, he envisioned a grandiose envelopment of Napoleon's right. "The approach march to Paris," explains General Janson of the German General Staff, "was thought to be concentric, instead it became eccentric, mainly because the Bohemian Army always slid to the left [west] and therefore lagged behind, although it had the shorter road on which to advance." To cover their own right, Schwarzenberg and Tsar Alexander penned their 7 February requests for Blücher to move General Kleist closer to Wittgenstein. Janson asserts that this request "was responsible for the ruin of the Silesian Army."[7]

On 10 February Vlasov's Cossacks reported that Napoleon led considerable forces north through Villenauxe to Sézanne, apparently to attack the Silesian Army. Before taking direct action, Schwarzenberg waited for confirmation. The next day he shifted his main body forty miles farther west from Troyes to Sens on the Yonne River. Apparently, Schwarzenberg never considered that Napoleon would attack the Allied army that he found actually marching on Paris, nor did he think Napoleon would seek a battle with the smaller of the two Allied armies. On 11 February the Austrian field marshal received confirmation that the emperor had launched an offensive against Blücher two days earlier. That same day Wittgenstein's VI Corps participated in the attack on Victor at Nogent-sur-Seine in conjunction with Wrede's V Corps. To relieve the pressure on Blücher, the Austrian commander ordered V and VI Corps to cross the Seine on the twelfth and assailed the French at Provins and Donnemarie-Dontilly. This relief came too late for the Silesian Army.[8] As General Unger notes, "halfway to Paris, Napoleon fell on it like a beast of prey and ripped it apart," reducing it by 14,000 men and forty-seven guns.[9]

After Schwarzenberg reopened the gap between the two armies, the left flank of the Silesian Army became increasingly exposed. Lacking cavalry, Blücher could not conduct reconnaissance in the actual direction of the danger. At Sézanne, Karpov's Cossacks quit their post too early and failed to report directly to the field marshal. This allowed the Poles to launch the failed night assault on Baye. Although concerned enough to move his headquarters seven miles east from Étoges to Vertus, the affair at Baye did not induce Blücher to summon Yorck and Sacken from their pursuit of Macdonald. Without eyes and ears, the Prussian should have postponed the pursuit of the marshal and concentrated his army.

If the request for Blücher to move Kleist closer to Wittgenstein "was responsible for the ruin of the Silesian Army," then Blücher shares the guilt for complying. In September 1813 he refused the Allied commander in chief and evaded the tsar; he should have done so again. Admittedly, providing flank coverage with a small army corps in February 1814 did not appear as bizarre as marching the army to Bohemia in September 1813, yet Blücher should have followed through with his plan to concentrate. In addition, ordering Kaptsevich and Olsufiev to follow Kleist made little sense, especially considering the inability to conduct reconnaissance when a degree of uncertainty existed. Instead of uniting the two Russian infantry corps with Yorck and Sacken, Blücher decided to move them south with Kleist to support the Bohemian Army. Blücher and his staff should have done all they could to unite the army as quickly as possible. Yet he froze on the eleventh and twelfth, becoming cautious at the wrong time. Even if Blücher marched west sooner than the fourteenth, Yorck's disobedience would have prevented the complete concentration of the army. Had that general obeyed, he could have united with Sacken on the eleventh. Together, the two would have possessed numbers superior to the French. The situation could have been very different if Napoleon found himself sandwiched on the Little Paris Highway between Yorck and Sacken, coming from the west, and Blücher with Kleist and Kaptsevich, advancing from the east.

Napoleon deserves much praise for the boldness of the Six Days Campaign. In terms of operations, he was again the general of 1796; his tired conscripts—many of them teenagers—fought like lions. By parading the prisoners and standards taken from the Silesian Army through the streets of Paris, he regained the political clout he lost at La Rothière. Confident that "the Silesian Army exists no more," as he boasted to Joseph, the master left Marmont's corps to monitor Blücher and turned to contend with Schwarzenberg, whose army closed on Paris.[10] Napoleon's failure to finish off Blücher and totally destroy the Silesian Army ranks as one of his greatest mistakes in 1814. With the end of that force, nothing would have stopped Schwarzenberg from conducting a general retreat across the Rhine. In turn, this would have allowed Napoleon to stabilize the situation in the Low Countries as well as Italy. Depending on how long the Allies sat idle in Germany, he may even have received the opportunity to chase Wellington across the Pyrenees. Thus, apologists for Blücher found a silver lining to the Six Days Campaign. According to his loyal Nostitz: "For Napoleon, the powerful exploitation of the advantages achieved at the expense of Field Marshal Blücher was perhaps the last favorable opportunity for him to avoid the fate that menacingly hung over his head. A total exploitation of the achieved advantages would have forced the Allies to compliantly submit to his demands." Yet he also maintains that without this campaign, which displayed Napoleon's "talents as a field commander to the highest degree by defeating five enemy corps in sequence, he probably would have accepted the peace offered to him at Châtillon." In either case, Napoleon would have remained on the French throne.[11]

Conversely, it is easy to criticize Blücher and pontificate the moves he should have made, yet the Six Days Campaign represents the first egregious mistake committed by him and his staff. The Prussian's zeal to destroy Macdonald—not march on Paris—clouded his judgment. After the Poles attempted the sneak attack at Braye, he should have concentrated the army until the situation to the south could be clarified. Gneisenau later lamented that he should have tried harder to convince Blücher to retreat across the Marne. Regardless of Blücher's culpability, Schwarzenberg's change of plans provided Napoleon this golden opportunity. That the Austrian did not take advantage of the opportunity provided by Blücher's drubbing irked the Prussian. His 16 February letter to Hardenberg reveals his thoughts: "My three corps of Yorck, Sacken, and Kleist all fought with Napoleon variously. Many men fell, but I have achieved my purpose and held the enemy here with his entire force for five days. That the Bohemian Army did not use this time when it faced no significant French forces is deplorable. The hour has come, a main battle must be delivered as soon as possible; we stand still and hesitate, we stir up everything and drive the people to desperation, and all rise against us in mass. A successful outcome cannot be doubted, but the good moment must not be squandered."[12]

Following the Six Days, Blücher's army marched after just two days of rest at Châlons, testament to Blücher's leadership, people skills, and ability to hold his army together. On 21 February the Silesian Army moved into position at Méry-sur-Seine next to Schwarzenberg's army and ready for combat. To avoid being part of the Austrian's retrograde movement, Blücher again separated from him. Again the Silesian Army rushed to the Marne, intent on reaching Paris. Yet the cautious and unorthodox Blücher of 1813 returned. Again he thwarted Napoleon's plans by sacrificing his line of communication through Fismes and Reims to Châlons. Regardless, the peril remained so great that he came within twelve hours of seeing his army again savagely beaten by the French at the Aisne. With a double superiority in manpower, Blücher continued to run. Three days after the fall of Soissons allowed the Silesian Army to safely escape north across the Aisne, his attempt to have the Russians bloody Napoleon's nose at Craonne on 7 March misfired completely. Only on the rock of Laon did Blücher feel comfortable accepting a *defensive* battle.[13] Rather than take the initiative, Marshal Vörwarts remained content with deflecting the emperor's blows on 9 and 10 March. Although possessing the numbers to inflict the same type of destruction on Napoleon that befell Marmont, Blücher cautiously refrained.

Throughout the 1814 campaign, Blücher struggled not so much with Napoleon, but with the effects of the Coalition's growing politicization. Not only diplomatic maneuvering between the coalition partners but also ongoing negotiations with the French subordinated Allied strategy to goals of national self-interest to a far greater degree than during the 1813 campaign. For example, on 24 February Schwarzenberg informed Blücher of a "compromise" he reached with Napoleon's chief of staff, Marshal Alexandre Berthier, to negotiate an armistice.[14] At this time over 180,000 Allied soldiers stood on an eighteen-mile stretch of the Seine between Méry-sur-Seine and Troyes facing Napoleon's 70,000 troops. Blücher just received permission from Tsar Alexander on behalf of King Frederick William and Kaiser Francis to conduct an offensive against Napoleon's left wing and communications.[15] Believing that the old Prussian threatened the chances of an armistice,

Schwarzenberg secured the tsar's support for a general retreat. For his part, Alexander consented because he did not want Blücher to reach Paris before him. Consequently, he pressured Frederick William, who directly ordered his field marshal to renounce his planned offensive and march east instead of west toward Paris.[16] On the same day, 24 February, Schwarzenberg informed Blücher that Napoleon rejected the proposed armistice, yet the retreat would continue.[17] The very next day the Allied commander in chief authorized the Prussian to commence his offensive, while the Bohemian Army continued its retrograde movement in response to "enemy forces that are gathering in southern France."[18] This made little difference as the Army of Silesia commenced its march on the twenty-fourth. Against this confusing backdrop, Schwarzenberg's caution, Blücher's boldness, and Napoleon's desperation extended the war many months longer than the imbalance of resources between the opposing sides should have allowed in modern "Napoleonic" warfare.

Although Blücher made critical operational mistakes in 1814, these must be attributed to the fact that he and Schwarzenberg remained miles apart operationally and strategically. Like Napoleon, Blücher placed all emphasis on achieving a decisive victory as quickly as possible and at any cost. Just as important, particularly for the 1815 campaign, he firmly believed in the necessity of cooperation to achieve the decisive victory. In 1814 he believed that the same cooperation between the Bohemian and Silesian Armies that produced Leipzig would again lead to decisive results in France. On the contrary, arguments in favor of the rapid conclusion of the war through either a bold offensive against Paris or a decisive battle with Napoleon's army had little effect on Schwarzenberg and the Austrians, who had neither political nor moral grounds to topple Napoleon. Austrian chief of staff Josef Wenzel Radetzky von Radetz, by far the best military mind in Schwarzenberg's headquarters, allowed his concerns over the internal state of the Austrian army to master his planning. Other influential personalities in Schwarzenberg's headquarters included his quartermaster general, the Saxon Karl Friedrich von Langenau, and the kaiser's childhood friend, Peter Duka von Kadar, who now served as the monarch's principal military advisor. Langenau has been described as "a man who was just as erudite as he was an impractical adherent of the old school, for which the experience of the Napoleonic Wars were ignored, and which looked at a battle as only a crude, dire expedient, unworthy of any educated field commander." Duka insisted on taking winter quarters on the right bank of the Rhine in order to begin a methodical invasion by besieging the enemy's frontier fortresses in 1814.[19] In terms of strength and proficiency, the Bohemian Army did little during this campaign.

Schwarzenberg himself viewed an advance on Paris as imprudent both militarily and politically. In his opinion, taking Paris would not necessarily end the war and could prove to be just as much a disaster for the Allies as Moscow had been for Napoleon. "Will we find peace there," he wrote his wife, "or will we plunge into further chaos? I believe the latter."[20] An advance on the capital could prompt Napoleon to sever Allied communications with Germany, an operation that would be facilitated by the numerous fortresses the French still held in the Allied rear such as Strasbourg, Metz, and Verdun. Should the emperor execute his famous *manoeuvre sur les derrière,* he could cut Allied supply lines in the middle of winter. To avoid such a setback, Schwarzenberg rejected Paris as the goal of an Allied offensive. Instead, he hoped to end the war through negotiation; if a further advance had to be made, it should be executed slowly and concentrically in unison with Wellington's army and the Armies of Italy and North Germany in order to close any gap that Napoleon could exploit to threaten their communications.[21] Rather than pin the French army and wage a decisive battle, the Austrians purposely paced the progress of the invasion to provide time to negotiate a peace that would keep France strong enough to serve Austria's needs in postwar Europe.[22]

Thus, the question: did the prudent General Backward submit to Marshal Vorwärts in 1814 and if so, why? Careful assessment suggests that sound reasoning based on Napoleonic (or what contemporaries called "modern") warfare instead of revenge and hatred guided Blücher's actions during the 1814 campaign. The ease of the Silesian Army's advance brought Blücher across the Marne River within three weeks of crossing the Rhine. As French resistance crumbled, he and Gneisenau sought to end the war by destroying Napoleon or marching on Paris. While a human desire for revenge cannot be discounted, they, like Napoleon, believed in seeking and achieving a decisive victory. Although both the Silesian and Bohemian Armies suffered incredible attrition from casualties, sickness, and strategic consumption, the Allies possessed a tremendous numerical advantage over Napoleon. Outnumbering the emperor four-to-one, the Allies would risk little if they sought a decisive engagement on French territory. Conversely, in a state as centralized as France, the fall of the national capital would paralyze the hinterlands—severe the head and the body will die. Thus, by suggesting a decisive battle with Napoleon, the Prussians offered a solution to ending the struggle based on "modern warfare." If that did not appeal to Allied headquarters, they provided an alternative that hearkened back to eighteenth-century warfare: the capture of a major geographic objective.

Where Blücher and Gneisenau did error was in their belief that Alexander would induce Schwarzenberg to operate according to such principles. Unfortunately for the tens of thousands who suffered and died during the 1814 campaign, the Austrians did not desire Napoleon's decisive defeat. In fact, Metternich preferred a strong Napoleonic France to counter Russia's increasing ambitions. He hoped to negotiate a peace settlement that would leave Napoleon on the French throne but not in control of an empire that included central Europe. With Metternich advising his every move, Schwarzenberg attempted to make clear to the Prussians that an advance on Paris remained inadvisable both militarily and politically. Austrian politics required Schwarzenberg to employ eighteenth-century principles to outmaneuver Napoleon and inflict a minor defeat on him, which in turn would convince him to end the conflict at the peace table by accepting Metternich's terms. Whether willing or not, Metternich forced Schwarzenberg to consider the consequences of any military operation on Austrian politics.

Blücher's own sense of honor as well as an unwarranted, blind faith in Schwarzenberg being a man of his word likewise cost the Army of Silesia dearly. In 1814 the Prussian held the Austrian in regard, just as he would Wellington in 1815. Throughout the fall campaign, Blücher did as much as possible to facilitate the operations of the Army of Bohemia. Granted, he refused the absurd orders to send part and then all of his army to Bohemia. Nevertheless, he viewed Schwarzenberg as a comrade who could be trusted. That in 1814 the Allied generalissimo would not keep his word and would place politics before military necessity never crossed his mind.

The significance of Blücher's second offensive against Paris cannot be underestimated. Accepting full responsibility for carrying the Allied war effort, he recognized the demands of the moment and wasted no time implementing a plan to restore the momentum of the campaign. On par in significance with the service he provided the Coalition by marching down the Elbe in late September 1813, his second offensive in 1814 prevented Schwarzenberg from further retreating by removing Napoleon's pressure on the Bohemian Army. Blücher and Gneisenau fully expected Napoleon to pursue the Silesian Army. Indeed, the emperor learned of Blücher's departure from the banks of the Seine during the course of the twenty-fifth but could not foresee its considerable implications. As Blücher predicted, Napoleon gave chase. Similar to October 1813, the master expected the Prussian to retreat along his line of communication. Instead of withdrawing eastward along the Marne and into the teeth of the French army, Blücher moved north across the Aisne, sacrificing his communications just as he in had in October 1813 by crossing the Saale. Even after Blücher's flight to Laon, Napoleon still had a chance to derail the Coalition. Had he defeated the Army of Silesia at Laon, it would have been forced to withdraw into Belgium. This may well have prompted Schwarzenberg to evacuate France as well. Instead, news of Blücher's victory at Laon encouraged the Austrian field marshal to resume the offensive.[23]

Sufficient documentary evidence exists to suggest that Blücher and Gneisenau did much to influence Alexander's decision to force the final drive on Paris.[24] "In the idea to go to Paris," notes Charles Stewart, "the Tsar was all the more reinforced by the reports and advice pushed upon him by Marshal Blücher and General Gneisenau."[25] "After I decisively defeated Napoleon at Laon," wrote Blücher, "I insisted against the opinion of the entourage of the monarchs that both armies should march directly on Paris; all of my adversaries maintained that Napoleon would march in our rear and set himself in communication with his fortresses and thus march against Mainz and Frankfurt. I insisted that we should take Paris and let Napoleon march wherever he wanted; nothing else would matter if we captured the capital. Tsar Alexander took my side and we marched on the great city."[26] In a letter to Clausewitz from Paris dated 28 April 1814, Gneisenau explained that "earlier, on 27 January, I advised Tsar Alexander that should he note tepidity in the advance [of the Bohemian Army], he should come to us, the Silesian Army, with his Russians and the Prussian Guard to advance on Paris in unison." More than once, and most notably during a council of war at Bar-sur-Aube on 25 February, the tsar threatened to accept Gneisenau's invitation. "One cried foul," continued Gneisenau.

"Now, he again made this suggestion and of course for the entire Bohemian Army. One knew nothing better to say. The diplomats had been cut off and sent back to Dijon. Schwarzenberg agreed and the march to Paris was decided."[27]

During the 1815 campaign, Napoleon smashed Blücher's army at Ligny, but two days later the old Prussian brought it to Waterloo. During the two-day interim, Blücher again evaded Napoleon and his subordinates by doing the bold and unorthodox: sacrificing his line of communication. Rather than retreat eastward to the Rhine along his line of communication, Blücher marched his army north to Wavre, ten miles east of Wellington's army.

This brings us to the two questions that the 1815 campaign raises: first, why did Blücher fight at Ligny on 16 June, and second, why did he support Wellington on the eighteenth? Turning to the first question, in the first decade of the twentieth century, Rudolf Friederich, a major assigned to Germany's Großen Generalstab and an instructor at Berlin's prestigious Kriegsakademie, attempted to identify the keys to Blücher's generalship when he published his contribution to the General Staff's massive nine-volume study of the 1813–15 wars against Napoleon titled *Geschichte der Befreiungskriege*. Friederich wrote the three volumes concerning the fall campaign of 1813, titled *Geschichte des Herbstfeldzuges 1813*. Aside from crafting a brilliant operational study of the campaign, the major provides erudite analysis, for the purpose of the overall work was to furnish German officers with an excellent learning tool. In his first volume, Friederich claims that Blücher established a "Prussian way of war" that was to be studied and emulated by German officers a century later. The key to this way of war was Blücher's concept of victory. Like Napoleon, he placed tremendous emphasis on the decisive battle and achieving a decisive victory as quickly as possible at any cost. Also like Napoleon, he measured victory and defeat only in terms of battlefield results. Deviating very little from the Corsican's art of war, the objective of Blücher's Prussian way of war was to make contact with the enemy as quickly as possible, concentrate all forces, deliver the decisive blow, and end the war. Thus, Blücher welcomed the opportunity for a decisive battle at Ligny. The chance that Wellington might arrive made the prospects all the better.

Regarding the second question, the answer is quite simple. First and foremost, Blücher had tremendous respect for the Duke of Wellington. Based on Wellington's record in Spain, Blücher believed that he had found a kindred spirit. Unlike Bernadotte or Schwarzenberg, in the Prussian's mind the duke was a man of his word who understood the concept of the decisive battle. Wellington's offer to support Blücher at Ligny provided an opportunity for a decisive battle, which was good enough for the Prussian despite his staff's suspicions. Conversely, Wellington based his decision to fight at Waterloo on Blücher's promise of support. Knowing that the duke's stand offered an opportunity to inflict a decisive defeat on Napoleon, Blücher brought the majority of his army to Waterloo. Consequently, his stand at Ligny and his march to Waterloo do not represent the rash, irrational actions of Marshal Forward, but instead were decisions based on experience and reality.

In the fall campaign of 1813, Blücher retreated before Napoleon on four occasions when his army was unsupported by other Coalition forces. Just as important, he understood that running from Napoleon would not bring about a decisive confrontation. Knowing that only through cooperation and mutual support could the Allies challenge the emperor, Blücher sought to forge these conditions.[28] Thus, he and his staff created the conditions that made the Kesselschlacht at Leipzig possible. In the 1814 campaign, he mistakenly thought the cooperation and mutual support between him and Schwarzenberg would continue. It did not, and neither a decisive battle nor the capture of Paris ended the war in January or February. Instead, the campaign dragged on, several bloody engagements occurred, and tens of thousands of men lost their lives in March and April. The lessons of 1813 and 1814 taught Blücher not to wait on others to create the conditions for a decisive battle. Likewise, he learned not to depend on complicated plans to establish these conditions. Thus, in 1815, with the two Allied armies so close together and cooperating with a general of Wellington's caliber, Blücher had no choice based on his experiences but to stand at Ligny and march to Waterloo. Although the French government continued the war for another month, the decisive battle at Waterloo did indeed end the war for Napoleon and his army.

Legacy

The fiery Blücher captured the imagination of not only the Prussians but also many other Germans, emerging as a true German hero in a century that inaugurated nationalism and romanticism. Poems and songs celebrated his feats. A German idiom that remained popular well into the twentieth century, *"ran wie Blücher"* ("charge like Blücher"), denoted very direct and aggressive action in war or otherwise. At Rostock on 26 August 1819, artist Johann Gottfried Schadow unveiled a monument to Blücher that he crafted in collaboration with Johann Wolfgang von Goethe.[29] On Blücher's death, the foremost German sculptor of the nineteenth-century, Christian Daniel Rauch, erected a statue of him at Breslau. In the 1820s Rauch also built a magnificent thirteen-foot-tall bronze statue of Blücher, which today stands on the historical Unter den Linden thoroughfare in Berlin. A fourth statue was erected in his memory at Kaub, the site where the field marshal crossed the Rhine on New Year's Day 1814, and remains there today. In the early 1820s Frederick William III commissioned a huge granite mausoleum to be built at the entrance to Krieblowitz. Unfortunately, the massive granite block required for the construction could not be transported to the village. Even after the engineers cut the block in half, it could not be moved from the quarry at Striegau (Strzegom) and lay in the adjacent field for twenty years. Finally, after King Frederick William IV arranged a meeting with Nostitz and Rauch to reconvene the project, construction began in 1846, and the magnificent structure was completed in 1853.

George Stephenson, a British engine wright at Killingworth Colliery, designed and named a prototype locomotive after Blücher in 1814. The Blücher, which could pull a train of thirty tons at a speed of four miles per hour up a gradient of 1 in 450, established Stephenson's reputation as an engine designer and launched his pivotal career as a railway developer. Later in the nineteenth century, a trick-taking card game called Napoleon, or Nap, that is related to euchre became popular in Great Britain. In the game a "Blücher" is a bid to win all five tricks. In addition to the locomotive and card game, a "Blucher" is a style of shoe similar to a derby, having a vamp made of a single piece of leather, or "one cut." Purportedly, the shoe derived its name after the field marshal commissioned a boot with side pieces lapped over the front in an effort to provide his troops with improved footwear. This design was adopted by armies across Europe.[30]

Three warships of the German navy have sailed under the name of Blücher. The first, a corvette built at Kiel, launched on 20

March 1877. Taken out of service after a boiler explosion in 1907, SMS *Blücher* ended her days as a coal freighter in Vigo, Spain. On 1 October 1908 the Imperial Navy christened its last armored cruiser, the SMS *Blücher*, at Kiel. During the First World War's 24 January 1915 battle of Dogger Bank, the *Blücher* took heavy fire from superior-armed British battlecruisers. Rear Admiral Franz von Hipper decided to sacrifice the *Blücher* to make good the escape of the rest of his squadron. Between 700 and 1,000 German seamen went down with the ship. Completed in September 1939 shortly after the outbreak of the Second World War, the German cruiser *Blücher* was the second of five *Admiral Hipper*–class heavy cruisers built after the Nazi government repudiated the limitations of the 1919 Treaty of Versailles. During the 1940 invasion of Norway, the *Blücher* led a flotilla of warships into the Oslofjord on the night of 8 April to seize Oslo, commencing the Battle of Drøbak Sound. Two eleven-inch coastal guns in the Oscarsborg Fortress engaged the ship at very close range, scoring two hits. Two torpedoes fired from a land-based battery struck the vessel, causing serious damage. After a magazine explosion, the ship slowly capsized and sank at 7:30 on the morning of the ninth with major loss of life. The wreck remains on the bottom of the Oslofjord.[31] A song, "Blücher," on the 2007 album *Ghost Opera* by the heavy-metal band Kamelot is dedicated to the story of the *Blücher* and her ill-fated mission. Later in the war the name was again used, this time to designate a wolfpack of eight German U-boats that operated from 13 July to 1 August 1942 during the Battle of the Atlantic. The Blücher wolfpack attacked the Freetown, Sierra Leone–Liverpool convoys SL-118 and SL-119, sinking six ships for a total of 41,984 gross register tons.

The Nazis and the Second World War also directly affected Blücher, or at least his remains. In 1937 the Nazis changed the name of Krieblowitz to Blüchersruh ("Blücher's resting place"), in part to honor the Prussian field marshal and in part because they thought Krieblowitz sounded too Slavic. In 1945 the rampaging soldiers of the Soviet Red Army overran Blüchersruhe and ransacked the schloß; Blücher's descendants fled for their lives. Not knowing the history of the field marshal or how much he loved his Russian soldiers, the Soviets viewed the mausoleum as just another German monument. They broke into the structure, desecrated the grave, and scattered Blücher's remains, reportedly using his skull as a soccer ball. After the war, the Poles took control of Silesia (as well as the rest of Prussia east of the Oder). Having no love for the Germans, the Poles did little to preserve or honor Blücher's memory. Sometime after the fall of communism in 1989, a Polish priest buried the bones that remained in the open grave in the catacomb of the church in Sośnica (Schosnitz), less than two miles from Krobielowice. Blücher's skull was never found. As of today, the mausoleum remains an empty, crumbling shell, but the schloß has been renovated and is used as a resort.

Just as interesting is the legacy that the German General Staff claimed for Blücher in the nineteenth and early twentieth centuries. In his 1900 work *Aufklärung und Armeeführung: Dargestellt an den Ereignissen bei der Schlesischen Armee im Herbst 1813,* the future deputy chief of the German General Staff during the First World War, Baron Hugo Friedrich Philipp Johann von Freytag-Loringhoven, wrote of the Army of Silesia in 1813: "By closer consideration, we become aware of how throughout the war its leaders many times conformed to principles that today are generally recognized, but which in the years of peace after 1815 fell into oblivion and only in the new era of warfare have again acquired prestige. It is the gradual development of a new way of war that we encounter by the Silesian Army in the fall campaign of 1813, a way of war that essentially helped lead to Napoleon's fall because it assimilated his own principles and still understood to expand on them."[32] According to Rob Citino, later generations of German staff officers found in the 1813 campaign an operational breakthrough that provided the conceptual link between the wars of Frederick the Great, Napoleon's principles of war, and the decisive Prussian campaigns of Helmuth von Moltke against the Austrians in 1866 and the French in 1870.[33] The concentric operations of separated bodies of the army stood at the heart of this new way of war.

While the German General Staff believed that the campaigns of the Silesian Army closed the intellectual gaps in their study of the evolution of the operational art of war, they also placed great emphasis on the unintellectual aspects of Blücher's leadership: aggression, hatred of the enemy, determination, strength of will, and ceaseless activity. The comment in his journal of the Rhineland campaigns concerning less thinking and more fighting became a revered doctrine in the German army. If remembered, his retreats were explained away as temporary inconveniences; the hard-charging, aggressive nature of Marshal Vorwärts received much more emphasis. Long after the historiographical debates over the evolution of operations ended, German military writers still focused on Blücher's style of leadership. "From Frederick the Great down to 1945," continues Citino, "the German officer who acted aggressively would be confident that he was acting in the best traditions of the service, and he could also be reasonably certain that the commander of the neighboring formation thought the same way. To sit and wait for the opponent's move was to be . . . Prince Hohenlohe at Jena."[34] In 1942 Dr. Eberhard Kessel published an article about the Prussian field marshal in the Wehrmacht's official journal, the *Militärwissenschaftliche Rundschau,* to celebrate Blücher's 200th birthday. With the Wehrmacht fighting for its life deep in Russia, the good professor reminded its commanders that the famed Prussian field marshal never bothered to ask "how strong is the enemy," but instead preferred the more direction question, "where is the enemy?"[35]

After the Second World War, the communist East Germans did as much as possible to tear down the few remaining symbols of old Prussia, yet the memory of Blücher officially survived and continued in the Soviet-dominated German Democratic Republic. Celebrated for having thrown off the yoke of Napoleon's western imperialism, the field marshal's name was given to the Blücher-Orden (Blücher Order) of the Nationale Volksarmee (National People's Army), or NVA. Established in 1965, the decoration was to be awarded for valor in time of war. Although the GDR minted a few hundred, not one of the six classes (bronze, silver, and gold medals; bronze, silver, and gold crosses) of the Blücher Order was ever awarded simply because the NVA never went to war. Because the army prohibited its military personnel from wearing Wehrmacht awards and decorations, the Iron Cross—by no means a Nazi invention—was replaced by an Occitan-like white cross, with a portrait of Blücher surrounded by a wreath of oak leaves in its center. Both portrait and oak leaves are colored according to the class of the decoration. The bronze cross is attached to a red ribbon with two yellow stripes on its edges, the silver class has a silver strip running along the center, while the gold class has a gold strip. Less pleasing to the eye is the medal, which is round and features a depiction of the front of the cross on it. Its ribbon is yellow with one blue stripe running down its center for the bronze class, two for the silver, and three for the gold. Incidentally, the Scharnhorst-Orden (Scharnhorst Order), established in 1966, was the highest decoration awarded by the NVA. The GDR viewed the progressive, reform-minded Scharnhorst as the theoretical father of the NVA. West Germany had no such awards, although the federal government did introduce new military decorations during the Cold War. German reunification led to the dissolution of the NVA and with it the Blücher Order. Although the modern Bundeswehr (Federal Defense Force) likewise bases its traditions in part on the Prussian reform movement led by Scharnhorst, not one of its awards is personified in honor of a hero of the Prusso-German military tradition.

Notes

Abbreviations

Add. Ms   British Manuscript Collection, London

BB   Gebhard Leberecht Blücher, 1st Prince of Wahlstatt, *Blüchers Briefe: Vervollständigte Sammlung des Generals E. v. Colomb*, ed. Wolfgang von Unger (Stuttgart, 1912).

BFA   Ehemals Mitteilungen aus dem Gräflichen Bülow Familien-Archiv zu Grünhoff, Baden-Baden, Ger.

CN   Napoléon I, emperor of the French, *La Correspondance de Napoléon Ier; publiée par ordre de l'empereur Napoléon III*, 32 vols. (Paris, 1858–69).

GStA PK   Geheimes Staatsarchiv Preußischer Kulturbesitz zu Berlin

ÖStA   Österreichisches Staatsarchiv, Kriegsarchiv, Vienna

RGVIA   Rossiiskii Gosudarstvennyi Voenno-Istoricheskii, Moscow

SHAT   Service Historique de l'Armée de Terre, Paris

Preface

1. Langeron, *Mémoires*, 208. The three assistants Langeron mentions are August von Gneisenau, Friedrich Karl von Müffling, and August Friedrich von der Goltz.

2. Friederich, *Herbstfeldzug 1813*, 1:227.

3. Langeron continues: "Blücher, Gneisenau, Muffling, etc., viewed my assignment to their army with a marked and unique repugnance because I was French; they did not know me personally, and some knowledge of my successes against the Turks could have weakened their prejudices against me; but I was French, and their hatred, their rage (if it is permissible to express oneself thus) against those who had so humiliated them on the battlefield and in the cabinets of the capitals, was such that it was impossible for them to make a single exception among the French nation. I had, moreover, a great fault amongst these men: I did not know a single word of German, which was a great inconvenience when serving with a Prussian army. Almost all of the Prussian officers spoke French, but General Blücher did not even understand it." *Mémoires*, 211.

4. Müffling, *Passages from My Life*, 296–97.

5. Nostitz, *Tagebuch*, 1:138.

6. Langeron, *Mémoires*, 210–11.

7. Friederich, *Herbstfeldzug 1813*, 1:229. Again, Blücher's correspondence, especially regarding how his operations would affect those of the other Allied armies, strongly suggests that he understood "strategic combinations."

8. Unger, *Blücher*, 2:246.

9. Friederich, *Herbstfeldzug 1813*, 1:226.

10. Otto Bleck's 1939 *Marschall Blücher* adds a little to Blücher's personal history.

11. Karl August Varnhagen von Ense's *Leben des Fürsten Blücher von Wahlstatt* (1826) attempts to follow both strains but, without the benefit of archival research, contains some flaws. Wilhelm Burckhardt's 1835 work, *Gebhard Leberecht von Blücher*, likewise attempts to include both, but at 127 pages the book is merely a survey. The same can be said of Carl Ludwig Bieske's 51-page *Der Feldmarschall Fürst Gebhard Leberecht Blücher*, but it does contain some interesting details and can be considered authoritative because Bieske was Blücher's doctor.

12. E. F. Henderson's *Blücher and the Uprising of Prussia against Napoleon, 1806–1815* (1911) cannot be considered a true biography because it lacks details on Blücher's early life. Also, Gneisenau's 1815 biography, *The Life and Campaigns of Field-Marshal Prince Blücher*, must be used with caution as it borders on hagiography. The same can be said of *Memoirs of Prince Blücher* (1932), which are actually the memoirs of Blücher's great-grandson Gebhard Leberecht, 4th Prince Blücher von Wahlstatt (1865–1931), which contain a fair amount of material about his namesake. Johannes Scheer's three-volume *Blücher: Seine Zeit und sein Leben* is much more about the time in which Blücher lived as opposed to a story of his life.

Chapter One

1. The Blücher family originally possessed the small Mecklenburg estate of Groß Renzow, but Gebhard's great-grandfather Ulrich Hans von Blücher (1624–90) lost it during the Thirty Years War as a penalty for serving in the Swedish cavalry. The Blüchers continued to live in Mecklenburg, but lacking an estate meant that the males had little choice but to pursue military careers. Gebhard's grandfather Siegfried Ulrich (1655–1701) died in the Netherlands serving in Mecklenburg's cavalry. Gebhard's father, Christian, joined a Mecklenburg cavalry regiment before transferring to the army of Hesse-Kassel.

2. In 1900 the thaler corresponded to 3 marks, and the mark at that time was worth 1,500 percent more than the German mark in 1996. Thus, 200,000 thaler in 1900 was equal to 9,000,000 marks in 1996. Therefore, approximately 200 years ago, 200,000 thaler were worth around 18,000,000 marks in 1996 and 12,000,000 U.S. dollars. As of 2012, 200,000 thaler was equal to 17,560,000 U.S. dollars. Based on these calculations, 200 thaler was equal to 1,756.39 U.S. dollars.

3. Wigger, *Feldmarschall Fürst Blücher*, 2.

4. Quoted in *BB*, v.

5. Unger, *Blücher*, 1:3–4.

6. "The letter is written in my own, unreadable handwriting, please excuse this to His Majesty." Blücher to Kleist, Münster, 25 July 1806, *BB*, 65.

7. *BB*, vii.

8. Unger, *Blücher*, 1:2–4.

9. Foreign and domestic issues moved the Swedes to join the coalition bent on destroying King Frederick II of Prussia. At the end of the Great Northern

War, Sweden and Prussia concluded the Treaty of Stockholm on 21 January 1720. Accordingly, Sweden ceded the part of Swedish Pomerania south of the Peene River and east of Peenestrom River to Prussia, including the islands of Usedom and Wollin, and the fortress of Stettin (Szczecin) as well as the towns of Damm (Dębowe) and Gollnow (Goleniów). Thirty-six years later the Hats faction (their name was derived from the tricorne worn by nobles and officers) that controlled the Swedish government believed Frederick would be defeated by Austria, Russia, and France and thus sought to recapture these Pomeranian possessions. Encouragement and promises of financial support came from France. Also, an attempt by the Swedish monarchy in 1756 to wrest control of the government from the Hats made the faction detest Swedish queen Louisa Ulrika, Frederick's sister and leader of the attempted royalist revolution. They saw Frederick's downfall as means to humiliate the queen and possibly destabilize the Swedish monarchy.

10. In September 1757 Swedish field marshal Mathias Alexander von Ungern-Sternberg commanded a force of 22,000 poorly supplied and ill-equipped troops (18,000 infantry and 4,000 cavalry) joined by 6,000 Mecklenburgers. Despite lacking the necessary funds for a campaign, Ungern-Sternberg prepared to commence an offensive against Berlin. With the main Prussian army in this theater—28,000 men under Field Marshal Johann von Lehwaldt—fighting the Russians in East Prussia, King Frederick II could mobilize only 10,000 *Lantbattalions* (militia) from Pomerania and Brandenburg under the command of General Heinrich von Manteuffel in defense. The Swedes invaded Prussian-Pomerania on the night of 12–13 September by crossing the Peene River and taking Demmin, Anklam, and Wolgast on the island of Usedom. After securing all of Usedom and taking the Prussian fort at Peenemünde, the Swedes assembled at Anklam and Swinemünde (Świnoujście) to launch a six-week campaign that resulted in the taking of the Pomeranian towns of Ückermünde, Pasewalk, and Prenzlau, the last being some seventy miles north of Berlin. But Ungern-Sternberg halted his offensive rather than continue south toward the capital or east to the fortress of Stettin. After the Russians withdrew from East Prussia, Frederick ordered Lehwaldt to drive the Swedes from Pomerania. Receiving these orders on 17 October, he immediately marched to Pomerania with 25,000 men. After learning of Lehwalt's approach, Ungern-Sternberg commenced the retreat on 12 November. The Swedes took positions north of the Peene, with detachments at Anklam and Demmin on the island of Wollin and at Peenemünde. After the main force continued the retreat toward Stralsund in early December, Ungern-Sternberg's posts along the Peene fell by month's end. Lehwaldt and Manteuffel retook most of Prussian Pomerania and captured 3,000 Swedes. By the end of the year, the invaders reached Rügen, leaving a garrison at Stralsund and a small force in the entrenchments at Peenemünde. Ungern-Sternberg relinquished command on 21 December to field marshal Fredrik von Rosen. Aside from occupying eastern Mecklenburg, Lehwaldt and Manteuffel took winter quarters in Swedish Pomerania, blockading its capital of Stralsund and remaining

in this position until 18 June 1758. At that time, a second Russian invasion of East Prussia forced the Prussians, now commanded by General Christoph II von Dohna-Schlodien, to march eastward. Meanwhile, Rosen had turned over his command to General Gustav David Hamilton. Archenholz, *Seven Years War in Germany*, 69–70, 101–103; Szabo, *Seven Years War in Europe*, 86, 92, 170–71, 224–25.

11. A *Pageninstitut* (page institute) was a lower military school for the sons of German nobles. After completing studies there, they attended a *Ritterakademie* (literally translated as "knight academy" but more analogous to a military academy).

12. The Bug rises between Hiddensee and Rügen but is connected to the northern part of the latter by a sliver of land. See Bug, Germany, http://www.geonames.org/2942043/bug.html.

13. Wigger, *Feldmarschall Fürst Blücher*, 3–4.

14. Parkinson and others incorrectly state the name of this regiment as the *Mörnerska hussarregementet* (Mörner Hussar Regiment). The unit did not use this name until 1801. Parkinson, *Hussar General*, 4–5.

15. See Szabo, *Seven Years War in Europe*, 225, 294.

16. Ibid., 296.

17. Wigger, *Feldmarschall Fürst Blücher*, 5.

18. Szabo, *Seven Years War in Europe*, 296–97.

19. Wigger, *Feldmarschall Fürst Blücher*, 5–7. Wigger claims that Belling participated in the skirmish.

20. Quoted in Blücher von Wahlstatt, *Memoirs*, 7. According to Burckhardt, a trooper of the Black Hussars by the name of Pfennig, an Austrian by birth, captured Blücher with the words, "what now, boy, you're already defeated." Pfennig then brought him to Belling. This account is not seconded in the other literature.*Gebhard Leberecht von Blücher*, 12. Bieske, Blücher's doctor, claims that Landeck, a Silesian, captured the teenager. *Feldmarschall Fürst Gebhard Leberecht Blücher*, 3.

21. Wigger, *Feldmarschall Fürst Blücher*, 6–7.

22. Ibid., 7.

23. Bieske, *Feldmarschall Fürst Gebhard Leberecht Blücher*, 3–4.

24. Wigger, *Feldmarschall Fürst Blücher*, 8; Haythornthwaite, *Frederick the Great's Army*, 34.

25. Bleck, *Marschall Blücher*, 10.

26. Henderson, *Blücher and the Uprising of Prussia*, 2–3.

27. Cavalry organization in the Frederician army contained an intermediary level between squadron and regiment called a battalion, which usually consisted of two to five squadrons.

28. GStA PK, VI HA Rep. 92 Nl. Blücher von Wahlstatt; Wigger, *Feldmarschall Fürst Blücher*, 7.

29. The *Rangliste* is reproduced in Bleck, *Marschall Blücher*, 11.

30. Quoted in Wigger, *Feldmarschall Fürst Blücher*, 8.

31. Ibid., 8.

32. Szabo, *Seven Years War in Europe*, 297–99.

33. Wigger, *Feldmarschall Fürst Blücher*, 9.

34. GStA PK, VI HA Rep. 92 Nl. Blücher von Wahlstatt.

35. Bleck, *Marschall Blücher*, 12.

36. Szabo, *Seven Years War in Europe*, 362–63.

37. Wigger, *Feldmarschall Fürst Blücher*, 10.

38. Szabo, *Seven Years War in Europe*, 414.

39. See ibid., 415; and Showalter, *Wars of Frederick the Great*, 319–20.

40. Bleck, *Marschall Blücher*, 12–13.

41. Quoted in Wigger, *Feldmarschall Fürst Blücher*, 11.

42. Varnhagen von Ense, *Blücher*, 10–11; Blücher von Wahlstatt, *Memoirs*, 8–9.

43. Bleck, *Marschall Blücher*, 13.

44. Wigger, *Feldmarschall Fürst Blücher*, 11.

45. Blasendorff, *Gebhard Leberecht von Blücher*, 14; Unger, *Blücher*, 1:14, 33–65.

46. Wigger, *Feldmarschall Fürst Blücher*, 18.

47. This region controlled more than 80 percent of Poland's foreign trade.

48. Wigger, *Feldmarschall Fürst Blücher*, 12.

49. On the western edge of Pomerelia, Lande Lauenburg und Bütow consisted of two districts centered on the towns of Lauenburg (Lębork) and Bütow (Bytów).

50. "Pro Memoria," Blücher to Frederick, Groß Raddow, 13 Aug. 1782, *BB*, 5.

51. GStA PK, VI HA Rep. 92 Nl. Blücher von Wahlstatt. Wigger maintains that Blücher's promotion did not come as a result of his action at Schneidemühl but because of a vacancy in the regiment. *Feldmarschall Fürst Blücher*, 12. Blücher thought otherwise: "I did not expect a promotion just because I defeated this group, but I was very happy to receive the grace of my monarch." "Pro Memoria," Blücher to Frederick, Groß Raddow, 13 Aug. 1782, *BB*, 5.

52. Blasendorff, *Gebhard Leberecht von Blücher*, 15.

53. Wigger states that despite an agreement between the Prussians and Poles, a confederate captain authorized the attack and "murder" of the Prussians at "Lubraniza," between Posen and Warsaw. Both Wigger and the headmaster at the Royal Bismarck Gymnasium at Pyritz, Dr. Carl Blasendorff, wrote that evidence later proved Blücher's assumption about the priest to be correct. Wigger, *Feldmarschall Fürst Blücher*, 14; Blasendorff, *Gebhard Leberecht von Blücher*, 15.

54. Bleck, *Marschall Blücher*, 13.

55. Blasendorff, *Gebhard Leberecht von Blücher*, 16.

56. Unger, *Blücher*, 1:65–67.

57. Wigger, *Feldmarschall Fürst Blücher*, 14.

58. Blücher to Frederick, Gresonse at Flatow, 9 June 1778, *BB*, 3. 1772.

59. Margrave Frederick William of Brandenburg-Schwedt (1700–1771) was the eldest son of Philip William (1669–1711), who in turn was the eldest son of Elector Frederick William I ("The Great Elector," 1620–88) and his second wife, Princess Sophia Dorothea of Schleswig-Holstein-Sonderburg-Glücksburg. To secure Philip William and his younger brothers (Albert Frederick, Charles, and Christian Louis, Johann Sebastian Bach's patron), Sophia had the Great Elector vest this line of the Hohenzollern dynasty with

land and the titles of Margrave of Brandenburg. After the 18 January 1701 coronation of his elder half-brother, Elector Frederick III, as Frederick I, king in Prussia, Philip William received the title of "Prince in Prussia, Margrave of Brandenburg." Upon Philip William's death in 1711, King Frederick assumed guardianship over Philip William's eleven-year-old son, Frederick William. When Frederick I died two years later, his son, King Frederick William I, assumed guardianship over the young margrave.

60. Unfortunately, Otto Bleck's contention that much uncertainty surrounds Blücher's dismissal remains true. Early historians such as Bieske, Burckhardt, Varnhagen von Ense, and Blasendorff, whom the modern writer Crepon follows, all claim that Blücher was arrested and imprisoned for nine months for challenging the king's decision to promote Jägersfeld. Wigger, however, makes no mention of an arrest. Varnhagen von Ense published his biography of Blücher in 1826, while Wigger published his in 1878 and Blasendorff in 1887. Unger, the German General Staff historian who published his two-volume biography of Blücher in 1907 and 1908, makes no mention of an arrest. But it is conceivable that either the documentary evidence was destroyed in the nineteenth century to protect Blücher's reputation or Unger simply ignored such evidence. Writing in 1943, and thus before the destruction of the General Staff archives during World War II, Görlitz claims that the documents state only that Blücher was cashiered. Bieske, *Feldmarschall Fürst Gebhard Leberecht Blücher*, 6; Burckhardt, *Gebhard Leberecht von Blücher*, 15; Varnhagen von Ense, *Blücher*, 13; Wigger, *Feldmarschall Fürst Blücher*, 14–15; Blasendorff, *Gebhard Leberecht von Blücher*, 17; Bleck, *Marschall Blücher*, 14; Görlitz, *Fürst Blücher*, 28–29; Unger, *Blücher*, 1:67–68; and Crepon, *Gebhard Leberecht von Blücher*, 64–65.

61. Unger, *Blücher*, 1:67–68.

62. Wigger, *Feldmarschall Fürst Blücher*, 15.

63. Unger, *Blücher*, 1:67–68. Unger does not believe that Lossow named Blücher because of the incident with the priest. Aside from Blücher, Second Lieutenant Franz Otton von Rexin was likewise listed as cashiered due to charges of poor performance and dishonest conduct (stealing a horse) in Poland. Bleck, *Marschall Blücher*, 14.

64. GStA PK, VI HA Rep. 92 Nl. Blücher von Wahlstatt.

65. Görlitz, *Fürst Blücher*, 29. Görlitz claims that Frederick harbored no resentment toward Blücher.

66. Wigger, *Feldmarschall Fürst Blücher*, 15.

67. Varnhagen von Ense, *Blücher*, 14.

68. Blücher to Frederick, Gresonse at Flatow, 9 June 1778, *BB*, 3.

69. Ibid.

70. King Frederick William I was such an enemy of the Freemasons that they remained underground until his death. Even the initiation of Crown Prince Frederick in 1738 was kept hidden from the "Potsdam Führer." Upon his death and Frederick's accession to the throne in 1740, the Freemasons received royal patronage, with the new king himself opening a lodge at Charlottenburg and initiating his brother, Prince Augustus William. By

1770, three grand lodges operated in Berlin: the Grand Lodge of the Three Globes, the Grand Lodge Royal York of Friendship, and the National Grand Lodge of Germany. Although Jews were denied membership, the Prussians led the rest of Europe in studying Freemasonry as a science. Frederick William II and Frederick William III both were Freemasons. Blücher remained an active member. In 1799 he joined the Zum hellen Licht Lodge at Hanau. Later he initiated his two sons and nine officers into the Pax Inimica Malis Lodge at Emmerich. From 1802 to 1806, he was grand master of the Zu Den Drey Balken Lodge at Münster, where he led at least 190 meetings. Mackey, *Encyclopedia of Freemasonry*, 2:814–15.

71. Wigger, *Feldmarschall Fürst Blücher*, 18.
72. Blücher to Frederick, Groß Raddow, 15 Jan. 1782, *BB*, 4.
73. Blücher to Frederick, Groß Raddow, 2 May 1782, *BB*, 4.
74. Quoted in Blücher, *Memoirs*, 11.
75. "Pro Memoria," Blücher to Frederick, Groß Raddow, 13 Aug. 1782, *BB*, 6.
76. Quoted in Blücher, *Memoirs*, 11.
77. Blücher to Frederick, Groß Raddow, 13 Oct. 1782, *BB*, 7.
78. Blücher to Frederick, Groß Raddow, 7 July 1783, *BB*, 7–8.
79. Blücher to Frederick, Groß Raddow, 16 Nov. 1785, *BB*, 10.
80. Blücher to Frederick, Groß Raddow, 14 Nov. 1783, *BB*, 8–9.
81. Wigger, *Feldmarschall Fürst Blücher*, 17–18.
82. Blücher to Frederick, Groß Raddow, 13 Jan. 1785, *BB*, 9.
83. Blücher to Frederick, Groß Raddow, 23 Jan. 1785, *BB*, 10.
84. Blücher to Frederick, Groß Raddow, 16 Nov. 1785, *BB*, 11. Frederick's treatment of Blücher and responses to his numerous entreaties captures perfectly the monarch's ill temper. Toward the end of his life, the great king became increasingly solitary, disparaging, and capricious.
85. Wigger, *Feldmarschall Fürst Blücher*, 23.
86. The second son of King George III of Great Britain and tutored in the art of soldiering by Frederick the Great himself, Frederick married Princess Frederica of Prussia, the oldest daughter of King Frederick William II, in 1791. It is not known how he and Blücher became friends.
87. Blasendorff, *Gebhard Leberecht von Blücher*, 25.
88. GStA PK, VI HA Rep. 92 Nl. Blücher von Wahlstatt; Wigger, *Feldmarschall Fürst Blücher*, 18–20; Varnhagen von Ense, *Blücher*, 16; Blasendorff, *Gebhard Leberecht von Blücher*, 27.
89. The Red Hussars recruited mainly in Saxony, Mecklenburg, West Prussia, and Danzig, though not in the German states of the Holy Roman Empire. It attracted numerous volunteers from Pomerania and Brandenburg. In its advertising, the regiment looked for hunters, butchers, and farm laborers familiar with handling horses and preferred "robust, healthy, fresh, and dapper chaps." Unger, *Blücher*, 1:78.
90. Ibid., 1:81–87.
91. Wigger, *Feldmarschall Fürst Blücher*, 20–21.
92. Unger, *Blücher*, 1:87–88.
93. Blasendorff, *Gebhard Leberecht von Blücher*, 28–29; Wigger, *Feldmarschall Fürst Blücher*, 21.

94. Unger, *Blücher*, 1:89–101.
95. GStA PK, VI HA Rep. 92 Nl. Blücher von Wahlstatt.
96 To fulfill his obligations to the Turks, Frederick William goaded the Swedes into directly confronting the Russians. In turn, the Russians spirited Denmark into declaring war on Sweden.
97. Although located in West Prussia, Danzig remained part of Poland after the First Partition thanks in part to the determined resistance of its defenders.
98. These Prussian "corps" were mere ad-hoc troop formations above the regimental level and should not be confused with the Napoleonic corps system.
99. Wigger, *Feldmarschall Fürst Blücher*, 23–24; Blasendorff, *Gebhard Leberecht von Blücher*, 32–33; Unger, *Blücher*, 1:107.
100. Blücher to Frederick William, Stolp, 2 May 1792, *BB*, 13–14.

Chapter Two

1. Blücher, *Kampagne Journal*, 44.
2. Blücher to the Fredrick William, Berlin, 3 Jan. 1793, *BB*, 12–13.
3. Blücher, *Kampagne Journal*, 44.
4. Blasendorff, *Gebhard Leberecht von Blücher*, 38–39. Blücher's adjutant, Goltz, and his *Kriegsrat* (military auditor), Friedrich Wilhelm Ribbentrop, primarily helped get the journal published. Aside from the journal, nothing written by Blücher himself in 1793 or 1794 survives.
5. Parkinson's entertaining but factually inaccurate work contains numerous errors. For example, he claims that this Brunswick was the twenty-two-year-old son of the Prussian commander in chief. *Hussar General*, 21.
6. This number included twelve infantry battalions, ten cuirassier squadrons, the 1st Battalion of Goltz Hussars, twenty-four guns, and a few heavy pieces.
7. Duke Frederick, a nephew of Frederick II as well as his chief aide, along with his older brother, Charles William Ferdinand, who commanded the main Prussian army along the Rhine, had been the darlings of the great king. After the Seven Years War, Duke Frederick conducted all major military exercises, with the old king observing at his side. General Unger describes the duke as "small, ugly, and deformed, but witty, and sharp with the tongue, pen, and pencil." Duke Frederick resented being subordinated to the Austrian Saxe-Coburg, who he considered to be an upstart with experience fighting only the inferior Turks. Unger, *Blücher*, 1:112.
8. Hochedlinger, *Austria's Wars*, 411. The British sought to gain Dunkirk to use as a base for their operations in Flanders as well as a bargaining chip in future peace negotiations.
9. Blücher, *Kampagne Journal*, 51–52. To the left (southeast) of the Prussians, Saxe-Coburg's line extended from Saint-Amand, passing Condé, Valenciennes, and Maubeuge, and extending through Namur to Luxemburg.
10. Ibid., 52–58.
11. Ibid., 60–61.
12. Blasendorff, *Gebhard Leberecht von Blücher*, 39.

13. Bleck, *Marschall Blücher*, 23.
14. Blücher, *Kampagne Journal*, 63–66.
15. Hochedlinger, *Austria's Wars*, 412. The French victory at Hondschoote on 6–8 September forced the Anglo-Hanoverians to raise the siege of Dunkirk.
16. Blücher, *Kampagne Journal*, 67–69.
17. For Blücher's activities up to 15 November, see ibid., 70–80.
18. Ibid., 80–82.
19. Ibid., 82–83.
20. Ibid., 84–85.
21. Ibid., 85–86.
22. Ibid., 86–87.
23. Ibid., 88.
24. Ibid., 88–92.
25. Ibid., 92–93.
26. Ibid., 95–96.
27. Ibid., 99.
28. Wigger, *Feldmarschall Fürst Blücher*, 24–25.
29. Blücher, *Kampagne Journal*, 97–99.
30. Ibid., 99–101.
31. Wigger, *Feldmarschall Fürst Blücher*, 25.
32. Blücher, *Kampagne Journal*, 102. Müffling was the father of Friedrich Karl Baron von Müffling, a future Prussian field marshal and chief of the General Staff. The younger Müffling served as Blücher's quartermaster general in the 1813 and 1814 campaigns and as the Prussian liaison at British headquarters in 1815. Although Blücher praised and repeatedly thanked the elder Müffling for his bravery and situational awareness during the 1794 campaign, he had a contentious relationship with the son. See Blücher, *Kampagne Journal*, 115.
33. Wigger, *Feldmarschall Fürst Blücher*, 24–25.
34. A gold coin, the karolin ("max d'or" or "Karl d'or"), was the Bavarian equivalent to the French Louis d'or (Louis from Gold) and the Prussian Friedrichsdor (Frederick from Gold). Blücher chose the Bavarian currency because that region of Germany, the Palatinate, was ruled by the Whittelsbach dynasty of Bavaria. The worth of one Karolin in 1794 equates to $1,534.71 in 2012. Ducats were smaller gold and silver coins used in many European countries. The worth of one dukat in 1794 equates to $767.36 in 2012.
35. Blücher, *Kampagne Journal*, 102–103.
36. Ibid., 103.
37. Unger, *Blücher*, 1:163–64.
38. St.-Cyr claims that this was a trap he purposefully set to destroy Blücher's hussars. *Mémoires sur les campagnes des armées du Rhin*, 2:108–14.
39. Blücher, *Kampagne Journal*, 106–107.
40. Ibid., 107–109.
41. Unger, *Blücher*, 1:165–66.
42. Blücher, *Kampagne Journal*, 108.

43. Here Blücher is referring to the hundreds of thousands of men who either volunteered for the French army in 1791 and 1792 or were conscripted in two drafts in 1793: the levy of 300,000 in the spring and the general levy that followed in August. These troops, known as the "blues" because many wore the blue coats of the French National Guard, did not receive the same amount of training as the professional soldiers, who wore the white coat of the traditional French army.
44. Blücher, *Kampagne Journal*, 108–109.
45. Quoted in Unger, *Blücher*, 1:168.
46. Blücher, *Kampagne Journal*, 109–11.
47. Ibid., 111.
48. St.-Cyr, *Mémoires sur les campagnes des armées du Rhin*, 2:10–13.
49. Phipps, *Armies of the First French Republic*, 2:128–29.
50. Unger, *Blücher*, 1:172–73.
51. The claim by Phipps that Blücher "was driven off" is absurd. See *Armies of the First French Republic*, 2:131.
52. Blücher, *Kampagne Journal*, 111–16.
53. Quoted in Unger, *Blücher*, 1:185
54. Blücher, *Kampagne Journal*, 116–18.
55. Phipps, *Armies of the First French Republic*, 2:130–31. Calling the victory at Kaiserslautern "complete" grossly exaggerated the truth. In fact, knowing of Möllendorf's numerical superiority, the French retreated southwest toward Pirmasens before the Prussians could attack.
56. Blücher, *Kampagne Journal*, 118–19.
57. Unger, *Blücher*, 1:176.
58. Ibid., 1:179.
59. Blücher, *Kampagne Journal*, 120–22.
60. Ibid., 122–23.
61. Ibid., 125.
62. Unger, *Blücher*, 1:182.
63. Blücher, *Kampagne Journal*, 126.
64. Unger, *Blücher*, 1:185.
65. Blücher, *Kampagne Journal*, 126.
66. For a detailed account of these operations, see St.-Cyr, *Mémoires sur les campagnes des armées du Rhin*, 2:16–44. See also Phipps, *Armies of the First French Republic*, 2:132.
67. Unger, *Blücher*, 1:187.
68. Blücher commanded a fairly large "detachment," consisting of the ten squadrons of the Red Hussars, a half-battery of horse artillery, and a brigade commanded by Prince George von Hohenlohe that contained the Manstein Grenadier Regiment, the Bila and Müffling Fusilier Regiments, one Jäger company, and half of a foot battery. Blücher, *Kampagne Journal*, 128.
69. St.-Cyr, *Mémoires sur les campagnes des armées du Rhin*, 2:49.
70. Phipps, *Armies of the First French Republic*, 2:133.
71. Blücher, *Kampagne Journal*, 132–33.
72. Ibid., 136.
73. Friedrich Ludwig Christian, commonly known as Louis Ferdinand (1772–1806), was the son of Prince August Ferdinand of Prussia (1730–1813), the

youngest brother of Frederick II. Not only was Louis Ferdinand the nephew of Frederick, but the army viewed him as the great king's military heir.

74. Blücher, *Kampagne Journal*, 137.

75. See St.-Cyr, *Mémoires sur les campagnes des armées du Rhin*, 2:76–89.

76. Unger, *Blücher*, 1:194. Bleck likewise claims that "as 'le roi rouge,' Blücher remained in the memory of the French." *Marschall Blücher*, 30.

77. Phipps, *Armies of the First French Republic*, 2:133.

78. Blücher, *Kampagne Journal*, 132–38.

79. Ibid., 142–44.

80. For this task, Blücher received his biggest command to date. Aside from his hussar regiment, Hohenlohe-Ingelfingen assigned him two fusilier battalions (Müffling's and Bila's), three Prussian Jäger companies, one Palatine Jäger battalion, three Palatine light-cavalry squadrons, and a half-battery of horse artillery as well as two Austrian Freikorps and one Austrian battery. Ibid., 144.

81. Wigger, *Feldmarschall Fürst Blücher*, 26.

82. On the modern map of Germany, Neukirchen is the town of Mehlingen.

83. Blücher, *Kampagne Journal*, 150.

84. Ibid., 151.

85. Ibid., 152.

86. Quoted in Unger, *Blücher*, 1:213.

87. Blücher, *Kampagne Journal*, 153.

88. Ibid., 154–56.

89. Ibid., 157.

90. Quoted in Unger, *Blücher*, 1:216.

91. Blücher, *Kampagne Journal*, 159–60.

92. Ibid., 161.

93. Ibid., 158.

94. Quoted in Unger, *Blücher*, 1:172.

95. Blücher to Breetz, Münster, 23 July 1796, *BB*, 25.

96. Wigger, *Feldmarschall Fürst Blücher*, 27.

97. Blücher's own figures state: "7 eight-pound cannon; 2 four-pound cannon; 2 eight-pound howitzers; 7 caissons; 5 flags; 1 general lieutenant, 137 officers, 3,327 men, and 1,134 horses." Blücher to Zastrow, Emden, 19 Sept. 1795, *BB*, 19.

98. Blücher, *Kampagne Journal*, 161. Forty-four noncommissioned officers received gold service medals while eighty-six soldiers received the silver service medals.

99. St.-Cyr, *Mémoires sur les campagnes des armées du Rhin*, 2:58.

100. Ibid., 2:115.

101. Blücher to Crown Prince Frederick William, Eberstadt near Gießen, 11 Feb. 1795, *BB*, 14.

Chapter Three

1. Blücher to Zastrow, Burgsteinfurt near Münster, 2 Nov. 1795, *BB*, 22–23.

2. Blücher to Frau v. d. S., day unknown, [?] Mar. 1795, *BB*, 15–16.

3. Blücher to Frau v. d. S., Riesenbeck, 1 Apr. 1795, *BB*, 16–17.

4. Wigger, *Feldmarschall Fürst Blücher*, 30–31, 34.
5. Blücher, *Memoirs*, 16.
6. Blücher, *Blücher in Briefen*, 5–7.
7. Blücher to Bonin, Münster, 4 Apr. 1796, *BB*, 25.
8. Blücher to Breetz, Münster, 23 July 1796, *BB*, 26.
9. Blücher to Zastrow, Emden, 19 Sept. 1795, *BB*, 17.
10. Wigger, *Feldmarschall Fürst Blücher*, 31. Other accounts claim that Blücher hurt the foot while riding. See Blasendorff, *Gebhard Leberecht von Blücher*, 48.
11. Blücher to Zastrow, Emden, 19 Sept. 1795, *BB*, 17.
12. Blasendorff, *Gebhard Leberecht von Blücher*, 48.
13. Blücher to Zastrow, Emden, 19 Sept. 1795, *BB*, 17–19.
14. Blücher to Zastrow, Burgsteinfurt near Münster, 2 Nov. 1795, *BB*, 20.
15. Ibid.
16. Wigger, *Feldmarschall Fürst Blücher*, 31.
17. Blücher to Zastrow, Burgsteinfurt near Münster, 2 Nov. 1795, *BB*, 21–22.
18. Ibid., 22.
19. Blücher to Bonin, Münster, 4 Apr. 1796, *BB*, 24.
20. Blücher to Breetz, Münster, 23 July 1796, *BB*, 26.
21. Blücher to Häse, Münster, 17 Oct. 1799, *BB*, 29.
22. Blücher to Zastrow, Münster, 27 Sept. 1797, *BB*, 28.
23. Blücher to Häse, Münster, 17 Oct. 1799, *BB*, 29–30.
24. Blücher to Bonin, Münster, 4 Apr. 1796, *BB*, 23–25.
25. Blücher to Breetz, Münster, 23 July 1796, *BB*, 26.
26. The term "heller" was used to describe German coins of small value, usually half a pfennig.
27. Blücher to Häse, Münster, 17 Oct. 1799, *BB*, 29–30.
28. Blücher to Kutscher, Emmerich, 19 Oct. 1800, *BB*, 31–32.
29. Prebendaries were clerics who have a role in the administration of a church or cathedral. A prebend was a type of benefice that provided income from a clerical estate.
30. Blücher to Köckritz, Berlin, 14 Mar. 1800, *BB*, 30.
31. Blücher to Geusau, Emden, 3 Nov. 1801, *BB*, 34.
32. Blücher to Geisler, Münster, 29 July 1802, *BB*, 34.
33. Wigger, *Feldmarschall Fürst Blücher*, 33–34. Private and professional business brought Blücher to Berlin shortly after the royal coronation. Wigger tells us that at this time Blücher came to know many of the influential persons of Prussia's new regime.

Chapter Four

1. Moreover, we have no insight of how Blücher viewed the overthrow of the French government in 1799 by General Bonaparte.
2. Unger, *Blücher*, 1:237.
3. Blücher to Geusau, Emden, 3 Nov. 1801, *BB*, 33–34.
4. Wigger, *Feldmarschall Fürst Blücher*, 36.
5. Bülow to Kutscher, Münster, 3 Dec. 1803, *BB*, 36.
6. Although responsible for the Treaty of Basel, Haugwitz disapproved of Frederick William III's neutral policy in the face of French expansion.

After the king refused his urgent advice in 1803 to demand the evacuation of Hanover by the French, he resigned. In his place Frederick William appointed Karl von Hardenberg in August 1804. It is unlikely that Blücher acted on some secret plan concocted with Haugwitz. By 1806, the general hated him, expressing his wish for Stein to be the foreign minister and for Haugwitz to " rot in hell." Blücher to Kleist, Münster, 23 July 1806, *BB*, 62.

7. Wigger, *Feldmarschall Fürst Blücher*, 36–37.
8. Bülow to Kutscher, Münster, 3 Dec. 1803, *BB*, 36–37.
9. Blücher to Kutscher, Münster, 10 Jan. 1804, *BB*, 39–40.
10. Blücher to Kutscher, Münster, 9 June 1804, *BB*, 44.
11. Blücher to Kutscher, Münster, 3 July 1804, *BB*, 44
12. Quoted in Wigger, *Feldmarschall Fürst Blücher*, 37.
13. Blücher to Kalckreuth, Potsdam, 23 Sept. 1804, *BB*, 46.
14. Wigger, *Feldmarschall Fürst Blücher*, 38–39.
15. Blücher to Kalckreuth, Potsdam, 23 Sept. 1804, *BB*, 46.
16. Blücher to Kutscher, Münster, 3 July 1804, *BB*, 44.
17. Wigger, *Feldmarschall Fürst Blücher*, 39,
18. Blücher to Kutscher, Münster, 5 Dec. 1804, *BB*, 48.
19. Blücher to Kutscher, Münster, 2 Feb. 1805, *BB*, 50.
20. Blücher to Kutscher, Münster, 21 May 1805, *BB*, 51.
21. Blücher to Knesebeck, Münster, 10 Nov. 1805, *BB*, 53.
22. Blücher to Knesebeck, Münster, 3 Dec. 1805, *BB*, 53.
23. Blücher to Knesebeck, Bayreuth, 20 Dec. 1805, *BB*, 53–54.
24. Wigger, *Feldmarschall Fürst Blücher*, 40.
25. Blücher to Knesebeck, Bayreuth, 29 Dec. 1805, *BB*, 55.
26. Wigger, *Feldmarschall Fürst Blücher*, 41.
27. Blücher to Knesebeck, Münster, 31 Mar. 1806, *BB*, 56.
28. Blücher to Frederick William, Münster, 2 July 1806, *BB*, 59.
29. Blücher to Frederick William, Münster, 12 July 1806, *BB*, 59.
30. Wigger, *Feldmarschall Fürst Blücher*, 41–42.
31. Blücher to Kleist, Münster, 22 July 1806, *BB*, 60.
32. Blücher to Kleist, Münster, 23 July 1806, *BB*, 61–62.
33. Blücher to Frederick William, Münster, 25 July 1806, *BB*, 63–65.
34. "I entrust you with a letter to His Majesty the King. Please place it in the highest hands. As the devoted servant of the King and as the general in command here, I saw it as necessary to give my opinion about the situation here. This is also the first and last time that I will talk politics. I just wanted to assure myself that I poured my heart out to the King, my Master. I do hope that it [the letter] will not be perceived as disgraceful because my intentions are genuine and pure." Blücher to Kleist, Münster, 25 July 1806, *BB*, 66.
35. Blücher to Brunswick, Münster, 16 Aug. 1806, *BB*, 67.
36. Blücher to Brüsewitz, Münster, 11 Sept. 1806, *BB*, 67.
37. Wigger, *Feldmarschall Fürst Blücher*, 46.
38. Blücher to Rüchel, Paderborn, 14 Sept. 1806, *BB*, 68.
39. Blücher to Rüchel, Paderborn, 18 Sept. 1806, *BB*, 68–69.
40. Blücher to Rüchel, Münster, 12 Sept. 1806, *BB*, 67.
41. Blücher to Vincke, Göttingen, 6 Oct. 1806, *BB*, 69.

42. Wigger, *Feldmarschall Fürst Blücher*, 46.
43. Blücher to Rüchel, Creuzburg, 8 Oct. 1806, *BB*, 69.
44. Blücher to Vincke, Creuzburg, 9 Oct. 1806, *BB*, 70.
45. Wigger, *Feldmarschall Fürst Blücher*, 47–48.
46. With cavalry screening the entire movement, V Corps led the left column followed by VII Corps at a distance of one day's march. Napoleon's I Corps formed the head of the center followed by III Corps. Leading the right column was IV Corps, followed by VI Corps. In the rear of the center column came the Reserve Cavalry and Imperial Guard. The spacing allotted the same distance between the head and rear of the center column—the northern and southern points of the diamond—as between the left and right columns—the eastern and western points. The genius of the bataillon carré is the flexibility it afforded. For example, if the enemy's main army took a position on Napoleon's left, then his left column immediately would become the head of the new center column, with the right column forming the rear. The head of the former center column would form the new right wing, while the rear of the former center column formed the new left wing.
47. Quoted in Unger, *Blücher*, 1:279.
48. Brunswick later died on 10 November at Altona, near Hamburg.
49. Quoted in Unger, *Blücher*, 1:295.
50. This account of the 1806 campaign is based on Unger, *Blücher*, 1:272–96; and Petre, *Napoleon's Conquest of Prussia*, 46, 68–70, 126, 150–64, 194–202, 218–49, 256–87.
51. Varnhagen von Ense, *Blücher*, 80–81.
52. Quoted in Unger, *Blücher*, 1:330.
53. Ibid., 1:329–30.
54. Varnhagen von Ense, *Bülow*, 70–72.

Chapter Five

1. Blücher to Hardenberg, Wolgast, [?] July 1807, *BB*, 81.
2. Shanahan, *Prussian Military Reforms*, 98. Kolberg, Graudenz (Grudziądz), Pillau (Baltiysk), Glatz (Kłodzko), Neiße (Nysa), Kosel (Kozanów), and Silberberg (Srebrna Góra) remained under Prussian control.
3. Varnhagen von Ense, *Bülow*, 76.
4. Blücher to Hardenberg, Wolgast, [?] July 1807, *BB*, 81.
5. Blücher to Gneisenau, [?] July 1807, *BB*, 81.
6. Unger, *Blücher*, 1:336.
7. Blücher to Gneisenau, Treptow, 3 Aug. 1807, *BB*, 85.
8. This document, titled "Entwurf zu einer Instruktion für die Untersuchungskommission der strafbaren Offiziere," is reproduced in full in Scharnhorst, *Private und dienstliche Schriften*, Nr. 380, 4:712–14.
9. Membership consisted of Prince William of Prussia; Generals Anton Wilhelm von L'Estocq, Ludwig August von Stutterheim, and Christoph Friedrich Otto von Diericke; Colonels Bülow, Ernst Wilhelm von Hamilton, and Ernst Julius Schuler von Senden; Lieutenant Colonels Gneisenau and Bronikowsky; Majors Christian Sigismund Ziehen, Ludwig August Friedrich Adolf Count von Chasot, and Otto Carl Lorenz von Pirch II; and Auditor General Johann Friedrich von Koenen. Ibid., Nr. 381, 4:715.

10. Blücher to Hardenberg, Treptow, 12 Aug. 1807, in Blücher, "Zwölf Blücherbriefe," 13:487–88.

11. Unger, *Blücher*, 1:337.

12. Feuchtwanger, *Prussia*, 114–15; Demeter, *German Officer Corps*, 13.

13. Proreform native Prussians Friedrich Wilhelm von Götzen (the Younger) and Major Leopold Hermann Ludwig von Boyen eventually joined their foreign-born colleagues on the Military Reorganization Commission, replacing the conservatives Borstell and Bronikowsky, while native Prussians Major Karl Wilhelm Georg von Grolman (purportedly one of the most radical reformers), Karl Friedrich Emil zu Dohna-Schlobitten (Scharnhorst's future son-in-law), Captain Carl Philipp Gottfried von Clausewitz (Scharnhorst's most gifted student), and Karl Ludwig von Tiedemann served as Scharnhorst's private staff.

14. Kitchen, *Military History of Germany*, 9. In 1803 Rüchel's adjutant, Major Karl Friedrich von dem Knesebeck, published a report suggesting that every year the army release 128,297 men and replace them with recruits who would later be released in the same manner to establish a substantial reserve of trained men. It is not known if Blücher was aware of this document. Scharnhorst would later present Knesebeck's essay to Frederick William III as the basis of the Krümper system.

15. Scharnhorst to Goltz, Memel, 8 Aug. 1807, Scharnhorst, *Private und dienstliche Schriften*, Nr. 338, 4:617–18.

16. Scharnhorst to Blücher, Königsberg, 28 Aug. 1808, ibid., Nr. 144, 5:234.

17. Blasendorff, *Gebhard Leberecht von Blücher*, 129–30.

18. Unger, *Blücher*, 1:334.

19. Blücher to Colomb, Treptow, 15 Aug. 1807, *BB*, 87.

20. Blücher to Colomb, Treptow, 26 Sept. 1807, *BB*, 90.

21. Koch, *History of Prussia*, 190.

22. Blasendorff, *Gebhard Leberecht von Blücher*, 130–31.

23. Unger, *Blücher*, 1:334.

24. Blücher to Beyme, Treptow, 9 Sept. 1807, *BB*, 88–89.

25. Blasendorff, *Gebhard Leberecht von Blücher*, 131–32; Unger, *Blücher*, 1:334–35.

26. Napoleon to Berthier, Fontainebleau, 24 Sept. 1807, *CN*, No. 13179, 16:55.

27. Blücher to Hardenberg, Treptow, 12 Aug. 1807, in Blücher, "Zwölf Blücherbriefe," 13:487.

28. Blücher to Colomb, Treptow, 26 Sept. 1807, *BB*, 90.

29. Blasendorff, *Gebhard Leberecht von Blücher*, 132; Unger, *Blücher*, 1:339.

30. Blücher to Hardenberg, Treptow, 12 Aug. 1807, in Blücher, "Zwölf Blücherbriefe," 13:488.

31. Blücher to Beyme, Treptow, 9 Sept. 1807, in ibid.

32. Blücher to Colomb, Treptow, 26 Sept. 1807, *BB*, 90.

33. Blücher to Beyme, Treptow, 9 Sept. 1807, in Blücher, "Zwölf Blücherbriefe," 13:489. Fritze married Major Count Adolf von der Schulenburg on 1 January 1804; he died of illness on 9 September 1813.

34. Unger, *Blücher*, 1:340.

35. Blücher to Goltz, Stargard, 4 Apr. 1809, *BB*, 94.

36. Blücher to Sprickmann, Treptow, 7 Sept. 1807, *BB*, 87–88.
37. Blücher to Beyme, Treptow, 9 Sept. 1807, in Blücher, "Zwölf Blücher-briefe," 13:489.
38. Blücher to Sprickmann, Treptow, 7 Sept. 1807, *BB*, 87–88.
39. Blasendorff, *Gebhard Leberecht von Blücher*, 134.
40. Blücher to Colomb, Treptow, 26 Sept. 1807, *BB*, 89–90.
41. Quoted in Blasendorff, *Gebhard Leberecht von Blücher*, 134.
42. Unger, *Blücher*, 1:338–39.
43. Quoted in Blasendorff, *Gebhard Leberecht von Blücher*, 133.
44. Blücher to Lottum, Treptow, 14 Mar. 1808, in Blücher, "Zwölf Blücher-briefe," 13:490.
45. Blücher to Colomb, Treptow, 25 Apr. 1808, *BB*, 91–92.
46. Quoted in Blasendorff, *Gebhard Leberecht von Blücher*, 135.
47. Unger, *Blücher*, 1:338.
48. Friedrich Wilhelm to Bülow, 22 June 1808, BFA, No. 12.
49. Varnhagen von Ense, *Blücher*, 83; Varnhagen von Ense, *Bülow*, 82; Unger, *Blücher*, 1:340.
50. Friedrich Wilhelm to Blücher, 24 Aug. 1808, BFA, No. 18.
51. Blasendorff, *Gebhard Leberecht von Blücher*, 137, 142.
52. Blücher to Goltz, Stargard, 4 Apr. 1809, *BB*, 93.
53. Blasendorff, *Gebhard Leberecht von Blücher*, 137.
54. Boyen, *Erinnerungen*, ed. Schmidt, 2:362–63.
55. Blasendorff, *Gebhard Leberecht von Blücher*, 137, 142.
56. Ibid., 138.
57. Scharnhorst to Bülow, Königsberg, 3 Dec. 1808, 23 Feb., 20 Mar., 2 and 16 May 1809, Scharnhorst, *Private und dienstliche Schriften*, Nrs. 205, 240, 321, 392, 408, 5:303, 358–59, 489–90, 573, 593–94.
58. Blasendorff, *Gebhard Leberecht von Blücher*, 139–40.
59. Blücher to Goltz, Stargard, 4 Apr. 1809, *BB*, 93–94.

Chapter Six

1. Blasendorff, *Gebhard Leberecht von Blücher*, 144.
2. Blücher to Frederick William, Stargard, early May 1809, *BB*, 95.
3. Duke Frederick William of Brunswick-Wolfenbüttel was the fourth son of the Duke of Brunswick.
4. For the definitive account of Schill's revolt, as well as those of Katte and Dörnberg, see Mustafa, *Long Ride*.
5. Blücher to Frederick William, Stargard, early May 1809, *BB*, 95–96.
6. Unger, *Blücher*, 1:342.
7. Mustafa, *Long Ride*, 55–57, 59, 92, 124–25.
8. In addition, in April the king received a report naming Scharnhorst as the leader of a plot to dethrone him. On these grounds, he ordered an investigation but later dropped the issue as unfounded. Lehmann, *Scharnhorst*, 2:277.
9. Blücher to Gneisenau, Stargard, 16 July 1809, *BB*, 103.
10. Mustafa, *Long Ride*, 92.
11. Blasendorff, *Gebhard Leberecht von Blücher*, 146.

12. Gneisenau to Götzen, Königsberg, [?] June 1809, in Griewank, *Gneisenau*, Nr. 55, 113–14.

13. Blücher to Gneisenau, Stargard, 16 July 1809, *BB*, 101.

14. Mustafa, *Long Ride*, 90.

15. Blücher to Frederick William, Stargard, May 1809, *BB*, 96–98.

16. Blücher to Bonin, Stargard, 6 June 1809, *BB*, 99.

17. Blücher to Götzen, Stargard, 14 June 1809, *BB*, 100.

18. This is a reference to the Battle of Raszyn on 19 April 1809 in the Grand Duchy of Warsaw. Although a tactical draw, the Poles and Saxons of Prince Joseph Poniatowski's army had to yield Warsaw to the Austrian army of Archduke Ferdinand.

19. Blücher to unnamed recipient, early June 1809, in Wigger, *Feldmarschall Fürst Blücher*, 88.

20. Unger, *Blücher*, 1:347.

21. Blücher to Bonin, Stargard, 6 June 1809, *BB*, 99.

22. Blücher to Gneisenau, Stargard, 16 July 1809, *BB*, 101.

23. Blasendorff, *Gebhard Leberecht von Blücher*, 146.

24. Gneisenau to Götzen, Königsberg, [?] June 1809, in Griewank, *Gneisenau*, Nr. 55, 113.

25. Mustafa, *Long Ride*, 108–12.

26. Blücher to Götzen, Stargard, 14 June 1809, *BB*, 100.

27. Mustafa, *Long Ride*, 124.

28. In a letter written sometime in July, Blücher explained his logic: "Regarding their [Schill's men] pardon, I already have written the King. Officers as well as noncommissioned officers and soldiers are blameless because Schill told them it was with royal approval that they cross the Elbe; as subordinates they acted in complete accordance with our service [regulations] by following the orders of their chief. When they later learned that it was not the will of the King, Schill declared that without hesitation he would shoot dead any individual who opposed his command." Quoted in Wigger, *Feldmarschall Fürst Blücher*, 93.

29. Blücher to Bonin, Stargard, 6 June 1809, *BB*, 100.

30. Blücher to Götzen, Stargard, 14 June 1809, *BB*, 100; Unger, 1:344; Mustafa, *Long Ride*, 125.

31. Blücher to Gneisenau, Stargard, 16 July 1809, *BB*, 102.

32. Mustafa, *Long Ride*, 127–29.

33. Blücher to Gneisenau, Stargard, 16 July 1809, *BB*, 102–103.

34. Gneisenau to Stein, Königsberg, 15 Feb.1809, in Griewank, *Gneisenau*, Nr. 51, 101.

35. Unger, *Blücher*, 1:346–47.

36. Gneisenau to Hardenberg, 2 Apr. 1809, *BB*, 109–10.

37. Blücher to Gneisenau, Stargard, 16 July 1809, *BB*, 101.

38. Sam Mustafa asserts that Blücher may have wanted Franz to leave Prussia because of his ties to Schill. *Long Ride*, 126. Blücher himself wrote, "You can easily guess why I have allowed Major Blücher to travel; he is my son: I know all the English princes, and I believe his arrival will make the best impression." Blücher to Gneisenau, Stargard, 16 July 1809, *BB*, 103.

39. Blücher to Götzen, Stargard, 16 July 1809, *BB*, 104.
40. Blücher to Gneisenau, Stargard, 16 July 1809, *BB*, 102–103.
41. Blücher to Götzen, Stargard, 19 July 1809, *BB*, 106. "Yesterday I sent to the King and put forward to him everything possible and requested that for God's sake he allow me to cross the Elbe with 16,000 men so that foreigners [French] do not exploit and exhaust our provinces on the opposite bank."
42. Blücher to Frederick William, Stargard, 18 July 1809, *BB*, 105–106.
43. Blücher to Bonin, Stargard, 20 July 1809, *BB*, 106.
44. Blasendorff, *Gebhard Leberecht von Blücher*, 148.
45. Unger, *Blücher*, 1:349.
46. Blücher to Götzen, Stargard, 2 Oct. 1809, *BB*, 109.
47. Quoted in Blasendorff, *Gebhard Leberecht von Blücher*, 144.
48. Blücher to Götzen, Stargard, 2 Oct. 1809, *BB*, 109.
49. Blücher to Bonin, Stargard, 9 Aug. 1809, *BB*, 106.
50. Blücher to Marwitz, Stargard, 12 Sept. 1809, *BB*, 107.
51. Quoted in Blasendorff, *Gebhard Leberecht von Blücher*, 152.
52. Unger, *Blücher*, 1:357.
53. Quoted in Blasendorff, *Gebhard Leberecht von Blücher*, 152–53.
54. Blücher to Götzen, Stargard, 2 Oct. 1809, *BB*, 108–109.
55. According to Blücher's response to Götzen, the latter learned of the treaty on 5 October. Blücher to Götzen, Stargard, 9 Oct. 1809, *BB*, 111.
56. Ibid.
57. "I also requested definitive instructions whether I should or should not allow reinforcements to reach Stettin and Küstrin, whose garrisons are currently weak, and whether it would be appropriate to seize the former; I hold it to be feasible." Ibid.
58. Blücher to Frederick William, Stargard, 9 Oct. 1809, *BB*, 109–11.
59. Blücher to Götzen, Stargard, 9 Oct. 1809, *BB*, 111–12.
60. The letters by both Götzen and Frederick William are quoted in Unger, *Blücher*, 1:352–54.
61. Blasendorff, *Gebhard Leberecht von Blücher*, 149.
62. Unger, *Blücher*, 1:353.
63. See Craig, *Politics of the Prussian Army*, 53–55.
64. Schroeder, *European Politics*, 451.
65. Unger, *Blücher*, 1:353.
66. Blücher to Gneisenau, Stargard, 16 July 1809, *BB*, 104.

Chapter Seven

1. Blasendorff, *Gebhard Leberecht von Blücher*, 150.
2. Shanahan, *Prussian Military Reforms*, 157.
3. Ibid., 158–59; Unger, *Blücher*, 1:354; Lehmann, *Scharnhorst*, 2:309.
4. Gneisenau to Franz von Blücher, 22 Oct. 1810, in Griewank, *Gneisenau*, Nr. 69, 153.
5. Unger, *Blücher*, 1:354.
6. Blücher to Katzler, Stargard, 9 June 1810, *BB*, 116.
7. Blücher to Eisenhart, Stargard, 21 Feb. 1811, *BB*, 125.
8. Blasendorff, *Gebhard Leberecht von Blücher*, 154–55.

9. Blücher to Boyen, Stargard, 20 Oct. 1810, *BB*, 122.
10. Blasendorff, *Gebhard Leberecht von Blücher*, 155.
11. Blücher to Eisenhart, Stargard, 6 June 1810, *BB*, 115.
12. Blücher to Eisenhart, Stargard, 14 June 1810, *BB*, 117.
13. Blücher to Katzler, Stargard, 9 June 1810, *BB*, 116.
14. Blücher to Eisenhart, Stargard, 15 July 1810, *BB*, 118.
15. Jany, *Geschichte der preussischen Heer*, 4:40; Shanahan, *Prussian Military Reforms*, 176.
16. See Shanahan, *Prussian Military Reforms*, 159–73.
17. Blücher to Boyen, Stargard, 18 Aug. 1810, *BB*, 119.
18. Blücher to Eisenhart, Stargard, 15 July 1810, *BB*, 118.
19. Blücher to Eisenhart, Stargard, 10 Sept. 1810, *BB*, 120.
20. Blücher to Bonin, Stargard, 10 Mar. 1811, *BB*, 126.
21. Quoted in Unger, *Blücher*, 1:356.
22. Quoted in Blasendorff, *Gebhard Leberecht von Blücher*, 164. Blassendorf claims that he found record of this incident in the archives at Kolberg.
23. Blücher to Hardenberg, Treptow, 16 Sept. 1811, *BB*, 144.
24. Unknown to Blücher, the British admiral, James Saumarez, received orders to be ready to provide all possible assistance to the Prussians should hostilities commence with France. As a result, Saumarez allowed corn and other supplies to slip through the British blockade to reach Kolberg. Muir, *Britain and the Defeat of Napoleon*, 188–89.
25. Unger, *Blücher*, 1:356.
26. Gneisenau to Chasot, May 1811, in Pertz and Delbrück, *Gneisenau*, 2:84.
27. Blücher to Eisenhart, Stargard, 22 July 1810, *BB*, 118.
28. Blücher to Boyen, Stargard, 20 Oct. 1810, *BB*, 121.
29. Blücher to Eisenhart, Stargard, 6 June 1810, *BB*, 116.
30. Blücher to Katzler, Stargard, 9 June 1810, *BB*, 116.
31. Blücher to Eisenhart, Stargard, 15 July 1810, *BB*, 118.
32. Blücher to Boyen, Stargard, 20 Oct. 1810, *BB*, 121.
33. Blücher to Eisenhart, Stargard, 22 Jan. 1811, *BB*, 124.
34. According to Shanahan, the Prussian cavalry regulations of 1812 were less worthy of praise than the new infantry tactics in part because Scharnhorst, an acknowledged artillery expert, knew little of the other arms beyond "an academic sense." *Prussian Military Reforms*, 184. The 1812 regulations called for three forms of attack—column, echelon, or line—placing emphasis on attack in column. All cavalry movements were to be synchronized with the infantry.
35. Blücher to Boyen, Stargard, 26 Sept. 1810, *BB*, 120.
36. Shanahan, *Prussian Military Reforms*, 140.
37. Blücher to Boyen, Stargard, 20 Oct. 1810, *BB*, 121–22.
38. Blücher to Boyen, Stargard, 15 Nov. 1810, *BB*, 122.
39. Blücher to Eisenhart, Stargard, 16 Nov. 1810, *BB*, 123.
40. The Bülow Family Archive contains the unpublished memoirs of Friederike von Auer titled "Erinnerungen aus der Jugendzeit für meine Kinder." Auer was Bülow's sister-in-law through her marriage to his wife's brother, Ludwig. Friederike recorded events from 1806 until 1816, living with

Bülow's wife during the 1813–15 campaigns. Her two handwritten journals remain in the possession of the Bülow von Dennewitz family. Pertinent copies have been provided for the author's use.

41. Blücher to Eisenhart, Stargard, 22 Jan. 1811, *BB*, 124.

42. Quoted in Unger, *Blücher*, 1:358.

43. Ibid.

44. Blücher to Boyen, Treptow, 4 May 1811, *BB*, 128.

45. Blücher to Yorck, Stargard, 23 Apr. 1811, *BB*, 127.

46. Unger, *Blücher*, 1:359.

47. Lehmann, Scharnhorst, 2:351; Shanahan, *Prussian Military Reforms*, 172–73.

48. Blücher to Bonin, Stargard, 10 Mar. 1811, *BB*, 126.

49. Blücher to Boyen, Treptow, 2 May 1811, *BB*, 127.

50. Lehmann, *Scharnhorst*, 2:357.

51. See Blasendorff, *Gebhard Leberecht von Blücher*, 162.

52. Blücher to Boyen, Treptow, 2 May 1811, *BB*, 127–28.

53. Unger, Blücher, 1:367.

54. Quoted in Blasendorff, *Gebhard Leberecht von Blücher*, 163.

55. Quoted in ibid., 162.

56. Unger, *Blücher*, 1:360–61.

57. Blücher to Boyen, Stargard, 21 Apr. 1811, *BB*, 126–27.

58. Blücher to Boyen, Stargard, 9 May 1811, *BB*, 128–29.

59. Blücher to Thile, Treptow, [?] Aug. 1811, *BB*, 138.

60. Unger, *Blücher*, 1:363.

61. Blücher to Thile, Treptow, [?] Aug. 1811, *BB*, 138.

62. Unger, *Blücher*, 1:360.

63. Shanahan, *Prussian Military Reforms*, 172–73.

64. Blücher to Bonin, Treptow, May or June 1811, *BB*, 130.

65. Quoted in Unger, *Blücher*, 1:361.

66. Blasendorff, *Gebhard Leberecht von Blücher*, 165.

67. Blücher to the Pomeranian government at Stargard, Treptow, 20 May 1811, *BB*, 129.

68. Blasendorff, *Gebhard Leberecht von Blücher*, 166.

69. Blücher never forgot occasions when his assessment of a situation appeared to have been correct. Referencing the crisis in 1803, he reminded Boyen: "I know that once I had attempted to disrupt the march of the French to Hanover and for this reason I traveled from Münster to Berlin and expressed my concern, but to my abject amazement I was told that this was nothing of importance, yet all of the misfortune suffered by Germany and the Prussian monarchy stemmed from this event, which at the time seemed so unimportant."

70. Blücher to Boyen, Treptow, 5 July 1811, *BB*, 130–31.

71. Quoted in Unger, *Blücher*, 1:362.

72. Blücher to Frederick William, Treptow, 25 July 1811, *BB*, 131–32.

73. Blücher to Frederick William, Treptow, 9 Aug. 1811, *BB*, 132–33.

74. Blücher to Hardenberg, Treptow, 12 Sept. 1811, *BB*, 143.

Chapter Eight

1. Blasendorff, *Gebhard Leberecht von Blücher*, 168–69.

2. Lehmann, *Scharnhorst*, 2:387.

3. Unger argues that "had Scharnhorst and Gneisenau given their advice over the construction of the fortifications, Blücher still would not have taken it, and would have arranged the particulars himself. He proceeded completely according to the idea of how he would conduct the defense." *Blücher*, 1:365.

4. Quoted in ibid., 1:364.

5. Blücher to Kleist, Treptow 8 Aug. 1811, *BB*, 132.

6. Blücher to Kleist, Treptow 18 Aug. 1811, *BB*, 133.

7. Blücher to Gneisenau, Treptow, 19 Aug. 1811, *BB*, 133–34. Just as Blücher finished writing this, a letter from Gneisenau reached his headquarters addressed to Franz Poppe, prompting Blücher to add in his own letter: "At this moment, your letter to Franz Poppe arrived. Be carefree, everything shall be ready! It pleases me to share the same views with you." These statements suggest that Blücher and Gneisenau agreed in principle on how to proceed at Kolberg as well as in regard to the French.

8. Ibid., 134–35.

9. Blasendorff, *Gebhard Leberecht von Blücher*, 171.

10. Blücher to Thile, Treptow, [?] Aug. 1811, *BB*, 137.

11. Blücher to Gneisenau, Treptow, [?] Aug. 1811, *BB*, 140.

12. Blücher to Thile, Treptow, [?] Aug. 1811, *BB*, 137.

13. "The terrain is generally to our advantage because both from Binnenfelde [to the east] as well as south of the camp, cavalry can operate and the advance of the enemy can be directed between the redoubts; also, on the other side of the Persante between Sellnow and Bork, the shoreline is useful for cavalry." Blücher to Gneisenau, Treptow, [?] Aug. 1811, *BB*, 139.

14. For the complete list of the fortifications Blücher planned to build, see Pertz and Delbrück, *Gneisenau*, 2:680–81.

15. Blücher to Thile, Treptow, [?] Aug. 1811, *BB*, 137.

16. Blücher to Gneisenau, Treptow, [?] Aug. 1811, *BB*, 139–40.

17. Blücher to Kleist, Treptow, 23 Aug. 1811, *BB*, 141.

18. Blücher to Gneisenau, Treptow, 22 Aug. 1811, *BB*, 140–41.

19. Blücher to Kleist, Treptow, 20 Aug. 1811, *BB*, 139.

20. Lehmann, *Scharnhorst*, 2:398.

21. Blücher to Gneisenau, Treptow, 22 Aug. 1811, *BB*, 140.

22. Blücher to Bonin, Treptow, 2 Sept. 1811, *BB*, 142.

23. Blücher to Thile, Treptow, [?] Aug. 1811, *BB*, 139.

24. Blücher to Gneisenau, Treptow, [?] Aug. 1811, *BB*, 141.

25. Bülow to Friedrich Wilhelm, 14 Aug. 1811, in Boyen, *Erinnerungen*, ed. Nippold, 2:128–29, 430–33.

26. Ranke, *Hardenberg*, 3:198.

27. In Boyen, *Erinnerungen*, ed. Nippold, 2:129.

28. Wigger, *Feldmarschall Fürst Blücher*, 104–105; Varnhagen von Ense, *Bülow*, 90–91.

29. Unger, *Blücher*, 1:367–68.

30. Scharnhorst to Yorck, 29 Aug. 1811, Linnebach, *Scharnhorsts Briefe*, 1:418–21.
31. Friederike von Auer, "Erinnerungen aus der Jugendzeit für meine Kinder," BFA, No. 17.
32. Blücher to Gneisenau, Treptow, 19 Aug. 1811, *BB*, 136.
33. Wigger, *Feldmarschall Fürst Blücher*, 104–105; Unger, *Blücher*, 1:367.
34. Bülow to Georg, 21 Oct. 1811, BFA, No. 18.
35. Bülow to Georg, 12 Dec. 1807, BFA, No. 19.
36. Blücher to Kleist, Treptow, 23 Aug. 1811, *BB*, 141–42.
37. Blücher to Bonin, Treptow, 2 Sept. 1811, *BB*, 142.
38. Wigger, *Feldmarschall Fürst Blücher*, 110.
39. Blücher to Hardenberg, Treptow, 12 Sept. 1811, *BB*, 143.
40. Quoted in Wigger, *Feldmarschall Fürst Blücher*, 110.
41. Ranke, *Hardenberg*, 3:199.
42. Wigger, *Feldmarschall Fürst Blücher*, 109–10.
43. Gneisenau to Hardenberg, Berlin, 22 Sept. 1811, in Griewank, *Gneisenau*, Nr. 80b, 177; Muir, *Britain and the Defeat of Napoleon*, 185.
44. Lehmann, *Scharnhorst*, 2:422; Muir, *Britain and the Defeat of Napoleon*, 186.
45. Blasendorff, *Gebhard Leberecht von Blücher*, 171; Unger, *Blücher*, 1:370.
46. Blücher to Hardenberg, Treptow, 12 Sept. 1811, *BB*, 142–43.
47. Ranke, *Hardenberg*, 3:199; Wigger, *Feldmarschall Fürst Blücher*, 111–12; Lehmann, *Scharnhorst*, 2:415; Blasendorff, *Gebhard Leberecht von Blücher*, 172; Unger, *Blücher*, 1:370, 375.
48. Blücher to Frederick William, Treptow, 4 Oct. 1811, *BB*, 144–45.
49. Blücher to Hardenberg, Treptow, 12 Oct. 1811, *BB*, 146.
50. Blücher to Gneisenau, Treptow, 12 Oct. 1811, *BB*, 147.
51. Quoted in Wigger, *Feldmarschall Fürst Blücher*, 113–14; Unger, *Blücher*, 1:371–72, 375; Blasendorff, *Gebhard Leberecht von Blücher*, 173.
52. Quoted in Unger, *Blücher*, 1:376.
53. Blücher to Gneisenau, Treptow, 12 Oct. 1811, *BB*, 146.
54. Wigger, *Feldmarschall Fürst Blücher*, 111.
55. Blücher to Hardenberg, Treptow, 12 Oct. 1811, *BB*, 145–46.
56. Wigger, *Feldmarschall Fürst Blücher*, 116; Blasendorff, *Gebhard Leberecht von Blücher*, 173.
57. Quoted in Wigger, *Feldmarschall Fürst Blücher*, 115.
58. Unger, *Blücher*, 1:376.
59. Quoted in Wigger, *Feldmarschall Fürst Blücher*, 116.
60. Wigger, *Feldmarschall Fürst Blücher*, 116–17; Blasendorff, *Gebhard Leberecht von Blücher*, 173–74; Unger, *Blücher*, 1: 376–77.
61. Unger, *Blücher*, 1:377.
62. Napoleon to Maret, Düsseldorf, 3 Nov. 1811, *CN*, No. 18234, 22:553.
63. Quoted in Wigger, *Feldmarschall Fürst Blücher*, 118.

Chapter Nine

1. Steffens, *Adventures on the Road to Paris*, 73.
2. Unger, *Blücher*, 2:2–3.

3. Ibid.
4. Ibid.
5. Pertz and Delbrück, *Gneisenau*, 2:520.
6. Unger, *Blücher*, 2:3.
7. Blücher to Frederick William, Breslau, 17 Nov. 1812, *BB*, 150.
8. Blasendorff, *Gebhard Leberecht von Blücher*, 177.
9. The best account of these events is provided by Droysen, *Yorck*, 1:336–77; and Henckel von Donnersmarck, *Erinnerungen*, 163–74. Supporting material can be found in Holleben and Caemmerer, *Geschichte des Frühjahrs-feldzuges 1813*, 1:86; Koch, *History of Prussia*, 195–96; and Maude, *Leipzig Campaign*, 50–52.
10. Lieven, *Russia against Napoleon*, 292.
11. Steffens, *Adventures on the Road to Paris*, 77.
12. Blücher to Scharnhorst, Breslau, 5 Jan. 1813, *BB*, 153.
13. Unger, *Blücher*, 2:6.
14. Blücher to Stein, Breslau, 25 Jan. 1813, *BB*, 153.
15. Blücher to Franz, Breslau, 26 Feb. 1813, *BB*, 153.
16. Blasendorff, *Gebhard Leberecht von Blücher*, 182.
17. Blücher to Franz, Breslau, 26 Feb. 1813, *BB*, 153–54.
18. Blasendorff, *Gebhard Leberecht von Blücher*, 182.
19. Bogdanovich, *Geschichte des Krieges im Jahre 1813*, 1a:71.
20. Blücher, *Blücher in Briefen*, 15.
21. Pertz and Delbrück, *Gneisenau*, 2:530.
22. Unger, *Blücher*, 2:6.
23. Quoted in Blasendorff, *Gebhard Leberecht von Blücher*, 182.
24. Blücher to Franz, Breslau, 5 Mar. 1813, *BB*, 154–55.
25. Blücher to Bonin, Breslau, 12 Mar. 1813, *BB*, 156.
26. Blücher to Franz, Breslau, 5 Mar. 1813, *BB*, 154–55.
27. Unger, *Blücher*, 2:8–9.
28. Blücher to Franz, Breslau, 5 Mar. 1813, *BB*, 155.
29. Holleben and Caemmerer, *Geschichte des Frühjahrsfeldzuges 1813*, 1:162–63; Unger, *Blücher*, 2:10.
30. Mikhailovsky-Danilevsky, *Denkwurdigkeiten*, 31–33.
31. Holleben and Caemmerer, *Geschichte des Frühjahrsfeldzuges 1813*, 1:163, 240–41.
32. Ibid.; Shanahan, *Prussian Military Reforms*, 206; Unger, *Blücher*, 2:12.
33. Blücher to Hake, Breslau, 11 Mar. 1813, *BB*, 155.
34. Specifically, Blücher's corps mustered at Gleiwitz (Gliwice), Oppeln (Opole), Ohlau (Olawa), Breslau, Neumarkt (Środa Śląska), Canth (Kąty Wrocławskie), Franconiastein (Ząbkowice Śląskie), Patschkau (Paczków), Leobschütz (Głubczyce), and Ratibor (Raciborz).
35. Frederick William to Blücher, 17 Mar. 1813, GStA PK, VI HA Rep. 92 Nl. Gneisenau, Nr. 18.
36. Holleben and Caemmerer, *Geschichte des Frühjahrsfeldzuges 1813*, 1:244; Pertz and Delbrück, *Gneisenau*, 2:546.
37. Quoted in Mikhailovsky-Danilevsky, *Denkwurdigkeiten*, 36.
38. Kutuzov to Blücher, Kalisch, 19 Mar. 1813, RGVIA, fond VUA, op. 16, delo 3921, I.96.

39. Grolman served as General Staff chief in 1814–19, Rühle in 1819–21, Müffling in 1821–29, and Krauseneck in 1829–49.

40. Steffens, *Adventures on the Road to Paris*, 82.

41. Clausewitz to Marie, Rochlitz, 9 Apr. 1813 in Schwartz, *Clausewitz*, 2:74.

42. Prince Frederick William Henry Augustus of Prussia (1779–1843) was the son of Frederick the Great's youngest brother, Prince Augustus Ferdinand; his older brother, Louis Ferdinand, was killed at Saalfeld in 1806. Both Louis Ferdinand and Augustus are often mistakenly referred to as brothers of Frederick William III.

43. Unger, *Blücher*, 2:11–12.

44. Most sources fail to describe the extent of the damage caused by Davout. Clausewitz provides an eyewitness report from shortly after the French blew the bridge: "The beautiful bridge, the most beautiful I have ever seen, is really so blown by the mines (not cannon), that no trace exists of two of the arches and one of the piers." Clausewitz to Marie, Dresden, 1 Apr. 1813, in Schwartz, *Clausewitz*, 2:72.

45. Holleben and Caemmerer, *Geschichte des Frühjahrsfeldzuges 1813*, 1:244–46.

46. Pertz and Delbrück, *Gneisenau*, 2:530–31.

47. Gneisenau to Hardenberg, Bunzlau, 24 Mar. 1813, in Griewank, *Gneisenau*, Nr. 108, 217–18.

48. Blücher to Hardenberg, Dresden, 30 Mar. 1813, in Blücher, "Aus Blüchers Korrespondenz," 157.

49. Blücher to Amalie, Dresden, 31 Mar. 1813, *BB*, 158.

50. Blücher to Hardenberg, Dresden, 30 Mar. 1813, in Blücher, "Aus Blüchers Korrespondenz," 157–58. Mikhailovsky-Danilevsky claims that while the Saxons greeted the Russians with "enthusiasm," the Prussians earned "hostile feelings." *Denkwurdigkeiten*, 52–53.

51. Quoted in Blasendorff, *Gebhard Leberecht von Blücher*, 185.

52. Bogdanovich, *Geschichte des Krieges im Jahre 1813*, 1a:98–99; Mikhailovsky-Danilevsky, *Denkwurdigkeiten*, 54.

53. Pertz and Delbrück, *Gneisenau*, 2:557.

54. Clausewitz to Marie, Penig, 4 Apr. 1813 in Schwartz, *Clausewitz*, 2:73.

55. Blücher to Amalie, Borna, 12 Apr. 1813, *BB*, 159–60.

56. Steffens, *Adventures on the Road to Paris*, 91.

57. Blasendorff, *Gebhard Leberecht von Blücher*, 186; Unger, *Blücher*, 2:18.

58. Blücher to Amalie, Altenburg, 22 Apr. 1813, GStA PK, VI HA Rep. 92 Nl. Blücher von Wahlstatt.

59. Holleben and Caemmerer, *Geschichte des Frühjahrsfeldzuges 1813*, 1:384–85.

60. Bogdanovich, *Geschichte des Krieges im Jahre 1813*, 1a:172.

61. See Mikhailovsky-Danilevsky, *Denkwurdigkeiten*, 64–70.

62. Pertz and Delbrück, *Gneisenau*, 2:581. None of Blücher's biographers mention this, nor do the historians of the German General Staff.

63. See Bogdanovich, *Geschichte des Krieges im Jahre 1813*, 1a:173.

64. Lieven, *Russia against Napoleon*, 313.

65. This letter is reproduced in full in Mikhailovsky-Danilevsky, *Denkwurdigkeiten*, 70.

66. Blücher to Frederick William, Altenburg, 29 Apr. 1813, GStA PK, VI HA Rep. 92 Nl. Gneisenau, 16.

67. Blücher to Boyen, [?] Apr. 1813, in Boyen, *Erinnerungen,* ed. Nippold, 3:303.
68. Blücher to a cavalry officer, Altenburg, 28 Apr. 1813, *BB,* 163–64.
69. Blücher to Amalie, Altenburg, 29 Apr. 1813, *BB,* 164.
70. Issued from Altenburg on 24 Apr. 1813 and quoted in Gneisenau, *Blücher,* 76–77.

Chapter Ten

1. Mikhailovsky-Danilevsky, *Denkwurdigkeiten,* 76.
2. Bogdanovich, *Geschichte des Krieges im Jahre 1813,* 1a:191; Pertz and Delbrück, *Gneisenau,* 2:587.
3. Parkinson's colorful and entertaining account of Lützen, particularly the sweeping cavalry charges led by Blücher, simply cannot be supported by the authoritative sources. He offers little documentation to support his interpretation of the battle. See Parkinson, *Hussar General,* 110–15.
4. Hüser, *Denkwürdigkeiten,* 112.
5. Varnhagen von Ense, *Blücher,* 103.
6. Clausewitz to Marie, Proschwitz, 8 May 1813, in Schwartz, *Clausewitz,* 2:80.
7. Blücher to Amalie, Borna, 4 May 1813, *BB,* 165.
8. Nauck's account is reproduced in full in Pertz and Delbrück, *Gneisenau,* 3:678.
9. Blasendorff, *Gebhard Leberecht von Blücher,* 189–90; Unger, *Blücher,* 2:25; Wigger, *Feldmarschall Fürst Blücher,* 136.
10. Berthezène, *Souvenirs militaires,* 2:237.
11. Much disagreement over when Scharnhorst received his wound can be found in the sources with many historians incorrectly placing the time much earlier in the day. According to Scharnhorst's own report, written on the night of 2/3 May, he was wounded between 6:00 and 7:00. Scharnhorst and Gneisenau, "Report over the Battle of Groß Görschen" or "Letter from an Officer of Blücher's Corps." Reproduced in full in Pertz and Delbrück, *Gneisenau,* 2:715.
12. Gneisenau to Caroline, Meißen, 6 May 1813, GStA PK, VI HA Rep. 92 Nl. Gneisenau, Paket Nr.18.
13. Clausewitz to Marie, 3 May 1813 in Schwartz, *Clausewitz,* 2:79.
14. Bogdanovich, *Geschichte des Krieges im Jahre 1813,* 1a:198–99; Vaudoncourt, *Histoire de la guerre,* 79.
15. Scheer, *Blücher,* 3:118.
16. Bogdanovich, *Geschichte des Krieges im Jahre 1813,* 1a:199. Unger and Görlitz each claim that the Russian cavalry refused to participate without the tsar's permission, which could not be secured in time. Unger, *Blücher,* 2:26; Görlitz, *Blücher,* 244.
17. According to Cathcart, the lack of moonlight made night movements impossible. *Commentaries,* 132.
18. Maude, *Leipzig Campaign,* 107.
19. Gneisenau to Caroline, Meißen, GStA PK, VI HA Rep. 92 Nl. Gneisenau, Paket Nr.18.
20. Clausewitz to Marie, 3 May 1813 in Schwartz, *Clausewitz,* 2:80.

21. Unger, *Blücher*, 2:27–28.

22. Holleben and Caemmerer, *Geschichte des Frühjahrsfeldzuges 1813*, 2:41.

23. Unger, *Blücher*, 2:28.

24. Blasendorff, *Gebhard Leberecht von Blücher*, 190–91.

25. Frederick William to Blücher, Groitzsch, 3 May 1813, in Blücher, *Blücher in Briefen*, 29.

26. Blücher to Amalie, Borna, 4 May 1813, *BB*, 165.

27. See Nauck's account in Pertz and Delbrück, *Gneisenau*, 3:678.

28. Steffens, *Adventures on the Road to Paris*, 98–99.

29. See in particular his letter to Yorck, informing the general that he had earned the Iron Cross, First Class for his part in the victorious battle. Droysen, *Yorck*, 2:66. According to Cathcart, Tsar Alexander also "spoke of the result as a victory gained on our side, and it was afterwards the fashion in the army to consider it as such." *Commentaries*, 135.

30. Nostitz, *Tagebuch*, 1:48–49.

31. Alexander to Blücher, Dresden, 5 May 1813, quoted in Blasendorff, *Gebhard Leberecht von Blücher*, 192.

32. Blücher to Amalie, Kumschütz, 15 May 1813, *BB*, 165.

33. Natzmer to Frederick William, Königsbrück, 10 May 1813, in Pertz and Delbrück, *Gneisenau*, 2:603. Unger also tells of "other old evils" that resurfaced. *Blücher*, 2:32. It is unclear whether these were mental or physical afflictions.

34. Nostitz, *Tagebuch*, 1:47.

35. Blücher to Amalie, Kumschütz, 15 May 1813, *BB*, 165–66.

36. Quoted in Blasendorff, *Gebhard Leberecht von Blücher*, 194.

37. Nostitz, *Tagebuch*, 1:48.

38. Maude, *Leipzig Campaign*, 135–36.

39. Josselson, *The Commander*, 172.

40. Fritz to Wilhelm, Goldberg, 25 May 1813, in Griewank, *Hohenzollernbriefe*, Nr. 40, 57.

41. Nostitz, *Tagebuch*, 1:49.

42. Steffens, *Adventures on the Road to Paris*, 102.

43. Unger, *Blücher*, 2:38.

44. Nostitz, *Tagebuch*, 1:49.

45. Steffens, *Adventures on the Road to Paris*, 103.

46. The account of 20 May has been derived from Blücher's after-action report, "Account of the Participation of General Blücher's Corps in the Battle of Bautzen on 20 and 21 May," dated 31 May 1813, which Müffling drafted, Gneisenau approved, and Blücher signed. The original Russian translation is in RGVIA, fond VUA, delo 3902, pt. 2, ll.73–74b. The report is reproduced in full in Pertz and Delbrück, *Gneisenau*, 2:619–20; in part in Unger, *Blücher*, 2:37–39. See also Plotho, *Der Krieg*, 1:160–63; Vaudoncourt, *Histoire de la guerre*, 93–95; Bogdanovich, *Geschichte des Krieges im Jahre 1813*, 1b:59–60; and Holleben and Caemmerer, *Geschichte des Frühjahrsfeldzuges 1813*, 2:212–16.

47. For details of the action during this part of the battle, see Bogdanovich, *Geschichte des Krieges im Jahre 1813*, 1b:67–68; and Vaudoncourt, *Histoire de la guerre*, 96.

48. Müffling, *Aus meinem Leben*, 40; Pertz and Delbrück, *Gneisenau*, 2:623.
49. "Account of the Participation of General Blücher's Corps in the Battle of Bautzen."
50. Gneisenau, *Blücher*, 119.
51. Bogdanovich, *Geschichte des Krieges im Jahre 1813*, 1b:69–70.
52. Gneisenau, *Blücher*, 120.
53. Pertz and Delbrück claim the French lost 4,000 men in the fighting at Preititz. *Gneisenau*, 2:624.
54. Nostitz, *Tagebuch*, 1:50.
55. Unger, *Blücher*, 2:41.
56. Mikhailovsky-Danilevsky, *Opisanie voiny 1813 goda*, 1: 210. The Russian eyewitness states that the Guard Artillery opened fire at 2:00.
57. Ibid.
58. Müffling, *Aus meinem Leben*, 42–43.
59. Pertz and Delbrück, *Gneisenau*, 2:629.
60. Bogdanovich, *Geschichte des Krieges im Jahre 1813*, 1b:76.
61. "The emperor [tsar] seemed to wish for an offensive movement," Robert Wilson recorded in his diary. "While the matter was under discussion, Blücher sent word that he was overpowered, and had ordered a retreat." Wilson, *Private Diary*, 2:19–20.
62. In an annotation on the bottom of page 76, the Russian officer who translated Bogdanovich's volumes to German, "A.S., a retired colonel of the Russian General Staff," claims to have heard Alexander utter these words at 4:00. Bogdanovich, *Geschichte des Krieges im Jahre 1813*, 1b:77.
63. Reiche, *Memoiren*, 1:283.
64. Stewart, *Narrative*, 49.
65. The account of 21 May has been derived from "Account of the Participation of General Blücher's Corps in the Battle of Bautzen"; Holleben and Caemmerer, *Geschichte des Frühjahrsfeldzuges 1813*, 2:207–40; Bogdanovich, *Geschichte des Krieges im Jahre 1813*, 1b:49–81; Plotho, *Der Krieg*, 1:164–72; Vaudoncourt, *Histoire de la guerre*, 95–98; and Droysen, *Yorck*, 2:252–53.
66. Blücher to Bonin, Strehlen, 24 June 1813, *BB*, 167.
67. Bogdanovich, *Geschichte des Krieges im Jahre 1813*, 1b:76; Droysen, *Yorck*, 2:94–95. Müffling states: "Our abandonment of the Kreckwitz Heights met with severe censure from all around the sovereigns, in which the tsar joined to a degree. Only our king, who tried but failed to get Wittgenstein to shift his left wing toward the center . . . , fully approved our retreat." *Aus meinem Leben*, 44.
68. Nostitz, *Tagebuch*, 1:51–52.
69. Lanrezac, *La Manoeuvre de Lützen*, 245.
70. Müffling, *Aus meinem Leben*, 40.
71. Bogdanovich, *Geschichte des Krieges im Jahre 1813*, 1b:93–94.
72. Osten-Sacken, *Militärische-Politische Geschichte des Befreiungskrieges*, 2:343. Lieven claims that by late May, the Russians "were also beginning to go hungry." *Russia against Napoleon*, 324.
73. Pertz and Delbrück, *Gneisenau*, 2:644–45.
74. Stewart, *Narrative*, 51. Cathcart describes the engagement as "one of the most brilliant cavalry affairs of modern days." *Commentaries*, 170.

75. The account of this engagement is derived from Zieten's after-action report, reproduced in full in Henckel von Donnersmarck, *Erinnerungen*, 197–98; and providing the most extensive coverage, Bogdanovich, *Geschichte des Krieges im Jahre 1813*, 1b:95–101.

76. Holleben and Caemmerer, *Geschichte des Frühjahrsfeldzuges 1813*, 2:258.

77. Quoted in Blasendorff, *Gebhard Leberecht von Blücher*, 197.

78. Macdonald to Berthier, 26 May 1813, SHAT, C^2 145.

79. Napoleon to Caulaincourt, Bunzlau, 26 May 1813, *CN*, No. 20052, 25:329–30.

80. Gneisenau to Caroline, 31 May 1813, GStA PK, VI HA Rep. 92 Nl. Gneisenau, Paket Nr. 21.

81. Wittgenstein to Bülow, Löwenberg, 25 May 1813, GStA PK, IV HA Rep. 15a Nr. 248.

82. Unger, *Blücher*, 2:48.

Chapter Eleven

1. Quoted in Blasendorff, *Gebhard Leberecht von Blücher*, 200. Stein wrote this letter to his wife on 18 June 1813.

2. Blücher to Bonin, Strehlen, 24 June 1813, *BB*, 167.

3. Nostitz, *Tagebuch*, 1:52.

4. Blücher to Hippel, Strehlen, July 1813, *BB*, 168.

5. Müffling, *Aus meinem Leben*, 53.

6. Steffens, *Adventures on the Road to Paris*, 107–108.

7. Blücher to Gneisenau, Strehlen, 29 June 1813, GStA PK, VI HA Rep. 92 Nl. Gneisenau, Paket Nr. 23.

8. Ibid.

9. Blücher to Gneisenau, Strehlen, 24 July 1813, GStA PK, VI HA Rep. 92 Nl. Gneisenau, Paket Nr. 23.

10. Ibid.; Droysen, *Yorck*, 2:110.

11. Müffling, *Aus meinem Leben*, 52.

12. Blücher to Hippel, Strehlen, July 1813, *BB*, 168.

13. Blücher to Gneisenau, Strehlen, 24 July 1813, GStA PK, VI HA Rep. 92 Nl. Gneisenau, Paket Nr. 23.

14. Ibid.

15. Blücher to Oppen, Strehlen, 24 July 1813, *BB*, 170.

16. Blücher to Hippel, Strehlen, July 1813, *BB*, 169.

17. Ibid., 168.

18. Bogdanovich, *Geschichte des Krieges im Jahre 1813*, 1b:275. On 9 August the 124,000 men and 402 guns of Kleist's II Corps, Wittgenstein's army corps, and the Russo-Prussian Guard and Reserve moved into the district of Landeshut and the County of Glatz along the Bohemian frontier, crossing the border on the eleventh.

19. Figures are drawn from Friederich, *Die Befreiungskriege*, 1:567–74, 85–90.

20. Nostitz, *Tagebuch*, 1:52–53.

21. Henderson, *Blücher and the Uprising of Prussia*, 114–15.

22. Maude, *Leipzig Campaign*, 159.

23. Müffling, *Aus meinem Leben*, 56.

24. Maude, *Leipzig Campaign*, 159.
25. Bogdanovich, *Geschichte des Krieges im Jahre 1813*, 1b:284.
26. Henderson, *Blücher and the Uprising of Prussia*, 116.
27. Friederich, *Die Befreiungskriege*, 1:224–25.
28. Droysen, *Yorck*, 2:106.
29. Maude, *Leipzig Campaign*, 159.
30. Bogdanovich, *Geschichte des Krieges im Jahre 1813*, 1b:283; Mikhailovsky-Danilevsky, *Denkwurdigkeiten*, 128.
31. Henderson, *Blücher and the Uprising of Prussia*, 115–16.
32. Craig, "Problems of Coalition Warfare," 28–29.
33. Freytag-Loringhoven, *Aufklärung und Armeeführung*, 3.
34. Bogdanovich, *Geschichte des Krieges im Jahre 1813*, 2a:17.
35. Lieven, *Russia against Napoleon*, 376.
36. Müffling, *Zur Kriegsgeschichte*, 2.
37. Unger, *Blücher*, 2:55–56.
38. Quoted in Droysen, *Yorck*, 2:117.
39. Bogdanovich, *Geschichte des Krieges im Jahre 1813*, 2a:18–19.
40. Müffling, *Zur Kriegsgeschichte*, 2–3.
41. This unit consisted of St. Priest's own VIII Infantry Corps, the 1st Dragoon Division, an additional dragoon brigade, and three Cossack regiments. Bogdanovich, *Geschichte des Krieges im Jahre 1813*, 2a:22.
42. Freytag-Loringhoven, *Aufklärung und Armeeführung*, 5.
43. Friederich, *Die Befreiungskriege*, 1:574–81.
44. Freytag-Loringhoven, *Aufklärung und Armeeführung*, 4–5. An additional thirty-eight battalions and seventeen squadrons garrisoned the fortresses and depots in Upper Silesia. Of these, a Landwehr detachment of eight battalions and twelve squadrons supported by four guns received the assignment of blockading Glogau after hostilities resumed.
45. Nostitz, *Tagebuch*, 1:53.
46. Steffens, *Adventures on the Road to Paris*, 109.
47. "Instructions," Dresden, 12 Aug. 1813, *CN*, No. 20360, 26:35.
48. After detaching forces to Italy and the Bavarian border, Napoleon did not think the Austrians would assemble more than 100,000 men in Bohemia to oppose him. "Instructions," Dresden, 12 Aug. June 1813, *CN*, No. 20360, 26:35.
49. Napoleon to Davout, Dresden, 8 Aug. 1813, *CN*, No. 20339, 26:13–16; Napoleon to Oudinot, Dresden, 12 Aug. 1813, ibid., No. 20364, 26:37–41.
50. Imperial forces in Silesia consisted of 130,000 men in fourteen divisions, each between 7,000–9,000 bayonets, and the 10,000 sabers of II Cavalry Corps.
51. Quoted in Freytag-Loringhoven, *Aufklärung und Armeeführung*, 42.
52. Maude, *Leipzig Campaign*, 175–76.
53. Napoleon to Berthier, Dresden, 15 Aug. 1813, *CN*, No. 20380, 26:61–62.
54. "Instructions," Dresden, 13 Aug. 1813, *CN*, No. 20373, 26:45–47.
55. Vaudoncourt, *Histoire de la guerre*, 139; Bogdanovich, *Geschichte des Krieges im Jahre 1813*, 2a:26.
56. Napoleon to Ney, Bautzen, 16 Aug. 1813, *CN*, No. 20389, 26:68–69.

57. Ibid., 68.
58. Bogdanovich, *Geschichte des Krieges im Jahre 1813*, 2(1):22.
59. Napoleon to Poniatowski, Bautzen, 16 Aug. 1813, *CN*, No. 20392, 26:70–71.
60. Napoleon to Macdonald, Bautzen, 16 Aug. 1813, *CN*, No. 20390, 26:69.
61. On 17 August Vandamme received orders to move I Corps from Dresden to Bautzen, from where it would proceed to Görlitz to form Napoleon's regular reserve. Berthier to Vandamme, Bautzen, 17 Aug. 1813, SHAT, C^{17} 179.
62. Napoleon to St.-Cyr, Bautzen, 17 Aug. 1813, *CN*, No. 20398, 26:77–78.
63. Napoleon to Ney, Görlitz, 19 Aug. 1813, *CN*, No. 20411, 26:95.
64. Vaudoncourt, *Histoire de la guerre*, 140; Bogdanovich, *Geschichte des Krieges im Jahre 1813*, 2a:27.
65. Napoleon to Berthier, Zittau, 20 Aug. 1813, *CN*, No. 20421, 26:103–104.

Chapter Twelve

1. Napoleon to Ney and Marmont, Görlitz, 2:00 P.M., 20 Aug. 1813, *CN*, No. 20425, 26:106.
2. Napoleon to Maret, Görlitz, 4:00 P.M., 20 Aug. 1813, *CN*, No. 20427, 26:107.
3. Napoleon to Macdonald, Lauban, 12:00 A.M., 21 Aug. 1813, *CN*, No. 20428, 26:107.
4. Napoleon to Macdonald, Görlitz, 3:00 P.M., 20 Aug. 1813, *CN*, No. 20426, 26:106; Napoleon to Ney and Marmont, Görlitz, 2:00 P.M., 20 Aug. 1813, *CN*, No. 20425, 26:106.
5. Odeleben, *Circumstantial Narrative*, 265.
6. Napoleon to Maret, Görlitz, 4:00 P.M., 20 Aug. 1813, *CN*, No. 20427, 26:107.
7. Napoleon to Ney, Lauban, 21 Aug. 1813, *CN*, No. 20435, 26:110.
8. Napoleon to Macdonald, Lauban, 12:00 A.M., 20 Aug. 1813, *CN*, No. 20428, 26:107; Napoleon to Berthier, Lauban, 21 Aug. 1813, ibid., No. 20429, 26:107–108; Friederich, *Herbstfeldzug 1813*, 1:264.
9. Berthier to Macdonald, Lauban, 5:00 A.M., 21 Aug. 1813, SHAT, C^{17} 179.
10. Disposition, 20 Aug. 1813, Add. Ms. 20,112.
11. Blücher to Frederick William, 20 Aug. 1813, GStA, PK, VI HA Rep. 92 Nl. Gneisenau, Nr. 16.
12. Freytag-Loringhoven, *Aufklärung und Armeeführung*, 34.
13. Gneisenau to Sacken, Hohlstein, 21 Aug. 1813, in Friederich, *Herbstfeldzug 1813*, 1:260–61.
14. Gneisenau's report to Hardenberg offers insight into the thought process at Blücher's headquarters. "On the 21st, the enemy wanted to engage us in a general battle (at Löwenberg). However, we committed only the advance guard and a portion of the Prince of Mecklenburg's brigade to the engagement. We held back our remaining masses, Russians and Prussians, and withdrew them to the region of the Gröditzberg unmolested because superior enemy forces advanced against General Sacken's position at Bunzlau and forced him to retreat." Gneisenau to Hardenberg, Jauer, 25 Aug. 1813, GSTA PK, I. HA Rep. 74 Staatskanzleramt O Ap. Nr. 9, Bd. 3.
15. Droysen, *Yorck*, 2:126.

16. Quoted in Unger, *Blücher*, 2:72.

17. Müffling, *Zur Kriegsgeschichte*, 21.

18. Gneisenau to Hardenberg, Jauer, 25 Aug. 1813, GSTA PK, I. HA Rep. 74 Staatskanzleramt O Ap. Nr. 9, Bd. 3.

19. Cathcart, *Commentaries*, 213–14.

20. Berthier to Ney, Löwenberg, 6:30 A.M., 22 Aug. 1813, SHAT, C^{17} 179.

21. Berthier to Macdonald, Lauriston, and Ney, Löwenberg, 6:30 A.M., 22 Aug. 1813, SHAT, C^{17} 179.

22. Odeleben, *Circumstantial Narrative*, 268–69.

23. Napoleon to St.-Cyr, Görlitz, 23 Aug. 1813, *CN*, No. 20445, 26:118–19.

24. Berthier to Corbineau, Löwenberg, 2:30 A.M.; Berthier to Marmont, Löwenberg, 4:30 A.M.; Berthier to Mouton and Mortier, Löwenberg, 3:00 A.M.; and Berthier to Latour-Maubourg, Löwenberg, 4:00 A.M., 23 Aug. 1813, SHAT, C^{17} 179.

25. Napoleon to Berthier, Löwenberg, 23 Aug. 1813, *CN*, No. 20442, 26:115–16.

26. Napoleon to Berthier, Löwenberg, 22 Aug. 1813, *CN*, Nos. 20440 and 20441, 26:114.

27. Napoleon to Berthier, Löwenberg, 23 Aug. 1813, *CN*, No. 20442, 26:115–16; Petre, *Napoleon's last Campaign*, 189–90.

28. The orders issued to the Army of the Bober for 23 August have been lost. The above is based on the operations that took place on that day. See Friederich, *Herbstfeldzug 1813*, 1:276.

29. Napoleon to Maret, Löwenberg, 22 Aug. 1813, *CN*, No. 20437, 26:112.

30. Napoleon to St.-Cyr and Vandamme, Görlitz, 23 Aug. 1813, *CN*, Nos. 20445 and 20446, 26:118–20.

31. See Leggiere, *Napoleon and Berlin*, 160–77.

32. Bernadotte to Blücher, Teltow, 24 Aug. 1813, Add. Ms. 20,112.

33. Müffling, *Zur Kriegsgeschichte*, 24; Bogdanovich, *Geschichte des Krieges im Jahre 1813*, 2a:33; Friederich, *Herbstfeldzug 1813*, 1:272.

34. Müffling, *Zur Kriegsgeschichte*, 24.

35. Blücher to Frederick William, Jauer, 23 Aug. 1813, GStA, PK, VI HA Rep. 92 Nl. Gneisenau, Nr. 16.

36. Freytag-Loringhoven, *Aufklärung und Armeeführung*, 55.

37. Unger, *Blücher*, 2:73.

38. Preliminary Disposition, 7:00 P.M., 24 Aug. 1813, Add. Ms 20,112.

39. Blücher to Amalie, Jauer, 25 Aug. 1813, *BB*, 174–75.

40. Disposition, 25 Aug. 1813, Add. Ms 20,112.

41. Freytag-Loringhoven, *Aufklärung und Armeeführung*, 66.

42. Henckel von Donnersmarck, *Erinnerungen*, 213; Friederich, *Herbstfeldzug 1813*, 1:291–92.

43. This statement is from Johann Friedrich Benzenberg to Gneisenau, 11 March 1817, quoted in Pertz and Delbrück, *Gneisenau*, 3:204.

44. Ordre de mouvement, Goldberg, 25 Aug. 1813, in Fabry, *Étude sur les opérations du maréchal Macdonald*, 50–51.

45. Gneisenau, *Blücher*, 162.

46. Unger, *Blücher*, 2:78.

47. Quoted in Gneisenau, *Blücher*, 163.

48. Gneisenau to Gibsone, Brechelshof, 26 Aug. 1813, GStA, PK, VI HA Rep. 92 Nl. Gneisenau, Nr. 21.

49. Sebastiani to Macdonald, 27 Aug. 1813, SHAT, C² 154.

50. Thinking Blücher would order a retreat, Langeron had sent his artillery to Jauer at the start of the battle.

51. Macdonald to Berthier, 27 Aug. 1813, SHAT, C² 154; Lauriston to Macdonald, 28 Aug. 1813, SHAT, C² 154; Müffling, *Aus meinem Leben*, 68; Fabry, *Étude sur les opérations du maréchal Macdonald*, 98–99.

52. Blücher to Frederick William, Goldberg, 28 Aug. 1813, GStA, PK, VI HA Rep. 92 Nl. Gneisenau, Nr. 16.

53. Gneisenau to Clausewitz, Goldberg, 28 Aug. 1813, GStA, PK, VI HA Rep. 92 Nl. Gneisenau, Nr. 21.

54. Blücher to Frederick William, Goldberg, 28 Aug. 1813, GStA, PK, VI HA Rep. 92 Nl. Gneisenau, Nr. 16.

55. Lieven, *Napoleon against Russia*, 387.

56. Pertz and Delbrück, *Gneisenau*, 3:212.

57. Gneisenau to a friend, Hohlstein, 29 Aug. 1813, reproduced in Pertz and Delbrück, *Gneisenau*, 3:242–43.

58. Friederich, *Herbstfeldzug 1813*, 1:339–40; Freytag-Loringhoven, *Aufklärung und Armeeführung*, 106–107.

59. Nostitz, *Tagebuch*, 1:59.

60. Blücher to Amalie, Löwenberg, 1 Sept. 1813, *BB*, 177.

61. Quoted in Friederich, *Herbstfeldzug 1813*, 1:342.

62. Tagesbefehl, Löwenberg, 1 Sept. 1813, in Pflugk-Harttung, *Das Befreiungsjahr 1813*, Nr. 221, 305–306.

63. Blücher to Amalie, Löwenberg, 1 Sept. 1813, *BB*, 176.

64. "Instructions," Duka [on behalf of Schwarzenberg] to Liechtenstein, Dux, 30 Aug. 1813, Add. Ms 20,112.

65. Blücher to Schwarzenberg Löwenberg, 2 Sept. 1813, ibid.

66. "Note sur la situation général de mes affairs," 30 Aug. 1813, *CN*, No. 20492, 26:153–57.

67. Napoleon to Berthier, Dresden, 3 Sept. 1813, *CN*, No. 20508, 26:165.

68. See Leggiere, *Napoleon and Berlin*, 189–228.

69. Friederich, *Herbstfeldzug 1813*, 2:247–48.

70. Odeleben, *Circumstantial Narrative*, 1:295–96.

71. Disposition for 7, 8, and 9 Sept. 1813, Add. Ms 20,112.

72. Blücher to Charles John, Rameritz, 9 Sept. 1813, ibid.

73. Blücher to Frederick William, Radmeritz, 11:00 A.M., 10 Sept. 1813, GStA, PK, VI HA Rep. 92 Nl. Gneisenau, Nr. 16.

74. Unger, *Blücher*, 2:89; Friederich, *Herbstfeldzug 1813*, 2:251–52.

75. Yorck von Wartenburg, *Napoleon as a General*, 2:281.

Chapter Thirteen

1. Blücher to Charles John, Hernnhut, 11 Sept. 1813, Add. Ms 20,112.

2. General Orders, 11 Sept. 1813, ibid.

3. Charles John to Blücher, Jüterbog, 9 Sept. 1813, SHAT, C¹⁷ 132.

4. Blücher to Alexander, Hernnhut, 11 Sept. 1813, reproduced in Lange, *Neithardt von Gneisenau*, 183–84.

5. Friederich, *Herbstfeldzug 1813*, 2:77.
6. Disposition, 13 Sept. 1813, Add. Ms 20,112.
7. Unger, *Blücher*, 2:92; Friederich, *Herbstfeldzug 1813*, 2:256–59; Leggiere, *Napoleon and Berlin*, 234.
8. Odeleben, *Circumstantial Narrative*, 1:306–307. Odeleben and thus Petre, who follows him, mistakenly state that the younger Blücher was captured on 11 September. Petre, *Napoleon's Last Campaign*, 284–85.
9. Napoleon to Berthier, Peterswalde, 5:00 A.M., 17 Sept. 1813, *CN*, No. 20574, 26:207.
10. Blücher to Amalie, Bautzen, 20 Sept. 1813, *BB*, 181–82.
11. Franz to Blücher, Dresden, 17 Sept. 1813, in Blasendorff, *Gebhard Leberecht von Blücher*, 218.
12. Blücher to Bonin, Bautzen, 22 Sept. 1813, *BB*, 182–83.
13. Quoted in Unger, *Blücher*, 2:94.
14. Macdonald to Berthier, 18 Sept. 1813, SHAT, C² 156.
15. Yorck von Wartenburg, *Napoleon as a General*, 2:321.
16. Napoleon to Poniatowski, Pirna, 11:00 A.M., 19 Sept. 1813, *CN*, No. 20594, 26:219.
17. Napoleon to Berthier, Pirna, 20 Sept. 1813, *CN*, No. 20602, 26:224.
18. Napoleon to Berthier, Pirna, 21 Sept. 1813, *CN*, No. 20607, 26:226.
19. Napoleon to Berthier, Dresden, 2:00 A.M., 22 Sept. 1813, *CN*, No. 20609, 26:227–28; Berthier to Macdonald, Dresden, 22 Sept. 1813, SHAT, C¹⁷ 180.
20. Napoleon to Macdonald, Dresden, 10:00 A.M., 22 Sept. 1813, *CN*, No. 20612, 26:229.
21. Quoted in Unger, *Blücher*, 2:93.
22. Napoleon to Maret, Großhartau, 22 Sept. 1813, *CN*, No. 20615, 26:232–33.
23. Ney to Berthier, Düben, 4:00 P.M., 22 Sept. 1813, SHAT, C² 156.
24. Napoleon to Murat, Großhartau, 23 Sept. 1813, *CN*, No. 20618, 26:236; Yorck von Wartenburg, *Napoleon as a General*, 2:323; Petre, *Napoleon's Last Campaign*, 291.
25. Blücher to Bonin, Bautzen, 22 Sept. 1813, *BB*, 182–83.
26. Disposition, 23 Sept. 1813, Add. Ms 20,112.
27. Pertz and Delbrück, *Gneisenau*, 371–72; Friederich, *Herbstfeldzug 1813*, 2:267–70.
28. Pertz and Delbrück, *Gneisenau*, 382–84.
29. Charles John to Blücher, Zerbst, 29 Sept. 1813, SHAT, C¹⁷ 132.
30. Blücher to Charles John, 30 Sept. 1813, reproduced in Fransecky, "Darstellung der Ereignisse bei der schlesischen Armee," 296.
31. Charles John to Blücher, Zerbst, 30 Sept. 1813, reproduced in ibid., 299.
32. Unger, *Blücher*, 2:98–99; Friederich, *Herbstfeldzug 1813*, 2:282–86.
33. Quoted in Unger, *Blücher*, 2:101–102.
34. Ibid., 2:102.
35. Friederich, *Herbstfeldzug 1813*, 2:303–304.
36. Blücher to Charles John, Bad Düben, 5 Oct. 1813, Add. Ms 20,112.
37. Charles John to Blücher, Dessau, 6 Oct. 1813, ibid.
38. Müffling, *Zur Kriegsgeschichte*, 63.
39. Friederich, *Herbstfeldzug 1813*, 2:313.

40. Charles John to Blücher, Dessau, 6 or 7 Oct. 1813, SHAT, C^{17} 133.
41. Friederich, *Herbstfeldzug 1813*, 2:316.
42. Müffling, *Zur Kriegsgeschichte*, 63.
43. Berthier to Souham, Dresden, 4:30 A.M., 3 Oct. 1813, SHAT, C^{17} 181.
44. Berthier to Chastel, Dresden, 4 Oct. 1813, ibid.
45. Napoleon to Macdonald, Dresden, 4 Oct. 1813, *CN*, No. 20693, 26:290.
46. Napoleon to Marmont, Dresden, 4 Oct. 1813, *CN*, No. 20694, 26:290–91.
47. Napoleon to Marmont, Dresden, 3:00 A.M., 5 Oct. 1813, *CN*, No. 20695, 26:291.
48. Napoleon to Berthier, Dresden, 3:00 A.M., 5 Oct. 1813, *CN*, No. 20697, 26:292.
49. Napoleon to Murat, Dresden, 3:00 A.M., 6 Oct. 1813, *CN*, No. 20703, 26:295.
50. Napoleon to Marmont, Dresden, 9:00 A.M., 6 Oct. 1813, *CN*, No. 20705, 26:296; Friederich, *Herbstfeldzug 1813*, 2:299–300, 374–75.
51. Notes, Dresden, 1:00 A.M., 7 Oct. 1813, *CN*, No. 20711, 26:299–300.
52. Napoleon to Murat, Dresden, 6:00 A.M., 7 Oct. 1813, *CN*, No. 20718, 26:304.
53. Friederich, *Herbstfeldzug 1813*, 2:316–17.
54. Napoleon to Murat, Wurzen, 9:00 A.M., 9 Oct. 1813, *CN*, No. 20735, 26:313–14.
55. Disposition, Bad Düben, 7 Oct. 1813, reproduced in Fransecky, "Darstellung der Ereignisse bei der schlesischen Armee," 333.
56. Charles John to Tauentzien, Zehbitz, 7 Oct. 1813, SHAT, C^{17} 133.
57. Unger, *Blücher*, 2:105.
58. Ibid., 2:106; Friederich, *Herbstfeldzug 1813*, 2:319–22; Charles John to Blücher, Zehbitz, 8 Oct. 1813, reproduced in Fransecky, "Darstellung der Ereignisse bei der schlesischen Armee," 342.
59. Müffling, *Zur Kriegsgeschichte*, 64.
60. Unger, *Blücher*, 2:106.
61. Blücher to Charles John, Bad Düben, 9 Oct. 1813, reproduced in Fransecky, "Darstellung der Ereignisse bei der schlesischen Armee," 342.
62. Müffling, *Zur Kriegsgeschichte*, 64–65. One officer from each corps staff was supposed to be sent to headquarters so that he could "transmit safely all urgent orders either by day or night. On the morning of the 9th, when this orderly officer from Sacken's corps should have taken the disposition to General Sacken, he was nowhere to be found, having already returned to his corps." Another officer had to be sent. He apparently lost his way, thus delivering the orders three hours late.
63. Unger, *Blücher*, 2:106; Yorck, *Droysen*, 202–203; Friederich, *Herbstfeldzug 1813*, 2:325–26.
64. Droysen, *Yorck*, 2:203.
65. Blücher to Charles John, Jeßnitz, 9 Oct. 1813, reproduced in Fransecky, "Darstellung der Ereignisse bei der schlesischen Armee," 346.
66. Unger, *Blücher*, 2:106.
67. Charles John to Blücher, Zehbitz, 9 Oct. 1813, reproduced in Fransecky, "Darstellung der Ereignisse bei der schlesischen Armee," 350.
68. Müffling, *Zur Kriegsgeschichte*, 66–67.
69. Ibid., 67.

70. Blücher to Charles John, Jeßnitz, 10 Oct. 1813, reproduced in Fransecky, "Darstellung der Ereignisse bei der schlesischen Armee," 350–51.
71. Unger, *Blücher*, 2:106.
72. Müffling, *Zur Kriegsgeschichte*, 67–68.
73. Charles John to Bülow, Zehbitz, 9 Oct. 1813, SHAT, C^{17} 133.
74. Müffling, *Zur Kriegsgeschichte*, 68–69; Müffling, *Aus meinem Leben*, 87.
75. Napoleon to Ney, Eilenburg, 4:30 A.M., 10 Oct. 1813, *CN*, No. 20740, 26:315–16.
76. Friederich, *Herbstfeldzug 1813*, 2:375.
77. Napoleon to Marmont, Eilenburg, 4:30 A.M., 10 Oct. 1813, *CN*, No. 20741, 26:316–17.
78. Berthier to Sebastiani, Bad Düben, 5:00 P.M., 10 Oct. 1813, SHAT, C^{17} 181.
79. Napoleon to Reynier, Bad Düben, 4:00 P.M., 10 Oct. 1813, *CN*, No. 20750, 26:324.
80. Napoleon to Berthier, Bad Düben, 5:00 P.M., 10 Oct. 1813, *CN*, No. 20752, 26:325.
81. Napoleon to Arrighi, Bad Düben, 4:00 P.M., 10 Oct. 1813, *CN*, No. 20749, 26:322–23.
82. Berthier to Marmont, Bad Düben, 6:30 P.M., 10 Oct. 1813, SHAT, C^{17} 181; Friederich, *Herbstfeldzug 1813*, 2:331.
83. Napoleon to Berthier, Bad Düben, 3:00 A.M., 11 Oct. 1813, *CN*, No. 20758, 26:327–28.
84. Napoleon to Maret, Bad Düben, 3:00 P.M., 10 Oct. 1813, *CN*, No. 20746, 26:320–21.
85. Müffling's 1827 work definitively states that the crown prince promised to construct a bridge at Wettin. *Zur Kriegsgeschichte*, 68.
86. Droysen, *Yorck*, 2:204.
87. In this example, Friederich's unbiased reporting must be acknowledged: "The omission to build the bridge at Wettin has been portrayed as a deliberate attempt to deceive Blücher in order to deny him a point of passage and thus force him 'to follow the North German Army and go in the direction that the crown prince previously failed to persuade him to take.' Examining the existing service letters with unprejudiced eyes, the crown prince appears to be completely innocent of this omission. Obviously, misunderstandings existed that emerged from a report from Vorontsov indicating the construction of a bridge at Wettin. It is not worth investigating the matter further as it is just typical to always give the worst possible interpretation to the efforts, actions, and omissions of the crown prince." Friederich, *Herbstfeldzug 1813*, 2:340.
88. Nostitz, *Tagebuch*, 1:66.
89. Müffling, *Zur Kriegsgeschichte*, 70.
90. Charles John to Blücher, Groß Weissand, 10 Oct. 1813, reproduced in Fransecky, "Darstellung der Ereignisse bei der schlesischen Armee," 354.
91. Charles John to Blücher, Rothenburg, 11 Oct. 1813, reproduced in ibid., 359.
92. Blücher to Alexander, Halle, 11 Oct. 1813, reproduced in ibid., 358.
93. Blücher to Charles John, Halle, 11 Oct. 1813, reproduced in ibid.

94. Charles John to Blücher, Rothenburg, 11 Oct. 1813, reproduced in ibid.
95. Droysen, *Yorck*, 2:205.
96. Friederich, *Herbstfeldzug 1813*, 2:337–38, 339–40.
97. Napoleon to Ney, Bad Düben, 10:30 A.M., 11 Oct. 1813, *CN*, No. 20761, 26:330.
98. Napoleon to Reynier, Bad Düben, 12:00 P.M., 11 Oct. 1813, *CN*, No. 20763, 26:331.
99. Napoleon to Ney, Bad Düben, 3:00 A.M., 12 Oct. 1813, *CN*, No. 20765, 26:332.
100. Napoleon to Maret, Bad Düben, 4:00 A.M., 12 Oct. 1813, *CN*, No. 20766, 26:333.
101. Napoleon to Ney, Bad Düben, 3:00 A.M., 12 Oct. 1813, *CN*, No. 20765, 26:332–33.
102. Napoleon to Reynier, Oudinot, and Marmont, Bad Düben, 4:00 A.M., 12 Oct. 1813, *CN*, Nos. 20766, 20769, and 20770, 26:334.
103. Yorck von Wartenburg, *Napoleon as a General*, 2:343.
104. Friederich, *Herbstfeldzug 1813*, 2:343–46.
105. Napoleon to Berthier, Bad Düben, 9:30 A.M., 12 Oct. 1813, *CN*, No. 20771, 26:336; "Notes sur la réunion des différents corps d'armée à Taucha," Bad Düben, 10:00 A.M., 12 Oct. 1813, *CN*, No. 20772, 26:336–38.
106. Napoleon to Marmont, Bad Düben, midnight, 12 Oct. 1813, *CN*, No. 20782, 26:344.
107. Napoleon to Macdonald, Bad Düben, 6:00 A.M., 13 Oct. 1813, *CN*, No. 20790, 26:349.
108. Schwarzenberg to Blücher, 13 Oct. 1813, ÖStA, FA 1537.
109. Unger, *Blücher*, 2:119–22.
110. Blücher to Amalie, Lützen, 20 Oct. 1813, *BB*, 188.
111. Blücher to Bonin, Lützen, 20 Oct. 1813, *BB*, 187.
112. Frederick William to Blücher, Leipzig, 20 Oct. 1813, in Blücher, *Blücher in Briefen*, 60.
113. Blücher to Amalie, Weißensee, 25 Oct. 1813, *BB*, 189.
114. Blücher to Amalie, Philippsthal, 30 Oct. 1813, *BB*, 189–90.
115. Blücher to Amalie, Gießen, 3 Nov. 1813, *BB*, 190–91.
116. Blücher to Bonin, Gießen, 4 Nov. 1813, *BB*, 192.
117. Quoted in Brett-James, *Europe against Napoleon*, 292–93.

Chapter Fourteen

1. Clausewitz, *Übersichtdes Feldzuges von 1814 in Frankreich*, 330–31.
2. Blücher to Hardenberg, 30 Jan. 1814, *BB*, 225.
3. Schwarzenberg to Blücher, Chaumont, 31 Jan. 1814, Add. Ms. 20,112; Bogdanovich, *Geschichte des Krieges*, 1:116.
4. Friederich, *Die Befreiungskriege*, 3:100.
5. According to Bogdanovich, the Allies captured a total of sixty-three guns. Plotho claims seventy-three guns, while Koch states the French lost fifty-four guns. Bogdanovich, *Geschichte des Krieges 1814*, 1:102; Plotho, *Der Krieg*, 3:126; Koch, *Campagne de 1814*, 1:186.

6. Berthier to Nansouty, Gérard, Ricard, Grouchy, Curial, Meunier, Rottembourg, Marmont, Victor, Defrance, Ruty, and Corbineau, 11:30 A.M., 1 Feb. 1814, SHAT, C¹⁷ 183.

7. Yorck von Wartenburg, *Napoleon as a General*, 2:383. "If the enemy had then imitated Napoleon's methods of pursuit, the campaign might have ended with this battle and, as Russia had been irrevocably lost to the conqueror on the Beresina, and Germany on the Elster, so France might have been lost to him on the Aube."

8. For the disorganization of the French army following the battle, see Marmont, *Mémoires*, 6:40.

9. Blücher to Bonin, 2 Feb. 1814, *BB*, 226.

10. Schwarzenberg to Blücher, Bar-sur-Aube, 3 Feb. 1814, Add. Ms. 20,112.

11. Napoleon to Clarke, Piney, 2 Feb. 1814, *CN*, No. 21169, 27:103.

12. Napoleon to Berthier, Troyes, 3:00 A.M., 5 Feb. 1814, *CN*, No. 21181, 27:111.

13. Napoleon to Joseph, Troyes, 3:00 P.M., 6 Feb. 1814, *CN*, No. 21190, 27:117.

14. Napoleon to Joseph, Nogent, 7 Feb. 1814, *CN*, Nos. 21195, 21203, 21204, and 21205, 27:121–22, 26–28; Napoleon to Marmont, Nogent, 7 Feb. 1814, *CN*, Nos. 21202 and 21203, 27:125–26.

15. In particular see Napoleon to Berthier, Nogent, 9 Feb. 1814, *CN*, No. 21221, 27:139–43.

16. Napoleon to Joseph, Nogent, 2:00 P.M., 9 Feb. 1814, *CN*, No. 21227, 27:147–49.

17. Yorck von Wartenburg, *Napoleon as a General*, 2:389.

18. Schwarzenberg to Blücher, Bar-sur-Aube, 3 Feb. 1814, Add. Ms. 20,112.

19. Disposition for 7–10 February, 6 Feb. 1814, GStA PK, VI HA Rep. 92 Nl. Gneisenau, Paket Nr. 18.

20. Sacken's army corps, 15,000 men; Olsufiev's IX Infantry Corps, 3,700; Yorck's I Corps, 16,000; Kleist's II Corps, 8,000; and Kaptsevich's X Infantry Corps, 7,000.

21. Blücher to Amalie, Vertus, 7 Feb. 1814, *BB*, 227–28.

22. Janson, *Feldzuges 1814*, 1:245–49.

23. Nostitz, *Tagebuch*, 1:102.

24. Ibid., 102–103; Unger, *Blücher*, 2:177.

25. Alexander to Blücher and Schwarzenberg to Blücher, Bar-sur-Seine, 6 Feb. 1814, Add. Ms. 20,112.

26. Alexander to Blücher and Schwarzenberg to Blücher, Bar-sur-Seine, 7 Feb. 1814, ibid.

27. Unger, *Blücher*, 2:179.

28. Blücher to Schwarzenberg, Champaubert, 9 Feb. 1814, Add. Ms. 20,112.

29. Janson, *Feldzuges 1814*, 1:253–54.

30. Blücher to Amalie, Étoges, 13 Feb. 1814, *BB*, 228.

31. Nostitz, *Tagebuch*, 1:97–98.

32. Janson, *Feldzuges 1814*, 1:260–85.

33. Unger, *Blücher*, 2:189; Janson, *Feldzuges in 1814*, 1:288–89.

34. Blücher to Hardenberg, Châlons, 16 Feb. 1814, *BB*, 230.

35. Schwarzenberg to Blücher, Bray-sur-Seine, 17 Feb. 1814, ÖStA KA, FA 1606, 434 and Add. Ms. 20,112.

36. Burghersch, *Operations of Allied Armies in 1813 and 1814*, 145–49.
37. Schwarzenberg to Blücher, Bray-sur-Seine, 18 Feb. 1814, ÖStA KA, FA 1606, 434 and Add. Ms. 20,112.
38. Blücher to Schwarzenberg, 19 Feb. 1814, Add. Ms. 20,112.
39. Janson, *Feldzuges in 1814*, 1:303–304.
40. Yorck von Wartenburg, *Napoleon as a General*, 2:398.
41. Schwarzenberg to Blücher, Troyes, 2:00 A.M., 21 Feb. 1814, Add. Ms. 20,112.
42. Janson, *Feldzuges in 1814*, 1:305–306.
43. Schwarzenberg to Blücher, Troyes, 11:00 P.M., 21 Feb. 1814, Add. Ms. 20,112.
44. Burghersch, *Operations of Allied Armies in 1813 and 1814*, 149–53.
45. Janson, *Feldzuges 1814*, 1:311.
46. Blücher to Schwarzenberg, Arcis-sur-Aube, 21 Feb. 1814, Add. Ms. 20,112.
47. Schwarzenberg to Blücher, Troyes, 23 Feb. 1814, ibid.
48. Alexander to Blücher, Bar-sur-Aube, 21 Feb. 1814, ibid.
49. Blücher to Alexander, Méry-sur-Seine, 23 Feb. 1814, *BB*, 231.
50. Mikhailovsky-Danilevsky, *History of the Campaign in France*, 198; Janson, *Feldzuges in 1814*, 1:313–14.
51. Plotho, *Der Krieg*, 3:265–66.
52. Burghersch, *Operations of Allied Armies in 1813 and 1814*, 186–87; Houssaye, *1814*, 106–107.
53. Plotho, *Der Krieg*, 3:269–76.
54. Napoleon to Joseph, Troyes, 4:00 P.M., 25 Feb. 1814, *CN*, No. 21367, 27:242.
55. Napoleon to Berthier, Troyes, 4:30 P.M., 25 Feb. 1814, *CN*, Nos. 21368 and 21369, 27:243.
56. Napoleon to Berthier, Troyes, 2:30 P.M., 26 Feb. 1814, *CN*, No. 21373, 27:244–45.
57. Napoleon to Clarke, Troyes, 26 Feb. 1814, *CN*, No. 21379, 27:248.
58. Napoleon to Clarke, Troyes, 26 Feb. 1814, *CN*, No. 21380, 27:249.
59. Napoleon to Berthier, Troyes, 5:00 P.M., 26 Feb. 1814, *CN*, No. 21384, 27:253–54.
60. Napoleon to Berthier, Troyes, 3:30 A.M., 27 Feb. 1814, *CN*, No. 21387, 27:255–56.
61. Napoleon to Berthier, Troyes, 7:00 A.M., 27 Feb. 1814, *CN*, No. 21390, 27:257.
62. Napoleon to Berthier, Troyes, 9:00 A.M., 27 Feb. 1814, *CN*, No. 21393, 27:258–59.
63. Napoleon to Caulaincourt, Troyes, 27 Feb. 1814, *CN*, No. 21397, 27:261.

Chapter Fifteen

1. Napoleon to Joseph, La Ferté-sous-Jouarre, 8:00 P.M., 1 Mar. 1814, *CN*, No. 21404, 27:266.
2. Napoleon to Clarke, La Ferté-sous-Jouarre, 2 Mar. 1814, *CN*, No. 21421, 27:278.
3. Napoleon to Berthier, La Ferté-sous-Jouarre, 2 Mar. 1814, *CN*, No. 21419, 27:276–77.
4. Napoleon to Joseph, La Ferté-sous-Jouarre, evening, 2 Mar. 1814, *CN*, No. 21420, 27:277.

5. Napoleon to Berthier, La Ferté-sous-Jouarre, 2 Mar. 1814, *CN*, No. 21419, 27:276–77.
6. Müffling, *Aus meinem Leben*, 145.
7. Berthier to Grouchy, Ney, and Victor, 3, 4 Mar. 1814, SHAT, C¹⁷ 184.
8. Napoleon to Clarke, Bézu-Saint-Germain, 4 Mar. 1814, *CN*, No. 21426, 27:280–81; Yorck von Wartenburg, *Napoleon as a General*, 2:401–402.
9. Houssaye, *1814*, 130.
10. Yorck von Wartenburg, *Napoleon as a General*, 2:402–403.
11. Berthier to Marmont, 4 Mar. 1814, SHAT, C¹⁷ 184.
12. Napoleon to Clarke, Bézu-Saint-Germain, 4 Mar. 1814, *CN*, No. 21426, 27:280–81.
13. Corbineau to Napoleon, 4, 5 Mar. 1814, Archives Nationales, AF IV, Carton 1670, Paris.
14. Napoleon to Joseph, Fismes, 4 Mar. 1814, *CN*, No. 21427, 27:281–82.
15. Napoleon to Joseph, La Ferté-sous-Jouarre, 3 Mar. 1814, *CN*, No. 21422, 27:278; Napoleon to Berthier, Fismes, 4 Mar. 1814, *CN*, No. 21429, 27:283.
16. Napoleon to Joseph, Fismes, 4 Mar. 1814, *CN*, No. 21427, 27:282.
17. Houssaye, *1814*, 158.
18. Napoleon to Berthier, Fismes, 4 Mar. 1814, *CN*, No. 21429, 27:283.
19. Nevertheless, many in the Silesian Army felt that the opening of Soissons saved them from destruction. "If the place had held out for twenty-four hours," recounts Langeron, "the Army of Silesia would have been crushed or at least lost all of its artillery." *Mémoires*, 410. Both Gneisenau and Müffling strove to dispel this idea. Long after Bülow's death, Müffling spewed his discontent: "In the negotiations at Soissons, a man was employed who had the reputation of being an overweening braggart and the notion he entertained of having done something quite extraordinary was supported by the opinion that had germinated in Bülow's corps that he had been the savior of the Field Marshal. Later, when letters arrived from the Grand [Bohemian] Army, everyone poured out congratulations that the Field Marshal and the brave Silesian Army had been so wonderfully saved from destruction by the surrender of Soissons. Gneisenau was so sensitive to this truly ridiculous rumor that he sought its origin and told me some time later that Bülow had used expressions in a report to the king that could only lead to the assumption that without the capitulation of Soissons, the Field Marshal would have been lost." *Aus Meinem Leben*, 148–49.
20. Napoleon to Joseph, Fismes, 4 Mar. 1814, *CN*, No. 21427, 27:281–82.
21. Friederike von Auer wrote in her unpublished memoirs that although their first meeting was cold, "the rough and open manner of the old soldier . . . soon allowed a calmer mood to set in. But with Gneisenau and Müffling it was different. Bülow could not reconcile either, and these two influential men always remained ill-disposed toward him." "Erinnerungen aus der Jugendzeit für meine Kinder," BFA, No. 127.
22. Müffling, *Aus Meinem Leben*, 146–47.
23. Reiche, *Memoiren*, 2:67.
24. Müffling, *Aus Meinem Leben*, 146.
25. Reiche, *Memoiren*, 2:67.
26. Müffling, *Aus Meinem Leben*, 146.

27. Bülow to Pauline, 5 Mar. 1814, BFA, No. 133.
28. Ibid.
29. For the account of this discussion, see Varnhagen von Ense, *Bülow*, 363. Like all Prussian field commanders, Bülow had a chief of staff, the gifted Boyen. Nevertheless, Boyen's role at corps headquarters remained more advisory that Gneisenau's role at army headquarters.
30. Bülow to Pauline, 5 Mar. 1814, BFA, No. 133.
31. Bülow shared these views. "We are all strong enough to be able to strike, if necessary, the French Grande Armée. Perhaps peace is closer than ever. We have heard that the commissioners are negotiating an armistice as well as the peace; what will now become of it we must await, but we are very strong on all points." Ibid.
32. Boyen to Gneisenau, 5 Mar. 1814, in Pertz-Delbrück, *Gneisenau*, 4:197.
33. Pertz-Delbrück, *Gneisenau*, 4:198.
34. Müffling, *Aus Meinem Leben*, 149–50.
35. Napoleon to Berthier, Fismes, 5 Mar. 1814, *CN*, Nos. 21432, 21434, and 21436, 27:284–87; Napoleon to Joseph, Fismes, 5 Mar. 1814, *CN*, Nos. 21438 and 21439, 27:288–89.
36. Yorck von Wartenburg, *Napoleon as a General*, 2:402–403.
37. Houssaye, *1814*, 163–69; Koch, *Mémoires*, 1:410–415; Vaudoncourt, *Histoire des campagnes de 1814 et 1815*, 2:23–29.
38. Napoleon to Berthier, Berry-au-Bac, 6 Mar. 1814, *CN*, No. 21448, 27:293.
39. Yorck von Wartenburg, *Napoleon as a General*, 2:405.
40. Napoleon to Joseph, Berry-au-Bac, noon, 6 Mar. 1814, *CN*, No. 21449, 27:293–94.
41. Napoleon to Joseph, Chavignon, 10 Mar. 1814, *CN*, No. 21460, 27:300.
42. Reiche, *Memoiren*, 2:68.
43. Napoleon to Berthier, Corbeny, 4:00 A.M., 7 Mar. 1814, *CN*, No. 21453, 27:296–97. Yorck's I Corps consisted of 13,500 men; Kleist's II Corps, 10,600; Bülow's III Corps, 16,900; Langeron's corps, 24,900; Sacken's corps, 12,700; and Wintzingerode's corps, 25,200: a total of 103,800 soldiers. St. Priest's corps of 2,400 Prussians and 3,000 Russians stood at Reims. As a result, Allied strength at the Battle of Laon totaled 98,400 men, of whom 38,000 did not participate in the combat. See Wagner, *Plane der Schlachten und Treffen*, 3:83. For a discussion over the strengths of the contending armies at Laon, see Petre, *Napoleon at Bay*, 115–16.
44. Blücher to Bonin, Laon, 10 Mar. 1814, *BB*, 232–33.
45. Blücher to L'Estoq, Laon, 10 Mar. 1814, *BB*, 232.
46. Blücher to Amalie, Laon, 10 Mar. 1814, *BB*, 231–32.
47. According to Tsar Alexander's secretary: "On that day, Blücher, who had been indisposed for some time, was suffering so violently from ague and an inflammation of the eyes that he was no longer master of his faculties. As a result, his chief of staff would not assume the responsibility of executing the order to advance which the field-marshal had given at midnight. He preferred to concentrate all of the troops at Laon when he saw Napoleon was renewing the battle in which Blücher was not in a situation to command in person." Mikhailovsky-Danilevsky, *History of the Campaign in France*, 244.

48. Müffling, *Aus Meinem Leben*, 172.
49. According to Müffling, "Gneisenau was besieged by his old friends to such a degree that it became very difficult for me to see him alone. . . . [T]he ideas forced on Gneisenau could have only originated in the political principle of sparing the Prussian troops, however misplaced it was here, when the issue was only to reap the fruits of a battle that was already won." Ibid., 167–68.
50. Ibid., 149–50.
51. According to the Russians: "Therefore, owing to the ailing state of Blücher, the French escaped a final overthrow. . . . Napoleon . . . succeeded in retiring without being molested." Mikhailovsky-Danilevsky, *History of the Campaign in France*, 244.
52. Napoleon to Joseph, Chavignon, 10 Mar. 1814, *CN*, No. 21460, 27:300–301; Koch, *Mémoires*, 1:418–19.
53. Napoleon to Joseph, Chavignon, 11 Mar. 1814, *CN*, No. 21461, 27:301.
54. Napoleon to Berthier, Soissons, 6:00 P.M. and 8:00 P.M., 12 Mar. 1814, *CN*, Nos. 21475 and 21476, 27:308–11.
55. Napoleon to Joseph, Reims, 14 Mar. 1814, *CN*, No. 21478, 27:311.
56. Janson, *Feldzuges 1814*, 2:203–204.
57. Yorck von Wartenburg, *Napoleon as a General*, 2:405.
58. Nostitz, *Tagebuch*, 1:128.
59. Blücher, *Blücher in Briefen*, 113–14.
60. Müffling, *Aus Meinem Leben*, 172.
61. Nostitz, *Tagebuch*, 1:127.
62. Müffling adds: "Various gossip could be heard in Bülow's corps [and] from the headquarters of the Crown Prince of Sweden, who had certainly talked a great deal of ridiculous nonsense after his arrival in Liège. It became known that he [Bernadotte] . . . still imagined that the French would call him to the throne of France in place of Napoleon." *Aus Meinem Leben*, 171. According to Varnhagen von Ense, Bülow later regretted his request. See *Bülow*, 380–83.
63. Plotho, *Der Krieg*, 3:355.
64. Nostitz, *Tagebuch*, 1:129.
65. Müffling, *Aus Meinem Leben*, 173–74.
66. Blücher to Schwarzenberg, Berry-au-Bac, 21 Mar. 1814, Add. Ms. 20,112.
67. Janson, *Feldzuges in 1814*, 1:229–32.
68. Nostitz, *Tagebuch*, 1:130.
69. Blücher to Amalie, Fismes, 21 or 22 Mar. 1814, *BB*, 235.
70. Nostitz, *Tagebuch*, 1:130.
71. Janson, *Feldzuges in 1814*, 2:231–32.
72. Quoted in Unger, *Blücher*, 2:232.
73. Janson, *Feldzuges in 1814*, 2:232.
74. Nostitz, *Tagebuch*, 1:131.
75. Perta and Delbrück, *Gneisenau*, 4:226.
76. Schwarzenberg to Blücher, Vitry-le-François, 24 Mar. 1814, Add. Ms. 20,112.
77. Blücher to Bonin, Paris, 30 Apr. 1814, *BB*, 240.
78. Nostitz, *Tagebuch*, 1:131.

79. Quoted in Unger, *Blücher*, 2:238.
80. Nostitz, *Tagebuch*, 1:136.
81. Unger, *Blücher*, 2:241.
82. Ibid., 239.
83. Nostitz, *Tagebuch*, 1:137.
84. Ibid., 137.
85. Blücher, *Blücher in Briefen*, 121.
86. Henderson, *Blücher and the Uprising of Prussia*, 257.
87. Blücher to Bonin, Paris, 30 Apr. 1814, *BB*, 240–41.
88. Quoted in Nostitz, *Tagebuch*, 1:137–38.
89. Blücher to Bonin, Paris, 30 Apr. 1814, *BB*, 241.
90. Quoted in Blücher, *Blücher in Briefen*, 123.
91. Blücher to Blücher-Altona, Paris, [?] May 1814, *BB*, 242.
92. Blücher to Frederick William, Paris, [?] Apr. 1814, *BB*, 235–36.
93. George, Prince Regent, to Blücher, Carlton House, 19 Apr. 1814, in Blücher, *Blücher in Briefen*, 124.
94. Blücher to Amalie, Paris, 28 Apr. 1814, *BB*, 239.
95. Blücher to Amalie, Boulogne, 3 June 1814, *BB*, 247.
96. Ibid., 246–47.
97. Blücher to Amalie, Paris, 16 May 1814, *BB*, 244.
98. Blücher to Amalie, Paris, 22 Apr. 1814, *BB*, 239.
99. Blücher to Blücher-Altona, Paris, [?] May 1814, *BB*, 242.
100. Blücher to Bonin, Paris, 30 Apr. 1814, *BB*, 241.
101. Blücher to Amalie, Paris, 16 May 1814, *BB*, 243–44.
102. Henderson, *Blücher and the Uprising of Prussia*, 259.
103. Blücher to Amalie, Paris, 6 May 1814, *BB*, 243.
104. Blücher to Amalie, Boulogne, 3 June 1814, *BB*, 246.
105. Blücher to Amalie, Paris, 28 Apr. 1814, *BB*, 239.
106. Blücher to Bonin, Paris, 30 Apr. 1814, *BB*, 241.
107. Blücher to Blücher-Altona, Paris, [?] May 1814, *BB*, 242.
108. Blücher to Amalie, Paris, 6 May 1814, *BB*, 243.
109. Blücher to Amalie, Boulogne, 3 June 1814, *BB*, 246.
110. William Henry, the Duke of Clarence, was the third son of George III and younger brother and successor to George IV. As William IV (1830–37), he was the last king and penultimate monarch of the House of Hanover.
111. Blücher to Amalie, Boulogne, 3 June 1814, *BB*, 245.
112. Blücher, *Memoirs of Prince Blücher*, 33.
113. Blücher to Amalie, London, 6 June 1814, *BB*, 246.
114. Blücher to Blücher-Altona, London, 30 June 1814, *BB*, 249.

Chapter Sixteen

1. Blücher, *Memoirs of Prince Blücher*, 33–34.
2. Blücher to Amalie, London, 6 June 1814, *BB*, 246.
3. Blücher, *Memoirs of Prince Blücher*, 33.
4. Ibid., 34–37; Henderson, *Blücher and the Uprising of Prussia*, 261–63; Blücher, *Blücher in Briefen*, 130–33.
5. Nostitz, *Tagebuch*, 1:34–35.

6. Blücher to Blücher-Altona, London, 30 June 1814, *BB*, 249.

7. Blücher to Amalie, Boulogne, 3 June 1814, *BB*, 245.

8. Blücher to Gneisenau, Berlin, late Aug. 1814, *BB*, 258.

9. Blücher to Blücher-Altona, Liège, 26 Apr. 1815, *BB*, 270.

10. The day after his death, doctors performed an autopsy and found "a chronic inflammation of the membranes covering the cerebral hemispheres," to which they attributed to Franz's derangement. "Unfortunately, this cause was completely overlooked by the physicians attending General Blücher, and a treatment was adopted that was rather calculated to aggravate than to allay the morbid irritation of the sensorium. This is all the more remarkable, as the French surgeons who treated the patient in 1813 . . . expressed their fears that at some future time the wounds to the head could cause a derangement of the intellect." All quotes of Franz's illness are from Wakely, *Lancet*, 2:829–31.

11. Blücher to Boyen, Berlin, 17 Feb. 1815, *BB*, 263; Blücher to Blücher-Altona, Liège, 26 Apr. 1815, *BB*, 269.

12. Blücher to Bülow, Fall 1814, *BB*, 253–54.

13. Blücher to Rüchel, Berlin, 27 Feb. 1815, *BB*, 263–64.

14. Houssaye, *1815*, 3. According to Houssaye, the general estimate of the Royal Army on 15 January 1815 was 192,675 men. This number does not include veterans, the gendarmerie, and household troops. He also gives Napoleon's estimate of the effective strength of the army on 20 March at 149,000 men.

15. Ollech, *Geschichte des Feldzuges von 1815*, 14.

16. Quoted in Unger, *Blücher*, 2:251.

17. Blücher to Blücher-Altona, Liège, 26 Apr. 1815, *BB*, 269.

18. Blücher to Amalie, Koblenz, 16 Apr. 1815, *BB*, 267.

19. Blücher to Amalie, Liège, 24 Apr. 1815, *BB*, 268–69.

20. Blücher to Arnim, Liège, 22 Apr. 1815, *BB*, 268.

21. Blücher to Hardenberg, Namur, 27 May 1815, *BB*, 274.

22. Blücher to Blücher-Altona, Liège, 26 Apr. 1815, *BB*, 269.

23. Blücher to Amalie, Liège, 5 May 1815, *BB*, 270–71.

24. Blücher to Amalie, Namur, 17 May 1815, *BB*, 270–72.

25. Blücher to Hardenberg, Namur, 2 June 1815, *BB*, 276.

26. "The cause of the mutiny," wrote Wellington after his meeting with Blücher on 3 May, "was the order to divide the corps, and that the Prussian part, in which the Guards were included, should take the oath of allegiance to the King of Prussia." Wellington to Clancarty, Brussels, 3 May 1815, *Wellington's Dispatches*, 12:346.

27. Quoted in Henderson, *Blücher and the Uprising of Prussia*, 276.

28. Blücher to Hardenberg, Namur, 2 June 1815, *BB*, 276.

29. Wellington to Clancarty, Brussels, 3 May 1815, *Wellington's Dispatches*, 12:346.

30. Quoted in Henderson, *Blücher and the Uprising of Prussia*, 278.

31. Blücher to Amalie, Namur, 3 June 1815, *BB*, 278.

32. Blücher to Hardenberg, Namur, 2 June 1815, *BB*, 276.

33. Blücher to Katharina, Namur, 3 June 1815, *BB*, 278.

34. No two accounts of the Saxon mutiny agree. See Unger, *Blücher*, 260–63; Lettow-Vorbeck, *Napoleons Untergang*, 1:491–509; Henderson, *Blücher and the Uprising of Prussia*, 275–78; and Hofschröer, *1815*, 1:50–52.
35. Blücher to Amalie, Liège, 5 May 1815, *BB*, 271.
36. Blücher to Frederick Augustus, Liège, 6 May 1815, *BB*, 271–72.
37. Blücher to Hardenberg, Namur, 27 May 1815, *BB*, 273–75.
38. Blücher to Hardenberg, Namur, 2 June 1815, *BB*, 276.
39. Blücher to Amalie, Namur, 3 June 1815, *BB*, 278.
40. Nostitz, *Tagebuch*, 2:11.
41. Wellington to Hardenberg, Brussels, 3 May 1815, *Wellington's Dispatches*, 12:346.
42. Wellington wrote to the Prince of Orange, Hardenberg, and Clancarty from Brussels on the night of 3 May. See *Wellington's Dispatches*, 12:345–46.
43. For comprehensive coverage of the 3 May meeting, see Hofschröer, *1815*, 1:116–18.
44. Blücher to Amalie, Namur, 17 May 1815, *BB*, 269.
45. Ollech, *Geschichte des Feldzuges von 1815*, 63.
46. Blücher to Amalie, Liège, 24 Apr. 1815, *BB*, 269.
47. See Lettow-Vorbeck, *Napoleons Untergang*, 1:179–86.
48. Müffling, *Geschichte des Feldzuges im Jahre 1815*, 219.
49. Blücher to Hardenberg, Namur, 27 May 1815, *BB*, 273.
50. Blücher to Hardenberg, Namur, 2 June 1815, *BB*, 277.
51. Blücher to Schwenke, Namur, 27 May 1815, *BB*, 274–75.
52. Gneisenau, *Blücher*, 401.
53. Blücher to Hardenberg, Namur, 2 June 1815, *BB*, 277.
54. Damitz, *Geschichte des Feldzuges 1815*, 1:37–39; Yorck von Wartenburg, *Napoleon as a General*, 2:428.
55. Blücher to Hardenberg, Namur, 2 June 1815, *BB*, 276–77.
56. Blücher to Blücher-Altona, Namur, 9 June 1815, *BB*, 279.
57. Blücher to Amalie, Namur, 3 June 1815, *BB*, 278.
58. Blücher to Hardenberg, Namur, 2 June 1815, *BB*, 277.
59. Blücher to Müffling, Namur, 11 June 1815, *BB*, 281.
60. Blücher to Blücher-Altona, Namur, 9 June 1815, *BB*, 279–80.
61. Blücher to Amalie, Namur, 3 June 1815, *BB*, 278.
62. Blücher to Hardenberg, Namur, 2 June 1815, *BB*, 277.
63. Blücher to Müffling, Namur, 11 June 1815, *BB*, 281.
64. Blücher to Blücher-Altona, Namur, 9 June 1815, *BB*, 280.
65. Gebhard Bernhard Carl (14 July 1799–8 March 1875) and Gustav Octavius Heinrich (3 August 1800–3 January 1866).
66. Blücher to Amalie, Namur, 3 June 1815, *BB*, 278.
67. Blücher to Amalie, Namur, 15 June 1815, *BB*, 282.
68. Yorck von Wartenburg, *Napoleon as a General*, 2:424–25.

Chapter Seventeen

1. Napoleon to Drouot, Paris, 7 June 1815, *CN*, No. 22031, 28:265–66.
2. Order of Movement, Beaumont, 14 June 1815, ibid., 281–86.
3. Napoleon to Joseph, Avenes, 14 June 1815, *CN*, No. 22050, 28:280.

4. Napoleon to Joseph, Charleroi, 9:00 P.M., 15 June 1815, *CN*, No. 22055, 28:286–87.

5. Charras, *Histoire de la campagne de 1815*, 1:85.

6. Yorck von Wartenburg, *Napoleon as a General*, 2:428–29.

7. Ollech, *Geschichte des Feldzuges von 1815*, 103.

8. Gneisenau, *Life and Campaigns of Blücher*, 406.

9. Blücher to Frederick William, Sombreffe, 11:30 P.M., 15 June 1815, in Ollech, *Geschichte des Feldzuges von 1815*, 106.

10. Ollech, *Geschichte des Feldzuges von 1815*, 123.

11. Hofschröer has conclusively debunked the story that in response to Wellington's reservations concerning Blücher's position at Ligny and its vulnerability to artillery fire, Gneisenau referred to the reverse-slope tactics the duke employed during the Peninsular War: "Our men like to see the enemy." *1815*, 1:233–42. For the origins of this myth, see Stanhope, *Notes of Conversations with the Duke of Wellington*, 108-110.

12. Napoleon to Grouchy, Charleroi, 16 June 1815, *CN*, No. 22059, 28:291–92.

13. Napoleon to Ney, Charleroi, 16 June 1815, *CN*, No. 22058, 28:289–91.

14. Damitz, *Geschichte des Feldzuges 1815*, 1:130.

15. Becke, *Napoleon and Waterloo*, 100.

16. Ollech, *Geschichte des Feldzuges von 1815*, 154–55.

17. On the Battle of Ligny, see Ollech, *Geschichte des Feldzuges von 1815*, 100–165; Damitz, *Geschichte des Feldzuges 1815*, 1:110–83; and Lettow-Vorbeck, *Napoleons Untergang*, 1:324–43.

18. Nostitz, *Tagebuch*, 2:31. For a thorough discussion, see also Hofschröer, *1815*, 1:325–27.

19. Ollech, *Geschichte des Feldzuges von 1815*, 106–107, 143.

20. Gneisenau to Zieten, Sombreffe, 15 June 1815, in Ollech, *Geschichte des Feldzuges von 1815*, 105.

21. Blücher to Schwarzenberg, 10:00 P.M., Sombreffe, 15 June 1815, in ibid.

22. Lettow-Vorbeck, *Napoleons Untergang*, 1:338.

23. Nostitz, *Tagebuch*, 2:31

24. Blücher to Gneisenau, Wavre, 17 June 1815, *BB*, 282.

25. Blücher to Katharina, Wavre, 17 June 1815, *BB*, 283.

26. Damitz, *Geschichte des Feldzuges 1815*, 1:183. Estimates of Blücher's losses at Ligny vary according to the source. American historian John C. Ropes placed Prussian casualties as high as 18,000 men, while French historian Houssaye cites them at 12,000. The German writer and contemporary August von Wagner also claims 12,000 casualties. Plotho, another German contemporary, maintains that Blücher lost 14,000 men. Ollech, citing Gneisenau's report, places the army's loss at 15,000 men. Becke wrote that Blücher lost 16,000 men. An English contemporary, William Siborne, claimed that Prussian losses totaled 12,000 for both the fifteenth and sixteenth. Müffling cited Prussian losses on both days at 20,900 men. Included in Müffling's figure are approximately 8,000 deserters; discrepancies likewise exist regarding this total. Gneisenau to Friedrich Wilhelm, 17 June 1815, in Ollech, *Geschichte des Feldzuges von 1815*, 163–64; Becke, *Napoleon and Waterloo*, 118; Houssaye, *1815*, 107; Müffling, *History of*

the *Campaign in the Year 1815*, 10; Plotho, *Der Krieg des verbündeten Europa gegen Frankreich*, 43; Ropes, *Campaign of Waterloo*, 159; Siborne, *History of the War*, 148; Wagner, *Plane der Schlachten und Treffen*, 4:47.

27. Malmesbury, *Letters of the First Earl of Malmesbury*, 2:447.
28. Wellington to Bathurst, 18 June 1815, Wellington, *Dispatches*, 12:479. See also Müffling, *History of the Campaign in the Year 1815*, 16.
29. Blücher to Bülow, 17 June 1815, BFA, No. 155. For Wellington's position, see Siborne, *History of the War*, 202–220.
30. Reproduced in Lettow-Vorbeck, *Napoleons Untergang*, 1:365.

Chapter Eighteen

1. Houssaye, *1815*, 125–26.
2. Ibid., 128.
3. Grouchy, *Relation succincte*, 19.
4. Houssaye, *1815*, 130.
5. Ibid., 130–31.
6. Siborne, *History of the War*, 185–86.
7. Kelly, *Battle of Wavre*, 90.
8. Soult to Grouchy, Le Caillou, 10:00 A.M., 18 June 1815, in Siborne, *History of the War*, 181.
9. Houssaye, *Waterloo*, 164–65.
10. Ollech, *Geschichte des Feldzuges von 1815*, 188–89.
11. Ibid., 189; Müffling, *Aus meinem Leben*, 184; Houssaye, *1815*, 163.
12. Müffling, *History of the Campaign in the Year 1815*, 18–19.
13. Ibid., 19–20; Gneisenau, *Life and Campaigns of Blücher*, 415.
14. Bülow to Friedrich Wilhelm, 19 June 1815, in Ollech, *Geschichte des Feldzuges*, 192–93.
15. Ollech, *Geschichte des Feldzuges*, 191–93; Treuenfeld, *Die Tage*, 413.
16. Treuenfeld, *Die Tage*, 413.
17. Plotho, *Der Krieg des Verbendeten Europa gegen Frankreich*, 65.
18. Müffling, *History of the Campaign in the Year 1815*, 29; Wagner, *Plane der Schlachten und Treffen*, 4:86.
19. Bülow to Friedrich Wilhelm, 19 June 1813, in Ollech, *Geschichte des Feldzuges*, 192.
20. Soult to Grouchy, 1:30 P.M., 18 June 1815, in Ropes, *Campaign of Waterloo*, 271.
21. Houssaye, *1815*, 190–91, 258–59; Becke, *Napoleon and Waterloo*, 257–59; Ropes, *Campaign of Waterloo*, 270–72.
22. Vivian to Siborne, 3 June 1839, in Siborne, *Waterloo Letters*, 151.
23. Seymore to Siborne, 21 Nov. 1842, in ibid., 20.
24. Houssaye, *1815*, 192–93.
25. Bülow to Friedrich Wilhelm, 19 June 1815, *Geschichte des Feldzuges*, 193.
26. Vivian to Siborne, n.d., in Siborne, *Waterloo Letters*, 161.
27. Siborne, *History of the War*, 323.
28. Houssaye, *1815*, 225.
29. Ibid., 233.
30. Quoted in Charras, *Histoire de la campagne de 1815*, 303–304.

31. Bergman, *Battle of Waterloo*, 60.
32. Houssaye, *1815*, 237–38.
33. "Report of the Prussian Army of the Lower Rhine," reproduced in Pertz and Delbrück, *Gneisenau*, 4:708.
34. Siborne, *History of the War*, 456.
35. Blücher to Amalie, Gemappe, 19 June 1815, *BB*, 283.
36. Blücher to Knesebeck, Gemappe, 19 June 1815, *BB*, 283.
37. Blücher to Amalie, Gosselies, 20 June 1815, *BB*, 284–85.
38. Blücher to Amalie, Châtillon-sur-Sambre, 23 June 1815, *BB*, 287.
39. Blücher to Stein, Noyelle-sur-Sambre, 22 June 1815, *BB*, 287.
40. Blücher to Hardenberg, Noyelle-sur-Sambre, 22 June 1815, *BB*, 285–86.
41. Blücher to Amalie, Châtillon-sur-Sambre, 23 June 1815, *BB*, 287.
42. Blücher to Dobschütz, Châtillon-sur-Sambre, 23 June 1815, *BB*, 288.
43. Siborne, *History of the War*, 494.
44. Blücher to Blücher-Altona, Hanape, 24 June 1815, *BB*, 288.
45. Gneisenau to Müffling, 27 June 1815, in Müffling, *Passages from My Life*, 272–73.
46. Lachouque, *Last Days of Napoleon*, 86–87; Kelly, *Battle of Wavre*, 147.
47. Wagner, *Plane der Schlachten und Treffen*, 4:118.
48. Batty, *An Historical Sketch*, 125; Becke, *Napoleon and Waterloo*, 273; Kelly, *Battle of Wavre*, 151.
49. Blücher to Amalie, Guivry near Noyon, 26 June 1815, *BB*, 289.
50. Blücher to Amalie, Compiègne, 27 June 1815, *BB*, 290.
51. Kelly, *Battle of Wavre*, 151; Müffling, *History of the Campaign*, 50.
52. Gneisenau, *Blücher*, 425.
53. Blücher's IV Corps reached Marly-la-Ville, with detachments at Le Bourget and Stains; I Corps camped at Nanteuil, with detachments at Le Plessis, Belleville, and Dammartin; and III Corps reached Crespy. Wellington placed his right wing at St. Just and his left at La Taulle, with units at Roye, Antheuil, Petit-Crevecoeur, Ressons, and Couchy.
54. Batty, *Historical Sketch*, 125; Ollech, *Geschichte des Feldzuges*, 330–34; Siborne, *History of the War*, 518-21.
55. For the measures to defend Paris, see Gallaher, *Iron Marshal*, 322; and Lachouque, *Last days of Napoleon*, 164.
56. Gallaher, *Iron Marshal*, 325; Ollech, *Geschichte des Feldzuges*, 365–73; Wagner, *Plane der Schlachten und Treffen*, 4:120.
57. Gallaher, *Iron Marshal*, 325; Plotho, *Der Krieg des verbündeten Europa gegen Frankreich*, 143.
58. Disposition for 2 July 1815, 1 July 1815, in Ollech, *Geschichte des Feldzuges*, 388; Müffling, *History of the Campaign*, 55; Wagner, *Plane der Schlachten und Treffen*, 4:123.
59. Blücher to Amalie, Genosse, 30 June 1815, *BB*, 290–91.
60. For Davout's considerations and preparations to attack the Prussians, see Gallaher, *Iron Marshal*, 321-25, 327–29. For the negotiations with the Prussians, see Houssaye, *1815*, 294.
61. Blücher to Amalie, St. Cloud, 3 July 1815, *BB*, 291.
62. Blücher to Amalie, Meudon, 3 July 1815, *BB*, 291.

63. For the capitulation of Paris, see Houssaye, *1815*, 285–302.
64. Blücher to Amalie, Paris, 9 July 1815, *BB*, 292–93.
65. Blücher to Frederick William, 24 June 1815, *BB*, 289.
66. Blücher to Goltz, St. Cloud, July 1815, *BB*, 293.
67. Blücher to Amalie, Paris, 4 Aug. 1815, *BB*, 299.
68. Blücher to Knesebeck, St. Cloud, 10 July 1815, *BB*, 294.
69. Blücher to Gneisenau, Rambouillet, 28 July 1815, *BB*, 297–98.
70. Blücher to Hardenberg, Rambouillet, 26 July 1815, *BB*, 297.
71. Blücher to Gneisenau, Rambouillet, 28 July 1815, *BB*, 298.
72. Blücher to Amalie, Paris, 4 Aug. 1815, *BB*, 299–300.
73. Blücher to Gneisenau, Rambouillet, 10 Aug. 1815, *BB*, 301.
74. Quoted in Blücher, *Blücher in Briefen*, 5–7.

Conclusion

1. One of Blücher's letters to Herr Häse, who rented and managed Groß Raddow, written while preparing to depart for the Dutch campaign, illustrates his hands-on style:

> Business and my indisposition prevent me from coming to Raddow. Because I would have stayed only a few hours anyway, I am leaving now: God bless, and from the bottom of my heart, good health. Raddow will remain in your hands and I know it is in good hands. Send whatever money you have left to me through the noncommissioned officer delivering this. Whatever you make in the future and don't need for the budget, give to Pastor Rebüser, who will pay part to my wife and invest the rest in bonds; as long as I am gone, I will take no money from Raddow. So the construction and the upkeep do not take too much money from the revenues, sell three *Schock* of lumber [180 pieces of wood] this winter. Try as much as possible to convert the cleared land into farmland. I will not tell you anything more about agriculture; you know it better than me. Herewith, I am also sending you a capable workhorse; in return, send me the old black gelding. Write me how the wheat is growing and if you have harvested the rye, and how much money it brings in, and how my sheep are doing. Should one of the people not follow orders tell me the name, and if it's a *Knecht* [worker] turn him over to the NCO who will bring him to me at Nörenberg. My wife will remain at Rummelsburg. If you can, send her between the harvests the horses with the green half-chaise; she will go to Wolpersnow, Raddow, and Schönwalde [the estate of her parents] for eight days; other people can drive her back. Once again, take care and stay well, remember me and believe me that I am your friend and servant.
>
> BLÜCHER TO HÄSE, Wusterbarth, 14 Aug. 1787, BB, 11.

2. Friederich, *Herbstfeldzug 1813*, 1:225–27.
3. Schwarzenberg to Blücher, Teplitz, 5 Sept. 1813, Add. Ms 20,112.
4. Unger, *Blücher*, 2:239.
5. Schwarzenberg to Marie Anna, 29 Jan. 1814, No. 271, in Schwarzenberg, *Briefe*, 370; Janson, *Feldzuges in 1814*, 1:162.
6. Schwarzenberg wrote Blücher on 4 February that "both the Bohemian Army and yours are sufficiently strong enough to engage the enemy that

we have before us. I believe that we must continue to proceed according to our earlier principles: weakly mask the front of the enemy, while the Bohemian Army operates in his right flank and your army in his left. Therefore, the enemy will be forced to operate against one of us and in general will be weaker than either of us. Should he break through the middle, he will lose his communications with Paris as well as with his flanks." Schwarzenberg penned this letter before receiving news of the attack on Liechtenstein. Schwarzenberg to Blücher, Vendeuvre-sur-Barse, 4 Feb. 1814, Add. Ms. 20,112.

7. Janson, *Feldzuges 1814*, 1:286.
8. On 13 February Schwarzenberg received Blücher's reports over the Army of Silesia's debacle. In response, the Allied generalissimo directed V and VI Corps thirty-five miles northeast from Provins and Donnemarie-Dontilly to Sézanne with orders to continue on another twenty-three miles to Sommesous and Arcis-sur-Aube. Both III Corps and the Russo-Prussian Guard and Reserve would follow. After news reached him that same night that Napoleon had ended the offensive against Blücher, Schwarzenberg cancelled these orders. Disposition for 14 and 15 February, Troyes, 13 Feb. 1814, Add. Ms. 20,112; Burghersh, *Operations of the Allied Armies*, 138–39.
9. Unger, *Blücher*, 2:187.
10. Napoleon to Joseph, farm of L'Epine-au-Bois, Ferme, 8:00 P.M., 11 Feb. 1814, *CN*, No. 21231, 27:150.
11. Nostitz, *Tagebuch*, 1:106.
12. Blücher to Hardenberg, Châlons, 16 Feb. 1814, *BB*, 229–30.
13. Unger, *Blücher*, 2:40–41.
14. Schwarzenberg to Blücher, Lusigny-sur-Barse, 24 Feb. 1814, Add. Ms. 20,112.
15. Alexander to Blücher, Bar-sur-Aube, 21 Feb. 1814, ibid.
16. Frederick William to Blücher, Vendeuvre-sur-Barse, 24 Feb. 1814, in Janson, *Feldzuges 1814*, 2:70.
17. Schwarzenberg to Blücher, Vendeuvre-sur-Barse, 24 Feb. 1814, Add. Ms. 20,112.
18. Schwarzenberg to Blücher, Bar-sur-Aube, 25 Feb. 1814, ibid.
19. Janson, *Geschichte des Feldzuges in 1814*, 1:3–5, 192.
20. Schwarzenberg to Marie Anna, 27 Jan. 1814, No. 270, in Schwarzenberg, *Briefe*, 370.
21. Pertz and Delbrück, *Gneisenau*, 4:35–36.
22. Clausewitz, *Übersicht des Feldzuges von 1814 in Frankreich*, 330–31.
23. Stewart, *Narrative*, 283.
24. Gneisenau also praised Stein for convincing Alexander to march on Paris and conclude peace there.
25. Quoted in Unger, *Blücher*, 2:233.
26. Blücher to Bonin, Paris, 30 Apr. 1814, *BB*, 240.
27. Gneisenau to Clausewitz, Paris, 28 Apr. 1814, GStA PK, VI HA Rep. 92 Nl. Gneisenau, Paket Nr. 21.
28. Blücher to Knesebeck, 1 Oct. 1813, *BB*, 184: "It pleases me uncommonly to see in the letter that you wrote to Gneisenau that one [Frederick William III] agrees with our decision to cross at Elster. If I find the crossing

at Mühlberg to be not very dangerous, I will cross. . . . Once we are across, I will thus put the bell on the cat and His Highness will have to go with us." In explaining the significance of crossing the Elbe at Wartenburg, Blücher wrote, "By far the trophies are not as significant as at the Katzbach; but the results of this victory must be great because now everything will cross the Elbe and the Grand Army can advance from Bohemia." Blücher to Bonin, 4 Oct. 1813, Unger, *Blüchers Brief*, 185.

29. Burckhardt, *Gebhard Leberecht von Blücher*, 127.

30. See Sternke, *Alles über Herrenschuhe*.

31. Binder and Schlünz, *Schwerer Kreuzer Blücher*, 90; Williamson, *German Heavy Cruisers*, 34.

32. Freytage-Loringhoven, *Aufklärung und Armeeführung*, iii.

33. Citino, *German Way of War*, 138–39.

34. Ibid., 141. See also Citino's discussion in *Death of the Wehrmacht*, 154–46.

35. Kessel, "Blücher," 303–13.

Bibliography

Archives

Berlin, Germany
Geheimes Staatsarchiv Preußischer Kulturbesitz zu Berlin

Baden-Baden, Germany
Ehemals Mitteilungen aus dem Gräflichen Bülow Familien-Archiv zu Grünhoff. Friedrich Wilhelm Graf Bülow von Dennewitz. Dokumentation in Briefen-Befehlen-Berichten. Gesammelt Übertragen und mit Anmerkungen Versehen von Joachim-Albrecht Graf Bülow von Dennewitz

Paris, France
Service Historique de l'Armée de Terre

Vienna, Austria
Österreichisches Staatsarchiv, Kriegsarchiv

Moscow, Russia
Rossiiskii Gosudarstvennyi Voenno-Istoricheskii

London, United Kingdom
British Manuscript Collection

Published Primary Sources

Batty, Robert. *An Historical Sketch of the Campaign of 1815, Illustrated by Plans of the Operations, and of the Battles of Quatre Bras, Ligny, and Waterloo. Second edition, considerably enlarged.* London, 1820.

Beauchamp, A. *Histoire des campagnes de 1814 et de 1815, ou histoire politique et militaire des deux invasions de la France, de l'entreprise de Bounaparte au mois de mars, de la chute totale de sa paissance, et de la double restauration du trône, jusqu'à la seconde paix de Paris, inclusivement. Seconde partie, comprenantle récit de tous les événemens survenus en france en 1815. Rédigée sur des matériaux authentiques au inedits.* 3 vols. Paris, 1817.

Berthezène, Pierre. *Souvenirs militaires de la république et de l'empire.* Paris, 1855.

Bieske, Carl Ludwig. *Der Feldmarschall Fürst Gebhard Leberecht Blücher von Wahlstatt.* Berlin, 1862.

Blücher, Gebhard Leberecht von. "Aus Blüchers Korrespondenz." Edited by Herman Granier. *Forschungen zur brandenburgischen-preußischen Geschichte* 26 (1913): 149–78.

——. *Blücher in Briefen aus den Feldzügen, 1813–15.* Edited by Wilhelm Günter Enno von Colomb. Stuttgart, 1876.

——. *Blüchers Briefe.* Edited by Wilhelm Capelle. Leipzig, 1915.

——. *Blüchers Briefe: Vervollständigte Sammlung des Generals E. v. Colomb.* Edited by Wolfgang von Unger. Stuttgart, 1912.

——. *Blücher's Kampagne Journal der Jahre 1793 und 1794.* Hamburg, 1796.

——. "Zwölf Blücherbriefe." Edited by Herman Granier. *Forschungen zur brandenburgischen-preußischen Geschichte* 12 (1900): 479–96.

Blücher von Wahlstatt, Gebhard Leberecht, 4th Prince of. *Memoirs of Prince Blücher.* Edited by Evelyn Mary Blücher von Wahlstatt and Wellesley William Desmond Mountjoy Chapman-Huston. London, 1932.

Boyen, Hermann v. *Erinnerungen aus dem Leben des General-Feldmarshalls Hermann von Boyen.* Edited by Friedrich Nippold. 3 vols. Leipzig, 1889–90.

——. *Erinnerungen aus dem Leben des General-Feldmarshalls Hermann von Boyen.* Edited by Dorothea Schmidt. 2 vols. Berlin, 1990.

Burckhardt, Wilhelm. *Gebhard Leberecht von Blücher preussischer Feldmarschall und Fürst von Wahlstatt: Nach Leben, Reden und Thaten geschildert.* Stuttgart, 1835.

Cathcart, George. *Commentaries on the War in Russia and Germany in 1812 and 1813.* London, 1850.

Clausewitz, C. *Der Feldzug 1812 in Rußland und die Befreiungskriege von 1812–15.* Berlin, 1906.

——. *Historical and Political Writings.* Translated and edited by P. Paret and D. Moran. Princeton, N.J., 1992.

——. *Übersichtdes Feldzuges von 1814 in Frankreich.* Vol. 7 of *Hinterlassene Werke des Generals Carl von Clausewitz über Krieg und Kriegführung.* 10 vols. Berlin, 1832–37.

Damitz, K. *Geschichte des Feldzuges von 1814.* 4 vols. Berlin, 1843.

——. *Geschichte des Feldzugs von 1815 in den Niederlanden und Frankreich als Beitrag zur Kriegsgeschichte der neuern Kriege.* 2 vols. Berlin, 1837–38.

Fain, A. J. F. *Manuscrit de mil huit cent quatorze, trouvé dans les voitures impériales prises à Waterloo, contenant l'histoire des six derniers mois du regne de Napoléon.* 4th ed. Paris, 1830.

Fane, J. [Lord Burghersh]. *Memoir of the Operations of the Allied Armies under Prince Schwarzenberg and Marshal Blücher, during the Later End of 1813, and the Year 1814.* London, 1822. Reprint, London, 1996.

Fezansac, Raymond. *Souvenirs militaires de 1804 à 1814.* Paris, 1870.

Gneisenau, August v. *Briefe August Neidhardts von Gneisenau. Eine Auswahl.* Edited by Koehler & Amelang Verlagsgesellschaft mbH München. Berlin, 2000.

——. *Gneisenau: Ein Leben in Briefen.* Edited by Karl Griewank. Leipzig, 1939.

——. *The Life and Campaigns of Field Marshal Prince Blücher.* London, 1815.

Grouchy, Emmanuel. *Relation succincte de la campagne de 1815 en Belgique, et notamment des mouvements, combats et opérations des troupes sous les ordres du Maréchal Grouchy, suivie de l'exposition de quelquesunes des causes de la perte de la bataille de Waterloo.* Paris, 1843.

Hellwald, F. J. H. *Der k.k. österreichische Feldmarschall Graf Radetzky : eine biographische Skizze nach den eigenen Dictaten und der Correspondenz des Feldmarschalls von einem österreichischen Veteranen.* Stuttgart, 1858.

Henckel von Donnersmarck, W. L. v. *Erinnerungen aus meinem Leben.* Leipzig, 1846.

Hüser, Heinrich v. *Denkwürdigkeiten aus dem Leben des Generals der Infanterie von Hüser.* Berlin, 1877.

Karl XIV, King of Sweden. *Recueil des ordres de mouvement proclamations et bulletins de S.A.R. le prince royal de suede, commandant en chef l'armée combinée du nord de l'Allemagne en 1813 et 1814.* Stockholm, 1838.

Koch, Frédéric. *Mémoires pour servir à l'histoire de la campagne de 1814.* Paris, 1819.

Langeron, Alexandre Louis Andrault. *Mémoires de Langeron, général d'infanterie dans l'armée russe. Campagnes de 1812, 1813, 1814.* Paris, 1902.

Linnebach, Karl, ed. *Scharnhorsts Briefe.* Vol. 1 of *Privatbriefe.* Leipzig, 1914. Reprint, with commentary by Heinz Stübig, Munich, 1980.

Malmesbury, James Harris. *A Series of Letters of the First Earl of Malmesbury, His Family, and Friends, from 1745 to 1820.* London, 1870.

Marmont, A. de. *Mémoires du Duc de Raguse.* 9 vols. Paris, 1857.

Martens, G. F. *Recueil de traités d'alliance, de paix, de trêve, de neutralité, de commerce, de limites, déchange, etc., et plusieurs autres actes servant à la connoissance des relations étrangères des puissances et états de l'Europe depuis 1761 jusqu'à présent.* 16 vols. Göttingen, 1817–42.

Marwitz, Friedrich v. d. *Aus dem Nachlaß Friedrich August Ludwig von der Marwitz.* 2 vols. Berlin, 1852.

Metternich, C. L. W. *Memoirs of Prince Metternich, 1773–1815.* 5 vols. Edited by R. Metternich. Translated by A. Napier. New York, 1970.

Mikhailovsky-Danilevsky, Aleksandr Ivanovich. *Denkwürdigkeiten aus dem Kriege von 1813.* Translated by Karl Goldhammer. Dorpat, 1837.

———. *History of the Campaign in France in the Year 1814.* London, 1840. Reprint, Cambridge, 1992.

———. *Opisanie voiny 1813 goda.* 2 vols. St. Petersburg, 1840.

Müffling, Friedrich Karl Ferdinand v. *Aus meinem Leben.* Berlin, 1851.

———. *Geschichte des Feldzugs der englisch-hannöversch-niederländischen und braunschweigischen Armee unter dem Herzog von Wellington und der preußischen unter dem Fürsten Blücher im Jahr 1815.* Stuttgart, 1815.

———. *History of the Campaign of the British, Dutch, Hanoverian, and Brunswick Armies, under the Command of the Duke of Wellington; and of the Prussians, under that of Prince Blücher of Wahlstatt, in the Year 1815.* London, 1816.

———. *Passages from My Life; Together with Memoirs of the Campaign of 1813 and 1814.* Translated and edited by Philip Yorke. London, 1853.

———. *A Sketch of the Battle of Waterloo. To Which Is Added Official Dispatches of Field-Marshal the Duke of Wellington; Field-Marshal Prince Blucher; and Reflections on the Battles of Ligny and Waterloo.* Brussels, 1850.

———. *Zur Kriegsgeschichte der Jahre 1813 und 1814. Die Feldzüge der schlesischen Armee unter dem Feldmarschall Blücher von der Beendigung des Waffenstillstandes bis zur Eroberung von Paris.* Berlin, 1827.

Napoléon I, emperor of the French. *La Correspondance de Napoléon Ier; publiée par ordre de l'empereur Napoléon III.* 32 vols. Paris, 1858–69.

Nostitz, August Ludwig Ferdinand v. *Das Tagebuch des Generals der Kavallerie Grafen von Nostitz.* 2 vols. Pt. 1 of *Kriegsgeschichtliche Einzelschriften.* 5 vols. Berlin, 1885.

Odeleben, E. O. v. *A Circumstantial Narrative of the Campaign in Saxony, in the Year 1813.* London, 1820.

———. *Napoleons Feldzug im Sachsen im Jahre 1813.* Dresden, 1816.

Osten-Sacken und Rhein, Ottomar v. *Militärisch-politische Geschichte des Befreiungskrieges im Jahre 1813.* 2 vols. Berlin, 1813.

Plotho, Carl v. *Der Krieg des verbündeten Europa gegen Frankreich im Jahre 1815.* Berlin 1818.

———. *Der Krieg in Deutschland und Frankreich in den Jahren 1813 und 1814.* 3 vols. Berlin, 1817.

Prittwitz, Karl Heinrich. *Beiträge zur Geschichte des Jahres 1813. Von einem höheren Offizier der Preußischen Armee.* 2 vols. Potsdam, 1843.

Quistorp, Barthold v. *Geschichte der Nord-Armee im Jahre 1813.* 3 vols. Berlin, 1894.

Reiche, Ludwig v. *Memoiren des königlichen preußischen Generals der Infanterie Ludwig von Reiche.* Edited by Louis von Weltzien. Leipzig, 1857.

Rochechouart, Louis Victor Léon. *Souvenirs sur la révolution, l'empire et la restauration.* Paris, 1933.

Scharnhorst, Gerhard v. *Private und dienstliche Schriften.* Edited by Johannes Kunisch and Michael Sikora. 6 vols. Köln, 2002–12.

———. *Scharnhorsts Briefe.* Edited by Karl Linnebach. Münich, 1914.

Scherbening, R. K. v., and K. W. Willisen, eds. *Die Reorganisation der Preußischen Armee nach dem Tilsiter Frieden.* 2 vols. Berlin, 1862–66.

Schwarzenberg, K. z. *Briefe des Feldmarschalls Fürsten Schwarzenberg an Seine Frau, 1799–1816.* Leipzig, 1913.

Siborne, H. T. *Waterloo Letters.* London, 1983.

Steffens, H. *Adventures on the Road to Paris, during the Campaigns of 1813–14.* London, 1848.

Stewart, Lord Londonderry, Lieutenant General Sir Charles William Vane. *Narrative of the War in Germany and France in 1813 and 1814.* London, 1830.

St.-Cyr, Laurent de Gouvion. *Mémoires sur les campagnes des armées du Rhin et de Rhin-et-Moselle Atlas des cartes et plans relatifs aux campagnes du Maréchal Gouvion St. Cyr aux armées du Rhin et de Rhin et Moselle pendant les années 1792, 1793, 1794, 1795, 1796 et 1797.* Paris, 1828.

Valentini, Georg v. *Der grosse Krieg.* 2 vols. Berlin, 1833.

———. *Lehre vom Kriege.* 2 vols. Berlin, 1835.

Varnhagen von Ense, Karl August. *Das Leben der Generals Gräfen Bülow von Dennewitz.* Berlin, 1853.

———. *Leben des Fürsten Blücher von Wahlstatt.* Berlin, 1933.

Vaudoncourt, Guillaume. *Histoire de la guerre soutenue par le Français en Allemagne en 1813*. Paris, 1819.

———. *Histoire des campagnes de 1814 et 1815 en France*. 5 vols. Paris, 1826.

Venturini, Carl. *Rußlands und Deutschlands Befreiungskriege von der Franzosen-Herrschaft unter Napoleon Buonaparte in den Jahren 1812–1815*. 4 vols. Altenburg, 1816–18.

Wagner, C. A. v. *Plane der Schlachten und Treffen von der preußischen Armee in den Feldzügen der Jahre 1813, 1814 und 1815*. Berlin, 1821.

Wakley, Thomas. *The Lancet for MDCCCXXXV–XXXVI*. 2 vols. London, 1835–36.

Wellington, Arthur Wellesley, Duke of. *The Dispatches of Field Marshal the Duke of Wellington: During his Various Campaigns in India, Denmark, Portugal, Spain, the Low Countries, and France, from 1799 to 1818*. London, 1837.

Wilson, Robert. *General Wilson's Journal, 1812–1814*. Edited by Antony Brett-James. London, 1964.

———. *Private Diary of Travels, Personal Services, and Public Events: During the Mission Employed with the European Armies in the Campaigns of 1812, 1813, 1814*. London, 1861.

Secondary Sources

Anderson, Eugene. *Nationalism and the Cultural Crises in Prussia, 1806–1815*. New York, 1976.

Archenholz, Johann Wilhelm v. *The History of the Seven Years War in Germany*. Frankfurt, 1843.

Atkinson, C. T. *A History of Germany, 1715–1815*. London, 1908.

Bailleu, Paul. "Haugwitz und Hardenberg." *Deutsche Rundschau* 20 (1879): 268–98.

Barton, D. Plunket. *Bernadotte: Prince and King, 1810–1844*. London, 1925.

Becke, Archibald Frank. *Napoleon and Waterloo: The Emperor's Campaign with the Armée du Nord, 1815. A Strategical and Tactical Study*. London, 1914.

Bernhardi, T. *Denkwürdigkeiten aus dem Leben des Kaiserlich Russischen Generals von der Infanterie Carl Friedrich Grafen von Toll*. 4 vols. Leipzig, 1856–66.

Binder, Frank, and Hans Hermann Schlünz. *Schwerer Kreuzer Blücher*. Herford, 1990.

Biro, Sydney. *The German Policy of Revolutionary France. A Study in French Diplomacy during the War of the First Coalition, 1792–1797*. 2 vols. Cambridge, 1957.

Blanning, T. C. W. "The Death and Transfiguration of Prussia." *Historical Journal* 29, no. 2 (1986): 433–59.

———. *The French Revolution in Germany: Occupation and Resistance in the Rhineland, 1792–1802*. Oxford, 1983.

———. *The Origins of the French Revolutionary Wars*. London, 1986.

Blasendorff, Carl. *Gebhard Leberecht von Blücher: mit Bild und Nachbild eines eigenhändigen Briefes*. Berlin, 1887.

Bleck, Otto. *Marschall Blücher: Ein Lebensbild*. Berlin, 1939.

Bogdanovich, Modest Ivanovich. *Geschichte des Krieges im Jahre 1813 für Deutschlands Unabhängigkeit. Nach den zuverläßigsten Quellen*. 2 vols. St. Petersburg, 1863–68.

———. *Geschichte des Krieges 1814 in Frankreich und des Sturzes Napoleon's I. Nach den zuverläßigsten Quellen*. Translated by G. Baumgarten. Leipzig, 1866.

Bowden, Scott. *Napoleon's Grande Armée of 1813*. Chicago, 1990.

Brett-James, Anthony. *Europe against Napoleon: The Leipzig Campaign, 1813, from Eyewitness Accounts*. London, 1970.

Caemmerer, Rudolf v. *Die Befreiungskrieg, 1813–1815: Ein Strategischer Überblick*. Berlin, 1907.

Chandler, David G. *The Campaigns of Napoleon*. New York, 1966.

Charras, Jean Baptiste Adolphe. *Histoire de la campagne de 1815: Waterloo*. Brussels, 1863.

———. *Histoire de la Guerre de 1813 en Allemagne. Derniers jours de la retraite, insurrection de l'Allemagne, armements, diplomatie, entrée en campagne*. 2nd ed. Paris, 1870.

Citino, Robert M. *Death of the Wehrmacht: The German Campaigns of 1942*. Lawrence, Kan., 2007.

———. *The German Way of War: From the Thirty Years' War to the Third Reich*. Lawrence, Kan., 2005.

Clément, Gérôme. *Campagne de 1813*. Paris, 1904.

Conrady, Emil v. *Leben und Wirken des Generals Carl von Grolman*. 3 vols. Berlin, 1933.

Craig, Gordon A. *The Politics of the Prussian Army: 1640–1945*. Oxford, 1956.

———. "Problems of Coalition Warfare: The Military Alliance against Napoleon, 1813–14." In *War, Politics, and Diplomacy: Selected Essays by Gordon Craig*. London, 1966.

Crepon, Tom. *Gebhard Leberecht von Blücher: Seine Leben, seine Kämpfe*. Rostock, 1999.

Demeter, Karl. *Das deutsche Heer und seine Offiziere*. Berlin, 1930.

———. *The German Officer Corps in Society and State, 1650–1945*. Translated by Angus Malcolm. New York, 1965.

Droysen, Johann. *Das Leben des Feldmarshalls Grafen Yorck von Wartenburg*. 2 vols. Leipzig, 1851.

Duffy, Christopher. *The Army of Frederick the Great*. New York, 1974.

———. *Frederick the Great: A Military Life*. London, 1985.

Dwyer, Philip. "The Politics of Prussian Neutrality, 1795–1806." *German History* 12 (1994): 351–74.

———. "Prussia and the Armed Neutrality: The Invasion of Hanover in 1801." *International History Review* 15 (1993): 661–87.

Fabry, Gabriel Joseph. *Étude sur les opérations de l'empereur, 5 septembre au 21 septembre 1813*. Paris, 1910.

———. *Étude sur les opérations du maréchal Macdonald du 22 août au 4 septembre, 1813: La Katzbach*. Paris, 1910.

———. *Étude sur les opérations du maréchal Oudinot du 15 août au 4 septembre: Groß Beeren*. Paris, 1910.

Feuchtwanger, E. J. *Prussia: Myth and Reality: The Role of Prussia in German History.* Chicago, 1970.

Fisher, H. A. L. *Napoleonic Statesmanship in Germany.* Oxford, 1903.

Ford, G. S. *Hanover and Prussia: A Study in Neutrality, 1795–1803.* New York, 1903.

————. *Stein and the Era of Reform in Prussia, 1807–1815.* Princeton, 1922. Reprint, Glouchester, 1965.

Foucart, P. J. *Bautzen: 20–21 mai 1813.* 2 vols. Paris, 1897.

Fransecky, Eduard Friedrich Karl v. "Darstellung der Ereignisse bei der schlesischen Armee." *Militair-Wochenblatt* (1844): 77–173, 205–316.

Freytag-Loringhoven, Hugo Friedrich Philipp Johann v. *Aufklärung und Armeeführung dargestellt an den Ereignissen bei der Schlesischen Armee im Herbst 1813: Eine Studie.* Berlin, 1900.

Friedrich, Rudolf v. "Die Aufassung der strategischen Lage seitens der Verbündeten am Schlusse des Waffenstillstandes von Poischwitz 1813." *Militair-Wochenblatt* (1902): 1–36.

————. *Die Befreiungskriege, 1813–1815.* 4 vols. Berlin, 1911–13.

————. *Geschichte des Herbstfeldzuges 1813.* 3 vols. Berlin, 1903–1906. In *Geschichte der Befreiungskriege, 1813–1815.* 9 vols. Berlin, 1903–1909.

————. "Die strategische Lage Napoleons am Schlusse des Waffenstillstandes von Poischwitz." *Militair-Wochenblatt* (1901): 1–36.

Gallaher, John. *The Iron Marshal: A Biography of Louis N. Davout.* Carbondale, Ill., 1976.

Görlitz, Walter. *Fürst Blücher von Wahlstatt.* Rostock, 1940.

————. *History of the German General Staff, 1657–1945.* Translated by Brian Battershaw. New York, 1954.

Griewank, Karl. "Hardenberg und die preußische Politik, 1804 bis 1806." *Forschungen zur brandenburgischen-preußischen Geschichte* 47 (1935): 227–308.

————. *Hohenzollernbriefe aus den Freiheitskriegen 1813–1815.* Leipzig, 1913.

Grunwald, Constantin de. *The Life of Baron Stein: Napoleon's Nemesis.* Translated by C. F. Atkinson. New York, 1936.

Hagen, William. "The Partitions of Poland and the Crises of the Old Regime in Prussia." *Central European History* 9 (1976): 115–28.

Hausherr, Hans. "Hardenberg und der Friede von Basel." *Historische Zeitschrift* 184 (1957): 292–335.

————. "Stein und Hardenberg." *Historische Zeitschrift* 190 (1960): 267–89.

Haythornthwaite, Philip. *Frederick the Great's Army.* Vol. 1, *Cavalry.* London, 1991.

Heidrich, Kurt. *Preußen im Kampfe gegen die französische Revolution bis zur zweiten Teilung Polens.* Berlin, 1908.

Henderson, Ernest F. *Blücher and the Uprising of Prussia against Napoleon, 1806–1815.* London, 1911.

Hochedlinger, Michael. *Austria's Wars of Emergence: War, State, and Society in the Habsburg Monarchy, 1683–1797.* Harlow, 2003.

Hofschröer, Peter. *1815: The Waterloo Campaign.* London, 1998–99.

Holleben, A. v., and R. v. Caemmerer. *Geschichte des Frühjahrsfeldzuges 1813 und seine Vorgeschichte.* 2 vols. Berlin, 1904–1909. In *Geschichte der Befreiungskriege, 1813–1815.* 9 vols. Berlin, 1903–1909.

Houssaye, H. *1814*. Paris, 1888. Reprint, Paris, 1986.

———. *1815*. Paris, 1889. Reprint, Paris, 1987.

Janson, A. *Geschichte des Feldzuges 1814 in Frankreich*. 2 vols. Berlin, 1903–1905. In *Geschichte der Befreiungskriege, 1813–1815*. 9 vols. Berlin, 1903–1909.

Jany, Curt. *Geschichte der königlichen preußischen Armee*. 4 vols. Berlin, 1929.

Josselson, Michael, and Diana Josselson. *The Commander: A Life of Barclay de Tolly*. Oxford, 1980.

Kelly, William Hyde. *The Battle of Wavre and Grouchy's Retreat*. London, 1905.

Kessel, Eberhard. "Blücher: Zum 200. Geburtstag am 16 Dezember." *Militärwissenschaftliche Rundschau* (1942): 303–13.

Kissinger, Henry. *A World Restored: Metternich, Castlereagh, and the Problems of Peace, 1812–22*. Boston, 1990.

Kitchen, Martin. *A Military History of Germany*. London, 1954.

Koch, H. W. *A History of Prussia*. New York, 1987.

Kraehe, Enno. *Metternich's German Policy*. 2 vols. Princeton, 1963.

Lachouque, H. *Napoleon en 1814*. Paris, 1959.

Lange, Fritz, ed. *Neithardt von Gneisenau: Schriften von und über Gneisenau*. Berlin, 1954.

Lanrezac, Charles Louis Marie. *La manoeuvre de Lützen 1813*. Paris, 1904.

Lefevbre de Behaine, F. *La Campagne de France*. 2 vols. Paris, 1913.

Leggiere, M. *Napoleon and Berlin: The Franco-Prussian War in North Germany, 1813*. Norman, 2002.

———. *The Fall of Napoleon*. Vol. 1, *The Allied Invasion of France*. Cambridge, 2007.

Lehmann, Max. *Freiherr vom Stein*. 3 vols. Leipzig, 1902–1905.

———. *Scharnhorst*. 2 vols. Leipzig, 1886–87.

Lettow-Vorbeck, Oscar v. *Napoleons Untergang 1815*. 2 vols. Berlin, 1904–1906. In *Geschichte der Befreiungskriege, 1813–1815*. 9 vols. Berlin, 1903–1909.

Lieven, Dominic. *Russia against Napoleon: The True Story of the Campaigns of War and Peace*. New York, 2010.

Mackey, Albert Gallatin. *Encyclopedia of Freemasonry*. 3 vols. Chicago, 1946.

Maude, F. N. *1806: The Jena Campaign*. New York, 1909.

———. *The Leipzig Campaign, 1813*. London, 1908.

Meinecke, Friedrich. *Das Leben des Generalfeldmarschalls Hermann von Boyen*. 2 vols. Stuttgart, 1896–99.

Mikaberidze, A. *The Russian Officer Corps in the Revolutionary and Napoleonic Wars, 1792–1815*. New York, 2005.

Muir, Rory. *Britain and the Defeat of Napoleon, 1807–1815*. London, 1996.

Mustafa, Sam. *The Long Ride of Major von Schill: A Journey through German History and Memory*. Lanham, 2008.

Nicolson, Harold. *The Congress of Vienna: A Study in Allied Unity*. New York, 1946.

Ollech, Karl Rudolf v. *Geschichte des Feldzuges von 1815 nach archivalischen Quellen*. Berlin, 1876.

Paret, Peter. *Clausewitz and the State*. Oxford, 1976.

————. *Yorck and the Era of Prussian Reform, 1807–1815.* Princeton, 1966.

Parkinson, Roger. *Clausewitz: A Biography.* New York, 1971.

————. *The Hussar General: The Life of Blücher, Man of Waterloo.* London, 1975.

Pertz, G. H. *Das Leben des Ministers Freiherrn vom Stein.* 6 vols. Berlin, 1849–55.

Pertz, G. H., and Hans Delbrück. *Das Leben des Feldmarschalls Grafen Neithardt von Gneisenau.* 5 vols. Berlin, 1864–80.

Petre, F. L. *Napoleon at Bay, 1814.* London, 1914. Reprint, London, 1977.

————. *Napoleon's Conquest of Prussia, 1806.* London, 1907. Reprint, London, 1993.

————. *Napoleon's Last Campaign in Germany, 1813.* London, 1912. Reprint, London, 1992.

Phipps, Ramsay Weston. *The Armies of the First French Republic and the Rise of the Marshals of Napoleon I.* 5 vols. London, 1926–39.

Pflugk-Harttung, Julius v. *Das Befreiungsjahr 1813: Aus den Akten des Geheimen Staatsarchivs.* Berlin, 1913.

Quintin, D., and B. Quintin. *Dictionnaire des colonels de Napoléon.* Paris, 1996.

Quistorp, B. *Geschichte der Nord-Armee im Jahre 1813.* 3 vols. Berlin, 1894.

Ranke, Leopold v. *Denkwürdigkeiten des Staatskanzlers Fürsten von Hardenberg.* 5 vols. Leipzig, 1877.

Roloff, G. *Politik und Kriegführung während des Krieges von 1814.* Berlin, 1891.

Ropes, John Codman. *The Campaign of Waterloo: A Military History.* New York, 1892.

Ross, S. *European Diplomatic History, 1789–1815: France against Europe.* New York, 1969.

Scherr, Johannes. *Blücher: Seine Zeit und sein Leben.* 3 vols. Leipzig, 1887.

Schroeder, Paul. *The Transformation of European Politics, 1763–1848.* Oxford, 1994.

Schwartz, Karl. *Leben des generals Carl von Clausewitz und der Frau Marie von Clausewitz geb. Gräfin von Brühl.* Berlin, 1878.

Seeley, J. R. *Life and Times of Stein or Germany and Prussia in the Napoleonic Age.* 3 vols. New York, 1969.

Shanahan, William. *Prussian Military Reforms, 1786–1813.* New York, 1945.

Sherwig, John. *Guineas and Gunpowder: British Foreign Aid in the Wars with France, 1793–1815.* Cambridge, 1969.

Showalter, Dennis E. "Hubertusberg to Auerstädt: The Prussian Army in Decline?" *German History* 12 (1994): 308–33.

————. "The Prussian Landwehr and Its Critics, 1813–1819." *Central European History* 4 (1971): 3–33.

————. *The Wars of Frederick the Great.* London, 1996.

Siborne, William. *History of the War in France and Belgium in 1815: Containing Minute Details of the Battles of Quatre-Bras, Ligny, Wavre, and Waterloo.* London, 1844.

Simms, Brendan. *The Impact of Napoleon: Prussian High Politics, Foreign Policy, and the Crises of the Executive, 1797–1806.* Cambridge, 1997.

———. "The Road to Jena: Prussian High Politics, 1804–1806." *German History* 12 (1994): 374–94.

Simon, Walter. *The Failure of the Prussian Reform Movement, 1807–1819.* Ithaca, 1955.

Six, Georges. *Dictionnaire Biographique des généraux et amiraux français de la révolution et de l'empire.* 2 vols. Paris, 1934.

Stamm-Kuhlmann, Thomas. *König in Preußens grosser Zeit: Friedrich Wilhelm III, der Melancholiker auf dem Thron.* Berlin, 1992.

Sternke, Helge. *Alles über Herrenschuhe.* Berlin, 2006.

Szabo, Franz. *The Seven Years War in Europe, 1756–1763.* New York, 2008.

Thiry, Jean. *Leipzig, 30 juin–7 novembre.* Paris, 1972.

Treuenfeld, Bruno. *Die Tage von Ligny und Belle-Alliance.* Hanover, 1880.

Unger, Wolfgang v. *Blücher.* 2 vols. Berlin, 1907–1908.

White, Charles E. *The Enlightened Soldier: Scharnhorst and the Militärische Gesellschaft in Berlin, 1801–1805.* Westport, Conn., 1989.

Wigger, Friedrich. *Feldmarschall Fürst Blücher von Wahlstatt.* Schwerin, 1878.

Williamson, Gordon. *German Heavy Cruisers, 1939–1945.* Oxford, 2003.

———. *The Iron Cross: A History, 1813–1957.* Denison, Tex., 1994.

Yorck von Wartenburg, Hans Ludwig David Maximilian, Graf. *Napoleon as a General.* 2 vols. Edited by Walter H. James. London, 1897–98.

Index